Drug abuse
sourcebook

Drug Abuse SOURCEBOOK

Fifth Edition

Health Reference Series

Fifth Edition

Drug Abuse SOURCEBOOK

Basic Consumer Health Information about the Abuse of Cocaine, Club Drugs, Marijuana, Inhalants, Heroin, Hallucinogens, and Other Illicit Substances and the Misuse of Prescription and Over-the-Counter Medications

Along with Facts and Statistics about Drug Use and Addiction, Treatment and Recovery, Drug Testing, Marijuana as Medicine, Drug Abuse Prevention and Intervention, Glossaries of Related Terms, and Directories of Resources for Additional Help and Information

OMNIGRAPHICS

615 Griswold, Ste. 901, Detroit, MI 48226

Bibliographic Note

Because this page cannot legibly accommodate all the copyright notices, the Bibliographic Note portion of the Preface constitutes an extension of the copyright notice.

* * *

Omnigraphics, Inc.
Editorial Services provided by Omnigraphics, Inc.,
a division of Relevant Information, LLC

Keith Jones, *Managing Editor*

* * *

ISBN 978-0-7808-1516-2
E-ISBN 978-0-7808-1517-9

Library of Congress Cataloging-in-Publication Data

Names: Omnigraphics, Inc., issuing body.

Title: Drug abuse sourcebook: basic consumer health information about the abuse of cocaine, club drugs, marijuana, inhalants, heroin, hallucinogens, and other illicit substances and the misuse of prescription and over-the-counter medications: along with facts and statistics about drug use and addiction, treatment and recovery, drug testing, drug abuse prevention and intervention, glossaries of related terms, and directories of resources for additional help and information.

Description: Fifth Edition. | Detroit, MI: Omnigraphics, 2016. | Series: Health reference series | Revised edition of Drug abuse sourcebook, 2014. | Includes bibliographical references and index.

Identifiers: LCCN 2016009649 (print) | LCCN 2016015613 (ebook) | ISBN 9780780815162 (hardcover: alk. paper) | ISBN 9780780815179 (ebook) | ISBN 9780780815179 (eBook)

Subjects: LCSH: Drug abuse--Prevention--Handbooks, manuals, etc. | Drug abuse--Treatment--Handbooks, manuals, etc. | Drug addiction--Treatment--Handbooks, manuals, etc.

Classification: LCC HV5801 .D724 2016 (print) | LCC HV5801 (ebook) | DDC 362.29--dc23

LC record available at https://lccn.loc.gov/2016009649

This book is printed on acid-free paper meeting the ANSI Z39.48 Standard. The infinity symbol that appears above indicates that the paper in this book meets that standard.

Printed in the United States

Table of Contents

Part II: Drug Abuse and Specific Populations

Part III: Drugs of Abuse

Part IV: The Causes and Consequences of Drug Abuse and Addiction

Part V: Drug Abuse Treatment and Recovery

Part VI: Drug Abuse Testing and Prevention

Part VII: Additional Help and Information

Preface

About This Book

Drug abuse remains a growing problem in the United States. A recent National Survey on Drug Use and Health (NSDUH) found that 27 million people aged 12 or older used an illicit drug in the past 30 days, which corresponds to about 1 in 10 Americans. The higher percentage of people who were current illicit drug users in the most recent survey appears to reflect trends in marijuana use. Nonmedical pain reliever use continued to be the second most common type of illicit drug use in the most recent survey, and while the percentage of people aged 12 or older who were current nonmedical users of pain relievers (1.6 percent) was lower than the percentages in past years, it was similar to the percentage in the previous year's survey. Abuse of tobacco, alcohol, and illicit drugs costs the nation more than $700 billion annually in costs related to crime, lost work productivity and health care according to the National Institute on Drug Abuse (NIDA).

Drug Abuse Sourcebook, Fifth Edition, provides updated information about the abuse of illegal drugs and the misuse of prescription and over-the-counter medications. It offers facts and statistics related to U.S. drug-using populations and presents details about specific drugs of abuse, including their health-related consequences, addiction potential, and other harms to individuals, their families, and communities. Drug treatment and recovery options are discussed, along with information on drug testing and drug-use prevention strategies for schools and others seeking help for themselves or a loved one. The book concludes with glossaries of terms related to drug abuse and directories of resources for additional help and information.

How to Use This Book

This book is divided into parts and chapters. Parts focus on broad areas of interest. Chapters are devoted to single topics within a part.

Part I: Facts and Statistics about Drug Abuse in the United States presents core data regarding the drug abuse problem and risks pertaining to the usage of illegal substances. It details the prevalence of drug abuse and the costs to society in terms of hospitalization, and treatment outcomes. It also discusses federal regulation of prescriptions, laws pertaining to illegal and legal drugs, and the current debate over medical and legalized marijuana. Statistics on substance abuse treatment is also provided.

Part II: Drug Abuse and Specific Populations describes drug use initiation and the effects of drug abuse on various groups of people, including children, adolescents, and women. It also addresses drug abuse in workplace, and it considers drug use in inmate, veteran, senior, and disabled populations.

Part III: Drugs of Abuse provides facts about illicit and misused substances, such as performance enhancers, inhalants, hallucinogens, dissociative drugs, narcotics, sedatives, stimulants and legally available substances, including anabolic steroids, marijuana, Rohypnol, ecstasy (MDMA), LSD, heroin, hydrocodone, cocaine, methamphetamine, tobacco, and many others. The part concludes with information about new and emerging drugs of abuse.

Part IV: The Causes and Consequences of Drug Abuse and Addiction explains the science behind addiction and what is known about the risk factors that can lead to drug dependency. Concerns related to prescription and over-the-counter drug abuse and drug interactions are addressed, in addition to the health, legal, financial, and social ramifications of drug abuse. The part also looks at the connection between substance abuse and infectious diseases, and it addresses related mental health issues, including suicide ideation.

Part V: Drug Abuse Treatment and Recovery offers suggestions for recognizing the existence of a drug problem and options for taking steps toward achieving and maintaining a healthy lifestyle, including intervention and detoxification. It provides details about various treatment approaches and reports on strategies for sustaining recovery. The part also discusses the legal rights of those in recovery and concerns related to the criminal justice system.

Part VI: Drug Abuse Testing and Prevention lays the groundwork for responses to drug abuse—in society, in schools, and especially in the home. It discusses ways parents can communicate with their children regarding drug abuse, and it addresses concerns about preventing drug abuse in the workplace. Drug testing and federal drug abuse prevention campaigns are also described.

Part VII: Additional Help and Information provides resources for readers seeking further assistance. It includes a glossary of terms related to drug abuse and a listing of street terms for common drugs of abuse. It concludes with directories of state substance abuse agencies and other organizations providing resources on drug abuse and addiction.

Bibliographic Note

This volume contains documents and excerpts from publications issued by the following U.S. government agencies: Bureau of Justice Statistics (BJS); Centers for Disease Control and Prevention (CDC); Family and Youth Services Bureau (FYSB); Federal Bureau of Investigation (FBI); National Institute of Justice (NIJ); National Institutes of Health (NIH); National Institute on Drug Abuse (NIDA); Office of Disease Prevention and Health Promotion (ODPHP); Substance Abuse and Mental Health Services Administration (SAMHSA); U.S. Department of Health and Human Services (HHS); U.S. Department of Veterans Affairs (VA); U.S. Drug Enforcement Administration (DEA); U.S. Food and Drug Administration (FDA); U.S. House of Representatives; WhiteHouse.gov; and Youth.gov.

About the Health Reference Series

The *Health Reference Series* is designed to provide basic medical information for patients, families, caregivers, and the general public. Each volume takes a particular topic and provides comprehensive coverage. This is especially important for people who may be dealing with a newly diagnosed disease or a chronic disorder in themselves or in a family member. People looking for preventive guidance, information about disease warning signs, medical statistics, and risk factors for health problems will also find answers to their questions in the *Health Reference Series*. The *Series*, however, is not intended to serve as a tool for diagnosing illness, in prescribing treatments, or as a substitute for the physician/patient relationship. All people concerned about medical symptoms or the possibility of disease are encouraged to seek professional care from an appropriate health care provider.

A Note about Spelling and Style

Health Reference Series editors use *Stedman's Medical Dictionary* as an authority for questions related to the spelling of medical terms and the *Chicago Manual of Style* for questions related to grammatical structures, punctuation, and other editorial concerns. Consistent adherence is not always possible, however, because the individual volumes within the *Series* include many documents from a wide variety of different producers, and the editor's primary goal is to present material from each source as accurately as is possible. This sometimes means that information in different chapters or sections may follow other guidelines and alternate spelling authorities.

Medical Review

Omnigraphics contracts with a team of qualified, senior medical professionals who serve as medical consultants for the *Health Reference Series*. As necessary, medical consultants review reprinted and originally written material for currency and accuracy. Citations including the phrase, "Reviewed (month, year)" indicate material reviewed by this team. Medical consultation services are provided to the *Health Reference Series* editors by:

Dr. Vijayalakshmi, MBBS, DGO, MD
Dr. Senthil Selvan, MBBS, DCH, MD

Our Advisory Board

We would like to thank the following board members for providing initial guidance on the development of this series:

- Dr. Lynda Baker, Associate Professor of Library and Information Science, Wayne State University, Detroit, MI
- Nancy Bulgarelli, William Beaumont Hospital Library, Royal Oak, MI
- Karen Imarisio, Bloomfield Township Public Library, Bloomfield Township, MI

- Karen Morgan, Mardigian Library, University of Michigan-Dearborn, Dearborn, MI
- Rosemary Orlando, St. Clair Shores Public Library, St. Clair Shores, MI

Health Reference Series *Update Policy*

The inaugural book in the *Health Reference Series* was the first edition of *Cancer Sourcebook* published in 1989. Since then, the *Series* has been enthusiastically received by librarians and in the medical community. In order to maintain the standard of providing high-quality health information for the layperson the editorial staff at Omnigraphics felt it was necessary to implement a policy of updating volumes when warranted.

Medical researchers have been making tremendous strides, and it is the purpose of the *Health Reference Series* to stay current with the most recent advances. Each decision to update a volume is made on an individual basis. Some of the considerations include how much new information is available and the feedback we receive from people who use the books. If there is a topic you would like to see added to the update list, or an area of medical concern you feel has not been adequately addressed, please write to:

Managing Editor
Health Reference Series
Omnigraphics, Inc.
615 Griswold, Ste. 901
Detroit, MI 48226

Part One

Facts and Statistics about Drug Abuse in the United States

Chapter 1

Prevalence of Illicit Drug Use and Substance Abuse

Summary

This national report summarizes findings from the 2014 National Survey on Drug Use and Health (NSDUH) on trends in the behavioral health of people aged 12 years old or older in the civilian, noninstitutionalized population of the United States. Results are provided by age subgroups. Substance use trends are presented for 2002 to 2014.

Illicit Drug Use

In 2014, 27.0 million people aged 12 or older used an illicit drug in the past 30 days, which corresponds to about 1 in 10 Americans (10.2%). This percentage in 2014 was higher than those in every year from 2002 through 2013. The illicit drug use estimate for 2014 continues to be driven primarily by marijuana use and the nonmedical use of prescription pain relievers, with 22.2 million current marijuana users aged 12 or older (i.e., users in the past 30 days) and 4.3 million people

---

This chapter contains text excerpted from the following sources: Text beginning with the heading "Summary" is excerpted from "Behavioral Health Trends in the United States: Results from the 2014 National Survey on Drug Use and Health," Substance Abuse and Mental Health Services Administration (SAMHSA), September 2015; Text beginning with the heading "Consequences of Illicit Drug Use in America" is excerpted from "Consequences of Illicit Drug Use in America," WhiteHouse.gov, April 2014.

aged 12 or older who reported current nonmedical use of prescription pain relievers.

The higher percentage of people who were current illicit drug users in 2014 than in prior years appears to reflect trends in marijuana use. The percentage of people aged 12 or older in 2014 who were current marijuana users (8.4 percent) also was greater than the percentages in 2002 to 2013. In addition, the estimate of current marijuana use was greater in 2014 than the estimates in 2002 to 2009 for young adults aged 18 to 25 and in 2002 to 2013 for adults aged 26 or older.

Although nonmedical pain reliever use continued to be the second most common type of illicit drug use in 2014, the percentage of people aged 12 or older in 2014 who were current nonmedical users of pain relievers (1.6 percent) was lower than the percentages in most years from 2002 to 2012, but it was similar to the percentage in 2013. Percentages for current nonmedical use of pain relievers also were lower in 2014 than in 2002 to 2011 for adolescents aged 12 to 17 and in 2002 to 2012 for young adults aged 18 to 25.

The use of many types of other illicit drugs has not increased in recent years. However, the percentage of people aged 12 or older in 2014 who were current heroin users was higher than the percentages in most years from 2002 to 2013.

Tobacco Use

In 2014, an estimated 66.9 million people aged 12 or older were current users of a tobacco product, including 55.2 million cigarette smokers. Across all age groups, tobacco use and cigarette use were lower in 2014 than in most years from 2002 to 2013. For example, about 1 in 8 adolescents aged 12 to 17 (13.0%) were current cigarette smokers in 2002. By 2014, about 1 in 20 adolescents (4.9%) were current smokers.

Alcohol Use

There were 139.7 million past month alcohol drinkers aged 12 or older in 2014, including 60.9 million who were binge alcohol users and 16.3 million who were heavy alcohol users. In 2014, the percentage of people aged 12 or older who were past month alcohol users (52.7%) was similar to the percentages in 2009 through 2013. The percentage of people aged 12 or older in 2014 who were past month heavy alcohol users (6.2%) also was similar to the percentages in 2011 through 2013. However, estimates of binge drinking among people aged 12 or older did not change over the period from 2002 to 2014 (23.0 percent in 2014).

Underage alcohol use (i.e., among people aged 12 to 20) and binge and heavy use among young adults aged 18 to 25 have declined over time but remain a concern. In 2014, 22.8 percent of underage people were current alcohol users, 13.8 percent were binge alcohol users, and 3.4 percent were heavy alcohol users. These percentages were lower than the percentages in 2002 to 2012, but they were similar to the percentages in 2013. Among young adults aged 18 to 25, the percentages who were binge or heavy alcohol users in 2014 were lower than those in 2002 to 2012. Nevertheless, more than one third of young adults in 2014 were binge alcohol users (37.7%), and about 1 in 10 were heavy alcohol users (10.8%).

Substance Use Disorders

Approximately 21.5 million people aged 12 or older in 2014 had a substance use disorder (SUD) in the past year, including 17.0 million people with an alcohol use disorder, 7.1 million with an illicit drug use disorder, and 2.6 million who had both an alcohol use and an illicit drug use disorder. The percentage of people aged 12 or older in 2014 who had an SUD (8.1%) was similar to the percentages in 2011 to 2013, but it was lower than those in 2002 through 2010. Percentages of adolescents aged 12 to 17 and young adults aged 18 to 25 who had an alcohol use disorder, marijuana use disorder, or pain reliever use disorder in 2014 were lower than the percentages in several or all years from 2002 to 2012.

Consequences of Illicit Drug Use in America

Drug Deaths

- According to the Centers for Disease Control and Prevention, 40,393 people died of drug-induced causes in 2010, the latest year for which data are available. The number of drug-induced deaths has grown from 19,128 in 1999, or from 6.8 deaths per 100,000 population to 12.9 in 2010. (These include causes directly involving drugs, such as accidental poisoning or overdoses, but do not include accidents, homicides, AIDS, and other causes indirectly related to drugs.)
- There is a drug-induced death in the United States every 13 minutes.
- Compared to other causes of preventable deaths, drug-induced causes exceeded the 31,328 deaths from injuries due to firearms and the 25,692 alcohol-induced deaths recorded in 2010. In the

same year, 38,364 deaths were classified as suicides and 16,259 deaths as homicides.

Drugged Driving

- From a national roadside survey in 2007, one in eight (12.4%) of weekend night time drivers tested positive for at least one illicit drug.
- Based on a self-report survey in 2012, approximately 10.2 million Americans aged 16 or older reported driving under the influence of an illicit drug.
- In 2012, more than one in three drivers (38%) killed in motor vehicle crashes who were tested for drugs and the results known, tested positive for at least one medication or illicit drug.
- Among high school seniors in 2013, one in 9 (11.7%) reported that in the two weeks prior to their interview, they had driven a vehicle after smoking marijuana.

Children

Annual averages for 2002 to 2007 indicate that over 8.3 million youth under 18 years of age, or almost one in eight youth (11.9%), lived with at least one parent who was dependent on alcohol or an illicit drug in the past year. Of these, About 2.1 million youth lived with a parent who was dependent on or abused illicit drugs, and almost 7.3 million lived with a parent who was dependent on or abused alcohol.

School Performance

- Among youth in school who reported an average grade of "D" or worse, one in four were current marijuana users, whereas fewer than one in ten (9.1%) of those who reported an average grade better than "D" were current marijuana users.
- College students who use prescription stimulant medications non-medically typically have lower grade point averages, are more likely to be heavy drinkers and users of other illicit drugs, and are more likely to meet diagnostic criteria for dependence on alcohol and marijuana, skip class more frequently, and spend less time studying.

Economic Costs

The economic cost of drug abuse in the United States was estimated at $193 billion in 2007, the last available estimate. This value represents both the use of resources to address health and crime consequences as well as the loss of potential productivity from disability, premature death, and withdrawal from the legitimate workforce.

Addiction and Treatment

- In 2012, 23.1 million persons aged 12 or older needed treatment for an illicit drug or alcohol use problem (8.9 percent of persons in that age group). Of these, 8.0 million persons (or 3.1%) needed treatment for illicit drug problems, with or without alcohol.
- Of the 23.5 million persons needing substance use treatment, 2.5 million received treatment at a specialty facility in the past year, and of the 8.0 million needing drug treatment, 1.5 million received specialty treatment.
- Over the past 10 years, there have been approximately one million drug treatment admissions recorded annually. Treatment admissions with opioids as the primary drug are the largest component. Treatment for heroin has been approximately 25 percent of drug treatment admissions annually over the past 10 years. Treatment admissions for non-heroin opioids such as prescription painkillers, has risen from under 5% in 2002 to over 15% by 2011.

Acute Health Effects

In 2011, an estimated 2.5 million visits to emergency departments in US hospitals were associated with drug misuse or abuse, including over 1.3 million (1,252,500) visits involving an illicit drug. Nonmedical use of pharmaceuticals was involved in over 1.4 million ED visits. Cocaine was involved in 505,224 visits, marijuana was involved in 455,668 visits, heroin was involved in 258,482 visits, and stimulants (including amphetamines and methamphetamine) were involved in 159,840 visits.

Criminal Justice Involvement

- According to a 2013 study of arrestees in 5 major metropolitan areas across the country, drug use among the arrestee population is much higher than in the general United States population. The percentage of booked arrestees testing positive for at least one illicit drug ranged from 63% to 83%. The most common substances present during tests, in descending order, are marijuana, cocaine, opiates (primarily metabolites of heroin or morphine), and methamphetamine. Many arrestees tested positive for more than one illegal drug at the time of arrest. Similar results were found in earlier studies conducted in additional locations across the country.

- According to a 2004 survey of inmates in correctional facilities, 32 percent of state inmates and 26 percent of federal prisoners reported that they used drugs at the time of the offense.

Environmental Impact and Dangers

- There are significant environmental impacts from clandestine methamphetamine drug labs, including chemical toxicity, risk of fire and explosion, lingering effects of toxic waste, and potential injuries. The number of domestic meth lab incidents, which includes dumpsites, active labs, and chemical/glassware set-ups, dropped dramatically in response to the Combat Meth Epidemic Act, (CMEA) of 2005, from nearly 24,000 in 2005 to nearly 7,000 in 2007. However, traffickers are devising methods to avoid the CMEA restrictions and domestic meth lab incidents are rising again, reaching 912,700 in 2012.
- Coca and poppy cultivation in the Andean jungle is significantly damaging the environment in the region. The primary threats to the environment are deforestation caused by clearing the fields for cultivation, soil erosion, and chemical pollution from insecticides and fertilizers. Additionally, the lab process of converting coca and poppy into cocaine and heroin has adverse effects on the environment.
- Mexican drug trafficking organizations have been operating on public lands in the United States to cultivate marijuana, with serious consequences for the environment and public safety. Propane tanks and other trash from illicit marijuana growers litter the remote areas of park lands from California to Tennessee. Growers often use a cocktail of pesticides and fertilizers many times stronger than what is used on residential lawns to cultivate their crop. These chemicals leach out quickly, killing native

insects and other organisms directly. Fertilizer runoff contaminates local waterways and aids in the growth of algae and weeds. The aquatic vegetation in turn impedes water flows that are critical to maintaining biodiversity in wetlands and other sensitive environments.

Chapter 2

Injection Drug Use and Related Risk Behaviors

Injected Drugs and HIV Risks

Injected drugs are drugs that are introduced into the bloodstream using a needle and syringe. Sharing drug preparation or injecting equipment ("works") can expose you to HIV-infected blood. If you share works with someone who is HIV-positive, that person's blood can stay on needles or spread to the drug solution.

In that case, you can inject HIV directly into your body

- Using blood-contaminated syringes to prepare drugs
- Reusing bottle caps, spoons, or other containers ("cookers") to dissolve drugs into water and to heat drugs solutions.
- Reusing water.
- Reusing small pieces of cotton or cigarette filters ("cottons") to filter out particles that could block the needle

---

This chapter contains text excerpted from the following sources: Text beginning with the heading "Injected Drugs and HIV Risks" is excerpted from "Substance Abuse/Use," U.S. Department of Health and Human Services (HHS), January 14, 2014; Text under the heading "Why Does Heroin Use Create Special Risk for Contracting HIV/AIDS and Hepatitis B and C?" is excerpted from "Heroin," National Institute on Drug Abuse (NIDA), November 2014; Text under the heading "Frequently Asked Questions" is excerpted from "Substance Abuse/Use," U.S. Department of Health and Human Services (HHS), January 14, 2014.

"Street sellers" of syringes may repackage used syringes and sell them as sterile syringes. For this reason, people who inject drugs should get syringes from reliable sources of sterile syringes, such as pharmacies or needle-exchange programs.

It is important to know that sharing a needle or syringe for any use, including skin popping and injecting steroids, hormones, or silicone, can put you at risk for HIV and other blood-borne infections.

How Can I Reduce My Risk of HIV Infection?

If you are injecting drugs and believe you cannot stop using yet, here are some other things that will reduce your risk of getting HIV or transmitting it to others:

- Never use or "share" syringes (needles), water, "works," or drug preparation equipment that has already been used by someone else.
- Use a new, sterile syringe each time you prepare and inject drugs. You can get clean needles from pharmacies or syringe services programs (often also called needle-exchange programs).
- Only use syringes that come from a reliable source (e.g., pharmacies or syringe exchange programs).
- Use sterile water to prepare drugs, such as water that has been boiled for 5 minutes or clean water from a reliable source (such as fresh tap water).
- Use a new or disinfected container ("cooker") and a new filter ("cotton") each time you prepare drugs.
- Before you inject, clean the injection site with a new alcohol swab.
- Safely dispose of syringes after one use.

Also, if you engage in sexual activity, reduce your sexual risk factors for HIV infection.

The Importance of HIV Testing for People Who Use Drugs

The Centers for Disease Control and Prevention (CDC) and the U.S. Preventive Services Task Force recommend that people who inject drugs or engage in other behaviors that put them at increased risk get tested for HIV at least once every year. (CDC also recommends that sexual partners of those who inject drugs also get tested at least once per year.)

Why Does Heroin Use Create Special Risk for Contracting HIV/AIDS and Hepatitis B and C?

Heroin use increases the risk of being exposed to HIV, viral hepatitis, and other infectious agents through contact with infected blood or body fluids (e.g., semen, saliva) that results from the sharing of syringes and injection paraphernalia that have been used by infected individuals or through unprotected sexual contact with an infected person. Snorting or smoking does not eliminate the risk of infectious disease like hepatitis and HIV/AIDS because people under the influence of drugs still engage in risky sexual and other behaviors that can expose them to these diseases.

Injection drug users (IDUs) are the highest-risk group for acquiring hepatitis C (HCV) infection and continue to drive the escalating HCV epidemic: Each IDU infected with HCV is likely to infect 20 other people. Of the 17,000 new HCV infections occurring in the United States in 2010, over half (53%) were among IDUs. Hepatitis B (HBV) infection in IDUs was reported to be as high as 20 percent in the United States in 2010, which is particularly disheartening since an effective vaccine that protects against HBV infection is available. There is currently no vaccine available to protect against HCV infection.

Drug use, viral hepatitis and other infectious diseases, mental illnesses, social dysfunctions, and stigma are often co-occuring conditions that affect one another, creating more complex health challenges that require comprehensive treatment plans tailored to meet all of a patient's needs. For example, NIDA-funded research has found that drug abuse treatment along with HIV prevention and community-based outreach programs can help people who use drugs change the behaviors that put them at risk for contracting HIV and other infectious diseases. They can reduce drug use and drug-related risk behaviors such as needle sharing and unsafe sexual practices and, in turn, reduce the risk of exposure to HIV/AIDS and other infectious diseases. Only through coordinated utilization of effective antiviral therapies coupled with treatment for drug abuse and mental illness can the health of those suffering from these conditions be restored.

Frequently Asked Questions

Can I Get HIV from Sharing Needles or Drug Equipment?

Yes. Used needles and equipment (or "works") can have HIV-infected blood on or inside them. If they do, you put that blood—and possibly HIV—directly into your body when you use them to inject or prepare your drugs. Only sterile equipment carries no risk of HIV contamination. If you inject drugs, (including steroids, insulin, etc.) don't share used needles or equipment with anyone.

Where Can I Go to Find Drug Treatment or Rehab?

You can use the HIV/AIDS Prevention and Services (www.//locator.aids.gov) to find a substance abuse treatment facility, as well as HIV testing sites and other services.

If I'm Not Ready to Quit, How Can I Protect Myself from HIV?

Quitting or getting into rehab is the best way to reduce your drug-related risk of getting HIV. But if you're not ready to quit, you can at least protect yourself and others from HIV and other diseases by using clean equipment if you inject drugs. Syringe services programs let you turn in your used needles and equipment for clean ones. They can also give you information on where you can get help to quit drugs. To find a needle exchange or syringe services program near you, use the Harm Reduction Coalition's Interactive Harm Reduction Resources Locator. Even though some service organizations provide syringe services, it may not be legal in a particular jurisdiction so be sure to check before participating in the program.

Do Syringe Services Programs Increase Drug Use?

No. National and international studies show that syringe services programs **do not** increase drug use. The research also shows that syringe services programs are very effective in decreasing blood-borne illnesses (like HIV and hepatitis) among injection drug users when they are included as part of medical and substance abuse treatment and prevention services. Syringe services programs protect injection drug users' sexual partners or children, who could otherwise be at risk for HIV infection. These programs also serve as important doorways to health information, treatment, and rehab. Because of the overwhelming evidence that they do not increase drug use and because of their clear effectiveness in decreasing HIV and other diseases.

Chapter 3

Drug Abuse and Related Hospitalization Costs

Chapter Contents

Section 3.1

Substance Abuse Cost to Society

This section contains text excerpted from the following sources: Text under the heading "Costs of Substance Abuse" is excerpted from "Trends and Statistics," National Institute on Drug Abuse (NIDA), August 2015; Text beginning with the heading "Excessive Drinking Costs" is excerpted from "Excessive Drinking Costs U.S. $223.5 Billion," Centers for Disease Control and Prevention (CDC), April 17, 2014; Text under the heading "Alcohol Misuse" is excerpted from "Workplace Health Promotion," Centers for Disease Control and Prevention (CDC), October 23, 2013.

Costs of Substance Abuse

Abuse of tobacco, alcohol, and illicit drugs is costly to our Nation, exacting more than $700 billion annually in costs related to crime, lost work productivity and health care.

Table 3.1. Costs of Substance Abuse

	Health Care	Overall
Tobacco	$130 billion	$295 billion
Alcohol	$25 billion	$224 billion
Illicit Drugs	$11 billion	$193 billion

Excessive Drinking Costs

Excessive alcohol consumption is known to kill about 88,000 people in the United States each year, but a study released by the CDC and The Lewin Group shows that it has a huge impact on our wallets as well.

The cost of excessive alcohol consumption in the United States reached **$223.5 billion** in 2006 or about **$1.90 per drink**. Almost three-quarters of these costs were due to **binge drinking**. Binge drinking is defined as consuming four or more alcoholic beverages per occasion for women or five or more drinks per occasion for men, and is the most common form of excessive alcohol consumption in the United States.

The researchers found that the cost of excessive drinking was quite far-reaching, reflecting the effect this dangerous behavior has on many aspects of the drinker's life and on the lives of those around them. The costs largely resulted from losses in **workplace productivity** (72% of the total cost), **healthcare** expenses for problems caused by excessive drinking (11% of total), law enforcement and other **criminal justice** expenses related to excessive alcohol consumption (9% of total), and **motor vehicle crash** costs from impaired driving (6% of the total).

The study analyzed national data from multiple sources to estimate the costs due to excessive drinking in 2006, the most recent year for which data were available. The study did not consider a number of other costs such as those because of pain and suffering among either the excessive drinker or others that were affected by their drinking, and thus may be an underestimate. Nevertheless, the researchers estimated that excessive drinking cost **$746 for every man, woman**, and **child** in the United States in 2006.

What You Need to Know about Binge Drinking?

- Binge drinking is reported by about 18% of U.S. adults.
- Binge drinking is most common among men, 18-to 34-year-olds, white people, and people with household incomes of $75,000 or more.
- Most binge drinkers are not alcohol dependent.

How Can We Prevent Excessive Alcohol Consumption and Reduce Its Economic Costs?

Communities can use evidence-based strategies, such as those recommended by the Community Preventive Services Task Force to prevent excessive drinking. These include:

- Increasing alcohol excise taxes.
- Reducing alcohol outlet density.
- Reducing the days and hours of alcohol sales.
- Holding alcohol retailers liable for injuries or damage done by their intoxicated or underage customers.

By implementing these evidence-based strategies, we can reduce excessive alcohol consumption and the many health and social costs related to it.

Alcohol Misuse

Alcohol misuse can result in a number of adverse health and social consequences.

- More than 700,000 Americans receive alcoholism treatment every day, but there is growing recognition that alcoholism (i.e., alcohol dependence or addition) represents only one end of the spectrum of "alcohol misuse"
- There are approximately 79,000 deaths attributable to excessive alcohol use each year in the United States

Many problem drinkers have medical or social problems attributable to alcohol (i.e., alcohol misuse or "excessive drinking") without typical signs of dependence, and other drinkers are at risk for future problems due to chronic alcohol consumption or frequent binges. Non-dependent drinkers who misuse alcohol account for the majority of alcohol-related disability and death in the general population.

Alcohol misuse is associated with high costs to employers including absenteeism, decreased productivity (due to poor work performance), turnover, accidents, and increased healthcare costs.

- The cost of alcohol misuse in the United States was estimated to be $185 billion in 1998. About $16 billion of this amount was spent on medical care for alcohol-related complications (not including fetal alcohol syndrome [FAS]), $7.5 billion was spent on specialty alcohol treatment services, and $2.9 billion was spent on FAS treatment. The remaining costs ($134 billion) were due to lost productivity. Lost productivity due to alcohol-related deaths and disabilities impose a greater economic burden than do healthcare costs
- Over 15% of U.S. workers report being impaired by alcohol at work at least one time during the past year, and 9% of workers reported being hung-over at work

Section 3.2

Drug-Related Hospital Emergency Room Visits

This section includes text excerpted from "Highlights of the 2011 Drug Abuse Warning Network (DAWN) Findings on Drug-Related Emergency Department Visits," Substance Abuse and Mental Health Services Administration (SAMHSA), February 22, 2013.

Overview

In 2011, there were 5.1 million drug-related ED visits About one half (49%, or 2.5 million visits) were attributed to drug misuse or abuse with a nearly equal number (45%, or 2.3 million visits) attributed to adverse drug reactions. Among visits involving drug misuse or abuse, 1.4 million visits involved pharmaceuticals, and 1.3 million involved illicit drugs. Visits involving use of illicit drugs were relatively stable from 2004 (991,640 visits) to 2009 (974, 392 visits) but increased from 2009 to 2011 (1,252,500 visits). The trend in visits involving misuse or abuse of pharmaceuticals displayed a steady upward climb from 2004 (626,470 visits) through 2011 (1,428,145 visits). Visits involving adverse reactions to drugs increased from 1,250,377 visits in 2005 to 2,287,271 visits in 2009; however, no increases occurred between 2009 and 2011 (2,301,059 visits).

Patient Demographics and Visit Characteristics

Slightly more than 80 percent of drug-related ED visits were made by adults aged 21 or older, 48 percent were male, 24 percent resulted in the patient being admitted to the hospital, and 66 percent involved a single drug. Among visits involving misuse or abuse of drugs, 82 percent were made by adults aged 21 or older, 56 percent were made by males, 25 percent resulted in the patient being admitted to the hospital, and 51 percent involved a single drug. Visits for adverse reactions typically involved a single drug (82%), and one fifth of patients were admitted to the hospital (21%). Visits for accidental ingestions typically involved patients aged 20 or younger, the majority (86%)

involved a single drug, and a small portion (10%) were admitted to the hospital.

Visits Involving Illicit Drugs

In 2011, there were 402.0 ED visits per 100,000 population involving illicit drugs. The most commonly involved drug was cocaine, with 162.1 visits per 100,000 population. This was closely followed by marijuana, which was involved in 146.2 visits per 100,000 population. Other drugs had lower rates: heroin (83.0 visits per 100,000 population), illicit stimulants (predominately amphetamines and methamphetamine; 51.3 visits per 100,000 population), and other illicit drugs (predominately PCP and various hallucinogens; 42.1 visits per 100,000 population).

Trends

ED visits involving use of illicit drugs were relatively stable from 2004 (991,640 visits) to 2009 (974,392 visits) but increased from 2009 to 2011 (1,252,500 visits). Between 2009 and 2011, the rate of visits involving illicit stimulants increased 68 percent, the rate of visits involving other illicit drugs (e.g., PCP, hallucinogens) rose 60 percent, and the rate of visits involving marijuana rose 19 percent. Cocaine and heroin involvement changed in neither the long term from 2004 to 2011 nor the short term from 2009 to 2011.

Age

Figure 3.1. depicts the rates of ED visits per 100,000 population for the major illicit drug categories among patients aged 12 to 17, aged 18 to 20, and aged 21 to 24. Rates of visits for heroin, cocaine, and illicit stimulants rose for each successively older age group. Visits involving marijuana were less common among patients aged 12 to 17 (240.2 visits per 100,000 population) compared with the older age groups, but there was no difference between those aged 18 to 20 (443.8 visits per 100,000 population) and those aged 21 to 24 (446.9 visits per 100,000 population).

Visits Involving Synthetic Cannabinoids

Synthetic cannabinoids first appeared in DAWN records in 2009, but there were too few visits to be reported. By 2010, ED visits involving synthetic cannabinoids rose to a reportable level for the Nation

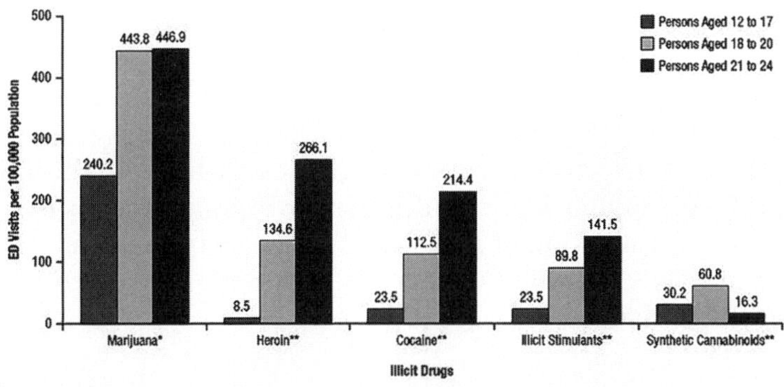

* The differences between those aged 12 to 17 and the two older age groups were statistically significant at the .05 level.
**All differences between age groups were statistically significant at the .05 level.
Source: 2011 SAMHSA Drug Abuse Warning Network (DAWN).

Figure 3.1. *Rates of Emergency Department Visits Involving Illicit Drugs among Patients Aged 12 to 24 per 100,000 Population, by Age Group: 2011*

(3.7 visits per 100,000 population). By 2011, there were 9.2 visits per 100,000 population involving synthetic cannabinoids across all age groups—about a 150 percent increase (data not shown). The rate of visits involving synthetic cannabinoids was highest among patients aged 18 to 20 (60.8 visits per 100,000 population), followed by patients aged 12 to 17 (30.2 visits per 100,000 population).

Visits Involving Misuse or Abuse of Pharmaceuticals

In 2011, there were 458.3 ED visits per 100,000 population involving misuse or abuse of pharmaceuticals. The most commonly involved drugs were anti-anxiety and insomnia medications (160.9 visits per 100,000 population) and narcotic pain relievers (134.8 visits per 100,000 population).

Among visits involving anti-anxiety and insomnia medications, alprazolam (e.g., Xanax®) was the most common at 49.4 visits per 100,000 population, followed by clonazepam (e.g., Klonopin®) at 24.6 visits, lorazepam (e.g., Ativan®) at 16.2 visits, and zolpidem (e.g., Ambien®) at 11.9 visits. Oxycodone products were the narcotic pain relievers most commonly involved in ED visits (175,229 visits, or 56.2 visits per 100,000 population). Involvement of hydrocodone, methadone, and morphine products followed oxycodone with 31.2, 24.3, and 12.3 visits per 100,000 population, respectively. Narcotic pain relievers and anti-anxiety and insomnia medications are often not specifically identified by drug or brand name in the ED records, so the actual involvement of specific drugs is likely higher than reported here.

Other types of drugs with measurable involvement included antidepressants (34.8 visits per 100,000 population) and antipsychotics (24.5 visits per 100,000 population). Drug classes with fewer than 20 visits per 100,000 population included cardiovascular medications (17.8 visits), muscle relaxants (17.0 visits), respiratory medications (15.0 visits), and central nervous system (CNS) stimulants (e.g., Adderall®, Ritalin®; 14.5 visits).

Trends

The rate of ED visits involving misuse or abuse of pharmaceuticals increased 114 percent from 214.0 visits per 100,000 population in 2004 to 458.3 visits per 100,000 population in 2011. CNS stimulants experienced the largest change in involvement with a 292 percent increase. The rate of visits involving anti-anxiety and insomnia medications increased 124 percent. Other drug groups experiencing lower increases included respiratory medications (76%), antipsychotics (71%), muscle relaxants (71%), cardiovascular medications (63%), and anticonvulsants (51%). An exception to the general upward trend occurred for visits involving antidepressants, where involvement remained stable from 2004 to 2011.

In respect to shorter term trends between 2009 and 2011, overall involvement of pharmaceuticals increased by about 13 percent. Only two drug groups showed significant increases from 2009 to 2011: visits involving anti-anxiety and insomnia medications increased 14 percent overall (although no single drug had a significant increase), and visits involving CNS stimulants increased 78 percent.

Age

Figure 3.2. depicts the rates of ED visits per 100,000 population for the major pharmaceutical drugs among patients aged 12 to 17, aged 18 to 20, and aged 21 to 24 in 2011. Rates of visits for narcotic pain relievers and anti-anxiety and insomnia medications rose for each successively older age group. The rate of visits involving CNS stimulants for those aged 12 to 17 was similar to that for those aged 18 to 20 but lower than the rate for those aged 21 to 24. Visits involving antipsychotics were less common among patients aged 12 to 17 than among patients in older age groups, but there was no difference between the two older age groups.

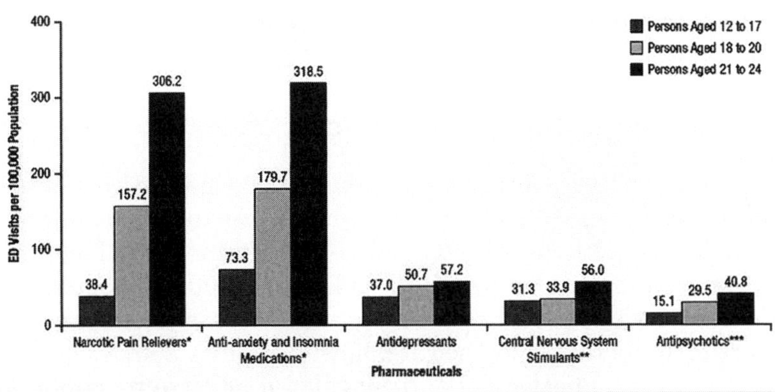

* All differences between age groups were statistically significant at the .05 level.
** The difference between patients aged 12 to 17 and those aged 21 to 24 was statistically significant at the .05 level.
*** The differences between patients age 12 to 17 and the two older age groups were statistically significant at the .05 level.
Source: 2011 SAMHSA Drug Abuse Warning Network (DAWN).

Figure 3.2. *Rates of Emergency Department Visits Involving Misuse or Abuse of Pharmaceuticals among Patients Aged 12 to 24 per 100,000 Population, by Age Group: 2011*

Visits Involving Alcohol

Involvement of alcohol is documented for all ED visits that also involve pharmaceuticals or illicit drugs. Also, because alcohol is considered an illicit drug for minors, visits involving "alcohol only" are included in DAWN for those aged 20 or younger. For the population aged 20 or younger, the rate of ED visits involving alcohol (with or without other drugs) is 215.8 visits per 100,000 population. The majority of those visits involved alcohol only (134.6 visits per 100,000 population). The rate of visits involving alcohol and other drugs was 238.9 visits per 100,000 population for patients aged 21 or older and 81.3 visits per 100,000 population for patients younger than 21. There have been no long-or short-term changes in the rate of visits involving drugs in combination with alcohol, or in visits for alcohol only (for those aged 20 or younger).

Visits Involving Accidental Ingestion of Drugs

ED visits involving accidental ingestion of drugs are most common among children aged 5 or younger, for whom the rate was 317.8 visits per 100,000 population in 2011. In the long term, this represents a 49 percent increase over visits occurring in 2004 (213.9 ED visits per 100,000 population). Involvement of narcotic pain relievers and anti-anxiety and insomnia medications increased from 2004 to

2011(data not shown). No significant increases occurred from 2009 to 2011.

Visits Involving Adverse Reactions to Drugs

ED visits involving adverse reactions to pharmaceuticals taken as prescribed or indicated increased 84 percent between 2005 and 2011, from 1,250,377 visits in 2005 to 2,301,059 visits in 2011. The rate for adverse reactions ranged from 423.1 visits per 100,000 population in 2005 to 738.5 visits in 2011—a 75 percent increase. There have been no short-term increases in the rate, however, since 2009.

In 2011, the highest rates of drug-related adverse reactions were found among patients aged 65 or older, with 1,525.8 visits per 100,000 population (data not shown). Cardiovascular medications are often involved in adverse reactions for patients aged 65 or older (273.1 visits per 100,000 population). Other common drugs for older adults were anticoagulants (215.9 visits per 100,000 population aged 65 or older), drugs to treat infections (225.5 visits), narcotic pain relievers (135.8 visits), drugs to treat diabetes (128.9 visits), and cancer drugs (128.8 visits). Visits involving anticoagulants, narcotic pain relievers, and diabetes drugs decreased (ranging from 19 to 38 percent decreases) from 2009 to 2011.

Section 3.3

Deaths from Drug Overdoses

This section includes text excerpted from "Increases in Drug and Opioid Overdose Deaths—United States, 2000–2014," Centers for Disease Control and Prevention (CDC), January 1, 2016.

Increases in Drug and Opioid Overdose Deaths—United States, 2000–2014

The United States is experiencing an epidemic of drug overdose (poisoning) deaths. Since 2000, the rate of deaths from drug overdoses has increased 137%, including a 200% increase in the rate of overdose deaths involving opioids (opioid pain relievers and heroin). CDC analyzed recent multiple cause-of-death mortality data to examine current trends and characteristics of drug overdose deaths, including the types of opioids associated with drug overdose deaths.

During 2014, a total of 47,055 drug overdose deaths occurred in the United States, representing a 1-year increase of 6.5%, from 13.8 per 100,000 persons in 2013 to 14.7 per 100,000 persons in 2014. The rate of drug overdose deaths increased significantly for both sexes, persons aged 25–44 years and ≥55 years, non-Hispanic whites and non-Hispanic blacks, and in the Northeastern, Midwestern, and Southern regions of the United States. Rates of opioid overdose deaths also increased significantly, from 7.9 per 100,000 in 2013 to 9.0 per 100,000 in 2014, a 14% increase.

Historically, CDC has programmatically characterized all opioid pain reliever deaths (natural and semisynthetic opioids, methadone, and other synthetic opioids) as "prescription" opioid overdoses. Between 2013 and 2014, the age-adjusted rate of death involving methadone remained unchanged; however, the age-adjusted rate of death involving natural and semisynthetic opioid pain relievers, heroin, and synthetic opioids, other than methadone (e.g., fentanyl) increased 9%, 26%, and 80%, respectively. The sharp increase in deaths involving synthetic opioids, other than methadone, in 2014 coincided with law enforcement reports of increased availability of illicitly manufactured fentanyl, a synthetic opioid; however, illicitly manufactured fentanyl cannot be distinguished from prescription fentanyl in death certificate data. These findings indicate that the opioid overdose epidemic is worsening. There is a need for continued action to prevent opioid abuse, dependence, and death, improve treatment capacity for opioid use disorders, and reduce the supply of illicit opioids, particularly heroin and illicit fentanyl.

The National Vital Statistics System multiple cause-of-death mortality files were used to identify drug overdose deaths. Drug overdose deaths were classified using the *International Classification of Disease, Tenth Revision* (ICD-10), based on the ICD-10 underlying cause-of-death codes X40–44 (unintentional), X60–64 (suicide), X85 (homicide), or Y10–Y14 (undetermined intent). Among the deaths with drug overdose as the underlying cause, the type of opioid involved is indicated by the following ICD-10 multiple cause-of-death codes: opioids (T40.0, T40.1, T40.2, T40.3, T40.4, or T40.6); natural and semisynthetic opioids (T40.2); methadone (T40.3); synthetic opioids, other than methadone (T40.4); and heroin (T40.1). Some deaths involve more than one type of opioid; these deaths were included in the rates for each category (e.g., a death involving both a synthetic opioid and heroin would be included in the rates for synthetic opioid deaths and in the rates for heroin deaths). Age-adjusted death rates were calculated by applying age-specific death rates to the 2000 U.S standard population age distribution. Significance testing was based on the z-test at a significance level of 0.05.

During 2014, 47,055 drug overdose deaths occurred in the United States. Since 2000, the age-adjusted drug overdose death rate has more than doubled, from 6.2 per 100,000 persons in 2000 to 14.7 per 100,000 in 2014. The overall number and rate of drug overdose deaths increased significantly from 2013 to 2014, with an additional 3,073 deaths occurring in 2014, resulting in a 6.5% increase in the age-adjusted rate. From 2013 to 2014, statistically significant increases in drug overdose death rates were seen for both males and females, persons aged 25–34 years, 35–44 years, 55–64 years, and ≥65 years; non-Hispanic whites and non-Hispanic blacks; and residents in the Northeast, Midwest and South Census Regions.

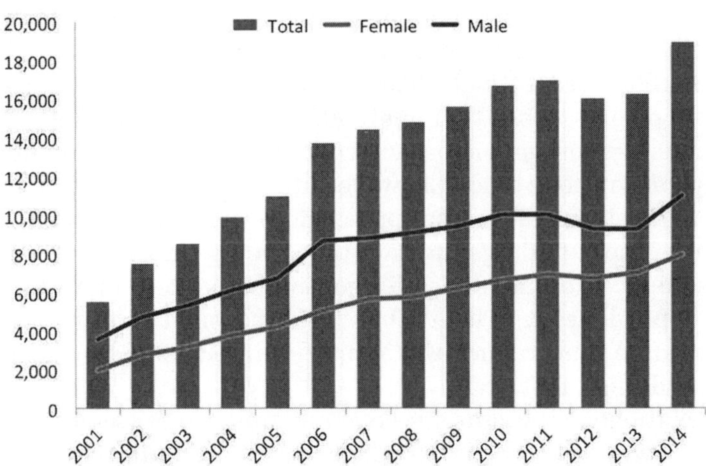

Figure 3.3. *National Overdose Deaths—Number of Deaths from Prescription Opioid Pain Relievers.*

In 2014, the five states with the highest rates of drug overdose deaths were West Virginia (35.5 deaths per 100,000), New Mexico (27.3), New Hampshire (26.2), Kentucky (24.7) and Ohio (24.6). States with statistically significant increases in the rate of drug overdose deaths from 2013 to 2014 included Alabama, Georgia, Illinois, Indiana, Maine, Maryland, Massachusetts, Michigan,

New Hampshire, New Mexico, North Dakota, Ohio, Pennsylvania, and Virginia.

In 2014, 61% (28,647, data not shown) of drug overdose deaths involved some type of opioid, including heroin. The age-adjusted rate of drug overdose deaths involving opioids increased significantly from 2000 to 2014, increasing 14% from 2013 (7.9 per 100,000) to 2014 (9.0). From 2013 to 2014, the largest increase in the rate of drug overdose deaths involved synthetic opioids, other than methadone (e.g., fentanyl and tramadol), which nearly doubled from 1.0 per 100,000 to 1.8 per 100,000. Heroin overdose death rates increased by 26% from 2013 to 2014 and have more than tripled since 2010, from 1.0 per 100,000 in 2010 to 3.4 per 100,000 in 2014. In 2014, the rate of drug overdose deaths involving natural and semisynthetic opioids (e.g., morphine, oxycodone, and hydrocodone), 3.8 per 100,000, was the highest among opioid overdose deaths, and increased 9% from 3.5 per 100,000 in 2013. The rate of drug overdose deaths involving methadone, a synthetic opioid classified separately from other synthetic opioids, was similar in 2013 and 2014.

Chapter 4

Understanding the Legal Use of Controlled Substances

Chapter Contents

Section 4.1

Schedule Classifications for Controlled Substances

This section includes text excerpted from "Drugs of Abuse," U.S. Drug Enforcement Administration (DEA), September 4, 2015.

Schedule Classifications for Controlled Substances

Whether the substance is an immediate precursor of a substance already controlled. The CSA allows inclusion of immediate precursors on this basis alone into the appropriate schedule and thus safeguards against possibilities of clandestine manufacture. After considering the above listed factors, the Administrator must make specific findings concerning the drug or other substance. This will determine into which schedule the drug or other substance will be placed.

These schedules are established by the CSA. They are as follows:

Schedule I

- The drug or other substance has a high potential for abuse.
- The drug or other substance has no currently accepted medical use in treatment in the United States.
- There is a lack of accepted safety for use of the drug or other substance under medical supervision.
- Examples of Schedule I substances include heroin, gamma hydroxybutyric acid (GHB), lysergic acid diethylamide (LSD), marijuana, and methaqualone.

Schedule II

- The drug or other substance has a high potential for abuse.
- The drug or other substance has a currently accepted medical use in treatment in the United States or a currently accepted medical use with severe restrictions.

- Abuse of the drug or other substance may lead to severe psychological or physical dependence.
- Examples of Schedule II substances include morphine, phencyclidine (PCP), codeine, methadone, hydrocodone, fentanyl, and methamphetamine.

Schedule III

- The drug or other substance has less potential for abuse than the drugs or other substances in Schedules I and II.
- The drug or other substance has a currently accepted medical use in treatment in the United States.
- Abuse of the drug or other substance may lead to moderate or low physical dependence or high psychological dependence.
- Anabolic steroids, codeine and hydrocodone products with aspirin or Tylenol®, and some barbiturates are examples of Schedule III substances.

Schedule IV

- The drug or other substance has a low potential for abuse relative to the drugs or other substances in Schedule III.
- The drug or other substance has a currently accepted medical use in treatment in the United States.
- Abuse of the drug or other substance may lead to limited physical dependence or psychological dependence relative to the drugs or other substances in Schedule III.
- Examples of drugs included in Schedule IV are alprazolam, clonazepam, and diazepam.

Schedule V

- The drug or other substance has a low potential for abuse relative to the drugs or other substances in Schedule IV.
- The drug or other substance has a currently accepted medical use in treatment in the United States.
- Abuse of the drug or other substances may lead to limited physical dependence or psychological dependence relative to the drugs or other substances in Schedule IV.

- Cough medicines with codeine are examples of Schedule V drugs.

When the U.S.Drug Enforcement Administration (DEA) Administrator has determined that a drug or other substance should be controlled, decontrolled, or rescheduled, a proposal to take action is published in the Federal Register. The proposal invites all interested persons to file comments with the DEA and may also request a hearing with the DEA. If no hearing is requested, the DEA will evaluate all comments received and publish a final order in the Federal Register, controlling the drug as proposed or with modifications based upon the written comments filed. This order will set the effective dates for imposing the various requirements of the CSA.

If a hearing is requested, the DEA will enter into discussions with the party or parties requesting a hearing in an attempt to narrow the issue for litigation. If necessary, a hearing will then be held before an Administrative Law Judge. The judge will take evidence on factual issues and hear arguments on legal questions regarding the control of the drug.

Depending on the scope and complexity of the issues, the hearing may be brief or quite extensive. The Administrative Law Judge, at the close of the hearing, prepares findings of fact and conclusions of law and a recommended decision that is submitted to the DEA Administrator. The DEA Administrator will review these documents, as well as the underlying material, and prepare his/her own findings of fact and conclusions of law (which may or may not be the same as those drafted by the Administrative Law Judge). The DEA Administrator then publishes a final order in the Federal Register either scheduling the drug or other substance or declining to do so.

Once the final order is published in the Federal Register, interested parties have 30 days to appeal to a U.S. Court of Appeals to challenge the order. Findings of fact by the Administrator are deemed conclusive if supported by "substantial evidence." The order imposing controls is not stayed during the appeal, however, unless so ordered by the Court.

Section 4.2

Prescriptions for Controlled Substances

This section includes text excerpted from "Controlled Substance Integrity—Documentation From Drop-Off to Pickup," Centers for Medicare and Medicaid Services (CMS), February 2016.

Abuse of Controlled Substances

The abuse of controlled substances in the United States and their diversion to individuals for whom they were not prescribed is a seemingly uphill battle for health care professionals, law enforcement, and policymakers. The crisis extends beyond our country's borders. The Global Burden of Disease Study 2010 is the first of its kind to assess the worldwide burden of disease attributable to illicit drug use and dependence. The study demonstrated that opioid dependence was the primary contributor to illicit drug-related deaths worldwide. In addition, the United States was one of the top four countries in the world with the highest rate of burden. From 1999–2010, opioid-related deaths in the United States dramatically increased in number, according to the Centers for Disease Control and Prevention (CDC). The number of deaths parallels the 300 percent increase in sales of opioid prescriptions during that same time.

While pharmacists routinely use their professional judgment when determining whether to fill prescriptions for controlled substances, added scrutiny is required to prevent diversion to the illicit drug market. Pharmacists are responsible for dispensing prescription drugs appropriately while intercepting prescriptions that are not issued by authorized prescribers for lawful medicinal purposes. As the primary gatekeepers between prescriptions and access to controlled substances, pharmacists are strategically positioned to ensure that all requirements are met in order to comply with State and Federal regulations. This section provides information that assists with compliance, appropriate validation, and documentation of a prescription for a controlled substance as well as the corresponding recordkeeping requirements related to distribution from the time the prescription is dropped off to the time it is picked up.

Drop-Off

Patient Identification

Verification that a prescription has been issued to a valid patient is one of the first steps to ensure the integrity of a prescription for a controlled substance. Patient identification is an important dispensing consideration, so identification issues may occur at drop-off, at pickup, or both. It is considered good practice for a patient to provide identification when the patient is not known to the pharmacy staff. This practice will help prevent fraud, waste, and abuse in the pharmacy, including, for example, the fraudulent use of another's identity to obtain drugs under a false claim for a Federal benefit. Medicaid law requires that a reasonable effort be made by the pharmacist to obtain, record, and maintain identifying information on individuals receiving prescription drug benefits under the program.

The Drug Enforcement Administration's (DEA) Office of Diversion Control explains that pharmacists must require "every purchaser of a controlled substance not known to him or her to furnish suitable identification" when dispensing controlled substances that are not prescription drugs. Nearly half of all States go a step further—as of August 31, 2010, 22 States required patient identification prior to dispensing a prescription for any controlled substance. Individual pharmacies may choose to establish a policy requiring photo identification as well. Examples of forms of identification that are typically acceptable include a valid driver's license or similar State-issued photo identification card, a military identification card, or a passport.

A prescription drug monitoring program (PDMP, or just PMP) is a State-sponsored prescription drug database that provides a unified system for sharing patients' prescription information between health care practitioners, pharmacists, and members of law enforcement who are authorized to use the system. In addition, some States that require pharmacies to record a patient's proof of identity and other personally identifiable information in the State's PDMP. How PDMPs are used, when they must be queried, what information is recorded, and who may access the information varies from State to State as do the reporting requirements. As of January 2016, 30 States are participating members in the National Association of Boards of Pharmacy's PMP InterConnect, which allows those with access to a State's PDMP to search other member States' PDMPs for patients who may be doctor shopping across State lines.

In addition, some States that require verification of a patient's identity require the pharmacy to record a patient's identifiable information in the State's Prescription Drug Monitoring Program (PDMP). PDMPs are State sponsored prescription drug databases that provide a unified system for sharing patients' prescription information between healthcare practitioners, pharmacists, and members of law enforcement who are authorized to use the system. How PDMPs are utilized, when they must be queried, what information is recorded, and who may access the information varies from State to State as do the reporting requirements.

In addition to verification of a patient's identity, pharmacy personnel should exercise professional judgment regarding the type of information provided by the patient prior to filling the prescription. According to the DEA, common characteristics of a drug abuser include:

- Patient provides suspect answers for medical history or allergies;
- Patient claims to be from out of town;
- Patient claims to have no regular doctor;
- Patient claims to have no health insurance;
- Patient has an unusually high level of knowledge of controlled substances; and
- Patient claims that only a particular medication is effective.

Pharmacy technicians and interns should document any of the above information on the prescription hard copy when a customer drops off the prescription. Pharmacists should review this information to determine if there needs to be further investigation.

Prescription Requirements

Performing a thorough inspection of the prescription hard copy is essential to ensure controlled substance integrity. This step may help identify a prescription that has been photocopied or altered. Since October 1, 2008, Federal law has required that printed prescriptions issued to Medicaid patients comply with three characteristics to be considered tamper-resistant. Prescriptions must have:

1. One or more industry-recognized features designed to prevent unauthorized copying of a completed or blank prescription form;

2. One or more industry-recognized features designed to prevent the erasure or modification of information written on the prescription pad by the prescriber; and
3. One or more industry-recognized features designed to prevent the use of counterfeit prescription forms.

In addition to ensuring that a prescription is issued on a tamper-resistant prescription blank for Medicaid patients and that the prescription has not been altered or tampered with, pharmacy personnel should ensure that the prescription contains all required information.

A valid prescription for a controlled substance must contain all of the following:

- Patient's full name and address;
- Drug name, strength, dosage form;
- Quantity or amount prescribed;
- Number of refills authorized (if any);
- Directions for use;
- Practitioner's name and address; and
- Practitioner's DEA registration number.

Federal law mandates that a prescription for a controlled substance be signed and dated on the day it is issued by the prescriber.

Federal law mandates that a prescriber sign and date a prescription for a controlled substance on the day he or she issues it. There is no Federal limit on when a written C-II prescription expires. However, some States, such as Louisiana, have established expiration rules on such prescriptions. Even though U.S. Code does not allow refill of C-II prescriptions, the DEA generally allows a provider to issue multiple subsequent prescriptions for C-II substances.

Prescribing Authority

In addition to verifying that the prescription blank appears valid and contains all required information, the pharmacist should recognize whether the practitioner has authority to prescribe the controlled substance in the State where the prescription was written. A June 2013 report released by the U.S. Department of Health and Human Services, Office of Inspector General (HHS-OIG) found that in 2009, tens of thousands of prescriptions (including 29,212 prescriptions for controlled substances) were inappropriately ordered nationwide by individuals who did not have the authority to prescribe medications and were paid for under Medicare Part D. This finding was based on a comparison of prescriptions found in CMS prescription drug event (PDE) database with the qualifications of prescribers as reflected in CMS National Plan and Provider Enumeration System (NPPES) database.

Using this data, HHS-OIG identified the top four types of providers that had prescribed Part D drugs without authority: dietitians and nutritionists; audiologists or other hearing- and speech-related service providers; massage therapists; and athletic trainers. In its comments on the report, CMS noted that "the instances identified by OIG are likely due to administrative data input and maintenance issues affecting database accuracy and reliability." While there is some question about the extent of prescribing without authority, CMS and HHS-OIG are in agreement that guidance is needed to identify and investigate apparent instances of prescribing without authority.

Effective June 1, 2010, mid-level practitioners were granted Federal prescribing authority. Mid-level practitioners provide care to patients while working under the supervision of a physician and may include physician assistants, nurse practitioners, and nurse anesthetists just to name a few. A mid-level practitioner may be authorized to prescribe controlled substances depending on the regulations of the State in which he or she practices. To ensure that a practitioner is prescribing within the scope of practice designated by Federal and State law, pharmacy technicians and pharmacists should be familiar with the prescribing scope of all practitioners, including mid-level practitioners in their State.

Pharmacy personnel should be familiar with the Code of Federal Regulations, which states that a pharmacist has the corresponding responsibility to ensure that a prescription for a controlled substance is issued in the "usual course" of business for the prescriber and for a "legitimate medical purpose."

Electronic Prescribing

A Federal rule to allow for e-prescribing of controlled substances became effective June 1, 2010. Prescribers have the choice of writing prescriptions for controlled substances manually or electronically, and pharmacies may receive, dispense, and store electronic prescriptions electronically; however e-prescribing of controlled substances is not permitted in any State. Pharmacists and technicians should be familiar with their State's e-prescribing regulatory requirements. The DEA requires registrants to be in compliance with all State and Federal laws. When State laws are more restrictive than Federal laws, registrants must comply with the more stringent State requirements

Multiple Schedule II Prescriptions

In certain instances, a prescriber may determine that it is appropriate to issue multiple prescriptions for Schedule II (C-II) substances to a patient. Federal law permits a prescriber to issue "multiple prescriptions authorizing the patient to receive a total of up to a 90-day supply." The prescriber must date and sign each sequential prescription on the day it is issued and must indicate the earliest date that each prescription may be filled by annotating a "dispense after" date on each prescription blank. To ensure compliance, pharmacy personnel should make certain that any prescription that contains a "dispense after" notation is not filled until the date designated on the C-II prescription.

The November 2007 Final Rule related to the issuance of multiple C-II prescriptions conflicted with previous regulations with respect to permissible changes to C-II prescriptions by pharmacists. Until this matter is resolved by the DEA, pharmacists should exercise professional judgment and comply with State and Federal regulations regarding changes that may be made to C-II prescriptions.

Changes to Controlled Substance Prescriptions by Pharmacists

Perform a careful inspection of the controlled substance prescription to ensure it does not contain any errors or require further clarification prior to filling. Only the following information may be changed on a Schedule III–V controlled substance prescription after consultation with the prescriber:

- Patient's address;
- Drug strength;
- Quantity to be dispensed;
- Directions for use;
- Issue date;
- Dosage form; and
- Generic substitution.

Pharmacists are prohibited from making any changes to the patient's name, the controlled substance prescribed (except for generic substitution), or the prescriber's signature. If any of the required information for a controlled substance is missing, or if the prescriber must be contacted to obtain or clarify any information prior to filling the prescription, the information should be documented on the prescription hard copy.

A good practice is to record the date the information was obtained, the name of the prescriber or authorized agent (if applicable) who provided the required information, and the initials of the dispensing pharmacist on the prescription hard copy. When clarifying an electronic prescription for a controlled substance, pharmacists should print a hard copy on which to record the required information, re-scan the prescription, and store the hard copy in a manner that complies with Federal requirements.

Drug Utilization Review

Prior to dispensing any prescription, a pharmacist should perform a drug utilization review of the patient's medication history. Pay particular attention to duplicate therapies, early refills, recent filling of drugs with antagonistic effects, and multiple prescribers for controlled substances. Also be aware of drugs commonly misused for "bridging." In the outpatient setting, bridging may involve the inappropriate use of prescription drugs by an abuser to reduce the severity of physiologic withdrawal symptoms associated with the abused substance of choice until the next high can be achieved. Although bridging is more traditionally associated with the pharmaceutical management of patients residing in substance abuse treatment centers, bridging in the outpatient setting may be considered misuse.

Substances commonly involved in bridging may include methadone, buprenorphine, buprenorphine/naloxone, gabapentin, and tramadol. In addition, performing a routine review of previously documented patient notes and a review of the patient's medication history may alert the pharmacist to prior suspicious activity. This may include things such as a history of frequent early refill requests, lost or spilled medication, or corresponding follow-up communication notes with prescribers.

Partial Fills

Federal law permits partial filling of Schedule III, IV, and V controlled substance prescriptions. In addition, the number of times the prescription is refilled may exceed the originally authorized number of refills so long as the total quantity of medication dispensed does not exceed the total quantity authorized on the original prescription. Record documentation of each partial filling of Schedules III, IV, and V prescriptions in the same manner as a refill.

Partial filling of C-II controlled substances is also permitted in certain situations. For example, a partial filling is permissible if the pharmacy is unable to supply the full quantity to the patient at the time the prescription is presented or called in for an emergency. The dispensing pharmacist must document the date, time, and partial quantity dispensed on the original C-II prescription hard copy. Federal law stipulates that any unfilled balance of the C-II prescription may be dispensed to the patient only within 72 hours of the first partial filling. If the remaining balance is either not filled or unable to be filled within 72 hours, the pharmacist must notify the prescriber, the remaining balance on the prescription must be forfeited, and no further quantities may be dispensed to the patient without a new prescription.

A partial filling of a C-II prescription is also permitted when the patient either resides in a long-term care facility or has been medically diagnosed with a terminal illness. A prescription that meets either of these criteria is valid for a maximum of 60 days from the date it was issued by the prescriber, and the medication may be dispensed in single units. To be in compliance, ensure that evidence of terminal illness or residency in a long-term care facility is documented on the original prescription hard copy. Documentation of each partial filling of a Schedule II, III, IV, and V prescription should be recorded in the same manner as a refill.

According to the Code of Federal Regulations: "For each partial filling, the dispensing pharmacist shall record on the back of the prescription (or on another appropriate record, uniformly maintained, and readily retrievable) the date of the partial filling, quantity dispensed, remaining quantity authorized to be dispensed, and the identification of the dispensing pharmacist."

Controlled Substance Refill Requests

In 2012, the DEA issued a letter of clarification to the legal counsel for Omnicare, Inc., (Omnicare) regarding the practice of sending refill reminders to prescribers on behalf of a patient for a controlled substance. The DEA determined that Omnicare was not complying with the Controlled Substances Act (CSA) because it was utilizing refill reminder notification forms that were prepopulated with all information, and only a prescriber's signature was required to make the prescription valid. In the letter, the DEA explicitly states that the intent of the CSA is to ensure that "every prescription for a controlled substance must be predicated on a determination by an individual practitioner that the dispensing of the controlled substance is for a legitimate medical purpose by a practitioner acting in the usual course of professional practice." In this instance, the DEA determined that Omnicare had acted as an unauthorized "agent" for the physician and the subsequent submission of such requests was a violation of the CSA.

Although the Federal law has not changed, the $50 million settlement agreement that Omnicare reached with the DEA for this and other violations caught the attention of pharmacists, pharmacies, State pharmacy boards, and pharmacy associations nationwide. Retail and long-term care pharmacies may not submit a refill request to a practitioner for a controlled substance prescription that is in the format of a partially or fully prepopulated prescription template because the pharmacy is not an authorized "agent" of the prescriber. A reminder notification that contains a blank prescription template that the prescriber must complete is acceptable. Pharmacy personnel should assess controlled substance refill request procedures to ensure that the process and any associated forms comply with the CSA.

Pickup

Patient Counseling

Section 4401 of the Omnibus Budget Reconciliation Act of 1990 (OBRA '90) dramatically impacted the delivery of pharmaceutical care and the interaction between patient and pharmacist. OBRA '90 was initially established to improve therapeutic outcomes of Medicaid recipients and includes three key pharmaceutical components:

1. A prospective drug review of the patient's profile.
2. Maintenance of essential patient and drug therapy information.
3. Provision of medication counseling for all Medicaid patients.

To ensure compliance and as a condition of receiving Federal Medicaid funds, each State was required to establish standards. According to the National Health Law Program (NHeLP), as of 2010, 48 States had enacted laws that require patient counseling or an offer to counsel. Although OBRA '90 was initially established to improve the therapeutic outcomes of Medicaid patients, the application of State-mandated patient counseling requirements extends to non-Medicaid patients.

All patients are entitled to the same standard of care with regard to patient counseling.

OBRA'90 patient counseling standards include:

- Name of the drug (brand name, generic, or other descriptive information);
- Intended use and expected action;
- Route, dosage form, dosage, and administration schedule;
- Common severe side effects or adverse effects or interactions and therapeutic contraindications that may be encountered, including how to avoid them and the action required if they occur;
- Techniques for self-monitoring of drug therapy;
- Proper storage;
- Potential drug-drug interactions or drug-disease contraindications;
- Prescription refill information; and
- Action to be taken in the event of a missed dose.

Many States have unique requirements for: counseling when the patient is not in the pharmacy; the distribution of supplemental written materials; and notification to the patient when a generic substitution has been made.

Pharmacy personnel are responsible for compliance with all patient counseling regulations in the States in which they practice. Patient counseling is an important part of health care delivery, especially since pharmacists have a "corresponding responsibility" to monitor patient use of prescription medications, especially controlled substances. Unfortunately, pharmacy counseling rates are consistently below 50 percent in surveys of the practice.

Documentation at the time a prescription is picked up is an important final step to ensure integrity when prescriptions for controlled substances are dispensed. Pharmacists and pharmacy technicians have a responsibility to ensure positive patient identification when prescriptions for a controlled substance are picked up. This measure helps prevent fraud, waste, and abuse, such as identity theft to obtain drugs under a false claim for a Federal benefit. State identification requirements and PDMP reporting requirements may vary. Pharmacists and pharmacy technicians should familiarize themselves with the regulations established by the State and corresponding compliance.

Key Points

Pharmacists, pharmacy interns, and pharmacy technicians should integrate the following aspects when handling prescriptions for controlled substances:

- Confirm the patient's identity;
- Verify that the prescription contains all required information;
- Confirm the prescriber has authority to prescribe the medication;
- Document any changes made to the original prescription as permitted by law;
- Perform a drug utilization review;
- Properly document full or partial dispensing(s);
- Verify that refill request forms comply with Federal and State requirements;
- Comply with patient counseling requirements;
- Collect patient signature to record the pickup of the medication; and
- Report required information to the State PDMP.

Section 4.3

Purchasing Prescribed Controlled Substances over the Internet

This section contains text excerpted from the following sources: Text beginning with the heading "Key Data about Online Sales of Prescription Medicines" is excerpted from "Key Data about Online Sales Of Prescription Medicines" U.S. House of Representatives, February 27, 2014; Text beginning with the heading "The Possible Dangers of Buying Medicines over the Internet" is excerpted from "The Possible Dangers of Buying Medicines over the Internet," U.S. Food and Drug Administration (FDA), January 16, 2015.

Key Data about Online Sales of Prescription Medicines

- There are believed to be between 35,000–50,000 active online drug sellers in operation. Often, these companies sell medicine without requiring a doctor's evaluation.
- More than 96 percent of drug seller websites reviewed by the National Associations of Boards of Pharmacies do not meet pharmacy laws and practice standards.
- 50 percent of the prescription medicines sold online by websites that hide their physical address are counterfeit.
- Large rogue Internet drug sellers can generate between $1 million and $2.5 million in sales each month.
- Online pharmacies have increased their market footprint, growing to an estimated $11 billion in sales in 2009.
- Patients have been harmed and in some cases killed by unsafe medicines purchased from illegitimate sources on the Internet.
- A U.S. study found that 85 percent the 159 websites surveyed that offer controlled substances did not require a prescription.
- During the forth quarter of 2011, pharmacy spam constituted 31 percent of all spam.

Examples of Patients Harmed by Medications Purchased Online

These are just a couple of illustrations, of the serious and growing global problem of illegal online drug sellers.

1. On June 3, 2011, an emergency room doctor, from Texas, suffered a stroke from ingesting counterfeit Alli from www.2day-dietshopping.com. The counterfeit Alli was produced using the controlled substance sibutramine, rather than the approved ingredient orlistat, and then shipped to the United States for redistribution.
2. On April 4, 2012, a mother and son in Los Angeles were looking for cold medication. They purchased and fell victim to a counterfeit drug "vitamin injection." The victim's heart rate increased rapidly, experienced severe headaches, dramatic weight loss, pass-outs and numbness in lips. The victim was eventually hospitalized.

Law Enforcement Actions Involving Illegal Online Drug Sellers

A few examples of recent U.S. and international law enforcement actions involving online drug sales:

1. On March 27, 2013, nine defendants were sentenced for their roles in illegally distributing controlled substances to customers who bought the drugs from illicit Internet pharmacies. The defendants were also collectively ordered to forfeit more than $94 million in illegal proceeds. Drug Enforcement Administration Acting Special Agent in Charge Bruce C. Balzano stated, "Prescription drug abuse has risen to alarming levels, often times leaving a trail of devastation behind and negatively impacting our communities. The individuals sentenced this week were involved in online pharmacy schemes that were illegally distributing controlled substances."
2. On March 27, 2013, three men and one woman have been sentenced in relation to the illegal online supply of prescription only and counterfeit medicines. This follows an undercover operation by the Medicines and Healthcare products Regulatory Agency (MHRA). Searches of the homes of those involved uncovered stashes of counterfeit medication and generic prescription only medicine. This included Viagra, Cialis,

diazepam and methadone. A study of a computer also showed email traffic between Andrew Luxton, Samantha Steed, Carl Willis and others indicating the previous supply of illegitimate medicine.

3. On June 27, 2013 the U.S. Food and Drug Administration (FDA) reported the successful execution of Operation Pangea VI, a law enforcement initiative resulting in the elimination of 1,677 websites selling illegal prescription drugs. In partnership with the Department of Justice, FDA's Office of Criminal Investigations, Interpol, and authorities from nearly 100 countries took action against 9,600 websites. Dangerous drugs valued at $41 million were seized.

The Possible Dangers of Buying Medicines over the Internet

The FDA wants to warn consumers about the possible dangers of buying medicines over the Internet. Some websites sell prescription and over-the-counter drugs that may not be safe to use and could put people's health at risk.

So how can you protect yourself? FDA says that consumers should know how to recognize a legal Internet pharmacy and how to buy medicines online safely.

Don't Be Deceived

Buying prescription and over-the-counter drugs on the Internet from a company you don't know means you may not know exactly what you're getting.

There are many websites that operate legally and offer convenience, privacy, and safeguards for purchasing medicines. But there are also many "rogue websites" that offer to sell potentially dangerous drugs that have not been checked for safety or effectiveness. Though a rogue site may look professional and legitimate, it could actually be an illegal operation.

These rogue sites often sell unapproved drugs, drugs that contain the wrong active ingredient, drugs that may contain too much or too little of the active ingredient, or drugs that contain dangerous ingredients.

For example, FDA purchased and analyzed several products that were represented online as Tamiflu (oseltamivir). One of the orders, which arrived in an unmarked envelope with a postmark from India, consisted of unlabeled, white tablets. When analyzed by FDA, the tablets were found to contain talc and acetaminophen, but none of the active ingredient oseltamivir.

FDA also became aware of a number of people who placed orders over the Internet for one of the following products:

- Ambien (zolpidem tartrate)
- Xanax (alprazolam)
- Lexapro (escitalopram oxalate)
- Ativan (lorazepam)

Instead of receiving the drug they ordered, several customers received products containing what was identified as foreign versions of Haldol (haloperidol), a powerful anti-psychotic drug. As a result, these customers needed emergency medical treatment for symptoms such as difficulty in breathing, muscle spasms, and muscle stiffness—all problems that can occur with haloperidol.

Other websites sell counterfeit drugs that may look exactly like real FDA-approved medicines, but their quality and safety are unknown.

Signs of a Trustworthy Website

- It's located in the United States.
- It's licensed by the state board of pharmacy where the website is operating. A list of these boards is available at the website of the National Association of Boards of Pharmacy.
- It has a licensed pharmacist available to answer your questions.
- It requires a prescription for prescription medicines from your doctor or another health care professional who is licensed to prescribe medicines.
- It provides contact information and allows you to talk to a person if you have problems or questions.

Another way to check on a website is to look for the National Association of Boards of Pharmacy's (NABP) Verified Internet Pharmacy Practice Sites™ Seal, also known as the VIPPS® Seal.

This seal means that the Internet pharmacy is safe to use because it has met state licensure requirements, as well as other NABP criteria. Visit the VIPPS website to find legitimate pharmacies that carry the VIPPS® seal.

Signs of an Unsafe Website

- It sends you drugs with unknown quality or origin.
- It gives you the wrong drug or another dangerous product for your illness.
- It doesn't provide a way to contact the website by phone.
- It offers prices that are dramatically lower than the competition.
- It may offer to sell prescription drugs without a prescription—this is against the law!
- It may not protect your personal information.

Know Your Medicines

Before you get any new medicine for the first time, talk to a health care professional such as your doctor or pharmacist about any special steps you need to take to fill your prescription.

Any time you get a prescription refilled

- check the physical appearance of the medicine (color, texture, shape, and packaging)
- check to see if it smells and tastes the same when you use it
- alert your pharmacist or whoever is providing treatment to anything that is different

Be aware that some drugs sold online

- are too old, too strong, or too weak
- aren't FDA-approved
- aren't made using safe standards
- aren't safe to use with other medicines or products
- aren't labeled, stored, or shipped correctly
- may be counterfeit

Counterfeit Drugs

Counterfeit drugs are fake or copycat products that can be difficult to identify.

The deliberate and fraudulent practice of counterfeiting can apply to both brand name and generic products, where the identity of the source is often mislabeled in a way that suggests it is the authentic approved product.

Counterfeit drugs may

- be contaminated
- not help the condition or disease the medicine is intended to treat
- lead to dangerous side effects
- contain the wrong active ingredient
- be made with the wrong amounts of ingredients
- contain no active ingredients at all or contain too much of an active ingredient
- be packaged in phony packaging that looks legitimate

For example, counterfeit versions of the FDA-approved weight loss drug Xenical, which contains the active ingredient orlistat, recently were obtained by three consumers from two different websites.

Laboratory analysis showed that the capsules that the consumers received contained the wrong active ingredient, sibutramine.

Sibutramine is the active ingredient of a different medicine called Meridia, a prescription drug also approved by FDA to help obese people lose weight and maintain weight loss. In addition, sibutramine is classified as a controlled substance by the Drug Enforcement Administration because of its potential for abuse and misuse.

Using medicine that contains an active ingredient that wasn't prescribed by your licensed health care provider may be harmful.

FDA continues to proactively protect consumers from counterfeit drugs. The agency is working with drug manufacturers, wholesalers, and retailers to identify and prevent counterfeit drugs. FDA also is exploring the use of modern technologies and other measures that will make it more difficult for counterfeit drugs to get mixed up with, or deliberately substituted for, safe and effective medicines.

How to Protect Yourself

- Only buy from state-licensed pharmacy websites located in the United States.
- Don't buy from websites that sell prescription drugs without a prescription.

- Don't buy from websites that offer to prescribe a drug for the first time without a physical exam by your doctor or by answering an online questionnaire.
- Check with your state board of pharmacy or the National Association of Boards of Pharmacy to see if an online pharmacy has a valid pharmacy license and meets state quality standards.
- Look for privacy and security policies that are easy to find and easy to understand.
- Don't give any personal information—such as a social security number, credit card information, or medical or health history—unless you are sure the website will keep your information safe and private.
- Use legitimate websites that have a licensed pharmacist to answer your question.
- Make sure that the website will not sell your personal information, unless you agree.

Section 4.4

Is Marijuana Medicine?

This section contains text excerpted from the following sources: Text beginning with the heading "What Is Medical Marijuana?" is excerpted from "DrugFacts: Is Marijuana Medicine?" National Institute on Drug Abuse (NIDA), July, 2015; Text beginning with the heading "Is Marijuana Medicine?" is excerpted from "The Dangers and Consequences of Marijuana Abuse," U.S. Drug Enforcement Administration (DEA), May 2014.

What Is Medical Marijuana?

The term medical marijuana refers to using the whole unprocessed marijuana plant or its basic extracts to treat a disease or symptom. The U.S. Food and Drug Administration (FDA) has not recognized or approved the marijuana plant as medicine.

However, scientific study of the chemicals in marijuana, called cannabinoids, has led to two FDA-approved medications that contain cannabinoid chemicals in pill form. Continued research may lead to more medications.

Because the marijuana plant contains chemicals that may help treat a range of illnesses or symptoms, many people argue that it should be legal for medical purposes. In fact, a growing number of states have legalized marijuana for medical use.

Is Marijuana Medicine?

Scientists and researchers contend that the marijuana plant contains several chemicals that may prove useful for treating a range of illnesses or symptoms, leading many people to argue that it should be made legally available for medical purposes. Marijuana is currently categorized as a Schedule I drug under the Controlled Substances Act (CSA), This classification does not interfere with allowing research, and for those drugs formulated with the plant or its crude extracts from being reviewed and approved by the FDA. The fact is much research is being done. The National Institute on Drug Abuse (NIDA) and DEA have fostered research on marijuana for many years.

According to NIDA:

- Scientific study of the active chemicals in marijuana, called cannabinoids, has led to the development of two FDA-approved medications already, and is leading to the development of new pharmaceuticals that harness the therapeutic benefits of cannabinoids while minimizing or eliminating the harmful side effects (including the "high") produced by eating or smoking the leaves.
- Cannabinoids are a large family of chemicals related to delta-9-tetrahydrocannabinol (THC), marijuana's main psychoactive (mind-altering) ingredient. In addition to THC, the marijuana plant contains over 100 other cannabinoids.
- Currently two main cannabinoids of interest therapeutically are THC and cannabidiol (CBD), found in varying ratios within the marijuana plant. THC stimulates appetite and reduces nausea (and there are already approved THC-based medications for these purposes), and it may also decrease pain, inflammation, and spasticity. CBD is a nonpsychoactive cannabinoid that may also be useful in reducing pain and inflammation, controlling epileptic seizures, and possibly even treating psychosis and addictions.

- An FDA–approved drug called Dronabinol (Marinol®) contains THC and is used to treat nausea caused by chemotherapy and wasting disease (extreme weight loss) caused by AIDS. Another FDA-approved drug called Nabilone (Cesamet®) contains a synthetic cannabinoid similar to THC and is used for the same purposes. Both are available through a doctor's prescription and come in pill or capsule form.
- Sativex®, an oromuscosal spray for treatment of spasticity due to multiple sclerosis, is already approved for use in other countries. Sativex® contains equal parts THC and CBD. Sativex® is now in Phase III clinical trials in the U.S. to establish its effectiveness and safety in treating cancer pain.
- Although it has not yet undergone clinical trials to establish its effectiveness and safety (necessary to obtain FDA approval), a CBD-based drug called Epidiolex® has recently been created to treat certain forms of childhood epilepsy."

Although there have been many stories in the media about CBD and the benefits achieved by its use, all these stories are anecdotal. Dr. Elson So, President of the American Epilepsy Society asks that the "professional and lay community do not make treatment decisions that are not based on sound research." In his letter to the Miami Herald, Dr. So points out that there is currently a lack of scientific evidence for the use of marijuana as treatment for epilepsy. It is not yet known if it is a safe and efficacious treatment. "In addition, there is little known about the long term effects of using marijuana on infants and children on memory, learning and behavior." "The lack of information does not mean that it is an ineffective treatment – but let's be sure that it is and learn how to use it correctly."

DEA has always supported ongoing research into potential medicinal uses of marijuana's active ingredients. As of May 2014:

- There are 237 researchers registered with DEA to perform studies with marijuana, marijuana extracts, and non-tetrahydrocannabinol marijuana derivatives that exists in the plant, such as cannabidiol and cannabinol.
- Studies include evaluation of abuse potential, physical/psychological effects, adverse effects, therapeutic potential, and detection.
- Sixteen of these registered researchers are approved to conduct research with smoked marijuana on human subjects.

Organizers behind the "medical" marijuana movement did not really concern themselves with marijuana as a medicine–they just saw it as a means to an end, which is the legalization of marijuana for recreational purposes. They did not deal with ensuring that the product meets the standards of modern medicine: quality, safety and efficacy. There is no standardized composition or dosage; no appropriate prescribing information; no quality control; no accountability for the product; no safety regulation: no way to measure its effectiveness (besides anecdotal stories); and no insurance coverage.

DEA and the Federal Government are not alone in viewing how drugs should become medicines, the negative ramifications of the current processes engaged in by some of the states, and the harms that we are doing to our youth by continuing to allow and accept popular vote as a method of determining what medicine is.

- The **American Medical Association (AMA)** in November 2013, amended their position on cannabis, stating that "cannabis is a dangerous drug and as such is a public health concern; sale of cannabis should not be legalized; public health based strategies, rather than incarceration should be utilized in the handling of individuals possessing cannabis for personal use; and that additional research should be encouraged."
- The **American Society of Addiction Medicine's (ASAM)** public policy statement on "Medical Marijuana," clearly rejects smoking as a means of drug delivery. ASAM further recommends that "all cannabis, cannabis-based products and cannabis delivery devices should be subject to the same standards applicable to all other prescription medication and medical devices, and should not be distributed or otherwise provided to patients" without FDA approval. ASAM also "discourages state interference in the federal medication approval process." ASAM continues to support these policies, and has also 5 stated that they do not "support proposals to legalize marijuana anywhere in the United States."
- The **American Cancer Society (ACS)** "is supportive of more research into the benefits of cannabinoids. Better and more effective treatments are needed to overcome the side effects of cancer and its treatment. However, the ACS does not advocate the use of inhaled marijuana or the legalization of marijuana."

- The **American Glaucoma Society (AGS)** has stated that "although marijuana can lower the intraocular pressure, the side effects and short duration of action, coupled with the lack of evidence that its use alters the course of glaucoma, preclude recommending this drug in any form for the treatment of glaucoma at the present time."
- The **Glaucoma Research Foundation (GRF)** states that "the high dose of marijuana necessary to produce a clinically relevant effect on intraocular pressure in people with glaucoma in the short term requires constant inhalation, as much as every three hours. The number of significant side effects generated by long-term use of marijuana or long-term inhalation of marijuana smoke make marijuana a poor choice in the treatment of glaucoma. To date, no studies have shown that marijuana—or any of its approximately 400 chemical components—can safely and effectively lower intraocular pressure better than the variety of drugs currently on the market."
- The **American Academy of Pediatrics (AAP)** believes that "any change in the legal status of marijuana, even if limited to adults, could affect the prevalence of use among adolescents." While it supports scientific research on the possible medical use of cannabinoids as opposed to smoked marijuana, it opposes the legalization of marijuana.
- The **American Academy of Child and Adolescent Psychiatry (AACAP)** "is concerned about the negative impact of medical marijuana on youth. Adolescents are especially vulnerable to the many adverse development, cognitive, medical, psychiatric, and addictive effects of marijuana." Of greater concern to the AACAP is that "adolescent marijuana users are more likely than adult users to develop marijuana dependence, and their heavy use is associated with increased incidence and worsened course of psychotic, mood, and anxiety disorders." "The "medicalization" of smoked marijuana has distorted the perception of the known risks and purposed benefits of this drug." Based upon these concerns, the "AACAP opposes medical marijuana dispensing to adolescents."
- The **National Multiple Sclerosis Society (NMSS)** has stated that "based on studies to date—and the fact that long-term use of marijuana may be associated with significant, serious side effects—it is the opinion of the NMSS's Medical Advisory

Board that there are currently insufficient data to recommend marijuana or its derivatives as a treatment for MS symptoms. Research is continuing to determine if there is a possible role for marijuana or its derivatives in the treatment of MS. In the meantime, other well tested, FDA-approved drugs are available to reduce spasticity."

- The **National Association of School Nurses (NASN)** consensus it that marijuana is properly categorized as a Schedule I substance under the Controlled Substances Act and 6 concurs with DEA that "the clear weight of the currently available evidence supports this classification, including evidence that smoked marijuana has a high potential for abuse, has no accepted medicinal value in treatment in the United States, and evidence that there is a general lack of accepted safety for its use even under medical supervision." NASN also supports of the position of the AAP that "any change in the legal status of marijuana, even if limited to adults, could affect the prevalence of use among adolescents."
- The **American Psychiatric Association (APA)** states that there is no current scientific evidence that marijuana is in any way beneficial for treatment of any psychiatric disorder. Current evidence supports, at minimum, a strong association of cannabis use with the onset of psychiatric disorders. Adolescents are particularly vulnerable to harm due to the effects of cannabis on neurological development. The APA does support further research of cannabis-derived substances as medicine, facilitated by the federal government, and if scientific evidence supports the use for treatment of specific conditions, the approval process should go through the FDA and in no way be authorized by ballot initiatives.

Section 4.5

Overview of the Medical Marijuana Debate

This section contains text excerpted from the following sources: Text beginning with the heading "Taking a Science-Informed Approach to Medical Marijuana" is excerpted from "Taking a Science-Informed Approach to Medical Marijuana," National Institute on Drug Abuse (NIDA), April 28, 2015; Text under the heading "Why Is the Federal Government Opposed to Medical Marijuana?" is excepted from "Answers to Frequently Asked Questions about Marijuana," WhiteHouse.gov, December 19, 2011. Reviewed April 2016.

Taking a Science-Informed Approach to Medical Marijuana

Opinion on marijuana has changed dramatically in the United States. The public increasingly perceives it as a benign substance, and there is growing interest in its potential medicinal uses. Already almost half of the states have medical marijuana laws, and congressional bills have recently been proposed that would reschedule the drug to reduce hindrances to research and facilitate marijuana's use as medicine.

Advocates tout marijuana as a miracle drug with a wide range of potential therapeutic uses, while public health voices raise alarms about its dangers if made more widely available. The science justifying either position is often not as robust or clear as its partisans would wish. Marijuana's impact on lung cancer remains unclear, for instance, but so does its actual range of medicinal benefits. The urgent need for more research is something all sides in the current marijuana debate can agree on. Policy changes around marijuana will need to be informed, as much as possible, by science.

There is solid evidence that the main psychoactive ingredient in marijuana, THC, is effective at controlling nausea and boosting appetite. There is also some preliminary evidence that THC or related cannabinoid compounds such as cannabidiol (CBD) may also have uses in treating autoimmune diseases, inflammation, pain, seizures and psychiatric disorders, including substance use disorders. Despite claims of marijuana's usefulness in treating posttraumatic stress disorder, supporting data is minimal, and studies have not investigated whether symptoms may worsen after treatment is discontinued.

We do not yet know all the ways chronic treatment with marijuana or marijuana-derived compounds could affect people who are rendered vulnerable either by their illnesses or by their age. We also don't know how medical marijuana laws will affect other aspects of public health and safety. For example, wider medical marijuana use could potentially impact driver safety, as both laboratory and epidemiological research link recent marijuana use to increased accident risk, likely reflecting marijuana's disruptive effects on motor coordination and time perception.

Impact on Teenagers

Perhaps the biggest public health concern around medical marijuana liberalization and legalization concerns the potential impact on teenagers, who could have greater access to it as a drug of abuse and who may increasingly see marijuana as a "safe, natural" medicine rather than a harmful intoxicant. Although there is still much to learn about marijuana's impact on the developing brain, the existing science paints a picture of lasting adverse consequences when the drug is used heavily prior to the completion of brain maturation in young adulthood. In teens, marijuana appears to impair cognitive development, may lower IQ and may precipitate psychosis in individuals with a genetic vulnerability.

Most states currently don't allow medical marijuana for children, but they too are vulnerable. Accidental ingestion of marijuana edibles by children has increased in Colorado since marijuana was decriminalized for medicinal use in 2009. Also potentially concerning is the possibility of increased prenatal exposure if women self-treat with marijuana to control nausea associated with pregnancy. Research suggests prenatal exposure could have adverse consequences for children's future health and brain development. There is as yet no research on the potential effects of secondhand marijuana smoke on children growing up in households where parents smoke.

Even in conditions for which THC, CBD or other cannabinoid constituents of the marijuana plant prove to be medically beneficial, consumption of the marijuana plant itself or its crude extracts via smoking, vaporizing or eating is unlikely to be the most effective, reliable or safe way for patients to obtain these benefits. Laboratory research is ongoing to better understand how cannabinoids work in the brain and body and hopefully guide development of safe, reliable therapeutic compounds that have a minimum of adverse side effects.

Existing Medications

Two THC-based medications, dronabinol and nabilone, are already approved by the Food and Drug Administration to treat nausea caused by chemotherapy and to boost appetite in patients with AIDS wasting syndrome. The United Kingdom, Canada and several European countries have approved a drug called nabiximols (Sativex), containing THC and CBD, as a medication for spasticity caused by multiple sclerosis (MS) and, in Canada, for MS- and cancer-related pain. Despite its success in reducing pain and spasticity, it has not received approval in the United States, and recent evidence has found impairments in cognition in users.

CBD on its own is not psychoactive and it actually mitigates the "high" produced by THC; it has been studied as a potential antipsychotic drug, and ongoing trials are testing its efficacy as an antiseizure agent. Some parents of children with severe forms of pediatric epilepsy have claimed that high-CBD (and low-THC) marijuana extracts control their children's seizures better than existing medicines. The maker of Sativex has recently created a CBD-based drug called Epidiolex to treat children with these conditions, and is in the process of conducting initial small-scale trials. Evidence so far shows that CBD is only effective in controlling seizures in a small subset of patients.

As public approval for medical marijuana grows, we need to ensure that our policy decisions are science-based and not swayed by the enthusiastic claims made widely in the media or on the Internet. We need to support and encourage increased research on marijuana's potential benefits and conduct intensified research on the cannabinoid system to inform the development of safe, FDA-approvable drugs. But the existing science on marijuana's adverse effects on youth demands we also proceed with caution in making policy changes that could result in increased use of or exposure to marijuana by young people.

Why Is the Federal Government Opposed to Medical Marijuana?

It is the Federal government's position that marijuana be subjected to the same rigorous clinical trials and scientific scrutiny that the U.S. Food and Drug Administration (FDA) applies to all other new medications, a comprehensive process designed to ensure the highest standards of safety and efficacy.

It is this rigorous FDA approval process, not popular vote, that should determine what is, and what is not medicine. The raw marijuana plant, which contains nearly 500 different chemical compounds, has not met the safety and efficacy standards of this process. According to the Institute of Medicine (IOM), smoking marijuana is an unsafe delivery system that produces harmful effects.

The FDA has, however, recognized and approved the medicinal use of isolated components of the marijuana plant and related synthetic compounds. Dronabinol is one such synthetically produced compound, used in the FDA-approved medicine Marinol, which is already legally available for prescription by physicians whose patients suffer from nausea and vomiting related to cancer chemotherapy and wasting (severe weight loss) associated with AIDS. Another FDA-approved medicine, Cesamet, contains the active ingredient Nabilone, which has a chemical structure similar to THC, the active ingredient of marijuana. And Sativex, an oromucosal spray approved in Canada, the UK, and other parts of Europe for the treatment of multiple sclerosis spasticity and cancer pain, is currently in late-stage clinical trials with the FDA. It combines THC and another active ingredient in marijuana, cannabidiol (CBD), and provides therapeutic benefits without the "high" from the drug.

A number of States have passed voter referenda or legislative actions allowing marijuana to be made available for a variety of medical conditions upon a licensed prescriber's recommendation, despite such measures' inconsistency with the scientific thoroughness of the FDA approval process. But these state actions are not, and never should be, the primary test for declaring a substance a recognized medication. Physicians routinely prescribe medications with standardized modes of administration that have been shown to be safe and effective at treating the conditions that marijuana proponents claim are relieved by smoking marijuana. Biomedical research and medical judgment should continue to determine the safety and effectiveness of prescribed medications.

Chapter 5

Regulations Regarding Controlled Substances

Chapter Contents

Section 5.1

The Controlled Substances Act

This section includes text excerpted from "Drugs of Abuse," U.S. Drug Enforcement Administration (DEA), 2015.

Controlling Drugs or Other Substances through Formal Scheduling

The Controlled Substances Act (CSA) places all substances which were in some manner regulated under existing federal law into one of five schedules. This placement is based upon the substance's medical use, potential for abuse, and safety or dependence liability. The Act also provides a mechanism for substances to be controlled (added to or transferred between schedules) or decontrolled (removed from control). The procedure for these actions is found in Section 201 of the Act.

Proceedings to add, delete, or change the schedule of a drug or other substance may be initiated by the Drug Enforcement Administration (DEA), the Department of Health and Human Services (HHS), or by petition from any interested party, including:

- The manufacturer of a drug
- A medical society or association
- A pharmacy association
- A public interest group concerned with drug abuse
- A state or local government agency
- An individual citizen

When a petition is received by the DEA, the agency begins its own investigation of the drug. The DEA also may begin an investigation of a drug at any time based upon information received from law enforcement laboratories, state and local law enforcement and regulatory agencies, or other sources of information.

Once the DEA has collected the necessary data, the DEA Administrator, by authority of the Attorney General, requests from HHS a scientific and medical evaluation and recommendation as to whether the drug or other substance should be controlled or removed from control. This request is sent to the Assistant Secretary for Health of HHS.

The Assistant Secretary, by authority of the Secretary, compiles the information and transmits back to the DEA: a medical and scientific evaluation regarding the drug or other substance, a recommendation as to whether the drug should be controlled, and in what schedule it should be placed.

The medical and scientific evaluations are binding on the DEA with respect to scientific and medical matters and form a part of the scheduling decision.

Once the DEA has received the scientific and medical evaluation from HHS, the Administrator will evaluate all available data and make a final decision whether to propose that a drug or other substance should be removed or controlled and into which schedule it should be placed.

If a drug does not have a potential for abuse, it cannot be controlled. Although the term "potential for abuse" is not defined in the CSA, there is much discussion of the term in the legislative history of the Act. The following items are indicators that a drug or other substance has a potential for abuse:

1. There is evidence that individuals are taking the drug or other substance in amounts sufficient to create a hazard to their health or to the safety of other individuals or to the community.

2. There is significant diversion of the drug or other substance from legitimate drug channels.

3. Individuals are taking the drug or other substance on their own initiative rather than on the basis of medical advice from a practitioner.

4. The drug is a new drug so related in its action to a drug or other substance already listed as having a potential for abuse to make it likely that the drug will have the same potential for abuse as such drugs, thus making it reasonable to assume that there may be significant diversions from legitimate channels, significant use contrary to or without medical advice, or that it has a substantial capability of creating hazards to the health of the user or to the safety of the community. Of course, evidence of actual abuse of a substance is indicative that a drug has a potential for abuse.

In determining into which schedule a drug or other substance should be placed, or whether a substance should be decontrolled or rescheduled, certain factors are required to be considered.

These factors are listed in Section 201 (c), of the CSA as follows:

1. The drug's actual or relative potential for abuse.
2. Scientific evidence of the drug's pharmacological effect, if known. The state of knowledge with respect to the effects of a specific drug is, of course, a major consideration. For example, it is vital to know whether or not a drug has a hallucinogenic effect if it is to be controlled due to that effect. The best available knowledge of the pharmacological properties of a drug should be considered.
3. The state of current scientific knowledge regarding the substance. Criteria (2) and (3) are closely related. However, (2) is primarily concerned with pharmacological effects and (3) deals with all scientific knowledge with respect to the substance.
4. Its history and current pattern of abuse. To determine whether or not a drug should be controlled, it is important to know the pattern of abuse of that substance.
5. The scope, duration, and significance of abuse. In evaluating existing abuse, the DEA Administrator must know not only the pattern of abuse, but whether the abuse is widespread.
6. What, if any, risk there is to the public health. If a drug creates dangers to the public health, in addition to or because of its abuse potential, then these dangers must also be considered by the Administrator.
7. The drug's psychic or physiological dependence liability. There must be an assessment of the extent to which a drug is physically addictive or psychologically habit forming.
8. Whether the substance is an immediate precursor of a substance already controlled. The CSA allows inclusion of immediate precursors on this basis alone into the appropriate schedule and thus safeguards against possibilities of clandestine manufacture. After considering the above listed factors, the Administrator must make specific findings concerning the drug or other substance. This will determine into which schedule the drug or other substance will be placed. These schedules are established by the CSA.

Section 5.2

Combat Methamphetamine Epidemic Act

This section includes text excerpted from "Legal Requirements for the Sale and Purchase of Drug Products Containing Pseudoephedrine, Ephedrine, and Phenylpropanolamine," U.S. Food and Drug Administration (FDA), July 30, 2014.

Legal Requirements for the Sale and Purchase of Drug Products Containing Pseudoephedrine, Ephedrine, and Phenylpropanolamine

The Combat Methamphetamine Epidemic Act of 2005 has been incorporated into the Patriot Act signed by President Bush on March 9, 2006. The act bans over-the-counter sales of cold medicines that contain the ingredient pseudoephedrine, which is commonly used to make methamphetamine. The sale of cold medicine containing pseudoephedrine is limited to behind the counter. The amount of pseudoephedrine that an individual can purchase each month is limited and individuals are required to present photo identification to purchase products containing pseudoephedrine. In addition, stores are required to keep personal information about purchasers for at least two years.

What Was FDA's Announcement?

The U.S. Food and Drug Administration (FDA) has announced new legal requirements for the legal sale and purchase of drug products containing pseudoephedrine, ephedrine, and phenylpropanolamine required by the Combat Methamphetamine Epidemic Act of 2005. This new law calls for a comprehensive system of controls regarding the distribution and sale of drug products that can be used in the illicit production of methamphetamine.

What Is the Combat Methamphetamine Epidemic Act of 2005?

The Combat Methamphetamine Epidemic Act of 2005 has been included in the Patriot Bill signed by the President on March 9, 2006. The Act would ban over-the-counter sales of cold medicines that contain ingredients that are commonly used to make methamphetamine such as pseudoephedrine.

Who Has Responsibility for Enforcement of the Act?

The Drug Enforcement Administration (DEA).

What Is Pseudoephedrine?

Pseudoephedrine is a drug found in both prescription and over-the-counter products used to relieve nasal or sinus congestion caused by the common cold, sinusitis, hay fever, and other respiratory allergies. It can also be used illegally to produce methamphetamine.

What Is Methamphetamine?

Methamphetamine is a powerful, highly addictive stimulant. It is manufactured in covert, illegal laboratories throughout the United States. Methamphetamine can be ingested by swallowing, inhaling, injecting or smoking. The side effects, which arise from the use and abuse of methamphetamine, include irritability, nervousness, insomnia, nausea, depression, and brain damage.

Does This Mean I Need a Prescription from My Doctor to Buy Pseudoephedrine?

No. The Act allows for the sale of pseudoephedrine only from locked cabinets or behind the counter. The law:

- limits the monthly amount any individual could purchase
- requires individuals to present photo identification to purchase such medications
- requires retailers to keep personal information about these customers for at least two years after the purchase of these medicines.

When Will This Law Take Effect?

This law became effective September on 30, 2006.

Does the Requirements of This Law Affect Combination Products, or Just Products That Contain Pure Pseudoephedrine?

The requirements of this law will affect all products that contain ingredients pseudoephedrine, phenylpropanolamine, and ephedrine.

I Still See Sudafed PE on the Shelves. Is This Different from Regular Sudafed?

Yes, Sudafed PE is different from Sudafed. Sudafed contains the active ingredient Pseudoephedrine, while the active ingredient in Sudafed PE is Phenylephrine. In response to the issue of misuse of pseudoephedrine-containing products, many companies are voluntarily re-formulating their products to exclude phenylpropanolamine, ephedrine, and pseudoephedrine.

What Are All the Products That Include the Ingredients Affected by This New Law?

The FDA recommends that consumers read the labels of OTC drug products to determine if the product contains pseudoephedrine, ephedrine, or phenylpropanolamine. FDA believes this to be the most accurate method for determining the contents of OTC products rather than providing an incomplete or out-of-date list of products that may have already been reformulated and no longer contain these ingredients.

Products Containing Pseudoephedrine Are Already Considered Prescription Controlled Substances in My State. Does This New Law Change That Status?

In response to the misuse of methamphetamine, many state governments have issued regulations controlling the sale of these products. This should not effect the restrictions already placed in your state.

Have Chronic Sinus Problems. Will I Be Limited from Getting the Amount of Pseudoephedrine I Need?

Yes, with this new law there will be limits on the number of tablets of ephedrine, pseudoephedrine, or phenylpropanolamine that can be purchased in a 30-day period. As there a many different dosages and formulations of these products, you should ask your pharmacist how much you will be allowed to purchase over a 30-day period for specific product you use.

How Will This Change the Way Pseudoephedrine Is Sold?

The Act requires that each regulated seller ensure that:

- Customers do not have direct access to the product before the sale is made.

- A written or electronic "logbook" listing sales is kept that identifies the products by name, quantity sold, names and addresses of purchasers, and the dates and times of the sales.
- There is a limit on the amount that can be purchased in a single day and in a month.

What Does "Behind-The-Counter" Mean?

The Act defines "behind-the-counter" as placement of the product to ensure that customers do not have direct access to the product before the sale is made. In other words, placement may be in a secure location in the pharmacy prescription-filling area or in a locked cabinet that is located in the area of the facility to which customers do have direct access. In all cases, the seller will deliver the product directly into the custody of the buyer.

Will Training Be Required for Personnel Responsible for Selling Pseudoephedrine?

Companies selling products containing pseudoephedrine are required to submit to the Attorney General a statement regarding self-certification and training on the new law.

What about a Sample Size Package Containing Only 1-2 Pills of Pseudoephedrine Like Those Often Sold at Gas Stations or Grocery Stores?

The Act exempts the requirements of a "logbook" to any purchase by an individual of a single sales package if that package contains not more than 60 milligrams of pseudoephedrine. These single dose packages have to remain behind the counter.

What Will Be Required to Purchase Pseudoephedrine?

In order to purchase pseudoephedrine:
Buyers must:

- Present a photo identification card issued by the State or the Federal Government or a document that is considered acceptable by the seller
- Enter into the logbook their information such as name, address, date and time of sale, and signature

Sellers must:

- Verify the logbook entries, and enter in the name of the product and quantity sold

What If I Have Other Questions about Pseudoephedrine or This New Law?

If you have further questions regarding pseudoephedrine, phenylpropanolamine, ephedrine, or any medications, please contact the Division of Drug Information in the FDA's Center for Drug Evaluation and Research (CDER) at: 888-INFOFDA (888-463-6332), or send an email to: druginfo@fda.hhs.gov

Chapter 6

Substance Abuse Treatment Statistics

Chapter Contents

Section 6.1

Treatment Received for Substance Abuse

This section includes text excerpted from "Results from the 2013 National Survey on Drug Use and Health: Summary of National Findings," Substance Abuse and Mental Health Services Administration (SAMHSA), September 2014.

Treatment for a Substance Use Problem

Estimates described in this section refer to treatment received for illicit drug or alcohol use, or for medical problems associated with the use of illicit drugs or alcohol. This includes treatment received in the past year at any location, such as a hospital (inpatient), rehabilitation facility (outpatient or inpatient), mental health center, emergency room, private doctor's office, prison or jail, or a self-help group, such as Alcoholics Anonymous or Narcotics Anonymous. Persons could report receiving treatment at more than one location. Specialty treatment includes treatment only at a hospital (inpatient), a rehabilitation facility (inpatient or outpatient), or a mental health center.

Individuals who reported receiving substance use treatment but were missing information on whether the treatment was specifically for alcohol use or illicit drug use were not counted in estimates of either illicit drug use treatment or alcohol use treatment; however, they were counted in estimates for "drug or alcohol use" treatment.

- In 2013, 4.1 million persons aged 12 or older (1.5% of the population) received treatment for a problem related to the use of alcohol or illicit drugs. Of these, 1.3 million received treatment for the use of both alcohol and illicit drugs, 0.9 million received treatment for the use of illicit drugs but not alcohol, and 1.4 million received treatment for the use of alcohol but not illicit drugs. (Note that estimates by substance do not sum to the total number of persons receiving treatment because the total includes persons who reported receiving treatment but did not report for which substance the treatment was received.)

- The rate and the number of persons in the population aged 12 or older receiving any substance use treatment within the past year remained stable between 2012 (1.5% and 4.0 million) and 2013 (1.5% and 4.1 million). The rate and number of persons receiving any substance use treatment within the past year in 2002 were 1.5% and 3.5 million. The rate in 2002 was similar to that in 2013, but the number of persons who received substance use treatment in 2002 was lower than that in 2013.
- In 2013, among the 4.1 million persons aged 12 or older who received treatment for alcohol or illicit drug use in the past year, 2.3 million persons received treatment at a self-help group, and 1.8 million received treatment at a rehabilitation facility as an outpatient. The numbers of persons who received treatment at other locations were 1.2 million at a mental health center as an outpatient, 1.0 million at a rehabilitation facility as an inpatient, 879,000 at a hospital as an inpatient, 770,000 at a private doctor's office, 603,000 at an emergency room, and 263,000 at a prison or jail. None of these estimates changed significantly between 2012 and 2013. The number of persons receiving treatment at a private doctor's office was lower in 2002 (523,000) than in 2013.
- In 2013, 2.5 million persons aged 12 or older reported receiving treatment for alcohol use during their most recent treatment in the past year, 845,000 persons received treatment for marijuana use, and 746,000 persons received treatment for pain relievers. Estimates for receiving treatment for the use of other drugs were 584,000 for cocaine, 526,000 for heroin, 461,000 for stimulants, 376,000 for tranquilizers, and 303,000 for hallucinogens. None of these estimates changed significantly between 2012 and 2013. The numbers of persons aged 12 or older who received their most recent treatment in the past year for alcohol, marijuana, cocaine, hallucinogens, inhalants, and sedatives were similar in 2002 and 2013. However, the number of persons who received treatment for tranquilizers increased from 2002 (197,000 persons) to 2013 (376,000 persons).
- The number who received treatment for heroin increased from 277,000 persons in 2002 to 526,000 persons in 2013. The number who received treatment for nonmedical use of prescription pain relievers increased from 2002 (360,000 persons) to 2013 (746,000 persons). The number who received treatment for stimulants

increased from 268,000 persons in 2002 to 461,000 persons in 2013. (Note that respondents could indicate that they received treatment for more than one substance during their most recent treatment.)

Need for and Receipt of Specialty Treatment

This section discusses the need for and receipt of treatment for a substance use problem at a "specialty" treatment facility. Specialty treatment is defined as treatment received at any of the following types of facilities: hospitals (inpatient only), drug or alcohol rehabilitation facilities (inpatient or outpatient), or mental health centers. It does not include treatment at an emergency room, private doctor's office, self-help group, prison or jail, or hospital as an outpatient. An individual is defined as needing treatment for an alcohol or drug use problem if he or she met the DSM-IV (APA, 1994) diagnostic criteria for alcohol or illicit drug dependence or abuse in the past 12 months or if he or she received specialty treatment for alcohol use or illicit drug use in the past 12 months.

In this section, an individual needing treatment for an illicit drug use problem is defined as receiving treatment for his or her drug use problem only if he or she reported receiving specialty treatment for illicit drug use in the past year. Thus, an individual who needed treatment for illicit drug use but received specialty treatment only for alcohol use in the past year or who received treatment for illicit drug use only at a facility not classified as a specialty facility was not counted as receiving treatment for illicit drug use.

Similarly, an individual who needed treatment for an alcohol use problem was counted as receiving alcohol use treatment only if the treatment was received for alcohol use at a specialty treatment facility. Individuals who reported receiving specialty substance use treatment but were missing information on whether the treatment was specifically for alcohol use or drug use were not counted in estimates of specialty drug use treatment or in estimates of specialty alcohol use treatment; however, they were counted in estimates for "drug or alcohol use" treatment.

In addition to questions about symptoms of substance use problems that are used to classify respondents' need for treatment based on DSM-IV criteria, NSDUH includes questions asking respondents about their perceived need for treatment (i.e., whether they felt they needed treatment or counseling for illicit drug use or alcohol use). In this report, estimates for perceived need for treatment are discussed only for persons who were classified as needing treatment (based on DSM-IV criteria) but did not receive treatment at a specialty facility. Similarly, estimates for whether a person made an effort to get treatment are discussed only for persons who felt the need for treatment and did not receive it.

Illicit Drug or Alcohol Use Treatment and Treatment Need

- In 2013, 22.7 million persons aged 12 or older needed treatment for an illicit drug or alcohol use problem (8.6% of persons aged 12 or older). The number in 2013 was similar to the numbers in 2002 to 2012 (ranging from 21.6 million to 23.6 million). The rate in 2013 was similar to the rates in 2011 (8.4%) and 2012 (8.9%), but it was lower than the rates in 2002 to 2010 (ranging from 9.2 to 9.8%).
- In 2013, 2.5 million persons (0.9% of persons aged 12 or older and 10.9% of those who needed treatment) received treatment at a specialty facility for an illicit drug or alcohol problem. The number in 2013 was similar to the numbers in 2002 (2.3 million) and in 2004 through 2012 (ranging from 2.3 million to 2.6 million), and it was higher than the number in 2003 (1.9 million). The rate in 2013 was not different from the rates in 2002 to 2012 (ranging from 0.8 to 1.0%).
- In 2013, 20.2 million persons (7.7% of the population aged 12 or older) needed treatment for an illicit drug or alcohol use problem but did not receive treatment at a specialty facility in the past year. The number in 2013 was similar to the numbers in 2002 to 2012 (ranging from 19.3 million to 21.1 million). The rate in 2013 was similar to the rates in 2010 to 2012 (ranging from 7.5 to 8.1%), but it was lower than the rates in 2002 to 2009 (ranging from 8.3 to 8.8%).
- Of the 2.5 million persons aged 12 or older who received specialty substance use treatment in 2013, 875,000 received treatment for alcohol use only, 936,000 received treatment for illicit drug use only, and 547,000 received treatment for both alcohol and illicit drug use. These estimates in 2013 were similar to the estimates in 2012 and 2002.
- Among persons in 2013 who received their most recent substance use treatment at a specialty facility in the past year, 41.7 percent reported using private health insurance as a source of

payment for their most recent specialty treatment, 40.6 percent reported using their "own savings or earnings," 29.0 percent reported using Medicaid, 29.0 percent reported using public assistance other than Medicaid, 26.8 percent reported using Medicare, and 23.0 percent reported using funds from family members. None of these estimates changed significantly between 2012 and 2013.

- In 2013, among the 20.2 million persons aged 12 or older who were classified as needing substance use treatment but not receiving treatment at a specialty facility in the past year, 908,000 persons (4.5%) reported that they perceived a need for treatment for their illicit drug or alcohol use problem. Of these 908,000 persons who felt they needed treatment but did not receive treatment in 2013, 316,000 (34.8%) reported that they made an effort to get treatment, and 592,000 (65.2%) reported making no effort to get treatment. These estimates were stable between 2012 and 2013.
- The rate and the number of youths aged 12 to 17 who needed treatment for an illicit drug or alcohol use problem in 2013 (5.4% and 1.3 million) were lower than those in 2012 (6.3% and 1.6 million), 2011 (7.0% and 1.7 million), 2010 (7.5% and 1.8 million), and 2002 (9.1% and 2.3 million). Of the 1.3 million youths who needed treatment in 2013, 122,000 received treatment at a specialty facility (about 9.1% of the youths who needed treatment), leaving about 1.2 million who needed treatment for a substance use problem but did not receive it at a specialty facility.
- Based on 2010-2013 combined data, commonly reported reasons for not receiving illicit drug or alcohol use treatment among persons aged 12 or older who needed and perceived a need for treatment but did not receive treatment at a specialty facility were (a) not ready to stop using (40.3%), (b) no health coverage and could not afford cost (31.4%), (c) possible negative effect on job (10.7%), (d) concern that receiving treatment might cause neighbors/community to have a negative opinion (10.1%), (e) not knowing where to go for treatment (9.2%), and (f) no program having type of treatment (8.0%).
- Based on 2010-2013 combined data, among persons aged 12 or older who needed but did not receive illicit drug or alcohol use treatment, felt a need for treatment, and made an effort to receive treatment, commonly reported reasons for not receiving

treatment were (a) no health coverage and could not afford cost (37.3%), (b) not ready to stop using (24.5%), (c) did not know where to go for treatment (9.0%), (d) had health coverage but did not cover treatment or did not cover cost (8.2%), and (e) no transportation or inconvenient (8.0%).

Illicit Drug Use Treatment and Treatment Need

- In 2013, the number of persons aged 12 or older needing treatment for an illicit drug use problem was 7.6 million (2.9% of the total population). The number in 2013 was similar to the number in each year from 2002 through 2012 (ranging from 7.2 million to 8.1 million). The rate of persons needing treatment for an illicit drug use problem in 2013 was lower than the rates in 2002 (3.3%) and 2004 (3.3%), but it was similar to the rates in 2012 and 2003 (3.1% in each year) and in 2005 to 2011 (ranging from 2.8 to 3.2%).
- Of the 7.6 million persons aged 12 or older who needed treatment for an illicit drug use problem in 2013, 1.5 million (0.6% of the total population and 19.5% of persons who needed treatment) received treatment at a specialty facility for an illicit drug use problem in the past year. The number in 2013 was similar to the numbers in 2012 (1.5 million), 2002 (1.4 million), and in 2004 to 2011 (ranging from 1.2 million to 1.6 million), but it was higher than the number in 2003 (1.1 million). The rate in 2013 was similar to the rates in 2002 to 2012 (ranging from 0.5 to 0.6%).
- There were 6.1 million persons (2.3% of the total population) who needed but did not receive treatment at a specialty facility for an illicit drug use problem in 2013. The number in 2013 was similar to the numbers in 2002 to 2012 (ranging from 5.8 million to 6.6 million). The rate in 2013 was similar to the rates in 2006 to 2012 (ranging from 2.3 to 2.5%), but it was lower than the rates in 2002 to 2005 (ranging from 2.6 to 2.8%).
- Of the 6.1 million persons aged 12 or older who needed but did not receive specialty treatment for illicit drug use in 2013, 395,000 (6.4%) reported that they perceived a need for treatment for their illicit drug use problem, and 5.7 million did not perceive a need for treatment. The number of persons in 2013 who needed treatment for an illicit drug use problem but did not perceive a need for treatment was similar to the number in

2012 (5.9 million). However, the number of persons who needed treatment and perceived a need for treatment for an illicit drug problem in 2013 was lower than the number in 2012 (588,000 persons).

- Of the 395,000 persons aged 12 or older in 2013 who felt a need for treatment for use of illicit drugs, 148,000 reported that they made an effort to get treatment, and 247,000 reported making no effort to get treatment. These estimates in 2013 for making or not making an effort to get treatment were similar to those in 2012.
- In 2013, among youths aged 12 to 17, 908,000 persons (3.6%) needed treatment for an illicit drug use problem, but only 90,000 received treatment at a specialty facility (10.0% of youths aged 12 to 17 who needed treatment), leaving 817,000 youths who needed treatment but did not receive it at a specialty facility. These estimates in 2013 were similar to those in 2012, except that the number and the rate of youths who needed treatment for an illicit drug use problem in 2013 were lower than those in 2012 (1.0 million and 4.2%).
- Among persons aged 12 or older who needed but did not receive illicit drug use treatment and felt they needed treatment (based on 2010-2013 combined data), the commonly reported reasons for not receiving treatment were (a) no health coverage and could not afford cost (42.1%), (b) not ready to stop using (27.5%), (c) concern that receiving treatment might cause neighbors/community to have negative opinion (15.9%), (d) possible negative effect on job (15.2%), (e) not knowing where to go for treatment (12.8%), and (f) having health coverage that did not cover treatment or did not cover the cost (9.6%).

Alcohol Use Treatment and Treatment Need

In 2013, the number of persons aged 12 or older needing treatment for an alcohol use problem was 18.0 million (6.9% of the population aged 12 or older). The number in 2013 was similar to the numbers in 2010 to 2012 (ranging from 17.4 million to 18.6 million) and in 2002, 2003, and 2008 (ranging from 18.2 million to 19.1 million). However, the number in 2013 was lower than the numbers in 2004 to 2007 and in 2009 (ranging from 19.4 million to 19.6 million). The rate in 2013 (6.9%) was similar to the rates in 2011 (6.8%) and 2012 (7.0%), but it was lower than the rates in 2002 to 2010 (ranging from 7.3 to 8.0%).

- Among the 18.0 million persons aged 12 or older who needed treatment for an alcohol use problem in 2013, 1.4 million (0.5% of the total population and 7.9% of the persons who needed treatment for an alcohol use problem) received alcohol use treatment at a specialty facility. The number and the rate of the need and receipt of treatment at a specialty facility for an alcohol use problem in 2013 did not change significantly since 2002 (ranging from 1.3 million to 1.7 million and from 0.5 to 0.7%).
- The number of persons aged 12 or older who needed but did not receive treatment at a specialty facility for an alcohol use problem in 2013 (16.6 million) was similar to the numbers in 2002 (17.1 million), 2003 (16.9 million), and from 2008 to 2012 (ranging from 15.9 million to 17.7 million), but it was lower than the numbers from 2004 to 2007 (ranging from 17.8 million to 18.0 million). The rate in 2013 (6.3% of the population aged 12 or older) was similar to the rates in 2010 to 2012 (ranging from 6.2 to 6.7%), but it was lower than the rates in 2002 to 2009 (ranging from 7.0 to 7.4%).
- Among the 16.6 million persons aged 12 or older who needed but did not receive specialty treatment for an alcohol use problem in 2013, 554,000 persons (3.3%) felt they needed treatment for their alcohol use problem. The number and rate in 2013 were similar to those in 2012 (665,000 persons and 4.0%) and 2002 (761,000 persons and 4.5%). Of the 554,000 persons in 2013 who perceived a need for treatment for an alcohol use problem but did not receive specialty treatment, 353,000 did not make an effort to get treatment, and 201,000 made an effort but were unable to get treatment.
- The number and the rate of youths aged 12 to 17 who needed treatment for an alcohol use problem in 2013 (735,000 and 3.0%) were lower than those in 2012 (889,000 and 3.6%). Of the youths in 2013 who needed treatment for an alcohol use problem, only 73,000 received treatment at a specialty facility (0.3% of all youths and 10.0% of youths who needed treatment). These estimates were similar to those in 2012. The number and the rate of youths who needed but did not receive treatment for an alcohol use problem in 2013 (662,000 and 2.7%) were lower than those in 2012 (814,000 and 3.3%).
- Among persons aged 12 or older who needed but did not receive illicit drug use treatment and felt they needed treatment (based

on 2010-2013 combined data), the commonly reported reasons for not receiving treatment were (a) no health coverage and could not afford cost (42.1%), (b) not ready to stop using (27.5%), (c) concern that receiving treatment might cause neighbors/community to have negative opinion (15.9%), (d) possible negative effect on job (15.2%), (e) not knowing where to go for treatment (12.8%), and (f) having health coverage that did not cover treatment or did not cover the cost (9.6%).

Section 6.2

Increase in Treatment Admissions for Prescription Pain Medicine Abuse

This section includes text excerpted from "America's Addiction to Opioids: Heroin and Prescription Drug Abuse," National Institute on Drug Abuse (NIDA), May 14, 2014.

Abuse of Prescription Opioids: Scope and Impact

Prescription opioids are one of the three main broad categories of medications that present abuse liability, the other two being stimulants and central nervous system (CNS) depressants.

Several factors are likely to have contributed to the severity of the current prescription drug abuse problem. They include drastic increases in the number of prescriptions written and dispensed, greater social acceptability for using medications for different purposes, and aggressive marketing by pharmaceutical companies. These factors together have helped create the broad "environmental availability" of prescription medications in general and opioid analgesics in particular.

The total number of opioid pain relievers prescribed in the United States has skyrocketed in the past 25 years. The number of prescriptions for opioids (like hydrocodone and oxycodone products) have escalated from around 76 million in 1991 to nearly 207 million in 2013, with the United States their biggest consumer globally, accounting for almost 100 percent of the world total for hydrocodone (e.g., Vicodin) and 81 percent for oxycodone (e.g., Percocet).

This greater availability of opioid (and other) prescribed drugs has been accompanied by alarming increases in the negative consequences related to their abuse. For example, the estimated number of emergency department visits involving nonmedical use of opioid analgesics increased from 144,600 in 2004 to 305,900 in 2008; treatment admissions for primary abuse of opiates other than heroin increased from one percent of all admissions in 1997 to five percent in 2007; and overdose deaths due to prescription opioid pain relievers have more than tripled in the past 20 years, escalating to 16,651 deaths in the United States in 2010.

In terms of abuse and mortality, opioids account for the greatest proportion of the prescription drug abuse problem. Deaths related to prescription opioids began rising in the early part of the 21st century. By 2002, death certificates listed opioid analgesic poisoning as a cause of death more commonly than heroin or cocaine.

The Effects of Opioid Abuse on the Brain and Body

Opioid pain relievers are sometimes diverted for nonmedical use by patients or their friends, or sold in the street. In 2012, over five percent of the U.S. population aged 12 years or older used opioid pain relievers nonmedically. The public health consequences of opioid pain reliever abuse are broad and disturbing. For example, abuse of prescription pain relievers by pregnant women can result in a number of problems in newborns, referred to as neonatal abstinence syndrome (NAS), which increased by almost 300 percent in the United States between 2000 and 2009. This increase is driven in part by the high rate of opioid prescriptions being given to pregnant women. In the United States, an estimated 14.4 percent of pregnant women are prescribed an opioid during their pregnancy.

Prescription opioid abuse is not only costly in economic terms (it has been estimated that the nonmedical use of opioid pain relievers costs insurance companies up to $72.5 billion annually in health-care costs) but may also be partly responsible for the steady upward trend in poisoning mortality. In 2010, there were 13,652 unintentional deaths from opioid pain reliever (82.8 percent of the 16,490 unintentional deaths from all prescription drugs), and there was a five-fold increase in treatment admissions for prescription pain relievers between 2001 and 2011 (from 35,648 to 180,708, respectively). In the same decade, there was a tripling of the prevalence of positive opioid tests among drivers who died within one hour of a crash.

Section 6.3

Predictors of Substance Abuse Treatment Completion

This section includes text excerpted from "Treatment Episode Data Set (TEDS) 2011," Substance Abuse and Mental Health Services Administration (SAMHSA), May 2014.

Treatment Completion or Transfer to Further Treatment

Completion/transfer rates were generally similar within admission characteristics, but varied widely by service type. Treatment completion/transfer rates ranged from 35 percent among discharges aged 12 and older from outpatient medication-assisted opioid therapy to 77 percent among discharges aged 12 and older from detoxification, while the largest variation by admission characteristic was for primary substance, ranging from 51 percent for marijuana to 66 percent for alcohol.

Some general observations can be made about the completion/transfer rate for all discharges aged 12 and older combined:

- The treatment completion/transfer rate increased with education
- For known primary substance of abuse, the treatment completion/transfer rates were highest for alcohol (66%), followed by stimulants and cocaine (62% and 55% respectively)
- The treatment completion/transfer rate was higher among those who were employed than among those who were unemployed or not in the labor force
- The treatment completion/transfer rate was lower among non-Hispanic Blacks or those of Hispanic origin (55% and 58%, respectively) than among non-Hispanic Whites (60%)

Treatment Completion by Service Type

The treatment completion rate was 44 percent for discharges aged 12 and older from all service types combined. For the individual service types, treatment was completed by:

- 67 percent of discharges from detoxification
- 54 percent of discharges from short-term residential treatment
- 53 percent of discharges from hospital residential treatment
- 52 percent of discharges from medication-assisted opioid detoxification
- 45 percent of discharges from long-term residential treatment
- 37 percent of discharges from outpatient treatment
- 33 percent of discharges from intensive outpatient treatment
- 12 percent of discharges from outpatient medication-assisted opioid therapy

Part Two

Drug Abuse and Specific Populations

Chapter 7

Initiation of Drug Abuse

Chapter Contents

Section 7.1

Estimates of Drug Use Initiation

This section contains text excerpted from the following sources: Text beginning with the heading "Age of Substance Use Initiation among Treatment Admissions Aged 18 to 30" is excerpted from "Age of Substance Use Initiation among Treatment Admissions Aged 18 to 30," Substance Abuse and Mental Health Services Administration (SAMHSA), July 17, 2014; Text beginning with the heading "Initiation of Drug and Substance Use" is excerpted from "Risk and Protective Factors and Initiation of Substance Use: Results from the 2014 National Survey on Drug Use and Health," Substance Abuse and Mental Health Services Administration (SAMHSA), October 2015.

Age of Substance Use Initiation among Treatment Admissions Aged 18 to 30

Initiating substance use during childhood or adolescence is linked to substantial long-term health risks. Early (aged 12 to 14) to late (aged 15 to 17) adolescence is generally regarded as a critical risk period for the initiation of alcohol use, with multiple studies showing associations between age at first alcohol use and the occurrence of alcohol abuse or dependence.

Moreover, there is evidence across a range of other substances—including marijuana, cocaine, other psychostimulants, and inhalants—that the risk of developing dependence or abuse is greater for individuals who initiate use of these substances in adolescence or early adolescence than for those who initiate use during adulthood. For example, 2012 National Survey on Drug Use and Health data indicate that among those adults who first tried marijuana at the age of 14 or younger, 13.2 percent were classified with illicit drug dependence or abuse; this percentage was 6 times higher than that for adults who first used marijuana at the age of 18 or older. In fact, among adolescents, the transition from initiation to regular use of alcohol, marijuana, and other drugs often occurs within 3 years.

Examining patterns in the age of drug or alcohol initiation among persons in treatment for substance abuse may increase understanding of the characteristics of those who initiate substance use during their childhood or adolescence and highlight potential ways to optimize prevention and treatment efforts.

Initiation of Drug and Substance Use

This section focuses on trends in the number of people who were recent initiates for a substance (e.g., the number of people aged 12 or older who were recent initiates of marijuana use). Information on changes in the number of recent initiates over time can be useful to policymakers and program planners for anticipating future needs for medical and behavioral health services both in the short term and in the longer term. For example, decreases in the number of people who have initiated use of cigarettes might translate over time into fewer new cases of people with chronic bronchitis, emphysema, heart disease, or lung cancer. In contrast, increases in the number of people who have initiated use of substances such as heroin could signal future needs for emergency medical services, treatment for infectious diseases such as hepatitis, or substance use treatment.

This section also presents trends in the average age at first use among recent initiates for use of a substance. Although trends in the numbers of initiates are shown for initiates aged 12 or older as well as by age group, trends in the average age at first use in this report are limited to all past year initiates aged 12 to 49 to avoid having the averages be influenced by extreme values. For example, a small number of people who started using a substance at very late ages could artificially inflate the average age at first use among all initiates. Figure 7.3 provides an overview of the numbers of past year initiates in 2014 for the majority of substances that are discussed in this section.

The illicit drugs with the largest number of recent initiates in 2014 were marijuana (2.6 million new users), pain relievers (1.4 million new users), and tranquilizers (1.1million new users). In addition, there were 4.7 million new users of alcohol, 2.2 million people who tried a cigarette for the first time in the past year, and 1.0 million people who first used smokeless tobacco in the past year.

Initiation of Marijuana Use

In 2014, about 2.6 million people aged 12 or older used marijuana for the first time within the past 12 months. This averages to about 7,000 new marijuana users each day. In 2014, the average age at first marijuana use among recent marijuana initiates aged 12 to 49 was 18.5 years. Although new marijuana users aged 12 to 49 initiated

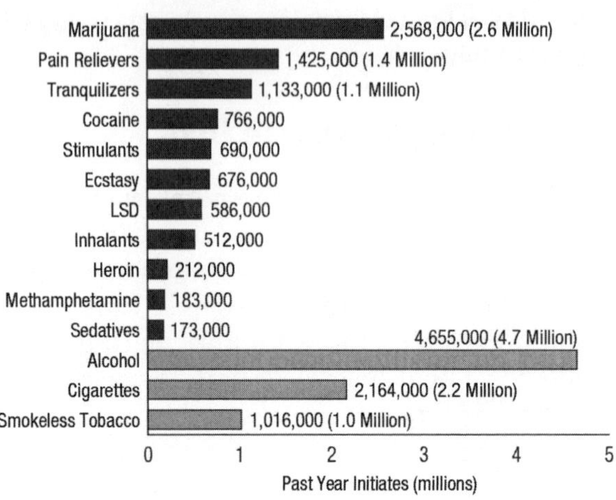

Figure 7.1. *Numbers of Past Year Initiates of Selected Substances among People Aged 12 or Older: 2014*

use on average in their late teens, these trend data suggest that new users on average were initiating use at a somewhat later age in 2014 compared with initiation in some earlier years.

By Age Group

In 2014, an estimated 1.2 million adolescents aged 12 to 17 used marijuana for the first time in the past year, which translates to approximately 3,300 adolescents initiating marijuana use each day. About 1.1 million to 1.4 million adolescents per year in 2002 to 2013 were recent marijuana initiates.

There were 1.1 million young adults aged 18 to 25 in 2014 who initiated marijuana use in the past year, or an average of about 3,000 recent initiates per day in this age group.

An estimated 271,000 adults aged 26 or older in 2014 also initiated marijuana use in the past year.

Initiation of Nonmedical Pain Reliever Use

In 2014, the number of recent initiates for nonmedical use of pain relievers (1.4 million) was second only to the number of marijuana initiates. The number of people aged 12 or older who used pain relievers nonmedically for the first time within the past year averages to about

3,900 initiates per day. The average age at first nonmedical use of pain relievers among recent pain reliever initiates aged 12 to 49 was 21.2 years.

By Age Group

In 2014, an estimated 489,000 adolescents aged 12 to 17 used pain relievers nonmedically for the first time in the past year. This averages to approximately 1,300 adolescents each day who initiated nonmedical use of pain relievers.

There were 574,000 young adults aged 18 to 25 and 362,000 adults aged 26 or older in 2014 who initiated nonmedical use of pain relievers in the past year. These numbers average to about 1,600 young adults and about 1,000 adults aged 26 or older who initiated nonmedical use of pain relievers each day.

Initiation of Nonmedical Tranquilizer Use

About 1.1 million people aged 12 or older in 2014 used tranquilizers nonmedically for the first time within the past year (Figure 7.3). This averages to about 3,100 initiates per day. The average age at first nonmedical use of tranquilizers among recent tranquilizer initiates aged 12 to 49 was 23.4 years.

By Age Group

In 2014, an estimated 254,000 adolescents aged 12 to 17, 440,000 young adults aged 18 to 25, and 439,000 adults aged 26 or older used tranquilizers nonmedically for the first time in the past year. Thus, about 700 adolescents, 1,200 young adults, and 1,200 adults aged 26 or older initiated nonmedical use of tranquilizers per day in 2014.

Initiation of Nonmedical Stimulant Use and Methamphetamine Use

In 2014, approximately 690,000 people aged 12 or older used stimulants nonmedically, and 183,000 used methamphetamine for the first time within the past year. These estimated numbers of initiates in 2014 average to about 1,900 initiates per day for nonmedical use of stimulants and to about 500 initiates per day for methamphetamine use.

In 2014, the average age at first use of stimulants among recent initiates aged 12 to 49 was 21.6 years. The average age at first methamphetamine use in 2014 among recent methamphetamine initiates aged 12 to 49 was 22.0 years.

By Age Group

In 2014, an estimated 183,000 adolescents aged 12 to 17, 356,000 young adults aged 18 to 25, and 152,000 adults aged 26 or older used stimulants nonmedically for the first time in the past year. For methamphetamine, 51,000 adolescents, 67,000 young adults, and 65,000 adults aged 26 or older were recent initiates in 2014.

Initiation of Nonmedical Sedative Use

In 2014, approximately 173,000 people aged 12 or older used sedatives nonmedically for the first time within the past year. In 2014, the average age at first nonmedical use of sedatives among recent initiates aged 12 to 49 was 21.4 years.

By Age Group

In 2014, an estimated 59,000 adolescents aged 12 to 17, 64,000 young adults aged 18 to 25, and 50,000 adults aged 26 or older used sedatives nonmedically for the first time in the past year.

Initiation of Cocaine Use

In 2014, there were 766,000 people aged 12 or older who used cocaine for the first time in the past year. This averages to approximately 2,100 cocaine initiates per day. In 2014, the average age at first cocaine use among recent cocaine initiates aged 12 to 49 was 21.8 years.

By Age Group

In 2014, an estimated 117,000 adolescents aged 12 to 17 used cocaine for the first time in the past year. Also in 2014, 501,000 young adults aged 18 to 25 and 148,000 adults aged 26 or older initiated cocaine use in the past year.

Initiation of Crack Cocaine Use

There were 109,000 recent crack cocaine initiates aged 12 or older in 2014. The average age at first crack use among recent crack initiates aged 12 to 49 was 26.4 years.

By Age Group

In 2014, an estimated 11,000 adolescents aged 12 to 17, 54,000 young adults aged 18 to 25, and 44,000 adults aged 26 or older used crack for the first time in the past year.

Initiation of Heroin Use

In 2014, there were 212,000 people aged 12 or older who used heroin for the first time within the past year. On average, this represents roughly 600 people initiating heroin use each day. The average age at first heroin use among recent heroin initiates aged 12 to 49 was 28.0 years.

By Age Group

In 2014, an estimated 13,000 adolescents aged 12 to 17, 75,000 young adults aged 18 to 25, and 124,000 adults aged 26 or older used heroin for the first time in the past year.

Initiation of Hallucinogen Use

In 2014, there were 936,000 people aged 12 or older who had used hallucinogens for the first time in the past year. This averages to about 2,600 new hallucinogen users each day. The average age at first hallucinogen use among recent hallucinogen initiates aged 12 to 49 was 19.3 years.

By Age Group

In 2014, an estimated 258,000 adolescents aged 12 to 17, 608,000 young adults aged 18 to 25, and 70,000 adults aged 26 or older used hallucinogens for the first time in the past year.

Initiation of LSD Use

There were 586,000 people aged 12 or older in 2014 who were past year initiates of LSD. On average, this represents roughly 1,600 people initiating LSD use each day. The average age at first LSD use among recent initiates aged 12 to 49 was 19.7 years.

Initiation of Ecstasy Use

In 2014, there were 676,000 past year initiates of Ecstasy aged 12 or older in 2014, which averages to about 1,900 people who initiated Ecstasy use each day. The average age at first Ecstasy use among recent Ecstasy initiates aged 12 to 49 was 21.0 years.

By Age Group

In 2014, an estimated 125,000 adolescents aged 12 to 17, 448,000 young adults aged 18 to 25, and 104,000 adults aged 26 or older used Ecstasy for the first time in the past year.

Initiation of Inhalant Use

In 2014, there were 512,000 people aged 12 or older who had used inhalants for the first time within the past 12 months, which averages to about 1,400 people who initiated inhalant use each day. The average age at first inhalant use among recent inhalant initiates aged 12 to 49 was 18.2 years.

By Age Group

In 2014, an estimated 271,000 adolescents aged 12 to 17 used inhalants for the first time in the past year. This averages to approximately 700 adolescents who initiated use of inhalants each day. There were 157,000 young adults aged 18 to 25 in 2014 who initiated use of inhalants in the past year.

Initiation of Alcohol Use

About 4.7 million people aged 12 or older in 2014 used alcohol for the first time within the past year. This averages to approximately 12,800 initiates per day. The average age at first alcohol use among recent alcohol initiates aged 12 to 49 was 17.3 years.

By Age Group

In 2014, an estimated 2.3 million adolescents aged 12 to 17 used alcohol for the first time in the past year, which averages to approximately 6,400 adolescents initiating alcohol use each day. Also in 2014, 2.2 million young adults aged 18 to 25 and 95,000 adults aged 26 or older initiated alcohol use in the past year.

Initiation of Cigarette Use

In 2014, about 2.2 million people aged 12 or older smoked cigarettes for the first time within the past 12 months. This averages to about 5,900 new cigarette smokers every day. The average age at first cigarette use among recent cigarette initiates aged 12 to 49 was 18.6 years.

By Age Group

In 2014, an estimated 838,000 adolescents aged 12 to 17 used cigarettes for the first time in the past year, which averages to approximately 2,300 adolescents each day who initiated cigarette use. Also,

1.2 million young adults aged 18 to 25 in 2014 initiated cigarette use in the past year, which translates to about 3,200 young adults each day who initiated cigarette use. Among adults aged 26 or older in 2014, 144,000 initiated cigarette use in the past year.

Initiation of Smokeless Tobacco Use

About 1.0 million people aged 12 or older in 2014 initiated use of smokeless tobacco in the past year. This averages to about 2,800 people who initiated smokeless tobacco use each day. The average age at first smokeless tobacco use among recent smokeless tobacco initiates aged 12 to 49 was 19.0 years

By Age Group

In 2014, an estimated 431,000 adolescents aged 12 to 17 used smokeless tobacco for the first time in the past year, which averages to approximately 1,200 adolescents who initiated smokeless tobacco use each day. There were 468,000 young adults aged 18 to 25 in 2014 who initiated smokeless tobacco use in the past year, or about 1,300 new initiates each day. Among adults aged 26 or older in 2014, 117,000 initiated smokeless tobacco use in the past year.

Section 7.2

Dependence Following Drug Use Initiation

This section includes text excerpted from "Results from the 2013 National Survey on Drug Use and Health: Summary of National Findings," Substance Abuse and Mental Health Services Administration (SAMHSA), September 2014.

Dependence or Abuse Following Drug Use Initiation

- In 2013, an estimated 21.6 million persons aged 12 or older were classified with substance dependence or abuse in the past year (8.2% of the population aged 12 or older). Of these, 2.6 million were classified with dependence or abuse of both alcohol and illicit drugs, 4.3 million had dependence or abuse of illicit drugs but not alcohol, and 14.7 million had dependence or abuse of alcohol but not illicit drugs. Overall, 17.3 million had alcohol dependence or abuse, and 6.9 million had illicit drug dependence or abuse.

The annual number of persons with substance dependence or abuse in 2013 (21.6 million) was similar to the number in each year from 2002 through 2012 (ranging from 20.6 million to 22.7 million).

- The rate of persons aged 12 or older who had substance dependence or abuse in 2013 (8.2 percent) was similar to the rates in 2011 (8.0%) and 2012 (8.5%), but it was lower than the rate in each year from 2002 through 2010 (ranging from 8.8 to 9.4%).

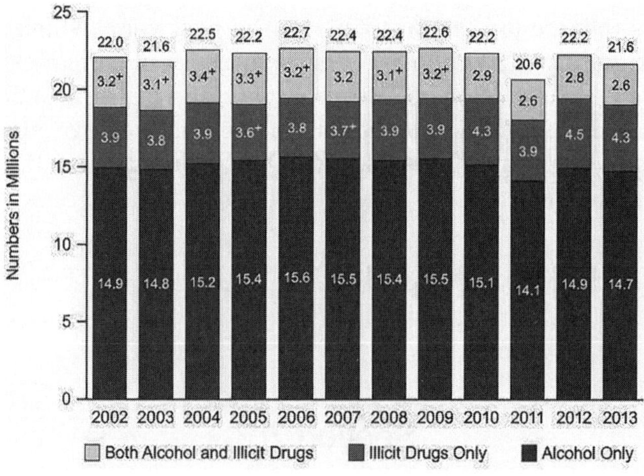

Figure 7.2. *Substance Dependence or Abuse in the Past Year among Persons Aged 12 or Older: 2002-2013*

- In 2013, 6.6 percent of the population aged 12 or older had alcohol dependence or abuse, which was similar to the rates in 2011 (6.5%) and 2012 (6.8 percent), but it was lower than the rate in each year from 2002 through 2010 (ranging from 7.1 to 7.8%).
- The rate of persons aged 12 or older who had illicit drug dependence or abuse in 2013 (2.6 percent) was similar to the rate in 2012 (2.8%) and in each year since 2005 (ranging from 2.5 to 2.9%), but it was lower than the rates in 2002 to 2004 (ranging from 2.9 to 3.0%).

- Marijuana was the illicit drug with the largest number of persons with past year dependence or abuse in 2013, followed by pain relievers, then by cocaine. Of the 6.9 million persons aged 12 or older who were classified with illicit drug dependence or abuse in 2013, 4.2 million persons had marijuana dependence or abuse (representing 1.6% of the total population aged 12 or older, and 61.4% of all those classified with illicit drug dependence or abuse), 1.9 million persons had pain reliever dependence or abuse, and 855,000 persons had cocaine dependence or abuse.
- The number of persons who had marijuana dependence or abuse in 2013 (4.2 million) was similar to the number in 2012 (4.3 million) and in each year from 2002 through 2011 (ranging from 3.9 million to 4.5 million). The rate of marijuana dependence or abuse in 2013 (1.6%) was lower than the rates in 2002 (1.8%) and 2004 (1.9%). Otherwise, the rate in 2013 was similar to the rates in prior years (ranging from 1.6 to 1.8%).

Age at First Use

- In 2013, among adults aged 18 or older, age at first use of marijuana was associated with illicit drug dependence or abuse. Among those who first tried marijuana at age 14 or younger, 11.5 percent were classified with illicit drug dependence or abuse, which was higher than the 2.6 percent of adults who had first used marijuana at age 18 or older.
- Among adults, age at first use of alcohol was associated with alcohol dependence or abuse. In 2013, among adults aged 18 or older who first tried alcohol at age 14 or younger, 15.4 percent were classified with alcohol dependence or abuse, which was higher than the 3.8 percent of adults who had first used alcohol at age 18 or older.
- Adults aged 21 or older who had first used alcohol before age 21 were more likely than adults who had their first drink at age 21 or older to be classified with alcohol dependence or abuse. In particular, adults aged 21 or older who had first used alcohol at age 14 or younger were more likely to be classified with alcohol dependence or abuse than adults who had their first drink at age 21 or older.

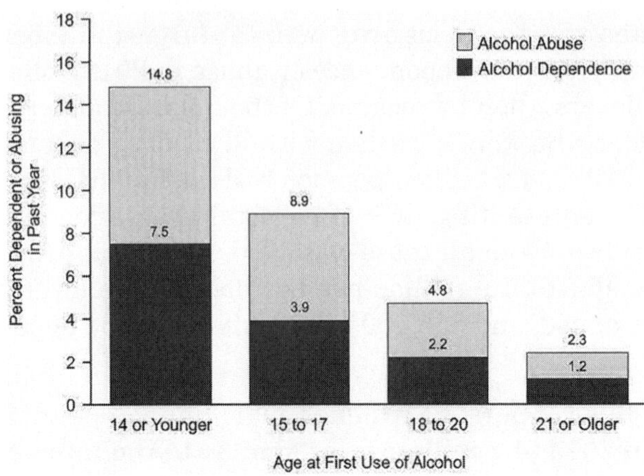

Figure 7.3. *Alcohol Dependence or Abuse in the Past Year among Adults Aged 21 or Older, by Age at First Use of Alcohol: 2013*

Age

- Rates of substance dependence or abuse were associated with age. In 2013, the rate of substance dependence or abuse among adults aged 18 to 25 (17.3%) was higher than that among adults aged 26 or older (7.0%), followed by youths aged 12 to 17 (5.2%). From 2002 to 2013, the rate decreased for youths aged 12 to 17 (from 8.9 to 5.2%) and for young adults aged 18 to 25 (from 21.7 to 17.3%).
- The rate of alcohol dependence or abuse among youths aged 12 to 17 was 2.8 percent in 2013, which was lower than the rates of 3.4 percent in 2012 and 5.9 percent in 2002. Among young adults aged 18 to 25, the rate of alcohol dependence or abuse was 13.0 percent in 2013, which also was lower than the rates of 14.3 percent in 2012 and 17.7 percent in 2002. Among adults aged 26 or older, the rates were not significantly different between 2012 (5.9%) and 2013 (6.0%) and between 2002 (6.2%) and 2013.
- The rate of illicit drug dependence or abuse among youths aged 12 to 17 was 3.5 percent in 2013, which was lower than the rates in 2012 (4.0%), 2011 (4.6%), 2010 (4.7%), and 2002 (5.6%). Among young adults aged 18 to 25, the rate of illicit drug dependence or abuse was 7.4 percent in 2013, which was similar to the rates in 2012 (7.8%), 2011 (7.5%), and 2010 (7.9%). Among adults aged 26 or older, the rate of illicit drug dependence or abuse remained stable between 2012 (1.8%) and 2013 (1.7%) and between 2002 (1.8%) and 2013.

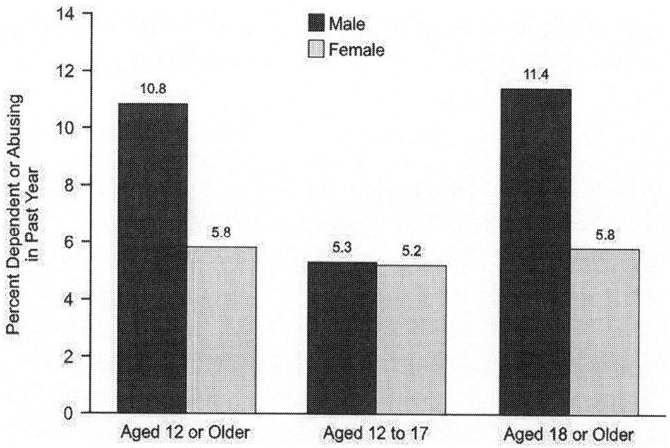

Figure 7.4. *Substance Dependence or Abuse in the Past Year, by Age and Gender: 2013*

Gender

- As was the case from 2002 through 2012, the rate of substance dependence or abuse for males aged 12 or older in 2013 was greater than the rate for females (10.8 vs. 5.8%). Among youths aged 12 to 17, however, the rate of substance dependence or abuse among males in 2013 (5.3%) was similar to the rate among their female counterparts (5.2%).

Race / Ethnicity

- In 2013, among persons aged 12 or older, the rate of substance dependence or abuse was 4.6 percent among Asians, 7.4 percent among blacks, 8.4 percent among whites, 8.6 percent among Hispanics, 10.9 percent among persons reporting two or more races, 11.3 percent among Native Hawaiians or Other Pacific Islanders, and 14.9 percent among American Indians or Alaska Natives. Except for Native Hawaiians or Other Pacific Islanders, the rate for Asians was lower than the rates for the other racial/ethnic groups.

Education

- In 2013, rates of illicit drug or alcohol dependence or abuse among adults aged 26 or older were not associated with levels of educational attainment. Among this group, rates of illicit drug or alcohol dependence or abuse were 6.4 percent for those who graduated from high school but had no further education, 7.2 percent for college graduates, 7.3 percent for those who did not graduate from high school, and 7.4 percent for those with some college education but no degree.

- Among adults aged 26 or older in 2013, rates of alcohol dependence or abuse also were not associated with levels of educational attainment. Rates of alcohol dependence or abuse for this age group were 5.4 percent for those who graduated from high school but had no further education, 5.7 percent for those who did not graduate from high school, 5.9 percent for those with some college education but no degree, and 6.6 percent for college graduates.
- However, rates of illicit drug dependence or abuse were associated with levels of educational attainment among adults aged 26 or older in 2013. Adults aged 26 or older who were college graduates had a lower rate of illicit drug dependence or abuse (0.9%) than those who did not graduate from high school (2.5%), those with some college education but no degree (2.1%), and those who graduated from high school but had no further education (1.9%).

Employment

- Rates of substance dependence or abuse were associated with current employment status in 2013. A higher percentage of unemployed adults aged 18 or older were classified with dependence or abuse (15.2%) than were full-time employed adults (9.5%) or part-time employed adults (9.3%).
- Over half of the adults aged 18 or older with substance dependence or abuse were employed full time in 2013. Of the 20.3 million adults who were classified with dependence or abuse, 11.3 million (55.7%) were employed full time.

Criminal Justice Populations

- In 2013, adults aged 18 or older who were on parole or a supervised release from jail during the past year had a higher rate of illicit drug or alcohol dependence or abuse (34.3%) than their counterparts who were not on parole or supervised release during the past year (8.4%).
- In 2013, probation status was associated with substance dependence or abuse. The rate of substance dependence or abuse was

35.0 percent among adults who were on probation during the past year, which was higher than the rate among adults who were not on probation during the past year (8.0%).

Geographic Area

- In 2013, rates of illicit drug or alcohol dependence or abuse among persons aged 12 or older were 8.9 percent in the West, 8.3 percent in the Northeast, 8.2 percent in the Midwest, and 7.8 percent in the South.
- Rates for illicit drug or alcohol dependence or abuse among persons aged 12 or older in 2013 were similar in large metropolitan areas (8.6%) and small metropolitan areas (8.4%), but were higher than in nonmetropolitan areas (6.6%).

Chapter 8

The Effect of Adult Substance Abuse on Children

Chapter Contents

Section 8.1

Concerns about Drug Abuse during Pregnancy

This section contains text excerpted from the following sources: Text beginning with the heading "Using Drugs When Pregnant Harms the Baby" is excerpted from "Using Drugs When Pregnant Harms the Baby," National Institute on Drug Abuse (NIDA), September 26, 2013; Text under the heading "Tobacco, Drug Use in Pregnancy Can Double Risk of Stillbirth" is excerpted from "Tobacco, Drug Use in Pregnancy Can Double Risk of Stillbirth," National Institutes of Health (NIH), December 11, 2013; Text under the heading "How Does Heroin Use Affect Pregnant Women?" is excerpted from "How Does Heroin Use Affect Pregnant Women?" National Institute on Drug Abuse (NIDA), November 2014.

Using Drugs When Pregnant Harms the Baby

Did you know that using alcohol, cigarettes, and illegal drugs during pregnancy can harm the mother and her baby? Everything a pregnant woman eats, drinks, or takes affects the baby. Using drugs can hurt the baby's growth or even cause the baby to get sick.

Cigarettes: Pregnant women who smoke expose their babies to nicotine and the dangerous chemicals in cigarettes. If the mother smokes, her baby may:

- Be born early
- Develop an addiction to nicotine
- Have breathing and behavioral problems
- Die before it is born or in the first year of life

Secondhand smoke can also be harmful to a baby. The baby is more likely to develop problems breathing, ear infections, and cavities.

Alcohol: Drinking alcohol while pregnant can cause babies to be born with illnesses. These children may:

- Have problems seeing and hearing

- Be born too small
- Struggle with eating and sleeping
- Have problems in school with learning and paying attention

Illegal drugs: Pregnant women who use illegal drugs like marijuana, cocaine, Ecstasy, meth, or heroin can cause lifelong harm to their babies. Drug use can cause babies to:

- Be born early
- Grow slowly
- Have withdrawal symptoms, including fever, vomiting, poor sleep, and shaking
- Have heart problems or a stroke
- Suffer lifelong disabilities

If you have been using drugs and think you might be pregnant, stop using the drug and talk to a doctor as soon as possible. (Exception: If you use heroin and you are pregnant, you will need to see a doctor to help you gradually get off the drug—if you stop too suddenly, it can harm the baby.) There are programs that can help teen moms stop using drugs and get healthy for their babies.

Tobacco, Drug Use in Pregnancy Can Double Risk of Stillbirth

Smoking tobacco or marijuana, taking prescription painkillers, or using illegal drugs during pregnancy is associated with double or even triple the risk of stillbirth, according to research funded by the National Institutes of Health.

Researchers based their findings on measurements of the chemical byproducts of nicotine in maternal blood samples; and cannabis, prescription painkillers and other drugs in umbilical cords. Taking direct measurements provided more precise information than did previous studies of stillbirth and substance use that relied only on women's self-reporting. The study findings appear in the journal Obstetrics and Gynecology.

The study enrolled women between March 2006 and September 2008 in five geographically defined areas delivering at 59 hospitals participating in the Stillbirth Collaborative Research Network. Women who experienced a stillbirth and those who gave birth to a live infant participated in the study. The researchers tested blood samples at delivery from the two groups of women and the umbilical cords from their deliveries to measure the exposure to the fetus. They also asked participants to self-report smoking and drug use during pregnancy.

The researchers tested the women's blood for cotinine, a derivative of nicotine, and tested fetal umbilical cords for evidence of several types of drugs. They looked for evidence of the stimulants cocaine and amphetamine; prescription painkillers, such as morphine and codeine, and marijuana. These tests reflect exposure late in pregnancy. Among the women who had experienced a stillbirth, more than 80 percent showed no traces of cotinine and 93 percent tested negative for the other drugs. In comparison, about 90 percent of women who gave birth to a live infant tested tobacco-free and 96 percent tested negative for other drugs.

Based on the blood test results and women's own responses, the researchers calculated the increased risk of stillbirth for each of the substances they examined:

- Tobacco use—0.8 to 2.8 times greater risk of stillbirth, with the highest risk found among the heaviest smokers
- Marijuana use—2.3 times greater risk of stillbirth
- Evidence of any stimulant, marijuana or prescription painkiller use—2.2 times greater risk of stillbirth
- Passive exposure to tobacco—2.1 times greater risk of stillbirth

The researchers noted that they could not entirely separate the effects of smoking tobacco from those of smoking marijuana. Only a small number of women tested positive for prescription painkiller use, but there was a trend towards an association of these drugs with an elevated stillbirth risk.

How Does Heroin Use Affect Pregnant Women?

Heroin use during pregnancy can result in neonatal abstinence syndrome (NAS). NAS occurs when heroin passes through the placenta to the fetus during pregnancy, causing the baby to become dependent along with the mother. Symptoms include excessive crying, fever, irritability, seizures, slow weight gain, tremors, diarrhea, vomiting, and possibly death. NAS requires hospitalization and treatment with medication (often morphine) to relieve symptoms; the medication is gradually tapered off until the baby adjusts to being opioid-free.

Methadone maintenance combined with prenatal care and a comprehensive drug treatment program can improve many of the outcomes associated with untreated heroin use for both the infant and mother, although infants exposed to methadone during pregnancy typically require treatment for NAS as well.

A recent NIDA-supported clinical trial demonstrated that buprenorphine treatment of opioid-dependent mothers is safe for both the unborn child and the mother. Once born, these infants require less morphine and shorter hospital stays as compared to infants born of mothers on methadone maintenance treatment. Research also indicates that buprenorphine combined with naloxone (compared to a morphine taper) is equally safe for treating babies born with NAS, further reducing side effects experienced by infants born to opioid-dependent mothers.

Section 8.2

Negative Consequences of Prenatal Exposure to Drugs

This section includes text excerpted from "Substance Use in Women," National Institute on Drug Abuse (NIDA), July 2015.

Substance Use While Pregnant and Breastfeeding

Research shows that use of tobacco, alcohol, or illicit drugs or abuse of prescription drugs by pregnant women can have severe health consequences for infants. This is because many substances pass easily through the placenta, so substances that a pregnant woman takes also, to some degree, reach the baby. Recent research shows that smoking tobacco or marijuana, taking prescription pain relievers, or using illegal drugs during pregnancy is associated with double or even triple the risk of stillbirth.

Regular drug use can produce dependence in the newborn, and the baby may go through withdrawal upon birth. Most research in this area has focused on the effects of opioid misuse (prescription pain relievers or heroin). However, more recent data has shown that use of alcohol, barbiturates, benzodiazepines, and caffeine during pregnancy may also cause the infant to show withdrawal symptoms at birth. The type and severity of an infant's withdrawal symptoms depend on the drug(s) used, how long and how often the birth mother used, how her body breaks the drug down, and whether the infant was born full term or prematurely.

Symptoms of drug withdrawal in a newborn can develop immediately or up to 14 days after birth and can include:

- blotchy skin coloring
- diarrhea
- excessive or high-pitched crying
- abnormal sucking reflex
- fever
- hyperactive reflexes
- increased muscle tone
- irritability
- poor feeding
- rapid breathing
- increased heart rate
- seizures
- sleep problems
- slow weight gain
- stuffy nose and sneezing
- sweating
- trembling
- vomiting

Effects of using some drugs could be long-term and possibly fatal to the baby:

- low birth weight
- birth defects

- small head circumference
- premature birth
- sudden infant death syndrome (SIDS)

Illegal Drugs

Marijuana

More research needs to be done on how marijuana use during pregnancy could impact the health and development of infants, given changing policies about access to marijuana, as well as significant increases over the last decade in the number of pregnant women seeking substance use disorder treatment for marijuana use.

There is no human research connecting marijuana use to the chance of miscarriage, although animal studies indicate that the risk for miscarriage increases if marijuana is used early in pregnancy. Some associations have been found between marijuana use during pregnancy and future developmental and hyperactivity disorders in children. Evidence is mixed as to whether marijuana use by pregnant women is associated with low birth rate or premature birth, although long-term use may elevate these risks. Longitudinal studies found marijuana to be associated with reduced length at birth, but it did not affect weight or head circumference.

It was also found that exposed fetuses had significantly reduced body weight and length, even when the data were adjusted to account for maternal alcohol consumption and smoking. Pregnant women are strongly discouraged from using marijuana, given its potential to negatively impact the developing brain. Children prenatally exposed to marijuana functioned above average on the Bayley Scale of Infant Development (BSID) at 9 months, but third-trimester marijuana use was associated with decreased BSID mental scores. Follow-up assessment of these children at age 10 found that prenatal marijuana exposure was associated with higher levels of behavior problems. A review of existing data reported that although global IQ is unaffected by prenatal marijuana exposure, aspects of executive function appear to be negatively associated with prenatal exposure in children beyond the toddler stage.

Some women report using marijuana to treat severe nausea associated with their pregnancy; however, there is no research confirming that this is a safe practice, and it is generally not recommended. Women considering using medical marijuana while pregnant should not do so without checking with their healthcare providers.

Animal studies have shown that moderate concentrations of delta-9-tetrahydrocannabinol (or THC, the main psychoactive ingredient in marijuana), when administered to mothers while pregnant or nursing, could have long-lasting effects on the child, including increasing stress responsivity and abnormal patterns of social interactions. Animal studies also show learning deficits in prenatally exposed individuals.

Human research has shown that some babies born to women who used marijuana during their pregnancies display altered responses to visual stimuli, increased trembling, and a high-pitched cry, which could indicate problems with neurological development. In school, marijuana-exposed children are more likely to show gaps in problem-solving skills, memory, and the ability to remain attentive. More research is needed, however, to disentangle marijuana-specific effects from those of other environmental factors that could be associated with a mother's marijuana use, such as an impoverished home environment or the mother's use of other drugs. Prenatal marijuana exposure is also associated with an increased likelihood of a person using marijuana as a young adult, even when other factors that influence drug use are considered.

Prenatal marijuana exposure is also associated with an increased likelihood of a person using marijuana as a young adult, even when other factors that influence drug use are considered.

Very little is known about **marijuana use and breastfeeding**. One study suggests that moderate amounts of THC find their way into breast milk when a nursing mother uses marijuana. Some evidence shows that exposure to THC through breast milk in the first month of life could result in decreased motor development at 1 year of age. There have been no studies to determine if exposure to THC during nursing is linked to effects later in the child's life. With regular use, THC can accumulate in human breast milk to high concentrations. Because a baby's brain is still forming, THC consumed in breast milk could affect brain development. Given all these uncertainties, nursing mothers are discouraged from using marijuana. New mothers using medical marijuana should be vigilant about coordinating care between the doctor recommending their marijuana use and the pediatrician caring for their baby.

Stimulants (Cocaine, Amphetamines and Methamphetamine)

Some may recall news items about "crack babies," a term coined in the 1980s to describe babies born to mothers who smoked **cocaine** while pregnant. These babies were initially predicted to suffer from severe, irreversible cognitive and behavioral consequences, including reduced intelligence and social skills. These purported effects turned out to be somewhat exaggerated. However, it is not completely known how a pregnant woman's cocaine use affects her child, since cocaine-using women are more likely to also use other drugs such as alcohol, to have poor nutrition, or to not seek prenatal care. All of these factors can affect a developing fetus, making it difficult to isolate the effects of cocaine.

Research does show, however, that pregnant women who use cocaine are at higher risk for maternal migraines and seizures, premature membrane rupture, and placental abruption (separation of the placental lining from the uterus). Pregnancy is accompanied by normal cardiovascular changes, and cocaine abuse exacerbates these changes—sometimes leading to serious problems with high blood pressure (hypertensive crises), spontaneous miscarriage, preterm labor, and difficult delivery. Babies born to mothers who use cocaine during pregnancy may also have low birth weight and smaller head circumferences, and are shorter in length than babies born to mothers who do not use cocaine. They also show symptoms of irritability, hyperactivity, tremors, high-pitched cry, and excessive sucking at birth. These symptoms may be due to the effects of cocaine itself, rather than withdrawal, since cocaine and its metabolites are still present in the baby's body up to 5 to 7 days after delivery.

Other studies dispute many previously reported severe effects of prenatal exposure of cocaine on the offspring. It was found in a study that the most consistent effects were small size and less-than-optimal motor performance. In another study, no evidence of the previously reported devastating effects of prenatal cocaine exposure was found. A cohort of cocaine-exposed infants was followed from birth to age 6; although they found lower weight and head circumference, they found no difference in developmental scores between cocaine-exposed and non–cocaine exposed infants. However, other evidence suggests that children exposed to cocaine during the first trimester were smaller on all growth parameters at 7 and 10 years of age compared with children who were not exposed to cocaine. This longitudinal analysis indicated that the disparity in growth between both groups did not converge over time.

A study reported that the quality of the caregiving environment was the strongest independent predictor of cognitive outcomes among children exposed to cocaine. Nonetheless, the effects of cocaine on the fetus may be dose and timing dependent, and significant cocaine use during pregnancy, with or without other drug use, is associated with negative consequences for the offspring and the mother. Birth weight, length, and head circumference of infants with high exposure to cocaine differed from those with low or no exposure. Heavily cocaine-exposed infants were found to have more jitteriness and attention problems than infants with light or no exposure to cocaine and lower auditory comprehension than unexposed infants. Evidence suggests that subtle deficits exist in cognitive and attentional processes in cocaine-exposed preschool and 6-year-old children. In addition, infants exposed to cocaine during pregnancy had more infections, including hepatitis and HIV/AIDS exposure.

Much is still unknown about the effects of prenatal cocaine exposure. However, cocaine use by a pregnant woman should be viewed as an indication of multiple medical and social risk factors; her ability to access prenatal care, gain supportive and effective case management services, and obtain substance abuse treatment can make all the difference in outcome.

Exposure to **amphetamines** in utero has been associated with both short- and long-term effects, including abnormal fetal growth, withdrawal symptoms after birth, and impaired neurological development in infancy and childhood. Both animal and human studies have shown that fetal exposure to amphetamines increases the risk of reduced fetal growth, cardiac anomalies, and cleft lip and palate. Unfortunately, knowledge of the effects of **methamphetamine** during pregnancy is limited. While there is evidence of increased rates of premature delivery, placental abruption, reduced fetal growth, and heart abnormalities, studies are confounded by other issues, including polysubstance abuse among participants and methodological issues in the research design.

In one study, which took into account several confounding variables, findings suggest that methamphetamine exposure in utero is associated with decreased growth and smaller gestational age for exposed neonates. Pregnant women who use methamphetamine have a greater risk of preeclampsia (high blood pressure and possible organ damage). Their babies are more likely to be smaller and to have low birth weight. In a large, longitudinal study of children prenatally exposed to methamphetamine, exposed children had increased emotional reactivity and anxiety/depression, were more withdrawn, had problems with attention, and showed cognitive problems that could lead to poorer academic outcomes.

MDMA (Ecstasy, Molly)

What little research exists on the effects of MDMA use in pregnancy suggests that prenatal MDMA exposure may cause learning, memory, and motor problems in the baby. More research is needed on this topic.

Opioids

Opioid use in pregnant women presents a difficult situation because of the many medical complications of opioid use, such as infections passed to the fetus by the use of contaminated needles. Obstetric complications in pregnant women who use opioids often are compounded by lack of prenatal care. Complications include spontaneous abortion, premature labor and delivery, premature rupture of membranes, preeclampsia (high blood pressure during pregnancy), abruptio placentae, and intrauterine death. The fetus is at risk for morbidity and mortality because of episodes of maternal withdrawal.

Reviews of several studies recommend methadone maintenance treatment (MMT) as the only treatment for the management of opioid dependence during pregnancy because, when methadone is provided within a treatment setting that includes comprehensive care, obstetric and fetal complications, including neonatal morbidity and mortality, can be reduced. Effective MMT prevents the onset of withdrawal, reduces or eliminates drug craving, and blocks the euphoric effects of illicit self-administered opioids. The use of methadone in pregnancy prevents erratic maternal opioid levels and protects the fetus from repeated episodes of withdrawal. Because needle use is eliminated, MMT reduces the risk of infectious diseases. The mandatory link to prenatal care, frequent contact with program staff, and elimination of the stress of obtaining opioids daily to feel “normal” are additional benefits from MMT.

Reviews of the literature note that studies consistently have found that fetuses exposed to opioids (i.e., heroin and methadone) have lower birth weights than unexposed fetuses and usually undergo neonatal abstinence syndrome (NAS) at birth. NAS is a generalized disorder characterized by signs and symptoms of central nervous system irritability, gastrointestinal dysfunction, respiratory distress, vomiting, and fever, among other symptoms. NAS can be more severe and prolonged with methadone exposure than heroin exposure, but with appropriate pharmacotherapy, NAS can be treated effectively.

Although findings among studies are diverse, most suggest that methadone-exposed infants and children through age 2 function well within the normal range of development and that methadone-exposed children between ages 2 and 5 do not differ in cognitive function from a population that was not drug exposed and was of comparable socioeconomic and racial background. Data suggest that such psychosocial factors as environment and parenting can have as much of an effect on development as prenatal exposure to opioids.

In more recent years, buprenorphine treatment has been examined as an alternative to maintenance therapy for opioid dependence during pregnancy. Nonetheless, research is limited and only two randomized, double-blind studies have been conducted comparing methadone with buprenorphine

Heroin

Heroin use during pregnancy can result in neonatal abstinence syndrome (NAS). NAS occurs when heroin passes through the placenta to the fetus during pregnancy, causing the baby to become dependent on opioids. Symptoms include excessive crying, high-pitched cry, irritability, seizures, and gastrointestinal problems, among others. NAS requires hospitalization of the affected infant and possibly treatment with morphine or methadone to relieve symptoms; researchers have also studied buprenorphine for this purpose. The medication is gradually tapered off until the baby adjusts to being opioid-free.

Medications

Prescription and Over-the-Counter (OTC) Drugs

Pregnancy can be a confusing time for pregnant women facing many choices about legal drugs, like tobacco and alcohol, as well as prescription and over-the-counter (OTC) drugs that may affect their baby. These are difficult issues for researchers to study because scientists cannot give potentially dangerous drugs to pregnant women. Here are some of the known facts about popular medications and pregnancy:

There are more than 6 million pregnancies in the United States every year, and pregnant women take an average of three to five prescription drugs while pregnant. The U.S. Food and Drug Administration recently issued new rules on drug labeling to provide clearer instructions for pregnant and nursing women, including a summary of the risks of use during pregnancy and breastfeeding, a discussion of the data supporting the summary, and other information to help prescribers make safe decisions.

Even so, we know little about the effects of taking most medications during pregnancy. This is because pregnant women are often not included in studies to determine safety of new medications before they come on the market. A recent study shows that use of short-acting prescription opioids such as oxycodone during pregnancy, especially when combined with tobacco and/or certain antidepressant medications, is associated with an increased likelihood of neonatal abstinence syndrome (NAS) in the infant.

Although some prescription and OTC medications are safe to take during pregnancy, a pregnant woman should tell her doctor about all prescription medications, OTC cold and pain medicines, and herbal or dietary supplements she is taking or planning to take. This will allow her doctor to weigh the risks and benefits of a medication during pregnancy. In some cases, the doctor may recommend the continued use of specific medications, even though they could have some impact on the fetus. Suddenly stopping the use of a medication may be more risky for both the mother and baby than continuing to use the medication while under a doctor's care. This could also include medications to treat substance use disorders.

Some prescription and OTC medications are generally compatible with breastfeeding, and the American Academy of Pediatrics maintains a list of such substances. Others, such as some anti-anxiety and antidepressant medications, have unknown effects, so mothers who are using these medications should consult with their doctor before breastfeeding. Nursing mothers should contact their infant's health care provider if their infants show any of these reactions to the breast milk: diarrhea, excessive crying, vomiting, skin rashes, loss of appetite, or sleepiness.

Other Substances

Alcohol

Above all other drugs, alcohol is the most common teratogen (any agent that interrupts development or causes malformation in an embryo or fetus) in pregnancy. Alcohol use while pregnant can result in Fetal Alcohol Spectrum Disorders (FASD), a general term that includes Fetal Alcohol Syndrome, partial Fetal Alcohol Syndrome, alcohol-related disorders of brain development, and alcohol-related birth defects. These effects can last throughout life, causing difficulties with motor coordination, emotional control, schoolwork, socialization, and holding a job.

Fetal alcohol exposure occurs when a woman drinks while pregnant. Alcohol can disrupt fetal development at any stage during a pregnancy—including at the earliest stages before a woman even knows she is pregnant. In utero, alcohol use is associated with an increased risk of spontaneous abortion and increased rates of prematurity and abruptio placentae (premature separation of the placenta from the uterus). A study found that women who consumed five or more drinks per week were three times as likely to deliver a stillborn baby compared with those who had fewer than one drink per week.

Maternal alcohol use during pregnancy contributes to a wide range of effects on exposed offspring, known as fetal alcohol spectrum disorders (FASDs), and the most serious consequence is fetal alcohol syndrome (FAS). FAS is characterized by abnormal facial features, growth deficiencies, and central nervous system problems. Symptoms can include hyperactivity and attention problems, learning and memory deficits, and problems with social and emotional development. Infants who show only some of these features were previously identified as having fetal alcohol effects (FAE). Since 1996, the term FAE has been replaced by alcohol related birth defects (ARBD), partial fetal alcohol syndrome (pFAS), and alcohol-related neurodevelopmental disorder. Children with ARBD have problems with major and sensory organs, as well as structural abnormalities; children with ARND have central nervous system abnormalities. Despite alcohol-related birth defects being completely preventable, FASDs are the most common non-hereditary causes of mental retardation.

There is currently little research into how a nursing mother's alcohol use might affect her breastfed baby. What science suggests is that, contrary to folklore, alcohol does not increase a nursing mother's milk production, and it may disrupt the breastfed child's sleep cycle. The American Academy of Pediatrics recommends that alcohol drinking should be minimized during the months a woman nurses and daily intake limited to no more than 2 ounces of liquor, 8 ounces of wine, or two average beers for a 130-pound woman. In this case, nursing should take place at least 2 hours after drinking to allow the alcohol to be reduced or eliminated from the mother's body and milk. This will minimize the amount of alcohol passed to the baby.

Another risk factor associated with alcohol exposure in utero is the potential of substance use disorders. An association of early-onset of alcohol disorders among children exposed to alcohol prenatally was found; this association was more pronounced with early pregnancy exposure. While little is known about the prevalence of FASD among individuals with substance use disorders, this co-occurring condition is likely to further challenge recovery effects.

Nicotine (Tobacco Products and E-Cigarettes)

Almost 16 percent of pregnant women in the United States have smoked in the past month. Carbon monoxide and nicotine from tobacco smoke may interfere with the oxygen supply to the fetus. Nicotine also readily crosses the placenta, and concentrations of this drug in the blood of the fetus can be as much as 15 percent higher than in the mother.

Smoking during pregnancy increases the risk for certain birth defects, premature birth, miscarriage, and low birth weight and is estimated to have caused 1,015 infant deaths annually from 2005 through 2009. Women who smoke tobacco increase their chances of ectopic pregnancy (development of a fetus outside the uterus), premature rupture of membranes, abruptio placentae, placenta previa, and preeclampsia. Newborns of smoking mothers also show signs of stress and drug withdrawal consistent with what has been reported in infants exposed to other drugs. In some cases, smoking during pregnancy may be associated with sudden infant death syndrome (SIDS), as well as learning and behavioral problems and an increased risk of obesity in children.

Children of parents who smoke heavily can be affected adversely in their auditory, language, and cognitive performance; hyperactivity and attention deficit disorders are also common, according to the literature. In addition, smoking more than one pack a day during pregnancy nearly doubles the risk that the affected child will become addicted to tobacco if that child starts smoking. Even a mother's secondhand exposure to cigarette smoke can cause problems; such exposure is associated with premature birth and low birth weight, for example. The U.S. Department of Health and Human Services provides resources specifically designed to help pregnant women quit smoking.

Recent research provides strong support that nicotine is a gateway drug, making the brain more sensitive to the effects of other drugs such as cocaine. This shows that pregnant women who use nicotine may be affecting their baby's brain in ways they may not anticipate. Because e-cigarettes typically also contain nicotine, those products may also pose a risk to the baby's health.

Similar to pregnant women, nursing mothers are also advised against using tobacco. New mothers who smoke should be aware that nicotine is passed through breast milk, so tobacco use can impact the infant's brain and body development—even if the mother never smokes near the baby. There is also evidence that the milk of mothers who smoke smells and may taste like cigarettes. It is unclear whether this will make it more likely that exposed children may find tobacco flavors/smells more appealing later in life.

Secondhand Smoke

Newborns exposed to secondhand smoke are at greater risk for SIDS, respiratory illnesses (asthma, respiratory infections, and bronchitis), ear infections, cavities, and increased medical visits and hospitalizations. If a woman smokes and is planning a pregnancy, the ideal time to seek smoking cessation help is before she becomes pregnant

Section 8.3

Drug Endangered Children

This section contains text excerpted from the following sources: Text under the heading "Exposure to Drugs or Alcohol Abuse" is excerpted from "Exposure to Drugs or Alcohol Abuse," Youth.gov, June 12, 2013; Text beginning with the heading "Parental Drug Use as Child Abuse" is excerpted from "Parental Drug Use as Child Abuse," U.S. Department of Health and Human Services (HHS), April 2015; Text beginning with the heading "The Relationship Between Substance Use Disorders and Child Maltreatment" is excerpted from "Parental Substance Use and the Child Welfare System," U.S. Department of Health and Human Services (HHS), October 2014.

Exposure to Drugs or Alcohol Abuse

The Federal Interagency Task Force for Drug Endangered Children defines **drug-endangered children** in this way:

A drug endangered child is a person, under the age of 18, who lives in or is exposed to an environment where drugs, including pharmaceuticals, are illegally used, possessed, trafficked, diverted, and/or manufactured and, as a result of that environment: the child experiences, or is at risk of experiencing, physical, sexual, or emotional abuse; the child experiences, or is at risk of experiencing, medical, educational, emotional, or physical harm, including harm resulting or possibly resulting from neglect; or the child is forced to participate in illegal or sexual activity in exchange for drugs or in exchange for money likely to be used to purchase drugs.

Children of incarcerated parents are more likely to have faced exposure to drug and alcohol abuse in their homes than other children.

Parental Drug Use as Child Abuse

Abuse of drugs or alcohol by parents and other caregivers can have negative effects on the health, safety, and well-being of children. Approximately 47 States, the District of Columbia, Guam, and the U.S. Virgin Islands have laws within their child protection statutes that address the issue of substance abuse by parents. Two areas of concern are the harm caused by prenatal drug exposure and the harm caused to children of any age by exposure to illegal drug activity in their homes or environment.

Children Exposed to Illegal Drug Activity

There is increasing concern about the negative effects on children when parents or other members of their households abuse alcohol or drugs or engage in other illegal drug-related activity, such as the manufacture of methamphetamines in home-based laboratories. Many States have responded to this problem by expanding the civil definition of child abuse or neglect to include this concern. Specific circumstances that are considered child abuse or neglect in some States include:

- Manufacturing a controlled substance in the presence of a child or on premises occupied by a child
- Exposing a child to, or allowing a child to be present where, chemicals or equipment for the manufacture of controlled substances are used or stored
- Selling, distributing, or giving drugs or alcohol to a child
- Using a controlled substance that impairs the caregiver's ability to adequately care for the child
- Exposing a child to the criminal sale or distribution of drugs

Approximately 34 States and the U.S. Virgin Islands address in their criminal statutes the issue of exposing children to illegal drug activity. For example, in 20 States the manufacture or possession of methamphetamine in the presence of a child is a felony, while in 10 States, the manufacture or possession of any controlled substance in the presence of a child is considered a felony. Nine States have enacted enhanced penalties for any conviction for the manufacture of methamphetamine when a child was on the premises where the crime occurred.

Exposing children to the manufacture, possession, or distribution of illegal drugs is considered child endangerment in 11 States. The exposure of a child to drugs or drug paraphernalia is a crime in eight States and the Virgin Islands. In North Carolina and Wyoming, selling or giving an illegal drug to a child by any person is a felony.

The Relationship between Substance Use Disorders and Child Maltreatment

It is difficult to provide precise, current statistics on the number of families in child welfare affected by parental substance use or dependency since there is no ongoing, standardized, national data collection on the topic. In a 1999 report to Congress, the U.S. Department of Health and Human Services (HHS) reported that studies showed that between one-third and two-thirds of child maltreatment cases were affected by substance use to some degree. More recent research reviews suggest that the range may be even wider. The variation in estimates may be attributable, in part, to differences in the populations studied and the type of child welfare involvement (e.g., reports, substantiation, out-of-home placement); differences in how substance use (or substance abuse or substance use disorder) is defined and measured; and variations in State and local child welfare policies and practices for case documentation of substance abuse.

Children of Parents with Substance Use Disorders

An estimated 12 percent of children in this country live with a parent who is dependent on or abuses alcohol or other drugs. Based on data from the period 2002 to 2007, the National Survey on Drug Use and Health (NSDUH) reported that 8.3 million children under 18 years of age lived with at least one substance-dependent or substance-abusing parent. Of these children, approximately 7.3 million lived with a parent who was dependent on or abused alcohol, and about 2.2 million lived with a parent who was dependent on or abused illicit drugs. While many of these children will not experience abuse or neglect, they are at increased risk for maltreatment and entering the child welfare system. For more than 400,000 infants each year (about 10 percent of all births), substance exposure begins prenatally. State and local surveys have documented prenatal substance use as high as 30 percent in some populations.

Based on NSDUH data from 2011 and 2012, approximately 5.9 percent of pregnant women aged 15 to 44 were current illicit drug users. Younger pregnant women generally reported the greatest substance use, with rates approaching 18.3 percent among 15- to 17-year-olds. Among pregnant women aged 15 to 44 years old, about 8.5 percent reported current alcohol use, 2.7 percent reported binge drinking, and 0.3 percent reported heavy drinking.

Parental Substance Abuse as a Risk Factor for Maltreatment and Child Welfare Involvement

Parental substance abuse is recognized as a risk factor for child maltreatment and child welfare involvement. Research shows that children with parents who abuse alcohol or drugs are more likely to experience abuse or neglect than children in other households. One longitudinal study identified parental substance abuse as one of five key factors that predicted a report to child protective services (CPS) for abuse or neglect. Once a report is substantiated, children of parents with substance use issues are more likely to be placed in out-of-home care and more likely to stay in care longer than other children.

The National Survey of Child and Adolescent Well-Being (NSCAW) estimates that 61 percent of infants and 41 percent of older children in out-of-home care are from families with active alcohol or drug abuse. According to data in the Adoption and Foster Care Analysis and Reporting System (AFCARS), parental substance abuse is frequently reported as a reason for removal, particularly in combination with neglect. For almost 31 percent of all children placed in foster care in 2012, parental alcohol or drug use was the documented reason for removal, and in several States that percentage surpassed 60 percent.

Nevertheless, many caregivers whose children remain at home after an investigation also have substance abuse issues. NSCAW found that the need for substance abuse services among in-home caregivers receiving child welfare services was substantially higher than that of adults nationwide (29 percent as compared with 20 percent, respectively, for parents ages 18 to 25, and 29 percent versus 7 percent for parents over age 26).

Role of Co-occurring Issues

While the link between substance abuse and child maltreatment is well documented, it is not clear how much is a direct causal connection and how much can be attributed to other co-occurring issues. National data reveal that slightly more than one-third of adults with substance use disorders have a co-occurring mental illness. Research on women with substance abuse problems shows high rates of posttraumatic stress disorder (PTSD), most commonly stemming from a history of childhood physical and/ or sexual assault.

Many parents with substance abuse problems also experience social isolation, poverty, unstable housing, and domestic violence. These co-occurring issues may contribute to both the substance use and the child maltreatment. Evidence increasingly points to a critical role of stress and reactions within the brain to stress, which can lead to both drug-seeking activity and inappropriate caregiving.

Impact of Parental Substance Use on Children

The way parents with substance use disorders behave and interact with their children can have a multifaceted impact on the children. The effects can be both indirect (e.g., through a chaotic living environment) and direct (e.g., physical or sexual abuse). Parental substance use can affect parenting, prenatal development, and early childhood and adolescent development. It is important to recognize, however, that not all children of parents with substance use issues will suffer abuse, neglect, or other negative outcomes.

Parenting

A parent's substance use disorder may affect his or her ability to function effectively in a parental role. Ineffective or inconsistent parenting can be due to the following:

- Physical or mental impairments caused by alcohol or other drugs
- Reduced capacity to respond to a child's cues and needs
- Difficulties regulating emotions and controlling anger and impulsivity
- Disruptions in healthy parent-child attachment
- Spending limited funds on alcohol and drugs rather than food or other household needs
- Spending time seeking out, manufacturing, or using alcohol or other drugs
- Incarceration, which can result in inadequate or inappropriate supervision for children
- Estrangement from family and other social supports

Family life for children with one or both parents that abuse drugs or alcohol often can be chaotic and unpredictable. Children's basic needs—including nutrition, supervision, and nurturing—may go unmet, which can result in neglect. These families often experience a number of other problems—such as mental illness, domestic violence, unemployment, and housing instability—that also affect parenting and contribute to high levels of stress. A parent with a substance abuse disorder may be unable to regulate stress and other emotions, which can lead to impulsive and reactive behavior that may escalate to physical abuse.

Different substances may have different effects on parenting and safety. For example, the threats to a child of a parent who becomes sedated and inattentive after drinking excessively differ from the threats posed by a parent who exhibits aggressive side effects from methamphetamine use. Dangers may be posed not only from use of illegal drugs, but also, and increasingly, from abuse of prescription drugs (pain relievers, anti-anxiety medicines, and sleeping pills). Polysubstance use (multiple drugs) may make it difficult to determine the specific and compounded effects on any individual. Further, risks for the child's safety may differ depending upon the level and severity of parental substance use and associated adverse effects.

Prenatal and Infant Development

The effects of parental substance use disorders on a child can begin before the child is born. Maternal drug and alcohol use during pregnancy have been associated with premature birth, low birth weight, slowed growth, and a variety of physical, emotional, behavioral, and cognitive problems. Research suggests powerful effects of legal drugs, such as tobacco, as well as illegal drugs on prenatal and early childhood development.

Fetal alcohol spectrum disorders (FASD) are a set of conditions that affect an estimated 40,000 infants born each year to mothers who drank alcohol during pregnancy. Children with FASD may experience mild to severe physical, mental, behavioral, and/or learning disabilities, some of which may have lifelong implications (e.g., brain damage, physical defects, attention deficits). In addition, increasing numbers of newborns—approximately 3 per 1,000 hospital births each year—are affected by neonatal abstinence syndrome (NAS), a group of problems that occur in a newborn who was exposed prenatally to addictive illegal or prescription drugs.

The full impact of prenatal substance exposure depends on a number of factors. These include the frequency, timing, and type of substances used by pregnant women; co-occurring environmental deficiencies; and the extent of prenatal care. Research suggests that some of the negative outcomes of prenatal exposure can be improved by supportive home environments and positive parenting practices.

Chapter 9

Adolescent Drug Abuse

Chapter Contents

Section 9.1

Trends in Adolescent Drug Abuse

This section includes text excerpted from "Drug Use Trends Remain Stable or Decline among Teens," National Institute on Drug Abuse (NIDA), December 16, 2015.

Drug Use Trends Remain Stable or Decline among Teen

NIH's 2015 Monitoring the Future survey shows long term decline in illicit drug use, prescription opioid abuse, cigarette and alcohol use among the nation's youth.

The 2015 Monitoring the Future survey (MTF) shows decreasing use of a number of substances, including cigarettes, alcohol, prescription opioid pain relievers, and synthetic cannabinoids ("synthetic marijuana"). Other drug use remains stable, so including marijuana, with continued high rates of daily use reported among 12th graders, and ongoing declines in perception of its harms.

The MTF survey measures drug use and attitudes among eighth, 10th, and 12th graders, and is funded by the National Institute on Drug Abuse (NIDA), part of the National Institutes of Health. The survey has been conducted by researchers at the University of Michigan at Ann Arbor since 1975.

For the first time, daily marijuana use exceeds daily tobacco cigarette use among 12th graders. Daily marijuana use for this group remained relatively stable at 6 percent, compared to 5.5 percent reporting daily cigarette smoking (down from 6.7 percent in 2014).

Areas of concern are the high rate of daily marijuana smoking seen among high school students, because of marijuana's potential deleterious effects on the developing brains of teenagers, and the high rates of overall tobacco products and nicotine containing e-cigarettes usage.

Other Highlights from the 2015 Survey

Drugs

- Use of many illicit drugs has trended down. Among high school seniors, 23.6 percent report using an illicit drug in the past month, with 7.6 percent reporting they used an illicit drug other than marijuana.

- Perception of marijuana use as risky continues to decline, with 31.9 percent of seniors saying regular use could be harmful, compared to 36.1 percent last year.
- Past year use of synthetic cannabinoids ("synthetic marijuana") is at 5.2 percent for 12th graders, down significantly from 11.4 in 2011, the first year it was measured in the survey.
- Past year use of heroin, typically very low among teens, is at an all-time low at 0.3 percent for eighth graders, and 0.5 for 10th and 12th graders.
- Use of MDMA (also known as Ecstasy or Molly), inhalants, and LSD are generally stable or down. In 2015, 3.6 percent of seniors reported past year use of MDMA, compared to 5 percent in 2014.
- Non-medical use of the prescription amphetamine Adderall, typically given for ADHD, remains high at 7.5 percent among 12th graders.
- Use of prescription opioids continues its downward trend, with 4.4 percent of high school seniors reporting non-medical use of Vicodin (hydrocodone and acetaminophen), down from a peak of 10.5 percent in 2003.
- Most teens abusing prescription opioids report getting them from friends or family members. However, one-third report getting them from their own prescriptions, underscoring the need to monitor teens taking opioids and evaluate prescribing practices.

Percent of Students Reporting Use of Marijuana in Past Year, by Grade

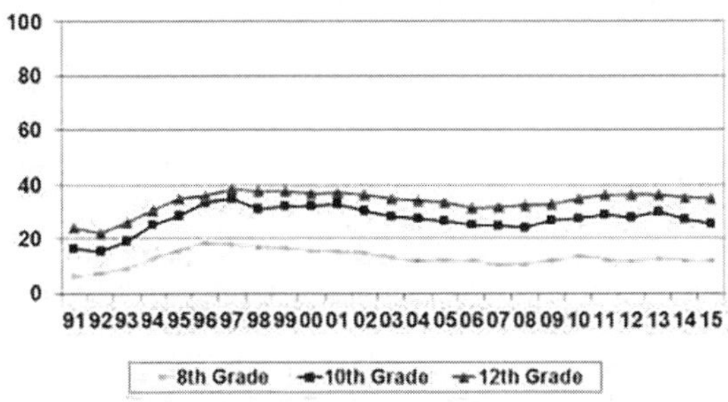

Figure 9.1. *Percent of students reporting use of marijuana in past year, by grade*

Tobacco

- Cigarette smoking rates have greatly declined among teens in recent years. For example, among 10th graders, there has been a 54.9 percent drop in daily smoking in just five years, reported at just 3 percent this year compared to 6.6 percent five years ago.
- However, rates of use of other tobacco products, while not significantly changed from 2014, remain high with 12th graders, reporting rates of past year use of hookah and small cigars of 19.8 percent and 15.9 percent, respectively.
- More than 75 percent of high school seniors view smoking a pack or more a day as harmful, compared to 51.3 percent in 1975, first year of the survey.
- As e-cigarettes are currently unregulated, there is limited data on what chemicals teens are actually smoking. However, when asked what they inhaled the last time they used an e-cigarette, only about 20 percent said they were using nicotine. Most say they inhaled flavoring alone and many admitted they were unsure what they inhaled. In fact, about 13 percent of eighth graders who use e-cigarettes said they did not know what was in the device they used. Furthermore, some products labeled nicotine-free may actually contain nicotine.
- Roughly twice as many boys as girls report using e-cigarettes (21.5% to 10.9%).

Alcohol

- Alcohol use continues its gradual downward trend among teens, with significant changes seen in the past five years in nearly all measures.
- Binge drinking (described as having five or more drinks in a row within the past two weeks) is 17.2 percent among seniors, down from 19.4 percent last year and down from peak rates in 1998 at 31.5 percent.
- 37.7 percent of 12th graders say they have been drunk in the past year, compared to 41.4 percent in 2014 and 53.2 percent in 2001, when rates were highest for that group.

- High school seniors see a distinction in potential harmfulness between one or two drinks nearly every day (21.5 percent) versus four to five drinks nearly every day (59.1 percent).

Overall, 44,892 students from 382 public and private schools participated in this year's MTF survey. Since 1975, the survey has measured drug, alcohol, and cigarette use and related attitudes in 12th graders nationwide. Eighth and 10th graders were added to the survey in 1991. Survey participants generally report their drug use behaviors across three time periods: lifetime, past year, and past month. Questions are also asked about daily cigarette and marijuana use.

Section 9.2

Understanding the Risk Factors and Reasons Why Adolescents Try Drugs and Alcohol

This section includes text excerpted from "Principles of Adolescent Substance Use Disorder Treatment: A Research-Based Guide," National Institute on Drug Abuse (NIDA), January 2014.

Why Do Adolescents Take Drugs?

Adolescents experiment with drugs or continue taking them for several reasons, including:

- **To fit in:** Many teens use drugs "because others are doing it"—or they think others are doing it—and they fear not being accepted in a social circle that includes drug-using peers.
- **To feel good:** Abused drugs interact with the neurochemistry of the brain to produce feelings of pleasure. The intensity of this euphoria differs by the type of drug and how it is used.
- **To feel better:** Some adolescents suffer from depression, social anxiety, stress-related disorders, and physical pain. Using drugs may be an attempt to lessen these feelings of distress. Stress especially plays a significant role in starting and continuing

drug use as well as returning to drug use (relapsing) for those recovering from an addiction.

- **To do better:** Ours is a very competitive society, in which the pressure to perform athletically and academically can be intense. Some adolescents may turn to certain drugs like illegal or prescription stimulants because they think those substances will enhance or improve their performance.
- **To experiment:** Adolescents are often motivated to seek new experiences, particularly those they perceive as thrilling or daring.

Principles of Adolescent Substance Use Disorder Treatment

People are most likely to begin abusing drugs*—including tobacco, alcohol, and illegal and prescription drugs—during adolescence and young adulthood.‡

By the time they are seniors, almost 70 percent of high school students will have tried alcohol, half will have taken an illegal drug, nearly 40 percent will have smoked a cigarette, and more than 20 percent will have used a prescription drug for a nonmedical purpose. There are many reasons adolescents use these substances, including the desire for new experiences, an attempt to deal with problems or perform better in school, and simple peer pressure. Adolescents are "biologically wired" to seek new experiences and take risks, as well as to carve out their own identity. Trying drugs may fulfill all of these normal developmental drives, but in an unhealthy way that can have very serious long-term consequences.

Many factors influence whether an adolescent tries drugs, including the availability of drugs within the neighborhood, community, and school and whether the adolescent's friends are using them. The family environment is also important: Violence, physical or emotional abuse, mental illness, or drug use in the household increase the likelihood an adolescent will use drugs. Finally, an adolescent's inherited genetic vulnerability; personality traits like poor impulse control or a high need for excitement; mental health conditions such as depression, anxiety, or ADHD; and beliefs such as that drugs are "cool" or harmless make it more likely that an adolescent will use drugs.

The teenage years are a critical window of vulnerability to substance use disorders, because the brain is still developing and malleable (a property known as neuroplasticity), and some brain areas are less mature than others. The parts of the brain that process feelings of reward and pain—crucial drivers of drug use—are the first to mature during childhood. What remains incompletely developed during the teen years are the prefrontal cortex and its connections to other brain regions. The prefrontal cortex is responsible for assessing situations, making sound decisions, and controlling our emotions and impulses; typically this circuitry is not mature until a person is in his or her mid-20s.

The adolescent brain is often likened to a car with a fully functioning gas pedal (the reward system) but weak brakes (the prefrontal cortex). Teenagers are highly motivated to pursue pleasurable rewards and avoid pain, but their judgment and decision-making skills are still limited. This affects their ability to weigh risks accurately and make sound decisions, including decisions about using drugs. For these reasons, adolescents are a major target for prevention messages promoting healthy, drug-free behavior and giving young people encouragement and skills to avoid the temptations of experimenting with drugs.

Most teens do not escalate from trying drugs to developing an addiction or other substance use disorder; however, even experimenting with drugs is a problem. Drug use can be part of a pattern of risky behavior including unsafe sex, driving while intoxicated, or other hazardous, unsupervised activities. And in cases when a teen does develop a pattern of repeated use, it can pose serious social and health risks, including:

- school failure
- problems with family and other relationships
- loss of interest in normal healthy activities
- impaired memory
- increased risk of contracting an infectious disease (like HIV or hepatitis C) via risky sexual behavior or sharing contaminated injection equipment
- mental health problems—including substance use disorders of varying severity
- the very real risk of overdose death

How Drug Use Can Progress to Addiction?

Different drugs affect the brain differently, but a common factor is that they all raise the level of the chemical dopamine in brain circuits that control reward and pleasure.

The brain is wired to encourage life-sustaining and healthy activities through the release of dopamine. Everyday rewards during adolescence—such as hanging out with friends, listening to music, playing sports, and all the other highly motivating experiences for teenagers—cause the release of this chemical in moderate amounts. This reinforces behaviors that contribute to learning, health, well-being, and the strengthening of social bonds.

Drugs, unfortunately, are able to hijack this process. The "high" produced by drugs represents a flooding of the brain's reward circuits with much more dopamine than natural rewards generate. This creates an especially strong drive to repeat the experience. The immature brain, already struggling with balancing impulse and self-control, is more likely to take drugs again without adequately considering the consequences. If the experience is repeated, the brain reinforces the neural links between pleasure and drug-taking, making the association stronger and stronger. Soon, taking the drug may assume an importance in the adolescent's life out of proportion to other rewards.

The development of addiction is like a vicious cycle: chronic drug use not only realigns a person's priorities but also may alter key brain areas necessary for judgment and self-control, further reducing the individual's ability to control or stop their drug use. This is why, despite popular belief, willpower alone is often insufficient to overcome an addiction. Drug use has compromised the very parts of the brain that make it possible to "say no."

Not all young people are equally at risk for developing an addiction. Various factors including inherited genetic predispositions and adverse experiences in early life make trying drugs and developing a substance use disorder more likely. Exposure to stress (such as emotional or physical abuse) in childhood primes the brain to be sensitive to stress and seek relief from it throughout life; this greatly increases the likelihood of subsequent drug abuse and of starting drug use early. In fact, certain traits that put a person at risk for drug use, such as being impulsive or aggressive, manifest well before the first episode of drug use and may be addressed by prevention interventions during childhood. By the same token, a range of factors, such as parenting that is nurturing or a healthy school environment, may encourage healthy development and thereby lessen the risk of later drug use.

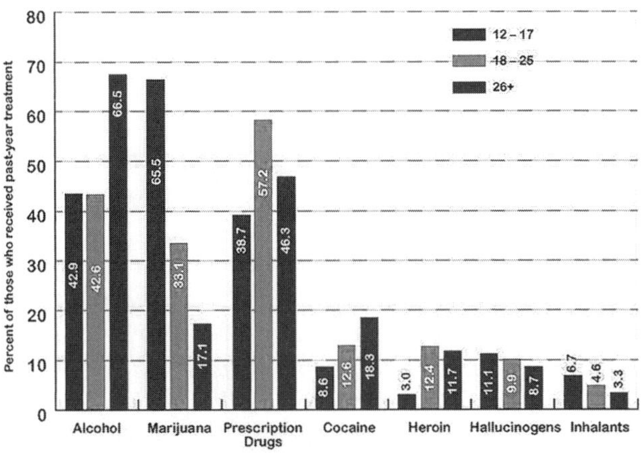

Figure 9.2. *Adolescents Differ from Adults in Substances Most Abused*

Drug use at an early age is an important predictor of development of a substance use disorder later. The majority of those who have a substance use disorder started using before age 18 and developed their disorder by age 20. The likelihood of developing a substance use disorder is greatest for those who begin use in their early teens. For example, 15.2 percent of people who start drinking by age 14 eventually develop alcohol abuse or dependence (as compared to just 2.1 percent of those who wait until they are 21 or older), and 25 percent of those who begin abusing prescription drugs at age 13 or younger develop a substance use disorder at some time in their lives. Tobacco, alcohol, and marijuana are the first addictive substances most people try. Data collected in 2012 found that nearly 13 percent of those with a substance use disorder began using marijuana by the time they were 14.

When substance use disorders occur in adolescence, they affect key developmental and social transitions, and they can interfere with normal brain maturation. These potentially lifelong consequences make addressing adolescent drug use an urgent matter. Chronic marijuana use in adolescence, for example, has been shown to lead to a loss of IQ that is not recovered even if the individual quits using in adulthood.

Impaired memory or thinking ability and other problems caused by drug use can derail a young person's social and educational development and hold him or her back in life. The serious health risks of drugs compound the need to get an adolescent who is abusing drugs into treatment as quickly as possible. Also, adolescents who are abusing drugs are likely to have other issues such as mental health problems accompanying and possibly contributing to their substance use, and these also need to be addressed. Unfortunately, less than one third of adolescents admitted to substance abuse treatment who have other mental health issues receive any care for their conditions.

* *In this section, the terms drugs and substances are used interchangeably to refer to tobacco, alcohol, illegal drugs, and prescription medications used for nonmedical reasons.*

‡ *Specifying the period of adolescence is complicated because it may be defined by different variables, and policymakers and researchers may disagree on the exact age boundaries. For purposes of this section, adolescents are considered to be people between the ages of 12 and 17.*

For purposes of this section, the term addiction refers to compulsive drug seeking and use that persists even in the face of devastating consequences; it may be regarded as equivalent to a severe substance use disorder as defined by the Diagnostic and Statistical Manual of Mental Disorders, Fifth Edition (DSM-5, 2013). The spectrum of substance use disorders in the DSM-5 includes the criteria for the DSM-4 diagnostic categories of abuse and dependence.

Section 9.3

Adolescent Marijuana Use Increases over Alcohol and Tobacco

This section includes text excerpted from "Alcohol, Tobacco, and Prescription Drug Use by Teens Declines; Level of Youth with Major Depressive Episodes Remains High," WhiteHouse.gov, September 29, 2015.

The Substance Abuse and Mental Health Services Administration's (SAMHSA) latest National Survey on Drug Use and Health (NSDUH) report shows progress in reducing some forms of substance use—especially among adolescents. Substance use levels in many areas, however, have remained relatively constant. Mental illness levels have also remained constant over time, but adolescents are experiencing higher levels of depression than in past years.

SAMHSA issued its 2014 NSDUH report on mental and substance use disorders as part of the kick off for the 26th annual observance of National Recovery Month. Recovery Month broadens public awareness to the fact that behavioral health is essential to health, prevention works, treatment for substance use and mental disorders is effective, and people can and do recover from these disorders.

With regard to substance use, the report found some areas of progress, particularly among adolescents. For example, the percentage of adolescents aged 12 to 17 who were current (past month) tobacco users declined by roughly half from 15.2 percent in 2002 to 7.0 percent in 2014. Similarly, the level of adolescents engaged in past month illegal alcohol use dropped from 17.6 percent to 11.5 percent over the same period. The level of current nonmedical users of prescription pain relievers decreased from 3.2 percent in 2002 to 1.9 percent in 2014 among adolescents aged 12 to 17.

Marijuana continues to be the most commonly used illicit drug. In 2014, roughly 8.4 percent of Americans age 12 and older were current users of marijuana—up from 7.5 percent in 2013. Marijuana use is especially growing among those aged 26 and older—from 5.6 percent in 2013 to 6.6 percent in 2014. The percentage of adolescents who were current marijuana users in 2014 (7.4 percent) was similar to recent years.

Although the survey shows nonmedical pain reliever use continues to be the second most common type of illicit drug use, the percentage of people aged 12 or older in 2014 who were current nonmedical users of pain relievers (1.6 percent) was lower than in most years since 2002, and about the same as in 2013. However, current heroin use increased from 0.1 percent of the population age 12 and older in 2013 to 0.2 in 2014.

Overall, the use of illicit drugs—including marijuana—among Americans aged 12 and older increased from 9.4 percent in 2013 to 10.2 percent in 2014. This was driven particularly by the increase in adult marijuana use.

The report also shows that about 43.6 million adults aged 18 or older experienced some form of mental illness in the past year. It also shows that 6.6 percent of the adult population and 11.4 percent of adolescents aged 12 to 17 (2.8 million adolescents) experienced major depressive episodes in the past year. Among adults, these levels are roughly consistent with levels seen in recent years. There was a higher percentage of youth with a major depressive episode in 2014 than in each year from 2004 and 2012—similar to the 2013 estimate. Youth who experienced a major depressive episode in the past year were more likely than other youth to have used any illicit drugs in the past year.

Section 9.4

Bullying and Youth Substance Use

This section includes text excerpted from "What Do Bullying and Youth Substance Use Have in Common? More than You Might Think," U.S. Department of Health and Human Services (HHS), January 29, 2013.

On the surface, bullying and youth substance use may seem like separate problems. However, from research, we know that kids who use drugs or alcohol are at risk for other problem behaviors during their teen years. Recent findings confirm previous studies that found links between bullying and substance use. In a recent study, researchers found that middle and high school students who bully their peers or are bully-victims (bully others and are also bullied) are more likely than students who aren't involved in bullying to use alcohol, cigarettes, and marijuana.

Bullying and substance use among kids have shared risk and protective factors. Prevention efforts can lessen these risk factors and strengthen protective factors in a child's life. If a problem has already surfaced, learn to recognize the warning signs of bullying and being bullied, underage alcohol use, and drug use to intervene before the problem becomes worse.

But let's rewind: how do you know which risk and protective factors to focus on?

Family

Close parent-child relationships are vital for a child's well-being. When families can talk openly, kids can talk about their problems more easily. Additionally, clear, consistent discipline—without being too extreme or physical—helps kids understand that certain behaviors, like bullying and substance use, are unacceptable and that there are consequences for those actions. Finally, showing empathy and helping kids form positive values helps keep them from bullying others and using drugs or alcohol. Children whose parents use drugs and alcohol are also at risk.

Peers

Peers and friends are important for social and personal growth. However, kids who spend time with other kids who bully or use alcohol and drugs are more likely to engage in those activities. The same goes for children who have trouble interacting with their peers.

Parent supervision and involvement, such as getting to know your child's friends, can help a young person avoid behavioral problems by making wise decisions about the company he or she keeps.

Academic Performance

Doing well in school and being enthusiastic about learning are protective factors for youth substance use and bullying. Poor grades and disinterest in school are just the opposite—they put a child at risk for those same behaviors.

Individual Characteristics

Parents and teachers should be on the lookout for aggressive behavior, especially if they see it at an early age, because it's an indicator that a child could become involved in drugs, alcohol, and/or bullying. Teachers and families should also seek opportunities to recognize and reinforce children's abilities and accomplishments—self-esteem, competencies, and skills are characteristics that "protect" a child.

Environmental Characteristics

Our environments play an important part in shaping who we become. Young people who are surrounded by substance use, crime, poverty, and violence at home or in their neighborhoods are more likely to turn to bullying and drug or alcohol use. Community and policy initiatives are essential to remove and prevent environmental risk factors that affect youth. Explore prevention resources and tools, and take the first step toward tackling these issues in your community.

Chapter 10

Drug Use among College Students

Drug and Alcohol Use in College-Age Adults

2014 Monitoring the Future College Students and Adults Survey Results

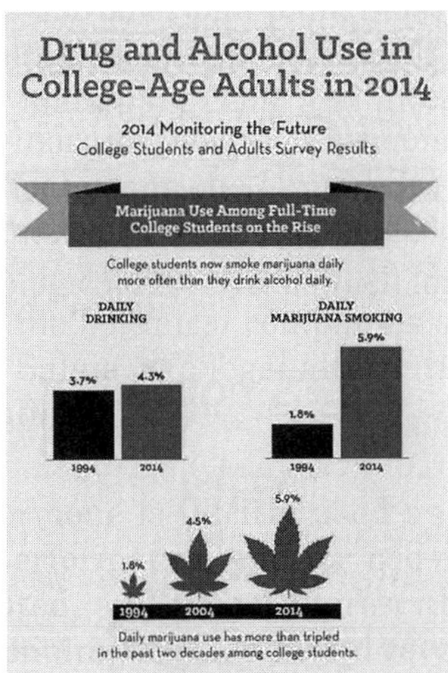

Figure 10.1. *Marijuana Use among Full-Time College Students on the Rise*

This chapter includes text excerpted from "Drug and Alcohol Use in College-Age Adults in 2014," National Institute on Drug Abuse (NIDA), December 2015.

- College students now smoke marijuana daily more often than they drink alcohol daily
- Daily drinking: 3.7 percent in 1994 and 4.3 percent in 2014
- Daily marijuana smoking: 1.8 percent 1994 and 5.9 percent in 2014.
- Daily marijuana use has more than tripled in the past two decades among college students with 1.8 percent smoking marijuana daily in 1994, 4.5 percent in 2004, and 5.9 percent in 2014

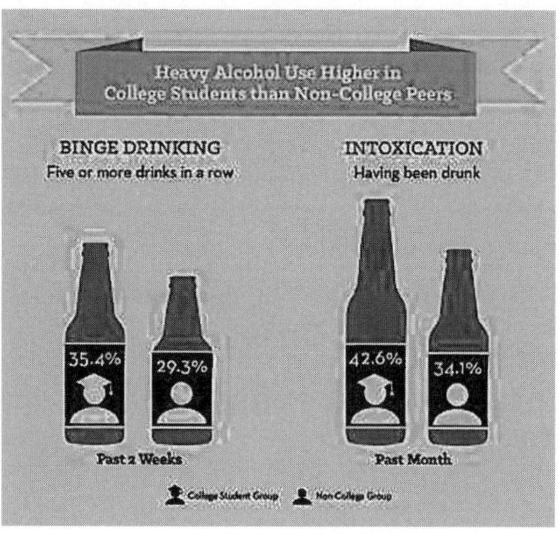

Figure 10.2. *Heavy Alcohol Use Higher in College Students than Non-College Peers*

- Binge drinking (five or more drinks in a row): 35.4 percent of college students and 29.3 percent of non-college peers in the past 2 weeks.
- Intoxication (having been drunk): 42.6 percent of college students and 34.1 percent of non-college peers in the past month.
- Four times more non-college young adults smoke half a pack of cigarettes or more daily than full-time college students.
- Cigarettes (past-month use): 12.9 percent of college students and 24.6 percent of non-college peers
- E-cigarettes (past-month use): 9.7 percent of college students and 15.4 percent of non-college peers

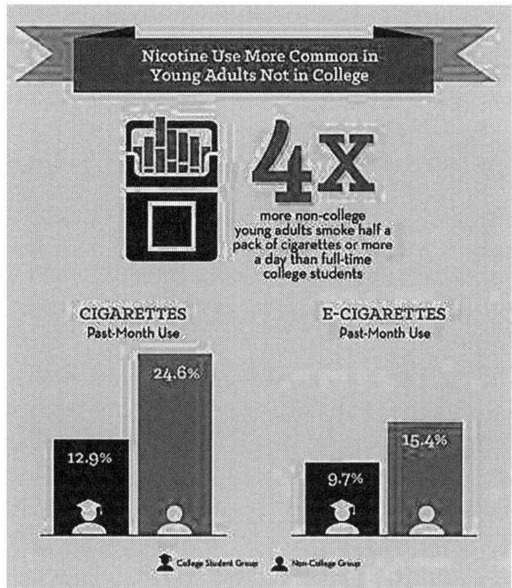

Figure 10.3. *Nicotine Use More Common in Young Adults Not in College*

- Past-year Adderall use: 10.7 percent in 2013 and 9.6 percent in 2014
- Past-year cocaine use: 2.7 percent in 2013 and 4.4 percent in 2014

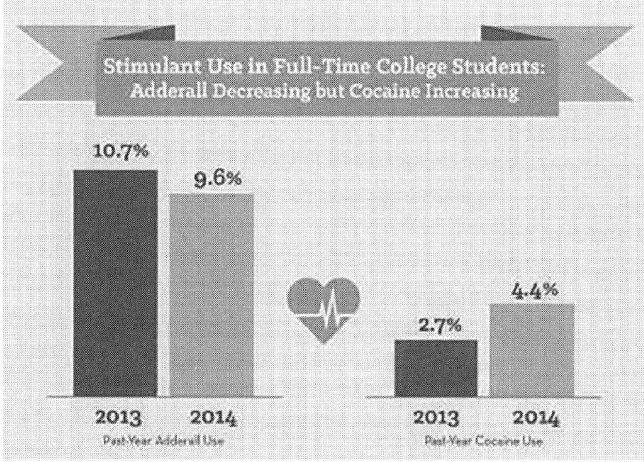

Figure 10.4. *Stimulant Use in Full-Time College Students*

Chapter 11

Substance Abuse Issues of Concern to Women

Chapter Contents

Section 11.1

Substance Use in Women

This section contains text excerpted from the following sources: Text beginning with the heading "Sex and Gender Differences in Substance Use" is excerpted from "DrugFacts: Substance Use in Women," National Institute on Drug Abuse (NIDA), September 2015; Text beginning with the heading "Substance Use in Women and Men" is excerpted from text from "Substance Use in Women and Men," National Institute on Drug Abuse (NIDA), January 2016.

Sex and Gender Differences in Substance Use

Women may face unique issues when it comes to substance use, in part influenced by:

- sex—differences based on biology
- gender—differences based on culturally defined roles for men and women

Scientists who study substance use have discovered special issues related to hormones, menstrual cycle, fertility, pregnancy, breastfeeding, and menopause that can impact women's struggles with drug use. In addition, women themselves describe unique reasons for using drugs, including controlling weight, fighting exhaustion, coping with pain, and self-treating mental health problems.

Science has also found that:

- Women use substances differently than men, such as using smaller amounts of certain drugs for less time before they become addicted.
- Women can respond to substances differently. For example, they may have more drug cravings and may be more likely to relapse after treatment. This could be affected by a woman's menstrual cycle.
- Sex hormones can make women more sensitive than men to the effects of some drugs.

- Women who use drugs may also experience more physical effects on their heart and blood vessels.
- Brain changes in women who use drugs can be different from those in men.
- Women may be more likely to go to the emergency room or die from overdose or other effects of certain substances.
- Women who are victims of domestic violence are at increased risk of substance use.
- Divorce, loss of child custody, or the death of a partner or child can trigger women's substance use or other mental health disorders.
- Women who use certain substances may be more likely to have panic attacks, anxiety, or depression.
- 15.8 million women (or 12.9%) ages 18 or older have used illicit drugs in the past year.

Substance Use While Pregnant and Breastfeeding

Substance use during pregnancy can be risky to the woman's health and that of her children in both the short and long term. Use of some substances can increase the risk of miscarriage and can cause migraines, seizures, or high blood pressure in the mother, which may affect the baby. In addition, the risk of stillbirth is two to three times greater in women who smoke tobacco or marijuana, take prescription pain relievers, or use illegal drugs during pregnancy.

When a woman uses substances regularly during pregnancy, the baby may go through withdrawal after birth, a condition called neonatal abstinence syndrome (NAS). Research has shown that NAS can occur with a pregnant woman's use of opioids, alcohol, caffeine, and some prescription sedatives. The type and severity of a baby's withdrawal symptoms depend on the drug(s) used, how long and how often the mother used, how her body breaks down the drug, and if the baby was born full term or prematurely.

Also, substance use by the pregnant mother can lead to long-term and even fatal effects, including:

- low birth weight
- birth defects
- small head size

- premature birth
- sudden infant death syndrome
- developmental delays
- problems with learning, memory, and emotional control

4.6 million women (or 3.8%) ages 18 and older have misused prescription drugs in the past year.

Every 3 minutes, a woman goes to the emergency room for prescription painkiller misuse or abuse.

Smoking tobacco during pregnancy is estimated to have caused 1,015 infant deaths per year from 2005 through 2009.

Some substances, such as marijuana, alcohol, nicotine, and certain medicines, can be found in breast milk. However, little is known about the long-term effects on a child who is exposed to these substances through the mother's milk. Scientists do know that teens who use drugs while their brains are still developing could be damaging their brain's learning abilities. Therefore, similar risks for brain problems could exist for drug-exposed babies. Given the potential of all drugs to affect a baby's developing brain, women who are breastfeeding should talk with a healthcare provider about all of their substance use.

Sex and Gender Differences in Drug Treatment

It is important to note that treatment for substance use disorders in women may progress differently than for men. Women report using some substances for a shorter period of time when they enter treatment. However, women's substance use tends to progress more quickly from first use to addiction. Withdrawal may also be more intense for women. In some cases, women respond differently than men to certain treatments. For instance, nicotine replacement (patch or gum) does not work as well for women as for men.

If a pregnant woman attempts to withdraw suddenly from addictive drugs and alcohol without medical help, she can put the baby at risk.

It can be hard for any person with a substance use disorder to quit. But women in particular may be afraid to get help during or after pregnancy due to possible legal or social fears and lack of child care while in treatment. Women in treatment often need support for handling the burdens of work, home care, child care, and other family responsibilities.

Specific programs can help pregnant women safely stop drug use and also provide prenatal care. Certain types of treatment have shown positive results, especially if they provide services such as child care, parenting classes, and job training. Medicines can help treat opioid use disorders in pregnant women, although some babies still need treatment for withdrawal symptoms. However, outcomes are better for the baby if the mother takes treatment medicine during pregnancy than if she continues to use opioids.

Substance Use in Women and Men

Figure 11.1. *Substance use in Women and Men*

Women:

- develop disorder more quickly
- more anxiety disorders
- more panic attacks

Men:

- more severe disorder
- more antisocial personality disorders
- more of other substance use problems

Prescription Pain Medicines

Women are less likely to misuse or abuse prescription pain medicines. Four million women report past-year misuse. Five million men report past-year misuse.

Figure 11.2. *Treatment For Sleeping Aid Misuse*

Treatment for Sleeping Aid Misuse

Women are more likely to seek treatment for misuse of barbiturates. Fifty-five percent of past-year treatment admissions for barbiturate misuse are women. Forty-five percent of past-year treatment admissions for barbiturate misuse are men.

Quitting Nicotine

Nicotine replacement options, such as the patch or gum, are less effective for women than for men. Quit rates after 6 months on the nicotine patch were 14.7 percent for women and 20.1 percent for men.

Section 11.2

Patterns and Prevalence of Substance Use among Women

This section includes text excerpted from "Substance Abuse Treatment: Addressing the Specific Needs of Women," Substance Abuse and Mental Health Services Administration (SAMHSA), 2015.

- **Narrowing of the Gender Gap:** In comparing male and female rates of alcohol use across 10 years, there is significant evidence of the gender gap narrowing. Overall, younger adult females are more likely to mirror male patterns of alcohol and illicit drug use than older females. This shrinking gender gap for alcohol and drug use has been noted across ethnic groups, especially among younger women.
- **People of Introduction and Relationship Status:** Women are more likely to be introduced to and initiate alcohol and drug use through significant relationships including boyfriends, spouses, partners, and relatives. According to the National Center on Addiction and Substance Abuse and Columbia University (CASA) research report, females are often introduced to substances in a more private setting. In addition, marital status plays an important role as a protective factor in the development of substance use disorders.
- **Drug Injection and Relationships:** Even though women are less likely to inject drugs than men, research suggests that women accelerate to injecting at a faster rate than men. When women inject drugs for the first time, they are more likely than men who are first-time injectors to be introduced to this form of administration by a sexual partner. Women are more likely to be involved with a sexual partner who also injects. While various personality and interpersonal factors influence needle sharing among women, women are more likely to inject with and borrow needles and equipment from their partner, spouse, or boyfriend. Among women who use with their sexual partners, a division of labor where men are responsible for obtaining, purchasing,

and injecting the drug for them was highlighted in a study. Thus, needle sharing and drug using with a sexual partner may engender a sense of emotional intimacy among women or reflect inequity of power in the relationship. Other "people of introduction" besides sexual partners are groups that are predominantly female. While women may initiate drug injection through relational means, it is important to recognize that some women are as likely to initiate drug injection on their own.

- **Earlier Patterns Reflect Later Problems:** Drinking low to moderate levels of alcohol in early adulthood is a predictor of later heavy drinking and alcohol-related substance use disorders among women. In addition to amount of alcohol intake, frequency of use appears positively associated with risk of alcohol dependence, particularly for women. Females who begin smoking at a young age are more likely to initiate alcohol and drug use than females who do not smoke.
- **Responsibilities and Pattern of Use:** Women are more likely to temporarily alter their pattern of use in response to caregiver responsibilities. As an example, women are likely to curtail or establish abstinence of alcohol and illicit drugs while pregnant, even though they are as likely to resume use later on. In addition, some women report that they use stimulants to help meet expectations associated with family responsibilities.
- **Progression and Consequences of Use:** Women experience an effect called telescoping, whereby they progress faster than men from initial use to alcohol and drug-related consequences even when using a similar or lesser amount of substances. While extensive research is available pertaining to the telescoping effect of alcohol and alcohol-related consequences among women, more recent research supports a preliminary finding—a similar pattern of rapid progression for illicit drugs. While women have a greater biological vulnerability to the adverse consequences of substance use, it is important to note that variations in progression and the biopsychosocial consequences of substance use may also be linked to socioeconomic status, racial/ethnic differences, and age. As an example, African Americans generally begin regular alcohol use later than most population groups yet demonstrate more rapid transition from initiation of use to abuse.

Section 11.3

What Women Need to Know about Date Rape Drugs

This section includes text excerpted from "Date Rape Drugs Fact Sheet," U.S. Department of Health and Human Services (HHS), July 16, 2012. Reviewed April 2016.

What Are Date Rape Drugs?

These are drugs that are sometimes used to assist a sexual assault. Sexual assault is any type of sexual activity that a person does not agree to. It can include touching that is not okay; putting something into the vagina; sexual intercourse; rape; and attempted rape. These drugs are powerful and dangerous. They can be slipped into your drink when you are not looking. The drugs often have no color, smell, or taste, so you can't tell if you are being drugged. The drugs can make you become weak and confused—or even pass out—so that you are unable to refuse sex or defend yourself. If you are drugged, you might not remember what happened while you were drugged. Date rape drugs are used on both females and males.

The three most common date rape drugs are:

- **Rohypnol.** Rohypnol is the trade name for flunitrazepam. Abuse of two similar drugs appears to have replaced Rohypnol abuse in some parts of the United States. These are: clonazepam (marketed as Klonopin in the U.S. and Rivotril in Mexico) and alprazolam (marketed as Xanax). Rohypnol is also known as:
  - Circles
  - Forget Pill
  - LA Rochas
  - Lunch Money
  - Mexican Valium
  - Mind Erasers
  - Poor Man's Quaalude
  - R-2
  - Rib
  - Roach
  - Roach-2
  - Roches

    - Roofies
    - Roopies
    - Rope
    - Rophies
    - Ruffies
    - Trip-and-Fall
    - Whiteys

- **GHB**, which is short for gamma hydroxybutyric acid. GHB is also known as:
    - Bedtime Scoop
    - Cherry Meth
    - Easy Lay
    - Energy Drink
    - G
    - Gamma 10
    - Georgia Home Boy
    - G-Juice
    - Gook
    - Goop
    - Great Hormones
    - Grievous Bodily Harm (GBH)
    - Liquid E
    - Liquid Ecstasy
    - Liquid X
    - PM
    - Salt Water
    - Soap
    - Somatomax
    - Vita-G
- **Ketamine**, also known as:
    - Black Hole
    - Bump
    - Cat Valium
    - Green
    - Jet
    - K
    - K-Hole
    - Kit Kat
    - Psychedelic Heroin
    - Purple
    - Special K
    - Super Acid

These drugs also are known as "club drugs" because they tend to be used at dance clubs, concerts, and "raves."

The term "date rape" is widely used. But most experts prefer the term "drug-facilitated sexual assault." These drugs also are used to help people commit other crimes, like robbery and physical assault. They are used on both men and women. The term "date rape" also can be misleading because the person who commits the crime might not be dating the victim. Rather, it could be an acquaintance or stranger.

What Do the Drugs Look Like?

- Rohypnol comes as a pill that dissolves in liquids. Some are small, round, and white. Newer pills are oval and green-gray in color. When slipped into a drink, a dye in these new pills makes clear liquids turn bright blue and dark drinks turn cloudy. But this color change might be hard to see in a dark drink, like cola or dark beer, or in a dark room. Also, the pills with no dye are still available. The pills may be ground up into a powder.
- GHB has a few forms: a liquid with no odor or color, white powder, and pill. It might give your drink a slightly salty taste. Mixing it with a sweet drink, such as fruit juice, can mask the salty taste.
- Ketamine comes as a liquid and a white powder.

What Effects Do These Drugs Have on the Body?

These drugs are very powerful. They can affect you very quickly and without your knowing. The length of time that the effects last varies. It depends on how much of the drug is taken and if the drug is mixed with other drugs or alcohol. Alcohol makes the drugs even stronger and can cause serious health problems—even death.

Rohypnol

The effects of Rohypnol can be felt within 30 minutes of being drugged and can last for several hours. If you are drugged, you might look and act like someone who is drunk. You might have trouble standing. Your speech might be slurred. Or you might pass out. Rohypnol can cause these problems:

- Muscle relaxation or loss of muscle control
- Difficulty with motor movements
- Drunk feeling
- Problems talking
- Nausea
- Can't remember what happened while drugged
- Loss of consciousness (black out)
- Confusion
- Problems seeing

- Dizziness
- Sleepiness
- Lower blood pressure
- Stomach problems
- Death

GHB

GHB takes effect in about 15 minutes and can last 3 or 4 hours. It is very potent: A very small amount can have a big effect. So it's easy to overdose on GHB. Most GHB is made by people in home or street "labs." So, you don't know what's in it or how it will affect you. GHB can cause these problems:

- Relaxation
- Drowsiness
- Dizziness
- Nausea
- Problems seeing
- Loss of consciousness (black out)
- Seizures
- Can't remember what happened while drugged
- Problems breathing
- Tremors
- Sweating
- Vomiting
- Slow heart rate
- Dream-like feeling
- Coma
- Death

Ketamine

Ketamine is very fast-acting. You might be aware of what is happening to you, but unable to move. It also causes memory problems.

Later, you might not be able to remember what happened while you were drugged. Ketamine can cause these problems:

- Distorted perceptions of sight and sound
- Lost sense of time and identity
- Out of body experiences
- Dream-like feeling
- Feeling out of control
- Impaired motor function
- Problems breathing
- Convulsions
- Vomiting
- Memory problems
- Numbness
- Loss of coordination
- Aggressive or violent behavior
- Depression
- High blood pressure
- Slurred speech

Are These Drugs Legal in the United States?

Some of these drugs are legal when lawfully used for medical purposes. But that doesn't mean they are safe. These drugs are powerful and can hurt you. They should only be used under a doctor's care and order.

- Rohypnol is not legal in the United States. It is legal in Europe and Mexico, where it is prescribed for sleep problems and to assist anesthesia before surgery. It is brought into the United States illegally.
- Ketamine is legal in the United States for use as an anesthetic for humans and animals. It is mostly used on animals. Veterinary clinics are robbed for their ketamine supplies.
- GHB was recently made legal in the United States to treat problems from narcolepsy (a sleep disorder). Distribution of GHB for this purpose is tightly restricted.

Is Alcohol a Date Rape Drug? What About Other Drugs?

Any drug that can affect judgment and behavior can put a person at risk for unwanted or risky sexual activity. Alcohol is one such drug. In fact, alcohol is the drug most commonly used to help commit sexual assault. When a person drinks too much alcohol:

- It's harder to think clearly.
- It's harder to set limits and make good choices.
- It's harder to tell when a situation could be dangerous.
- It's harder to say "no" to sexual advances.
- It's harder to fight back if a sexual assault occurs.
- It's possible to blackout and to have memory loss.

The club drug "ecstasy" (MDMA) has been used to commit sexual assault. It can be slipped into someone's drink without the person's knowledge. Also, a person who willingly takes ecstasy is at greater risk of sexual assault. Ecstasy can make a person feel "lovey-dovey" towards others. It also can lower a person's ability to give reasoned consent. Once under the drug's influence, a person is less able to sense danger or to resist a sexual assault.

Even if a victim of sexual assault drank alcohol or willingly took drugs, the victim is not at fault for being assaulted. You cannot "ask for it" or cause it to happen.

How Can I Protect Myself from Being a Victim?

- Don't accept drinks from other people.
- Open containers yourself.
- Keep your drink with you at all times, even when you go to the bathroom.
- Don't share drinks.
- Don't drink from punch bowls or other common, open containers. They may already have drugs in them.
- If someone offers to get you a drink from a bar or at a party, go with the person to order your drink. Watch the drink being poured and carry it yourself.
- Don't drink anything that tastes or smells strange. Sometimes, GHB tastes salty.

- Have a nondrinking friend with you to make sure nothing happens.
- If you realize you left your drink unattended, pour it out.
- If you feel drunk and haven't drunk any alcohol—or, if you feel like the effects of drinking alcohol are stronger than usual—get help right away.

Are There Ways to Tell If I Might Have Been Drugged and Raped?

It is often hard to tell. Most victims don't remember being drugged or assaulted. The victim might not be aware of the attack until 8 or 12 hours after it occurred. These drugs also leave the body very quickly. Once a victim gets help, there might be no proof that drugs were involved in the attack. But there are some signs that you might have been drugged:

- You feel drunk and haven't drunk any alcohol—or, you feel like the effects of drinking alcohol are stronger than usual.
- You wake up feeling very hung over and disoriented or having no memory of a period of time.
- You remember having a drink, but cannot recall anything after that.
- You find that your clothes are torn or not on right.
- You feel like you had sex, but you cannot remember it.

What Should I Do If I Think I've Been Drugged and Raped?

- Get medical care right away. Call 911 or have a trusted friend take you to a hospital emergency room. Don't urinate, douche, bathe, brush your teeth, wash your hands, change clothes, or eat or drink before you go. These things may give evidence of the rape. The hospital will use a "rape kit" to collect evidence.
- Call the police from the hospital. Tell the police exactly what you remember. Be honest about all your activities. Remember, nothing you did—including drinking alcohol or doing drugs—can justify rape.
- Ask the hospital to take a urine (pee) sample that can be used to test for date rape drugs. The drugs leave your system quickly.

Rohypnol stays in the body for several hours, and can be detected in the urine up to 72 hours after taking it. GHB leaves the body in 12 hours. Don't urinate before going to the hospital.

- Don't pick up or clean up where you think the assault might have occurred. There could be evidence left behind—such as on a drinking glass or bed sheets.
- Get counseling and treatment. Feelings of shame, guilt, fear, and shock are normal. A counselor can help you work through these emotions and begin the healing process. Calling a crisis center or a hotline is a good place to start. One national hotline is the **National Sexual Assault Hotline at 800-656-HOPE.**

Section 11.4

Prescription Painkiller Overdoses among Women

This section includes text excerpted from "Prescription Painkiller Overdoses," Centers for Disease Control and Prevention (CDC), July 2, 2013.

Prescription Painkiller Overdoses

About 18 women die every day of a prescription painkiller overdose in the U.S. more than 6,600 deaths in 2010. Prescription painkiller overdoses are an under-recognized and growing problem for women.

Although men are still more likely to die of prescription painkiller overdoses (more than 10,000 deaths in 2010), the gap between men and women is closing. Deaths from prescription painkiller overdose among women have risen more sharply than among men; since 1999 the percentage increase in deaths was more than 400% among women compared to 265% in men. This rise relates closely to increased prescribing of these drugs during the past decade. Healthcare providers can help improve the way painkillers are prescribed while making sure women have access to safe, effective pain treatment.

When prescribing painkillers, healthcare providers can

- Recognize that women are at risk of prescription painkiller overdose.*
- Follow guidelines for responsible prescribing, including screening and monitoring for substance abuse and mental health problems.
- Use prescription drug monitoring programs to identify patients who may be improperly obtaining or using prescription painkillers and other drugs.

*"Prescription painkillers" refers to opioid or narcotic pain relievers, including drugs such as Vicodin (hydrocodone), OxyContin (oxycodone), Opana (oxymorphone), and methadone.

Problem

Prescription Painkiller Overdoses Are a Serious and Growing Problem among Women.

- More than 5 times as many women died from prescription painkiller overdoses in 2010 as in 1999.
- Women between the ages of 25 and 54 are more likely than other age groups to go to the emergency department from prescription painkiller misuse or abuse. Women ages 45 to 54 have the highest risk of dying from a prescription painkiller overdose.*
- Non-Hispanic white and American Indian or Alaska Native women have the highest risk of dying from a prescription painkiller overdose.
- Prescription painkillers are involved in 1 in 10 suicides among women.

*Death data include unintentional, suicide, and other deaths. Emergency department visits only include suicide attempts if an illicit drug was involved in the attempt.

The Prescription Painkiller Problem Affects Women in Different Ways than Men.

- Women are more likely to have chronic pain, be prescribed prescription painkillers, be given higher doses, and use them for longer time periods than men.

- Women may become dependent on prescription painkillers more quickly than men.
- Women may be more likely than men to engage in "doctor shopping" (obtaining prescriptions from multiple prescribers).
- Abuse of prescription painkillers by pregnant women can put an infant at risk. Cases of neonatal abstinence syndrome (NAS)—which is a group of problems that can occur in newborns exposed to prescription painkillers or other drugs while in the womb—grew by almost 300% in the US between 2000 and 2009.

What Can be done

Federal Government Is

- Tracking prescription drug overdose trends to better understand the epidemic.
- Educating healthcare providers and the public about prescription drug misuse, abuse, suicide, and overdose, and the risks for women.
- Developing and evaluating programs and policies that prevent and treat prescription drug abuse and overdose, while making sure patients have access to safe, effective pain treatment.
- Working to improve access to mental health and substance abuse treatment through implementation of the Affordable Care Act.

Healthcare Providers Can

- Recognize that women can be at risk of prescription drug overdose.
- Discuss pain treatment options, including ones that do not involve prescription drugs.
- Discuss the risks and benefits of taking prescription painkillers, especially during pregnancy. This includes when painkillers are taken for chronic conditions.
- Follow guidelines for responsible painkiller prescribing, including:
    - Screening and monitoring for substance abuse and mental health problems.

- Prescribing only the quantity needed based on appropriate pain diagnosis.
- Using patient-provider agreements combined with urine drug tests for people using prescription painkillers long term.
- Teaching patients how to safely use, store, and dispose of drugs.
- Avoiding combinations of prescription painkillers and benzodiazepines (such as Xanax and Valium) unless there is a specific medical indication.

- Talk with pregnant women who are dependent on prescription painkillers about treatment options, such as opioid agonist therapy.
- Use prescription drug monitoring programs (PDMPs)—electronic databases that track all controlled substance prescriptions in the state—to identify patients who may be improperly using prescription painkillers and other drugs.

States Can

- Take steps to improve PDMPs, such as real time data reporting and access, integration with electronic health records, proactive unsolicited reporting, incentives for provider use, and interoperability with other states.
- Identify improper prescribing of painkillers and other prescription drugs by using PDMPs and other data.
- Increase access to substance abuse treatment, including getting immediate treatment help for pregnant women.
- Consider steps that can reduce barriers (such as lack of childcare) to substance abuse treatment for women.

Women Can

- Discuss all medications they are taking (including over-the-counter) with their healthcare provider.
- Use prescription drugs only as directed by a healthcare provider, and store them in a secure place.
- Dispose of medications properly, as soon as the course of treatment is done. Do not keep prescription medications around "just in case."

- Help prevent misuse and abuse by not selling or sharing prescription drugs. Never use another person's prescription drugs.
- Discuss pregnancy plans with their healthcare provider before taking prescription painkillers.
- Get help for substance abuse problems (1-800- 662-HELP); call Poison Help (1-800-222-1222) for questions about medicines.

Chapter 12

Substance Abuse in the Workplace

How Substance Use Affects Workplace

Substance use negatively affects U S. industry through lost productivity, workplace accidents and injuries, employee absenteeism, low morale, and increased illness. U.S. companies lose billions of dollars a year because of employees alcohol and drug use and related problems. Research shows that the rate of substance use varies by occupation and industry.

The National Survey on Drug Use and Health (NSDUH) gathers information about substance use and dependence or abuse. NSDUH defines illicit drugs as marijuana/hashish, cocaine (including crack), inhalants, hallucinogens, heroin, or prescription-type drugs used nonmedically. Heavy alcohol use is defined as drinking five or more drinks on the same occasion (i.e., at the same time or within a couple of hours

---

This chapter contains text excerpted from the following sources: Text beginning with the heading "How Substance Use Affects Workplace" is excerpted from "Substance Use and Substance Use Disorder by Industry," Substance Abuse and Mental Health Services Administration (SAMHSA), April 16, 2015; Text beginning with the heading "Addressing Employee Substance Abuse" is excerpted from "Drug Use Awareness—For Managers/Supervisors," U.S. Department of Health and Human Services (HHS), September 2013; Text beginning with the heading "Health-Related Programs for Alcohol and Substance Misuse" is excerpted from "Alcohol and Substance Misuse," Centers for Disease Control and Prevention (CDC), October 23, 2013.

of each other) on 5 or more days in the past 30 days. NSDUH also includes a series of questions to assess symptoms of dependence on or abuse of alcohol or illicit drugs during the past year. These questions are used to classify persons as dependent on or abusing substances based on criteria in the fourth edition of the *Diagnostic and Statistical Manual of Mental Disorders* (DSM-IV). In this chapter, dependence on or abuse of alcohol or illicit drugs is referred to as a "substance use disorder."

To enhance the statistical power and analytic capability and ensure consistency in time frames across all of the updated reports, 5-year time periods were chosen. This chapter uses combined data from the 2008 to 2012 surveys from The *CBHSQ Report* to present estimates of substance use behaviors (past month illicit drug use and past month heavy alcohol use) and past year substance use disorder among persons aged 18 to 64 who are employed full time by industry category.

Full-time employment is defined as working 35 or more hours per week and working in the past week or having a job despite not working in the past week. NSDUH includes questions to assess the type of business or industry in which these respondents worked. Using the North American Industry Classification System (NAICS) developed by the U.S. Census Bureau, 19 major industry groupings were identified.

The analyses includes comparisons of the 2008 to 2012 rates of illicit drug use and heavy alcohol use across industries and comparisons of the 2008 to 2012 rates with the 2003 to 2007 rates within each industry. For this report, testing for differences across industry groupings included two phases. First, differences across industries were assessed by making pair-wise comparisons between industries (e.g., the rates for each industry were compared with those of every other industry) to identify whether any industry had significantly higher rates than all other industries.

A second test was conducted to assess whether significant differences between industries were the result of differences in the age and gender composition of the industry. Previous research has shown that males have higher substance use rates than females and adults aged 18 to 25 have higher substance use rates than older adults. As a result, male-dominated or youth-dominated industries could have higher substance use rates at the overall level, but when the industry's age and gender distribution was taken into account, the industry might not differ from other industries.

Substance Use by Industry Category

Rates of substance use behaviors and substance use disorder varied across industry groupings. The overall rate of past month heavy alcohol use among full-time workers aged 18 to 64 was 8.7 percent. Rates of past month heavy alcohol use ranged from 17.5 percent among workers in the mining industry to 4.4 percent among workers in the healthcare and social assistance industry.

The overall rate of past month illicit drug use among full-time workers aged 18 to 64 was 8.6 percent. Rates of past month illicit drug use ranged from 19.1 percent among workers in the accommodations and food services industry to 4.3 percent among workers in the public administration industry. These findings remained true even when controlling for gender and age differences across industries.

The overall rate of past year substance use disorder among full-time workers aged 18 to 64 was 9.5 percent. Rates of past year substance use disorder ranged from 16.9 percent among workers in the accommodations and food services industry to 5.5 percent among workers in the educational services industry. Although the accommodations and food services industry group had the highest rate of past year substance use disorder, this finding did not remain true after controlling for age and gender distributions. This indicates that the high rate can be attributed to the demographic composition of the accommodation and food services industry.

Addressing Employee Substance Abuse

Recognizing an employee's drug use isn't always easy. When one of your employees has a problem with alcohol or drugs, it can impact the whole work group. Problems can appear in areas such as meeting deadlines, team communication and morale, accidents, absenteeism and more.

The adverse economic impact of employee drug use on employers is well documented. So it's important to learn not only your organization's policies on substance abuse, but how to be aware of the signs of drug and alcohol use in your employees. Drawing upon available expert support can help you be better equipped to deal with such challenges.

Remember that you can always get prompt assistance in dealing with employee performance issues. Your program is in place to provide you with responsive professional support for your specific workplace challenges.

Warning Signs of Drug Use

As a manager, it always pays to be observant. And while you want to recognize good performance, it's also important to be on the lookout for possible negative trends. When an employee is having a problem with drugs, you're likely to see the following types of behavior changes:

- Abrupt declines in attendance, quality and output of work
- General attitude changes and/or irritability
- Withdrawal from responsibility
- Decline in physical appearance and grooming
- Difficulty with concentration and/or memory
- Impaired performance on the job—such as errors in judgment—affecting the quality of work or endangering safety
- Wearing of sunglasses at inappropriate times to hide dilated or constricted pupils
- A change in the employee's social group, and possibly an association with known substance abusers
- Unusual borrowing of money from friends and coworkers
- Requests for leave around payday
- Theft of small items from the workplace
- Excessive breaks during the workday

When changes in employee behavior begin to affect performance, it's time to intervene.

Workplace Impact of Drug Use—How to Respond

The statistics on the impact of drug use on the American workplace can be startling. Studies show that business owners in the U.S. lose an estimated $100 billion per year because of substance abuse. More than sixty percent of adults know people who have gone to work under the influence of drugs or alcohol. These and many other such statistics indicate the prevalence of the problem.

Impact on Coworkers

A drug problem doesn't just hurt the employee. Often coworkers are asked to pick up the slack when an impaired colleague is absent.

Coworkers may end up taking on extra assignments and working longer hours. This can lead to long-term resentments and increased stress at work. Also, the safety of coworkers can be put at risk if a drug user is under the influence at work.

How Should a Manager Respond?

If you spot the warning signs of substance use in an employee, there are several steps to take. First, document the behaviors and actions that may indicate trouble. There are checklists available to help you name specific behaviors and actions. Write down your specific observations about the employee's performance. Confirm these observations with another supervisor if possible.

Then it's time to confront the employee about what you have observed. In a "constructive confrontation," calmly and firmly address the performance issues with the employee without getting into personal problems or acting judgmental. Before your meeting, it may help to call and consult with an experienced counselor (24/7) to help you prepare. Finally, offer support. Refer to your employee assistance program (EAP) and how it can help. Emphasize the confidentiality of the program and how EAP usage will not block someone's career path.

Health-Related Programs for Alcohol and Substance Misuse

Employee programs refer to activities that include active employee involvement, such as classes, seminars or competitions. Employee programs are frequently provided on-site at the workplace.

Employee Assistance Programs (EAPs) can offer information and referral services for employees with alcohol or drug use problems

Several behaviors regarding job performance indicate a high likelihood that an employee has problematic alcohol or drug use:

- A pattern of poor quality or poor quantity of work
- Attendance problems
- Problems related to interaction with clients or customers
- Employees may self-identify that their misuse behaviors are causing problems
- When these problems are identified the employee can be referred to the EAP for additional assessment

Support education programs through an EAP or health promotion program

- Employees need education on recognizing signs and symptoms of misuse in themselves and others
- Worksite health fairs, education campaigns and EAP brochures should include information on alcohol and substance misuse and specific information on obtaining confidential counseling and referral through EAP programs
- Additionally, support can be provided through programs such as Alcoholics Anonymous or Al-Anon, and the availability of counseling, diagnosis and treatment services

Worksite health promotion such as physical activity or nutrition programs can reduce alcohol and drug misuse

Encouraging healthy behaviors is an appropriate adjunct to standard therapies for substance misuse. See the workplace implementation descriptions for physical activity, nutrition, and obesity.

Health-Related Policies for Alcohol and Substance Misuse

Workplace policies promote a corporate "culture of good health."

Alcohol- and drug-free workplace policies discourage substance misuse

- Key principles to develop a well-defined alcohol- and drug-free workplace policy include:
- Drug free policies are publicized and employees are clear that substance misuse is never permitted in the workplace
- Workplace health promotion programs include education on substance misuse
- EAP services include assessment, counseling, and referral for employees regarding substance misuse

In high performance job settings, workplace policies require alcohol and drug testing

- As part of workplaces "rules of conduct" or "fitness for duty" regulations, supervisors are often empowered to discipline or remove an employee from the job on the suspicion of drinking.

In these settings the protocol for testing and follow up should be well defined and clear to all employees

- For example, alcohol testing is mandated for the transportation industry through Federal regulations. Alcohol testing is most commonly used in other workplace settings when cause is established, particularly in response to on-the-job accidents. In such cases, alcohol testing is critical in establishing possible culpability, especially if injuries have occurred. When alcohol tests are positive, case dispositions may vary according to company policy, ranging from dismissal to the offering of counseling or treatment under the auspices of an EAP

Policies for worksite health promotion such as physical activity or nutrition programs can reduce alcohol and drug misuse

See health-related policies for obesity, high blood pressure, tobacco use, physical activity, and nutrition.

Health Benefits for Alcohol and Substance Misuse

Employee health benefits are part of an overall compensation package and affect an employee's willingness to seek preventive services and clinical care.

Provide coverage for screening and counseling to reduce alcohol misuse

- The United States Preventive Services Task Force recommends screening and counseling in clinical settings for people who misuse alcohol (i.e., patients who drink in excess of NIAAA guidelines)
- Brief counseling in clinical settings can reduce consumption among drinkers who misuse alcohol who do not meet the criteria for alcohol dependence. Each dollar invested in screening and brief counseling saves $4 in healthcare costs
- Routine measurement of biochemical markers (i.e., screening) is not recommended in asymptomatic persons
- Pregnant women should be advised to limit or cease drinking during pregnancy
- All persons who use alcohol should be counseled about the dangers of operating a motor vehicle or performing other potentially dangerous activities after drinking alcohol

Provide coverage for screening for depression in clinical practices

- Other mental health disorders frequently co-occur with alcohol and drug misuse problems. For people struggling with co-occurring mental health and substance misuse disorders, physical safety and overall health risk are greater; the impairment of life skills is greater; and the chances for successful treatment are much less
- Mental health problems often predate substance misuse problems by 4-6 years; alcohol or other drugs may be used as a form of self-medication to alleviate the symptoms of the mental health disorder
- In some cases, substance misuse precedes the development of mental health problems. For instance, anxiety and depression may be brought on as a response to stressors from broken relationships, lost employment, and other situations directly related to a drug-using lifestyle
- A person with a substance misuse problem should be screened and treated as needed for depression and other mental health problems

Environmental support for alcohol and substance misuse

Environmental support provides a worksite physically designed to encourage good health.

Environmental support for worksite health promotion such as physical activity or nutrition programs can reduce alcohol and drug misuse

See environmental support recommendations for obesity, high blood pressure, physical activity and nutrition.

Chapter 13

Veterans and Drug Abuse

Veterans and Substance Use Problems

Members of the armed forces are not immune to the substance use problems that affect the rest of society. Although illicit drug use is lower among U.S. military personnel than among civilians, heavy alcohol and tobacco use, and especially prescription drug abuse, are much more prevalent and are on the rise.

The stresses of deployment during wartime and the unique culture of the military account for some of these differences. Zero-tolerance policies and stigma pose difficulties in identifying and treating substance use problems in military personnel, as does lack of confidentiality that deters many who need treatment from seeking it.

Those with multiple deployments and combat exposure are at greatest risk of developing substance use problems. They are more apt to engage in new-onset heavy weekly drinking and binge drinking, to suffer alcohol- and other drug-related problems, and to have greater prescribed use of behavioral health medications. They are also more likely to start smoking or relapse to smoking.

This chapter contains text excerpted from the following sources: Text beginning with the heading "Veterans and Substance Use Problems" is excerpted from "DrugFacts: Substance Abuse in the Military," National Institute on Drug Abuse (NIDA), March 2013; Text beginning with the heading "PTSD and Substance Abuse in Veterans" is excerpted from "PTSD and Substance Abuse in Veterans," U.S. Department of Veterans Affairs (VA), August 13, 2015.

Illicit and Prescription Drugs

According to the 2008 Department of Defense (DoD) Survey of Health Related Behaviors among Active Duty Military Personnel, just 2.3 percent of military personnel were past-month users of an illicit drug, compared with 12 percent of civilians. Among those age 18–25 (who are most likely to use drugs), the rate among military personnel was 3.9 percent, compared with 17.2 percent among civilians.

A policy of zero tolerance for drug use among DoD personnel is likely one reason why illicit drug use has remained at a low level in the military for 2 decades. The policy was instituted in 1982 and is currently enforced by frequent random drug testing; service members face dishonorable discharge and even criminal prosecution for a positive drug test.

However, in spite of the low level of illicit drug use, abuse of prescription drugs is higher among service members than among civilians and is on the increase. In 2008, 11 percent of service members reported misusing prescription drugs, up from 2 percent in 2002 and 4 percent in 2005. Most of the prescription drugs misused by service members are opioid pain medications.

The greater availability of these medications and increases in prescriptions for them may contribute to their growing misuse by service members. Pain reliever prescriptions written by military physicians quadrupled between 2001 and 2009—to almost 3.8 million. Combat-related injuries and the strains from carrying heavy equipment during multiple deployments likely play a role in this trend.

Drinking and Smoking

Alcohol use is also higher among men and women in military service than among civilians. Almost half of active duty service members (47 %) reported binge drinking in 2008—up from 35 percent in 1998. In 2008, 20 percent of military personnel reported binge drinking every week in the past month; the rate was considerably higher—27 percent—among those with high combat exposure.

In 2008, 30 percent of all service members were current cigarette smokers—comparable to the rate for civilians (29%). However, as with alcohol use, smoking rates are significantly higher among personnel who have been exposed to combat.

Suicides and Substance Use

Suicide rates in the military were traditionally lower than among civilians in the same age range, but in 2004 the suicide rate in the U.S.

Army began to climb, surpassing the civilian rate in 2008. Substance use is involved in many of these suicides. The 2010 report of the Army Suicide Prevention Task Force found that 29 percent of active duty Army suicides from fiscal year (FY) 2005 to FY 2009 involved alcohol or drug use; and in 2009, prescription drugs were involved in almost one third of them.

Addressing the Problem

A 2012 report prepared for the DoD by the Institute of Medicine (IOM Report) recommended ways of addressing the problem of substance use in the military, including increasing the use of evidence-based prevention and treatment interventions and expanding access to care. The report recommends broadening insurance coverage to include effective outpatient treatments and better equipping healthcare providers to recognize and screen for substance use problems so they can refer patients to appropriate, evidence-based treatment when needed. It also recommends measures like limiting access to alcohol on bases.

The IOM Report also notes that addressing substance use in the military will require increasing confidentiality and shifting a cultural climate in which drug problems are stigmatized and evoke fear in people suffering from them.

Branches of the military have already taken steps to curb prescription drug abuse. The Army, for example, has implemented changes that include limiting the duration of prescriptions for opioid pain relievers to 6 months and having a pharmacist monitor a soldier's medications when multiple prescriptions are being used.

NIDA and other government agencies are currently funding research to better understand the causes of drug abuse and other mental health problems among military personnel, veterans, and their families and how best to prevent and treat them.

PTSD and Substance Abuse in Veterans

Some people try to cope with their Posttraumatic Stress Disorder (PTSD) symptoms by drinking heavily, using drugs, or smoking too much. People with PTSD have more problems with drugs and alcohol both before and after getting PTSD. Also, even if someone does not have a problem with alcohol before a traumatic event, getting PTSD increases the risk that he or she will develop a drinking or drug problem.

Eventually, the overuse of these substances can develop into Substance Use Disorder (SUD), and treatment should be given for both PTSD and SUD to lead to successful recovery. The good news is that treatment of co-occurring (happening at the same time) PTSD and SUD works.

How Common Is Co-Occurring PTSD and SUD in Veterans?

Studies show that there is a strong relationship between PTSD and SUD, in both civilian and military populations, as well as for both men and women.

Specific to Veterans:

- More than 2 of 10 Veterans with PTSD also have SUD.
- War Veterans with PTSD and alcohol problems tend to be binge drinkers. Binges may be in response to bad memories of combat trauma.
- Almost 1 out of every 3 Veterans seeking treatment for SUD also has PTSD.
- The number of Veterans who smoke (nicotine) is almost double for those with PTSD (about 6 of 10) versus those without a PTSD diagnosis (3 of 10).
- In the wars in Iraq and Afghanistan, about 1 in 10 returning soldiers seen in VA have a problem with alcohol or other drugs.

How Can Co-Occurring PTSD and SUD Create Problems?

If someone has both PTSD and SUD, it is likely that he or she also has other health problems (such as physical pain), relationship problems (with family and/or friends), or problems in functioning (like keeping a job or staying in school). Using drugs and/or alcohol can make PTSD symptoms worse.

For example:

- PTSD may create sleep problems (trouble falling asleep or waking up during the night). You might "medicate" yourself with alcohol or drugs because you think it helps your sleep, but drugs and alcohol change the quality of your sleep and make you feel less refreshed.
- PTSD makes you feel "numb," like being cut off from others, angry and irritable, or depressed. PTSD also makes you feel like

you are always "on guard." All of these feelings can get worse when you use drugs and alcohol.

- Drug and alcohol use allows you to continue the cycle of "avoidance" found in PTSD. Avoiding bad memories and dreams or people and places can actually make PTSD last longer. You cannot make as much progress in treatment if you avoid your problems.
- You may drink or use drugs because it distracts you from your problems for a short time, but drugs and alcohol make it harder to concentrate, be productive, and enjoy all parts of your life.

VA has made it easier to get help. It is important to know that treatment can help and you are not alone.

What Treatments Are Offered for Co-Occurring PTSD and SUD?

Evidence shows that in general people have improved PTSD and SUD symptoms when they are provided treatment that addresses both conditions. This can involve any of the following (alone or together):

- Individual or group cognitive behavioral treatments (CBT)
- Specific psychological treatments for PTSD, such as Cognitive Processing Therapy (CPT) or Prolonged Exposure (PE)
- Behavioral couples therapy with your spouse or significant other
- Medications that may help you manage the PTSD or SUD symptoms

Talk with your provider about treatment for specific symptoms like pain, anger, or sleep problems.

What Should I Do If I Think I Have Co-Occurring PTSD and SUD?

The first step is to talk to a health professional and ask for more information about treatment options. Each VA medical center has an SUD-PTSD Specialist trained in treating both conditions to reach the best health outcomes. If there are signals you are at risk for both disorders, you will be encouraged to talk with a provider about how to best support your recovery. There are treatment resources at every VA medical center. The VA wants you to have the best possible care for co-occurring PTSD and SUD.

- Find a VA PTSD Program
- Find a VA SUD Program

If you continue to be troubled or distracted by your experiences for more than three months or have questions about your drinking or drug use, learn more about treatment options. Life can be better! Talk to a VA or other health professional to discuss choices for getting started.

Chapter 14

Drug Abuse in Other Populations

Chapter Contents

Section 14.1

Inmate Populations and Substance Abuse

This section includes text excerpted from "Principles of Drug Abuse Treatment for Criminal Justice Populations," National Institute on Drug Abuse (NIDA), April 2014.

Why Do People Involved in the Criminal Justice System Continue Abusing Drugs?

The answer to this perplexing question spans basic neurobiological, psychological, social, and environmental factors. The repeated use of addictive drugs eventually changes how the brain functions. Resulting brain changes, which accompany the transition from voluntary to compulsive drug use, affect the brain's natural inhibition and reward centers, causing the addicted person to use drugs in spite of the adverse health, social, and legal consequences. Craving for drugs may be triggered by contact with the people, places, and things associated with prior drug use, as well as by stress. Forced abstinence (when it occurs) is not treatment, and it does not cure addiction. Abstinent individuals must still learn how to avoid relapse, including those who may have been abstinent for a long period of time while incarcerated.

Potential risk factors for released offenders include pressures from peers and family members to return to drug use and a criminal lifestyle. Tensions of daily life—violent associates, few opportunities for legitimate employment, lack of safe housing, and even the need to comply with correctional supervision conditions—can also create stressful situations that can precipitate a relapse to drug use.

Research on how the brain is affected by drug abuse promises to teach us much more about the mechanics of drug-induced brain changes and their relationship to addiction. Research also reveals that with effective drug abuse treatment, individuals can overcome persistent drug effects and lead healthy, productive lives.

Why Should Drug Abuse Treatment Be Provided to Offenders?

The case for treating drug abusing offenders is compelling. Drug abuse treatment improves outcomes for drug abusing offenders and has beneficial effects for public health and safety. Effective treatment decreases future drug use and drug-related criminal behavior, can improve the individual's relationships with his or her family, and may improve prospects for employment. In addition, it can save lives: A retrospective study of more than 30,000 Washington State inmates found that during the first 2 weeks after release, the risk of death among former inmates was more than 12 times that among other residents, with drug overdose being the leading cause.

Outcomes for substance abusing individuals can be improved when criminal justice personnel work in tandem with treatment providers on drug abuse treatment needs and supervision requirements. Treatment needs that can be assessed after arrest include substance abuse severity, mental health problems, and physical health. Defense attorneys, prosecutors, and judges need to work together during the prosecution and sentencing phases of the criminal justice process to determine suitable treatment programs that meet the offender's needs.

Through drug courts, diversion programs, pretrial release programs that are conditional on treatment, and conditional probation with sanctions, the offender can participate in community-based drug abuse treatment while under criminal justice supervision. In some instances, the judge may recommend that the offender participate in treatment while serving jail or prison time or require it as part of continuing correctional supervision post-release.

Section 14.2

Substance Use Disorders in People with Disabilities

This section includes text excerpted from "Substance Use Disorders in People With Physical and Sensory Disabilities," Substance Abuse and Mental Health Services Administration (SAMHSA), August 2011. Reviewed April 2016.

Substance Use Disorders in People with Physical and Sensory Disabilities

Approximately 23 million people in the United States, including people with disabilities, need treatment for substance use disorders

(SUDs), a major behavioral health disorder. In addition, more than 24 million adults in the United States experienced serious psychological distress in 2006. People with and without disabilities may face many of the same barriers to substance abuse treatment, such as lacking insurance or sufficient funds for treatment services, or feeling they do not need treatment.

In addition, people with disabilities may face other barriers to SUD treatment, particularly finding treatment facilities that are fully accessible. Vocational rehabilitation (VR) counselors, vocational education providers, and others who work with people with disabilities report that their clients with SUDs have less successful vocational outcomes than clients without SUDs.

To improve outcomes, it is important that clients with disabilities and SUDs receive services for both conditions and that the disabilities do not prevent clients from receiving treatment for SUDs. This In *Brief* is intended to help people who work with people with physical and sensory disabilities—hearing loss, deafness, blindness, and low vision—to better understand SUDs and assist their clients in finding accessible SUD treatment services.

What Is an SUD?

Substance use disorder is a broad term that encompasses abuse of and dependence on drugs or alcohol. It includes using illegal substances, such as heroin, marijuana, or methamphetamines, and using legal substances, such as prescription or over-the-counter medications, in ways not prescribed or recommended.

SUDs Harm People with Disabilities

It is difficult to estimate the number of people with physical disabilities who have SUDs. Some studies suggest that people with disabilities have higher rates of legal and illegal substance use than the general population, whereas other studies show lower rates. Although debate exists among researchers about the prevalence of SUDs among people with disabilities, there is agreement that active SUDs can seriously harm the health and quality of life of individuals with disabilities. An active SUD can:

- Interfere with successful engagement in rehabilitation services.
- Interact with prescribed medications; alcohol, for example, can interfere with antiseizure medications.

- Impede coordination and muscle control.
- Impair cognition.
- Reduce the ability to follow self-care regimens.
- Contribute to social isolation, poor communication, and domestic strife.
- Contribute to poor health, secondary disabling conditions, or the hastening of disabling diseases (e.g., cirrhosis, depression, bladder infections).
- Inhibit educational advancement.
- Lead to job loss, underemployment, and housing instability.

Women with Disabilities and SUDs

Across all age groups, more women than men are disabled. Women with co-occurring disabilities and SUDs are at high risk for experiencing physical abuse and domestic violence.

One study of people with disabilities and SUDs found that 47 percent of women reported histories of physical, sexual, or domestic violence, compared with 20 percent of men with disabilities reporting abuse experiences. In the same study, 37 percent of women reported sexual abuse, compared with 7 percent of men.

Another study found that 56 percent of women with disabilities reported abuse, with 89 percent of these reporting multiple abusive incidents. What is more, being a victim of physical or sexual abuse is a risk factor for SUD.

SUD Risk Factors and Warning Signs

For some people, drug or alcohol abuse is a direct or indirect cause of their disability, for example, by their becoming intoxicated and then falling or causing a car crash. Without SUD treatment, people who had SUDs before sustaining a disability will likely continue to use substances afterward. Other people may have developed SUDs after using substances such as pain medications or alcohol to cope with aspects of their disability or to cope with social isolation or depression.

Numerous signs may suggest the presence of an active SUD. These include, but are not limited to:

- Dilated or constricted pupils.
- Slurred speech.

- Inability to focus, visually or cognitively.
- Unsteady gait.
- Blackouts.
- Insomnia.
- Irritability or agitation.
- Depression, anxiety, low self-esteem, resentment.
- Odor of alcohol on breath.
- Excessive use of aftershave or mouthwash (to mask the odor of alcohol).
- Mild tremor.
- Nasal irritation (suggestive of cocaine insufflation).
- Eye irritation (suggestive of exposure to marijuana smoke)
- Odor of marijuana on clothing.
- Abuse of drugs or alcohol by family members.
- Many missed appointments with VR, job interviews, and the like.
- Difficulty learning new tasks.
- Attention deficits.
- Lack of initiative.

Some manifestations of certain disabilities may be difficult to distinguish from the signs of SUDs mentioned above. For example, people with multiple sclerosis may have an unsteady gait, slurred speech, and memory impairment. Other signs, such as depression or anxiety, may indicate a different, distinct behavioral health condition.

Screening for SUDs

Screening is not the same as diagnosing; it simply indicates whether further evaluation by an SUD professional is indicated. The National Institute on Alcohol Abuse and Alcoholism (NIAAA) developed a single-question screening tool for alcohol use disorder. Clients should also be screened for illicit drug use and prescription medication abuse. VR professionals, physical therapists, and others may benefit from training on how to administer screening and assessment tools.

Single-Question Screening Test

Ask men: "How many times in the past year have you had 5 or more drinks in a day?"

Ask women: "How many times in the past year have you had 4 or more drinks in a day?"

A response of more than 1 day is considered positive.

No screening tools have been validated in Deaf populations. If possible, clients who exhibit warning signs or symptoms should be screened for SUDs. If screening is not possible or if the screening is positive, the client should be referred to an SUD treatment provider for further assessment.

Some clients may benefit from a brief intervention (a discussion of 5 minutes or less) to prevent their substance use from becoming an SUD.

Types of SUD Services

SUD services include:

- *Prevention education*—information in various formats that helps people understand the risks of substance use.
- *In depth assessment*—an evaluation by a treatment provider to determine whether an SUD is present and, if so, what level of care is needed and what treatment options are available.
- *Outpatient or inpatient detoxification*—medically supervised withdrawal from alcohol or drugs.
- *Outpatient treatment*—psychosocial interventions and individual and group counseling on substance use.
- *Medication-assisted treatment and counseling*—methadone, buprenorphine, and other medications for opioid dependence or acamprosate, disulfiram, and naltrexone for alcohol use disorders; medication assisted treatment works best if combined with psychosocial counseling interventions.
- *Residential programs*—short- and long-term structured living to help people re-enter their community.

In addition, people in recovery often attend mutual-help groups, such as Alcoholics Anonymous (AA), Narcotics Anonymous (NA), and SMART (Self Management and Recovery Training) Recovery to share experiences and support one another's recovery efforts. Many meetings of AA and NA that are wheelchair accessible are identified in meeting lists. Online meetings are an option for those who are Deaf and hard of hearing, people with visual disabilities, or people who live in locations without accessible meetings. Some AA groups will pay for a sign language interpreter or make use of sign language interpreters who are in recovery themselves.

Accessible SUD Treatment Facilities

Despite requirements of the Americans with Disabilities Act (ADA), studies suggest that many treatment facilities are not fully accessible to people with disabilities. Examples of physical barriers include doors and hallways too narrow for wheelchairs, uneven flooring, non-functioning elevators, and a reliance on signage to provide directions, which leaves people with low or no vision without a means to find their way through facilities.

Many other types of barriers exist. Some SUD treatment administrators believe that their facilities are more accessible than they actually are. Of various types of healthcare providers, outpatient SUD treatment providers are among the least likely to report that their services are accessible to people with disabilities or that they have had training on mobility impairments.

Comparatively little information is available on how many people with disabilities have been denied SUD treatment because of physical barriers in the treatment facility itself. One survey of 174 SUD treatment providers in Virginia found that 87 percent of people with multiple sclerosis, 75 percent of people with muscular dystrophy, and 67 percent of people with spinal cord injuries who sought services were denied SUD treatment services because of physical barriers at the treatment facility.

Barriers to Treatment for People Who Are Blind or Visually Impaired

A survey of VR counselors and SUD treatment providers found that barriers to SUD treatment for people who are blind or visually impaired are formidable. Frequently identified barriers are presented below:

- Negative attitudes and prejudices about people with SUDs. Some VR professionals regarded people with SUDs and disabilities as "not worthy" of SUD treatment, particularly if outcomes are perceived as poor for people with these two co-occurring conditions.
- Lack of staff training. SUD counselors reported a need to learn about working with people who are blind, and VR counselors report a need to learn about SUDs in their clients.

- Inaccessible methods and materials. Many facilities that provide SUD services reported that they are "handicapped accessible" if they provide ramps for clients. But people who are visually impaired require Braille signs and other navigational features and alternatives to sight-based counseling treatment activities like films and booklets to have genuine accessibility to treatment services.

Survey respondents noted it is important to identify which agency will coordinate comprehensive client care. Respondents also commonly mentioned that, because there are no formal mechanisms for shared communication and case management, SUD and VR services providers may not know how to manage cases and work together across fields to provide services for their clients.

Treatment Innovations for People Who Are Deaf or Hard of Hearing

Few fully accessible SUD treatment services exist for people who are Deaf. Specialty treatment facilities for people who are Deaf exist, but the number has declined in the last decade. In 2009, only five providers in the United States offered inpatient SUD services especially for people who are Deaf, and four provided outpatient treatment.

A national survey in 2008 by SAMHSA found that 27 percent of opioid treatment facilities offered interpretation services for people who are Deaf or hard of hearing. However, there are numerous barriers to providing fully accessible mainstream SUD treatment to people who are Deaf, including cultural and linguistic barriers, lack of local SUD treatment providers trained to work with people who are Deaf, lack of American Sign Language interpreters, inability of people who are Deaf to participate in group counseling (a mainstay of SUD treatment), increased costs associated with making treatment accessible to people who are Deaf, and more.

One way to fill the treatment gap is to advocate telehealth SUD treatment services for people who are Deaf. Telehealth technology, such as electronic mailing lists and video conferencing, can connect people who are Deaf to appropriate SUD specialists across the country, and it can be adapted for an array of SUD services, from recovery support after treatment to mutual-help groups. Telehealth could also be used to train more people who are Deaf to be SUD counselors. One promising model piloted by Wright State University is Deaf off Drugs and Alcohol (DODA), a program for Ohio residents that supplements local SUD treatment with Internet- and video-based case management, group therapy, individual therapy, and follow up.

Section 14.3

Seniors and Drug Abuse

This section contains text excerpted from the following sources: Text in this section begins with excerpts from "Specific Populations and Prescription Drug Misuse and Abuse," Substance Abuse and Mental Health Services Administration (SAMHSA), October 27, 2015; Text beginning with the heading "Overview of the Problem" is excerpted from "Prescription Medication Misuse and Abuse Among Older Adults," Substance Abuse and Mental Health Services Administration (SAMHSA), 2012. Reviewed April 2016; Text under the heading "Prescription Drug Abuse Among Older Adults" is excerpted "Older Adults," National Institute on Drug Abuse (NIDA), November 2014.

According to the National Institute on Drug Abuse (NIDA), as of 2014, prescription drug misuse or abuse is increasing among people in their fifties.

Older adults are likely to experience more problems with relatively small amounts of medications because of increased medication sensitivity, and slower metabolism and elimination. Older adults are at higher risk for medication misuse than the general population because of their elevated rates of pain, sleep disorders/insomnia, and anxiety. They also may experience cognitive decline, which could lead to improper use of medications.

- The combination of alcohol and medication misuse has been estimated to affect up to 19% of older Americans.
- Approximately 25% of older adults use prescription psychoactive medications that have a potential to be misused and abused.
- Older adults are more likely to take prescribed psychoactive medications for longer periods of time than younger adults.

Overview of the Problem

Prescription medication misuse and abuse are growing public health problems among older adults; these problems are associated with many serious consequences, and often go unrecognized. Misuse of prescription medications, also referred to as nonmedical use of prescription drugs, is estimated to increase from 1.2 percent (911,000) in 2001 to 2.4 percent (2.7 million) in 2020—a 100 percent increase—among older adults.

This problem is growing because of the size of the baby boom population as well as the boomers greater acceptance of and experiences with using prescription medications and illicit drugs. One indicator of this growth is emergency department (ED) visits involving medication misuse and abuse; from 2004 to 2008, there was a 121 percent increase in ED visits involving prescription medication misuse by older Americans.

Problematic prescription medication use by older adults is usually unintentional, and most misused medications are obtained legally through prescriptions. However, unintentional prescription medication misuse can progress to abuse if an older adult continues to use a medication for the desirable effects it provides. Furthermore, tolerance and physical dependence can develop in some older adults when certain psychoactive medications, such as benzodiazepines, are taken regularly at the therapeutic appropriate dose for brief periods.

Prevalence of the Problem

Few studies have specifically examined the prevalence and nature of medication misuse and abuse, and the results of those studies have been mixed. These studies have varied in their definitions of substance misuse or abuse from the very broad (e.g., general medication management problems such as wrong medication or dose or lack of adherence) to the very specific (e.g., the *Diagnostic and Statistical Manual of Mental Disorders* [DSM]). Depending on the definition, estimates of the prevalence of medication misuse, abuse, and dependence among older adults range from 1 percent to 26 percent. One study found that up to 11 percent of women older than age 60 misuse prescription medications.

Nature of the Problem

Older adults are among those most vulnerable to medication misuse and abuse because they use more prescription and over-the-counter (OTC) medications than other age groups. They are likely to experience more problems with relatively small amounts of medications because of increased medication sensitivity as well as slower metabolism and elimination. Older adults are at high risk for medication misuse due to conditions like pain, sleep disorders/insomnia, and anxiety that commonly occur in this population.

They are, therefore, more likely to receive prescriptions for psychoactive medications with misuse and abuse potential, such as opioid analgesics for pain and central nervous system depressants like benzodiazepines for sleep disorders and anxiety. Approximately 25 percent of older adults use prescription psychoactive medications that have a potential to be misused and abused. Older adults are more likely to use psychoactive medications for longer periods than younger adults. Longer periods of use increases the risk of misuse and abuse. In addition to concerns regarding misuse of medications alone, the combination of alcohol and medication misuse has been estimated to affect up to 19 percent of older Americans.

Definitions of Proper Use, Misuse, Abuse, and Dependence

DSM-IV has defined the continuum of use of psychoactive prescription medications as follows:

- Proper use—Taking only medications that have been prescribed, for the reasons the medications are prescribed, in the correct dosage, and for the correct duration
- Misuse (by patient)
  - Dose level more than prescribed
  - Longer duration than prescribed
  - Use for purposes other than prescribed
  - Use in conjunction with other medications or alcohol
  - Skipping doses/hoarding drug
- Misuse (by practitioner)
  - Prescription for inappropriate indication
  - Prescription for unnecessary high dose
  - Failure to monitor or fully explain appropriate use
- Abuse (by patient)
  - Use resulting in declining physical or social function
  - Use in risky situations (hazardous use)

    - Continued use despite adverse social or personal consequences
- Dependence
    - Use resulting in tolerance or withdrawal symptoms
    - Unsuccessful attempts to stop or control use
    - Preoccupation with attaining or using the drug

Misuse and abuse are distinct from medication mismanagement problems, such as forgetting to take medications, and confusion or lack of understanding about proper use. Medication mismanagement problems can also have serious consequences for older adults, but they have different risk factors and typically require different types of interventions.

Who is at Risk for Psychoactive Prescription Medication Misuse and Abuse?

A number of factors have been associated with an increased risk of psychoactive prescription medication misuse/abuse among older adults:

- Female gender
- Social isolation
- History of substance abuse
- A mental health disorder, particularly depression

Older women are at higher risk because they are more likely to use psychoactive medications, especially benzodiazepines. This use may be associated with divorce, widowhood, lower income, poorer health status, depression, and/or anxiety. Impact of the Problem on Older Adults The potential health consequences of psychoactive medication misuse are numerous. Prolonged use of psychoactive medications, especially benzodiazepines, has been associated with depression and cognitive decline. Benzodiazepine use is associated with confusion, falls, and hip fractures in older adults.

Use of opioid analgesics can lead to excessive sedation, respiratory depression, and impairment in vision, attention, and coordination as well as falls among older persons. Other negative effects of psychoactive medication misuse and abuse are loss of motivation, memory problems, family or marital discord, new difficulties with activities of daily living, declines in personal grooming and hygiene, and withdrawal from family, friends, and normal social activities.

What Are Psychoactive Medications?

Psychoactive substances act primarily on the central nervous system, where they affect brain function resulting in changes in mood, cognition, behavior, and consciousness as well as block the perception of pain. Some psychoactive substances also produce euphoric effects by acting on the pleasure center of the brain.

The two classes of psychoactive prescription medications that are most problematic among older adults are opioid analgesics (also known as narcotic analgesics) used for the treatment of pain and benzodiazepines (also referred to as sedatives or tranquilizers) used primarily for the treatment of anxiety/nervousness and insomnia. Listed below are common opioid analgesics and benzodiazepines.

These medications are frequently prescribed to older adults, have a high dependence and abuse potential, and interact with alcohol leading to many negative consequences. Pain relievers were the type of medication most commonly involved (43.5 %) in older adults' ED visits involving medication misuse, followed by medications for anxiety and insomnia (31.8 %).

Common Benzodiazepines for Anxiety, Nervousness, and Insomnia

- Alprazolam (Xanax®)
- Clorazepate (Tranxene®)
- Diazepam (Valium®)
- Estazolam (ProSom®)
- Flurazepam (Dalmane®)
- Lorazepam (Ativan®)
- Oxazepam (Serax®)
- Quazepam (Doral®)
- Temazepam (Restoril®)
- Triazolam (Halcion®)

Common Opioid Analgesics for Pain

- Codeine (Tylenol #3®, Empirin® and Fiorinol® with codeine, Robitussin A-C®)
- Oxycodone (OxyContin®, Percocet®, Percodan®)
- Hydrocodone (Vicodin®, Lortab®, Lorcet®, Tussionex®)
- Morphine (MS Contin®, Roxanol®, Kadian®, Avinza®)

- Meperidine (Demerol®)
- Triazolam (Halcion®)
- Hydromorphone (Dilaudid®)
- Fentanyl (Duragesic®, Actiq®)
- Tramadol (Ultram®)
- Methadon

Prescription Drug Abuse Among Older Adults

Persons aged 65 years and older comprise only 13 percent of the population, yet account for more than one-third of total outpatient spending on prescription medications in the United States. Older patients are more likely to be prescribed long-term and multiple prescriptions, and some experience cognitive decline, which could lead to improper use of medications. Alternatively, those on a fixed income may abuse another person's remaining medication to save money.

The high rates of comorbid illnesses in older populations, age-related changes in drug metabolism, and the potential for drug interactions may make any of these practices more dangerous than in younger populations. Further, a large percentage of older adults also use OTC medicines and dietary supplements, which (in addition to alcohol) could compound any adverse health consequences resulting from prescription drug abuse.

Part Three

Drugs of Abuse

Chapter 15

Drugs Used as Performance Enhancers

Chapter Contents

Section 15.1

Anabolic Steroids

This section contains text excerpted from the following sources: Text beginning with the heading "What Are Anabolic Steroids?" is excerpted from "Anabolic Steroids," National Institute on Drug Abuse (NIDA), March 10, 2016; Text beginning with the heading "Which Drugs Cause Similar Effects?" is excerpted from "Drugs of Abuse," U.S. Drug Enforcement Administration (DEA), 2015.

What Are Anabolic Steroids?

Also known as: Anabolic-androgenic steroids, "roids," or "juice"

Common brand names: Androsterone, Oxandrin, Dianabol, Winstrol, Deca-durabolin, and Equipoise

Anabolic steroids are man-made substances related to testosterone (male sex hormone). Doctors use anabolic steroids to treat hormone problems in men, delayed puberty, and muscle loss from some diseases.

Bodybuilders and athletes may use anabolic steroids to build muscles and improve athletic performance, often taking doses much higher than would be prescribed for a medical condition. Using them this way is not legal—or safe.

Anabolic steroids are only one type of steroid. Other types of steroids include cortisol, estrogen, and progesterone. These are different chemicals and do not have the same effects.

What Do They Look Like?

Steroids are available in: Tablets and capsules, sublingual-tablets, liquid drops, gels, creams, transdermal patches, subdermal implant pellets, and water-based and oil-based injectable solutions

The appearance of these products varies depending on the type and manufacturer.

How Are Anabolic Steroids Abused?

When people take steroids without a doctor's prescription or in ways other than as prescribed, they are abusing steroids.

Some people who abuse steroids take pills; others use needles to inject steroids into their muscles.

How Do Anabolic Steroids Affect the Brain?

Anabolic steroids affect a part of the brain called the limbic system, which controls mood. Long-term steroid abuse can lead to aggressive behavior and extreme mood swings. This is sometimes referred to as "roid rage."

Steroids can also lead to feeling paranoid (like someone or something is out to get you), jealousy, delusions (belief in something that is not true), and feeling invincible (like nothing can hurt you).

What Are the Other Effects of Anabolic Steroids?

Abuse of anabolic steroids has been linked with serious health problems. They include:

- High blood pressure
- Changes in blood cholesterol (increases in "bad" cholesterol or low-density lipoprotein [LDL], decreases in "good" cholesterol or high-density lipoprotein [HDL])
- Enlarged heart
- Heart attack or stroke (even in young people)
- Liver disease, including cancer
- Kidney problems or failure
- Severe acne

Males

- Breast growth and shrinking of testicles
- Low sperm count/infertility (unable to have children)
- Increased risk for prostate cancer

Females

- Voice deepening
- Growth of facial hair
- Male-pattern baldness

- Changes in or end of menstrual cycle/getting your period
- Enlargement of clitoris

In addition, if teens abuse anabolic steroids, they may never achieve their full height because anabolic steroids can stop growth in the middle of puberty.

Can You Get Addicted to Anabolic Steroids?

Yes. Addiction to steroids is different compared to other drugs of abuse, because users don't become high when using. People who do become addicted keep using steroids despite bad effects on their bodies and lives. Also, people who abuse steroids typically spend large amount of time and money obtaining the drugs, which is another sign they may be addicted.

When they stop using steroids, people can experience withdrawal symptoms such as feeling depressed, mood swings, feeling tired or restless, loss of appetite, being unable to sleep (insomnia), and the desire to take more steroids. Depression can be very dangerous, because it sometimes leads people to think of or attempt suicide (killing themselves). If not treated, some symptoms of depression that are linked with anabolic steroid withdrawal have lasted for a year or more after the person stops taking the drugs.

NIDA has two education programs for players on high school sports teams. In the Athletes Training and Learning to Avoid Steroids (ATLAS—for guys) and Athletes Targeting Healthy Exercise and Nutrition Alternatives (ATHENA—for girls) programs, coaches and sports team leaders talk about how steroids and other illegal drugs can affect sports performance, and they teach how to say no to offers of drugs. They also discuss how strength training and eating healthy foods can help teens build their bodies without the use of steroids. Later, special trainers teach the players proper weightlifting skills.

If you see or hear about someone abusing steroids, talk to a coach, teacher, or other trusted adult.

What Are Their Overdose Effects?

Anabolic steroids are not associated with overdoses. The adverse effects a user would experience develop from the use of steroids over time.

Can You Die If You Abuse Anabolic Steroids?

Yes. Although it is rare, there are a few ways steroid abuse can cause death.

- **Heart attacks and strokes.** Steroid use can lead to a condition called atherosclerosis, in which fat builds up inside arteries and makes it hard for blood to flow. When blood flow to the heart is blocked, a heart attack can occur. If blood flow to the brain is blocked, a stroke can occur.
- **HIV.** People who inject anabolic steroids using needles may share dirty drug injection equipment that can spread serious viral infections such as HIV/AIDS or hepatitis (a liver disease).

How Many Teens Abuse Anabolic Steroids?

See the most recent statistics on teen drug use from NIDA's Monitoring the Future study below:

Table 15.1. Monitoring the Future Study: Trends in Prevalence of Steroids for 8th Graders, 10th Graders, and 12th Graders

Drug	Time Period	8th Graders	10th Graders	12th Graders
Steroids	Lifetime	1	1.2	2.3
	Past Year	0.5	0.7	1.7
	Past Month	0.3	0.4	1

Which Drugs Cause Similar Effects?

There are several substances that produce effects similar to those of anabolic steroids. These include human growth hormone (HHG), clenbuterol, gonadotropins, and erythropoietin.

What Is Their Legal Status in the United States?

Anabolic steroids are Schedule III substances under the Controlled Substances Act. Only a small number of anabolic steroids are approved for either human or veterinary use. Steroids may be prescribed by a licensed physician for the treatment of testosterone deficiency, delayed puberty, low red blood cell count, breast cancer, and tissue wasting resulting from AIDS.

Section 15.2

Clenbuterol

This section includes text excerpted from "Clenbuterol," U.S. Drug Enforcement Administration (DEA), November 2013.

Introduction

Clenbuterol is a potent, long-lasting bronchodilator that is prescribed for human use outside of the United States. It is abused generally by bodybuilders and athletes for its ability to increase lean muscle mass and reduce body fat (i.e.,fever, repartitioning effects). However, clenbuterol is also associated with significant adverse cardiovascular and neurological effects.

Licit Uses

In the United States, clenbuterol is not approved for human use; it is only approved for use in horses. In 1998, the U.S. Food and Drug Administration (FDA) approved the clenbuterol-based Ventipulmin Syrup, manufactured by Boehringer Ingelheim Vetmedica, Inc., as a prescription-only drug for the treatment of airway obstruction in horses (0.8-3.2 μg/kg twice daily). This product is not intended for human use or for use in food-producing animals.

Outside the United States, clenbuterol is available by prescription for the treatment of bronchial asthma in humans. It is available in tablets (0.01 or 0.02 mg per tablet) and liquid and preparations. The recommended dosage is 0.02–0.03 mg twice daily.

Chemistry and Pharmacology

Clenbuterol is a beta2-adrenergic agonist. Stimulation of the beta2-adrenergic receptors on bronchial smooth muscle produces bronchodilation. However, clenbuterol like other beta-adrenergic agonists, can produce adverse cardiovascular and neurological effects, such as heart palpitations, muscle tremors, and nervousness. Activation of beta-adrenergic receptors also accounts for clenbuterol's ability to increase lean muscle mass and reduce body fat, although the downstream mechanisms by which it does so yet to be clearly defined.

After ingestion, clenbuterol is readily absorbed (70–80%) and remains in the body for a while (25–39 hours). As a result of its long half life, the adverse effects of clenbuterol are often prolonged.

Illicit Uses

Clenbuterol is abused for its ability to alter composition by reducing body fat and increasing skeletal muscle mass. It is typically abused by athletes and bodybuilders at a dose of 60–120 μg per day. It is often used in combination with other performance enhancing drugs, such as anabolic steroids and growth hormone.

It is also illicitly administered to livestock for its repartitioning effects. This has resulted in several outbreaks of acute illness in Spain, France, Italy, China, and Portugal 0.5–3 hours after individuals ingested liver and meat containing clenbuterol residues. The symptoms, which included increased heart rate, nervousness, headache, muscular tremor, dizziness, nausea, vomiting, fever, and chills, typically resolved within 2 to 6 days. Consequently, the United States and Europe actively monitor urine and tissue samples from livestock for the presence of clenbuterol.

There have also been reports of clenbuterol-tainted heroin and cocaine. Although no deaths were attributed to the clenbuterol exposures, the individuals were hospitalized for up to several days due to clenbuterol intoxication.

User Population

Clenbuterol is typically abused by athletes. It is thought to be more popular among female athletes as repartitioning effects are not associated with the typical androgenic side effects (i.e., facial hair, deepening of the voice, and thickening of the skin) of anabolic steroids. Professional athletes in several different sports have tested positive for clenbuterol. Clenbuterol is also marketed and abused for weight-loss purposes.

Illicit Distribution

Clenbuterol is readily available on the Internet as tablets, syrup, and an injectable formulation. The drug is purportedly obtained by illegal importation from other countries where it is approved for human use. According to the National Forensic Laboratory Information System (NFLIS) and the System to Retrieve Information from Drug Evidence (STRIDE), 16 exhibits were identified as clenbuterol in 2011, 13 exhibits were identified in 2012 and two exhibits were identified in the first quarter 2013. The relatively small numbers of drug seizures are likely a result of low enforcement priority due to the non-controlled status of clenbuterol in the United States.

Control Status

Clenbuterol is currently not under the Controlled Substances Act (CSA). However, clenbuterol is listed by the World Anti-Doping Agency and the International Olympic Committee as a performance enhancing drug. Therefore, athletes are barred from its use.

Section 15.3

Human Growth Hormone (hGH)

This section includes text excerpted from "Human Growth Hormone," U.S. Drug Enforcement Administration (DEA), August 2013.

Introduction

Human growth hormone (hGH) is a naturally occurring polypeptide hormone secreted by the pituitary gland and is essential for body growth. Daily secretion of hGH increases throughout childhood, peaking during adolescence, and steadily declining thereafter. In 1985, synthetic hGH was developed and approved by the FDA for specific uses. However, it is commonly abused by athletes, bodybuilders, and aging adults for its ability to increase muscle mass and decrease body fat, as well as its purported potential to improve athletic performance and reverse the effects of aging.

Licit Use

Several FDA-approved injectable hGH preparations are available by prescription from a supervising physician for clearly and narrowly defined indications. In children, hGH is approved for the treatment of poor growth due to Turner's syndrome, Prader-Willi syndrome, and chronic renal insufficiency, hGH insufficiency/deficiency, for children born small for gestational age, and for idiopathic short stature. Accepted medical uses in adults include the treatment of the wasting syndrome of AIDS and hGH deficiency. The recommended dosage is 40 μg/kg/day for children and 25 μg/kg/day for adults. The FDA-approved injectable formulations are available as liquid preparations, or as powder with a diluent for reconstitution.

Chemistry and Pharmacology

Using recombinant DNA technology, two forms of synthetic hGH were developed, somatropin and somatrem. Synthetic hGH also is chemically indistinguishable from the naturally occurring hormone in blood and urine tests.

hGH binds to growth hormone receptors present on cells throughout the body. hGH functions to regulate body composition, fluid homeostasis, glucose and lipid metabolism, skeletal muscle and bone growth, and possibly cardiac functioning. Sleep, exercise, and stress all increase the secretion of hGH.

The use of hGH is associated with several adverse effects including edema, carpal tunnel syndrome, joint pain, muscle pain, and abnormal skin sensations (e.g., numbness and tingling). It may also increase the growth of preexisting malignant cells, and increase the possibility of developing diabetes.

hGH is administered by subcutaneous or intramuscular injection. The circulating half-life of hGH is relatively short half-life (20–30 minutes), while its biological half-life is much longer (9–17 hours) due to its indirect effects.

Illicit Uses

Human growth hormone is illicitly used as an anti-aging agent, to improve athletic performance, and for bodybuilding purposes. It is marketed, distributed, and illegally prescribed off-label to aging adults to replenish declining hGH levels and reverse age-related bodily deterioration. It is also abused for its ability to alter body composition by reducing body fat and increasing skeletal muscle mass. It is often used in combination with other performance enhancing drugs, such as anabolic steroids. Athletes also use it to improve their athletic performance, although the ability of hGH to increase athletic performance is debatable.

Abuser Population

Athletes, bodybuilders, and aging adults are the primary abusers of hGH. Because the illicit use of synthetic hGH is difficult to detect, its use in sports is believed to be widespread. Over the past few years, numerous professional athletes have admitted to using hGH. Bodybuilders, as well as celebrities also purportedly use it for its ability to alter body composition. Aging adults looking to reverse the effects of aging are increasingly using synthetic hGH.

Illicit Distribution

The illicit distribution of hGH occurs as the result of physicians illegally prescribing it for off-label uses, and for the treatment of FDA-approved medical conditions without examination and supervision. Illicit distribution also involves diverted hGH obtained through theft, smuggled hGH illegally imported from other countries, and counterfeit hGH.

The illicit distribution of injectable synthetic hGH formulations is thought to be primarily through Internet pharmacies, as well as wellness and anti-aging clinics and websites. Internet pharmacies are often partnered with a physician willing to write prescriptions for a fee without a physical examination. Individuals may also obtain hGH without a prescription through the black market. hGH is often marketed with other performance enhancing drugs (e.g., anabolic steroids).

According to DEA's National Forensic Laboratory Information System (NFLIS) and the System to Retrieve Information from Drug Evidence (STRIDE), law enforcement officials submitted five hGH exhibits to federal, state and local forensic laboratories in 2011 and one in 2012. In the first quarter of 2013, there have been no reports of hGH in NFLIS or STRIDE. Various oral preparations (e.g., sprays and pills) purported to contain hGH are also marketed and distributed. However, hGH is only available in the injectable form. The hGH molecule is too large for absorption across the lining of the oral mucosa and the hormone is digested by the stomach before absorption can occur.

Control Status

Human growth hormone is not controlled under the Controlled Substances Act (CSA). However, as part of the 1990 Anabolic Steroids

Control Act, the distribution and possession, with the intent to distribute, of hGH "for any use...other than the treatment of a disease or other recognized medical condition, where such use has been authorized by the Secretary of Health and Human Services...and pursuant to the order of a physician..." was criminalized as a five-year felony under the penalties chapter of the Food, Drug, and Cosmetics Act of the FDA. hGH is listed by the World Anti-Doping Agency and the International Olympic Committee as a performance enhancing drug barring athletes from using it.

Chapter 16

Cannabinoids

What Is Marijuana?

Also known as: "weed," "pot," "bud," "grass," "herb," "Mary Jane," "MJ," "reefer," "skunk," "boom," "gangster," "kif," "chronic," and "ganja"

Marijuana is a mixture of the dried and shredded leaves, stems, seeds, and flowers of *Cannabis sativa*—the hemp plant. The mixture can be green, brown, or gray. Stronger forms of the drug include sinsemilla, hashish ("hash" for short), and hash oil.

Of the more than 500 chemicals in marijuana, delta-9-tetrahydrocannabinol, known as THC, is responsible for many of the drug's psychotropic (mind-altering) effects. It's this chemical that changes how the brain works, distorting how the mind perceives the world.

Legal Issues

It is illegal to buy, sell, or carry marijuana under Federal law. The Federal Government considers marijuana a Schedule I substance—having no medicinal uses and high risk for abuse. However, across the United States, marijuana state laws for adult use are changing. A growing number of states have passed laws allowing the use of marijuana as a treatment for certain medical conditions.

This chapter contains text excerpted from the following sources: Text beginning with the heading "What Is Marijuana?" is excerpted from "Marijuana," National Institute on Drug Abuse (NIDA), March 10, 2016; Text beginning with the heading "What If a Person Wants to Quit Using Marijuana?" is excerpted from "Marijuana: Facts for Teens," National Institute on Drug Abuse (NIDA), May 2015.

In addition, four states and the District of Columbia have legalized marijuana for adult recreational use. Because of concerns over the possible harm to the developing teen brain and the risk of driving under the influence, marijuana use by people under age 21 is prohibited in all states.

Strength and Potency

The amount of THC in marijuana has increased over the past few decades. In the early 1990's, the average THC content was about 3.74 percent for marijuana and 7.5 percent for sinsemilla. In 2013, it was almost 10 percent for marijuana and 16 percent for sinsemilla in 2013. Scientists don't yet know what this increase in potency means for a person's health. It could be that users take in higher amounts of THC, or they may adjust how they consume marijuana (like smoke or eat less) to compensate for the greater potency.

Hash Oil

The honey-like resin from the marijuana plant has 3 to 5 times more THC than the plant itself. Smoking it (also called "dabbing") can deliver dangerous amounts of THC to users, and has led some people to the emergency room. People have been burned in fires and explosions caused by attempts to remove hash oil using butane (lighter fluid).

How Is Marijuana Used?

Marijuana is commonly smoked using pipes, water pipes called "bongs," or hand-rolled cigarettes called "joints" or "nails." It is sometimes also combined with tobacco in partially hollowed-out cigars, known as "blunts." Recently vaporizers, that use heat without burning to produce a vapor, have increased in popularity. Marijuana can also be brewed as tea or mixed with food, sometimes called edibles.

In addition, concentrated resins containing high doses of marijuana's active ingredients, including honey-like "hash oil," waxy "budder," and hard amber-like "shatter," are increasingly popular among both recreational and medical users.

How Does Marijuana Affect the Brain?

The main chemical in marijuana that affects the brain is delta-9-tetrahydrocannabinol (THC). When marijuana is smoked, THC quickly passes from the lungs into the bloodstream, which carries it to organs throughout the body, including the brain. As it enters the brain, THC attaches to cells, or neurons, with specific kinds of receptors called cannabinoid receptors. Normally, these receptors are activated by chemicals that occur naturally in the body. They are part of a communication network in the brain called the endocannabinoid system. This system is important in normal brain development and function.

Most of the cannabinoid receptors are found in parts of the brain that influence pleasure, memory, thinking, concentration, sensory and time perception, and coordinated movement. Marijuana triggers an increase in the activity of the endocannabinoid system, which causes the release of dopamine in the brain's reward centers, creating the pleasurable feelings or "high." Other effects include changes in perceptions and mood, lack of coordination, difficulty with thinking and problem solving, and disrupted learning and memory.

Certain parts of the brain have a lot of cannabinoid receptors. These areas are the hippocampus, the cerebellum, the basal ganglia, and the cerebral cortex. The functions that these brain areas control are the ones most affected by marijuana:

- **Learning and memory.** The hippocampus plays a critical role in certain types of learning. Disrupting its normal functioning can lead to problems studying, learning new things, and recalling recent events. A recent study followed people from age 13 to 38 and found that those who used marijuana a lot in their teens had up to an 8 point drop in IQ, even if they quit in adulthood.
- **Coordination.** THC affects the cerebellum, the area of our brain that controls balance and coordination, and the basal ganglia, another part of the brain that helps control movement. These effects can influence performance in such activities as sports, driving, and video games.
- **Judgment.** Since THC affects areas of the frontal cortex involved in decision making, using it can cause you to do things you might not do when you are not under the influence of drugs—such as engaging in risky sexual behavior, which can lead to sexually transmitted diseases (STDs) like HIV, the virus that causes AIDS—or getting in a car with someone who's been drinking or is high on marijuana.

When marijuana is smoked, its effects begin almost immediately and can last from 1 to 3 hours. Decision making, concentration, and memory can suffer for days after use, especially in regular users.

If marijuana is consumed in foods or beverages, the effects of THC appear later—usually in 30 minutes to 1 hour—but may last for many hours.

Long-term, regular use of marijuana—starting in the teen years—may impair brain development and lower IQ, meaning the brain may not reach its full potential.

What Are the Other Effects of Marijuana?

The changes that take place in the brain when a person uses marijuana can cause serious health problems and affect a person's daily life.

Effects on Health

Within a few minutes after inhaling marijuana smoke, a person's heart rate speeds up, the bronchial passages (the pipes that let air in and out of your lungs) relax and become enlarged, and blood vessels in the eyes expand, making the eyes look red. While these and other effects seem harmless, they can take a toll on the body.

- **Increased heart rate.** When someone uses marijuana, heart rate—normally 70 to 80 beats per minute—may increase by 20 to 50 beats per minute or, in some cases, even double. This effect can be greater if other drugs are taken with marijuana. The increased heart rate forces the heart to work extra hard to keep up.
- **Respiratory (lung and breathing) problems.** Smoke from marijuana irritates the lungs, causing breathing and lung problems among regular users similar to those experienced by people who smoke tobacco—like a daily cough and a greater risk for lung infections such as pneumonia. While research has not found a strong association between marijuana and lung cancer, many people who smoke marijuana also smoke cigarettes, which do cause cancer. And, some studies have suggested that smoking marijuana could make it harder to quit cigarette smoking.
- **Increased risk for mental health problems.** Marijuana use has been linked with depression and anxiety, as well as suicidal thoughts among adolescents. In addition, research has suggested that in people with a genetic risk for developing schizophrenia, smoking marijuana during adolescence may increase the risk for developing psychosis and developing it at an earlier age. Researchers are still learning exactly what the relationship is between these mental health problems and marijuana use.

- **Increased risk of problems for an unborn baby.** Pregnant women who use marijuana may risk changing the developing brain of the unborn baby. These changes could contribute to problems with attention, memory, and problem solving.

Effects on School and Social Life

The effects of marijuana on the brain and body can have a serious impact on a person's life.

- **Reduced school performance.** Students who smoke marijuana tend to get lower grades and are more likely to drop out of high school than their peers who do not use. The effects of marijuana on attention, memory, and learning can last for days or weeks. These effects have a negative impact on learning and motivation. In fact, people who use marijuana regularly for a long time are less satisfied with their lives and have more problems with friends and family compared to people who do not use marijuana.
- **Impaired driving.** It is unsafe to drive while under the influence of marijuana. Marijuana affects a number of skills required for safe driving—alertness, concentration, coordination, and reaction time—so it's not safe to drive high or to ride with someone who's been smoking. Marijuana makes it hard to judge distances and react to signals and sounds on the road. Marijuana is the most common illegal drug involved in auto fatalities. High school seniors who smoke marijuana are 2 times more likely to receive a traffic ticket and 65% more likely to get into an accident than those who don't smoke. In 2011, among 12th graders, 12.5% reported that within the past 2 weeks they had driven after using marijuana. And combining marijuana with drinking even a small amount of alcohol greatly increases driving danger, more than either drug alone.
- **Potential gateway to other drugs**. Most young people who use marijuana do not go on to use other drugs. However, those who use marijuana, alcohol, or tobacco during their teen years are more likely to use other illegal drugs. It isn't clear why some people do go on to try other drugs, but researchers have a few theories. The human brain continues to develop into the early 20s. Exposure to addictive substances, including marijuana, may cause changes to the developing brain that make other drugs more appealing. Animal research supports this possibility—for

example, early exposure to marijuana makes opioid drugs (like Vicodin or heroin) more pleasurable. In addition, someone who uses marijuana is more likely to be in contact with people who use and sell other drugs, increasing the risk for being encouraged or tempted to try them. Finally, people at high risk for using drugs may use marijuana first because it is easy to get (like cigarettes and alcohol).

Can You Get Addicted to Marijuana?

Yes, marijuana is addictive. A user may feel the urge to smoke marijuana again and again to re-create the "high." Repeated use could lead to addiction—which means the person has trouble controlling their drug use and often cannot stop even though they want to.

An estimated nine percent of people who use marijuana will become dependent; people who begin using marijuana before the age of 18 are 4–7 times more likely to become addicted than adults.

It is estimated that about 1 in 6 people who start using as a teen, and 25 percent to 50 percent of those who use it every day, become addicted to marijuana. What causes one person to become addicted to marijuana and another not to depends on many factors—including their family history (genetics), the age they start using, whether they also use other drugs, their family and friend relationships, and whether they take part in positive activities like school or sports (environment).

People who use marijuana may also feel withdrawal when they stop using the drug. Withdrawal symptoms may include:

- Irritability
- Sleeplessness
- Lack of appetite, which can lead to weight loss
- Anxiety
- Drug cravings

These effects can last for several days to a few weeks after drug use is stopped. Relapse (returning to the drug after you've quit) is common during this period because people also crave the drug to relieve these symptoms.

Can You Die If You Use Marijuana?

It is very unlikely for a person to overdose and die from marijuana use. However, people can and do injure themselves and die because of marijuana's effects on judgment, perception, and coordination, for example, when driving under the influence of the drug. Also, people can experience extreme anxiety (panic attacks) or psychotic reactions (where they lose touch with reality and may become paranoid).

How Many Teens Use Marijuana?

Marijuana is the most common illicit drug used in the United States by teens as well as adults. The growing belief by young people that marijuana is a safe drug may be the result of recent public discussions about medical marijuana and the public debate over the drug's legal status. In addition, some teens believe marijuana cannot be harmful because it is "natural." But not all natural plants are good for you—take tobacco, for example.

Table 16.1. Monitoring the Future Study: Trends in Prevalence of Marijuana/ Hashish for 8th Graders, 10th Graders, and 12th Graders; 2015 (in percent)*

Drug	Time Period	8th Graders	10th Graders	12th Graders
Marijuana/ Hashish	Lifetime	15.5	[31.10]	44.7
	Past Year	11.8	25.4	34.9
	Past Month	6.5	14.8	21.3
	Daily	1.1	3	6

**Data in brackets indicate statistically significant change from the previous year.*

What If a Person Wants to Quit Using Marijuana?

Researchers are testing different ways to help marijuana users stay off the drug, including some medications. Current treatment programs focus on counseling and group support systems. There are also a number of programs designed especially to help teenagers.

Isn't Marijuana Sometimes Used as a Medicine?

A number of states have passed laws allowing marijuana for medical use, but the U.S. Food and Drug Administration (FDA) has not approved the marijuana plant to treat any diseases. Even so, the marijuana plant contains ingredients that could have important medical uses. Currently, the FDA has approved two pill versions of THC to treat nausea in cancer chemotherapy patients and to stimulate appetite in some patients with AIDS. Also, a new product that is a chemically controlled mixture of THC and cannabidiol (another chemical found in the marijuana plant) is available in several countries outside the United States as a mouth spray. However, it's important to remember that because marijuana is usually smoked into the lungs and has ingredients that can vary from plant to plant, its health risks may outweigh its value as a treatment. Scientists continue to investigate safe ways that patients can use THC and other marijuana ingredients as medicine.

Chapter 17

Date Rape Drugs / Club Drugs

Chapter Contents

Section 17.1

Introduction to Club Drugs

This section contains text excerpted from the following sources: Text beginning with the heading "Club Drugs (GHB, Ketamine, and Rohypnol)" is excerpted from "DrugFacts," National Institute on Drug Abuse (NIDA), December 2014; Text under the heading "So What Can You Do to Avoid Date Rape Drugs?" is excerpted from "What Are Date Rape Drugs and How Do You Avoid Them?" National Institute on Drug Abuse (NIDA), March 16, 2015.

Club Drugs (GHB, Ketamine, and Rohypnol)

Club drugs are a pharmacologically heterogeneous group of psychoactive drugs that tend to be abused by teens and young adults at bars, nightclubs, concerts, and parties. Gamma hydroxybutyrate (GHB), Rohypnol, ketamine, as well as MDMA (ecstasy) and methamphetamine are some of the drugs included in this group.

- GHB (Xyrem) is a central nervous system (CNS) depressant that was approved by the U.S. Food and Drug Administration (FDA) in 2002 for use in the treatment of narcolepsy (a sleep disorder). This approval came with severe restrictions, including its use only for the treatment of narcolepsy, and the requirement for a patient registry monitored by the FDA. GHB is also a metabolite of the inhibitory neurotransmitter gamma-aminobutyric acid (GABA). It exists naturally in the brain, but at much lower concentrations than those found when GHB is abused.
- Rohypnol (flunitrazepam) use began gaining popularity in the United States in the early 1990s. It is a benzodiazepine (chemically similar to sedative-hypnotic drugs such as Valium or Xanax), but it is not approved for medical use in this country, and its importation is banned.
- Ketamine is a dissociative anesthetic, mostly used in veterinary practice.

How Are Club Drugs Abused?

- GHB and Rohypnol are available in odorless, colorless, and tasteless forms that are frequently combined with alcohol and other beverages. Both drugs have been used to commit sexual assaults (also known as "date rape," "drug rape," "acquaintance rape," or "drug-assisted" assault) due to their ability to sedate and incapacitate unsuspecting victims, preventing them from resisting sexual assault.
- GHB is usually ingested orally, either in liquid or powder form, while Rohypnol is typically taken orally in pill form. Recent reports, however, have shown that Rohypnol is being ground up and snorted.
- Both GHB and Rohypnol are also abused for their intoxicating effects, similar to other CNS depressants.
- GHB also has anabolic effects (it stimulates protein synthesis) and has been used by bodybuilders to aid in fat reduction and muscle building.
- Ketamine is usually snorted or injected intramuscularly.

How Do Club Drugs Affect the Brain?

- GHB acts on at least two sites in the brain: the $GABA_B$ receptor and a specific GHB binding site. At high doses, GHB's sedative effects may result in sleep, coma, or death
- Rohypnol, like other benzodiazepines, acts at the $GABA_A$ receptor. It can produce anterograde amnesia, in which individuals may not remember events they experienced while under the influence of the drug.
- Ketamine is a dissociative anesthetic, so called because it distorts perceptions of sight and sound and produces feelings of detachment from the environment and self. Ketamine acts on a type of glutamate receptor (NMDA receptor) to produce its effects, which are similar to those of the drug PCP. Low-dose intoxication results in impaired attention, learning ability, and memory. At higher doses, ketamine can cause dreamlike states and hallucinations; and at higher doses still, ketamine can cause delirium and amnesia.

Addictive Potential

- Repeated use of GHB may lead to withdrawal effects, including insomnia, anxiety, tremors, and sweating. Severe withdrawal reactions have been reported among patients presenting from an overdose of GHB or related compounds, especially if other drugs or alcohol are involved.
- Like other benzodiazepines, chronic use of Rohypnol can produce tolerance, physical dependence, and addiction.
- There have been reports of people binging on ketamine, a behavior that is similar to that seen in some cocaine—or amphetamine—dependent individuals. Ketamine users can develop signs of tolerance and cravings for the drug.

What Other Adverse Effects Do Club Drugs Have on Health?

Uncertainties about the sources, chemicals, and possible contaminants used to manufacture many club drugs make it extremely difficult to determine toxicity and associated medical consequences. Nonetheless, we do know that:

- Coma and seizures can occur following use of GHB. Combined use with other drugs such as alcohol can result in nausea and breathing difficulties. GHB and two of its precursors, gamma butyrolactone (GBL) and 1,4 butanediol (BD), have been involved in poisonings, overdoses, date rapes, and deaths.
- Rohypnol may be lethal when mixed with alcohol and/or other CNS depressants.
- Ketamine, in high doses, can cause impaired motor function, high blood pressure, and potentially fatal respiratory problems.

What Treatment Options Exist?

There is very little information available in the scientific literature about treatment for persons who abuse or are dependent upon club drugs.

- There are no GHB detection tests for use in emergency rooms, and as many clinicians are unfamiliar with the drug, many GHB incidents likely go undetected. According to case reports, however, patients who abuse GHB appear to present both a mixed picture of severe problems upon admission and a good response to treatment, which often involves residential services.

- Treatment for Rohypnol follows accepted protocols for any benzodiazepine, which may consist of a 3- to 5-day inpatient detoxification program with 24-hour intensive medical monitoring and management of withdrawal symptoms, since withdrawal from benzodiazepines can be life-threatening.
- Patients with a ketamine overdose are managed through supportive care for acute symptoms, with special attention to cardiac and respiratory functions.

How Widespread Is Club Drug Abuse?

The 2014 Monitoring the Future Survey has reported consistently low levels of abuse of these club drugs since they were added to the survey. For GHB and ketamine, this occurred in 2000; for Rohypnol, 1996. According to results of the MTF survey, 1.0 percent of 12th-grade students reported past-year use of GHB, a statistically significant decrease from peak year use of 2.0 percent in 2004. GHB use among 8th- and 10th-grade students was not reported.

Past-year use of ketamine was reported by 1.4 percent of 12th-graders in 2014. This also represents a significant decrease from the peak year of 2002, in which 2.6 percent reported past-year use.

For Rohypnol, 0.3 percent of 8th-graders, 0.5 percent of 10th-graders, and 0.7 percent of 12th-graders reported past-year use, also down from peak use in 1996 for 8th graders (1.0%), 1997 for 10th graders (1.3%), and 2002 and 2004 for 12th-graders (1.6%).

So What Can You Do to Avoid Date Rape Drugs?

Date rape, also known as "drug-facilitated sexual assault," is any type of sexual activity that a person does not agree to. It may come from someone you know, may have just met, and/or thought you could trust.

Date rape drugs can make people become physically weak or pass out. This is why people who want to rape someone use them, because they leave individuals unable to protect themselves.

If you are at a party where people are drinking alcohol, you should be aware that there could be predators hoping to make you drunk or vulnerable. No matter what you are drinking, even if it's sodas or juice, people can slip drugs in your drinks—so pour all drinks yourself and never leave them unattended (even if you have to take them into the bathroom with you).

Also, be sure to stick with your friends—there's safety in numbers.

But even if you leave your drink or leave your friends behind, know this for certain: if you are drugged and taken advantage of, it's *not* your fault.

Bottom line: People who date rape other people are committing a crime.

Section 17.2

Gamma Hydroxybutyrate (GHB)

This section includes text excerpted from "Drugs of Abuse," U.S. Drug Enforcement Administration (DEA), 2015.

What Is GHB?

Gamma-Hydroxybutyric acid (GHB) is another name for the generic drug sodium oxybate. Xyrem® (which is sodium oxybate) is the trade name of the U.S. Food and Drug Administration (FDA)-approved prescription medication.

Analogues that are often substituted for GHB include GBL (gamma butyrolactone) and 1,4 BD (also called just "BD"), which is 1,4-butanediol. These analogues are available legally as industrial solvents used to produce polyurethane, pesticides, elastic fibers, pharmaceuticals, coatings on metal or plastic, and other products. They are also are sold illicitly as supplements for bodybuilding, fat loss, reversal of baldness, improved eyesight, and to combat aging, depression, drug addiction, and insomnia.

GBL and BD are sold as "fish tank cleaner," "ink stain remover," "ink cartridge cleaner" and "nail enamel remover" for approximately $100 per bottle—much more expensive than comparable products. Attempts to identify the abuse of GHB analogues are hampered by the fact that routine toxicological screens do not detect the presence of these analogues.

What Is Its Origin?

GHB is produced illegally in both domestic and foreign clandestine laboratories. The major source of GHB on the street is through clandestine synthesis by local operators. At bars or "rave" parties, GHB is typically sold in liquid form by the capful or "swig" for $5 to $25 per cap. Xyrem® has the potential for diversion and abuse like any other pharmaceutical containing a controlled substance.

GHB has been encountered in nearly every region of the country.

What Are Common Street Names?

Common street names include:

- Easy Lay, G, Georgia Home Boy, GHB, Goop, Grievous Bodily Harm, Liquid Ecstasy, Liquid X, and Scoop

What Does It Look Like?

GHB is usually sold as a liquid or as a white powder that is dissolved in a liquid, such as water, juice, or alcohol. GHB dissolved in liquid has been packaged in small vials or small water bottles. In liquid form, GHB is clear and colorless and slightly salty in taste.

How Is It Abused?

GHB and its analogues are abused for their euphoric and calming effects and because some people believe they build muscles and cause weight loss.

GHB and its analogues are also misused for their ability to increase libido, suggestibility, passivity, and to cause amnesia (no memory of events while under the influence of the substance)—traits that make users vulnerable to sexual assault and other criminal acts. GHB abuse became popular among teens and young adults at dance clubs and "raves" in the 1990s and gained notoriety as a date rape drug. GHB is taken alone or in combination with other drugs, such as alcohol (primarily), other depressants, stimulants, hallucinogens, and marijuana.

The average dose ranges from 1 to 5 grams (depending on the purity of the compound, this can be 1–2 teaspoons mixed in a beverage). However, the concentrations of these "home-brews" have varied so much that users are usually unaware of the actual dose they are drinking.

What Is Its Effect on the Mind?

GHB occurs naturally in the central nervous system in very small amounts. Use of GHB produces Central Nervous System (CNS) depressant effects including:

- Euphoria, drowsiness, decreased anxiety, confusion, and memory impairment

GHB can also produce both visual hallucinations and—paradoxically—excited and aggressive behavior. GHB greatly increases the CNS depressant effects of alcohol and other depressants.

What Is Its Effect on the Body?

GHB takes effect in 15 to 30 minutes, and the effects last 3 to 6 hours. Low doses of GHB produce nausea. At high doses, GHB overdose can result in:

- Unconsciousness, seizures, slowed heart rate, greatly slowed breathing, lower body temperature, vomiting, nausea, coma, and death

Regular use of GHB can lead to addiction and withdrawal that includes:

- Insomnia, anxiety, tremors, increased heart rate and blood pressure, and occasional psychotic thoughts

Currently, there is no antidote available for GHB intoxication. GHB analogues are known to produce side effects such as:

- Topical irritation to the skin and eyes, nausea, vomiting, incontinence, loss of consciousness, seizures, liver damage, kidney failure, respiratory depression, and death

What Are Its Overdose Effects?

GHB overdose can cause death.

Which Drugs Cause Similar Effects?

GHB analogues are often abused in place of GHB. Both GBL and BD metabolize to GHB when taken and produce effects similar to GHB.

CNS depressants such as barbiturates and methaqualone also produce effects similar to GHB.

What Is Its Legal Status in the United States?

GHB is a Schedule I controlled substance, meaning that it has a high potential for abuse, no currently accepted medical use in treatment in the United States, and a lack of accepted safety for use under medical supervision. GHB products are Schedule III substances under the Controlled Substances Act. In addition, GBL is a List I chemical.

It was placed on Schedule I of the Controlled Substances Act in March 2000. However, when sold as GHB products (such as Xyrem®), it is considered Schedule III, one of several drugs that are listed in multiple schedules.

Section 17.3

Ketamine

This section includes text excerpted from "Drugs of Abuse," U.S. Drug Enforcement Administration (DEA), 2015.

What Is Ketamine?

Ketamine is a dissociative anesthetic that has some hallucinogenic effects. It distorts perceptions of sight and sound and makes the user feel disconnected and not in control. It is an injectable, short-acting anesthetic for use in humans and animals. It is referred to as a "dissociative anesthetic" because it makes patients feel detached from their pain and environment.

Ketamine can induce a state of sedation (feeling calm and relaxed), immobility, relief from pain, and amnesia (no memory of events while under the influence of the drug). It is abused for its ability to produce dissociative sensations and hallucinations. Ketamine has also been used to facilitate sexual assault.

What Is Its Origin?

Ketamine is produced commercially in a number of countries, including the United States. Most of the ketamine illegally distributed in the United States is diverted or stolen from legitimate sources, particularly veterinary clinics, or smuggled into the United States from Mexico.

Distribution of ketamine typically occurs among friends and acquaintances, most often at raves, nightclubs, and at private parties; street sales of ketamine are rare.

What Are Common Street Names?

Common street names include:

- Cat Tranquilizer, Cat Valium, Jet K, Kit Kat, Purple, Special K, Special La Coke, Super Acid, Super K, and Vitamin K

What Does It Look Like?

Ketamine comes in a clear liquid and a white or off-white powder. Powdered ketamine (100 milligrams to 200 milligrams) typically is packaged in small glass vials, small plastic bags, and capsules as well as paper, glassine, or aluminum foil folds.

How Is It Abused?

Ketamine, along with the other "club drugs," has become popular among teens and young adults at dance clubs and "raves." Ketamine is manufactured commercially as a powder or liquid. Powdered ketamine is also formed from pharmaceutical ketamine by evaporating the liquid using hot plates, warming trays, or microwave ovens, a process that results in the formation of crystals, which are then ground into powder.

Powdered ketamine is cut into lines known as bumps and snorted, or it is smoked, typically in marijuana or tobacco cigarettes. Liquid ketamine is injected or mixed into drinks. Ketamine is found by itself or often in combination with MDMA, amphetamine, methamphetamine, or cocaine.

What Is Its Effect on the Mind?

Ketamine produces hallucinations. It distorts perceptions of sight and sound and makes the user feel disconnected and not in control. A "Special K" trip is touted as better than that of LSD or PCP because its hallucinatory effects are relatively short in duration, lasting approximately 30 to 60 minutes as opposed to several hours.

Slang for experiences related to Ketamine or effects of Ketamine include:

- "K-land" (refers to a mellow and colorful experience)
- "K-hole" (refers to the out-of-body, near death experience)
- "Baby food" (users sink into blissful, infantile inertia)
- "God" (users are convinced that they have met their maker)

The onset of effects is rapid and often occurs within a few minutes of taking the drug, though taking it orally results in a slightly slower onset of effects. Flashbacks have been reported several weeks after ketamine is used. Ketamine may also cause agitation, depression, cognitive difficulties, unconsciousness, and amnesia.

What Is Its Effect on the Body?

A couple of minutes after taking the drug, the user may experience an increase in heart rate and blood pressure that gradually decreases over the next 10 to 20 minutes. Ketamine can make users unresponsive to stimuli. When in this state, users experience:

- Involuntarily rapid eye movement, dilated pupils, salivation, tear secretions, and stiffening of the muscles

This drug can also cause nausea.

What Are Its Overdose Effects?

An overdose can cause unconsciousness and dangerously slowed breathing.

Which Drugs Cause Similar Effects?

Other hallucinogenic drugs such as LSD, PCP, and mescaline can cause hallucinations. There are also several drugs such as GHB, Rohypnol and other depressants that are misused for their amnesiac or sedative properties to facilitate sexual assault.

What Is Its Legal Status in the United States?

Since the 1970s, ketamine has been marketed in the United States as an injectable, short-acting anesthetic for use in humans and animals. In 1999, ketamine including its salts, isomers, and salts of isomers, became a Schedule III non-narcotic substance under the Federal Controlled Substances Act. It has a currently acceptable medical use but some potential for abuse, which may lead to moderate or low physical dependence or high psychological dependence.

Section 17.4

Rohypnol

This section includes text excerpted from "Drugs of Abuse," U.S. Drug Enforcement Administration (DEA), 2015.

What Is Rohypnol®?

Rohypnol® is a trade name for flunitrazepam, a central nervous system (CNS) depressant that belongs to a class of drugs known as benzodiazepines. Flunitrazepam is also marketed as generic preparations and other trade name products outside of the United States.

Like other benzodiazepines, Rohypnol® produces sedative hypnotic, anti-anxiety, and muscle relaxant effects. This drug has never been approved for medical use in the United States by the Food and Drug Administration. Outside the United States, Rohypnol® is commonly prescribed to treat insomnia. Rohypnol® is also referred to as a "date rape" drug.

What Is Its Origin?

Rohypnol® is smuggled into the United States from other countries, such as Mexico.

What Are Common Street Names?

Common street names include:

- Circles, Forget Pill, Forget-Me-Pill, La Rocha, Lunch Money Drug, Mexican Valium, Pingus, R2, Reynolds, Roach, Roach 2,

Roaches, Roachies, Roapies, Robutal, Rochas Dos, Rohypnol, Roofies, Rophies, Ropies, Roples, Row-Shay, Ruffies, and Wolfies

What does it look like?

Prior to 1997, Rohypnol® was manufactured as a white tablet (0.5-2 milligrams per tablet), and when mixed in drinks, was colorless, tasteless, and odorless. In 1997, the manufacturer responded to concerns about the drug's role in sexual assaults by reformulating the drug. Rohypnol® is now manufactured as an oblong olive green tablet with a speckled blue core that when dissolved in light-colored drinks will dye the liquid blue. However, generic versions of the drug may not contain the blue dye.

How Is It Abused?

The tablet can be swallowed whole, crushed and snorted, or dissolved in liquid. Adolescents may abuse Rohypnol® to produce a euphoric effect often described as a "high." While high, they experience reduced inhibitions and impaired judgment.

Rohypnol® is also abused in combination with alcohol to produce an exaggerated intoxication.

In addition, abuse of Rohypnol® may be associated with multiple-substance abuse. For example, cocaine addicts may use benzodiazepines such as Rohypnol® to relieve the side effects (e.g., irritability and agitation) associated with cocaine binges.

Rohypnol® is also misused to physically and psychologically incapacitate women targeted for sexual assault. The drug is usually placed in the alcoholic drink of an unsuspecting victim to incapacitate them and prevent resistance to sexual assault. The drug leaves the victim unaware of what has happened to them.

What Is Its Effect on the Mind?

Like other benzodiazepines, Rohypnol® slows down the functioning of the CNS producing:

- Drowsiness (sedation), sleep (pharmacological hypnosis), decreased anxiety, and amnesia (no memory of events while under the influence of the substance)

Rohypnol® can also cause:

- Increased or decreased reaction time, impaired mental functioning and judgment, confusion, aggression, and excitability

What Is Its Effect on the Body?

Rohypnol® causes muscle relaxation. Adverse physical effects include

- Slurred speech, loss of motor coordination, weakness, headache, and respiratory depression

Rohypnol also can produce physical dependence when taken regularly over a period of time.

What Are Its Overdose Effects?

High doses of Rohypnol®, particularly when combined with CNS depressant drugs such as alcohol and heroin, can cause severe sedation, unconsciousness, slow heart rate, and suppression of respiration that may be sufficient to result in death.

Which Drugs Cause Similar Effects?

Drugs that cause similar effects include GHB (gamma hydroxybutyrate) and other benzodiazepines such as alprazolam (e.g., Xanax®), clonazepam (e.g., Klonopin®), and diazepam (e.g., Valium®).

What Is Its Legal Status in the United States?

Rohypnol® is a Schedule IV substance under the Controlled Substance Act. Rohypnol® is not approved for manufacture, sale, use or importation to the United States. It is legally manufactured and marketed in many countries. Penalties for possession, trafficking, and distribution involving one gram or more are the same as those of a Schedule I drug.

Chapter 18

Hallucinogenic Drugs

Chapter Contents

Section 18.1

Introduction to Hallucinogens

This section includes text excerpted from "DrugFacts: Hallucinogens," National Institute on Drug Abuse (NIDA), January 2016.

What Are Hallucinogens?

Hallucinogens are a diverse group of drugs that alter perception (awareness of surrounding objects and conditions), thoughts, and feelings. They cause hallucinations, or sensations and images that seem real though they are not. Hallucinogens can be found in some plants and mushrooms (or their extracts) or can be human-made. People have used hallucinogens for centuries, mostly for religious rituals. Common hallucinogens include the following:

- **Ayahuasca** is a tea made from one of several Amazonian plants containing *dimethyltryptamine* (DMT), the primary mind-altering ingredient. Ayahuasca is also known as Hoasca, Aya, and Yagé.
- **DMT** is a powerful chemical found in some Amazonian plants. Manufacturers can also make DMT in a lab. The drug is usually a white crystalline powder. A popular name for DMT is Dimitri.
- ***D-lysergic acid diethylamide*** **(LSD)** is one of the most powerful mood-changing chemicals. It is a clear or white odorless material made from lysergic acid, which is found in a fungus that grows on rye and other grains. LSD has many other names, including Acid, Blotter, Dots, and Yellow Sunshine.
- **Peyote (mescaline)** is a small, spineless cactus with mescaline as its main ingredient. Peyote can also be synthetic. Buttons, Cactus, and Mesc are common names for peyote.
- **4-phosphoryloxy-N,N-dimethyltryptamine (psilocybin)** comes from certain types of mushrooms found in tropical and subtropical regions of South America, Mexico, and the United States. Other names for psilocybin include Little Smoke, Magic Mushrooms, Purple Passion, and Shrooms.

Some hallucinogens also cause users to feel out of control or disconnected from their body and environment. Common examples include the following:

- ***Dextromethorphan*** **(DXM)** is a cough suppressant and mucus-clearing ingredient in some over-the-counter cold and cough medicines (syrups, tablets, and gel capsules). Robo is another popular name for DXM.
- **Ketamine** is used as a surgery anesthetic for humans and animals. Much of the ketamine sold on the streets comes from veterinary offices. While available as an injectable liquid, manufacturers mostly sell it as a powder or as pills. Other names for ketamine include K, Special K, or Cat Valium.
- ***Phencyclidine*** **(PCP)** was developed in the 1950s as a general anesthetic for surgery. It's no longer used for this purpose due to serious side effects. While PCP can be found in a variety of forms, including tablets or capsules, liquid and white crystal powder are the most common forms. PCP has various other names, such as Angel Dust, Hog, Love Boat, and Peace Pill.
- ***Salvia divinorum*** **(salvia)** is a plant common to southern Mexico and Central and South America. Other names for salvia are Diviner's Sage, Maria Pastora, Sally-D, and Magic Mint.

How Do Hallucinogens Affect the Brain?

Research suggests that hallucinogens work at least partially by temporarily disrupting communication between brain chemical systems throughout the brain and spinal cord. Some hallucinogens interfere with the action of the brain chemical serotonin, which regulates:

- mood
- sensory perception
- sleep
- hunger
- body temperature
- sexual behavior
- muscle control

Other hallucinogens interfere with the action of the brain chemical glutamate, which regulates:

- pain perception
- responses to the environment
- emotion
- learning and memory

Short-Term Effects

The effects of hallucinogens can begin within 20 to 90 minutes and can last as long as 6 to 12 hours. Salvia's effects are more short-lived, appearing in less than 1 minute and lasting less than 30 minutes. Hallucinogen users refer to the experiences brought on by these drugs as "trips," calling the unpleasant experiences "bad trips."

Along with hallucinations, other short-term general effects include:

- increased heart rate
- nausea
- intensified feelings and sensory experiences
- changes in sense of time (for example, time passing by slowly)

Specific short-term effects of some hallucinogens include:

- increased blood pressure, breathing rate, or body temperature
- loss of appetite
- dry mouth
- sleep problems
- mixed senses (such as "seeing" sounds or "hearing" colors)
- spiritual experiences
- feelings of relaxation or detachment from self/environment
- uncoordinated movements
- excessive sweating
- panic
- *paranoia*—extreme and unreasonable distrust of others
- *psychosis*—disordered thinking detached from reality

Long-Term Effects

Little is known about the long-term effects of hallucinogens. Researchers do know that ketamine users may develop symptoms that include ulcers in the bladder, kidney problems, and poor memory. Repeated use of PCP can result in long-term effects that may continue for a year or more after use stops, such as:

- speech problem
- memory loss
- weight loss
- anxiety
- depression and suicidal thoughts

Though rare, long-term effects of some hallucinogens include the following:

- **Persistent psychosis**—a series of continuing mental problems, including:
    - visual disturbances
    - disorganized thinking
    - paranoia
    - mood changes
- **Flashbacks**—recurrences of certain drug experiences. They often happen without warning and may occur within a few days or more than a year after drug use. In some users, flashbacks can persist and affect daily functioning, a condition known as *hallucinogen persisting perceptual disorder* (HPPD). These people continue to have hallucinations and other visual disturbances, such as seeing trails attached to moving objects.
- Symptoms that are sometimes mistaken for other disorders, such as stroke or a brain tumor

What Are Other Risks of Hallucinogens?

Other risks or health effects of many hallucinogens remain unclear and need more research. Known risks include the following:

- Some psilocybin users risk poisoning and possibly death from using a poisonous mushroom by mistake.
- High doses of PCP can cause seizures, coma, and death, though death more often results from accidental injury or suicide during PCP intoxication. Interactions between PCP and depressants

such as alcohol and benzodiazepines (prescribed to relieve anxiety or promote sleep—alprazolam [Xanax®], for instance) can also lead to coma.

- Some bizarre behaviors resulting from hallucinogens that users display in public places may prompt public health or law enforcement personnel intervention.
- While hallucinogens' effects on the developing fetus are unknown, researchers do know that mescaline in peyote may affect the fetus of a pregnant woman using the drug.

Are Hallucinogens Addictive?

Evidence indicates that certain hallucinogens can be addictive or that people can develop a tolerance to them. Use of some hallucinogens also produces tolerance to other similar drugs.

For example, LSD is not considered an addictive drug because it doesn't cause uncontrollable drug-seeking behavior. However, LSD does produce tolerance, so some users who take the drug repeatedly must take higher doses to achieve the same effect. This is an extremely dangerous practice, given the unpredictability of the drug. In addition, LSD produces tolerance to other hallucinogens, including psilocybin.

On the other hand, PCP is a hallucinogen that can be addictive. People who stop repeated use of PCP experience drug cravings, headaches, and sweating as common withdrawal symptoms.

Scientists need more research into the tolerance or addiction potential of hallucinogens.

How Can People Get Treatment for Addiction to Hallucinogens?

There are no government-approved medications to treat addiction to hallucinogens. While inpatient and/or behavioral treatments can be helpful for patients with a variety of addictions, scientists need more research to find out if behavioral therapies are effective for addiction to hallucinogens.

Section 18.2

Synthetic Drugs: 2C-I and 2C-T-7 (Blue Mystic)

This section contains text excerpted from the following sources: Text beginning with the heading "4-Iodo-2,5-Dimethoxyphenethylamine" is excerpted from "4-Iodo-2,5-Dimethoxyphenethylamine," U.S. Drug Enforcement Administration (DEA), May 2013; Text beginning with the heading "2,5-Dimethoxy-4-(N)-Propylthiophenethylamine" is excerpted from "2,5-Dimethoxy-4-(N)-Propylthiophenethylamine," U.S. Drug Enforcement Administration (DEA), May 2013.

4-Iodo-2,5-Dimethoxyphenethylamine

Street Names: 2C-I, i

Introduction

4-Iodo-2,5-dimethoxyphenethylamine (2C-I, 4-iodo-2,5-DMPEA) is a synthetic drug abused for its hallucinogenic effects.

Licit Uses

2C-I has no approved medical uses in the United States.

Chemistry and Pharmacology

4-Iodo-2,5-dimethoxyphenethylamine is closely related to the phenethylamine hallucinogens, 1-(4-bromo-2, 5-dimethoxyphenyl)-2-aminopropane (DOB) and 2,5-dimethoxy-4-methylamphetamine (DOM). Like DOM and DOB, 2C-I displays high affinity for central serotonin receptors. 2C-I selectively binds to the 5-HT receptor system.

Drug discrimination studies in animals indicate that 2C-I produces discriminative stimulus effects that are similar to those of several Schedule I hallucinogens such as lysergic acid diethylamide (LSD), N,N-dimethyltryptamine (DMT) and methylene-dioxymethamphetamine (MDMA). In rats trained to discriminate LSD, DMT or MDMA from saline, 2C-I fully substituted for these Schedule I hallucinogens.

In humans, 2C-I produces dose dependent psychoactive effects. User reports have mentioned oral doses between 3 and 25 mg, producing LSD-like hallucinations and visual distortions, and MDMA-like empathy. Onset of subjective effects following 2C-I ingestion is around 40 minutes with peak effects occurring at approximately 2 hours. Effects of 2C-I can last up to 8 hours. Various users reported delayed desired effects compared to related drugs, which may result in some users taking additional doses or other drugs which may increase the risk of toxicity or accidental over dosage.

Radioimmunoassay detection system that is commonly used for testing amphetamine and hallucinogens is not expected to detect 2C-I. In the Marquis Reagent Field Test, 2C-I produces a dark green to black color.

Illicit Uses

2C-I is abused for its hallucinogenic effects. 2C-I is taken orally in tablet or capsule forms or snorted in its powder form. It has also been found impregnated on small squares of blotter paper for oral administration, which is a technique often seen for the distribution and abuse of LSD. The drug has been misrepresented by distributors and sold as other hallucinogens such as MDMA and LSD.

User Population

2C-I is used by the same population as those using "Ecstasy" and other club drugs, high school and college students, and other young adults in dance and nightlife settings.

Illicit Distribution

2C-I is distributed as capsules, tablets, in powder form, or in liquid form. DEA identified occurrences of the drug being purchased through Internet retailers. In one instance, it was purchased in powder form through the Internet and encapsulated for retail, at a street value of $6 per capsule. In Europe, 2C-I has often been seized in tablet form with an 'i' logo which may be to signify that it is not ecstasy (MDMA).

The National Forensic Laboratory Information System (NFLIS) is a DEA database that collects scientifically verified data on drug items and cases submitted to and analyzed by state and local forensic laboratories. The System to Retrieve Information from Drug Evidence (STRIDE) provides information on drug seizures reported to and analyzed by DEA laboratories. From 2007 to 2012, 353 exhibits have been identified as 2C-I by federal, state, and local forensic laboratories in 33 states. In 2010, there were 61 2C-I reports. There were 95 2C-I reports in 2011 and 73 reports in 2012.

Control Status

The Controlled Substances Act (CSA) lists 2C-I in Schedule I.

2,5-Dimethoxy-4-(N)-Propylthiophenethylamine

Street Names: 2C-T-7, Blue Mystic, T7, Beautiful, Tripstay, Tweety-Bird Mescaline

Licit Uses

2C-T-7 is not approved for marketing by the Food and Drug Administration and is not sold legally in the United States.

Chemistry and Pharmacology:

2,5-Dimethoxy-4-(n)-propylthiophenethylamine (2C-T-7), is a phenethylamine hallucinogen that is structurally related to the Schedule I phenethylamine hallucinogens, 4-bromo-2, 5-dimethoxyphenethylamine (2C-B, Nexus) and mescaline. Based on structural similarly to these compounds, the pharmacological profile of 2C-T-7 is expected to be qualitatively similar to these hallucinogens.

Drug discrimination studies in animals indicate that 2C-T-7 produces discriminative stimulus effects similar to those of several Schedule I hallucinogens. In rat strained to discriminate 2,5-dimethoxy-4-methyl-amphetamine (DOM), 2C-T-7 fully substituted for DOM and was slightly less potent than 2C-B in eliciting DOM-like effects. 2C-T-7 was also shown to share some commonality with LSD; it partially substituted for LSD up to doses that severely disrupted performance in rats trained to discriminate LSD. 2C-T-7 can also function as a discriminative stimulus in rats. Rats readily learned to discriminate 2C-T-7 from saline. When either 2C-B or LSD was substituted for 2C-T-7, each elicited 2C-T-7-like discriminative stimulus effects.

The subjective effects of 2C-T-7, like those of 2C-B and DOM, appear to be mediated through central serotonin receptors. 2C-T-7 selectively binds to the 5-HT receptor system.

According to one published case report, 2C-T-7 abuse has been associated with convulsions in humans.

Illicit Uses

2C-T-7 is abused orally and intranasally for its hallucinogenic effects. Information from a website about a variety of illicit drugs has suggested that 2C-T-7 produce effects similar to those of 2C-B. This information is based on individuals self-administering 2C-T-7 illicitly and self-reporting the effects. Its effects include visual hallucination, mood lifting, sense of well being, emotionality, volatility, increased appreciation of music, and psychedelic ideation. The oral and intranasal doses recommended on this website are 10-50 mg and 5-10 mg, respectively. 2C-T-7's onset and duration of actions are dependent upon the route of administration.

Following oral administration, onset and duration of effects are 1 to 2.5 hours and 5 to 7 hours, respectively. After intranasal administration, the onset of action and duration of effects are 5 to 15 minutes and 2 to 4 hours, respectively.

User Population

Young adults are the main abusers of 2C-T-7.

Illicit Distribution

The National Forensic Laboratory Information System (NFLIS) is a DEA database that collects scientifically verified data on drug items and cases submitted to and analyzed by state and local forensic laboratories. The System to Retrieve Information from Drug Evidence (STRIDE) provides information on drug seizures reported to and analyzed by DEA laboratories. From January 2007 to December 2012, 51 reports, identified as 2C-T-7, were submitted to federal, state, and local forensic laboratories. During this time, law enforcement officials encountered 2C-T-7 in 13 states; 28 of the 51 reports were encountered in the state of Florida.

2C-T-7 was being purchased over the Internet from a company located in Indiana. This site was traced to an individual who had been selling large quantities of this substance since January 2000. Sales through this Internet site were thought to be the major sources of 2C-T-7 in the United States. One clandestine laboratory was identified in Las Vegas, Nevada as the supplier of2C-T-7 to the individual in Indiana. 2C-T-7 has been sold under the street names Blue Mystic, T7, Beautiful,Tweety-Bird Mescaline or Tripstay.

Control Status

2C-T-7 has been placed in Schedule I of the Controlled Substances Act.

Section 18.3

Alpha-Methyltryptamine (Spirals)

This section includes text excerpted from "Alpha-Methyltryptamine," U.S. Drug Enforcement Administration (DEA), April 2013.

Introduction

Alpha-methyltryptamine (AMT) is a tryptamine derivative and shares many pharmacological similarities with those of Schedule I hallucinogens such as alpha-ethyltryptamine, N,N-dimethyltryptamine, psilocybin, and LSD. Since 1999, AMT has become popular among drug abusers for its hallucinogenic-like effects. In the 1960s, following extensive clinical studies on AMT as a possible antidepressant drug, the Upjohn Company concluded that AMT was a toxic substance and produces psychosis.

Licit Uses

AMT has no currently accepted medical uses in treatment in the United States.

Chemistry/Pharmacology

The hydrochloride salt of AMT is a white crystalline powder.

AMT, similar to several other Schedule I hallucinogens, binds with moderate affinities to serotonin (5-HT) receptors (5-HT1 and 5-HT2). AMT inhibits the uptake of monoamines especially 5-HT and is a potent inhibitor of monoamine oxidase (MAO) (especially MAO-A), an enzyme critical for the metabolic degradation of monoamines, the brain chemicals important for sensory, emotional and other behavioral functions. AMT has been shown to produce locomotor stimulant effects in animals. It has been hypothesized that both 5-HT and dopamine systems mediate the stimulant effects of AMT. In animals, AMT produces behavioral effects that are substantially similar to those of 1-(2,5-dimethoxy-4-methylphenyl)-2-aminopropane (DOM) and methylene-dioxymethamphetamine (MDMA), both Schedule I hallucinogens, in animals.

In humans, AMT elicits subjective effects including hallucinations. It has an onset of action of about 3 to 4 hours and duration of about 12 to 24 hours, but may produce an extended duration of 2 days in some subjects. Subjects report uncomfortable feelings, muscular tension, nervous tension, irritability, restlessness, unsettled feeling in stomach, and the inability to relax and sleep. AMT can alter sensory perception and judgment and can pose serious health risks to the user and the general public. Abuse of AMT led to two emergency department admissions and one death. AMT increases blood pressure and heart rate, dilates pupils, and causes deep tendon reflexes and impairs coordination.

Illicit Uses

AMT is abused for its hallucinogenic effects and is used as substitute for MDMA. It is often administered orally as either powder or capsules at doses ranging from 15-40 mg. Other routes of administration include smoking and snorting.

User Population

Youth and young adults are the main abusers of AMT. Internet websites are a source that high school students and United States soldiers have used to obtain and abuse AMT.

Illicit Distribution

The National Forensic Laboratory Information System is a DEA database that collects scientifically verified data on drug items and cases submitted to and analyzed by state and local forensic laboratories. The System to Retrieve Information from Drug Evidence (STRIDE) provides information on drug seizures reported to and analyzed by DEA laboratories. According to the System to Retrieve Information from Drug Evidence (STRIDE) data, the first recorded submission by law enforcement to DEA laboratories of a drug exhibit containing AMT occurred in 1999.

NFLIS and STRIDE indicate that reports of AMT by federal, state, and local forensic laboratories increased from 10 in 2002 to 31 in 2003. In the years after temporary scheduling of AMT in 2003, the number of reports declined. In 2004, there were six reports and in 2005, there were two reports. From 2006 to 2011, NFLIS and STRIDE indicated a total of five AMT reports in those databases. However, in 2012, the number of AMT reports in NFLIS and STRIDE increased to 25. AMT has been illicitly available from United States and foreign chemical companies and from Internet websites. Additionally, there is evidence of attempted clandestine production of AMT.

Control Status

The Drug Enforcement Administration (DEA) placed AMT temporarily in Schedule I of the Controlled Substances Act (CSA) on April 4, 2003, pursuant to the temporary scheduling provisions of the CSA (68 FR 16427). On September 29, 2004, AMT was permanently controlled as a Schedule I substance under the CSA (69 FR 58050).

Section 18.4

N, N-Dimethyltryptamine (DMT)

This section includes text excerpted from "N,N-Dimethyltryptamine," U.S. Drug Enforcement Administration (DEA), January 2013.

Introduction

N,N-Dimethyltryptamine (DMT) is the prototypical indolethylamine hallucinogen. The history of human experience with DMT probably goes back several hundred years since DMT usage is associated with a number of religious practices and rituals. As a naturally occurring substance in many species of plants, DMT is present in a number of South American snuffs and brewed concoctions, like Ayahuasca. In addition, DMT can be produced synthetically. The original synthesis was conducted by a British chemist, Richard Manske, in 1931.

DMT gained popularity as a drug of abuse in the 1960s and was placed under federal control in Schedule I when the Controlled Substances Act was passed in 1971. Today, it is still encountered on the illicit market along with a number of other tryptamine hallucinogens.

Licit Use

DMT has no approved medical use in the United States but can be used by researchers under a Schedule I research registration that requires approval from both DEA and the Food and Drug Administration.

Pharmacology

Administered alone, DMT is usually snorted, smoked or injected because the oral bioavailability of DMT is very poor unless it is combined with a substance that inhibits its metabolism. For example, in ayahuasca, the presence of harmala alkaloids (harmine, harmaline, tetrahydro-harmaline) inhibits the enzyme, monoamine oxidase which normally metabolizes DMT. As a consequence, DMT remains intact long enough to be absorbed insufficient amounts to affect brain function and produce psychoactive effects.

In clinical studies, DMT was fully hallucinogenic at doses between 0.2 and 0.4 mg/kg. The onset of DMT effects is very rapid but usually resolves within 30 to 45 minutes. Psychological effects include intense visual hallucinations, depersonalization, auditory distortions and an altered sense of time and body image. Physiological effects include hypertension, increased heart rate, agitation, seizures, dilated pupils, nystagmus (involuntary rapid rhythmic movement of the eye), dizziness and ataxia (muscular incoordination). At high doses, coma and respiratory arrest have occurred.

Illicit Use

DMT is used for its psychoactive effects. The intense effects and short duration of action are attractive to individuals who want the psychodelic experience but do not choose to experience the mind altering perceptions over an extended period of time as occurs with other hallucinogens, like LSD. DMT is generally smoked or consumed orally in brews like Ayahuasca.

Illicit Distribution

DMT is found in a number of plant materials and can be extracted or synthetically produced in clandestine labs. Like other hallucinogens, Internet sales and distribution have served as the source of drug supply in this country. According to the National Forensic Laboratory Information System (NFLIS) and the System to Retrieve Information from Drug Evidence (STRIDE), there were 540 DMT reports from Federal, state and local forensic laboratories in 2011. From January to June 2012, there were 338 DMT reports. According to STRIDE and NFLIS, illicit use of DMT has been encountered in most states and the District of Columbia.

Control Status

DMT is controlled in Schedule I of the Controlled Substances Act.

Section 18.5

Ecstasy (MDMA)

This section contains text excerpted from the following sources: Text beginning with the heading "What Is MDMA (Ecstasy or Molly)?" is excerpted from "MDMA (Ecstasy or Molly)," National Institute on Drug Abuse (NIDA), March 7, 2016; Text beginning with the heading "Which Drugs Cause Similar Effects?" is excerpted from "Drugs of Abuse," U.S. Drug Enforcement Administration (DEA), 2015.

What Is MDMA (Ecstasy or Molly)?

Also known as: "Ecstasy," "Molly," "E," "XTC," "X," "Adam," "hug," "beans," "clarity," "lover's speed," and "love drug"

MDMA, short for 3,4-methylenedioxymethamphetamine, is most commonly known as "Ecstasy" or "Molly." It is a man made drug that produces energizing effects similar to the stimulant class amphetamines as well as psychedelic effects, similar to the hallucinogen mescaline. MDMA is known as a "club drug" because of its popularity in the nightclub scene, at "raves" (all-night dance parties), and music festivals or concerts.

MDMA is a Schedule I substance, which means that it is considered by the U.S. Federal government to have no medical benefit and a high potential for abuse. However, researchers continue to investigate the possible medical benefits for patients with posttraumatic stress disorder (PTSD) and terminal cancer patients with anxiety.

How Is MDMA Used?

Most people who use MDMA take it in a pill, tablet, or capsule. The pills can be different colors and sometimes have cartoon-like images on them. Some people take more than one pill at a time, called "bumping." The popular term "Molly" (slang for "molecular") refers to the pure crystalline powder form of MDMA, usually sold in capsules.

Researchers have found that much of the Ecstasy used today contains other drugs in addition to MDMA, which themselves can be harmful. Makers of MDMA might add caffeine, dextromethorphan (found in some cough syrups), amphetamines, PCP, or cocaine to the pills, tablets, or capsules. Frequently, they substitute other chemicals for MDMA, such as synthetic cathinones, the chemicals in "bath salts."

MDMA's effects generally last from 3 to 6 hours. It is common for users to take a second dose of the drug as the effects of the first dose begin to fade. Some users may also take MDMA along with other drugs.

How Does MDMA Affect the Brain?

Once the pill or capsule is swallowed, it takes about 15 minutes for MDMA to enter the bloodstream and reach the brain. MDMA produces its effects by increasing the activity of three neurotransmitters (the chemical messengers of brain cells): serotonin, dopamine, and norepinephrine.

The serotonin system plays a role in controlling our mood, aggression, sexual activity, sleep, and feeling of pain. The extra serotonin that is released by MDMA likely causes mood-lifting effects in users. People who use MDMA might feel very alert, or "hyper," at first. Some lose a sense of time and have other changes in perception, such as a more intense sense of touch. Serotonin also triggers the release of the hormones oxytocin and vasopressin, which play a role in feelings of love, sexual arousal, and trust. This may be why users report feeling a heightened sense of emotional closeness and empathy.

Some users experience negative effects. They may become anxious and agitated, become sweaty, have chills, or feel faint or dizzy.

Even those who don't feel negative effects during use can experience negative aftereffects. These aftereffects are caused by the brain no longer having enough serotonin after the surge that was triggered by using MDMA. Days or even weeks after use, people can experience confusion, depression, sleep problems, drug craving, and anxiety.

Effects of Long-Term Use

Researchers are not sure if MDMA causes long-term brain changes in people, or whether the effects are reversible when someone stops using the drug. However, studies have shown that some heavy MDMA users experience problems that are long lasting, including confusion, depression, and problems with memory and attention.

What Is Its Effect on the Body?

Users of MDMA experience many of the same effects and face many of the same risks as users of other stimulants such as cocaine and amphetamines. These include increased motor activity, alertness, heart rate, and blood pressure.

The changes that take place in the brain with MDMA use affect the user in other ways as well. These include:

- Increases in heart rate and blood pressure
- Muscle tension
- Teeth clenching
- Nausea (feeling sick)
- Blurred vision
- Faintness
- Chills or sweating
- Higher body temperature (can lead to serious heart, liver, or kidney problems)
- Increased risk for unsafe sex

High doses of MDMA can interfere with the ability to regulate body temperature, resulting in a sharp increase in body temperature (hyperthermia), leading to liver, kidney and cardiovascular failure.

Severe dehydration can result from the combination of the drug's effects and the crowded and hot conditions in which the drug is often taken.

Studies suggest chronic use of MDMA can produce damage to the serotonin system. It is ironic that a drug that is taken to increase pleasure may cause damage that reduces a person's ability to feel pleasure.

Because MDMA does not always break down in the body, it can interfere with its own metabolism. This can cause harmful levels of the drug to build up in the body if it is taken repeatedly within short periods of time. High levels of the drug in the bloodstream can increase the risk for seizures and affect the heart's ability to beat normally.

Can You Get Addicted to MDMA?

Researchers don't yet know. What is known is that MDMA targets the same neurotransmitters that are targeted by other addictive drugs. Researchers are still working to understand MDMA's addictive properties. But, some users experience:

- Dependence—continued use despite understanding the harm it can cause
- Withdrawal—symptoms that occur after regular use of the drug is reduced or stopped, such as fatigue, loss of appetite, depression, and trouble concentrating
- Tolerance—the need for more of the drug to get the same "high" feeling

How Many Teens Use MDMA?

Table 18.1. Monitoring the Future Study: Trends in Prevalence of MDMA for 8th Graders, 10th Graders, and 12th Graders; 2015 (in percent)*

Drug	Time Period	8th Graders	10th Graders	12th Graders
MDMA	Lifetime	2.3	[3.80]	[5.90]
	Past Year	1.4	[2.40]	[3.60]
	Past Month	0.5	0.9	1.1

**Data in brackets indicate statistically significant change from the previous year.*

What Are Its Overdose Effects?

In high doses, MDMA can interfere with the body's ability to regulate temperature. On occasions, this can lead to a sharp increase in body temperature (hyperthermia), resulting in liver, kidney, and cardiovascular system failure, and death. Because MDMA can interfere with its own metabolism (that is, its break down within the body), potentially harmful levels can be reached by repeated drug use within short intervals.

Can You Die from MDMA Use?

Yes, you can die from MDMA use. MDMA can cause problems with the body's ability to regulate temperature, particularly when it is used in active, hot settings (like dance parties or concerts). On rare occasions, this can lead to a sharp rise in body temperature (known as hyperthermia), which can cause liver, kidney, or heart failure or even death.

Which Drugs Cause Similar Effects?

No one other drug is quite like MDMA, but MDMA produces both amphetamine-like stimulation and mild mescaline-like hallucinations.

What Is Its Legal Status in the United States?

MDMA is a Schedule I drug under the Controlled Substances Act, meaning it has a high potential for abuse, no currently accepted medical use in treatment in the United States, and a lack of accepted safety for use under medical supervision.

Section 18.6

Foxy

This section includes text excerpted from "5-Methoxy-N,N-Diisopropyltryptamine," U.S. Drug Enforcement Administration (DEA), April 2013.

5-Methoxy-N,N-Diisopropyltryptamine

Street Names: Foxy, or Foxy methoxy

Introduction

5-methoxy-N,N-diisopropyltryptamine (5-MeO-DIPT) is a tryptamine derivative and shares many similarities with Schedule I tryptamine hallucinogens such as alpha-ethyltryptamine, N,N-dimethyltryptamine, N,N-diethyltryptamine, bufotenine, psilocybin and psilocin. Since 1999, 5-MeO-DIPT has become popular among drug abusers. This substance is abused for its hallucinogenic effects.

Licit Uses

5-MeO-DIPT has no accepted medical uses in treatment in the United States.

Chemistry/Pharmacology

5-MeO-DIPT is a tryptamine derivative. The hydrochloride salt of 5-MeO-DIPT is a white crystalline powder. In animal behavioral studies, 5-MeO-DIPT has been shown to produce behavioral effects that are substantially similar to those of 1-(2,5-dimethoxy-4-methylphenyl)-2-aminopropane (DOM) and lysergic acid diethylamide (LSD), both Schedule I hallucinogens.

In humans, 5-MeO-DIPT elicits subjective effects including hallucinations similar to those produced by several Schedule I hallucinogens such as 2C-B and 4-ethyl-2,5-dimethoxyphenyl-isopropylamine (DOET). The threshold dose of 5-MeO-DIPT to produce psychoactive effects is 4 mg, while effective doses range from 6 to 20 mg. 5-MeO-DIPT produces effects with an onset of 20 to 30 minutes and with peak effects occurring between 1 to 1.5 hours after administration. Effects last about 3 to 6 hours. Initial effects include mild nausea, muscular hyperreflexia, and dilation of pupils. Other effects include relaxation associated with emotional enhancement, talkativeness and behavioral disinhibition. High doses of 5-MeO-DIPT produce abstract eyes-closed imagery. 5-MeO-DIPT alters sensory perception and judgment and can pose serious health risks to the user and the general public. Abuse of 5-MeO-DIPT led to at least one emergency department admission.

Illicit Uses

5-MeO-DIPT is abused for its hallucinogenic-like effects and is used as a substitute for MDMA. It is often administered orally as either powder, tablets or capsules at doses ranging from 6–20 mg. Other routes of administration include smoking and snorting. Tablets often bear imprints commonly seen on MDMA tablets (spider and alien head logos) and vary in color. Powder in capsules was found to vary in colors.

User Population

Youth and young adults are the main abusers of 5-MeO-DIPT.

Illicit Distribution

The National Forensic Laboratory Information System (NFLIS) is a DEA database that collects scientifically verified data on drug items and cases submitted to and analyzed by state and local forensic laboratories. The System to Retrieve Information from Drug Evidence (STRIDE) provides information on drug seizures reported to and analyzed by DEA laboratories. According to NFLIS and STRIDE, 5-MeO-DIPT drug reports increased sharply from 72 in 2010 to 3,271 in 2011 and then decreased to 1,525 in 2012.5-MeO-DIPT has been illicitly available from United States and foreign chemical companies and from individuals through the Internet. There is some evidence of the attempted clandestine production of 5-MeO-DIPT.

Control Status

The Drug Enforcement Administration (DEA) temporarily placed 5-MeO-DIPT in Schedule I of the Controlled Substances Act (CSA) on April 4, 2003, pursuant to the temporary scheduling provisions of the CSA (68 FR 16427). On September 29, 2004, 5-MeO-DIPT was permanently controlled as a Schedule I substance under the CSA (69 FR 58050).

Section 18.7

LSD

This section includes text excerpted from "Drugs of Abuse," U.S. Drug Enforcement Administration (DEA), 2015.

What Is LSD?

Lysergic acid diethylamide (LSD) is a potent hallucinogen that has a high potential for abuse and currently has no accepted medical use in treatment in the United States.

What Is Its Origin?

LSD is produced in clandestine laboratories in the United States.

What Are Common Street Names?

Common names for LSD include:

- Acid, Blotter Acid, Dots, Mellow Yellow, and Window Pane

What Does It Look Like?

LSD is sold on the street in tablets, capsules, and occasionally in liquid form. It is an odorless and colorless substance with a slightly bitter taste. LSD is often added to absorbent paper, such as blotter paper, and divided into small decorated squares, with each square representing one dose.

How Is It Abused?

LSD is abused orally.

What Is Its Effect on the Mind?

During the first hour after ingestion, users may experience visual changes with extreme changes in mood. While hallucinating, the user may suffer impaired depth and time perception accompanied by distorted perception of the shape and size of objects, movements, colors, sound, touch and the user's own body image.

The ability to make sound judgments and see common dangers is impaired, making the user susceptible to personal injury. It is possible for users to suffer acute anxiety and depression after an LSD "trip" and flashbacks have been reported days, and even months, after taking the last dose.

What Is Its Effect on the Body?

The physical effects include:

- Dilated pupils, higher body temperature, increased heart rate and blood pressure, sweating, loss of appetite, sleeplessness, dry mouth, and tremors

What Are Its Overdose Effects?

LSD's effects are similar to other hallucinogens, such as PCP, mescaline, and peyote.

What Is Its Legal Status in the United States?

LSD is a Schedule I substance under the Controlled Substances Act. Schedule I substances have a high potential for abuse, no currently accepted medical use in treatment in the United States, and a lack of accepted safety for use under medical supervision.

Section 18.8

Mescaline (Peyote)

This section includes text excerpted from "Drugs of Abuse," U.S. Drug Enforcement Administration (DEA), 2015.

What Are Peyote and Mescaline?

Peyote is a small, spineless cactus. The active ingredient in peyote is the hallucinogen mescaline.

What Is Its Origin?

From earliest recorded time, peyote has been used by natives in northern Mexico and the southwestern United States as a part of their religious rites. Mescaline can be extracted from peyote or produced synthetically.

What Are Common Street Names?

Common street names include:

- Buttons, Cactus, Mesc, and Peyoto

What Does It Look Like?

The top of the peyote cactus is referred to as the "crown" and consists of disc-shaped buttons that are cut off.

How Is It Abused?

The fresh or dried buttons are chewed or soaked in water to produce an intoxicating liquid. Peyote buttons may also be ground into a powder that can be placed inside gelatin capsules to be swallowed, or smoked with a leaf material such as cannabis or tobacco.

What Is Its Effect on the Mind?

Abuse of peyote and mescaline will cause varying degrees of:

- Illusions, hallucinations, altered perception of space and time, and altered body image

Users may also experience euphoria, which is sometimes followed by feelings of anxiety.

What Is Its Effect on the Body?

Following the consumption of peyote and mescaline, users may experience:

- Intense nausea, vomiting, dilation of the pupils, increased heart rate, increased blood pressure, a rise in body temperature that causes heavy perspiration, headaches, muscle weakness, and impaired motor coordination

Which Drugs Cause Similar Effects?

Other hallucinogens like LSD, psilocycbin (mushrooms), and PCP

What is its legal status in the United States?

Peyote and Mescaline are Schedule I substances under the Controlled Substances Act, meaning that they have a high potential for abuse, no currently accepted medical use in treatment in the United States, and a lack of accepted safety for use under medical supervision.

Section 18.9

Psilocybin

This section includes text excerpted from "Drugs of Abuse," U.S. Drug Enforcement Administration (DEA), 2015.

What Is Psilocybin?

Psilocybin is a chemical obtained from certain types of fresh or dried mushrooms.

What Is Its Origin?

Psilocybin mushrooms are found in Mexico, Central America, and the United States.

What Are Common Street Names?

Common street names include:

- Magic Mushrooms, Mushrooms, and Shrooms

What Does It Look Like?

Mushrooms containing psilocybin are available fresh or dried and have long, slender stems topped by caps with dark gills on the underside. Fresh mushrooms have white or whitish-gray stems; the caps are dark brown around the edges and light brown or white in the center. Dried mushrooms are usually rusty brown with isolated areas of off-white.

How Is It Abused?

Psilocybin mushrooms are ingested orally. They may also be brewed as a tea or added to other foods to mask their bitter flavor.

What Is Its Effect on the Mind?

The psychological consequences of psilocybin use include hallucinations and an inability to discern fantasy from reality. Panic reactions and psychosis also may occur, particularly if a user ingests a large dose.

What Is Its Effect on the Body?

The physical effects include:

- Nausea, vomiting, muscle weakness, and lack of coordination

What Are Its Overdose Effects?

Effects of overdose include:

- Longer, more intense "trip" episodes, psychosis, and possible death

Abuse of psilocybin mushrooms could also lead to poisoning if one of the many varieties of poisonous mushrooms is incorrectly identified as a psilocybin mushroom.

Which Drugs Cause Similar Effects?

Psilocybin effects are similar to other hallucinogens, such as mescaline and peyote.

What Is Its Legal Status in the United States?

Psilocybin is a Schedule I substance under the Controlled Substances Act, meaning that it has a high potential for abuse, no currently accepted medical use in treatment in the United States, and a lack of accepted safety for use under medical supervision.

Section 18.10

Toonies (Nexus, 2C-B)

This section includes text excerpted from "4-Bromo-2,5-Dimethoxyphenethylamine," U.S. Drug Enforcement Administration (DEA), May 2013.

4-Bromo-2,5-Dimethoxyphenethylamine

Street Names: 2C-B, Nexus, 2's, Toonies, Bromo, Spectrum, Venus

Introduction

4-Bromo-2,5-dimethoxyphenethylamine (2C-B, 4-bromo-2,5-DMPEA) is a synthetic Schedule I hallucinogen. It is abused for its hallucinogenic effects primarily as a club drug in the rave culture and "circuit" party scene.

Licit Uses

2C-B has no approved medical uses in the United States.

Chemistry and Pharmacology

4-Bromo-2,5-dimethoxyphenethylamine is closely related to the phenylisopropylamine hallucinogen 1-(4-bromo-2, 5-dimethoxyphenyl)-2-aminopropane (DOB) and is referred to as alpha-desmethyl DOB. 2C-B produces effects similar to 2,5-dimethoxy-4-methylamphetamine (DOM) and DOB. 2C-B displays high affinity for central serotonin receptors. 2C-B produces dose-dependent psychoactive effects. Threshold effects are noted at approximately 4 mg of an oral dose; the user becomes passive and relaxed and is aware of an integration of sensory perception with emotional states. There is euphoria with increased body awareness and enhanced receptiveness of visual, auditory, olfactory, and tactile sensation. Oral doses of 8 to 10 mg produce stimulant effects and cause a full intoxicated state. Doses in the range of 20 to 40 mg produce LSD-like hallucinations. Doses greater than 50 mg have produced extremely fearful hallucinations and morbid delusions. Onset of subjective effects following 2C-B ingestion is between 20 to 30 minutes with peak effects occurring at 1.5 to 2 hours. Effects of 2C-B can last up to 8 hours.

Radioimmunoassay detection system that is commonly used for testing amphetamine and hallucinogens does not detect 2C-B. In the Marquis Reagent Field Test-902, 2C-B produces a bright green color. 2C-B is the only known drug to produce a bright green color when using this test.

Illicit Uses

2C-B is abused for its hallucinogenic effects. 2C-B is abused orally in tablet or capsule forms or snorted in its powder form. The drug has been misrepresented by distributors and sold as other hallucinogens such as MDMA and LSD. Some user's abuse 2C-B in combination with LSD (referred to as a "banana split") or MDMA (called a "party pack").

User Population

2C-B is used by the same population as those using "Ecstasy" and other club drugs, high school and college students, and other young adults who frequent "rave" or "techno" parties.

Illicit Distribution

2C-B is distributed as tablets, capsules, or in powder form. Usually sold as MDMA, a single dosage unit of 2C-B typically sells for $10 to $30 per tablet. The illicit source of 2C-B currently available on the street has not been identified by DEA. Prior to its control, DEA seized both clandestine laboratories and illicit "repacking shops." As the name implies, these shops would repackage and reformulate the doses of the tablets prior to illicit sales. According to the System to Retrieve Information from Drug Evidence (STRIDE) data, the first recorded submission by law enforcement to DEA forensic laboratories of a drug exhibit containing 2C-B occurred in 1986.

The National Forensic Laboratory Information System (NFLIS) is a DEA database that collects scientifically verified data on drug items and cases submitted to and analyzed by state and local forensic laboratories. The STRIDE database provides information on drug seizures reported to and analyzed by DEA laboratories. From 2007 to 2012, 2C-B has been encountered by law enforcement in 37 states. Law enforcement officials submitted 89 exhibits identified as 2C-B to federal, state, and local forensic laboratories in 2010, 66 exhibits in 2011, and 74 exhibits in 2012.

Control Status

The Drug Enforcement Administration placed 2C-B in Schedule I of the Controlled Substances Act (CSA).

Chapter 19

Dissociative Drugs

Chapter Contents

Section 19.1

Dextromethorphan (DXM)

This section includes text excerpted from "Drugs of Abuse," U.S. Drug Enforcement Administration (DEA), 2015.

What Is DXM?

Dextromethorphan (DXM) is a cough suppressor found in more than 120 over-the counter (OTC) cold medications, either alone or in combination with other drugs such as analgesics (e.g., acetaminophen), antihistamines (e.g., chlorpheniramine), decongestants (e.g., pseudoephedrine), and/or expectorants (e.g., guaifenesin). The typical adult dose for cough is 15 or 30 mg taken three to four times daily. The cough-suppressing effects of DXM persist for 5 to 6 hours after ingestion. When taken as directed, side-effects are rarely observed.

What Is Its Origin?

DXM abusers can obtain the drug at almost any pharmacy or supermarket, seeking out the products with the highest concentration of the drug from among all the OTC cough and cold remedies that contain it. DXM products and powder can also be purchased on the Internet.

What Are Common Street Names?

Common street names includes:

- CCC, Dex, DXM, Poor Man's PCP, Robo, Rojo, Skittles, Triple C, and Velvet.

What Does It Look Like?

DXM can come in the form of:

- cough syrup, tablets, capsules, or powder

How Is It Abused?

DXM is abused in high doses to experience euphoria and visual and auditory hallucinations. Abusers take various amounts depending on their body weight and the effect they are attempting to achieve. Some abusers ingest 250 to 1,500 milligrams in a single dosage, far more than the recommended therapeutic dosages described above.

Illicit use of DXM is referred to on the street as "Robotripping," "skittling," or "dexing." The first two terms are derived from the products that are most commonly abused, Robitussin and Coricidin HBP. DXM abuse has traditionally involved drinking large volumes of the OTC liquid cough preparations. More recently, however, abuse of tablet and gel capsule preparations has increased.

These newer, high-dose DXM products have particular appeal for abusers. They are much easier to consume, eliminate the need to drink large volumes of unpleasant-tasting syrup, and are easily portable and concealed, allowing an abuser to continue to abuse DXM throughout the day, whether at school or work.

DXM powder, sold over the Internet, is also a source of DXM for abuse. (The powdered form of DXM poses additional risks to the abuser due to the uncertainty of composition and dose.) DXM is also distributed in illicitly manufactured tablets containing only DXM or mixed with other drugs such as pseudoephedrine and/ or methamphetamine.

DXM is abused by individuals of all ages, but its abuse by teenagers and young adults is of particular concern. This abuse is fueled by DXM's OTC availability and extensive "how to" abuse information on various web sites.

What Is Its Effect on the Mind?

Some of the many psychoactive effects associated with high-dose DXM include:

- Confusion, inappropriate laughter, agitation, paranoia, and hallucinations.

Other sensory changes, including the feeling of floating and changes in hearing and touch. Long-term abuse of DXM is associated with severe psychological dependence.

What Is Its Effect on the Body?

DXM intoxication involves:

- Over-excitability, lethargy, loss of coordination, slurred speech, sweating, hypertension, and involuntary spasmodic movement of the eyeballs

The use of high doses of DXM in combination with alcohol or other drugs is particularly dangerous, and deaths have been reported. Approximately 5-10% of Caucasians are poor DXM metabolizers and at increased risk for overdoses and deaths. DXM taken with antidepressants can be life threatening.

OTC products that contain DXM often contain other ingredients such as acetaminophen, chlorpheniramine, and guaifenesin that have their own effects, such as:

- Liver damage, rapid heart rate, lack of coordination, vomiting, seizures, and coma

To circumvent the many side effects associated with these other ingredients, a simple chemical extraction procedure has been developed and published on the Internet that removes most of these other ingredients in cough syrup.

What Are Its Overdose Effects?

DXM overdose can be treated in an emergency room setting and generally does not result in severe medical consequences or death. Most DXM-related deaths are caused by ingesting the drug in combination with other drugs. DXM-related deaths also occur from impairment of the senses, which can lead to accidents.

Which Drugs Cause Similar Effects?

Depending on the dose, DXM can have effects similar to marijuana or Ecstasy. In high doses its out-of-body effects are similar to those of Ketamine or PCP.

What Is Its Legal Status in the United States?

DXM is a legally marketed cough suppressant that is neither a controlled substance nor a regulated chemical under the Controlled Substances Act.

Section 19.2

PCP and Analogs

This section includes text excerpted from "Phencyclidine," U.S. Drug Enforcement Administration (DEA), January 2013.

Phencyclidine

Street Names: PCP, Angel Dust, Supergrass, Boat, Tic Tac, Zoom, Shermans

Introduction

After a decline in abuse during the late 1980s and 1990s, the abuse of phencyclidine (PCP) has increased slightly in recent years. Street names include Angel Dust, Hog, Ozone, Rocket Fuel, Shermans, Wack, Crystal and Embalming Fluid. Street names for PCP combined with marijuana include Killer Joints, Super Grass, Fry, Lovelies, Wets, and Waters.

Licit Uses

PCP was developed in the 1950s to be used as an intravenous anesthetic in the United States, but its use was discontinued due to the high incidence of patients experiencing postoperative delirium with hallucinations. PCP is no longer produced or used for medical purposes in the United States.

Chemistry and Pharmacology

Phencyclidine, 1-(1-phencyclohexyl) piperidine, is a white crystalline powder which is readily soluble in water or alcohol. PCP is classified as a hallucinogen. PCP is a "dissociative" drug; it induces distortion of sight and sound and produces feelings of detachment.

PCP's effects include sedation, immobility, amnesia, and marked analgesia. The effects of PCP vary by the route of administration and dose. The intoxicating effects can be produced within 2 to 5 minutes after smoking and 30 to 60 minutes after swallowing. PCP intoxication may last from 4 to 8 hours; some users report experiencing subjective effects from 24 to 48 hours after using PCP. Low to moderate doses (1 to 5 mg) induce feelings of detachment from surroundings and self, numbness, slurred speech and loss of coordination accompanied by a sense of strength and invulnerability. A blank stare, rapid and involuntary eye movements are the more observable effects. Catatonic posturing, resembling that observed with schizophrenia, is also produced. Higher doses of PCP produce hallucinations. Physiological effects include increased blood pressure, rapid and shallow breathing, elevated heart rate and elevated temperature.

Chronic use of PCP can result in dependency with a withdrawal syndrome upon cessation of the drug. Chronic abuse of PCP can impair memory and thinking. Other effects of long-term use include persistent speech difficulties, suicidal thoughts, anxiety, depression, and social withdrawal.

Illicit Uses

PCP is abused for its mind altering effects. It can be abused by snorting, smoking or swallowing. Smoking is the most common method of abusing PCP. Leafy material such as mint, parsley, oregano, tobacco, or marijuana is saturated with PCP, and subsequently rolled into a cigarette and smoked. A marijuana joint or cigarette dipped in liquid PCP is known as a "dipper." PCP is typically used in small quantities; 5 to 10 mg is an average dose.

User Population

PCP is predominantly abused by young adults and high school students. In 2010, there was an estimated 53,542 emergency department visits associated with PCP use, according to Drug Abuse Warning Network (New DAWN ED). This is a significant increase from an estimated 37,266 PCP-associated visits in 2008. The American Association of Poison Control Centers (AAPCC) National Poison Data System reports 747 PCP exposure case mentions and 350 single exposures in 2010. According to the 2011 National Survey on Drug Use and Health (NSDUH), 6.1 million (2.4%) individuals in the U.S., aged 12 and older, reported using PCP in their lifetime. The Monitoring the Future (MTF) survey indicates that PCP use among 12th graders in the past year increased from 1.0% in 2010 to 1.3% in 2011 and then decreased to 0.9% in 2012.

Illicit Distribution

PCP is available in powder, crystal, tablet, capsule, and liquid forms. It is most commonly sold in powder and liquid forms. Tablets sold as MDMA (Ecstasy) occasionally are found to contain PCP. Prices for PCP range from $5-$15 per tablet, $20-$30 for a gram of powder PCP, and $200-$300 for an ounce of liquid PCP. The "dipper" sells for $10-$20 each.

According to the System to Retrieve Information from Drug Evidence (STRIDE) and the National Forensic Laboratory Information System (NFLIS), 5,374 PCP reports were from Federal, state, and local forensic laboratories in 2011. In the first six months of 2012, there were 2,748 PCP reports from forensic laboratories.

Control Status

On January 25, 1978, PCP was transferred from Schedule III to Schedule II under the Controlled Substances Act.

Section 19.3

Salvia Divinorum

This section contains text excerpted from the following sources: Text beginning with the heading "What Is Salvia?" is excerpted from "Salvia," National Institute on Drug Abuse (NIDA), March 10, 2016; Text beginning with the heading "Which Drugs Cause Similar Effects?" is excerpted from "Drugs of Abuse," U.S. Drug Enforcement Administration (DEA), 2015.

What Is Salvia?

Also known as: "shepherdess's herb," "diviner's sage," "seer's sage," "Maria pastora," "magic mint," and "Sally-D"

Salvia (*Salvia divinorum*) is an herb in the mint family found in southern Mexico. The main active ingredient in salvia, salvinorin A, changes the chemistry in the brain, causing hallucinations (seeing something that seems real but isn't). The effects are short lived, but may be very intense and frightening.

Although salvia is not illegal according to Federal law, several states and countries have passed laws to regulate its use. The Drug Enforcement Administration lists salvia as a drug of concern that poses risk to people who use it.

How Is Salvia Used?

Usually, people chew fresh *S. divinorum* leaves or drink their extracted juices. The dried leaves of *S. divinorum* also can be smoked in rolled cigarettes, inhaled through water pipes (hookahs), or vaporized and inhaled.

How Does Salvia Affect the Brain?

Researchers are studying salvia to learn exactly how it acts in the brain to produce its effects. What is currently known is that salvinorin A, the main active ingredient in salvia, attaches to parts of nerve cells called kappa opioid receptors. (Note: These receptors are different from the ones involved with opioid drugs, such as heroin and morphine.)

The effects of salvinorin A are described as intense but short lived, generally lasting for less than 30 minutes. People who use salvia generally have hallucinations—they see or feel things that aren't really there. They also have changes in vision, mood and body sensations, emotional swings, and feelings of detachment (disconnected from their environment). There are reports of people losing contact with reality—being unable to tell the difference between what's real and what's not. Many of these effects raise concern about the dangers of driving under the influence of salvia.

What Are the Other Effects of Salvia?

Physical and other effects of saliva use have not been fully studied. There have been reports that the drug causes loss of coordination, dizziness, and slurred speech.

In addition, we also don't know the long-term effects of using the drug. However, recent studies with animals showed that salvia harms learning and memory.

Can You Get Addicted to Salvia?

It's not clear if using salvia leads to addiction. More studies are needed to learn whether it has addictive properties.

What Are Its Overdose Effects?

Adverse physical effects may include lack of coordination, dizziness, and slurred speech.

Can You Die If You Use Salvia?

It is not clear whether there have been any deaths associated with salvia. However, because we do not know all of salvia's effects, it is a drug that authorities are watching carefully.

How Many Teens Use Salvia?

Table 19.1. Monitoring the Future Study: Trends in Prevalence of Salvia for 8th Graders, 10th Graders, and 12th Graders; 2015 (in percent)

Drug	Time Period	8th Graders	10th Graders	10th Graders
Salvia	Past Year	0.7	1.2	1.9

Which Drugs Cause Similar Effects?

When Salvia divinorum is chewed or smoked, the hallucinogenic effects elicited are similar to those induced by other Schedule hallucinogenic substances.

What Is Its Legal Status in the United States?

Neither Salvia divinorum nor its active constituent Salvinorin A has an approved medical use in the United States. Salvia is not controlled under the Controlled Substances Act. Salvia divinorum is, however, controlled by a number of states. Since Salvia is not controlled by the CSA, some online botanical companies and drug promotional sites have advertised Salvia as a legal alternative to other plant hallucinogens like mescaline.

Chapter 20

Inhalants

What Are Inhalants?

Also known as: "laughing gas" (nitrous oxide), "snappers" (amyl nitrite), "poppers" (amyl nitrite and butyl nitrite), "whippets" (fluorinated hydrocarbons), "bold" (nitrites), and "rush" (nitrites)

Inhalants are chemicals found in ordinary household or workplace products that people inhale on purpose to get "high." Because many inhalants can be found around the house, people often don't realize that inhaling their fumes, even just once, can be very harmful to the brain and body and can lead to death. In fact, the chemicals found in these products can change the way the brain works and cause other problems in the body.

Although different inhalants cause different effects, they generally fall into one of four categories.

Volatile solvents are liquids that become a gas at room temperature. They are found in:

- Paint thinner, nail polish remover, degreaser, dry-cleaning fluid, gasoline, and contact cement

---

This section contains text excerpted from the following sources: Text beginning with the heading "What Are Inhalants?" is excerpted from "Inhalants," National Institute on Drug Abuse (NIDA), March 10, 2016; Text beginning with the heading "Which Drugs Cause Similar Effects?" is excerpted from "Drugs of Abuse," U.S. Drug Enforcement Administration (DEA), 2015.

- Some art or office supplies, such as correction fluid, felt-tip marker fluid, and electronic contact cleaner

Aerosols are sprays that contain propellants and solvents. They include:

- Spray paint, hairspray, deodorant spray, vegetable oil sprays, and fabric protector spray

Gases may be in household or commercial products, or used in the medical field to provide pain relief. They are found in:

- Butane lighters, propane tanks, whipped cream dispensers, and refrigerant gases
- Anesthesia, including ether, chloroform, halothane, and nitrous oxide (commonly called "laughing gas").

Nitrites are a class of inhalants used mainly to enhance sexual experiences. Organic nitrites include amyl, butyl, and cyclohexyl nitrites and other related compounds. Amyl nitrite was used in the past by doctors to help with chest pain and is sometimes used today to diagnose heart problems. Nitrites now are prohibited by the Consumer Product Safety Commission but can still be found, sold in small bottles labeled as "video head cleaner," "room odorizer," "leather cleaner," or "liquid aroma."

How Are Inhalants Used?

People who use inhalants breathe in the fumes through their nose or mouth, usually by:

- "Sniffing" or "snorting" fumes from containers
- Spraying aerosols directly into the nose or mouth
- Sniffing or inhaling fumes from substances sprayed or placed into a plastic or paper bag ("bagging")
- "Huffing" from an inhalant-soaked rag stuffed in the mouth
- Inhaling from balloons filled with nitrous oxide

Because the "high" lasts only a few minutes, people who use inhalants often try to make the feeling last longer by inhaling repeatedly over several hours.

How Do Inhalants Affect the Brain?

The lungs absorb inhaled chemicals into the bloodstream very quickly, sending them throughout the brain and body. Nearly all inhalants (except nitrites) produce a pleasurable effect by slowing down brain activity. Nitrites, in contrast, expand and relax blood vessels.

Short-Term Effects

Within seconds, users feel intoxicated and experience effects similar to those of alcohol, such as slurred speech, lack of coordination, euphoria (a feeling of intense happiness), and dizziness. Some users also experience lightheadedness, hallucinations (seeing things that are not really there), and delusions (believing something that is not true). If enough of the chemical is inhaled, nearly all solvents and gases produce anesthesia—a loss of sensation—and can lead to unconsciousness.

The high usually lasts only a few minutes, causing people to continue the high by inhaling repeatedly, which is very dangerous. Repeated use in one session can cause a person to lose consciousness and possibly even die.

With repeated inhaling, many users feel less inhibited and less in control. Some may feel drowsy for several hours and have a headache that lasts a while.

Long-Term Effects

Inhalants often contain more than one chemical. Some chemicals leave the body quickly, but others stay for a long time and get absorbed by fatty tissues in the brain and central nervous system. Over the long term, the chemicals can cause serious problems:

- **Damage to nerve fibers**. Long-term inhalant use can break down the protective sheath around certain nerve fibers in the brain and elsewhere in the body. When this happens, nerve cells are not able to send messages as well, which can cause muscle spasms and tremors or even permanent trouble with basic actions like walking, bending, and talking. These effects are similar to what happens to people with multiple sclerosis.
- **Damage to brain cells.** Inhalants also can damage brain cells by preventing them from getting enough oxygen. The effects of this condition, also known as brain hypoxia, depend on the area of the brain affected. The hippocampus, for example, is

responsible for memory, so someone who repeatedly uses inhalants may be unable to learn new things or may have a hard time carrying on simple conversations. If the cerebral cortex is affected, the ability to solve complex problems and plan ahead will be compromised. And, if the cerebellum is affected, it can cause a person to move slowly or be clumsy.

What Are the Other Effects of Inhalants?

Regular use of inhalants can cause serious harm to vital organs and systems besides the brain. Inhalants can cause:

- Heart damage
- Liver failure
- Muscle weakness
- Aplastic anemia—the body produces fewer blood cells
- Nerve damage, which can lead to chronic pain

Damage to these organs is not reversible even when the person stops abusing inhalants.

What Is Their Effect on the Body?

Inhaled chemicals are rapidly absorbed through the lungs into the bloodstream and quickly distributed to the brain and other organs. Nearly all inhalants produce effects similar to anesthetics, which slow down the body's function. Depending on the degree of abuse, the user can experience slight stimulation, feeling of less inhibition or loss of consciousness.

Within minutes of inhalation, the user experiences intoxication along with other effects similar to those produced by alcohol. These effects may include slurred speech, an inability to coordinate movements, euphoria, and dizziness. After heavy use of inhalants, abusers may feel drowsy for several hours and experience a lingering headache.

Additional symptoms exhibited by long-term inhalant abusers include:

- Weight loss, muscle weakness, disorientation, inattentiveness, lack of coordination, irritability, depression, and damage to the nervous system and other organs

Some of the damaging effects to the body may be at least partially reversible when inhalant abuse is stopped; however, many of the effects from prolonged abuse are irreversible.

Prolonged sniffing of the highly concentrated chemicals in solvents or aerosol sprays can induce irregular and rapid heart rhythms and lead to heart failure and death within minutes. There is a common link between inhalant use and problems in school—failing grades, chronic absences, and general apathy. Other signs include:

- Paint or stains on body or clothing; spots or sores around the mouth; red or runny eyes or nose; chemical breath odor; drunk, dazed, or dizzy appearance; nausea; loss of appetite; anxiety; excitability; and irritability

Effects of Specific Chemicals

Depending on the type of inhalant used, the harmful health effects will differ. Below is a list of some of the harmful effects of inhalants.

- Amyl nitrite, butyl nitrite (Poppers, video head cleaner)
    - Sudden sniffing death
    - Weakened immune system
    - Damage to red blood cells (interfering with oxygen supply to vital tissues)
- Benzene (Gasoline)
    - Bone marrow damage
    - Weakened immune system
    - Increased risk of leukemia (a form of cancer)
    - Reproductive system complications
- Butane, propane (Lighter fluid, hair and pain strays)
    - Sudden sniffing death from heart effects
    - Serious burn injuries
- Freon (difluoroethane substitutes) (Refrigerant and aerosol propellant)
    - Sudden sniffing death
    - Breathing problems and death (from sudden cooling of airways)
    - Liver damage
- Methylene chloride (Paint thinners and removers, degreasers)
    - Reduced ability of blood to carry oxygen to the brain and body

- Changes to heart muscle and heartbeat
- Nitrous oxide, hexane ("Laughing gas")
    - Death from lack of oxygen to the brain
    - Altered perception and motor coordination
    - Loss of sensation
    - Spasms
    - Blackouts caused by blood pressure changes
    - Depression of heart muscle functioning
- Toluene (Gasoline, paint thinners and removers, correction fluid)
    - Brain damage (loss of brain tissue, impaired thinking, loss of coordination, limb spasms, hearing and vision loss)
    - Liver and kidney damage
- Tricholoroethylene (Spot removers, degreasers)
    - Sudden sniffing death
    - Liver disease
    - Reproductive problems
    - Hearing and vision loss

Signs of Inhalant Use

Sometimes you can see signs that tell you a person is abusing inhalants, such as:

- Chemical odors on breath or clothing
- Paint or other stains on the face, hands, or clothing
- Hidden empty spray paint or solvent containers, or rags or clothing soaked with chemicals
- Drunk or disoriented actions
- Slurred speech
- Nausea (feeling sick) or loss of appetite and weight loss
- Confusion, inattentiveness, lack of coordination, irritability, and depression

Can You Get Addicted to Inhalants?

It isn't common, but addiction can happen. Some people, particularly those who use inhalants a lot and for a long time, report a strong need to continue using inhalants. Using inhalants over and over again can cause mild withdrawal when stopped. In fact, research in animal models shows that toluene can affect the brain in a way that is similar to other drugs of use (e.g., amphetamines). Toluene increases dopamine activity in reward areas of the brain, and the long-term disruption of the dopamine system is one of the key factors leading to addiction.

What Are Their Overdose Effects?

Because intoxication lasts only a few minutes, abusers try to prolong the high by continuing to inhale repeatedly over the course of several hours, which is a very dangerous practice. With successive inhalations, abusers may suffer loss of consciousness and/or death.

"Sudden sniffing death" can result from a single session of inhalant use by an otherwise healthy young person. Sudden sniffing death is particularly associated with the abuse of butane, propane, and chemicals in aerosols.

Inhalant abuse can also cause death by asphyxiation from repeated inhalations, which lead to high concentrations of inhaled fumes displacing the available oxygen in the lungs, suffocation by blocking air from entering the lungs when inhaling fumes from a plastic bag placed over the head, and choking from swallowing vomit after inhaling substances.

Can You Die If You Use Inhalants?

Yes, using inhalants can cause death, even after just one use, by:

- Sudden sniffing death—heart beats quickly and irregularly, and then suddenly stops (cardiac arrest)
- Asphyxiation—toxic fumes replace oxygen in the lungs so that a person stops breathing
- Suffocation—air is blocked from entering the lungs when inhaling fumes from a plastic bag placed over the head
- Convulsions or seizures—abnormal electrical discharges in the brain
- Coma—the brain shuts down all but the most vital functions

- Choking—inhaling vomit after inhalant use
- Injuries—accidents, including driving, while intoxicated

How Many Teens Use Inhalants?

Inhalants are often among the first drugs that young adolescents use. In fact, they are one of the few classes of drugs that are used more by younger adolescents than older ones. Inhalant use can become chronic and continue into adulthood.

Table 20.1. Monitoring the Future Study: Trends in Prevalence of Inhalants for 8th Graders, 10th Graders, and 12th Graders; 2015 (in percent)*

Drug	Time Period	8th Graders	10th Graders	12th Graders
Inhalants	Lifetime	[9.40]	[7.20]	5.7
	Past Year	4.6	2.9	1.9
	Past Month	2	1.2	0.7

**Data in brackets indicate statistically significant change from the previous year.*

Which Drugs Cause Similar Effects?

Most inhalants produce a rapid high that is similar to the effects of alcohol intoxication.

What Is Their Legal Status in the United States?

The common household products that are misused as inhalants are legally available for their intended and legitimate uses. Many state legislatures have attempted to deter youth who buy legal products to get high by placing restriction on the sale of these products to minors.

Chapter 21

Narcotics (Opioids)

Chapter Contents

Section 21.1

Introduction to Narcotics

This section contains text excerpted from the following sources: Text beginning with the heading "What Are Narcotics?" is excerpted from "Drugs of Abuse," U.S. Drug Enforcement Administration (DEA), 2015; Text beginning with the heading "Can You Die If You Abuse Opioids?" is excerpted from "Prescription Pain Medications (Opioids)," National Institute on Drug Abuse (NIDA), March 10, 2016.

What Are Narcotics?

Also known as "opioids," the term "narcotic" comes from the Greek word for "stupor" and originally referred to a variety of substances that dulled the senses and relieved pain. Though some people still refer to all drugs as "narcotics," today "narcotic" refers to opium, opium derivatives, and their semi-synthetic substitutes. A more current term for these drugs, with less uncertainty regarding its meaning, is "opioid." Examples include the illicit drug heroin and pharmaceutical drugs like OxyContin®, Vicodin®, codeine, morphine, methadone, and fentanyl.

What Is Their Origin?

The poppy papaver somniferum is the source for all natural opioids, whereas synthetic opioids are made entirely in a lab and include meperidine, fentanyl, and methadone. Semi-synthetic opioids are synthesized from naturally occurring opium products, such as morphine and codeine, and include heroin, oxycodone, hydrocodone, and hydromorphone. Teens can obtain narcotics from friends, family members, medicine cabinets, pharmacies, nursing homes, hospitals, hospices, doctors, and the Internet.

What Are Common Street Names?

Street names for various narcotics/opioids include:

- Smack, Horse, Mud, Brown Sugar, Junk, Black Tat, Big H, Paregoric, Dover's Powder, MPTP (New Heroin), Hilbilly Heroin, Lean or Purple Drank, OC, Ox, Oxy, Oxycotton, Sippin Syrup

What Do They Look Like?

Narcotics/opioids come in various forms, including:

- Tablets, capsules, skin patches, powder, chunks in varying colors (from white to shades of brown and black), liquid form for oral use and injection, syrups, suppositories, and lollipops

How Are They Abused?

Narcotics/opioids can be swallowed, smoked, sniffed, or injected.

What Is Their Effect on the Mind?

Besides their medical use, narcotics/opioids produce a general sense of well-being by reducing tension, anxiety, and aggression. These effects are helpful in a therapeutic setting but contribute to the drugs' abuse. Narcotic/opioid use comes with a variety of unwanted effects, including drowsiness, inability to concentrate, and apathy.

Psychological Dependence

Use can create psychological dependence. Long after the physical need for the drug has passed, the addict may continue to think and talk about using drugs and feel overwhelmed coping with daily activities. Relapse is common if there are no changes to the physical environment or the behavioral motivators that prompted the abuse in the first place.

What Is Their Effect on the Body?

Narcotics/opioids are prescribed by doctors to treat pain, suppress cough, cure diarrhea, and put people to sleep. Effects depend heavily on the dose, how it's taken, and previous exposure to the drug. Negative effects include slowed physical activity, constriction of the pupils, flushing of the face and neck, constipation, nausea, vomiting, and slowed breathing.

As the dose is increased, both the pain relief and the harmful effects become more pronounced. Some of these preparations are so potent that a single dose can be lethal to an inexperienced user. However, except in cases of extreme intoxication, there is no loss of motor coordination or slurred speech.

Physical Dependence and Withdrawal

Physical dependence is a consequence of chronic opioid use, and withdrawal takes place when drug use is discontinued. The intensity and character of the physical symptoms experienced during withdrawal are directly related to the particular drug used, the total daily dose, the interval between doses, the duration of use and the health and personality of the user. These symptoms usually appear shortly before the time of the next scheduled dose.

Early withdrawal symptoms often include watery eyes, runny nose, yawning, and sweating. As the withdrawal worsens, symptoms can include restlessness, irritability, loss of appetite, nausea, tremors, drug craving, severe depression, vomiting, increased heart rate and blood pressure, and chills alternating with flushing and excessive sweating However, without intervention, the withdrawal usually runs its course, and most physical symptoms disappear within days or weeks, depending on the particular drug.

What Are Their Overdose Effects?

Overdoses of narcotics are not uncommon and can be fatal. Physical signs of narcotics/opioid overdose include constricted (pinpoint) pupils, cold clammy skin, confusion, convulsions, extreme drowsiness, and slowed.

Which Drugs Cause Similar Effects?

With the exception of pain relief and cough suppression, most central nervous system depressants (like barbiturates, benzodiazepines, and alcohol) have similar effects, including slowed breathing, tolerance, and dependence.

What Is Their Legal Status in the United States?

Narcotics/opioids are controlled substances that vary from Schedule I to Schedule V, depending on their medical usefulness, abuse potential, safety, and drug dependence profile. Schedule I narcotics, like heroin, have no medical use in the U.S. and are illegal to distribute, purchase, or use outside of medical research.

Can You Die If You Abuse Opioids?

Yes. In fact, taking just 1 large dose could cause serious breathing problems that lead to death. In 2014, opioid pain relievers accounted for close to 19,000 deaths in the United States. If you compare it to 2001, when 5,500 people died from an overdose of opioid pain relievers, you can see how dramatically deaths have increased in the last decade. Among young people, males are much more likely to overdose from opioid abuse than are females. In 2014, among young people ages 15–24, three out of every four deaths from an overdose of pain relievers is a male.

The risk for overdose and death are increased when opioids are combined with alcohol or other drugs, especially depressants such as Benzodiazepines.

There is an "opioid antagonist" medication, Naloxone, which can reverse the effects of opioid overdose and prevent death if it is given in time. Doctors can prescribe Naloxone to people who abuse opioid drugs in the hopes that a friend or family could deliver the drug in the event of an overdose. Naloxone is also commonly carried by emergency responders including police officers and EMTs.

How Many Teens Abuse Opioids?

NIDA's Monitoring the Future study collects data on teen abuse of two types of prescription opioids—Vicodin and OxyContin:

Table 21.1. Monitoring the Future Study: Trends in Prevalence of Various Drugs for 8th Graders, 10th Graders, and 12th Graders; 2015 (in percent)

Drug	Time Period	8th Graders	10th Graders	12th Graders
Vicodin	Past Year	0.9	2.5	4.4
OxyContin	Past Year	0.8	2.6	3.7

Section 21.2

Buprenorphine

This section includes text excerpted from "Buprenorphine," U.S. Drug Enforcement Administration (DEA), July 2013.

Introduction

Buprenorphine was first marketed in the United States in 1985 as a Schedule V narcotic analgesic. Initially, the only available buprenorphine product in the United States had been a low-dose (0.3 mg/ml) injectable formulation under the brand name, Buprenex®. Diversion, trafficking and abuse of other buprenorphine products have occurred in Europe and other areas of the world.

In October 2002, the U.S. Food and Drug Administration (FDA) approved two buprenorphine products (Suboxone® and Subutex®) for the treatment of narcotic addiction. Both products are high dose (2 mg and 8 mg) sublingual (under the tongue) tablets: Subutex® is a single entity buprenorphine product and Suboxone® is a combination product with buprenorphine and naloxone in a 4:1 ratio, respectively. After reviewing the available data and receiving a Schedule III recommendation from the Department of Health and Human Services (DHHS), the DEA placed buprenorphine and all products containing buprenorphine into Schedule III in 2002. Since 2003, diversion, trafficking and abuse of buprenorphine have become more common in the United States. In June 2010, FDA approved an extended release transdermal film containing buprenorphine (Butrans®) for the management of moderate to severe chronic pain in patients requiring a continuous, extended period, around-the-clock opioid analgesic.

Licit Uses

Buprenorphine is intended for the treatment of pain(Buprenex®) and opioid addiction (Suboxone® and Subutex®). In 2001, 2005, and 2006, the Narcotic Addict Treatment Act was amended to allow qualified physicians, under certification of the DHHS, to prescribe Schedule

III-V narcotic drugs (FDA approved for the indication of narcotic treatment) for narcotic addiction, up to 30 patients per physician at any time, outside the context of clinic-based narcotic treatment programs (Pub.L. 106-310). This limit was increased to 100 patients per physician, who meet the specified criteria, under the Office of National Drug Control Policy Reauthorization Act (P.L. 69-469, ONDCPRA), which became effective on December 29, 2006.

Suboxone® and Subutex® are the only treatment drugs that meet the requirement of this exemption. Currently, there are nearly 15,700 physicians who have been approved by the Substance Abuse and Mental Health Services Administration (SAMHSA) and the DEA for office-based narcotic buprenorphine treatment. Of those physicians, approximately 13,150 were approved to treat up to 30 patients per provider and about 2,500 were approved to treat up to 100 patients. More than 3,000 physicians have submitted their intention to treat up to 100 patients per provider.

IMS Health TM National Prescription Audit Plus indicates that 9.3 million buprenorphine prescriptions were dispensed in the U.S. in 2012. From January to March 2013, 2.5 million buprenorphine prescriptions were dispensed.

Chemistry/Pharmacology

Buprenorphine has a unique pharmacological profile. It produces the effects typical of both pure mu agonists (e.g.,morphine) and partial agonists (e.g., pentazocine) depending on dose, pattern of use and population taking the drug. It is about 20–30 times more potent than morphine as an analgesic; and like morphine it produces dose-related euphoria, drug liking, papillary constriction, respiratory depression and sedation. However, acute, high doses of buprenorphine have been shown to have a blunting effect on both physiological and psychological effects due to its partial opioid activity.

Buprenorphine is a long-acting (24–72 hours) opioid that produces less respiratory depression at high doses than other narcotic treatment drugs. However, severe respiratory depression can occur when buprenorphine is combined with other central nervous system depressants, especially benzodiazepines. Deaths have resulted from this combination. The addition of naloxone in the Suboxone® product is intended to block the euphoric high resulting from the injection of this drug by non-buprenorphine maintained narcotic abusers.

User Population

In countries where buprenorphine has gained popularity as a drug of abuse, it is sought by a wide variety of narcotic abusers: young naive individuals, non-addicted opioid abusers, heroin addicts and buprenorphine treatment clients.

Illicit Uses

Like other opioids commonly abused, buprenorphine is capable of producing significant euphoria. Data from other countries indicate that buprenorphine has been abused by various routes of administration (sublingual, intranasal and injection) and has gained popularity as a heroin substitute and as a primary drug of abuse. Large percentages of the drug abusing populations in some areas of France, Ireland, Scotland, India, Nepal, Bangladesh, Pakistan, and New Zealand have reported abusing buprenorphine by injection and in combination with a benzodiazepine.

The National Forensic Laboratory Information System (NFLIS) is a DEA database that collects scientifically verified data on drug items and cases submitted to and analyzed by state and local forensic laboratories. The System to Retrieve Information from Drug Evidence (STRIDE) provides information on drug seizures reported to and analyzed by DEA laboratories. In 2012, federal, state and local forensic laboratories identified 10,804. In the first quarter of 2013, 1,905 buprenorphine exhibits were identified.

According to the Drug Abuse Warning Network (DAWNED), an estimated 21,483 emergency department visits were associated with nonmedical use of buprenorphine in 2011, nearly five times the 4,440 estimated number of buprenorphine ED visits in 2006. The American Association of Poison Control Centers Annual Report indicates that U.S. poison centers recorded 3,625 case mentions and three deaths involving toxic exposure from buprenorphine in 2011.

Control Status

Buprenorphine and all products containing buprenorphine are controlled in Schedule III of the Controlled Substances Act.

Section 21.3

Fentanyl

This section contains text excerpted from the following sources: Text beginning with the heading "Introduction" is excerpted from "Fentanyl," U.S. Drug Enforcement Administration (DEA), March 2015; Text under the heading "Surge in Fentanyl Overdose Deaths" is excerpted from "Surge in Fentanyl Overdose Deaths," National Institute on Drug Abuse (NIDA), July 10, 2015.

Introduction

Fentanyl is a potent synthetic opioid. It was introduced into medical practice as an intravenous anesthetic under the trade name of Sublimaze in the 1960s.

Licit Uses

In 2013 and 2014, there were 6.75 million and 6.64 million fentanyl prescriptions, respectively, dispensed in the U.S. (IMS Health™). Fentanyl pharmaceutical products are currently available in the dosage forms of oral transmucosal lozenges, commonly referred to as the fentanyl "lollipops" (Actiq®), effervescent buccal tablets (Fentora™), transdermal patches (Duragesic®), and injectable formulations. Oral transmucosal lozenges and effervescent buccal tablets are used for the management of breakthrough cancer pain in patients who are already receiving opioid medication for their underlying persistent pain. Transdermal patches are used in the management of chronic pain in patients who require continuous opioid analgesia.

Fentanyl citrate injections are administered intravenously, intramuscularly, spinally or epidurally for potent analgesia and anesthesia. Fentanyl is frequently used in anesthetic practice for patients undergoing heart surgery or for patients with poor heart function. Because of a concern about deaths and overdoses resulting from fentanyl transdermal patches (Duragesic® and generic version), on July 15, 2005, the Food and Drug Administration issued safety warnings and reiterated the importance of strict adherence to the guidelines for the proper use of these products.

Chemistry and Pharmacology

Fentanyl is about 100 times more potent than morphine as an analgesic. It is a μ-opioid receptor agonist with high lipid solubility and a rapid onset and short duration of effects. Fentanyl rapidly crosses the blood-brain barrier. It is similar to other μ-opioid receptor agonists (like morphine oroxycodone) in its pharmacological effects and produces analgesia, sedation, respiratory depression, nausea, and vomiting. Fentanyl appears to produce muscle rigidity with greater frequency than other opioids. Unlike some μ-opioid receptor agonists, fentanyl does not cause histamine release and has minimal depressant effects on the heart.

Illicit Uses

Fentanyl is abused for its intense euphoric effects. Fentanyl can serve as a direct substitute for heroin in opioid dependent individuals. However, fentanyl is a very dangerous substitute for heroin because it is much more potent than heroin and results in frequent overdoses that can lead to respiratory depression and death.

Fentanyl patches are abused by removing the contents from the patches and then injecting or ingesting these contents. Patches have also been frozen, cut into pieces and placed under the tongue or in the cheek cavity for drug absorption through the oral mucosa. Used patches are attractive to abusers as a large percentage of fentanyl remains in these patches even after a 3-day use. Fentanyl oral transmucosal lozenges and fentanyl injectables are also diverted and abused.

Abuse of fentanyl initially appeared in mid-1970s and has increased in recent years. There have been reports of deaths associated with abuse of fentanyl products.

According to the Drug Abuse Warning Network (DAWN), emergency department visits associated with nonmedical use of fentanyl increased from an estimated 15,947 in 2007 to an estimated 20,034 in 2011.

According to the Florida Department of Law Enforcement Medical Examiners 2013 Annual Report, fentanyl was identified in 251 deceased persons in Florida in 2012 and increased 16.3% to being identified in 292 deceased persons in 2013. Of the 292 decedents with fentanyl identified, fentanyl caused the death in 185 of those persons (63.4%), which is a 36% increase from 2012.

Illicit Distribution

Fentanyl is diverted via pharmacy theft, fraudulent prescriptions, and illicit distribution by patients and registrants (physicians and pharmacists). Theft has also been identified at nursing homes and other long-term care facilities. According to the National Forensic Laboratory Information System (NFLIS), 668 items/exhibits were identified as fentanyl in 2012 and 942 in 2013 by federal, state and local forensic laboratories in the United States. In 2014, the number of fentanyl reports increased significantly to 3,344.

Clandestine Manufacture

From April 2005 to March 2007, an outbreak of fentanyl overdoses and deaths occurred. The Centers for Disease Control and Prevention (CDC)/Drug Enforcement Administration (DEA) surveillance system reported 1,013 confirmed non-pharmaceutical fentanyl-related deaths. Most of these deaths occurred in Delaware, Illinois, Maryland, Michigan, Missouri, New Jersey, and Pennsylvania. Consequently, DEA immediately undertook the development of regulations to control the precursor chemicals used by the clandestine laboratories to illicitly manufacture fentanyl.

In 2007, DEA published an Interim Final Rule to designate N-phenethyl-4-piperidone (NPP)–a precursor to fentanyl, as a List 1 chemical. After the control of NPP, the number of fentanyl-related deaths continually declined. DEA also completed a scheduling action of designating another chemical precursor, 4-anilino-N-phenethyl-4-pipe ridine (ANPP) as a Schedule II immediate precursor in 2010.

Control Status

Fentanyl is a Schedule II substance under the Controlled Substances Act.

Surge in Fentanyl Overdose Deaths

A surge in overdose deaths related to fentanyl, an opioid 30 to 50 times more potent than heroin, has prompted Baltimore health officials to launch a public health campaign to raise awareness among drug users. Hundreds of people have overdosed on fentanyl across the nation since 2013, often as a result of using heroin that has been laced with the much stronger substance. A quarter of drug overdose deaths in Maryland now involve fentanyl, up from 4 percent in 2013. Opioid overdose can stop a person's respiration, and fentanyl can have this effect very quickly. Other parts of the country such as Detroit and surrounding suburbs are also seeing major surges in fentanyl use and fentanyl-related deaths. In some cases users are unknowingly taking fentanyl in what they believe to be pure heroin, but a growing number of opioid users are deliberately taking fentanyl.

Fentanyl and other opioid overdoses can be reversed if the drug naloxone (Narcan) is administered promptly. In a growing number of states, naloxone is being distributed to injection drug users and other laypersons to use in the event of overdose. For example, Baltimore's Staying Alive Drug Overdose Prevention and Response plan issues naloxone and training in its use.

Section 21.4

Heroin

This section contains text excerpted from the following sources: Text beginning with the heading "What Is Heroin?" is excerpted from "Heroin," National Institute on Drug Abuse (NIDA), March 10, 2016; Text beginning with the heading "The Connection between Pain Medications and Heroin" is excerpted from "The Connection Between Pain Medications and Heroin," National Institute on Drug Abuse (NIDA), March 10, 2016; Text beginning with the heading "Which Drugs Cause Similar Effects?" is excerpted from "Drugs of Abuse," U.S. Drug Enforcement Administration (DEA), 2015.

What Is Heroin?

Also known as: "Smack," "Junk," "H," "Black tar," "Ska," and "Horse"

Heroin is a type of opioid drug that is partly man made and partly natural. It is made from morphine, a psychoactive (mind-altering) substance that occurs naturally in the resin of the opium poppy plant. Heroin's color and look depend on how it is made and what else it may be mixed with. It can be white or brown powder or a black, sticky substance called "black tar heroin."

Heroin is becoming an increasing concern in areas where lots of people abuse prescription opioid painkillers, like OxyContin and Vicodin. They may turn to heroin since it produces a similar high but is cheaper and easier to obtain. Nearly half of young people who inject heroin surveyed in recent studies reported abusing prescription opioids before starting to use heroin.

How Is Heroin Used?

Heroin is mixed with water and injected with a needle. It can also be smoked or snorted.

How Does Heroin Affect the Brain?

When heroin enters the brain, it is converted back into morphine. It then binds to molecules on cells known as opioid receptors. These receptors are located in many areas of the brain and body, especially areas involved in the perception of pain and pleasure.

Short-term effects of heroin include a rush of good feelings and clouded thinking. For the first several hours after taking heroin, people want to sleep, and their heart rate and breathing slow down. When the drug wears off, people may feel a strong urge to take more.

Regular heroin use changes the functioning of the brain. Using heroin repeatedly can result in:

- Tolerance—more of the drug is needed to achieve the same "high"
- Dependence—the need to continue use of the drug to avoid withdrawal symptoms
- Addiction—a devastating brain disease where, without proper treatment, people can't stop using drugs even when they really want to and even after it causes terrible consequences to their health and other parts of their lives

What Are the Other Effects of Heroin?

The changes that take place in the brain from heroin use have effects on the rest of the body. Some of these effects are quite serious. In 2011, more than 250,000 visits to a hospital emergency department involved heroin.

Heroin use can cause:

- Feeling sick to the stomach and throwing up
- Severe itching
- Slowed (or even stopped) breathing

- Increased risk of HIV and hepatitis (a liver disease) through shared needles
- Coma—a deep state of unconsciousness

In addition to the effects of the drug itself, heroin bought on the street often contains a mix of substances, some of which can be toxic and can clog the blood vessels leading to the lungs, liver, kidney, or brain. This can cause permanent damage to those organs.

Can You Get Addicted to Heroin?

Yes, heroin is very addictive. It enters the brain quickly, causing a fast, intense high. Because users can develop a tolerance, people who use heroin need to take more and more of it to get the same effect, and eventually they may need to keep taking the drug just to feel normal. It is estimated that about 23 percent of individuals who use heroin become addicted. For those who use heroin repeatedly (over and over again), addiction is very likely. Once a person becomes addicted to heroin, seeking and using the drug becomes their main goal in life.

The number of people addicted to heroin doubled from 214,000 in 2002 to 517,000 in 2013.

When someone is addicted to heroin and stops using it, he or she may experience:

- Muscle and bone pain
- Cold flashes with chills
- Throwing up
- Inability to sleep
- Restlessness
- Kicking movements
- Strong craving for the drug

Fortunately, treatment can help an addicted person stop using and stay off heroin. Medicines can help with cravings that occur after quitting, helping a person to take control of their health and their lives.

Can You Die If You Use Heroin?

Yes, heroin slows, and sometimes stops, breathing, and this can kill a person. Dying in this way is known as overdosing. Deaths from drug overdoses have been increasing since the early 1990s—fueled most recently by a surge in heroin use. In 2014, more than 10,000 people in the United States died from a heroin overdose. Compare that with 2001, when just 1,800 people overdosed on heroin and died. For young people (ages 15 to 24), the increases are greater, with 1,300 young people dying from heroin overdose in 2014 as compared with 212 people who died in 2001 from a heroin overdose. Signs of a heroin overdose are slow breathing, blue lips and fingernails, cold damp skin, and shaking. People who might be overdosing should be taken to the emergency room right away.

How Many Teens Use Heroin?

For the most recent statistics on heroin use among teens, see the results below from NIDA's Monitoring the Future study.

Table 21.2. Monitoring the Future Study: Trends in Prevalence of Heroin for 8th Graders, 10th Graders, and 12th Graders; 2015 (in percent)

Drug	Time Period	8th Graders	10th Graders	12th Graders
Heroin	Lifetime	[0.50]	0.7	0.8
	Past Year	[0.30]	0.5	0.5
	Past Month	0.1	0.2	0.3

The Connection between Pain Medications and Heroin

More and more young people are using heroin these days, and sometimes they start using it because they've gotten addicted to prescription painkillers.

One study showed that people who abuse painkillers like OxyContin are 19 times more likely to start using heroin. The study also found that 8 out of 10 people who started using heroin abused painkillers first.

Heroin and painkillers belong to the same class of drugs: Opioids. Opioids attach to specific molecules called opioid receptors, which are found on nerve cells in the brain, spinal cord, intestines, and other organs. When painkillers or heroin attach to these receptors, they can decrease the feeling of pain. Opioids can also cause a person to feel relaxed and happy, which can lead some people to abuse the drugs.

Opioids have many negative effects. Painkillers and heroin can cause sleepiness, constipation, and, depending on the amount taken, affect a person's ability to breathe properly. In fact, taking just one large dose of painkillers or heroin could cause a person's breathing to stop, sometimes killing them.

Why do people switch from painkillers to heroin? In an effort to cut down on painkiller abuse, changes have been made to laws and prescription drug tracking systems. Because it's getting harder to get painkillers, people may turn to heroin because it is cheaper and easier to get.

The Danger in Abusing Painkillers or Heroin

Not everyone who abuses painkillers starts using heroin, but even painkiller abuse alone can hurt you. Opioid drugs of all kinds can be very addictive. Addiction is a disease where you feel like you need to use a drug even if that drug is hurting you and messing up your life. Addiction is caused by chemical changes in the brain after drug use.

When someone is addicted to painkillers or heroin, it is very difficult for them to stop using the drug. People trying to stop using opioids after they are addicted may have withdrawal. Some of the effects of opioid withdrawal are restlessness, muscle and bone pain, trouble sleeping, diarrhea, vomiting, cold flashes with goosebumps, and uncontrollable leg movements.

What Are Its Overdose Effects?

Because heroin abusers do not know the actual strength of the drug or its true contents, they are at a high risk of overdose or death. The effects of a heroin overdose are:

- Slow and shallow breathing, blue lips and fingernails, clammy skin, convulsions, coma, and possible death

Which Drugs Cause Similar Effects?

Other opioids such as OxyContin®, Vicodin®, codeine, morphine, methadone, and fentanyl can cause similar effects as heroin.

What Is Its Legal Status in the United States?

Heroin is a Schedule I substance under the Controlled Substances Act meaning that it has a high potential for abuse, no currently accepted medical use in treatment in the United States, and a lack of accepted safety for use under medical supervision.

Section 21.5

Hydrocodone

This section includes text excerpted from "Hydrocodone," U.S. Drug Enforcement Administration (DEA), October 2014.

Introduction

Since 2009, hydrocodone has been the second most frequently encountered opioid pharmaceutical in drug evidence submitted to federal, state, and local forensic laboratories as reported by DEA's National Forensic Laboratory Information System (NFLIS) and System to Retrieve Information from Drug Evidence (STRIDE).

Licit Uses

Hydrocodone is an antitussive (cough suppressant) and narcotic analgesic agent for the treatment of moderate to moderately severe pain. Studies indicate that hydrocodone is as effective, or more effective, than code in for cough suppression and nearly equipotent to morphine for pain relief.

Hydrocodone is the most frequently prescribed opiate in the United States with more than 136 million prescriptions for hydrocodone-containing products dispensed in 2013 and with nearly 65.5 million dispensed in the first six months of 2014 (IMS Health™). There are several hundred brand name and generic hydrocodone products marketed, most of which are combination products. The most frequently prescribed combination is hydrocodone and acetaminophen (Vicodin®, Lortab®).

Chemistry/Pharmacology

Hydrocodone [4, 5α-epoxy-3-methoxy-17-methyl-morphinan-6-onetartrate (1:1) hydrate (2:5), dihydrocodeinone] is a semi-synthetic opioid most closely related to codeine in structure and morphine in producing opiate-like effects. The first report, that hydrocodone produces euphoria and habituation symptoms, was published in 1923.

The first report of hydrocodone dependence and addiction was published in 1961.

Illicit Uses

Hydrocodone is abused for its opioid effects. Widespread diversion via bogus call-in prescriptions, altered prescriptions, theft, and illicit purchases from Internet sources are made easier by the present controls placed on hydrocodone products. Hydrocodone pills are the most frequently encountered dosage form in illicit traffic. Hydrocodone is generally abused orally, often in combination with alcohol.

Of particular concern is the prevalence of illicit use of hydrocodone among school-aged children. The 2013 Monitoring the Future Survey reports that 1.4%, 4.6% and 5.3% of 8th, 10th, and 12th graders, respectively, used Vicodin® for non medical purposes in the past year.

The American Association of Poison Control Centers (AAPCC) reports that in 2012, there were 29,391 total exposures and 36 deaths associated with hydrocodone in the United States. The 2013 National Survey on Drug Use and Health (NSDUH) reports that 24.4 million people in the U.S. population, aged 12 and older, used hydrocodone for non medical purposes in their lifetime, compared to 25.7 million in 2012. There was a significant decrease in reports of lifetime nonmedical use among those aged 12 to 17 and aged 18 to 25, compared to 2012.

According to the Drug Abuse Warning Network (DAWN ED), an estimated 82,480 emergency department visits were associated with nonmedical use of hydrocodone in 2011. This number of ED visits represents a 107% significant increase from the number of ED visits reported in 2004 (39,846). The Florida Department of Law Enforcement reported 431 deaths as being related to hydrocodone from January to June 2013,an 8.8% increase from the previous six months (396 deaths, July– December 2012). Of these 431 deaths, 158 of them were determined to be caused by hydrocodone.

As with most opiates, abuse of hydrocodone is associated with tolerance, dependence, and addiction. The co-formulation with acetaminophen carries an additional risk of liver toxicity when high, acute doses are consumed. Some individuals who abuse very high doses of acetaminophen-containing hydrocodone products may be spared this liver toxicity if they have been chronically taking these products and have escalated their dose slowly over a long period of time.

User Population

Every age group has been affected by the relative ease of hydrocodone availability and the perceived safety of these products by medical prescribers. Sometimes viewed as a "white collar" addiction, hydrocodone abuse has increased among all ethnic and economic groups.

Illicit Distribution

Hydrocodone has been encountered in tablets, capsules, and liquid form in the illicit market. However, hydrocodone tablets with the co-ingredient, acetaminophen, is the most frequently encountered form. Hydrocodone is not typically found to be clandestinely produced; diverted pharmaceuticals are the primary source of the drug for abuse purposes. Doctor shopping, altered or fraudulent prescriptions, bogus call-in prescriptions, diversion by some physicians and pharmacists, and drug theft are also major sources of the diverted drug.

The National Forensic Laboratory Information System (NFLIS) is a DEA database that collects scientifically verified data on drug items and cases submitted to and analyzed by state and local forensic laboratories. The System to Retrieve Information from Drug Evidence (STRIDE) provides information on drug seizures reported to and analyzed by DEA laboratories. In 2013, there were 34,961 hydrocodone reports identified in the NFLIS and STRIDE systems, a decrease from 41,401 reports in 2012.

Control Status

The DEA published in the Federal Register the final rule placing hydrocodone (in bulk, single entity products, and combinations) in Schedule II of the CSA. This rule is effective as of October 6, 2014.

Section 21.6

Hydromorphone

This section includes text excerpted from "Drugs of Abuse," U.S. Drug Enforcement Administration (DEA), 2015.

What Is Hydromorphone?

Hydromorphone belongs to a class of drugs called "opioids," which includes morphine. It has an analgesic potency of two to eight times that of morphine, but has a shorter duration of action and greater sedative properties.

What Is Its Origin?

Hydromorphone is legally manufactured and distributed in the United States. However, abusers can obtain hydromorphone from forged prescriptions, "doctor-shopping," theft from pharmacies, and from friends and acquaintances.

What Are the Street Names?

Common street names include:

- D, Dillies, Dust, Footballs, Juice, and Smack

What Does It Look Like?

Hydromorphone comes in:

- Tablets, rectal suppositories, oral solutions, and injectable formulations

How Is It Abused?

Users may abuse hydromorphone tablets by ingesting them. Injectable solutions, as well as tablets that have been crushed and dissolved in a solution may be injected as a substitute for heroin.

What Is Its Effect on the Mind?

When used as a drug of abuse, and not under a doctor's supervision, hydromorphone is taken to produce feelings of euphoria, relaxation, sedation, and reduced anxiety. It may also cause mental clouding, changes in mood, nervousness, and restlessness. It works centrally (in the brain) to reduce pain and suppress cough. Hydromorphone use is associated with both physiological and psychological dependence.

What Is Its Effect on the Body?

Hydromorphone may cause:

- Constipation, pupillary constriction, urinary retention, nausea, vomiting, respiratory depression, dizziness, impaired coordination, loss of appetite, rash, slow or rapid heartbeat, and changes in blood pressure

What Are Its Overdose Effects?

Acute overdose of hydromorphone can produce:

- Severe respiratory depression, drowsiness progressing to stupor or coma, lack of skeletal muscle tone, cold and clammy skin, constricted pupils, and reduction in blood pressure and heart rate

Severe overdose may result in death due to respiratory depression.

Which Drugs Cause Similar Effects?

Drugs that have similar effects include:

- Heroin, morphine, hydrocodone, fentanyl, and oxycodone

What Is Its Legal Status in the United States?

Hydromorphone is a Schedule II drug under the Controlled Substances Act with an accepted medical use as a pain reliever. Hydromorphone has a high potential for abuse and use may lead to severe psychological or physical dependence.

Section 21.7

Methadone

This section includes text excerpted from "Drugs of Abuse," U.S. Drug Enforcement Administration (DEA), 2015.

What Is Methadone?

Methadone is a synthetic (man-made) narcotic.

What Is Its Origin?

German scientists synthesized methadone during World War II because of a shortage of morphine. Methadone was introduced into the United States in 1947 as an analgesic (Dolophinel).

What Are Common Street Names?

Common street names include:

- Amidone, Chocolate Chip Cookies, Fizzies, Maria, Pastora, Salvia, Street Methadone, and Wafer

What Does It Look Like?

Methadone is available as a tablet, disc, oral solution, or injectable liquid. Tablets are available in 5 mg and 10 mg formulations. As of January 1, 2008, manufacturers of methadone hydrochloride tablets 40 mg (dispersible) have voluntarily agreed to restrict distribution of this formulation to only those facilities authorized for detoxification and maintenance treatment of opioid addiction, and hospitals. Manufacturers will instruct their wholesale distributors to discontinue supplying this formulation to any facility not meeting the above criteria.

How Is It Abused?

Methodone can be swallowed or injected.

What Is Its Effect on the Mind?

Abuse of methadone can lead to psychological dependence.

What Is Its Effect on the Body?

When an individual uses methadone, he/she may experience physical symptoms like sweating, itchy skin, or sleepiness. Individuals who abuse methadone risk becoming tolerant of and physically dependent on the drug. When use is stopped, individuals may experience withdrawal symptoms including:

- Anxiety, muscle tremors, nausea, diarrhea, vomiting, and abdominal cramps

What Are Its Overdose Effects?

The effects of a methadone overdose are:

- Slow and shallow breathing, blue fingernails and lips, stomach spasms, clammy skin, convulsions, weak pulse, coma, and possible death

Which Drugs Cause Similar Effects?

Although chemically unlike morphine or heroin, methadone produces many of the same effects.

What Is Its Legal Status in the United States?

Methadone is a Schedule II drug under the Controlled Substances Act. While it may legally be used under a doctor's supervision, its non-medical use is illegal.

Section 21.8

Morphine

This section includes text excerpted from "Drugs of Abuse," U.S. Drug Enforcement Administration (DEA), 2015.

What Is Morphine?

Morphine is a non-synthetic narcotic with a high potential for abuse and is the principal constituent of opium. It is one of the most effective drugs known for the relief of severe pain.

What Is Its Origin?

In the United States, a small percentage of the morphine obtained from opium is used directly for pharmaceutical products. The remaining morphine is processed into codeine and other derivatives.

What Are Common Street Names?

Common street names include:

- Dreamer, Emsel, First Line, God's Drug, Hows, M.S., Mister Blue, Morf, Morpho, and Unkie

What Does It Look Like?

Morphine is marketed under generic and brand name products, including:

- MS-Contin®, Oramorph SR®, MSIR®, Roxanol®, Kadian®, and RMS®

How Is It Abused?

Traditionally, morphine was almost exclusively used by injection, but the variety of pharmaceutical forms that it is marketed as today support its use by oral and other routes of administration.

Forms include:

- Oral solutions, immediate-and sustained-release tablets and capsules, suppositories, and injectable preparations

Those dependent on morphine prefer injection because the drug enters the blood stream more quickly.

What Is Its Effect on the Mind?

Morphine's effects include euphoria and relief of pain. Chronic use of morphine results in tolerance and physical and psychological dependence.

What Is Its Effect on the Body?

Morphine use results in relief from physical pain, decrease in hunger, and inhibition of the cough reflex.

What Are Its Overdose Effects?

Overdose effects include:

- Cold, clammy skin, lowered blood pressure, sleepiness, slowed breathing, slow pulse rate, coma, and possible death

Which Drugs Cause Similar Effects?

Drugs causing similar effects as morphine include:

- Opium, codeine, heroin, methadone, hydrocodone, fentanyl, and oxycodone

What Is Its Legal Status in the United States?

Morphine is a Schedule II narcotic under the Controlled Substances Act.

Section 21.9

Oxycodone

This section includes text excerpted from "Drugs of Abuse," U.S. Drug Enforcement Administration (DEA), 2015.

What Is Oxycodone?

Oxycodone is a semi-synthetic narcotic analgesic and historically has been a popular drug of abuse among the narcotic abusing population.

What Is Its Origin?

Oxycodone is synthesized from thebaine, a constituent of the poppy plants.

What Are Common Street Names?

Common street names include:

- Hillbilly Heroin, Kicker, OC, ox, Roxy, Perc, and oxy

What Does It Look Like?

Oxycodone is marketed alone as OxyContin® in 10, 20, 40 and 80 mg controlled-release tablets and other immediate-release capsules like 5 mg OxyIR®. It is also marketed in combination products with aspirin such as Percodan® or acetaminophen such as Roxicet®.

How Is It Abused?

Oxycodone is abused orally or intravenously. The tablets are crushed and sniffed or dissolved in water and injected. Others heat a tablet that has been placed on a piece of foil then inhale the vapors.

What Is Its Effect on the Mind?

Euphoria and feelings of relaxation are the most common effects of oxycodone on the brain, which explains its high potential for abuse.

What Is Its Effect on the Body?

Physiological effects of oxycodone include:

- Pain relief, sedation, respiratory depression, constipation, papillary constriction, and cough suppression. Extended or chronic use of oxycodone containing acetaminophen may cause severe liver damage.

What Are Its Overdose Effects?

Overdose effects include:

- Extreme drowsiness, muscle weakness, confusion, cold and clammy skin, pinpoint pupils, shallow breathing, slow heart rate, fainting, coma, and possible death

Which Drugs Cause Similar Effects?

Drugs that cause similar effects to Oxycodone include:

- opium, codeine, heroin, methadone, hydrocodone, fentanyl, and morphine

What Is Its Legal Status in the United States?

Oxycodone products are in Schedule II of the federal Controlled Substances Act of 1970.

Section 21.10

Opium

This section includes text excerpted from "Drugs of Abuse," U.S. Drug Enforcement Administration (DEA), 2015.

What Is Opium?

Opium is a highly addictive non-synthetic narcotic that is extracted from the poppy plant, Papaver somniferum. The opium poppy is the key source for many narcotics, including morphine, codeine, and heroin.

What Is Its Origin?

The poppy plant, Papaver somniferum, is the source of opium. It was grown in the Mediterranean region as early as 5,000 B.C., and has since been cultivated in a number of countries throughout the world. The milky fluid that seeps from its incisions in the unripe seed pod of this poppy has been scraped by hand and air-dried to produce what is known as opium.

A more modern method of harvesting for pharmaceutical use is by the industrial poppy straw process of extracting alkaloids from the mature dried plant (concentrate of poppy straw). All opium and poppy straw used for pharmaceutical products are imported into the United States from legitimate sources in regulated countries.

What Are Common Street Names?

Common street names include:

- Ah-pen-yen, Aunti, Aunti Emma, Big O, Black Pill, Chandoo, Chandu, Chinese Molasses, Chinese Tobacco, Dopium, Dover's Powder, Dream Gun, Dream Stick, Dreams, Easing Powder, Fi-do-nie, Gee, God's Medicine, Gondola, Goric, Great Tobacco, Guma, Hop/hops, Joy Plant, Midnight Oil, Mira, O, O.P., Ope, Pen Yan, Pin Gon, Pox, Skee, Toxy, Toys, When-shee, Ze, and Zero

What Does It Look Like?

Opium can be a liquid, solid, or powder, but most poppy straw concentrate is available commercially as a fine brownish powder.

How Is It Abused?

Opium can be smoked, intravenously injected, or taken in pill form. Opium is also abused in combination with other drugs. For example, "Black" is a combination of marijuana, opium, and methamphetamine, and "Buddha" is potent marijuana spiked with opium.

What Is Its Effect on the Mind?

The intensity of opium's euphoric effects on the brain depends on the dose and route of administration. It works quickly when smoked because the opiate chemicals pass into the lungs, where they are quickly absorbed and then sent to the brain. An opium "high" is very similar to a heroin "high"; users experience a euphoric rush, followed by relaxation and the relief of physical pain.

What Is Its Effect on the Body?

Opium inhibits muscle movement in the bowels leading to constipation. It also can dry out the mouth and mucous membranes in the nose. Opium use leads to physical and psychological dependence, and can lead to overdose.

What Are Its Overdose Effects?

Overdose effects include:

- Slow breathing, seizures, dizziness, weakness, loss of consciousness, coma, and possible death

Which Drugs Cause Similar Effects?

Drugs that cause similar effects include:

- Morphine, codeine, heroin, methadone, hydroquinone, fentanyl, and oxycodone

What Is Its Legal Status in the United States?

Opium is a Schedule II drug under the Controlled Substances Act. Most opioids are Schedule II, III, IV, or V drugs. Some drugs that are derived from opium, such as heroin, are Schedule I drugs.

Chapter 22

Sedatives (Depressants)

Chapter Contents

Section 22.1

Introduction to Depressants

This section contains text excerpted from the following sources: Text beginning with the heading "What Are Depressants?" is excerpted from "Prescription Depressant Medications," National Institute on Drug Abuse (NIDA), March 10, 2016; Text beginning with the heading "Which Drugs Cause Similar Effects?" is excerpted from "Drugs of Abuse," U.S. Drug Enforcement Administration (DEA), 2015.

What Are Depressants?

Also known as: barbs, reds, red birds, phennies, tooies, yellows, or yellow jackets, candy, downers, sleeping pills, or tranks, A-minus, or zombie pills

Depressants, sometimes referred to as central nervous system (CNS) depressants or tranquilizers, slow down (or "depress") the normal activity that goes on in the brain and spinal cord. Doctors often prescribe them for people who are anxious or can't sleep. Taken as prescribed by a doctor, they can be relatively safe and helpful. However, dependence and addiction are still potential risks when taking prescription depressants. These risks increase when these drugs are abused. Taking someone else's prescription drugs or taking the drugs to get "high" can cause serious, and even dangerous, problems.

Depressants can be divided into three primary groups: barbiturates, benzodiazepines, and sleep medications.

Types of Depressants

Table 22.1. Types of Depressants

Type	Conditions They Treat
Barbiturates • Mephobarbital (Mebaral) • Sodium pentobarbital (Nembutal)	• Seizure disorders • Anxiety and tension

Table 22.1. Continued

Type	Conditions They Treat
Benzodiazepines • Diazepam (Valium) • Alprazolam (Xanax) • Estazolam (ProSom) • Clonazepam (Klonopin) • Lorazepam (Ativan)	• Acute stress reactions • Panic attacks • Convulsions • Sleep disorders
Sleep Medications • Zolpidem (Ambien) • Zaleplon (Sonata) • Eszopiclone (Lunesta)	• Sleep disorders

How Are Depressants Abused?

Depressants usually come in pill or capsule form. People abuse depressants by taking them in a way that is not intended, such as:

- Taking someone else's prescription depressant medication.
- Taking a depressant medication in a way other than prescribed by their doctor.
- Taking a depressant for fun or to get high.
- Taking a depressant with other drugs or to counteract the effects of those drugs, such as stimulants.

How Do Depressants Affect the Brain?

Most depressants affect the brain by increasing the activity of gamma-aminobutyric acid (GABA), a chemical in the brain that sends messages between cells. The increased GABA activity in turn slows down brain activity. This causes a relaxing effect that is helpful to people with anxiety or sleep problems. Too much GABA activity, though, can be harmful.

What Are the Other Effects of Depressants?

As depressants slow down brain activity, they cause other effects:

- Slurred speech
- Shallow breathing, which can lead to overdose and even death.
- Sleepiness

- Disorientation
- Lack of coordination

These effects can lead to serious accidents or injuries. Abuse of depressants can also lead to physical dependence, another reason they should only be used as prescribed.

Depressants should not be combined with any medicine or substance that causes sleepiness, like prescription pain medicines, certain over-the-counter cold and allergy medicines, or alcohol. If combined, they can slow both the heart rate and breathing increasing the risk of overdose and death.

Can You Get Addicted to Depressants?

Yes. Abuse of depressants can lead to physical dependence, which is when the body gets used to the drug and a person can't stop taking it without feeling discomfort or even worse symptoms (withdrawal). It can also lead to addiction, which is when a person compulsively seeks and takes the drug, to the point of damaging their life.

Depressants work by slowing the brain's activity. During the first few days of taking a depressant, a person usually feels sleepy and uncoordinated. With continuing use, the body becomes used to these effects and they lessen. This is known as tolerance, which means a person has to take more of the drug to get the same initial effects.

When someone who is physically dependent on a depressant stops abruptly, the brain reacts strongly, even violently sometimes, because it is missing the chemicals it's come to depend on through repeated drug use. In some cases, the brain activity races out of control to the point where it causes seizures. Just like with illegal drugs, quitting depressants is hard and can be dangerous. Someone who is either thinking about stopping use, or who has stopped and is suffering withdrawal, should get medical treatment.

Can You Die If You Abuse Depressants?

Yes, you can die if you abuse depressants. Of the 25,700 deaths related to prescription drug overdose in 2014, more than 7,900 involved benzodiazepines (such as Valium and Xanax). Among young people, males are more likely to overdose from benzodiazepines than are females. In 2014, among young people ages 15–24, three out of every four deaths from an overdose of depressant prescription drugs is a male. The risk for overdose and death are increased when depressants are combined with alcohol or other drugs.

How Many Teens Abuse Depressants?

NIDA's Monitoring the Future study collects data on teen abuse of depressants, referring to the drugs as tranquilizers:

Table 22.2. Monitoring the Future Study: Trends in Prevalence of Tranquilizers for 8th Graders, 10th Graders, and 12th Graders; 2015 (in percent)

Drug	Time Period	8th Graders	10th Graders	12th Graders
Tranquilizers	Lifetime	3	5.8	6.9
	Past Year	1.7	3.9	4.7
	Past Month	0.8	1.7	2

What Is Their Effect on the Body?

Some depressants can relax the muscles. Unwanted physical effects include slurred speech, loss of motor coordination, weakness, headache, lightheadedness, blurred vision, dizziness, nausea, vomiting, low blood pressure, and slowed breathing.

Prolonged use of depressants can lead to physical dependence even at doses recommended for medical treatment. Unlike barbiturates, large doses of benzodiazepines are rarely fatal unless combined with other drugs or alcohol. But unlike the withdrawal syndrome seen with most other drugs of abuse, withdrawal from depressants can be life threatening.

What Are Their Overdose Effects?

High doses of depressants or use of them with alcohol or other drugs can slow heart rate and breathing enough to cause death.

Which Drugs Cause Similar Effects?

Some antipsychotics, antihistamines, and antidepressants produce sedative effects. Alcohol's effects are similar to those of depressants.

What Is Their Legal Status in the United States?

Most depressants are controlled substances that range from Schedule I to Schedule IV under the Controlled Substances Act, depending on their risk for abuse and whether they currently have an accepted medical use. Many of the depressants have FDA-approved medical uses. Rohypnol® is not manufactured or legally marketed in the United States.

Section 22.2

Barbiturates

This section includes text excerpted from "Drugs of Abuse," U.S. Drug Enforcement Administration (DEA), 2015.

What Are Barbiturates?

Barbiturates are depressants that produce a wide spectrum of central nervous system depression from mild sedation to coma. They have also been used as sedatives, hypnotics, anesthetics, and anticonvulsants.

Barbiturates are classified as:

- Ultrashort, Short, Intermediate, Long-acting

What Is Their Origin?

Barbiturates were first introduced for medical use in the 1900s, and today about 12 substances are in medical use.

What Are Common Street Names?

Common street names include:

- Barbs, Block Busters, Christmas Trees, Goof Balls, Pinks, Red Devils, Reds and Blues, and Yellow Jackets

What Do They Look Like?

Barbiturates come in a variety of multicolored pills and tablets. Abusers prefer the short-acting and intermediate barbiturates such as Amytal® and Seconal®.

How Are They Abused?

Barbiturates are abused by swallowing a pill or injecting a liquid form. Barbiturates are generally abused to reduce anxiety, decrease inhibitions, and treat unwanted effects of illicit drugs. Barbiturates can be extremely dangerous because overdoses can occur easily and lead to death.

What Is Their Effect on the Mind?

- Barbiturates cause mild euphoria, lack of inhibition, relief of anxiety, and sleepiness
- Higher doses cause impairment of memory, judgment, and coordination; irritability; and paranoid and suicidal ideation
- Tolerance develops quickly and larger doses are then needed to produce the same effect, increasing the danger of an overdose.

What Is Their Effect on the Body?

Barbiturates slow down the central nervous system and cause sleepiness.

What Are Their Overdose Effects?

Effects of overdose include shallow respiration, clammy skin, dilated pupils, weak and rapid pulse, coma, and possible death

Which Drugs Cause Similar Effects?

Drugs with similar effects include alcohol, benzodiazepines like Valium® and Xanax®, tranquilizers, sleeping pills, Rohypnol®, and GHB

What Is Their Legal Status in the United States?

Barbiturates are Schedule II, III, and IV depressants under the Controlled Substances Act.

Section 22.3

Benzodiazepines

This section includes text excerpted from "Drugs of Abuse," U.S. Drug Enforcement Administration (DEA), 2015.

What Are Benzodiazepines?

Benzodiazepines are depressants that produce sedation, induce sleep, relieve anxiety and muscle spasms, and prevent seizures.

What Is Their Origin?

Benzodiazepines are only legally available through prescription. Many abusers maintain their drug supply by getting prescriptions from several doctors, forging prescriptions, or buying them illicitly. Alprazolam and diazepam are the two most frequently encountered benzodiazepines on the illicit market.

What Are Common Street Names?

Common street names include Benzos and Downers.

What Do They Look Like?

The most common benzodiazepines are the prescription drugs Valium®, Xanax®, Halcion®, Ativan®, and Klonopin®. Tolerance can develop, although at variable rates and to different degrees. Shorter-acting benzodiazepines used to manage insomnia include estazolam (ProSom®), flurazepam (Dalmane®), temazepam (Restoril®), and triazolam (Halcion®). Midazolam (Versed®), a short-acting benzodiazepine, is utilized for sedation, anxiety, and amnesia in critical care settings and prior to anesthesia. It is available in the United States as an injectable preparation and as a syrup (primarily for pediatric patients).

Benzodiazepines with a longer duration of action are utilized to treat insomnia in patients with daytime anxiety. These benzodiazepines include alprazolam (Xanax®), chlordiazepoxide (Librium®), clorazepate (Tranxene®), diazepam (Valium®), halazepam (Paxipam®), lorzepam (Ativan®), oxazepam (Serax®), prazepam (Centrax®), and quazepam (Doral®). Clonazepam (Klonopin®), diazepam, and clorazepate are also used as anticonvulsants.

How Are They Abused?

Abuse is frequently associated with adolescents and young adults who take the drug orally or crush it up and snort it to get high. Abuse is particularly high among heroin and cocaine abusers.

What Is Their Effect on the Mind?

Benzodiazepines are associated with amnesia, hostility, irritability, and vivid or disturbing dreams.

What Is Their Effect on the Body?

Benzodiazepines slow down the central nervous system and may cause sleepiness.

What Are Their Overdose Effects?

Effects of overdose include shallow respiration, clammy skin, dilated pupils, weak and rapid pulse, coma, and possible death.

Which Drugs Cause Similar Effects?

Drugs that cause similar effects include alcohol, barbiturates, sleeping pills, and GHB.

What Is Their Legal Status in the United States?

Benzodiazepines are controlled in Schedule IV of the Controlled Substance Act.

Section 22.4

Kava

This section includes text excerpted from "Kava," U.S. Drug Enforcement Administration (DEA), January 2013.

Introduction

Kava, also known as Piper methysticum (in toxicatingpepper), is a perennial shrub native to the South Pacific Islands, including Hawaii. It is harvested for its rootstock, which contains the pharmacologically active compounds kavalactones.

The term kava also refers to the non-fermented, psychoactive beverage prepared from the rootstock. For many centuries, Pacific Island societies have consumed kava beverages for social, ceremonial, and medical purposes. Traditionally, kava beverages are prepared by chewing or pounding the rootstock to produce a cloudy, milky pulp that is then soaked in water before the liquid is filtered to drink. There is an increasing use of kava for recreational purposes. The reinforcing effects of kava include mild euphoria, muscle relaxation, sedation, and analgesia.

Licit Uses

In the United States, kava is sold as dietary supplements promoted as natural alternatives to anti-anxiety drugs and sleeping pills. An analysis of six kava clinical trials found that kava (60-200 mg of kavalactones/day) produced a significant reduction in anxiety compared to placebo. However, the FDA has not made a determination about the ability of dietary supplements containing kava to provide such benefits.

Kava dietary supplements are commonly formulated as tablets and capsules (30-90 percent kavalactones; 50-250 mg per capsule). Kava is also available as whole root, powdered root, extracts (powder, paste, and liquid), tea bags, and instant powdered drink mix. Kava is frequently found in products containing a variety of herbs or vitamins, or both.

A number of cases of liver damage (hepatitis and cirrhosis), and liver failure have been associated with commercial extract preparations of kava. In 2002, the FDA issued an advisory alerting consumers and health care providers to the potential risk of liver-related injuries associated with the use of kava dietary supplements.

Chemistry and Pharmacology

The pharmacologically active kavalactones are found in the lipid soluble resin of the kava rootstock. Of the 18 isolated and identified, yangonin, methysticin, dihydromethysticin, dihydro kawain, kawain, and desmethoxyyangoin are the six major kavalactones. Different varieties of kava plants possess varying concentrations of kavalactones.

The pharmacokinetics of the kavalactones has not been extensively studied. Kavalactones are thought to be relatively quickly absorbed in the gut. There may be differences in the bioavailability between each kavalactone.

The limbic structures, amygdala complex, and reticular formation of the brain appear to be the preferential sites of action of kavalactones. However, the exact molecular mechanisms of action are not clear.

Kava has the potential for causing drug interactions through the inhibition of CYP 450 enzymes that are responsible for the metabolism of many pharmaceutical agents and other herbal remedies. Chronic use of kava in large quantities may cause a dry scaly skin or yellow skin discoloration known as kava dermopathy. It may also cause liver toxicity, and extrapyramidal effects (e.g., tremor and abnormal body movement). Individuals may experience a numbing or tingling of the mouth upon drinking kava due to its local anesthetic action. High doses of kavalactones can also produce CNS depressant effects (e.g.,sedation and muscle weakness) that appear to be transient.

Illicit Uses

Information on the illicit use of kava in the U.S. is anecdotal. Based on information on the Internet, kava is being used recreationally to relax the body and achieve a mild euphoria. It is typically consumed as a beverage made from dried kava root powder, flavored and unflavored powdered extracts, and liquid extract dissolved in pure grain alcohol and vegetable glycerin. Individuals may consume 25 grams of kavalactones, which is about 125 times the daily dose in kava dietary supplements.

Intoxicated individuals typically have sensible thought processes and comprehensive conversations, but have difficulty coordinating movement and often fall asleep. Kava users do not exhibit the generalized confusion and delirium that occurs with high levels of alcohol intoxication. While kava alone does not produce the motor and cognitive impairments caused by alcohol, kava does potentiate both the perceived and measured impairment produced by alcohol.

The American Association of Poison Control Centers reported 42 case mentions and 21 single exposures associated with kavain 2010.

User Population

Information on user population in the U.S. is very limited. In the 1980s, kava was introduced to Australian Aboriginal communities where it quickly became a drug of abuse. It has become a serious social problem in regions of Northern Australia.

Distribution

Kava is widely available on the Internet. Some websites promoting and selling kava products also sell other uncontrolled psychoactive products such as Salvia divinorum and kratom. Several kava bars and lounges in the U.S. sell kava drinks. The National Forensic Laboratory Information System (NFLIS) and the System to Retrieve Information from Drug Evidence (STRIDE) do not indicate any kava reports.

Control Status: Kava is not a controlled substance in the U.S. Due to concerns of liver toxicity, many countries including Australia, Canada, France, Germany, Malaysia, Singapore, Switzerland, and the United Kingdom have placed regulatory controls on kava. These controls range from warning consumers of the dangers of taking kava to removing kava products from the marketplace.

Chapter 23

Stimulants

Chapter Contents

Section 23.1

Introduction to Stimulants

This section includes text excerpted from "Drugs of Abuse," U.S. Drug Enforcement Administration (DEA), 2015.

What Are Stimulants?

Stimulants speed up the body's systems. This class of drugs includes prescription drugs such as amphetamines [Adderall® and dexedrine®], methylphenidate [Concerta® and Ritalin®], diet aids [such as didrex®, Bontril®, Preludin®, Fastin®, Adipex P®, ionomin®, and Meridia®] and illicitly produced drugs such as methamphetamine, cocaine, and methcathinone.

What Is Their Origin?

Stimulants are diverted from legitimate channels and clandestinely manufactured exclusively for the illicit market.

What Are Common Street Names?

Common street names for stimulants include:

- Bennies, Black Beauties, Cat, Coke, Crank, Crystal, Flake, ice, Pellets, R-Ball, Skippy, Snow, Speed, Uppers, and Vitamin R

What Do They Look Like?

Stimulants come in the form of:

- Pills, powder, rocks, and injectable liquids

How Are They Abused?

Stimulants can be pills or capsules that are swallowed. Smoking, snorting, or injecting stimulants produces a sudden sensation known as a "rush" or a "flash."

Abuse is often associated with a pattern of binge use—sporadically consuming large doses of stimulants over a short period of time. Heavy users may inject themselves every few hours, continuing until they have depleted their drug supply or reached a point of delirium, psychosis, and physical exhaustion. During heavy use, all other interests become secondary to recreating the initial euphoric rush.

What Is Their Effect on the Mind?

When used as drugs of abuse and not under a doctor's supervision, stimulants are frequently taken to:

- Produce a sense of exhilaration, enhance self-esteem, improve mental and physical performance, increase activity, reduce appetite, extend wakefulness for prolonged period, and "get high"

Chronic, high-dose use is frequently associated with agitation, hostility, panic, aggression, and suicidal or homicidal tendencies. Paranoia, sometimes accompanied by both auditory and visual hallucinations, may also occur.

Tolerance, in which more and more drug is needed to produce the usual effects, can develop rapidly, and psychological dependence occurs. In fact, the strongest psychological dependence observed occurs with the more potent stimulants, such as amphetamine, methylphenidate, methamphetamine, cocaine and methcathinone.

Abrupt cessation is commonly followed by depression, anxiety, drug craving, and extreme fatigue, known as a "crash."

What Is Their Effect on the Body?

Stimulants are sometimes referred to as uppers and reverse the effects of fatigue on both mental and physical tasks. Therapeutic levels of stimulants can produce exhilaration, extended wakeful-ness, and loss of appetite. These effects are greatly intensified when large doses of stimulants are taken.

Taking too large a dose at one time or taking large doses over an extended period of time may cause such physical side effects as:

- Dizziness, tremors, headache, flushed skin, chest pain with palpitations, excessive sweating, vomiting, and abdominal cramps.

What Are Their Overdose Effects?

In overdose, unless there is medical intervention, high fever, convulsions, and cardiovascular collapse may precede death. Because accidental death is partially due to the effects of stimulants on the body's cardiovascular and temperature-regulating systems, physical exertion increases the hazards of stimulant use.

Which Drugs Cause Similar Effects?

Some hallucinogenic substances, such as Ecstasy, have a stimulant component to their activity.

What Is Their Legal Status in the United States?

A number of stimulants have no medical use in the United States but have a high potential for abuse. These stimulants are controlled in Schedule I. Some prescription stimulants are not controlled, and some stimulants like tobacco and caffeine don't require a prescription—though society's recognition of their adverse effects has resulted in a proliferation of caffeine-free products and efforts to discourage cigarette smoking.

Stimulant chemicals in over-the-counter products, such as ephedrine and pseudoephedrine can be found in allergy and cold medicine. As required by The Combat Methamphetamine Epidemic Act of 2005, a retail outlet must store these products out of reach of customers, either behind the counter or in a locked cabinet. Regulated sellers are required to maintain a written or electronic form of a logbook to record sales of these products. In order to purchase these products, customers must now show a photo identification issued by a state or federal government. They are also required to write or enter into the logbook: their name, signature, address, date, and time of sale. In addition to the above, there are daily and monthly sales limits set for customers.

Section 23.2

Amphetamine and Methylphenidate

This section includes text excerpted from "Drugs of Abuse," U.S. Drug Enforcement Administration (DEA), 2015.

What Are Amphetamines?

Amphetamines are stimulants that speed up the body's system. Many are legally prescribed and used to treat attention-deficit hyperactivity disorder (ADHD).

What Is Their Origin?

Amphetamine was first marketed in the 1930s as Benzedrine® in an over-the-counter inhaler to treat nasal congestion. By 1937 amphetamine was available by prescription in tablet form and was used in the treatment of the sleeping disorder, narcolepsy, and ADHD.

Over the years, the use and abuse of clandestinely produced amphetamines have spread. Today, clandestine laboratory production of amphetamines has mushroomed, and the abuse of the drug has increased dramatically.

What Are Common Street Names?

Common street names include:

- Bennies, Black Beauties, Crank, Ice, Speed, and Uppers

What Do They Look Like?

Amphetamines can look like pills or powder. Common prescription amphetamines include methylphenidate (Ritalin® or Ritalin SR®), amphetamine and dextroamphetamine (Adderall®), and dextroamphetamine (Dexedrine®).

How Are They Abused?

Amphetamines are generally taken orally or injected. However, the addition of "ice," the slang name of crystallized methamphetamine hydrochloride, has promoted smoking as another mode of administration. Just as "crack" is smokable cocaine, "ice" is smokable methamphetamine.

What Is Their Effect on the Mind?

The effects of amphetamines and methamphetamine are similar to cocaine, but their onset is slower and their duration is longer. In contrast to cocaine, which is quickly removed from the brain and is almost completely metabolized, methamphetamine remains in the central nervous system longer, and a larger percentage of the drug remains unchanged in the body, producing prolonged stimulant effects.

Chronic abuse produces a psychosis that resembles schizophrenia and is characterized by: Paranoia, picking at the skin, preoccupation with one's own thoughts, and auditory and visual hallucinations. Violent and erratic behavior is frequently seen among chronic abusers of amphetamines and methamphetamine.

What Is Their Effect on the Body?

Physical effects of amphetamine use include:

- Increased blood pressure and pulse rates, insomnia, loss of appetite, and physical exhaustion

What Are Their Overdose Effects?

Overdose effects include:

- Agitation, increased body temperature, hallucinations, convulsions, and possible death

Which Drugs Cause Similar Effects?

Drugs that cause similar effects include:

- Dexmethylphendiate, phentermine, benzphetamine, phendimetrazine, cocaine, crack, methamphetamine, and khat

What Is Their Legal Status in the United States?

Amphetamines are Schedule II stimulants, which means that they have a high potential for abuse and limited medical uses. Pharmaceutical products are available only through a prescription that cannot be refilled.

Section 23.3

Benzylpiperazine (BZP)

This section includes text excerpted from "N-Benzylpiperazine," U.S. Drug Enforcement Administration (DEA), March 2014.

Introduction

N-Benzylpiperazine (BZP) was first synthesized in 1944 as a potential antiparasitic agent. It was subsequently shown to possess antidepressant activity and amphetamine-like effects, but was not developed for marketing. The amphetamine-like effects of BZP attracted the attention of drug abusers. Since 1996, BZP has been abused by drug abusers; as evidenced by the encounters of this substance by law enforcement officials in various states and the District of Columbia. The Drug Enforcement Administration (DEA) placed BZP in schedule I of the Controlled Substances Act (CSA) because of its high abuse potential and lack of accepted medical use or safety.

Licit Uses

BZP is used as an intermediate in chemical synthesis. It has no known medical use in the United States.

Chemistry

BZP is an N-monosubstituted piperazine derivative available as either base or the hydrochloride salt. The base form is a slightly yellowish-green liquid. The hydrochloride salt is a white solid. BZP base is corrosive and causes burns. The salt form of BZP is an irritant to eyes, respiratory system and skin.

Pharmacology

Both animal studies and human clinical studies have demonstrated that the pharmacological effects of BZP are qualitatively similar to those of amphetamine. BZP has been reported to be similar to amphetamine in its effects on chemical transmission in brain. BZP fully mimics discriminative stimulus effects of amphetamine in animals. BZP is self-administered by monkeys indicating reinforcing effects. Subjective effects of BZP were amphetamine-like in drug-naive volunteers and in volunteers with a history of stimulant dependence. BZP acts as a stimulant in humans and produces euphoria and cardiovascular effects, namely increases in heart rate and systolic blood pressure. BZP is about 10 to 20 times less potent than amphetamine in producing these effects. Experimental studies demonstrate that the abuse, dependence potential, pharmacology and toxicology of BZP are similar to those of amphetamine. Public health risks of BZP are similar to those of amphetamine.

Illicit Uses

BZP is often abused in combination with 1- [3 (trifluoro-methyl) phenyl] piperazine (TFMPP), an on controlled substance. This combination has been promoted to the youth population as a substitute for 3, 4methylenedioxymethamphetamine (MDMA) at raves (all night dance parties). However, there are no clinical March 2014 DEA/OD/ODE studies that directly compared the behavioral effects of BZP to those of MDMA. BZP may also be abused alone for its stimulant effects. BZP is generally administered orally as either powder or tablets and capsules. Other routes of administration included smoking and snorting. In 2001, a report from University in Zurich, Switzerland described the death of a young female which was attributed to the combined use of BZP and MDMA. There have also been several life-threatening incidents that resulted in emergency department admissions following the ingestion of BZP.

User Population

Youth and young adults are the main abusers of BZP.

Illicit Distribution

According to DEA's System to Retrieve Information from Drug Evidence (STRIDE) and National Forensic Laboratory Information System (NFLIS), the number of reports submitted to federal, state, and local forensic laboratories and identified as BZP peaked in 2009 at 15,174 and decreased each year thereafter. In 2013, there were 2,548 BZP reports identified.

Illicit distributions occur through smuggling of bulk powder through drug trafficking organizations with connections to overseas sources of supply. The bulk powder is then processed into capsules and tablets. BZP is encountered as pink, white, off-white, purple, orange, tan, and mottle orange-brown tablets. These tablets bear imprints commonly seen on MDMA tablets such as housefly, crown, heart, butterfly, smiley face or bull's head logos and are often sold as "ecstasy." BZP has been found in powder or liquid form which is packaged in small convenience sizes and sold on the Internet.

Control Status

BZP was temporarily placed into schedule I of the CSA on September 20, 2002 (67 FR 59161). On March 18, 2004, the DEA published a Final Rule in the Federal Register permanently placing BZP in schedule I.

Section 23.4

Cocaine

This section contains text excerpted from the following sources: Text beginning with the heading "What Is Cocaine?" is excerpted from "Cocaine," National Institute on Drug Abuse (NIDA), March 10, 2016; Text beginning with the heading "What Is Its Effect on the Body?" is excerpted from "Drugs of Abuse," U.S. Drug Enforcement Administration (DEA), 2015.

What Is Cocaine?

Also known as: "coke," "Coca," "C," "snow," "flake," "blow," "bump," "candy," "Charlie," "rock," and "toot"

Cocaine is a powerfully addictive stimulant drug made from the leaves of the coca plant native to South America. Cocaine comes in two forms:

- **Powder cocaine** is a white powder (which scientists call a hydrochloride salt). Street dealers often mix cocaine with other substances like cornstarch, talcum powder, or sugar. They also mix cocaine with active drugs like procaine, a chemical that produces local anesthesia (a local anesthetic that causes you not to feel pain in a specific area of the body) and with other stimulants like amphetamines.

- **Crack** is a form of cocaine that has been processed to make a rock crystal that people smoke. The term "crack" refers to the cracking sound the rocks make when they are heated. To make crack, the powder cocaine is mixed with ammonia or baking soda and water and then heated to produce the crystal.

How Is Cocaine Used?

Powder cocaine can be snorted up the nose or mixed with water and injected with a needle. Sometimes, powder cocaine is rubbed on to gums or other tissues in the body. Crack is smoked in a small glass pipe. The crystal is heated to produce vapors that are absorbed into the blood through the lungs.

In order to keep the "high" going, people may take the drug repeatedly within a short period of time, at increasingly higher doses.

How Does Cocaine Affect the Brain?

Stimulants like cocaine change the way the brain works by changing the way nerve cells communicate. Nerve cells, called neurons, send messages to each other by releasing chemicals called neurotransmitters. These neurotransmitters attach to molecules on neurons called receptors.

There are many neurotransmitters, but dopamine is the main one that makes people feel good when they do something they enjoy, like eating a piece of chocolate cake or playing a video game. It is then recycled back into the cell that released it, thus shutting off the signal. Cocaine prevents the dopamine from being recycled, causing a buildup of the neurotransmitter in the brain. It is this flood of dopamine that causes cocaine's high. The drug can cause a feeling of intense pleasure and increased energy.

With repeated use, stimulants can disrupt how the brain's dopamine system works, reducing a person's ability to feel any pleasure at all. People may try to make up for it by taking more and more of the drug to feel the same pleasure.

After the "high" of the cocaine wears off, many people experience a "crash" and feel tired or sad for days. They also experience a strong craving to take cocaine again to try to feel better.

What Are the Other Effects of Cocaine?

The surge of dopamine in the brain affects the body in a variety of ways:

- Constricted blood vessels and dilated pupils
- Higher body temperature
- Higher blood pressure and faster heartbeat
- Feeling sick to the stomach
- Restlessness
- Decreased appetite and, over time, a loss of weight
- Inability to sleep
- Increased risk of heart attack or stroke due to high blood pressure
- Increased risk of HIV because of impaired judgment leading to risky sexual behavior
- Strange, unpredictable behavior, panic attacks, or paranoid psychosis (losing touch with reality)

How cocaine is used leads to different physical problems. For example, regularly snorting cocaine can lead to a hoarse voice, loss of the sense of smell, nosebleeds, and a constant runny nose. Cocaine taken by mouth can reduce blood flow in your intestines, leading to bowel problems. Injecting cocaine can increase a person's risk of getting HIV, hepatitis C (a liver disease), and other diseases transmitted by blood contact.

Can You Get Addicted to Cocaine?

Yes, repeated use can lead to addiction, a devastating brain disease where people can't stop using drugs even when they really want to and even after it causes terrible consequences to their health and other parts of their lives. Using cocaine over and over can cause tolerance to the drug. This means that it takes more of the drug for the user to get the same high felt when first using it.

Because a cocaine high usually doesn't last very long, people take it again and again to try to keep feeling good. Once addicted, people who are trying to quit taking cocaine might:

- Act nervous and restless

- Feel very sad and tired
- Have bad dreams
- Not trust people and things around them
- Feel a strong need to take cocaine

The right treatment, however, can help an addicted person control their cravings and stop using cocaine.

Can You Die If You Use Cocaine?

Yes. In 2014, more than 5,400 people died from a cocaine overdose. Males are much more likely to die in this way than are females. During the year, 3,900 males overdosed on cocaine, as compared with 1,500 females who died as a result of a cocaine overdose.

Cocaine can be deadly when taken in large doses or when mixed with other drugs or alcohol. Cocaine-related deaths are often a result of the heart stopping (cardiac arrest) followed by stopped breathing. Abusing cocaine with alcohol or other drugs increases these dangers, including the risk of overdose. For example, combining cocaine and heroin (known as a "speedball") puts a person at higher risk of death from an overdose.

In rare instances, sudden death can occur on the first use of cocaine or soon after.

How Many Teens Use Cocaine?

For the most recent statistics on cocaine use among teens, see the results below from NIDA's Monitoring the Future study.

Table 23.1. Monitoring the Future Study: Trends in Prevalence of Various Drugs for 8th Graders, 10th Graders, and 12th Graders; 2015 (in percent)

Drug	Time Period	8th Graders	10th Graders	12th Graders
Cocaine	Lifetime	1.6	2.7	4
	Past Year	0.9	1.8	2.5
	Past Month	0.5	0.8	1.1
Crack Cocaine	Lifetime	1	1.1	1.7
	Past Year	0.5	0.7	1.1
	Past Month	0.3	0.3	0.6

What Is Its Effect on the Body?

Physiological effects of cocaine include increased blood pressure and heart rate, dilated pupils, insomnia, and loss of appetite. The widespread abuse of highly pure street cocaine has led to many severe adverse health consequences such as:

- Cardiac arrhythmias, ischemic heart conditions, sudden cardiac arrest, convulsions, strokes, and death

In some users, the long-term use of inhaled cocaine has led to a unique respiratory syndrome, and chronic snorting of cocaine has led to the erosion of the upper nasal cavity.

Which Drugs Cause Similar Effects?

Other stimulants, such as methamphetamine, cause effects similar to cocaine that vary mainly in degree.

What Is Its Legal Status in the United States?

Cocaine is a Schedule II drug under the Controlled Substances Act, meaning it has a high potential for abuse and limited medical usage. Cocaine hydrochloride solution (4% and 10%) is used primarily as a topical local anesthetic for the upper respiratory tract. It also is used to reduce bleeding of the mucous membranes in the mouth, throat, and nasal cavities. However, better products have been developed for these purposes, and cocaine is rarely used medically in the United States.

Section 23.5

Khat

This section includes text excerpted from "Drugs of Abuse," U.S. Drug Enforcement Administration (DEA), 2015.

What Is Khat?

Khat is a flowering evergreen shrub that is abused for its stimulant-like effect. Khat has two active ingredients, cathine and cathinone.

What Is Its Origin?

Khat is native to East Africa and the Arabian Peninsula, where the use of it is an established cultural tradition for many social situations.

What Are Common Street Names?

Common street names for Khat include:

- Abyssinian Tea, African Salad, Catha, Chat, Kat, and Oat

What Does It Look Like?

Khat is a flowering evergreen shrub. Khat that is sold and abused is usually just the leaves, twigs, and shoots of the Khat shrub.

How Is It Abused?

Khat is typically chewed like tobacco, then retained in the cheek and chewed intermittently to release the active drug, which produces a stimulant-like effect. Dried Khat leaves can be made into tea or a chewable paste, and Khat can also be smoked and even sprinkled on food.

What Is Its Effect on the Mind?

Khat can induce manic behavior with:

- Grandiose delusions, paranoia, nightmares, hallucinations, and hyperactivity

Chronic Khat abuse can result in violence and suicidal depression.

What Is Its Effect on the Body?

Khat causes an immediate increase in blood pressure and heart rate. Khat can also cause a brown staining of the teeth, insomnia, and gastric disorders. Chronic abuse of Khat can cause physical exhaustion.

What Are Its Overdose Effects?

The dose needed to constitute an overdose is not known, however it has historically been associated with those who have been long-term chewers of the leaves. Symptoms of toxicity include:

- Delusions, loss of appetite, difficulty with breathing, and increases in both blood pressure and heart rate

Additionally, there are reports of liver damage (chemical hepatitis) and of cardiac complications, specifically myocardial infarctions. This mostly occurs among long-term chewers of khat or those who have chewed too large a dose.

Which Drugs Cause Similar Effects?

Khat's effects are similar to other stimulants, such as cocaine and methamphetamine.

What Is Its Legal Status in the United States?

The chemicals found in khat are controlled under the Controlled Substances Act. Cathine is a Schedule IV stimulant, and cathinone is a Schedule I stimulant under the Controlled Substances Act, meaning that it has a high potential for abuse, no currently accepted medical use in treatment in the United States, and a lack of accepted safety for use under medical supervision.

Section 23.6

Kratom

This section includes text excerpted from "Drugs of Abuse," U.S. Drug Enforcement Administration (DEA), 2015.

What Is Kratom?

Kratom is a tropical tree native to Southeast Asia. Consumption of its leaves produces both stimulant effects (in low doses) and sedative effects (in high doses), and can lead to psychotic symptoms and psychological addiction. The psychoactive ingredient is found in the leaves from kratom tree. These leaves are subsequently crushed and then smoked, brewed with tea, or placed into gel capsules. Also known as thang, kakuam, thom, ketum, and biak, kratom is more commonly abused in the Asia Pacific region than the United States.

How Is It Abused?

Mostly abused by oral ingestion in a pill form, kratom may also be dissolved and ingested as a tea or the kratom leave may be chewed.

What Are the Effects?

At low doses, kratom produces stimulant effects with users reporting increased alertness, physical energy, and talkativeness. At high doses, users experience sedative effects. Kratom consumption can lead to addiction. Several cases of psychosis resulting from use of kratom have been reported, where individuals addicted to kratom exhibited psychotic symptoms, including hallucinations, delusion, and confusion.

What Does It Do to Your Body?

Kratom's effects on the body include nausea, itching, sweating, dry mouth, constipation, increased urination, and loss of appetite. Long-term users of kratom have experienced anorexia, weight loss, insomnia, dry mouth, frequent urination, and constipation.

What Is Its Legal Status?

Kratom is not controlled under the Federal Controlled Substances Act; however, there may be some State regulations or prohibitions against the possession and use of kratom. There is no legitimate medical use for kratom in the United States. In addition, DEA has listed kratom as a Drug and Chemical of Concern.

Section 23.7

Methamphetamine

This section contains text excerpted from the following sources: Text beginning with the heading "What Is Methamphetamine (Meth)?" is excerpted from "Methamphetamine (Meth)," National Institute on Drug Abuse (NIDA), March 10, 2016; Text beginning with the heading "Which Drugs Cause Similar Effects?" is excerpted from "Drugs of Abuse," U.S. Drug Enforcement Administration (DEA), 2015.

What Is Methamphetamine (Meth)?

Also known as: "Meth," "Speed," "chalk," and "tina"; or for crystal meth, "ice," "crank," "glass," "fire," and "go fast"

Methamphetamine—known as "meth"—is a very addictive stimulant drug. Stimulants are a class of drugs that can boost mood, increase feelings of well-being, increase energy, and make you more alert—but they also have dangerous effects like raising heart rate and blood pressure.

Methamphetamine is a manmade, white, bitter-tasting powder. Sometimes it's made into a white pill or a shiny, white or clear rock called a crystal. Most of the meth used in the United States comes from "superlabs"—big illegal laboratories that make the drug in large quantities. But it is also made in small labs using cheap, over-the-counter ingredients such as pseudoephedrine, which is common in cold medicines. Other chemicals, some of them toxic, are also involved in making methamphetamine.

Methamphetamine is classified as a Schedule II drug, meaning it has high potential for abuse and is available only through a prescription that cannot be refilled. It is prescribed by a doctor in rare cases to treat attention deficit hyperactivity disorder and other conditions. In these cases, the dose is much lower than what is typically used for the purpose of getting high.

How Is Methamphetamine Used?

Methamphetamine is swallowed, snorted, injected with a needle, or smoked. "Crystal meth" is a large, usually clear crystal that is smoked in a glass pipe. Smoking or injecting the drug delivers it very quickly to the brain, where it produces an immediate and intense high. Because the feeling doesn't last long, users often take the drug repeatedly, in a "binge and crash" pattern.

How Does Methamphetamine Affect the Brain?

Methamphetamine causes a release of the neurotransmitter dopamine in the brain. The release of small amounts of dopamine makes a person feel pleasure when they do things like listen to music, play video games, or eat tasty food. Methamphetamine's ability to release dopamine very quickly in the brain produces the feelings of extreme pleasure, sometimes referred to as a "rush" or "flash," that many users experience. After the effects have worn off, the brain has less dopamine, which can lead to depression.

Regular use of methamphetamine causes chemical and molecular changes in the brain. The activity of the dopamine system changes, causing problems with movement and thinking. Some of these changes remain long after methamphetamine use has stopped. Although, some may reverse after a person is off the drug for a long period of time, perhaps more than a year, methamphetamine may destroy nerve cells that produce dopamine and another neurotransmitter called serotonin.

What Are the Other Effects of Methamphetamine?

The release of dopamine in the brain causes several physical effects, similar to those of other stimulants like cocaine. These include:

- Feeling very awake and active
- Fast heart rate and irregular heartbeat
- Higher blood pressure
- Higher body temperature
- Increased risk for HIV/AIDS or hepatitis (a liver disease) from unsafe sex and shared needles

Effects of Long-Term Use

Continued methamphetamine use may cause effects that last for a long time, even after a person quits using the drug. These effects include:

Anxiety and confusion

- Problems sleeping
- Mood swings
- Violent behavior
- Psychosis (hearing, seeing, or feeling things that are not there)
- Skin sores caused by scratching
- Severe weight loss
- Severe dental problems, known as "meth mouth"
- Problems with thinking, emotion, and memory

Can You Get Addicted to Methamphetamine?

Yes. Methamphetamine use can quickly lead to addiction. That's when a person seeks out the drug over and over, even after they want to stop and even after it has caused damage to their health and other parts of their life.

Methamphetamine causes tolerance—when a person needs to take more of it to get the same high. People who usually eat or snort meth might start to smoke or inject it to get a stronger, quicker high.

People who are trying to quit using methamphetamine might:

- Get really tired but have trouble sleeping.
- Feel angry or nervous.
- Feel depressed.
- Feel a very strong craving to use methamphetamine.

Can You Die If You Use Methamphetamine?

Yes, it is possible. Methamphetamine can raise your body temperature so much that you pass out. If not treated right away, this can cause death. Death can also occur from heart attack or stroke caused by the drug's effects on the neurotransmitter norepinephrine, which raises heart beat and blood pressure and constricts blood vessels.

How Many Teens Use Methamphetamine?

Table 23.2. Monitoring the Future Study: Trends in Prevalence of Methamphetamine for 8th Graders, 10th Graders, and 12th Graders; 2015 (in percent)*

Drug	Time Period	8th Graders	10th Graders	12th Graders
Methamphetamine	Lifetime	0.8	1.3	1
	Past Year	0.5	0.8	0.6
	Past Month	0.3	0.3	0.4

**Data in brackets indicate statistically significant change from the previous year.*

What Is Its Effect on the Body?

Taking even small amounts of meth can result in:

- Increased wakefulness, increased physical activity, decreased appetite, rapid breathing and heart rate, irregular heartbeat, increased blood pressure, and hyperthermia (overheating)

High doses can elevate body temperature to dangerous, sometimes lethal, levels, and cause convulsions and even cardiovascular collapse and death. Meth abuse may also cause extreme anorexia, memory loss, and severe dental problems.

What Are Its Overdose Effects?

High doses may result in death from stroke, heart attack, or multiple organ problems caused by overheating.

Which Drugs Cause Similar Effects?

Cocaine and potent stimulant pharmaceuticals, such as amphetamines and methylphenidate, produce similar effects.

What Is Its Legal Status in the United States?

Methamphetamine is a Schedule II stimulant under the Controlled Substances Act, which means that it has a high potential for abuse and limited medical use. It is available only through a prescription that cannot be refilled. Today there is only one legal meth product, Desoxyn®. It is currently marketed in 5-milligram tablets and has very limited use in the treatment of obesity and attention deficit hyperactivity disorder (ADHD).

Section 23.8

Caffeine

This section contains text excerpted from the following sources: Text beginning with the heading "What's the Most Widely Used Drug?" is excerpted from "The Buzz on Caffeine," National Institute on Drug Abuse (NIDA), March 14, 2016; Text beginning with the heading "Adolescent Caffeine Use and Cocaine Sensitivity" is excerpted from "Adolescent Caffeine Use and Cocaine Sensitivity," National Institute on Drug Abuse (NIDA), November 2014; Text beginning with the heading "Caffeine Powder" is excerpted text from "Caffeine Powder," National Institutes on Drug Abuse (NIDA), July 25, 2014.

What's the Most Widely Used Drug?

It's not marijuana—and no, it's not tobacco or alcohol either. Nine out of 10 Americans take it in some form every day, and it's not limited to adults.

Answer: Caffeine!

That's right, caffeine is a drug—a stimulant drug, to be exact. It's even possible to be physically dependent on it—which means that a person who is used to drinking lots of caffeinated beverages can experience withdrawal symptoms if they quit.

According to a recent study published by the American Academy of Pediatrics, nearly three-fourths (75%) of children, teens, and young adults use it daily too—in the form of soda, coffee, and energy drinks.

Caffeine: Breaking Down the Buzz

Caffeine has a perk-up effect because it blocks a brain chemical, adenosine, which causes sleepiness. On its own, moderate amounts of caffeine rarely cause harmful long-term health effects, although it is definitely possible to take too much caffeine and get sick as a result.

Consuming too much caffeine can make you feel jittery or jumpy—your heart may race and your palms may sweat, kind of like a panic attack. It may also interfere with your sleep, which is especially important while your brain is still developing.

Some caffeine drinks and foods will affect you more than others, because they contain very different amounts.

But it's more than just how much caffeine a beverage has that can make it harmful. Even though energy drinks don't necessarily have more caffeine than other popular beverages (that is, unless you take 8 ounces of 5-Hour Energy Shot, which has 400 milligrams!), it's the way they are sometimes used that worries health experts.

In 2011, of the 20,783 emergency room visits because of energy drinks, 42% were because the user combined them with other drugs (e.g., prescription drugs, alcohol, or marijuana).

Caffeine + Alcohol = Danger

Mixing alcohol and caffeine is serious business. As a stimulant, caffeine sort of has the opposite effect on the brain as alcohol, which is a depressant. But don't think the effects of each are canceled out! In fact, drinking caffeine doesn't reduce the intoxication effect of alcohol (that is, how drunk you become) or reduce its cognitive impairments (that is, your ability to walk or drive or think clearly). But it does reduce alcohol's sedation effects, so you feel more awake and probably drink for longer periods of time, and you may think you are less drunk than you really are.

That can be super dangerous. People who consume alcohol mixed with energy drinks are 3 times more likely to binge drink than people who do not report mixing alcohol with energy drinks.

Table 23.3. Monitoring the Future Study: Trends in Prevalence of Various Drugs for 8th Graders, 10th Graders, and 12th Graders; 2015 (in percent)

Caffeine Source	Caffeine Content
8 oz black tea	14–70 milligrams (mg)
12 oz cola	23–35 mg
8.4 oz Red Bull	75–80 mg
8 oz regular coffee	95–200 mg
1 cup semi-sweet chocolate chips	104 mg
2 oz 5-Hour Energy Shot	200–207 mg

Stay Away From Caffeine?

Drinking a cup of coffee, or eating a bar of chocolate, is usually not a big deal. But there are alternatives to caffeine if you're looking for an energy burst but don't want to get that jittery feeling caffeine sometimes causes. Here are a few alternatives you can try to feel energized without overdoing the caffeine:

- **Sleep**. This may sound obvious, but getting enough sleep is important. Teens need 9 hours of sleep a night.
- **Eat regularly**. When you don't eat, your glucose (sugar) levels drop, making you feel drained. Some people find it helpful to eat four or five smaller meals throughout the day instead of fewer big meals.
- **Drink enough water.** Since our bodies are more than two-thirds H_2O, we need at least 64 ounces of water a day.
- **Take a walk.** If you're feeling drained in the middle of the day, it helps to move around. Do sit-ups or jumping jacks. Go outside for a brisk walk or ride your bike.

Adolescent Caffeine Use and Cocaine Sensitivity

Caffeine is the most widely used stimulant in the world and use by adolescents has more than doubled since 1980. Chronic caffeine use produces greater tolerance in adolescents compared with adults, suggesting that caffeine may cause greater brain changes in young people. Caffeine consumption is also known to be correlated with increased risk for illicit drug use and substance use disorders (as noted in a recent editorial in Addiction)." Since caffeine effects brain areas and circuits where cocaine acts, this study explored whether caffeine use by adolescents can impact the brain's sensitivity to cocaine in adulthood.

In a new study, rats that were treated with caffeine in adolescence showed an increased sensitivity to cocaine as adults that was associated with altered dopamine signaling in brain reward pathway involved in addiction. These changes were not seen in animals that were given caffeine as adults. These results highlight that adolescent brains are still developing and can be impacted by substances in ways that are different from fully developed adult brains. Caffeine use by adolescents may prime the still developing brain for later use of other illicit drugs.

Caffeine Powder

The death of an Ohio high school senior caused by an overdose of powdered caffeine has prompted the FDA to issue a safety advisory about caffeine powders. Bulk bags of pure caffeine powder are readily available online, and these products may be attractive to young people looking for added caffeine stimulation or for help losing weight, but they are extremely dangerous. Just a teaspoon of pure caffeine powder is equivalent to about 25 cups of coffee—a lethal amount. Besides death, severe caffeine overdose can cause fast and erratic heartbeat, seizures, vomiting, diarrhea, and disorientation—symptoms much more extreme than those of drinking too much coffee or tea or consuming too many sodas or energy drinks.

Although caffeine is generally safe at the dosages contained in popular beverages, caffeine powder is so potent that safe amounts cannot be measured with ordinary kitchen measuring tools, making it very easy to overdose on them even when users are aware of their potency. The FDA thus recommends that consumers avoid caffeine powder altogether, and wishes to alert parents to the existence of these products and their hazards.

Chapter 24

Tobacco, Nicotine, and E-Cigarettes

What Are Tobacco, Nicotine, and E-Cigarette Products?

Cigarettes: Also known as: "smokes," "cigs," or "butts"

Smokeless tobacco: Also known as: "chew," "dip," "spit tobacco," "snus," or "snuff"

Hookah: Also known as: "waterpipe," "narghile," "shisha," "hubble-bubble," or "goza"

Tobacco is a leafy plant grown around the world, including in parts of the United States. There are many chemicals found in tobacco or created by burning it (as in cigarettes), but nicotine is the ingredient that can lead to addiction. Other chemicals produced by smoking, such as tar, carbon monoxide, acetaldehyde, and nitrosamines, also can cause harm to the body. For example, tar causes lung cancer and

---

This chapter contains text excerpted from the following sources: Text beginning with the heading "What Are Tobacco, Nicotine, and E-Cigarette Products?" is excerpted from "Tobacco, Nicotine, and E-Cigarettes," National Institute on Drug Abuse (NIDA), March 10, 2016; Text under the heading "Statistics and Trends" is excerpted from "Tobacco/Nicotine," National Institute on Drug Abuse (NIDA), August 2015; Text beginning with the heading "Are There Effective Treatments for Tobacco Addiction?" is excerpted from "DrugFacts: Cigarettes and Other Tobacco Products," National Institutes on Drug Abuse (NIDA), August 2015.

other serious diseases that affect breathing. Carbon monoxide causes heart problems, which is one reason why people who smoke are at high risk for heart disease.

Tobacco use is the leading preventable cause of disease, disability, and death in the United States. According to the Centers for Disease Control and Prevention (CDC), cigarettes cause more than 480,000 premature deaths in the United States each year—from smoking or exposure to secondhand smoke—about 1 in every 5 U.S. deaths, or 1,300 deaths every day. An additional 16 million people suffer with a serious illness caused by smoking. Thus, for every 1 person who dies from smoking, 30 more suffer from at least 1 serious tobacco-related illness.

How Are Tobacco and Nicotine Products Used?

Tobacco and nicotine products come in many forms. People either smoke, chew, or sniff them, or inhale their vapors.

- **Smoked tobacco products.**
    - Cigarettes (regular, light, and menthol). No evidence exists that "lite" or menthol cigarettes are safer than regular cigarettes.
    - Cigars and pipes.
    - Bidis and kreteks (clove cigarettes). Bidis are small, thin, hand-rolled cigarettes primarily imported to the United States from India and other Southeast Asian countries. Kreteks—sometimes referred to as clove cigarettes—contain about 60-80% tobacco and 20-40% ground cloves. Flavored bidis and kreteks are banned in the United States because of the ban on flavored cigarettes.
    - Hookahs or water pipes. Practiced for centuries in other countries, smoking hookahs has become popular among teens in the United States. Hookah tobacco comes in many flavors, and the pipe is typically passed around in groups. As with smoking cigarettes, water pipe smoking still delivers the addictive drug nicotine and is at least as toxic as cigarette smoking.
- **Smokeless tobacco products.** The tobacco is not burned with these products:
    - Chewing tobacco, which is placed between the cheek and gums.
    - Snuff, ground tobacco which can be sniffed if dried or placed between the cheek and gum.

    - Dip, moist snuff that is used like chewing tobacco.
    - Snus, a small pouch of moist snuff.
    - Dissolvable products, including lozenges, orbs, sticks, and strips.
- **Electronic cigarettes.** Also called e-cigarettes, electronic nicotine delivery systems, or e-cigs, electronic cigarettes are smokeless, battery-operated devices that deliver flavored nicotine to the lungs without burning tobacco (the usual source of nicotine). In most e-cigarettes, puffing activates the battery-powered heating device, which vaporizes the liquid in the cartridge. The resulting vapor is then inhaled (called "vaping").

How Do Tobacco and Nicotine Affect the Brain?

Like cocaine, heroin, and marijuana, nicotine increases levels of a neurotransmitter called dopamine. Dopamine is released normally when you experience something pleasurable like good food, your favorite activity, or spending time with people you care about. When a person uses tobacco products, the release of dopamine causes similar effects. This effect wears off quickly, causing people who smoke to get the urge to light up again for more of that good feeling, which can lead to addiction.

Studies suggest that other chemicals in tobacco smoke, such as acetaldehyde, may enhance the effects of nicotine on the brain.

When smokeless tobacco is used, nicotine is absorbed through the mouth tissues directly into the blood, where it goes to the brain. Even after the tobacco is removed from the mouth, nicotine continues to be absorbed into the bloodstream. Also, the nicotine stays in the blood longer for users of smokeless tobacco than for smokers.

What Are the Other Effects of Tobacco and Nicotine?

When nicotine enters the body, it initially causes the adrenal glands to release a hormone called epinephrine (adrenaline). The rush of adrenaline stimulates the body and causes an increase in blood pressure, heart rate, and breathing.

Most of the harm to the body is not from the nicotine, but from other chemicals contained in tobacco or produced when burning it—including carbon monoxide, tar, formaldehyde, cyanide, and ammonia. Tobacco use harms every organ in the body and can cause many problems. The health effects of smokeless tobacco are somewhat different from those of smoked tobacco. But for both types of tobacco products, the risks are real.

Smoking Tobacco Effects

- **Cancer.** Tobacco use can be blamed for about one-third of all cancer deaths, including 90% of lung cancer cases. Tobacco use is also linked with cancers of the mouth, pharynx, larynx, esophagus, stomach, pancreas, cervix, kidney, ureter, bladder, and bone marrow (leukemia).
- **Lung or respiratory problems.** Bronchitis (swelling of the air passages to the lungs), emphysema (damage to the lungs), and pneumonia have been linked with smoking.
- **Heart disease.** Smoking increases the risk for stroke, heart attack, vascular disease (diseases that affect the circulation of blood through the body), and aneurysm (a balloon-like bulge in an artery that can rupture and cause death).
- **Cataracts (an eye condition).** People who smoke can experience this clouding of the eye, which causes blurred vision.
- **Loss of sense of smell and taste.**
- **Lowered lung capacity.** People who smoke can't exercise or play sports for as long as they once did.
- **Aging skin and teeth.** After smoking for a long time, people find that their skin ages faster and their teeth discolor or turn brown.
- **Harm to the unborn baby of a pregnant woman who smokes.** Pregnant women who smoke are at increased risk for delivering their baby early or suffering a miscarriage, still birth, or experiencing other problems with their pregnancy. Smoking by pregnant women also may be associated with learning and behavior problems in children.
- **Accidental death from fires.** Smoking is the leading cause of fire-related deaths—more than 600 deaths each year.

Secondhand Smoke

For people who do not smoke, secondhand smoke—exposure to exhaled smoke and smoke given off by the burning end of tobacco products—increases the risk for many diseases. Each year, an estimated 58 million Americans are regularly exposed to secondhand smoke and more than 41,000 nonsmokers die from diseases caused by secondhand smoke exposure.

Inhaling secondhand smoke increases a person's risk for developing:

- **Heart disease.** Secondhand smoke increases the risk for heart disease by 25% to 30%. It is estimated to contribute to as many as 34,000 deaths related to heart disease.
- **Lung cancer.** People exposed to secondhand smoke increase their risk for lung cancer by 20% to 30%. About 7,300 lung cancer deaths occur per year among people who do not smoke.
- **Lung problems.** Secondhand smoke causes breathing problems in people who do not smoke, like coughing, phlegm, and lungs not working as well as they should.
- **Health problems for children.** Children exposed to secondhand smoke are at an increased risk for sudden infant death syndrome, lung infections, ear problems, and more severe asthma.

Smokeless Tobacco Effects

People who use smokeless tobacco products, such as chewing tobacco, snuff, or dip, are at risk for several health problems:

- **Tooth decay, gum problems, and mouth sores.** Smokeless tobacco increases the chance of getting cavities, gum disease, and sores in the mouth that can make eating and drinking painful.
- **Cancer.** Close to 30 chemicals in smokeless tobacco have been found to cause cancer. People who use smokeless tobacco are at increased risk for oral cancer (cancers of the mouth, lip, tongue, and pharynx) as well as esophageal and pancreatic cancers.
- **Other potential health problems.** Recent research shows smokeless tobacco may play a role in causing heart disease and stroke.

What about E-Cigarettes?

E-Cigarettes have emerged over the past decade and researchers in the early stage of investigating what the health effects are for people who use these products or who are exposed to the aerosol (vapor) secondhand.

E-Cigarettes are designed to deliver nicotine without the other chemicals produced by burning tobacco leaves. Puffing on the mouthpiece of the cartridge activates a battery-powered inhalation device (called a vaporizer). The vaporizer heats the liquid inside the cartridge which contains nicotine, flavors, and other chemicals. The heated liquid turns into an aerosol (vapor) which the user inhales—referred to as "vaping."

There are conflicting studies about whether or not e-cigarettes help smokers to quit. For tobacco cigarette smokers, e-cigarettes may be a safer alternative, if the goal is not to quit nicotine altogether. However, health experts have raised many questions about the safety of these products, particularly for teens:

- Testing of some e-cigarette products found the aerosol (vapor) to contain known cancer-causing and toxic chemicals, and particles from the vaporizing mechanism that may be harmful. The health effects of repeated exposure to these chemicals are not yet clear.
- There is animal research which shows that nicotine exposure may cause changes in the brain that make other drugs more rewarding. If this is true in humans, as some experts believe, it would mean that using nicotine would increase the risk of other drug use and for addiction.
- There is an established link between e-cigarette use and tobacco cigarette use in teens. Researchers are investigating this relationship. The concern is that e-cigarette use may serve as a "gateway" or introductory product for youth to try other tobacco products, including regular cigarettes, which are known to cause disease and lead to early death.
- The liquid in e-cigarettes can cause nicotine poisoning if someone drinks, sniffs, or touches it. Recently there has been a surge of poisoning cases in children under age 5. There is also concern for users changing cartridges and for pets.

Are E-Cigarettes Regulated?

The U.S. government's Food and Drug Administration (FDA) may start to regulate how e-cigarettes are made and sold. Currently, they only regulate e-cigarettes that have a therapeutic benefit, but at this time no products qualify. If the FDA moves to regulate all e-cigarettes, this will likely result in there being rules on safety, advertising, and warning labels, similar to those that currently govern tobacco cigarettes and other tobacco products. For now, e-cigarettes are not guaranteed to be safe. Consumers should not assume that the health claims made in advertisements by manufactures are scientifically proven.

Can You Get Addicted to Tobacco or Nicotine Products?

Yes. It is the nicotine in tobacco that is addictive. Each cigarette contains about 10 milligrams of nicotine. A person inhales only some of the smoke from a cigarette, and not all of each puff is absorbed in the lungs. Therefore, a person gets about 1 to 2 milligrams of the drug from each cigarette.

Studies of widely used brands of smokeless tobacco showed that the amount of nicotine per gram of tobacco ranged from 4.4 milligrams to 25.0 milligrams. Holding an average-size dip in your mouth for 30 minutes gives you as much nicotine as smoking 3 cigarettes. A 2-can-a-week snuff dipper gets as much nicotine as a person who smokes 1½ packs a day.

Whether a person smokes tobacco products or uses smokeless tobacco, the amount of nicotine absorbed in the body is enough to make someone addicted. When this happens, the person compulsively seeks out the tobacco even though he or she understands the harm it causes. Nicotine addiction can cause:

- **Tolerance.** Over the course of a day, someone who uses tobacco products develops tolerance—more nicotine is required to produce the same initial effects. Some of this tolerance is lost overnight. In fact, people who smoke often report that the first cigarette of the day is the strongest or the "best."
- **Withdrawal.** When people quit using tobacco products, they usually experience withdrawal symptoms, which often drive them back to tobacco use. Nicotine withdrawal symptoms include:
    - Irritability
    - Problems with thinking and paying attention
    - Sleep problems
    - Increased appetite
    - Craving, which may last 6 months or longer, and can be a major stumbling block to quitting

Treatments can help people who use tobacco products manage these symptoms and improve the likelihood of successfully quitting.

Most people (nearly 70%) who smoke want to quit. Most who try to quit on their own relapse—often within a week. However, most former smokers have had several failed quit attempts before they succeed.

Can You Die If You Use Tobacco and Nicotine?

Yes. Tobacco use (both smoked and smokeless tobacco use) is the leading preventable cause of death in the United States. It is a known cause of human cancer. Smoking tobacco also can lead to early death from heart disease, health problems in children, and accidental fires caused by dropped cigarettes. In addition, the nicotine in smokeless tobacco may increase the risk for sudden death from a condition where the heart does not beat properly (ventricular arrhythmias); as a result, the heart pumps little or no blood to the body's organs.

According to the Centers for Disease Control and Prevention (CDC), cigarette smoking results in more than 480,000 premature deaths in the United States each year—about 1 in every 5 U.S. deaths, or 1,300 deaths every day. On average, smokers die 10 years earlier than non-smokers. People who smoke are at increased risk of death from cancer, particularly lung cancer, heart disease, lung diseases, and accidental injury from fires started by dropped cigarettes.

How Many Teens Use Tobacco and Nicotine?

Smoking and smokeless tobacco use generally start during adolescence. Among people who use tobacco:

- Each day nearly 3,000 people younger than 18 years of age smoke their first cigarette.
- Every day an estimated 2,100 youth and young adults who have been occasional smokers become daily cigarette smokers.
- If smoking continues at the current rate among youth in this country, 5.6 million of today's Americans under the age of 18—or about 1 in every 13 young people—could die prematurely (too early) from a smoking-related illness.
- Most smokeless tobacco users will also smoke cigarettes at some time in their lives.
- Using smokeless tobacco remains a mostly male behavior. About 490,000 teens ages 12 to 17 are current smokeless tobacco users. Most of them, 85% are boys. That means, for every 100 teens who use smokeless tobacco, 85 of them are boys and 15 of them are girls.

Table 24.1. Monitoring the Future Study: Trends in Prevalence of Various Drugs for 8th Graders, 10th Graders, and 12th Graders; 2015 (in percent)*

Drug	Time Period	8th Graders	10th Graders	12th Graders
Cigarettes (any use)	Lifetime	13.3	[19.90]	[31.10]
	Past Month	[3.60]	[6.30]	[11.40]
	Daily	1.3	3	[5.50]
	1/2-pack+/day	0.4	1	2.1
E-cigarettes	Past Month	9.5	14	16.2
	Lifetime	8.6	12.3	13.2
Smokeless Tobacco	Past Month	3.2	4.9	6.1
	Daily	0.8	1.6	2.9

**Data in brackets indicate statistically significant change from the previous year.*

Statistics and Trends

Tobacco use is the leading preventable cause of disease, disability, and death in the United States. According to the Centers for Disease Control and Prevention (CDC), cigarette smoking results in more than 480,000 premature deaths in the United States each year—about in every 5 U.S. deaths—and an additional 16 million people suffer with a serious illness caused by smoking. In fact, for every one person who dies from smoking, about 30 more suffer from at least one serious tobacco-related illness.

Table 24.2. Monitoring the Future Study: Trends in Prevalence of Various Drugs for 8th Graders, 10th Graders, and 12th Graders; 2015 (in percent)*

Drug	Time Period	8th Graders	10th Graders	12th Graders
Cigarettes (any use)	Lifetime	13.3	[19.90]	[31.10]
	Past Month	[3.60]	[6.30]	[11.40]
	Daily	1.3	3	[5.50]
E-cigarettes	Past Month	9.5		14
Smokeless Tobacco	Lifetime	8.6	12.3	13.2
	Past Month	3.2	4.9	6.1
	Daily	0.8	1.6	2.9

Table 24.3. National Survey on Drug Use and Health: Trends in Prevalence of Various Drugs for Ages 12 or Older, Ages 12 to 17, Ages 18 to 25, and Ages 26 or Older; 2014 (in percent)*

Drug	Time Period	Ages 12 or Older	Ages 12 to 17	Ages 18 to 25	Ages 26 or Older
Cigarettes (any use)	Lifetime	61	14.2	56.1	67.5
	Past Year	24.8	8.9	37.7	24.6
	Past Month	20.8	4.9	28.4	21.5
Smokeless Tobacco	Lifetime	17.1	5.7	19.4	18.1
	Past Year	4.4	3.8	8.8	3.7
	Past Month	3.3	2	5.6	3

**Data in brackets indicate statistically significant change from the previous year.*

Are There Effective Treatments for Tobacco Addiction?

Tobacco addiction is a chronic disease that often requires multiple attempts to quit. Although some smokers are able to quit without help, many others need assistance. Both behavioral interventions (counseling) and medication can help smokers quit; but the combination of medication with counseling is more effective than either alone.

The U.S. Department of Health and Human Services (HHS) has established a national toll-free quitline, 800-QUIT-NOW, to serve as an access point for any smoker seeking information and assistance in quitting. NIDA's scientists are looking at ways to make smoking cessation easier by developing tools to make behavioral support available over the internet or through text-based messaging. In addition, NIDA is developing strategies designed to help vulnerable or hard-to-reach populations quit smoking.

Behavioral Treatments

Behavioral treatments employ a variety of methods to help smokers quit, ranging from self-help materials to counseling. These interventions teach people to recognize high-risk situations and develop coping strategies to deal with them.

Nicotine Replacement Treatments

Nicotine replacement therapies (NRTs) were the first pharmacological treatments approved by the U.S. Food and Drug Administration

(FDA) for use in smoking cessation therapy. Current FDA-approved NRT products include nicotine chewing gum, the nicotine transdermal patch, nasal sprays, inhalers, and lozenges. NRTs deliver a controlled dose of nicotine to a smoker in order to relieve withdrawal symptoms during the smoking cessation process. They are most successful when used in combination with behavioral treatments.

Other Medications

Bupropion and varenicline are two FDA-approved non-nicotine medications that have helped people quit smoking. Bupropion, a medication that goes by the trade name Zyban, was approved by the FDA in 1997, and Varenicline tartrate (trade name: Chantix) was approved in 2006. It targets nicotine receptors in the brain, easing withdrawal symptoms and blocking the effects of nicotine if people resume smoking.

Current Treatment Research

Scientists are currently developing new smoking cessation therapies. For example, they are working on a nicotine vaccine, which would block nicotine's reinforcing effects by causing the immune system to bind to nicotine in the bloodstream preventing it from reaching the brain. In addition, some medications already in use might work better if they are used together. Scientists are looking for ways to target several relapse symptoms at the same time—like withdrawal, craving and depression.

How Widespread Is Tobacco Use?

Monitoring the Future Survey

Current smoking rates among 8th-, 10th-, and 12th-grade students reached an all-time low in 2014. According to the Monitoring the Future survey, 4.0 percent of 8th-graders, 7.2 percent of 10th graders, and 13.6 percent of 12th-graders reported they had used cigarettes in the past month. Although unacceptably high numbers of youth continue to smoke, these numbers represent a significant decrease from peak smoking rates (21 percent in 8th-graders, 30 percent in 10th-graders, and 37 percent in 12th-graders) that were reached in the late 1990s.

The use of hookahs has also remained steady at high levels since its inclusion in the survey in 2010–past year use was reported by 22.9 percent of high school seniors. Meanwhile, past year use of small cigars has declined since 2010 yet remains high with 18.9 percent of 12th graders reporting past year use. Past-month use of smokeless tobacco in 2014 was reported by 3.0 percent of 8th graders, 5.3 percent of 10th graders, and 8.4 percent of 12th graders.

National Survey on Drug Use and Health (NSDUH)

In 2013, 25.5 percent of the U.S. population age 12 and older used a tobacco product at least once in the month prior to being interviewed. This figure includes 2 million young people aged 12 to 17 (7.8 percent of this age group). In addition, almost 55.8 million Americans (21.3 percent of the population) were current cigarette smokers; 12.4 million smoked cigars; more than 8.8 million used smokeless tobacco; and over 2.3 million smoked tobacco in pipes.

Chapter 25

New and Emerging Drugs of Abuse

Chapter Contents

Section 25.1

Introduction to Synthetic Drugs

This section contains text excerpted from the following sources: Text beginning with the heading "What Are Synthetic Cannabinoids?" is excerpted from "DrugFacts: Synthetic Cannabinoids," National Institute on Drug Abuse (NIDA), November 2015; Text beginning with the heading "Synthetic Drugs (a.k.a. K2, Spice, Bath Salts, Etc.)" is excerpted from "Office of National Drug Control Policy," WhiteHouse.gov, April 12, 2013.

What Are Synthetic Cannabinoids?

Synthetic cannabinoids refer to a growing number of man-made mind-altering chemicals that are either sprayed on dried, shredded plant material so they can be smoked (herbal incense) or sold as liquids to be vaporized and inhaled in e-cigarettes and other devices (liquid incense).

These chemicals are called cannabinoids because they are related to chemicals found in the marijuana plant. Because of this similarity, synthetic cannabinoids are sometimes misleadingly called "synthetic marijuana" (or "fake weed"), and they are often marketed as "safe," legal alternatives to that drug. In fact, they may affect the brain much more powerfully than marijuana; their actual effects can be unpredictable and, in some cases, severe or even life-threatening.

Synthetic cannabinoids are included in a group of drugs called "new psychoactive substances" (NPS). NPS are unregulated psychoactive (mind-altering) substances that have become newly available on the market and are intended to copy the effects of illegal drugs. Some of these substances may have been around for years but have reentered the market in altered chemical forms or due to renewed popularity.

Manufacturers sell these herbal incense products in colorful foil packages and sell similar liquid incense products, like other e-cigarette fluids, in plastic bottles. They market these products under a wide variety of specific brand names; in past years, K2 and Spice were common. Hundreds of other brand names now exist, such as Joker, Black Mamba, Kush, and Kronic.

For several years, synthetic cannabinoid mixtures have been easy to buy in drug paraphernalia shops, novelty stores, gas stations, and through the Internet. Because the chemicals used in them have a high potential for abuse and no medical benefit, authorities have made it illegal to sell, buy, or possess some of these chemicals. However, manufacturers try to sidestep these laws by changing the chemical formulas in their mixtures.

Easy access and the belief that synthetic cannabinoid products are "natural" and therefore harmless have likely contributed to their use among young people. Another reason for their use is that standard drug tests cannot easily detect many of the chemicals used in these products.

How Do People Use Synthetic Cannabinoids?

Users usually smoke the dried plant material sprayed with synthetic cannabinoids. Sometimes they mix the sprayed plant material with marijuana, or they brew it as tea. Other users buy synthetic cannabinoid products as liquids to vaporize them in e-cigarettes.

How Do Synthetic Cannabinoids Affect the Brain?

Synthetic cannabinoids act on the same brain cell receptors as delta-9-tetrahydrocannabinol (THC), the mind-altering ingredient in marijuana.

So far, there have been few scientific studies of the effects of synthetic cannabinoids on the human brain, but researchers do know that some of them bind more strongly than marijuana to the cell receptors affected by THC, and may produce much stronger effects. The resulting health effects can be unpredictable.

Because the chemical composition of many synthetic cannabinoid products is unknown and may change from batch to batch, these products are likely to contain substances that cause dramatically different effects than the user might expect.

Synthetic cannabinoid users report some effects similar to those produced by marijuana:

- elevated mood
- relaxation
- altered perception—awareness of surrounding objects and conditions

- symptoms of psychosis—delusional or disordered thinking detached from reality

Psychotic effects include:

- extreme anxiety
- confusion
- paranoia—extreme and unreasonable distrust of others
- hallucinations—sensations and images that seem real though they are not

What Are Some Other Health Effects of Synthetic Cannabinoids?

People who have used synthetic cannabinoids and have been taken to emergency rooms have shown severe effects including:

- rapid heart rate
- vomiting
- violent behavior
- suicidal thoughts

Synthetic cannabinoids can also raise blood pressure and cause reduced blood supply to the heart, as well as kidney damage and seizures. Use of these drugs is associated with a rising number of deaths.

Are Synthetic Cannabinoids Addictive?

Yes, synthetic cannabinoids can be addictive. Regular users trying to quit may have the following withdrawal symptoms:

- headaches
- anxiety
- depression
- irritability

Behavioral therapies and medications have not specifically been tested for treatment of addiction to these products.

Synthetic Drugs (a.k.a. K2, Spice, Bath Salts, Etc.)

Overview and History

- Synthetic cannabinoids, commonly known as "synthetic marijuana," "K2," or "Spice", are often sold in legal retail outlets as "herbal incense" or "potpourri", and synthetic cathinones are often sold as "bath salts" or "jewelry cleaner". They are labeled "not for human consumption" to mask their intended purpose and avoid U.S. Food and Drug Administration (FDA) regulatory oversight of the manufacturing process.
- Synthetic cannabinoids are man-made chemicals that are applied (often sprayed) onto plant material and marketed as a "legal" high. Users claim that synthetic cannabinoids mimic Δ9-tetrahydrocannabinol (THC), the primary psychoactive active ingredient in marijuana.
- Use of synthetic cannabinoids is alarmingly high, especially among young people. According to the 2012 Monitoring the Future survey of youth drug-use trends, one in nine 12th graders in America reported using synthetic cannabinoids in the past year. This rate, unchanged from 2011, puts synthetic cannabinoids as the second most frequently used illegal drug among high school seniors after marijuana.
- Synthetic cathinones are man-made chemicals related to amphetamines. Synthetic cathinone products often consist of methylenedioxypyrovalerone (MDPV), mephedrone, and methylone.
- The Administration has been working with Federal, Congressional, state, local, and non-governmental partners to put policies and legislation in place to combat this threat, and to educate people about the tremendous health risk posed by these substances.

A Rapidly Emerging Threat

- Synthetic cannabinoids laced on plant material were first reported in the U.S. in December 2008, when a shipment of "Spice" was seized and analyzed by U.S. Customs and Border Protection (CBP) in Dayton, Ohio.
- There is an increasingly expanding array of synthetic drugs available. 51 new synthetic cannabinoids were identified in

2012, compared to just two in 2009. Furthermore, 31 new synthetic cathinones were identified in 2012, compared to only four in 2009. In addition, 76 other synthetic compounds were identified in 2012, bringing the total number of new synthetic substances identified in 2012 to 158.

Risk to the Public Health

- The contents and effects of synthetic cannabinoids and cathinones are unpredictable due to a constantly changing variety of chemicals used in manufacturing processes devoid of quality controls and government regulatory oversight. Health warnings have been issued by numerous public health authorities and poison control centers describing the adverse health effects associated with the use of synthetic drugs.
- The effects of synthetic cannabinoids include severe agitation and anxiety, nausea, vomiting, tachycardia (fast, racing heartbeat), elevated blood pressure, tremors and seizures, hallucinations, dilated pupils, and suicidal and other harmful thoughts and/or actions.
- Similar to the adverse effects of cocaine, LSD, and methamphetamine, synthetic cathinone use is associated with increased heart rate and blood pressure, chest pain, extreme paranoia, hallucinations, delusions, and violent behavior, which causes users to harm themselves or others.

Section 25.2

Bath Salts

This section contains text excerpted from the following sources: Text beginning with the heading "What Are Bath Salts?" is excerpted from "Bath Salts," National Institute on Drug Abuse (NIDA), March 10, 2016; Text beginning with the heading "Which Drugs Cause Similar Effects?" is excerpted from "Drugs of Abuse," U.S. Drug Enforcement Administration (DEA), 2015.

What Are Bath Salts?

Also known as: "Bloom," "Cloud Nine," "Vanilla Sky," "White Lightning," and "Scarface"

"Bath salts" is the name given to a family of drugs that have one or more manmade chemicals related to cathinone. Cathinone is an amphetamine-like stimulant found naturally in the khat plant. Chemically, they are similar to other amphetamines such as methamphetamine and to **MDMA** (Ecstasy or Molly). Common manmade cathinones found in bath salts include 3,4-methylenedioxypyrovalerone (MDPV), mephedrone ("Drone," "Meph," or "Meow Meow"), and methylone, but there are many others.

Bath salts are usually white or brown crystal-like powder and are sold in small plastic or foil packages labeled "Not for Human Consumption." Sometimes labeled as "plant food"—or, more recently, as "jewelry cleaner" or "phone screen cleaner"—they are sold online and in drug product stores. These names or descriptions have nothing to do with the product. It's a way for the drug makers to avoid detection by the Drug Enforcement Administration or local police.

The man made cathinone products sold as "bath salts" should not be confused with Epsom salts (the original bath salts), which are made of a mineral mixture of magnesium and sulfate and are added to bathwater to help ease stress and relax muscles.

Use of bath salts sometimes causes severe intoxication (a person seems very drunk or "out of it") and dangerous health effects. There are also reports of people becoming psychotic (losing touch with reality) and violent. Although it is rare, there have been several cases where bath salts have been the direct cause of death.

In addition, people who believe they are taking drugs such as MDMA (Molly or Ecstasy) may be getting bath salts instead. Methylone, a common chemical in bath salts, has been substituted for MDMA in capsules sold as Molly in some areas.

Banning Bath Salts

At the end of the last decade, bath salts began to be gain in popularity in the United States and Europe as "legal highs." In October 2011, the Drug Enforcement Administration put an emergency ban on three common manmade cathinones until officials knew more about them. In July 2012, President Barack Obama signed legislation permanently making two of them—mephedrone and MDPV—illegal, along with several other manmade drugs often sold as marijuana substitutes (like Spice).

Although the law also bans chemically similar "analogues" of the named drugs, manufacturers have responded by making new drugs different enough from the banned substances to get around the law.

How Are Bath Salts Used?

Bath salts can be swallowed, snorted through the nose, inhaled, or injected with a needle. Snorting or injecting is the most harmful.

How Do Bath Salts Affect the Brain?

The man made cathinones in bath salts can produce feelings of joy and increased social interaction and sex drive. These chemicals can also cause people to feel paranoid and nervous and to have hallucinations (see or hear things that are not real). There is a lot we still don't know about how the different chemicals in bath salts affect the brain.

The energizing and often agitating effects reported in people who have taken bath salts are similar to the effects of other drugs like amphetamines and cocaine. These drugs raise the level of dopamine in brain paths that control reward and movement. Dopamine is the main neurotransmitter (a substance that passes messages between nerve cells) that makes people feel good when they do something they enjoy. A rush of dopamine causes feelings of joy and increased activity and can also raise heart rate and blood pressure.

A study in animals found that MDPV raises brain dopamine in the same way as cocaine but is at least 10 times stronger. If this is also true in people, it may account for the reason that MDPV is the most common manmade cathinone found in the blood and urine of patients admitted to emergency rooms after taking bath salts.

Additionally, the hallucinations often reported by users of bath salts are similar to the effects caused by other drugs such as MDMA or LSD. These drugs raise levels of the neurotransmitter serotonin.

What Are the Other Effects of Bath Salts?

In 2011, bath salts were reported in nearly 23,000 emergency room visits. Reports show bath salts users have needed help for heart problems (such as racing heart, high blood pressure, and chest pains) and symptoms like paranoia, hallucinations, and panic attacks.

Patients with the syndrome known as "excited delirium" from taking bath salts also may have dehydration, breakdown of muscle tissue attached to bones, and kidney failure. Intoxication from several manmade cathinones including MDPV, mephedrone, methedrone, and butylone has caused death among some users.

Another danger of bath salts is that these products may contain other ingredients that may cause their own harmful effects. There is no way to know what is in a dose of bath salts other than testing it in a lab.

Can You Get Addicted to Bath Salts?

Yes. Research shows and bath salts users have reported that the drugs cause an intense urge to use the drug again and that they are highly addictive. Frequent use may cause tolerance (a person needs to take more to feel the same effects), dependence, and strong withdrawal symptoms when not taking the drug.

Can You Die If You Use Bath Salts?

Yes. Intoxication from several manmade cathinones, including MDPV, mephedrone, methedrone, and butylone, has caused death among some users.

How Many Teens Use Bath Salts?

Bath salts have been involved in thousands of visits to the emergency room. In 2011 alone, there were 22,904 reports of bath salts use during emergency room visits. About two thirds of those visits involved bath salts in combination with other drugs.

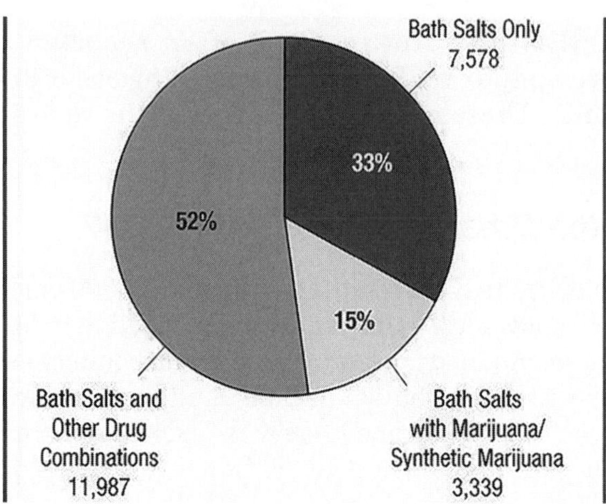

Figure 25.1. *Emergency Department Visits Involving Bath Salts*

Table 25.1. Monitoring the Future Study: Trends in Prevalence of Bath Salts for 8th Graders, 10th Graders, and 12th Graders; 2015 (in percent)

Drug	Time Period	8th Graders	10th Graders	12th Graders
Bath Salts	Past Year	0.4	0.7	1

What Is Their Effect on the Body?

Adverse or toxic effects associated with the abuse of cathinones, including synthetic cathinones, include rapid heartbeat; hypertension; hyperthermia; prolonged dilation of the pupil of the eye; breakdown of muscle fibers that leads to release of muscle fiber contents into bloodstream; teeth grinding; sweating; headaches; palpitations; seizures; as well as paranoia, hallucinations, and delusions.

What Are Their Overdose Effects?

In addition to effects above, reports of death from individuals abusing drugs in this class indicate the seriousness of the risk users are taking when ingesting these products.

Which Drugs Cause Similar Effects?

They cause effects similar to those of other stimulants such as methamphetamine, MDMA, and cocaine.

What Is Their Legal Status in the United States?

In July 2012, the U.S. Government passed Pub.L. 112- 144, the Synthetic Drug Abuse Prevention Act (SDAPA), that classified a number of synthetic substances under Schedule I of the Controlled Substances Act. SDAPA placed these substances in the most restrictive category of controlled substances. Cannabimimetic agents, including fifteen (15) synthetic cannabinoid compounds identified by name, two (2) synthetic cathinone compounds (mephedrone and MDPV), and nine (9) synthetic hallucinogens known as the 2C family, are now restricted by this law. In addition, methylone was permanently controlled by DEA through administrative process, and another ten (10) synthetic cathinones became subject to temporary control. Synthetic cathinones may be subject to prosecution under the Controlled Substance Analogue Enforcement Act which allows these dangerous substances to be treated as Schedule I controlled substances if certain criteria can be met.

Section 25.3

Spice/K2

This section contains text excerpted from the following sources: Text beginning with the heading "What Is Spice?" is excerpted from "Spice," National Institute on Drug Abuse (NIDA), March 10, 2016; Text beginning with the heading "What Are Its Overdose Effects?" is excerpted from "Drugs of Abuse," U.S. Drug Enforcement Administration (DEA), 2015.

What Is Spice?

Also known as: "K2," "fake weed," "Bliss," "Black Mamba," "Bombay Blue," "Genie," "Zohai," "Yucatan Fire," "Skunk," and "Moon Rocks"

Spice is a mix of herbs (shredded plant material) and man-made chemicals with mind-altering effects. It is often called "synthetic marijuana" or "fake weed" because some of the chemicals in it are similar to ones in marijuana; but its effects are sometimes very different from marijuana, and frequently much stronger.

Because the chemicals used in Spice have a high potential for abuse and no medical benefit, the Drug Enforcement Administration has made many of the active chemicals most frequently found in Spice illegal. However, the people who make these products try to avoid these laws by using different chemicals in their mixtures.

Spice is most often labeled "Not for Human Consumption" and disguised as incense. Sellers of the drug try to lead people to believe they are "natural" and therefore harmless, but they are neither. In fact, their actual effects can be unpredictable and, in some cases, severe or cause death.

How Is Spice Used?

Most people smoke Spice by rolling it in papers (like with marijuana or handmade tobacco cigarettes); sometimes, it is mixed with marijuana. Some users also make it as an herbal tea for drinking. Others buy Spice products as liquids to vaporize them in e-cigarettes.

How Does Spice Affect the Brain?

Some Spice users report feeling relaxed and having mild changes in perception. Users also report extreme anxiety, feeling like someone is out to get them (paranoia), and seeing or hearing things that aren't there (hallucinations).

Spice is a new drug and research is only just beginning to measure how it affects the brain. What is known is that the chemicals found in Spice attach to the same nerve cell receptors as THC, the main mind-altering ingredient in marijuana. Some of the chemicals in Spice, however, attach to those receptors more strongly than THC, which could lead to a much stronger and more unpredictable effect. Additionally, there are many chemicals that remain unidentified in products sold as Spice and it is therefore not clear how they may affect the user. Moreover, these chemicals are often being changed as the makers of Spice alter them to avoid the products being illegal.

What Are the Other Effects of Spice?

In 2011, Spice was mentioned by patients in the emergency room 28,531 times. This is a drastic increase over the 11,406 mentions in 2010. People who have had bad reactions to Spice report symptoms like:

- fast heart rate

- throwing up
- feeling anxious or nervous
- feeling confused
- violent behavior
- suicidal thoughts

Spice can also raise blood pressure and cause less blood to flow to the heart. In a few cases, it has been linked with heart attacks and death. People who use Spice a lot may have withdrawal and addiction symptoms.

We still do not know all the ways Spice may affect a person's health or how toxic it may be, but it is possible that there may be harmful heavy metal residues in Spice mixtures.

Can You Get Addicted to Spice?

Yes, Spice can be addictive. People who use Spice a lot may have withdrawal symptoms if they try to quit. This means they can't stop using it even when they really want to and even after it causes terrible consequences to their health and other parts of their lives. Withdrawal symptoms can include:

- headaches
- anxiety
- depression
- irritability

Can You Die If You Use Spice?

Yes. Spice use has been linked to a rising number of emergency department visits and to some deaths.

How Many Teens Use Spice?

Spice is the second-most popular illegal drug used by high school seniors (marijuana is the first). Easy access and the misperception that Spice is "natural" and safe have likely contributed to these high rates of use.

Table 25.2. Monitoring the Future Study: Trends in Prevalence of K2/ Spice (Synthetic Marijuana) for 8th Graders, 10th Graders, and 12th Graders; 2015 (in percent)

Drug	Time Period	8th Graders	10th Graders	12th Graders
K2/Spice (Synthetic Marijuana)	Past Year	3.1	4.3	5.2

What Are Its Overdose Effects?

Overdose deaths have been attributed to the abuse of synthetic cannabinoids, including death by heart attack. Acute kidney injury requiring hospitalization and dialysis in several patients reportedly having smoked synthetic cannabinoids has also been reported by the Center for Disease Control.

What Is Its Effect on the Body?

State public health and poison centers have issued warnings in response to adverse health effects associated with abuse of herbal incense products containing these synthetic cannabinoids. These adverse effects included tachycardia (elevated heart rate), elevated blood pressure, unconsciousness, tremors, seizures, vomiting, hallucinations, agitation, anxiety, pallor, numbness and tingling. This is in addition to the numerous public health and poison centers which have similarly issued warnings regarding the abuse of these synthetic cannabinoids.

What Is Its Legal Status in the United States?

These substances have no accepted medical use in the United States and have been reported to produce adverse health effects. Currently, 22 synthetic cannabinoids have been controlled either through legislation or regulatory action, Federally. Unfortunately DEA has identified over 75 additional synthetic cannabinoids that are not controlled but are currently appearing in the domestic marketplace, encountered by foreign agencies, or discussed on the Internet. The ease with which foreign entities can quickly develop and manufacture designer drugs on a large-scale in laboratories located outside of the United States creates challenges for the administrative scheduling option.

There are many synthetic cannabinoid substances that are being sold as “incense,” “potpourri” and other products that are not controlled substances. However, synthetic cannabinoids may be subject to prosecution under the Controlled Substance Analogue Enforcement Act which allows non-controlled drugs to be treated as Schedule I controlled substances if certain criteria can be met. The DEA has successfully investigated and prosecuted individuals trafficking and selling these dangerous substances using the Controlled Substance Analogue Enforcement Act.

Section 25.4

Flakka, Krokodil, N-Bomb, and Purple Drank

This section includes text excerpted from "Emergency Trends," National Institute on Drug Abuse (NIDA), December 2015.

"Flakka" (Alpha-PVP)"

Use of a dangerous synthetic cathinone drug called alpha-pyrrolidinopentiophenone (alpha-PDP), popularly known as "Flakka," is surging in Florida and is also being reported in other parts of the country, according to news reports.

Alpha-PVP is chemically similar to other synthetic cathinone drugs popularly called "bath salts," and takes the form of a white or pink, foul-smelling crystal that can be eaten, snorted, injected, or vaporized in an e-cigarette or similar device. Vaporizing, which sends the drug very quickly into the bloodstream, may make it particularly easy to overdose. Like other drugs of this type, alpha-PVP can cause a condition called "excited delirium" that involves hyperstimulation, paranoia, and hallucinations that can lead to violent aggression and self-injury. The drug has been linked to deaths by suicide as well as heart attack. It can also dangerously raise body temperature and lead to kidney damage or kidney failure.

"Krokodil"

"Krokodil," a toxic homemade opioid that has been used as a cheap heroin substitute in poor rural areas of Russia, has recently been featured in news reports alleging its appearance in parts of the United States. The CEWG is investigating, although the DEA has not yet confirmed any krokodil in this country.

Krokodil is a synthetic form of a heroin-like drug called desomorphine that is made by combining codeine tablets with various toxic chemicals including lighter fluid and industrial cleaners. Desomorphine has a similar effect to heroin in the brain, although it is more powerful and has a shorter duration. Krokodil gets its name from the scaly, gray-green dead skin that forms at the site of an injection. The flesh destroyed by krokodil becomes gangrenous, and, in some cases, limb amputation has been necessary to save a user's life.

"N-Bomb"

"N-bomb" refers to any of three closely related synthetic hallucinogens (25I-NBOMe, 25C-NBOMe, and 25B-NBOMe) that are being sold as legal substitutes for LSD or mescaline. Also called "legal acid," "smiles," or "25I," they are generally found as powders, liquids, soaked into blotter paper (like LSD) or laced on something edible.

These chemicals act on serotonin receptors in the brain, like other hallucinogens, but they are considerably more powerful even than LSD. Extremely small amounts can cause seizures, heart attack or arrested breathing, and death. At least 19 young people are reported to have died after taking 25I- 25C- or 25B-NBOMe between March 2012 and August 2013. People may ingest one of these drugs unknowingly, believing it to be LSD; a young man in one medical case report published in late 2014 experienced severe hallucinations and panic and attempted suicide after such an ingestion.

"Syrup," "Purple Drank," "Sizzurp," "Lean"

Drinking prescription-strength cough syrup containing codeine and promethazine mixed with soda was referenced frequently in some popular music beginning in the late 90s and has now become increasingly popular among youth in several areas of the country, according to recent CEWG data. Codeine is an opioid that can produce relaxation and euphoria when consumed in sufficient quantities. Promethazine is an antihistamine that also acts as a sedative. Users may also flavor the mixture with the addition of hard candies.

Codeine and other opioids present a high risk of fatal overdose due to their effect of depressing the central nervous system, which can slow or stop the heart and lungs. Mixing with alcohol greatly increases this risk. Deaths from prescription opioid medications now outnumber overdose deaths from all other drugs (including cocaine and heroin), and codeine-promethazine cough syrup has been linked to the overdose deaths of some prominent musicians.

Part Four

The Causes and Consequences of Drug Abuse and Addiction

Chapter 26

Understanding Drug Abuse and Addiction

Chapter Contents

Section 26.1

Drug Addiction Is a Chronic Disease

This section includes text excerpted from "Drugs, Brains, and Behavior: The Science of Addiction," National Institute on Drug Abuse (NIDA), July 2014.

Drug Abuse and Addiction

What Is Drug Addiction?

Addiction is defined as a chronic, relapsing brain disease that is characterized by compulsive drug seeking and use, despite harmful consequences. It is considered a brain disease because drugs change the brain—they change its structure and how it works. These brain changes can be long-lasting, and can lead to the harmful behaviors seen in people who abuse drugs.

Why Do People Take Drugs?

In general, people begin taking drugs for a variety of reasons:

- **To feel good**. Most abused drugs produce intense feelings of pleasure. This initial sensation of euphoria is followed by other effects, which differ with the type of drug used. For example, with stimulants such as cocaine, the "high" is followed by feelings of power, self-confidence, and increased energy. In contrast, the euphoria caused by opiates such as heroin is followed by feelings of relaxation and satisfaction.
- **To feel better**. Some people who suffer from social anxiety, stress-related disorders, and depression begin abusing drugs in an attempt to lessen feelings of distress. Stress can play a major role in beginning drug use, continuing drug abuse, or relapse in patients recovering from addiction.
- **To do better**. Some people feel pressure to chemically enhance or improve their cognitive or athletic performance, which can play a role in initial experimentation and continued abuse of

drugs such as prescription stimulants or anabolic/androgenic steroids.

- **Curiosity and "because others are doing it."** In this respect adolescents are particularly vulnerable because of the strong influence of peer pressure. Teens are more likely than adults to engage in risky or daring behaviors to impress their friends and express their independence from parental and social rules.

If Taking Drugs Makes People Feel Good or Better, What's the Problem?

When they first use a drug, people may perceive what seem to be positive effects; they also may believe that they can control their use. However, drugs can quickly take over a person's life. Over time, if drug use continues, other pleasurable activities become less pleasurable, and taking the drug becomes necessary for the user just to feel "normal." They may then compulsively seek and take drugs even though it causes tremendous problems for themselves and their loved ones. Some people may start to feel the need to take higher or more frequent doses, even in the early stages of their drug use. These are the telltale signs of an addiction.

Even relatively moderate drug use poses dangers. Consider how a social drinker can become intoxicated, get behind the wheel of a car, and quickly turn a pleasurable activity into a tragedy that affects many lives.

Is Continued Drug Abuse a Voluntary Behavior?

The initial decision to take drugs is typically voluntary. However, with continued use, a person's ability to exert self-control can become seriously impaired; this impairment in self-control is the hallmark of addiction. Brain imaging studies of people with addiction show physical changes in areas of the brain that are critical to judgment, decision making, learning and memory, and behavior control. Scientists believe that these changes alter the way the brain works and may help explain the compulsive and destructive behaviors of addiction.

Why Do Some People Become Addicted to Drugs, While Others Do Not?

As with any other disease, vulnerability to addiction differs from person to person, and no single factor determines whether a person will become addicted to drugs. In general, the more risk factors a person has, the greater the chance that taking drugs will lead to abuse and addiction. *Protective factors*, on the other hand, reduce a person's risk of developing addiction. Risk and protective factors may be either environmental (such as conditions at home, at school, and in the neighborhood) or biological (for instance, a person's genes, their stage of development, and even their gender or ethnicity).

Table 26.1. Risk and Protective Factors for Drug Abuse and Addiction

Risk Factors	Protective Factors
Aggressive behavior in childhood	Good self-control
Lack of parental supervision	Parental monitoring and support
Poor social skills	Positive relationships
Drug experimentation	Academic Competence
Availability of drugs at school	School anti-drug policies
Community poverty	Neighborhood pride

What Environmental Factors Increase the Risk of Addiction?

- **Home and Family**. The influence of the home environment, especially during childhood, is a very important factor. Parents or older family members who abuse alcohol or drugs, or who engage in criminal behavior, can increase children's risks of developing their own drug problems.
- **Peer and School**. Friends and acquaintances can have an increasingly strong influence during adolescence. Drug-using peers can sway even those without risk factors to try drugs for the first time. Academic failure or poor social skills can put a child at further risk for using or becoming addicted to drugs.

What Biological Factors Increase Risk of Addiction?

Scientists estimate that genetic factors account for between 40 and 60 percent of a person's vulnerability to addiction; this includes the effects of environmental factors on the function and expression of a person's genes. A person's stage of development and other medical conditions they may have are also factors. Adolescents and people with mental disorders are at greater risk of drug abuse and addiction than the general population.

What Other Factors Increase the Risk of Addiction?

- **Early Use**. Although taking drugs at any age can lead to addiction, research shows that the earlier a person begins to use drugs, the more likely he or she is to develop serious problems. This may reflect the harmful effect that drugs can have on the developing brain; it also may result from a mix of early social and biological vulnerability factors, including unstable family relationships, exposure to physical or sexual abuse, genetic susceptibility, or mental illness. Still, the fact remains that early use is a strong indicator of problems ahead, including addiction.
- **Method of Administration**. Smoking a drug or injecting it into a vein increases its addictive potential. Both smoked and injected drugs enter the brain within seconds, producing a powerful rush of pleasure. However, this intense "high" can fade within a few minutes, taking the abuser down to lower, more normal levels. Scientists believe this starkly felt contrast drives some people to repeated drug taking in an attempt to recapture the fleeting pleasurable state.

Section 26.2

Common Risk and Protective Factors for Drug Use

This section contains text excerpted from the following sources: Text in this section begins with excerpts from "Risk and Protective Factors and Initiation of Substance Use," Substance Abuse and Mental Health Services Administration (SAMHSA), October 2015; Text beginning with the heading "Risk and Protective Factors" is excerpted from "Risk and Protective Factors," Substance Abuse and Mental Health Services Administration (SAMHSA), October 2, 2015.

Substance use and abuse are major public health problems in the United States. Nevertheless, many individuals do not engage in substance use. Whether someone engages in substance use depends on the number and types of risk factors that are typically associated with an increased likelihood of substance use (e.g., perception of low risk of harm from using a substance, easy availability of substances) and protective factors that are typically associated with a decreased likelihood of substance use (e.g., exposure to prevention messages). Risk and protective factors include variables that reflect different domains of influence, including the individual, family, peer, school, community, and society.

Risk and Protective Factors

Many factors influence a person's chance of developing a mental and/or substance use disorder. Effective prevention focuses on reducing those risk factors, and strengthening protective factors, that are most closely related to the problem being addressed. Applying the Strategic Prevention Framework (SPF) helps prevention professionals identify factors having the greatest impact on their target population.

Risk factors are characteristics at the biological, psychological, family, community, or cultural level that precede and are associated with a higher likelihood of negative outcomes.

Protective factors are characteristics associated with a lower likelihood of negative outcomes or that reduce a risk factor's impact. Protective factors may be seen as positive countering events.

Some risk and protective factors are fixed: they don't change over time. Other risk and protective factors are considered variable and can change over time.

Variable risk factors include income level, peer group, adverse childhood experiences (ACEs), and employment status.

Individual-level risk factors may include a person's genetic predisposition to addiction or exposure to alcohol prenatally.

Individual-level protective factors might include positive self-image, self-control, or social competence.

Key Features of Risk and Protective Factors

Prevention professionals should consider these key features of risk and protective factors when designing and evaluating prevention interventions. Then, prioritize the risk and protective factors that most impact your community.

Risk and Protective Factors Exist in Multiple Contexts

All people have biological and psychological characteristics that make them vulnerable to, or resilient in the face of, potential behavioral health issues. Because people have relationships within their communities and larger society, each person's biological and psychological characteristics exist in multiple contexts. A variety of risk and protective factors operate within each of these contexts. These factors also influence one another.

Targeting only one context when addressing a person's risk or protective factors is unlikely to be successful, because people don't exist in isolation. For example:

- **In relationships**, risk factors include parents who use drugs and alcohol or who suffer from mental illness, child abuse and maltreatment, and inadequate supervision. In this context, parental involvement is an example of a protective factor.
- **In communities,** risk factors include neighborhood poverty and violence. Here, protective factors could include the availability of faith-based resources and after-school activities.
- **In society**, risk factors can include norms and laws favorable to substance use, as well as racism and a lack of economic opportunity. Protective factors in this context would include hate crime laws or policies limiting the availability of alcohol.

Risk and Protective Factors Are Correlated and Cumulative

Risk factors tend to be positively correlated with one another and negatively correlated to protective factors. In other words, people with some risk factors have a greater chance of experiencing even more risk factors, and they are less likely to have protective factors.

Risk and protective factors also tend to have a cumulative effect on the development—or reduced development—of behavioral health issues. Young people with multiple risk factors have a greater likelihood of developing a condition that impacts their physical or mental health; young people with multiple protective factors are at a reduced risk.

These correlations underscore the importance of:

- Early intervention
- Interventions that target multiple, not single, factors

Individual Factors Can Be Associated with Multiple Outcomes

- Though preventive interventions are often designed to produce a single outcome, both risk and protective factors can be associated with multiple outcomes. For example, negative life events are associated with substance use as well as anxiety, depression, and other behavioral health issues. Prevention efforts targeting a set of risk or protective factors have the potential to produce positive effects in multiple areas.

Risk and Protective Factors Are Influential over Time

Risk and protective factors can have influence throughout a person's entire lifespan. For example, risk factors such as poverty and family dysfunction can contribute to the development of mental and/or substance use disorders later in life. Risk and protective factors within one particular context—such as the family—may also influence or be influenced by factors in another context. Effective parenting has been shown to mediate the effects of multiple risk factors, including poverty, divorce, parental bereavement, and parental mental illness.

The more we understand how risk and protective factors interact, the better prepared we will be to develop appropriate interventions.

Universal, Selective, and Indicated Prevention Interventions

Not all people or populations are at the same risk of developing behavioral health problems. Prevention interventions are most effective when they are matched to their target population's level of risk. Prevention interventions fall into three broad categories:

- **Universal preventive interventions** take the broadest approach and are designed to reach entire groups or populations. Universal prevention interventions might target schools, whole communities, or workplaces.
- **Selective interventions** target biological, psychological, or social risk factors that are more prominent among high-risk groups than among the wider population. Examples include prevention education for immigrant families with young children or peer support groups for adults with a family history of substance use disorders.
- **Indicated preventive interventions** target individuals who show signs of being at risk for a substance use disorder. These

types of interventions include referral to support services for young adults who violate drug policies or screening and consultation for families of older adults admitted to hospitals with potential alcohol-related injuries.

Section 26.3

How Drugs Affect the Brain

This section includes text excerpted from "Brain and Addiction," National Institute on Drug Abuse (NIDA), March 7, 2016.

Your Brain

Your brain is who you are. It's what allows you to think, breathe, move, speak, and feel. It's just 3 pounds of gray-and-white matter that rests in your skull, and it is your own personal "mission control." Information from your environment—both outside (like what your eyes see and skin feels) and inside (like your heart rate and body temperature)—makes its way to the brain, which receives, processes, and integrates it so that you can survive and function under all sorts of changing circumstances and learn from experience. The brain is always working, even when you are sleeping.

The brain is made up of many parts that all work together as a team. Each of these different parts has a specific and important job to do.

When drugs enter the brain, they interfere with its normal processing and can eventually lead to changes in how well it works. Over time, drug use can lead to addiction, a devastating brain disease in which people can't stop using drugs even when they really want to and even after it causes terrible consequences to their health and other parts of their lives.

Drugs affect three primary areas of the brain:

- **The brain stem** is in charge of all the functions our body needs to stay alive—breathing, moving blood, and digesting food. It also links the brain with the spinal cord, which runs down the back and moves muscles and limbs as well as lets the brain know what's happening to the body.

- **The limbic system** links together a bunch of brain structures that control our emotional responses, such as feeling pleasure when we eat chocolate. The good feelings motivate us to repeat the behavior, which is good because eating is critical to our lives.
- **The cerebral cortex** is the mushroom-shaped outer part of the brain (the gray matter). In humans, it is so big that it makes up about three-fourths of the entire brain. It's divided into four areas, called lobes, which control specific functions. Some areas process information from our senses, allowing us to see, feel, hear, and taste. The front part of the cortex, known as the frontal cortex or forebrain, is the thinking center. It powers our ability to think, plan, solve problems, and make decisions.

How Does Your Brain Communicate?

The brain is a complex communications network of billions of neurons, or nerve cells. Networks of neurons pass messages back and forth thousands of times a minute within the brain, spinal column, and nerves. These nerve networks control everything we feel, think, and do. Understanding these networks helps in understanding how drugs affect the brain. The networks are made up of:

- **Neurons**

Your brain contains about 100 billion neurons—nerve cells that work nonstop to send and receive messages. Within a neuron, messages travel from the cell body down the axon to the axon terminal in the form of electrical impulses. From there, the message is sent to other neurons with the help of neurotransmitters.

- **Neurotransmitters—The Brain's Chemical Messengers**

To make messages jump from one neuron to another, the neuron creates chemical messengers, called neurotransmitters. The axon terminal releases neurotransmitters that travel across the space (called the synapse) to nearby neurons. Then the transmitter attaches to receptors on the nearby neuron.

- **Receptors—The Brain's Chemical Receivers**

As the neurotransmitter approaches the nearby neuron, it attaches to a special site on that neuron called a receptor. A neurotransmitter and its receptor operate like a key and lock, in that a very specific mechanism makes sure that each receptor will forward the right message only after interacting with the right kind of neurotransmitter.

- **Transporters—The Brain's Chemical Recyclers**

Once neurotransmitters do their job, they are pulled back into their original neuron by transporters. This recycling process shuts off the signal between the neurons.

How Do Drugs Affect Your Brain?

Drugs are chemicals. When someone puts these chemicals into their body, either by smoking, injecting, inhaling, or eating them, they tap into the brain's communication system and tamper with the way nerve cells normally send, receive, and process information. Different drugs—because of their chemical structures—work differently. We know there are at least two ways drugs work in the brain:

- Imitating the brain's natural chemical messengers
- Overstimulating the "reward circuit" of the brain

Some drugs, like marijuana and heroin, have chemical structures that mimic that of a neurotransmitter that naturally occurs in our bodies. In fact, these drugs can "fool" our receptors, lock onto them, and activate the nerve cells. However, they don't work the same way as a natural neurotransmitter, and the neurons wind up sending abnormal messages through the brain, which can cause problems both for our brains as well as our bodies.

Other drugs, such as cocaine and methamphetamine, cause nerve cells to release too much dopamine, which is a natural neurotransmitter, or prevent the normal recycling of dopamine. This leads to exaggerated messages in the brain, causing problems with communication channels. It's like the difference between someone whispering in your ear versus someone shouting in a microphone.

The "High" From Drugs / Pleasure Effect

Most drugs of abuse—nicotine, cocaine, marijuana, and others—affect the brain's "reward" circuit, which is part of the limbic system. Normally, the reward circuit responds to feelings of pleasure by releasing the neurotransmitter dopamine. Dopamine creates feelings of pleasure. Drugs take control of this system, causing large amounts of dopamine to flood the system. This flood of dopamine is what causes the "high" or intense excitement and happiness (sometimes called euphoria) linked with drug use.

The Repeat Effect

Our brains are wired to make sure we will repeat healthy activities, like eating, by connecting those activities with feeling good. Whenever this reward circuit is kick-started, the brain notes that something important is happening that needs to be remembered, and teaches us to do it again and again, without thinking about it. Because drugs of abuse come in and "hijack" the same circuit, people learn to use drugs in the same way.

After repeated drug use, the brain starts to adjust to the surges of dopamine. Neurons may begin to reduce the number of dopamine receptors or simply make less dopamine. The result is less dopamine signaling in the brain—like turning down the volume on the dopamine signal. Because some drugs are toxic, some neurons also may die.

As a result, the ability to feel any pleasure is reduced. The person feels flat, lifeless, and depressed, and is unable to enjoy things that once brought pleasure. Now the person needs drugs just to bring dopamine levels up to normal, and more of the drug is needed to create a dopamine flood, or "high"—an effect known as "tolerance."

Long-Term Effects

Drug use can eventually lead to dramatic changes in neurons and brain circuits. These changes can still be present even after the person has stopped taking drugs. This is more likely to happen when a drug is taken over and over.

Chapter 27

Prescription and Over-the-Counter Drug Abuse

Chapter Contents

Section 27.1

Prescription Drug Abuse

This section contains text excerpted from the following sources: Text under the heading "The Truth about Prescription Drugs" is excerpted from "During National Drug Facts Week: The Truth About Prescription Drugs," National Institute on Drug Abuse (NIDA), February 1, 2013; Text beginning with the heading "What Is Prescription Drug Abuse?" is excerpted from "Prescription Drugs," National Institute on Drug Abuse (NIDA), March 23, 2016.

The Truth about Prescription Drugs

Did you know that prescription and over-the-counter (OTC) drugs are the most commonly abused substances by high school seniors (after marijuana and alcohol)? Some medications have psychoactive (mind-altering) properties and, because of that, are sometimes abused—taken for reasons or in ways not intended by a doctor, or taken by someone with no prescription.

Sometimes, addiction comes from a lack of knowledge. For example, people often think that prescription and OTC drugs are safer than illicit drugs, but that's only true when they are taken exactly as prescribed and for the purpose intended. When abused, prescription and OTC drugs can be addictive and lead to other bad health effects, including overdose—especially when taken along with other drugs or alcohol.

What Is Prescription Drug Abuse?

Also known as:

Opioids: Hillbilly heroin, oxy, OC, oxycotton, percs, happy pills, vikes

Depressants: barbs, reds, red birds, phennies, tooies, yellows, yellow jackets; candy, downers, sleeping pills, tranks; A-minus, zombie pills

Stimulants: Skippy, the smart drug, Vitamin R, bennies, black beauties, roses, hearts, speed, uppers

Prescription drug abuse is when someone takes a medication that was prescribed for someone else or takes their own prescription in a way not intended by a doctor or for a different reason—like to get high.

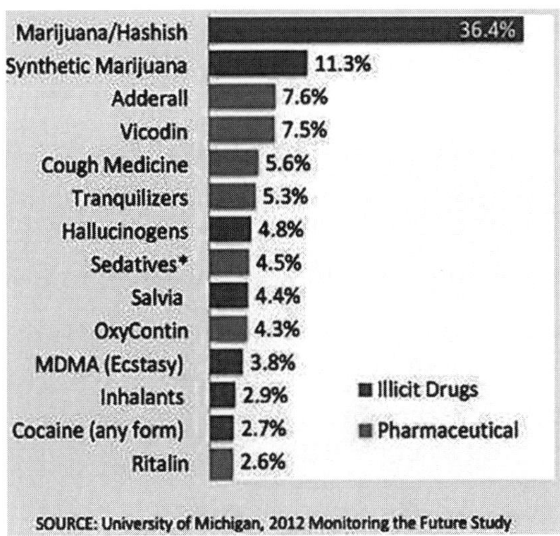

Figure 27.1. *Use Illicit Drugs and Pharmaceuticals among 12th Graders*

It has become a big health issue because of the dangers, particularly the danger of abusing prescription pain medications. For teens, it is a growing problem:

- After marijuana and alcohol, prescription drugs are the most commonly abused substances by Americans age 14 and older.
- Teens abuse prescription drugs for a number of reasons, such as to get high, to stop pain, or because they think it will help them with school work.
- Most teens get prescription drugs they abuse from friends and relatives, sometimes without the person knowing.
- Boys and girls tend to abuse some types of prescription drugs for different reasons. For example, boys are more likely to abuse prescription stimulants to get high, while girls tend to abuse them to stay alert or to lose weight.

When prescription drugs are taken as directed, they are usually safe. It requires a trained health care clinician, such as a doctor or nurse, to determine if the benefits of taking the medication outweigh any risks for side effects. But when abused and taken in different amounts or for different purposes than as prescribed, they affect the brain and body in ways very similar to illicit drugs.

When prescription drugs are abused, they can be addictive and put the person at risk for other harmful health effects, such as overdose (especially when taken along with other drugs or alcohol). And, abusing prescription drugs is illegal—and that includes sharing prescriptions with family members or friends.

Commonly Abused Prescription Drugs

There are three kinds of prescription drugs that are commonly abused.

- **Opioids**—painkillers like Vicodin, OxyContin, or codeine
- **Depressants**—like those used to relieve anxiety or help a person sleep, such as Valium or Xanax
- **Stimulants**—like those used for treating attention deficit hyperactivity disorder (ADHD), such as Adderall and Ritalin

But Aren't Prescription Drugs Safe?

Prescription drugs are often strong medications, which is why they require a prescription in the first place. When they are abused, they can be just as dangerous as drugs that are made illegally. Even when they are not abused, every medication has some risk for harmful effects, sometimes serious ones. Doctors consider the potential benefits and risks to each patient before prescribing medications and take into account a lot of different factors, described below. People who abuse drugs might not understand how these factors interact and put them at risk.

- **Personal information.** Doctors take into account a person's weight, how long they've been prescribed the medication, and what other medications they are taking. Someone abusing prescription drugs may overload their system or put themselves at risk for dangerous drug interactions that can cause seizures, coma, or even death.
- **Form and dose.** Doctors know how long it takes for a pill or capsule to dissolve in the stomach, release drugs to the blood, and reach the brain. When abused, prescription drugs may be taken in larger amounts or in ways that change the way the drug works in the body and brain, putting the person at greater risk for an overdose. For example, when people who abuse OxyContin crush and inhale the pills, a dose that normally works over the course of 12 hours hits the central nervous system all at once. This effect increases the risk for addiction and overdose.
- **Side effects.** Prescription drugs are designed to treat a specific illness or condition, but they often affect the body in other ways,

some of which can be dangerous. These are called side effects. For example, OxyContin stops pain, but it also causes constipation and sleepiness. Stimulants, such as Adderall, increase a person's ability to pay attention, but they also raise blood pressure and heart rate, making the heart work harder. These side effects can be worse when prescription drugs are not taken as prescribed or are abused in combination with other substances—including alcohol, other prescription drugs, and even over-the-counter drugs, such as cold medicines. For instance, some people mix alcohol and depressants, like Valium, both of which can slow breathing. This combination could stop breathing altogether.

How Are Prescription Drugs Abused?

People abuse prescription drugs by taking medication in a way that is not intended, such as:

- **Taking someone else's prescription medication.** Even when someone takes another person's medication for its intended purposes (such as to relieve pain, to stay awake, or to fall asleep) it is considered abuse.
- **Taking a prescription medication in a way other than prescribed.** Taking your own prescription in a way that it is not meant to be taken is also abuse. This includes taking more of the medication than prescribed or changing its form—for example, breaking or crushing a pill or capsule and then snorting the powder.
- **Taking a prescription medication to get high.** Some types of prescription drugs also can produce pleasurable effects or "highs." Taking the medication only for the purpose of getting high is considered prescription drug abuse.

How Does Prescription Drug Abuse Affect Your Brain?

In the brain, neurotransmitters such as **dopamine** send messages by attaching to receptors on nearby cells. The actions of these neurotransmitters and receptors cause the effects from prescription drugs. Each class of prescription drugs works a bit differently in the brain:

- **Prescription opioid pain medications** bind to molecules on cells known as opioid receptors—the same receptors that respond to **heroin**. These receptors are found on nerve cells in many areas of the brain and body, especially in brain areas involved in the perception of pain and pleasure.

- **Prescription stimulants**, such as Ritalin, have similar effects to **cocaine**, by causing a buildup of dopamine and norepinephrine.
- **Prescription depressants** make a person feel calm and relaxed in the same manner as the club drugs GHB and rohypnol.

What Are the Other Effects of Prescription Drugs?

Prescription drugs can cause dangerous short- and long-term health problems when they are not used as directed or when they are taken by someone other than the person they were prescribed for.

- Abusing **opioids** like oxycodone and codeine can cause you to feel sleepy, sick to your stomach, and constipated. At higher doses, opioids can make it hard to breathe properly and can cause overdose and death.
- Abusing **stimulants** like Adderall or Ritalin can make you feel paranoid (feeling like someone is going to harm you even though they aren't). It also can cause your body temperature to get dangerously high and make your heart beat too fast. This is especially likely if stimulants are taken in large doses or in ways other than swallowing a pill.
- Abusing **depressants** like barbiturates can cause slurred speech, shallow breathing, sleepiness, disorientation, and lack of coordination. People who abuse depressants regularly and then stop suddenly may experience seizures. At higher doses depressants can also cause overdose and death, especially when combined with alcohol.

Abusing depressants like barbiturates can cause slurred speech, shallow breathing, sleepiness, disorientation, and lack of coordination. People who abuse depressants regularly and then stop suddenly may experience seizures.

In addition, abusing over-the-counter drugs that contain DXM can also produce very dangerous effects.

Abuse of any of these types of medications can lead to addiction. And, abusing any type of drug that causes changes in your mood, perceptions, and behavior can affect judgment and willingness to take risks—putting you at greater risk for HIV and other sexually transmitted diseases (STDs).

Prescription drugs can increase risk for health problems when combined with other prescription medications, over-the-counter medicines, illicit drugs, or alcohol. For example, combining opioids (painkillers) with alcohol can make breathing problems worse and can lead to death.

Can You Get Addicted to Prescription Drugs?

Yes, prescription drugs that effects the brain, including opioid painkillers, stimulants, and depressants, may cause physical dependence that can turn into addiction.

Dependence happens because the brain and body adapt to having drugs in the system for a while. A person may need larger doses of the drug to get the same initial effects. This is known as "tolerance." When drug use is stopped, withdrawal symptoms can occur. Dependence is not the same as addiction, but it can contribute to a person developing an addiction. It is one of the many reasons why a person should only take (and stop taking) prescription drugs under a doctor's care.

Carefully following the doctor's instructions for taking a medication can make it less likely that someone will develop dependence or addiction, because the medication is prescribed in amounts and forms that are considered appropriate for that person. However, dependence and addiction are still potential risks when taking certain types of prescription drugs. These risks should be carefully weighed against the benefits of the medication and patients should communicate any issues or concerns to their doctor as soon as they arise.

Medications that affect the brain can change the way it works—especially when they are taken over an extended period of time or with escalating doses. They can change the reward system, making it harder for a person to feel good without the drug and possibly leading to intense cravings, which make it hard to stop using. This is no different from what can happen when someone takes illicit drugs—addiction is a real possibility. When a person is addicted to a drug, finding and using that drug can begin to feel like the most important thing—more important than family, friends, school, sports, or health.

Other kinds of medications that do not act in the brain, such as antibiotics used to treat infections, are not addictive.

Can You Die If You Abuse Prescription Drugs?

Yes. More than half of the drug overdose deaths in the United States each year are caused by prescription drug abuse. In the last decade, the number of deaths from abuse of prescription drugs has increased dramatically.

In 2001, 9,197 people died from a prescription drug overdose; that number jumped to 25,700 in 2014. The trend holds true for young people—close to 800 young people died as a result of a prescription drug overdose in 2001. In contrast, more than 2 times that—1,700 young people—died from an overdose in 2014. Close to 19,000 of all deaths from abuse of prescription drugs involved opioid painkillers and 7,900 involved a class of depressants known as benzodiazepines (some deaths include more than one type of drug).

Mixing different types of prescription drugs can be particularly dangerous. For example, benzodiazepines interact with opioids and increase the risk of overdose.

How Many Teens Abuse Prescription Drugs?

Prescription and over-the-counter drugs are the most commonly abused substances by Americans age 14 and older, after marijuana and alcohol.

Table 27.1. Monitoring the Future Study: Trends in Prevalence of Any Prescription Drug for 12th Graders; 2012–2015 (in percent)*

Drug	**Time Period**	**12th Graders**			
		2012	**2013**	**2014**	**2015**
Any Prescription Drug	Lifetime	21.2	21.5	[19.90]	**18.3**
	Past Year	14.8	15	[13.90]	**12.9**
	Past Month	7	7	6.4	**5.9**

** Data in brackets indicate statistically significant change from the previous year.*

Section 27.2

Causes and Prevalence of Prescription Drug Abuse

This section contains text excerpted from the following sources: Text under the heading "Risk Factors for Prescription Opioid Abuse and Overdose" is excerpted from "Risk Factors for Prescription Opioid Abuse and Overdose," Centers for Disease Control and Prevention (CDC), March 16, 2016; Text under the heading "Drivers and Challenges to Reform" is excerpted from "State Medicate Interventions for Preventing Prescription Drug Abuse and Overdose," Substance Abuse and Mental Health Services Administration (SAMHSA), October 1, 2014; Text beginning with the heading "Prescription Opioid Overdose Data" is excerpted from "Prescription Opioid Overdose Data," Centers for Disease Control and Prevention (CDC), March 12, 2016; Text beginning with the heading "Trends in Prescription Drug Abuse" is excerpted from "Trends in Prescription Drug Abuse," National Institute on Drug Abuse (NIDA), November 2014.

Risk Factors for Prescription Painkiller Abuse and Overdose

Research shows that some risk factors make people particularly vulnerable to prescription painkiller abuse and overdose, including:

- Obtaining overlapping prescriptions from multiple providers and pharmacies.
- Taking high daily dosages of prescription painkillers.
- Having mental illness or a history of alcohol or other substance abuse.
- Living in rural areas and having low income.

Medicaid Patients

- Inappropriate provider prescribing practices and patient use are substantially higher among Medicaid patients than among privately insured patients.

- In one study based on 2010 data, 40% of Medicaid enrollees with painkiller prescriptions had at least one indicator of potentially inappropriate use or prescribing:
    - overlapping painkiller prescriptions
    - overlapping painkiller and benzodiazepine prescriptions
    - long-acting or extended release prescription painkillers for acute pain and high daily doses

Drivers and Challenges to Reform

The causes of prescription drug abuse are diverse and intensely complex, presenting significant obstacles to comprehensive reform and requiring an equally diverse set of solutions. Among the primary causes of prescription drug abuse and misuse are inadequate chronic pain management, inconsistencies in clinical practice and insurance benefit coverage, the presence of a drug culture in the U.S. and the marketplace for illegally and fraudulently obtained prescription drugs, and a prevailing public perception of the relative safety of prescription medicines. Addressing these root causes requires a multi-level solution which includes participation from clinical providers, healthcare payers, and various state and federal agencies.

Prescription Opioid Overdose Data

Overdose deaths involving prescription opioids have quadrupled since 1999, and so have sales of these prescription drugs. From 1999 to 2014, more than 165,000 people have died in the U.S. from overdoses related to prescription opioids.

Opioid prescribing continues to fuel the epidemic. Today, at least half of all U.S. opioid overdose deaths involve a prescription opioid. In 2014, more than 14,000 people died from overdoses involving prescription opioids.

Most Commonly Overdosed Opioids

The most common drugs involved in prescription opioid overdose deaths include:

- Methadone
- Oxycodone (such as OxyContin®)
- Hydrocodone (such as Vicodin®)

Overdose Deaths

Among those who died from prescription opioid overdose between 1999 and 2014:

- Overdose rates were highest among people aged 25 to 54 years.
- Overdose rates were higher among non-Hispanic whites and American Indian or Alaskan Natives, compared to non-Hispanic blacks and Hispanics.
- Men were more likely to die from overdose, but the mortality gap between men and women is closing.

Additional Risks

Overdose is not the only risk related to prescription opioids. Misuse, abuse, and opioid use disorder (addiction) are also potential dangers.

- In 2014, almost 2 million Americans abused or were dependent on prescription opioids.
- As many as 1 in 4 people who receive prescription opioids long term for noncancer pain in primary care settings struggles with addiction.
- Every day, over 1,000 people are treated in emergency departments for misusing prescription opioids.

Trends in Prescription Drug Abuse

Adolescents and Young Adults

Abuse of prescription drugs is highest among young adults aged 18 to 25, with 5.9 percent reporting nonmedical use in the past month. Among youth aged 12 to 17, 3.0 percent reported past-month nonmedical use of prescription medications.

According to the 2010 MTF, prescription and OTC drugs are among the most commonly abused drugs by 12th graders, after alcohol, marijuana, and tobacco. While past-year nonmedical use of sedatives and tranquilizers decreased among 12th graders over the last 5 years, this is not the case for the nonmedical use of amphetamines or opioid pain relievers.

When asked how prescription opioids were obtained for nonmedical use, more than half of the 12th graders surveyed said they were given the drugs or bought them from a friend or relative. Interestingly, the number of students who purchased opioids over the Internet was negligible.

Youth who abuse prescription medications are also more likely to report use of other drugs. Multiple studies have revealed associations between prescription drug abuse and higher rates of cigarette smoking; heavy episodic drinking; and marijuana, cocaine, and other illicit drug use among adolescents, young adults, and college students in the United States.

Older Adults

Persons aged 65 years and older comprise only 13 percent of the population, yet account for more than one-third of total outpatient spending on prescription medications in the United States. Older patients are more likely to be prescribed long-term and multiple prescriptions, and some experience cognitive decline, which could lead to improper use of medications. Alternatively, those on a fixed income may abuse another person's remaining medication to save money.

The high rates of comorbid illnesses in older populations, age-related changes in drug metabolism, and the potential for drug interactions may make any of these practices more dangerous than in younger populations. Further, a large percentage of older adults also use OTC medicines and dietary supplements, which (in addition to alcohol) could compound any adverse health consequences resulting from prescription drug abuse.

Gender Differences

Overall, more males than females abuse prescription drugs in all age groups except the youngest (aged 12 to 17 years); that is, females in this age group exceed males in the nonmedical use of all psychotherapeutics, including pain relievers, tranquilizers, and stimulants. Among nonmedical users of prescription drugs, females 12 to 17 years old are also more likely to meet abuse or dependence criteria for psychotherapeutics.

Section 27.3

Cough and Cold Medicine (DXM and Codeine Syrup)

This section includes text excerpted from "Cough and Cold Medicine (DXM and Codeine Syrup)," National Institute on Drug Abuse (NIDA), March 10, 2016.

What Are Cough and Cold Medicines?

Also known as: robotripping, robo, tussin, triple c, dex, skittles, candy, velvet, and drank

Millions of Americans take cough and cold medicines each year to help with symptoms of colds, and when taken as instructed, these medicines can be safe and effective. However, several cough and cold medicines contain ingredients that are psychoactive (mind-altering) when taken in higher-than-recommended dosages, and some people may abuse them. These products also contain other ingredients that can add to the risks.

Two commonly abused cough and cold medicines are:

- **Cough syrups and capsules containing dextromethorphan (DXM).** These over-the-counter (OTC)—meaning they can be bought without a prescription—cough medicines are safe for stopping coughs during a cold if you take them as directed. Taking more than the recommended amount can produce euphoria (a relaxed pleasurable feeling) and dissociative effects (like you are detached from your body).
- **Promethazine-codeine cough syrup.** These prescription medications contain an opioid drug called codeine, which stops coughs, but when taken in higher doses produces euphoria.

How Are Cough and Cold Medicines Abused?

Cough and cold medicines are usually sold in liquid syrup, capsule, or pill form. They may also come in a powder. Young people are more likely to abuse cough and cold medicines containing DXM because these medicines can be purchased without a prescription. Some people mix promethazine-codeine cough syrup with soda or alcohol and flavor the mixture by adding hard candies.

How Do Cough and Cold Medicines Affect the Brain?

When cough and cold medicines are taken as directed, they safely treat symptoms caused by colds and flu. But when taken in higher quantities or when such symptoms aren't present, they may affect the brain in ways very similar to illegal drugs.

DXM acts on the same brain cell receptors as drugs like ketamine or PCP. A single high dose of DXM can cause hallucinations (imagined experiences that seem real). Ketamine and PCP are called "dissociative" drugs, which means they make you feel separated from your body or your environment, and they twist the way you think or feel about something or someone.

Codeine attaches to the same cell receptors as opioids like heroin. High doses of promethazine-codeine cough syrup can produce euphoria similar to that produced by other opioid drugs. Also, both codeine and promethazine depress activities in the central nervous system (brain and spinal cord), which produces calming effects.

Both codeine and DXM cause an increase in the amount of dopamine in the brain's reward pathway. Extra amounts of dopamine increase the feeling of pleasure and at the same time cause important messages to get lost, causing a range of effects from lack of motivation to serious health problems. Repeatedly seeking to experience that feeling can lead to addiction.

What Are the Other Effects of Cough and Cold Medicines?

DXM abuse can cause:

- Loss of coordination
- Numbness
- Feeling sick to the stomach
- Increased blood pressure
- Faster heart beat
- In rare instances, lack of oxygen to the brain, creating lasting brain damage, when DXM is taken with decongestants

Promethazine-codeine cough syrup can cause:

- Slowed heart rate
- Slowed breathing (high doses can lead to overdose and death)

Also, cough and cold medicines are even more dangerous when taken with alcohol or other drugs.

Can You Get Addicted to Cough and Cold Medicines?

Yes, high doses and repeated abuse of cough and cold medicines can lead to addiction. That's when a person seeks out and takes the drug over and over even though they know that it is causing problems with their health and their life.

Can You Die If You Abuse Cough and Cold Medicines?

Yes. Abuse of promethazine-codeine cough syrup slows down the central nervous system, which can slow or stop the heart and lungs. Mixing it with alcohol greatly increases this risk. Promethazine-codeine cough syrup has been linked to the overdose deaths of a few prominent musicians.

How Many Teens Abuse Cough and Cold Medicines?

NIDA's Monitoring the Future study collects data on teen abuse of cough medicines:

Table 27.2. Monitoring the Future Study: Trends in Prevalence of Cough Medicine (non-prescription) for 8th Graders, 10th Graders, and 12th Graders; 2015 (in percent)*

Drug	Time Period	8th Graders	10th Graders	12th Graders
Cough Medicine (non-prescription)	Past Year	1.6	3.3	4.6

**Data in brackets indicate statistically significant change from the previous year.*

Chapter 28

Drug Interactions

Drug Interactions: What You Should Know

There are more opportunities today than ever before to learn about your health and to take better care of yourself. It is also more important than ever to know about the medicines you take. If you take several different medicines, see more than one doctor, or have certain health conditions, you and your doctors need to be aware of all the medicines you take. Doing so will help you to avoid potential problems such as drug interactions.

Drug interactions may make your drug less effective, cause unexpected side effects, or increase the action of a particular drug. Some drug interactions can even be harmful to you. Reading the label every time you use a nonprescription or prescription drug and taking the time to learn about drug interactions may be critical to your health. You can reduce the risk of potentially harmful drug interactions and side effects with a little bit of knowledge and common sense. Drug interactions fall into three broad categories:

- **Drug-drug interactions** occur when two or more drugs react with each other. This drug-drug interaction may cause you to experience an unexpected side effect. For example, mixing a drug you take to help you sleep (a sedative) and a drug you take

---

This chapter includes text excerpted from "Drug Interactions: What You Should Know," U.S. Food and Drug Administration (FDA), September 25, 2013.

for allergies (an antihistamine) can slow your reactions and make driving a car or operating machinery dangerous.

- **Drug-food/beverage interactions** result from drugs reacting with foods or beverages. For example, mixing alcohol with some drugs may cause you to feel tired or slow your reactions.
- **Drug-condition interactions** may occur when an existing medical condition makes certain drugs potentially harmful. For example, if you have high blood pressure you could experience an unwanted reaction if you take a nasal decongestant.

Drug Interactions and Over-the-Counter Medicines

Over-the-counter (OTC) drug labels contain information about ingredients, uses, warnings and directions that is important to read and understand. The label also includes important information about possible drug interactions. Further, drug labels may change as new information becomes known. That's why it's especially important to read the label every time you use a drug.

- The "**Active Ingredients**" and "**Purpose**" sections list:
    - the name and amount of each active ingredient
    - the purpose of each active ingredient
- The "**Uses**" section of the label:
    - tells you what the drug is used for
    - helps you find the best drug for your specific symptoms
- The "**Warnings**" section of the label provides important drug interaction and precaution information such as
    - when to talk to a doctor or pharmacist before use
    - the medical conditions that may make the drug less effective or not safe
    - under what circumstances the drug should not be used
    - when to stop taking the drug
- The "**Directions**" section of the label tells you:
    - the length of time and the amount of the product that you may safely use
    - any special instructions on how to use the product

- The "**Other Information**" section of the label tells you:
    - required information about certain ingredients, such as sodium content, for people with dietary restrictions or allergies
- The "**Inactive Ingredients**" section of the label tells you:
    - the name of each inactive ingredient (such as colorings, binders, etc.)
- The "**Questions?**" or "Questions or Comments?" section of the label (if included):
    - provides telephone numbers of a source to answer questions about the product

Learning More About Drug Interactions

Talk to your doctor or pharmacist about the drugs you take. When your doctor prescribes a new drug, discuss all OTC and prescription drugs, dietary supplements, vitamins, botanicals, minerals and herbals you take, as well as the foods you eat. Ask your pharmacist for the package insert for each prescription drug you take. The package insert provides more information about potential drug interactions.

Before taking a drug, ask your doctor or pharmacist the following questions:

- Can I take it with other drugs?
- Should I avoid certain foods, beverages or other products?
- What are possible drug interaction signs I should know about?
- How will the drug work in my body?
- Is there more information available about the drug or my condition (on the Internet or in health and medical literature)?

Know how to take drugs safely and responsibly. Remember, the drug label will tell you:

- what the drug is used for
- how to take the drug
- how to reduce the risk of drug interactions and unwanted side effects

If you still have questions after reading the drug product label, ask your doctor or pharmacist for more information

Remember that different OTC drugs may contain the same active ingredient. If you are taking more than one OTC drug, pay attention to the active ingredients used in the products to avoid taking too much of a particular ingredient. Under certain circumstances—such as if you are pregnant or breast-feeding—you should talk to your doctor before you take any medicine. Also, make sure you know what ingredients are contained in the medicines you take. Doing so will help you to avoid possible allergic reactions.

Examples of Drug Interation Warnings

The following are examples of drug interaction warnings that you may see on certain OTC drug products. These examples do not include all of the warnings for the listed types of products and should not take the place of reading the actual product label.

Table 28.1. Drug Interaction Information

Category	Drug Interaction Information
Acid Reducers **H2 Receptor Antagonists** *(drugs that prevent or relieve heartburn associated with acid indigestion and sour stomach)*	**For products containing cimetidine, ask a doctor or pharmacist before use if you are:** • taking theophylline (oral asthma drug), warfarin (blood thinning drug), or phenytoin (seizure drug)
Antacids *(drugs for relief of acid indigestion, heartburn, and/or sour stomach)*	**Ask a doctor or pharmacist before use if you are:** • allergic to milk or milk products if the product contains more than 5 grams lactose in a maximum daily dose • taking a prescription drug **Ask a doctor before use if you have:** • kidney disease
Antiemetics *(drugs for prevention or treatment of nausea, vomiting, or dizziness associated with motion sickness)*	**Ask a doctor or pharmacist before use if you are:** • taking sedatives or tranquilizers **Ask a doctor before use if you have:** • a breathing problem, such as emphysema or chronic bronchitis

Table 28.1. Continued

Category	Drug Interaction Information
	• glaucoma • difficulty in urination due to an enlarged prostate gland **When using this product:** • avoid alcoholic beverages
Antihistamines *(drugs that temporarily relieve runny nose or reduce sneezing, itching of the nose or throat, and itchy watery eyes due to hay fever or other upper respiratory problems)*	**Ask a doctor or pharmacist before use if you are taking:** • sedatives or tranquilizers • a prescription drug for high blood pressure or depression **Ask a doctor before use if you have:** • glaucoma or difficulty in urination due to an enlarged prostate gland • breathing problems, such as emphysema, chronic bronchitis, or asthma **When using this product:** • alcohol, sedatives, and tranquilizers may increase drowsiness • avoid alcoholic beverages
Antitussives **Cough Medicine** *(drugs that temporarily reduce cough due to minor throat and bronchial irritation as may occur with a cold)*	**Ask a doctor or pharmacist before use if you are:** • taking sedatives or tranquilizers **Ask a doctor before use if you have:** • glaucoma or difficulty in urination due to an enlarged prostate gland
Ask a doctor before use if you: • have heart disease, high blood pressure, thyroid disease, diabetes, or difficulty in urination due to an enlarged prostate gland • have ever been hospitalized for asthma or are taking a prescription drug for asthma	
Laxatives *(drugs for the temporary relief of constipation)*	**Ask a doctor before use if you have:** • kidney disease and the laxative contains phosphates, potassium, or magnesium • stomach pain, nausea, or vomiting

Table 28.1. Continued

Category	Drug Interaction Information
Nasal Decongestants *(drugs for the temporary relief of nasal congestion due to a cold, hay fever, or other upper respiratory allergies)*	**Ask a doctor before use if you:** • have heart disease, high blood pressure, thyroid disease, diabetes, or difficulty in urination due to an enlarged prostate gland
Nicotine Replacement Products *(drugs that reduce withdrawal symptoms associated with quitting smoking, including nicotine craving)*	**Ask a doctor before use if you:** • have high blood pressure not controlled by medication • have heart disease or have had a recent heart attack or irregular heartbeat, since nicotine can increase your heart rate **Ask a doctor or pharmacist before use if you are:** • taking a prescription drug for depression or asthma (your dose may need to be adjusted) • using a prescription non-nicotine stop smoking drug **Do not use:** • if you continue to smoke, chew tobacco, use snuff, or use other nicotine-containing products
Nighttime Sleep Aids *(drugs for relief of occasional sleeplessness)*	**Ask a doctor or pharmacist before use if you are:** • taking sedatives or tranquilizers **Ask a doctor before use if you have:** • a breathing problem such as emphysema or chronic bronchitis • glaucoma • difficulty in urination due to an enlarged prostate gland **When using this product:** • avoid alcoholic beverages
Pain Relievers *(drugs for the temporary relief of minor body aches, pains, and headaches)*	**Ask a doctor before taking if you:** • consume three or more alcohol-containing drinks per day *(The following ingredients are found in different OTC pain relievers: acetaminophen, aspirin, ibuprofen, ketoprofen, magnesium salicylate, and naproxen. It is important to read the label of pain reliever products to learn about different drug interaction warnings for each ingredient.)*

Table 28.1. Continued

Category	Drug Interaction Information
Stimulants *(drugs that help restore mental alertness or wakefulness during fatigue or drowsines)*	**When using this product:** • limit the use of foods, beverages, and other drugs that have caffeine. Too much caffeine can cause nervousness, irritability, sleeplessness, and occasional rapid heart beat • be aware that the recommended dose of this product contains about as much caffeine as a cup of coffee
Topical Acne *(drugs for the treatment of acne)*	**When using this product:** • increased dryness or irritation of the skin may occur immediately following use of this product or if you are using other topical acne drugs at the same time. If this occurs, only one drug should be used unless directed by your doctor

Chapter 29

Legal, Financial, and Social Consequences of Drug Abuse

Chapter Contents

Section 29.1

Consequences of Drug Abuse

This section includes text excerpted from "Consequences of Illicit Drug Use in America," WhiteHouse.gov, April 2014.

Consequences of Illicit Drug Use in America

Drug Deaths

- According to the Centers for Disease Control and Prevention, 40,393 people died of drug-induced causes in 2010, the latest year for which data are available. The number of drug-induced deaths has grown from 19,128 in 1999, or from 6.8 deaths per 100,000 population to 12.9 in 2010. (These include causes directly involving drugs, such as accidental poisoning or overdoses, but do not include accidents, homicides, AIDS, and other causes indirectly related to drugs.)
- There is a drug-induced death in the U.S. every 13 minutes.
- Compared to other causes of preventable deaths, drug-induced causes exceeded the 31,328 deaths from injuries due to firearms and the 25,692 alcohol-induced deaths recorded in 2010. In the same year, 38,364 deaths were classified as suicides and 16,259 deaths as homicides.

Drugged Driving

- From a national roadside survey in 2007, one in eight (12.4%) of weekend nighttime drivers tested positive for at least one illicit drug.
- Based on a self-report survey in 2012, approximately 10.2 million Americans aged 16 or older reported driving under the influence of an illicit drug during the past year.
- In 2012, more than one in three drivers (38%) killed in motor vehicle crashes who were tested for drugs and the results known, tested positive for at least one medication or illicit drug.

- Among high school seniors in 2013, one in 9 (11.7%) reported that in the two weeks prior to their interview, they had driven a vehicle after smoking marijuana.

Children

Annual averages for 2002 to 2007 indicate that over 8.3 million youth under 18 years of age, or almost one in eight youth (11.9%), lived with at least one parent who was dependent on alcohol or an illicit drug in the past year. Of these, About 2.1 million youth lived with a parent who was dependent on or abused illicit drugs, and almost 7.3 million lived with a parent who was dependent on or abused alcohol.

School Performance

- Among youth in school who reported an average grade of "D" or worse, one in four were current marijuana users, whereas fewer than one in ten (9.1%) of those who reported an average grade better than "D" were current marijuana users
- College students who use prescription stimulant medications non-medically typically have lower grade point averages, are more likely to be heavy drinkers and users of other illicit drugs, and are more likely to meet diagnostic criteria for dependence on alcohol and marijuana, skip class more frequently, and spend less time studying.

Economic Costs

The economic cost of drug abuse in the U.S. was estimated at $193 billion in 2007, the last available estimate. This value represents both the use of resources to address health and crime consequences as well as the loss of potential productivity from disability, premature death, and withdrawal from the legitimate workforce.

Addiction and Treatment

- In 2012, 23.1 million persons aged 12 or older needed treatment for an illicit drug or alcohol use problem (8.9% of persons in that age group). Of these, 8.0 million persons (or 3.1%) needed treatment for illicit drug problems, with or without alcohol.

- Of the 23.5 million persons needing substance use treatment, 2.5 million received treatment at a specialty facility in the past year, and of the 8.0 million needing drug treatment, 1.5 million received specialty treatment.
- Over the past 10 years, there have been approximately one million drug treatment admissions recorded annually. Treatment admissions with opioids as the primary drug are the largest component. Treatment for heroin has been approximately 25% of drug treatment admissions annually over the past 10 years. Treatment admissions for non-heroin opioids such as prescription painkillers, has risen from under 5% in 2002 to over 15% by 2011.

Acute Health Effects

In 2011, an estimated 2.5 million visits to emergency departments in U.S. hospitals were associated with drug misuse or abuse, including over 1.3 million (1,252,500) visits involving an illicit drug. Nonmedical use of pharmaceuticals was involved in over 1.4 million ED visits. Cocaine was involved in 505,224 visits, marijuana was involved in 455,668 visits, heroin was involved in 258,482 visits, and stimulants (including amphetamines and methamphetamine) were involved in 159,840 visits.

Criminal Justice Involvement

- According to a 2013 study of arrestees in 5 major metropolitan areas across the country, drug use among the arrestee population is much higher than in the general U.S. population. The percentage of booked arrestees testing positive for at least one illicit drug ranged from 63 percent to 83 percent. The most common substances present during tests, in descending order, are marijuana, cocaine, opiates (primarily metabolites of heroin or morphine), and methamphetamine. Many arrestees tested positive for more than one illegal drug at the time of arrest. Similar results were found in earlier studies conducted in additional locations across the country.
- According to a 2004 survey of inmates in correctional facilities, 32 percent of state inmates and 26 percent of federal prisoners reported that they used drugs at the time of the offense.

Environmental Impact and Dangers

- There are significant environmental impacts from clandestine methamphetamine drug labs, including chemical toxicity, risk of fire and explosion, lingering effects of toxic waste, and potential injuries. The number of domestic meth lab incidents, which includes dumpsites, active labs, and chemical/glassware set-ups, dropped dramatically in response to the Combat Meth Epidemic Act, (CMEA) of 2005, from nearly 24,000 in 2005 to nearly 7,000 in 2007. However, traffickers are devising methods to avoid the CMEA restrictions and domestic meth lab incidents are rising again, reaching 912,700 in 2012.
- Coca and poppy cultivation in the Andean jungle is significantly damaging the environment in the region. The primary threats to the environment are deforestation caused by clearing the fields for cultivation, soil erosion, and chemical pollution from insecticides and fertilizers. Additionally, the lab process of converting coca and poppy into cocaine and heroin has adverse effects on the environment.
- Mexican drug trafficking organizations have been operating on public lands in the U.S. to cultivate marijuana, with serious consequences for the environment and public safety. Propane tanks and other trash from illicit marijuana growers litter the remote areas of park lands from California to Tennessee. Growers often use a cocktail of pesticides and fertilizers many times stronger than what is used on residential lawns to cultivate their crop. These chemicals leach out quickly, killing native insects and other organisms directly. Fertilizer runoff contaminates local waterways and aids in the growth of algae and weeds. The aquatic vegetation in turn impedes water flows that are critical to maintaining biodiversity in wetlands and other sensitive environments.

Section 29.2

Drugged Driving

This section contains text excerpted from the following sources: Text beginning with the heading "Driving under Influence" is excerpted from "DrugFacts: Drugged Driving," National Institute on Drug Abuse (NIDA), May 2015; Text beginning with the heading "Designated Drivers—You Are Not Alone" is excerpted from "Designated Drivers—You Are Not Alone," National Institute on Drug Abuse (NIDA), March 22, 2016.

Driving under Influence

Use of illegal drugs or misuse of prescription drugs can make driving a car unsafe—just like driving after drinking alcohol. Drugged driving puts not only the driver but also passengers and others who share the road at risk.

Why Is Drugged Driving Dangerous?

The effects of specific drugs differ depending on how they act in the brain. For example, marijuana can slow reaction time, impair judgment of time and distance, and decrease motor coordination. Drivers who have used cocaine or methamphetamine can be aggressive and reckless when driving. Certain kinds of sedatives, called benzodiazepines, can cause dizziness and drowsiness, which can lead to accidents.

Research studies have shown negative effects of marijuana on drivers, including an increase in lane weaving and poor reaction time and attention to the road. Use of alcohol with marijuana made drivers more impaired, causing even more lane weaving.

Scientists need to conduct more research to know how much of a drug impairs a person's driving ability. But even small amounts of some drugs can have a measurable effect. Some states have zero-tolerance laws for drugged driving. This means a person can face charges for driving under the influence (DUI) if there is any amount of drug in the blood or urine. It is important to note that many states are waiting for research to better define blood levels that indicate impairment, such as those they use with alcohol.

How Many People Take Drugs and Drive?

According to the 2013 National Survey on Drug Use and Health (NSDUH), an estimated 9.9 million people aged 12 or older (or 3.8% of teens and adults) reported driving under the influence of illicit drugs ("Illicit" refers to use of illegal drugs, including marijuana according to federal law, and misuse of prescription drugs.) during the year prior to being surveyed. This was lower than the rate in 2012 (3.9%). By comparison, in 2013, an estimated 28.7 million people (10.9%) reported driving under the influence of alcohol at least once in the past year.

The National Highway Traffic Safety Administration's (NHTSA) 2013-2014 National Roadside Survey found that more than 22 percent of drivers tested positive for illegal, prescription, or over-the-counter drugs. This was true for both weekday daytime and weekend nighttime drivers. But illegal drug use increased from daytime to nighttime while use of prescription drugs decreased. By comparison, 1.1 percent of drivers tested positive for alcohol during the daytime on weekdays, but 8.3 percent of drivers on weekend nights tested positive.

NSDUH data also show that men are more likely than women to drive under the influence of drugs or alcohol. And a higher percentage of young adults aged 18 to 25 drive after taking drugs or drinking than adults 26 or older.

How Often Does Drugged Driving Cause Accidents?

It is hard to measure how many accidents drugged driving causes. This is because:

- a good roadside test for drug levels in the body does not yet exist
- people are not usually tested for drugs if they are above the legal limit for alcohol because there is already enough evidence for a DUI charge
- many drivers who cause accidents are found to have both drugs and alcohol or more than one drug in their system, making it hard to know which substance had the greater effect

One NHTSA study found that in 2009, 18 percent of drivers killed in an accident tested positive for at least one drug—an increase from

13 percent in 2005. A 2010 study showed that 11.4 percent of fatal crashes involved a drugged driver.

Which Drugs Are Linked to Drugged Driving?

After alcohol, marijuana is the drug most often linked to drugged driving. Tests for detecting marijuana in drivers measure the level of delta-9-tetrahydrocannabinol (THC), marijuana's active ingredient, in the blood. In the 2013-2014 National Roadside Survey, 12.6 percent of drivers on weekend nights tested positive for THC. This was significantly higher than the 8.6 percent who tested positive in 2007.

A study of more than 3,000 fatally injured drivers in Australia showed that drivers with THC in their blood were much more likely to be at fault for an accident than drivers without drugs or alcohol in their system. This likelihood increased as the level of THC in the blood increased.

A 2010 nationwide study of fatal crashes found that 46.5 percent of drivers who tested positive for drugs had used a prescription drug, 36.9 percent had used marijuana, and 9.8 percent had used cocaine. The most common prescription drugs found were:

- alprazolam (Xanax®)—12.1 percent
- hydrocodone (Vicodin®)—11.1 percent
- oxycodone (OxyContin®)—10.2 percent
- diazepam (Valium®)—8.4 percent

Note that the study did not distinguish between legal and illicit use of the drugs.

In a small study of driver deaths in six states, 28.3 percent of drivers tested positive for drugs in 2010—12.2 percent for marijuana and 5.4 percent for opioids. These numbers were significantly higher than in 1999 when 16.6 percent of drivers tested positive—4.2 percent for marijuana and 1.8 percent for opioids.

Why Is Drugged Driving a Problem in Teens and Young Adults?

Motor vehicle crashes are the leading cause of death among young people aged 16 to 19. Teens are more likely than older drivers to underestimate or not recognize dangerous situations. They are also more likely to speed and allow less distance between vehicles. When lack of driving experience is combined with drug use, the results can be tragic.

Data from a 2011 survey of middle and high school students showed that in the 2 weeks before the survey, the number of 12th-grade students who had driven after using:

- marijuana was 12.4 percent
- other illicit drugs was 2.4 percent
- alcohol was 8.7 percent

A study of college students with access to a car found that 1 in 6 (about 17 percent) had driven under the influence of a drug other than alcohol at least once in the past year. Of those students, 57 to 67 percent did so at least three times and 27 to 37 percent at least 10 times. Marijuana was the most common drug used, followed by cocaine and prescription opioids.

Because drugged driving puts people at an increased risk for accidents, public health experts urge drug and alcohol users to develop social strategies to prevent them from getting behind the wheel of a car while impaired. Steps people can take include:

- offering to be a designated driver
- appointing a designated driver to take all car keys
- avoiding driving to parties where drugs and alcohol are present
- discussing the risks of drugged driving with friends in advance

Drugged Driving in Older Adults

- In 2010, more than one-quarter (26.2%) of drugged drivers in fatal accidents were 50 years of age or older, up from 14.4 percent in 1993.
- Illicit drug use in adults 50 to 59 years of age more than doubled from 3.4 percent in 2002 to 7.2 percent in 2010.
- Nine out of 10 people 65 years of age and older take one or more prescription drugs, and almost 40 percent take five or more.
- Mental decline in older adults can lead to taking a prescription drug more or less often than they should or in the wrong amount. Older adults also may not break down the drug in their system as quickly as younger people. These factors can lead to unintentional intoxication.

Designated Drivers—You Are Not Alone

A new survey from Mothers Against Drunk Driving (MADD) and Nationwide Insurance found that 3 out of 4 people use designated drivers (DD). The DD is the person who does not drink, use drugs, or even take medication that might impair their driving. By the way, the DD is NOT the least drunk person in the group—they are the ones who don't use any drug or alcohol at all at a party or event, even a little bit.

Why Do They Choose DDs?

Because they want to get home in one piece.

The MADD survey reveals that 75% of the people who volunteer to be the DD do so because they want to get home safely, and 85% ride with a sober driver for the same reason. Another reason for being or using a DD was not wanting to get in trouble with the law.

Problem Solved, Right?

Not quite. It's awesome that so many people understand the dangers of drunk driving and chose to use a DD. But there are still many who do not. While drunk driving deaths decreased by 2.5 percent from 2012 to 2013, they still account for 31 percent of overall traffic deaths, according to the National Highway Traffic Safety Administration (NHTSA). That's too many, considering drunk driving deaths are 100 percent preventable, 100 percent of the time. That's 32,719 deaths that could have been prevented in 2013.

What about Drugged Driving?

Driving after using other drugs is a real problem as well. An estimated 9.9 million people—or 3.8 percent of adolescents and adults—reported driving under the influence of illicit drugs during the year prior to being surveyed. The good news is that number has decreased a little.

Drugged driving, like drunk driving, causes traffic deaths. One NHTSA study found that in 2009, 18 percent of drivers killed in accidents tested positive for at least one drug.

What If I Need a DD?

Drinking alcohol and using drugs is a bad idea. But don't make things worse by driving or getting into a car with someone who has been using. The best thing to do is to choose a DD *before* the group goes out.

If you didn't plan ahead, or your DD flakes out and uses drugs or alcohol, then here are a few alternative ways to get home:

- Call a cab. Google it on your phone or call 411 to get the number. And always bring along a little extra cash just in case you need it.
- Contact your local safe ride program.
- Find out (in advance) what your community offers. Many have their own "safe driver" programs.
- Request a ride from a car service.
- Use public transportation if you are traveling in a group of two or more (safety in numbers).
- Call mom, dad, or a trusted adult. *Who knows? They might be less mad because you did the responsible thing.*
- Stay put. If you're at a friend's house, or near a friend's house, sleep it off and drive home in the morning.

Section 29.3

Drug Use and Crime

This section contains text excerpted from the following sources: Text beginning with the heading "Drug Use, Crime, and Incarceration" is excerpted from "Drug Addiction Treatment in the Criminal Justice System," National Institute on Drug Abuse (NIDA), April 2014; Text beginning with the heading "Drugs and Crime Relationship" is excerpted from "Drug Use And Crime," Bureau of Justice Statistics (BJS), October 22, 2013.

Drug Use, Crime, and Incarceration

The connection between drug use and crime is well known. Drug use is implicated in at least five types of drug-related offenses:

1. Offenses related to drug possession or sales
2. Offenses directly related to obtaining drugs (e.g., stealing to get money for drugs)

3. Offenses related to a lifestyle that includes association with other offenders or with illicit markets
4. Offenses related to abusive and violent behaviors, including domestic violence and sexual assault
5. Offenses related to driving while intoxicated or under the influence, which can include property damage, accidents, injuries, and fatalities.

Incarceration

Drug use and intoxication can impair judgment, resulting in criminal behavior, poor anger management, and violent behavior. Sometimes drug users steal money or property to be able to buy drugs. Often they will commit crimes while "high" on drugs, and many drug users are sent to jail or prison. In 2012, nearly 7 million adults were involved with the criminal justice system (State or Federal prisons, local jails), including nearly 5 million who were under probation or parole supervision. A 2004 survey by the U.S. Department of Justice (DOJ) estimated that about 70 percent of State and 64 percent of Federal prisoners regularly used drugs prior to incarceration. The study also showed that 1 in 4 violent offenders in State prisons committed their offenses under the influence of drugs.

Most prisoners serving time for drug-related crimes were not arrested for simple possession. Among sentenced prisoners under State jurisdiction in 2008, 18 percent were sentenced for drug offenses and only 6 percent were incarcerated for drug possession alone. Just over 4 percent (4.4%) were drug offenders with no prior sentences. In 2009 about half (51%) of Federal prisoners, who represent 13 percent of the total prison population, had a drug offense as the most serious offense. Federal data show that the vast majority (99.8%) of Federal prisoners sentenced for drug offenses were incarcerated for drug trafficking.

Simple possession is even less of a factor with crimes related to marijuana. Only one-tenth of 1 percent (0.1%) of State prisoners were marijuana possession offenders with no prior sentences.

Drug Use and Crime

Drugs are related to crime in multiple ways. Most directly, it is a crime to use, possess, manufacture, or distribute drugs classified as having a potential for abuse. Cocaine, heroin, marijuana, and amphetamines are examples of drugs classified to have abuse potential. Drugs are also related to crime through the effects they have on the user's behavior and by generating violence and other illegal activity in connection with drug trafficking. The following scheme summarizes the various ways that drugs and crime are related.

Drugs and Crime Relationship

- **Drug-defined offenses**. Violations of laws prohibiting or regulating the possession, distribution, or manufacture of illegal drugs. Example: Drug possession or use. Marijuana cultivation. Methamphetamine production. Cocaine, heroin, or marijuana sales.
- **Drug-related**. Offenses in which drug's pharmacologic effects contribute; offenses are motivated by the user's need for money to support continued use; and offenses connected to drug distribution itself. Example: Violent behavior resulting from drug effects. Stealing to get money to buy drugs. Violence against rival drug dealers.
- **Drug-using lifestyle.** Drug use and crime are common aspects of a deviant lifestyle. The likelihood and frequency of involvement in illegal activity is increased because drug users may not participate in the legitimate economy and are exposed to situations that encourage crime.

Section 29.4

Drug Use And Violence

This section contains text excerpted from the following sources: Text beginning with the heading "Drug Use and Violence: An Unhappy Relationship" is excerpted from Drug Use and Violence: An Unhappy Relationship," National Institute on Drug Abuse (NIDA), March 26, 2015; Text beginning with the heading "Connections between Drug Use and Violence, Trauma among Homeless Youth" is excerpted from "Research Roundup: Connections Between Drug Use and Violence, Trauma Among Homeless Youth," Family and Youth Services Bureau (FYSB), U.S. Department of Health and Human Services, October 13, 2015.

Drug Use and Violence: An Unhappy Relationship

Most of us have been in an argument. How far it goes and whether it escalates and turns violent depends on a lot of different factors—what the argument is about, the personalities of the people involved, where the fight takes place, and whether or not one or both people are under the influence of drugs and alcohol.

A NIDA-funded study looked at youth who were treated in an urban emergency department because of a violence-related injury. It turns out that not all drug use leads to the same kinds of violence. This study looked specifically at whether the violence was "dating violence" or "non-dating violence" and what impact, if any, the type of drug used made.

The researchers found that teens treated in the emergency department for an injury related to dating violence were more likely to be girls than boys. There were also differences in the types of drugs used before a dating violence incident vs. non-dating violence incidents.

For example, some youth tended to use alcohol alone or in combination with marijuana just before a non-dating violence incident occurred and tended to abuse prescription sedatives (Xanax or Valium) and/or opioids (like Vicodin and OxyContin) before a dating violence incident occurred.

This study tells us that the drug of choice may be different for boys and girls, and that girls are more likely than boys to experience dating violence. The drugs used may also be different depending on the situation (for example, being at home versus being at a bar or club). But more research is needed to learn how different drugs may make us more or less aggressive or more likely to be the victim of someone else who is using drugs or alcohol. Understanding more about this, and how gender and substance use factor into dating violence (and non-dating violence), will help public health educators develop programs to help teens who may end up in violent situations.

Connections between Drug Use and Violence, Trauma among Homeless Youth

In August, a study was shared that explored drinking and drug use among homeless youth as a way to detach from their experiences with violence on the street. Here, it is asked whether drug use is linked with youth's increased risk of witnessing, experiencing, or perpetrating violence or other traumatic events among strangers and those they know. Three recent studies examine the link between homeless young people's drug habits and multiple types of violence and trauma—including intimate partner violence, robbery, physical and sexual assault, loss of a loved one, drug overdose, and risky sexual behaviors.

Emerging Connections between Drug Use, Violence, and Traumatic Events

Researcher Kimberly Bender and her colleagues interviewed 601 homeless youth from Los Angeles, Denver, and Austin to ask about their recent substance use and experiences with violence. The researchers divided participants into three categories: those who rarely experienced or witnessed violence or traumatic events, including a drug overdose; those who witnessed threats, physical attacks, or the death of a close friend; and those who experienced or witnessed high levels of violence or traumatic events on a regular basis.

The study found that participants who witnessed or experienced violence more frequently used alcohol and drugs more than those with fewer encounters. The findings did not specify, however, whether drug use prompted or resulted from those occurrences. Because of the overlap between drug use and violence, the authors recommend that youth-serving agencies increase their screening for both, as well as related mental health symptoms. Ideally, they say, youth should receive treatment for victimization and substance abuse recovery at the same time.

For Some Drugs, a Stronger Link than Others

Despite the emerging connections between drug use and violence, few studies have explored the impact of specific types of drugs on relationship violence among homeless youth. Led by Robin Petering, researchers from the University of Southern California School of Social Work developed a questionnaire for 238 homeless youth who said they had been in a sexual relationship during the past year. Participants answered questions about whether they had used or experienced violence (or both) and if they had taken methamphetamine, powder cocaine, ecstasy, heroin, or crack cocaine in the last 30 days. Youth who reported using—or both using and experiencing—violence were more likely to have taken methamphetamine and/or ecstasy. Both drugs are classified as psychostimulants, the authors write, and prior studies have shown that they are linked to aggression.

Chapter 30

Health Consequences of Drug Addiction

Chapter Contents

Section 30.1

Poor Health Outcomes of Commonly Abused Drugs

This section contains text excerpted from the following sources: Text beginning with the heading "Health Effects of Commonly Abused Drugs," is excerpted from "Commonly Abused Drugs Charts," National Institute on Drug Abuse (NIDA), March 2016; Text under the heading "Alcohol" is excerpted from "Fact Sheets - Alcohol Use and Your Health," Centers for Disease Control and Prevention (CDC), February 29, 2016.

Health Effects of Commonly Abused Drugs

Most drugs of abuse can alter a person's thinking and judgment, leading to health risks, including addiction, drugged driving and infectious disease. Most drugs could potentially harm an unborn baby; pregnancy-related issues are listed below for drugs where there is enough scientific evidence to connect the drug use to specific negative effects.

Ayahuasca

Possible Health Effects

- **Short-term:** Strong hallucinations including perceptions of otherworldly imagery, altered visual and auditory perceptions; increased blood pressure; vomiting.
- **Long-term:** Unknown.
- **Other Health-related Issues:** Unknown.
- **In Combination with Alcohol:** Unknown.
- **Withdrawal Symptoms**: Unknown.

Cocaine

Possible Health Effects

- **Short-term**: Narrowed blood vessels; enlarged pupils; increased body temperature, heart rate, and blood pressure; headache;

abdominal pain and nausea; euphoria; increased energy, alertness; insomnia, restlessness; anxiety; erratic and violent behavior, panic attacks, paranoia, psychosis; heart rhythm problems, heart attack; stroke, seizure, coma.

- **Long-term**: Loss of sense of smell, nosebleeds, nasal damage and trouble swallowing from snorting; infection and death of bowel tissue from decreased blood flow; poor nutrition and weight loss from decreased appetite.
- **Other Health-related Issues:** Pregnancy: premature delivery, low birth weight, neonatal abstinence syndrome. Risk of HIV, hepatitis, and other infectious diseases from shared needles.
- **In Combination with Alcohol:** Greater risk of overdose and sudden death than from either drug alone.
- **Withdrawal Symptoms:** Depression, tiredness, increased appetite, insomnia, vivid unpleasant dreams, slowed thinking and movement, restlessness.

DMT

Possible Health Effects

- **Short-term**: Intense visual hallucinations, depersonalization, auditory distortions, and an altered perception of time and body image, usually resolving in 30-45 minutes or less. Physical effects include hypertension, increased heart rate, agitation, seizures, dilated pupils, involuntary rapid eye movements, dizziness, incoordination.
- **Long-term:** Unknown.
- **Other Health-related Issues:** At high doses, coma and respiratory arrest have occurred.
- **In Combination with Alcohol**: Unknown.
- **Withdrawal Symptoms:** Unknown.

GHB

Possible Health Effects

- **Short-term:** Euphoria, drowsiness, decreased anxiety, confusion, memory loss, hallucinations, excited and aggressive behavior, nausea, vomiting, unconsciousness, seizures, slowed heart rate and breathing, lower body temperature, coma, death.

- **Long-term**: Unknown.
- **Other Health-related Issues:** Sometimes used as a date rape drug.
- **In Combination with Alcohol:** Nausea, problems with breathing, greatly increased depressant effects.
- **Withdrawal Symptoms:** Insomnia, anxiety, tremors, sweating, increased heart rate and blood pressure, psychotic thoughts.

Heroin

Possible Health Effects

- **Short-term:** Euphoria; warm flushing of skin; dry mouth; heavy feeling in the hands and feet; clouded thinking; alternate wakeful and drowsy states; itching; nausea; vomiting; slowed breathing and heart rate.
- **Long-term:** Collapsed veins; abscesses (swollen tissue with pus); infection of the lining and valves in the heart; constipation and stomach cramps; liver or kidney disease; pneumonia.
- **Other Health-related Issues**: Pregnancy: miscarriage, low birth weight, neonatal abstinence syndrome. Risk of HIV, hepatitis, and other infectious diseases from shared needles.
- **In Combination with Alcohol:** Dangerous slowdown of heart rate and breathing, coma, death.
- **Withdrawal Symptoms**: Restlessness, muscle and bone pain, insomnia, diarrhea, vomiting, cold flashes with goose bumps ("cold turkey"), leg movements.

Inhalants

Possible Health Effects

- **Short-term:** Confusion; nausea; slurred speech; lack of coordination; euphoria; dizziness; drowsiness; disinhibition, lightheadedness, hallucinations/delusions; headaches; sudden sniffing death due to heart failure (from butane, propane, and other chemicals in aerosols); death from asphyxiation, suffocation, convulsions or seizures, coma, or choking.
    - Nitrites: enlarged blood vessels, enhanced sexual pleasure, increased heart rate, brief sensation of heat and excitement, dizziness, headache.

- **Long-term:** Liver and kidney damage; bone marrow damage; limb spasms due to nerve damage; brain damage from lack of oxygen that can cause problems with thinking, movement, vision, and hearing.
    - Nitrites: increased risk of pneumonia.
- **Other Health-related Issues:** Pregnancy: low birth weight, bone problems, delayed behavioral development due to brain problems, altered metabolism and body composition.
- **In Combination with Alcohol**: dangerously low blood pressure.
- **Withdrawal Symptoms:** Nausea, loss of appetite, sweating, tics, problems sleeping, and mood changes.

Ketamine

Possible Health Effects

- **Short-term:** Problems with attention, learning, and memory; dreamlike states, hallucinations; sedation; confusion and problems speaking; loss of memory; problems moving, to the point of being immobile; raised blood pressure; unconsciousness; slowed breathing that can lead to death.
- **Long-term:** Ulcers and pain in the bladder; kidney problems; stomach pain; depression; poor memory.
- **Other Health-related Issues:** Sometimes used as a date rape drug. Risk of HIV, hepatitis, and other infectious diseases from shared needles.
- **In Combination with Alcohol:** Increased risk of adverse effects.
- **Withdrawal Symptoms**: Unknown.

Khat

Possible Health Effects

- **Short-term**: Euphoria, increased alertness and arousal, increased blood pressure and heart rate, depression, inability to concentrate, irritability, loss of appetite, insomnia.
- **Long-term:** Tooth decay and gum disease; gastrointestinal disorders such as constipation, ulcers, stomach inflammation, and

increased risk of upper gastrointestinal tumors; cardiovascular disorders such as irregular heartbeat, decreased blood flow, and heart attack.

- **Other Health-related Issues**: In rare cases associated with heavy use: psychotic reactions such as fear, anxiety, grandiose delusions (fantastical beliefs that one has superior qualities such as fame, power, and wealth), hallucinations, and paranoia.
- **In Combination with Alcohol**: Unknown.
- **Withdrawal Symptoms:** Depression, nightmares, trembling, and lack of energy.

Kratom

Possible Health Effects

- **Short-term:** Sensitivity to sunburn, nausea, itching, sweating, dry mouth, constipation, increased urination, loss of appetite. Low doses: increased energy, sociability, alertness. High doses: sedation, euphoria, decreased pain.
- **Long-term:** Anorexia, weight loss, insomnia, skin darkening, dry mouth, frequent urination, constipation. Hallucination and paranoia with long-term use at high doses.
- **Other Health-related Issues:** Unknown.
- **In Combination with Alcohol**: Unknown.
- **Withdrawal Symptoms**: Muscle aches, insomnia, irritability, hostility, aggression, emotional changes, runny nose, jerky movements.

LSD

Possible Health Effects

- **Short-term:** Rapid emotional swings; distortion of a person's ability to recognize reality, think rationally, or communicate with others; raised blood pressure, heart rate, body temperature; dizziness and insomnia; loss of appetite; dry mouth; sweating; numbness; weakness; tremors; enlarged pupils.
- **Long-term:** Frightening flashbacks (called Hallucinogen Persisting Perception Disorder [HPPD]); ongoing visual disturbances, disorganized thinking, paranoia, and mood swings.

- **Other Health-related Issues:** Unknown.
- **In Combination with Alcohol**: May decrease the perceived effects of alcohol.
- **Withdrawal Symptoms**: Unknown.

Marijuana (Cannabis)

Possible Health Effects

- **Short-term:** Enhanced sensory perception and euphoria followed by drowsiness/relaxation; slowed reaction time; problems with balance and coordination; increased heart rate and appetite; problems with learning and memory; hallucinations; anxiety; panic attacks; psychosis.
- **Long-term:** Mental health problems, chronic cough, frequent respiratory infections.
- **Other Health-related Issues**: Youth: possible loss of IQ points when repeated use begins in adolescence. Pregnancy: babies born with problems with attention, memory, and problem solving.
- **In Combination with Alcohol:** Increased heart rate, blood pressure; further slowing of mental processing and reaction time.
- **Withdrawal Symptoms**: Irritability, trouble sleeping, decreased appetite, anxiety.

MDMA (Ecstasy / Molly)

Possible Health Effects

- **Short-term**: Lowered inhibition; enhanced sensory perception; confusion; depression; sleep problems; anxiety; increased heart rate and blood pressure; muscle tension; teeth clenching; nausea; blurred vision; faintness; chills or sweating; sharp rise in body temperature leading to liver, kidney, or heart failure and death.
- **Long-term:** Long-lasting confusion, depression, problems with attention, memory, and sleep; increased anxiety, impulsiveness, aggression; loss of appetite; less interest in sex.

- **Other Health-related Issues:** Unknown.
- **In Combination with Alcohol**: May increase the risk of cell and organ damage.
- **Withdrawal Symptoms**: Fatigue, loss of appetite, depression, trouble concentrating.

Mescaline (Peyote)

Possible Health Effects

- **Short-term:** Enhanced perception and feeling; hallucinations; euphoria; anxiety; increased body temperature, heart rate, blood pressure; sweating; problems with movement.
- **Long-term**: Unknown.
- **Other Health-related Issues:** Unknown.
- **In Combination with Alcohol:** Unknown.
- **Withdrawal Symptoms:** Unknown.

Methamphetamine

Possible Health Effects

- **Short-term:** Increased wakefulness and physical activity; decreased appetite; increased breathing, heart rate, blood pressure, temperature; irregular heartbeat.
- **Long-term:** Anxiety, confusion, insomnia, mood problems, violent behavior, paranoia, hallucinations, delusions, weight loss, severe dental problems ("meth mouth"), intense itching leading to skin sores from scratching.
- **Other Health-related Issues**: Pregnancy: premature delivery; separation of the placenta from the uterus; low birth weight; lethargy; heart and brain problems. Risk of HIV, hepatitis, and other infectious diseases from shared needles.
- **In Combination with Alcohol:** Masks the depressant effect of alcohol, increasing risk of alcohol overdose; may increase blood pressure and jitters.
- **Withdrawal Symptoms**: Depression, anxiety, tiredness.

Over-the-counter Cough / Cold Medicines (Dextromethorphan or DMX)

Possible Health Effects

- **Short-term**: Euphoria; slurred speech; increased heart rate, blood pressure, temperature; numbness; dizziness; nausea; vomiting; confusion; paranoia; altered visual perceptions; problems with movement; buildup of excess acid in body fluids.
- **Long-term:** Unknown.
- **Other Health-related Issues:** Breathing problems, seizures, and increased heart rate may occur from other ingredients in cough/cold medicines.
- **In Combination with Alcohol:** Increased risk of adverse effects.
- **Withdrawal Symptoms:** Unknown.

PCP

Possible Health Effects

- **Short-term**: Delusions, hallucinations, paranoia, problems thinking, a sense of distance from one's environment, anxiety. Low doses: slight increase in breathing rate; increased blood pressure and heart rate; shallow breathing; face redness and sweating; numbness of the hands or feet; problems with movement. High doses: lowered blood pressure, pulse rate, breathing rate; nausea; vomiting; blurred vision; flicking up and down of the eyes; drooling; loss of balance; dizziness; violence; suicidal thoughts; seizures, coma, and death.
- **Long-term**: Memory loss, problems with speech and thinking, depression, weight loss, anxiety.
- **Other Health-related Issues:** PCP has been linked to self-injury. Risk of HIV, hepatitis, and other infectious diseases from shared needles.
- **In Combination with Alcohol:** Increased risk of coma.
- **Withdrawal Symptoms**: Headaches, sweating.

Prescription Opioids

Possible Health Effects

- **Short-term**: Pain relief, drowsiness, nausea, constipation, euphoria, confusion, slowed breathing, death.
- **Long-term**: Unknown.
- **Other Health-related Issues:** Pregnancy: Miscarriage, low birth weight, neonatal abstinence syndrome. Older adults: higher risk of accidental misuse or abuse because many older adults have multiple prescriptions, increasing the risk of drug-drug interactions, and breakdown of drugs slows with age; also, many older adults are treated with prescription medications for pain. Risk of HIV, hepatitis, and other infectious diseases from shared needles.
- **In Combination with Alcohol**: Dangerous slowing of heart rate and breathing leading to coma or death.
- **Withdrawal Symptoms**: Restlessness, muscle and bone pain, insomnia, diarrhea, vomiting, cold flashes with goose bumps ("cold turkey"), leg movements.

Prescription Sedatives (Tranquilizers, Depressants)

Possible Health Effects

- **Short-term:** Drowsiness, slurred speech, poor concentration, confusion, dizziness, problems with movement and memory, lowered blood pressure, slowed breathing.
- **Long-term:** Unknown.
- **Other Health-related Issues:** Sleep medications are sometimes used as date rape drugs. Risk of HIV, hepatitis, and other infectious diseases from shared needles.
- **In Combination with Alcohol:** Further slows heart rate and breathing, which can lead to death.
- **Withdrawal Symptoms:** Must be discussed with a health care provider; barbiturate withdrawal can cause a serious abstinence syndrome that may even include seizures.

Prescription Stimulants

Possible Health Effects

- **Short-term:** Increased alertness, attention, energy; increased blood pressure and heart rate; narrowed blood vessels; increased blood sugar; opened-up breathing passages. High doses: dangerously high body temperature and irregular heartbeat; heart failure; seizures.

- **Long-term**: Heart problems, psychosis, anger, paranoia.
- **Other Health-related Issues**: Risk of HIV, hepatitis, and other infectious diseases from shared needles.
- **In Combination with Alcohol:** Masks the depressant action of alcohol, increasing risk of alcohol overdose; may increase blood pressure and jitters.
- **Withdrawal Symptoms:** Depression, tiredness, sleep problems.

Psilocybin

Possible Health Effects

- **Short-term:** Hallucinations, altered perception of time, inability to tell fantasy from reality, panic, muscle relaxation or weakness, problems with movement, enlarged pupils, nausea, vomiting, drowsiness.
- **Long-term:** Risk of flashbacks and memory problems.
- **Other Health-related Issues**: Risk of poisoning if a poisonous mushroom is accidentally used.
- **In Combination with Alcohol:** May decrease the perceived effects of alcohol.
- **Withdrawal Symptoms:** Unknown.

Rohypnol© (Flunitrazepam)

Possible Health Effects

- **Short-term:** Drowsiness, sedation, sleep; amnesia, blackout; decreased anxiety; muscle relaxation, impaired reaction time and motor coordination; impaired mental functioning and judgment; confusion; aggression; excitability; slurred speech; headache; slowed breathing and heart rate.
- **Long-term**: Unknown.
- **Other Health-related Issues**: Unknown.
- **In Combination with Alcohol:** Severe sedation, unconsciousness, and slowed heart rate and breathing, which can lead to death.

- **Withdrawal Symptoms:** Headache; muscle pain; extreme anxiety, tension, restlessness, confusion, irritability; numbness and tingling of hands or feet; hallucinations, delirium, convulsions, seizures, or shock.

Salvia

Possible Health Effects

- **Short-term**: Short-lived but intense hallucinations; altered visual perception, mood, body sensations; mood swings, feelings of detachment from one's body; sweating.
- **Long-term:** Unknown.
- **Other Health-related Issues:** Unknown.
- **In Combination with Alcohol:** Unknown.
- **Withdrawal Symptoms**: Unknown.

Steroids (Anabolic)

Possible Health Effects

- **Short-term:** Headache, acne, fluid retention (especially in the hands and feet), oily skin, yellowing of the skin and whites of the eyes, infection at the injection site.
- **Long-term**: Kidney damage or failure; liver damage; high blood pressure, enlarged heart, or changes in cholesterol leading to increased risk of stroke or heart attack, even in young people; aggression; extreme mood swings; anger ("roid rage"); paranoid jealousy; extreme irritability; delusions; impaired judgment.
- **Other Health-related Issues:** Males: shrunken testicles, lowered sperm count, infertility, baldness, development of breasts, increased risk for prostate cancer. Females: facial hair, male-pattern baldness, menstrual cycle changes, enlargement of the clitoris, deepened voice. Adolescents: stunted growth. Risk of HIV, hepatitis, and other infectious diseases from shared needles.
- **In Combination with Alcohol**: Increased risk of violent behavior.
- **Withdrawal Symptoms:** Mood swings; tiredness; restlessness; loss of appetite; insomnia; lowered sex drive; depression, sometimes leading to suicide attempts.

Synthetic Cannabinoids

Possible Health Effects

- **Short-term:** Increased heart rate; vomiting; agitation; confusion; hallucinations, anxiety, paranoia; increased blood pressure and reduced blood supply to the heart; heart attack.
- **Long-term**: Unknown.
- **Other Health-related Issues:** Use of synthetic cannabinoids has led to an increase in emergency room visits in certain areas.
- **In Combination with Alcohol:** Unknown.
- **Withdrawal Symptoms:** Headaches, anxiety, depression, irritability.

Synthetic Cathinones (Bath Salts)

Possible Health Effects

- **Short-term:** Increased heart rate and blood pressure; euphoria; increased sociability and sex drive; paranoia, agitation, and hallucinations; psychotic and violent behavior; nosebleeds; sweating; nausea, vomiting; insomnia; irritability; dizziness; depression; suicidal thoughts; panic attacks; reduced motor control; cloudy thinking.
- **Long-term**: Breakdown of skeletal muscle tissue; kidney failure; death.
- **Other Health-related Issues:** Risk of HIV, hepatitis, and other infectious diseases from shared needles.
- **In Combination with Alcohol**: Unknown.
- **Withdrawal Symptoms**: Depression, anxiety, problems sleeping, tremors, paranoia.

Tobacco

Possible Health Effects

- **Short-term**: Increased blood pressure, breathing, and heart rate.
- **Long-term**: Greatly increased risk of cancer, especially lung cancer when smoked and oral cancers when chewed; chronic

bronchitis; emphysema; heart disease; leukemia; cataracts; pneumonia.

- **Other Health-related Issues:** Pregnancy: miscarriage, low birth weight, premature delivery, stillbirth, learning and behavior problems.
- **In Combination with Alcohol:** Unknown.
- **Withdrawal Symptoms:** Irritability, attention and sleep problems, increased appetite.

Alcohol

Short-Term Health Risks

Excessive alcohol use has immediate effects that increase the risk of many harmful health conditions. These are most often the result of binge drinking and include the following:

- Injuries, such as motor vehicle crashes, falls, drownings, and burns.
- Violence, including homicide, suicide, sexual assault, and intimate partner violence.
- Alcohol poisoning, a medical emergency that results from high blood alcohol levels.
- Risky sexual behaviors, including unprotected sex or sex with multiple partners. These behaviors can result in unintended pregnancy or sexually transmitted diseases, including HIV.
- Miscarriage and stillbirth or fetal alcohol spectrum disorders (FASDs) among pregnant women.

Long-Term Health Risks

Over time, excessive alcohol use can lead to the development of chronic diseases and other serious problems including:

- High blood pressure, heart disease, stroke, liver disease, and digestive problems.
- Cancer of the breast, mouth, throat, esophagus, liver, and colon.
- Learning and memory problems, including dementia and poor school performance.

- Mental health problems, including depression and anxiety.
- Social problems, including lost productivity, family problems, and unemployment.
- Alcohol dependence, or alcoholism.

By not drinking too much, you can reduce the risk of these short- and long-term health risks.

Section 30.2

Substance Abuse and Medical Complications

This section includes text excerpted from "Drugs, Brains, and Behavior: The Science of Addiction," National Institute on Drug Abuse (NIDA), July 2014.

Addiction and Health

What Are the Medical Consequences of Drug Addiction?

People who suffer from addiction often have one or more accompanying medical issues, which may include lung or cardiovascular disease, stroke, cancer, and mental disorders. Imaging scans, chest X-rays, and blood tests show the damaging effects of long-term drug abuse throughout the body. For example, research has shown that tobacco smoke causes cancer of the mouth, throat, larynx, blood, lungs, stomach, pancreas, kidney, bladder, and cervix. In addition, some drugs of abuse, such as inhalants, are toxic to nerve cells and may damage or destroy them either in the brain or the peripheral nervous system.

The Impact of Addiction Can Be Far-Reaching

- Cardiovascular disease
- Stroke
- Cancer
- HIV/AIDS

- Hepatitis B and C
- Lung disease
- Mental disorders

Does Drug Abuse Cause Mental Disorders, or vice Versa?

Drug abuse and mental illness often co-exist. In some cases, mental disorders such as anxiety, depression, or schizophrenia may precede addiction; in other cases, drug abuse may trigger or exacerbate those mental disorders, particularly in people with specific vulnerabilities.

How Can Addiction Harm Other People?

Beyond the harmful consequences for the person with the addiction, drug abuse can cause serious health problems for others. Three of the more devastating and troubling consequences of addiction are:

- **Negative effects of prenatal drug exposure on infants and children.**

A mother's abuse of heroin or prescription opioids during pregnancy can cause a withdrawal syndrome (called neonatal abstinence syndrome, or NAS) in her infant. It is also likely that some drug-exposed children will need educational support in the classroom to help them overcome what may be subtle deficits in developmental areas such as behavior, attention, and thinking. Ongoing research is investigating whether the effects of prenatal drug exposure on the brain and behavior extend into adolescence to cause developmental problems during that time period.

- **Negative effects of secondhand smoke.**

Secondhand tobacco smoke, also called environmental tobacco smoke (ETS), is a significant source of exposure to a large number of substances known to be hazardous to human health, particularly to children. According to the Surgeon General's 2006 Report, The Health Consequences of Involuntary Exposure to Tobacco Smoke, involuntary exposure to secondhand smoke increases the risks of heart disease and lung cancer in people who have never smoked by 25–30 percent and 20–30 percent, respectively.

- **Increased spread of infectious diseases.**

Injection of drugs such as heroin, cocaine, and methamphetamine currently accounts for about 12 percent of new AIDS cases. Injection drug use is also a major factor in the spread of hepatitis C, a serious, potentially fatal liver disease. Injection drug use is not the only way that drug abuse contributes to the spread of infectious diseases. All drugs of abuse cause some form of intoxication, which interferes with judgment and increases the likelihood of risky sexual behaviors. This, in turn, contributes to the spread of HIV/AIDS, hepatitis B and C, and other sexually transmitted diseases.

What Are Some Effects of Specific Abused Substances?

- **Nicotine** is an addictive stimulant found in cigarettes and other forms of tobacco. Tobacco smoke increases a user's risk of cancer, emphysema, bronchial disorders, and cardiovascular disease. The mortality rate associated with tobacco addiction is staggering. Tobacco use killed approximately 100 million people during the 20th century, and, if current smoking trends continue, the cumulative death toll for this century has been projected to reach 1 billion.
- **Alcohol** consumption can damage the brain and most body organs. Areas of the brain that are especially vulnerable to alcohol-related damage are the cerebral cortex (largely responsible for our higher brain functions, including problem solving and decision making), the hippocampus (important for memory and learning), and the cerebellum (important for movement coordination).
- **Marijuana** is the most commonly abused illegal substance. This drug impairs short-term memory and learning, the ability to focus attention, and coordination. It also increases heart rate, can harm the lungs, and can increase the risk of psychosis in those with an underlying vulnerability.
- **Prescription medications**, including opioid pain relievers (such as OxyContin® and Vicodin®), anti-anxiety sedatives (such as Valium® and Xanax®), and ADHD stimulants (such as Adderall® and Ritalin®), are commonly misused to self-treat for medical problems or abused for purposes of getting high or (especially with stimulants) improving performance. However, misuse or abuse of these drugs (that is, taking them other than exactly as instructed by a doctor and for the purposes prescribed) can lead to addiction and even, in some cases, death. Opioid pain relievers, for instance, are frequently abused by being crushed and injected or snorted, greatly raising the risk of addiction and

overdose. Unfortunately, there is a common misperception that because medications are prescribed by physicians, they are safe even when used illegally or by another person than they were prescribed for.

- **Inhalants** are volatile substances found in many household products, such as oven cleaners, gasoline, spray paints, and other aerosols, that induce mind-altering effects; they are frequently the first drugs tried by children or young teens. Inhalants are extremely toxic and can damage the heart, kidneys, lungs, and brain. Even a healthy person can suffer heart failure and death within minutes of a single session of prolonged sniffing of an inhalant.
- **Cocaine** is a short-acting stimulant, which can lead users to take the drug many times in a single session (known as a "binge"). Cocaine use can lead to severe medical consequences related to the heart and the respiratory, nervous, and digestive systems.
- **Amphetamines,** including methamphetamine, are powerful stimulants that can produce feelings of euphoria and alertness. Methamphetamine's effects are particularly long-lasting and harmful to the brain. Amphetamines can cause high body temperature and can lead to serious heart problems and seizures.
- **MDMA** (Ecstasy or "Molly") produces both stimulant and mind-altering effects. It can increase body temperature, heart rate, blood pressure, and heart-wall stress. MDMA may also be toxic to nerve cells.
- **LSD** is one of the most potent hallucinogenic, or perception-altering, drugs. Its effects are unpredictable, and abusers may see vivid colors and images, hear sounds, and feel sensations that seem real but do not exist. Users also may have traumatic experiences and emotions that can last for many hours.
- **Heroin** is a powerful opioid drug that produces euphoria and feelings of relaxation. It slows respiration, and its use is linked to an increased risk of serious infectious diseases, especially when taken intravenously. People who become addicted to opioid pain relievers sometimes switch to heroin instead, because it produces similar effects and may be cheaper or easier to obtain.
- **Steroids**, which can also be prescribed for certain medical conditions, are abused to increase muscle mass and to improve

athletic performance or physical appearance. Serious consequences of abuse can include severe acne, heart disease, liver problems, stroke, infectious diseases, depression, and suicide.

- **Drug combinations**. A particularly dangerous and common practice is the combining of two or more drugs. The practice ranges from the co-administration of legal drugs, like alcohol and nicotine, to the dangerous mixing of prescription drugs, to the deadly combination of heroin or cocaine with fentanyl (an opioid pain medication). Whatever the context, it is critical to realize that because of drug–drug interactions, such practices often pose significantly higher risks than the already harmful individual drugs.

Section 30.3

Early-Onset, Regular Cannabis Use Is Linked to IQ Decline

This section includes text excerpted from "Early-Onset, Regular Cannabis Use Is Linked to IQ Decline," National Institute on Drug Abuse (NIDA), August 13, 2013.

Regular cannabis use that starts in adolescence strips away IQ, a NIDA-supported 25-year study of 1,000 individuals suggests. Study participants who initiated weekly cannabis use before age 18 dropped IQ points in proportion to how long they persisted in using the drug, while nonusers gained a fraction of a point.

Persistent cannabis users' cognitive difficulties were evident to friends and family and measurable on psychological tests. Moreover, among adolescent-onset users, quitting or cutting back did not fully eliminate the IQ loss. Drs. Madeline Meier, Terrie Moffitt, Avshalom Caspi, and colleagues at Duke University, King's College London, and the University of Otago, New Zealand, say their findings accord with other data that have suggested that cannabis use may harm the developing brain.

Cannabis Use Correlates with Cognitive Decline

The study participants were 1,037 people who were born in 1972 and 1973 in Dunedin, New Zealand, and enrolled as infants in the longitudinal Dunedin Multidisciplinary Health and Development Study. Their families represented the range of socioeconomic statuses in that region.

Dr. Meier and her team tested each participant's IQ four times up to age 13; asked about past-year cannabis use at ages 18, 21, 26, 32, and 38; and assessed IQ again at age 38. The researchers used the Wechsler Intelligence Scale for Children-Revised (WISC-R) and the Wechsler Adult Intelligence Scale-IV (WAIS-IV) to assess IQ in childhood and adulthood, respectively. The team averaged each participant's four childhood IQ scores and compared that number with his or her score at age 38.

Changes in the participants' IQ scores from childhood to age 38 correlated with the number of assessments at which they reported having used cannabis regularly (at least 4 times weekly). Those who reported regular use at 1 of the 5 drug assessments scored 3 IQ points lower, on average, at age 38 than they had in childhood; the scores of those who reported regular use at 3 or more assessments fell 5 points. In contrast, the scores of participants who reported no cannabis use throughout the study increased slightly. The researchers found similar correlations between participants' IQ trajectories and the number of assessments in which they met diagnostic criteria for cannabis dependence.

When researchers matched adolescent-onset and adult-onset cannabis users with equally persistent use, they saw greater IQ declines among the adolescent-onset users. In fact, whereas individuals who were dependent on cannabis before age 18 and in a total of 3 or more assessments lost 8 IQ points, on average, individuals who developed dependence as adults did not exhibit IQ declines in relation to their cannabis dependence.

The 8-point decline observed among the most persistent adolescent-onset users would move an individual who started at the 50th percentile with an IQ of 100 to the 29th percentile, says Dr. Meier. Such a drop could put a person at a disadvantage compared with his or her peers in terms of ability to get an education or find and hold a good job, she says.

Dr. Meier and colleagues also assessed a variety of specific mental functions at age 38, such as memory and processing speed, using a battery of tests. Dr. Moffitt notes that although she and her colleagues had expected to see impairments in memory, "all kinds of functions were impaired, across the board. Virtually every kind of brain function was involved: memory, processing speed, executive functions, verbal skills, attention, and so forth."

These deficits affected participants' daily functioning to an extent that was noticeable to people who knew them well. The researchers asked informants chosen by the participants themselves to provide information on the participants' mental capacities at age 38. The informants reported more memory and attention problems among cannabis users than among non-users who had started out with the same IQs in childhood.

Cannabis May Harm the Developing Brain

Dr. Meier and colleagues' findings suggest that IQ is particularly vulnerable to cannabis exposure in adolescence:

- Only adolescent-onset users evidenced significant IQ decline.
- Among all the study participants who initiated weekly cannabis use before age 18, there was little difference in average IQ loss between those who had reduced or stopped their use of the drug for a year or more by age 38, versus those who continued to use frequently.

During puberty, neurons and neurotransmitter systems mature and link up into refined neural networks. "We hypothesize that cannabis use may interrupt these changes. Animal studies also suggest that this is the case," Dr. Meier says. To strengthen this hypothesis, future imaging studies might look for structural changes or functional connectivity problems in the brains of adolescent cannabis users.

Dr. Meier and Dr. Moffitt and colleagues ruled out several potential alternative explanations for the observed correlations between cannabis and IQ decline. In a series of analyses, they showed that the correlation still remained after adjusting for participants' cannabis use in the last week before IQ testing, tobacco use, and dependence on alcohol and other drugs.

Fewer cannabis users than non-users in the study were educated beyond high school, and studies have correlated education with improvements in IQ. However, looking only at the study participants who had a high school diploma or less, the persistent cannabis users still showed greater IQ declines. Dr. Meier and Dr. Moffitt and colleagues suggest that cannabis use and fewer years of school could be reciprocally related. Effects of cannabis on the brain could result in poor academic performance and school dropout, which might produce further declines in brain functioning.

In response to suggestions from other researchers, the team examined whether the participants' socioeconomic status and personality factors might explain their results. These analyses disclosed little impact of these factors on the cannabis-IQ correlation.

Are the Changes Reversible?

The researchers say that further research is needed to learn whether cannabis-related impairments in the brain are reversible. However, they point to the current study's finding that stopping or reducing use did not completely restore IQ declines among adolescent-onset users.

"This study is important because we have precious little evidence on whether or not drug use leads to enduring changes in cognition," says Dr. Steven Grant, chief of the Clinical Neurosciences Branch within NIDA's Division of Clinical Neuroscience and Behavioral Research. "The issue is critical, because at stake are the individual's ability to benefit from current substance abuse therapies and recoup his or her full potential for a rich, fulfilling life."

Chapter 31

Hepatitis and Substance Abuse

What Is Hepatitis?

Hepatitis is an inflammation of the liver. It can be caused by a variety of toxins (such as drugs or alcohol), autoimmune conditions, or pathogens (including viruses, bacteria, or parasites). Viral hepatitis is caused by a family of viruses labeled A, B, C, D, and E; each has its own unique route of transmission and prognosis. Hepatitis B (HBV) and hepatitis C (HCV) are the most common viral hepatitis infections transmitted through the risky behaviors that drug users often engage in. Approximately 800,000–1.4 million people are living with HBV and 2.7–3.9 million people are living with HCV in the United States.

Left untreated, hepatitis can lead to cirrhosis (progressive deterioration and malfunction) of the liver and a type of liver cancer called hepatocellular carcinoma (HCC). In fact, HBV and HCV infections are the major risk factors for liver cancer worldwide—an estimated 22,000 people are expected to die from this disease in 2013 in the United States alone, a number that has been steadily increasing over the past several years and now exceeds deaths linked to human immunodeficiency virus. During the next 40–50 years, 1 million people with untreated chronic HCV infection will likely die from complications related to their HCV.

This chapter includes text excerpted from "Viral Hepatitis—A Very Real Consequence of Substance Use," National Institute on Drug Abuse (NIDA), May 2013.

What Is the Relationship between Drug Use and Viral Hepatitis?

Drug and alcohol use places individuals at particular risk for contracting viral hepatitis. Engaging in risky sexual behavior that often accompanies drug use places individuals at risk for contracting HBV, and less frequently HCV. Injection drug users (IDUs) are at high risk for contracting HBV and HCV from shared needles and other drug preparation equipment, which exposes them to bodily fluids from other infected people. Because of the compulsive nature of addiction, IDUs repeatedly engage in these unsafe behaviors, which can make them "super-spreaders" of the virus.

A recent study reported that each IDU infected with HCV is likely to infect about 20 others and that this rapid transmission of the disease occurs within the first three years of initial infection. Drug and alcohol use can also directly damage the liver, increasing risk for chronic liver disease and cancer among those infected with hepatitis. This underscores that early detection and treatment of hepatitis infections in IDUs and other drug users is paramount to protecting both the health of the individual and that of the community.

What Other Health Challenges Do IDUs with Hepatitis Have?

Injection drug users (IDUs) with hepatitis often suffer from several other health conditions at the same time, including mental illness and HIV/AIDS thus requiring care from multiple healthcare providers. Drug abuse treatment is critical for IDUs, as it can reduce risky behaviors that increase the chance of transmitting hepatitis. Research has shown that patients with hepatitis receiving medication-assisted therapy for their opioid addiction can be safely treated with antiviral medications. To enhance HCV care, NIDA is examining coordinated care models that utilize case managers to integrate HCV specialty care with primary care, substance abuse treatment, and mental health services so that these patients get treatment regimens that address all of their health care needs.

What Treatments Are Available for Viral Hepatitis?

Medications are available for the treatment of chronic HBV and HCV infection. For chronic HBV infection, there are several antiviral drugs (adefovir dipivoxil, interferon alfa-2b, pegylated interferon alfa-2a, lamivudine, entecavir, and telbivudine). People who are chronically infected with HBV require consistent medical monitoring to ensure that the medications are keeping the virus in check and that the disease is not progressing to liver damage or cancer.

There are also antiviral medications available for HCV treatment; however, not everyone needs or can benefit from treatment. Until recently, only two antiviral medications (pegylated interferon and ribavirin) were available to treat HCV infection. Although both are effective, serious side effects including depression and suicidal thoughts are experienced by some patients. Now, there are two new safer, direct-acting antiviral (DAA) medications available (boceprevir and telaprevir), which are administered by injection with pegylated interferon. This new treatment lasts between 12-48 weeks depending on the individual and cures HCV infection, unlike treatment for HIV which lasts a lifetime and does not rid the body of HIV.

Research on HCV antivirals continues, and several new promising medications that avoid the adverse events associated with pegylated interferon and can be administered orally (not injected) are in development.

Some people are able to clear the HCV virus (that is, rid it from their bodies) without medications. Recently, NIDA researchers have identified genes that are associated with spontaneous clearance of HCV. These genes also enable people who are unable to clear HCV on their own to respond more favorably to treatment medications. This information can be used to determine which patients can benefit most from HCV treatment. More studies must be done, but this is a first step to personalized medicine for the treatment of HCV.

How Do I Know If I Am Infected with Viral Hepatitis?

The number of new HBV and HCV infections has been declining in recent years, but the number of people living with chronic hepatitis infections is considerable, and deaths associated with untreated, chronic hepatitis infections have been on the rise. This is because most people don't know they are infected until the disease has begun to damage their liver, highlighting why screening for viral hepatitis is so important.

Initial screening for HBV or HCV involves antibody tests, which show whether you have been exposed to the hepatitis virus, although not necessarily whether you are still infected. A positive antibody test should then be followed up with a test that measures the amount of virus in your blood. If this follow-up test is positive, then you should seek advice from a physician that specializes in viral hepatitis treatment. Because screening for hepatitis is so critical for linking people who test positive to the care they need, NIDA is studying new rapid HCV antibody tests that can be used in drug treatment settings.

Chapter 32

HIV / AIDS and Drug Abuse

HIV / AIDS and Drug Abuse: Intertwined Epidemics

Drug abuse and addiction have been inextricably linked with HIV/AIDS since the beginning of the epidemic. The link has to do with heightened risk—both of contracting and transmitting HIV and of worsening its consequences.

No vaccine yet exists to protect a person from getting HIV, and there is no cure. However, HIV can be prevented and its transmission curtailed. Drug abuse treatment fosters both of these goals. HIV medications also help prevent HIV transmission and the progression of HIV to AIDS, greatly prolonging lives.

What Exactly Is HIV/AIDS?

HIV stands for human immunodeficiency virus. This virus severely damages the immune system and causes acquired immune deficiency syndrome, or AIDS, a condition that defeats the body's ability to protect itself against disease.

HIV inflicts this damage by infecting immune cells in our bodies called CD4 positive (CD4+) T cells—essential for fighting infections.

This chapter includes text excerpted from "DrugFacts: HIV/AIDS and Drug Abuse: Intertwined Epidemics," National Institute on Drug Abuse (NIDA), May 2012. Reviewed April 2016.

HIV converts the CD4+ T cells into "factories" that produce more of the HIV virus to infect other healthy cells, eventually destroying the CD4+ T cells.

As CD4+ T cells are lost and the immune system weakens, a person becomes more prone to illnesses and common infections. AIDS is diagnosed when a person has one or more of these infections and a CD4+ cell count of less than 200.

How Do Drugs Affect HIV?

Most people know that intravenous drug use and needle-sharing can transmit HIV; less known is the role that drug abuse in general plays. A person under the influence of certain drugs is more likely to engage in risky behaviors such as having unsafe sex with an infected partner. Indeed, the most common (but not only) way of contracting HIV is through unsafe sex. This includes "transactional" sex—trading sex for drugs or money.

Drug abuse and addiction can also worsen HIV symptoms, causing greater neuronal injury and cognitive impairment, for example.

Because of the strong link between drug abuse and the spread of HIV, drug abuse treatment can be an effective way to prevent the latter. People in drug abuse treatment, which often includes HIV risk reduction counseling, stop or reduce their drug use and related risk behaviors, including risky injection practices and unsafe sex.

Can Anyone Get HIV/AIDS?

Yes, anyone is vulnerable to contracting HIV. Although injecting and other drug users are at elevated risk, anyone who has unprotected sex could be exposed to the infection. In 2010, nearly 47,000 people were diagnosed with HIV. Among those newly diagnosed, nearly two-thirds occurred in men who have sex with men (MSM). One-half of all people living with HIV in 2008 were MSM.

How Is HIV Treated?

From the beginning of the HIV/AIDS epidemic in the early 1980s until the mid-1990s, HIV infection was almost guaranteed to result in death from AIDS. The number of deaths declined after 1996, when effective treatments were introduced.

HAART—highly active antiretroviral therapy—is a customized combination of different classes of medications that a physician prescribes to treat HIV. Although it cannot rid the body of the virus, HAART can control the amount of virus in the bloodstream (viral load), helping to delay the onset of symptoms and progression to AIDS, prolonging survival in people with HIV.

Why Is HIV Testing so Important?

A person infected with HIV may look and feel fine for many years and may not even be aware of the infection. In fact, the Centers for Disease Control and Prevention estimates that 1.2 million people are infected with HIV in the United States and that one in five people infected are unaware of it. HIV testing is critical and can help prevent spread of the infection—among those most at risk (e.g., people who abuse drugs) and in general. Getting tested is not complicated. Some tests can even provide results in 20 minutes, although testing is not accurate until about 6–8 weeks after exposure to HIV. That time is needed for HIV antibodies to form in amounts detectable by a standard HIV test.

Research shows that seeking out and testing high-risk populations and starting treatment for those who test positive prevents HIV transmission by decreasing viral load, infectivity (the ability to infect others), and subsequent illness—to the benefit of all.

Chapter 33

Mental Illness and Addiction

Chapter Contents

Section 33.1

Addiction and Mental Health Disorders

This section contains text excerpted from the following sources: Text beginning with the heading "Mental and Substance Use Disorders" is excerpted from "Mental and Substance Use Disorders," Substance Abuse and Mental Health Services Administration (SAMHSA), March 8, 2016; Text under the heading "Severe Mental Illness Tied to Higher Rates of Substance Use" is excerpted from "Severe Mental Illness Tied to Higher Rates of Substance Use," National Institute on Drug Abuse (NIDA), January 3, 2014.

Mental and Substance Use Disorders

Overview

Mental and substance use disorders affect people from all walks of life and all age groups. These illnesses are common, recurrent, and often serious, but they are treatable and many people do recover. Learning about some of the most common mental and substance use disorders can help people recognize their signs and to seek help.

According to SAMHSA's 2014 National Survey on Drug Use and Health (NSDUH) an estimated 43.6 million (18.1%) Americans ages 18 and up experienced some form of mental illness. In the past year, 20.2 million adults (8.4%) had a substance use disorder. Of these, 7.9 million people had both a mental disorder and substance use disorder, also known as co-occurring mental and substance use disorders.

Various mental and substance use disorders have prevalence rates that differ by gender, age, race, and ethnicity.

Mental Disorders

Mental disorders involve changes in thinking, mood, and/or behavior. These disorders can affect how we relate to others and make choices. Mental disorders take many different forms, with some rooted in deep levels of anxiety, extreme changes in mood, or reduced ability to focus or behave appropriately. Others involve unwanted, intrusive thoughts and some may result in auditory and visual hallucinations or false beliefs about basic aspects of reality. Reaching a level that can be formally diagnosed often depends on a reduction in a person's ability to function as a result of the disorder.

Anxiety disorders are the most common type of mental disorders, followed by depressive disorders. Different mental disorders are more likely to begin and occur at different stages in life and are thus more prevalent in certain age groups. Lifetime anxiety disorders generally have the earliest age of first onset, most commonly around age 6. Other disorders emerge in childhood, approximately 11% of children 4 to 17 years of age (6.4 million) have been diagnosed with attention deficit hyperactivity disorder (ADHD) as of 2011.

Schizophrenia spectrum and psychotic disorders emerge later in life, usually in early adulthood. Not all mental health issues first experienced during childhood or adolescence continue into adulthood, and not all mental health issues are first experienced before adulthood. Mental disorders can occur once, reoccur intermittently, or be more chronic in nature. Mental disorders frequently co-occur with each other and with substance use disorders. Because of this and because of variation in symptoms even within one type of disorder, individual situations and symptoms are extremely varied.

Serious Mental Illness

Serious mental illness among people ages 18 and older is defined at the federal level as having, at any time during the past year, a diagnosable mental, behavior, or emotional disorder that causes serious functional impairment that substantially interferes with or limits one or more major life activities. Serious mental illnesses include major depression, schizophrenia, and bipolar disorder, and other mental disorders that cause serious impairment. In 2014, there were an estimated 9.8 million adults (4.1%) ages 18 and up with a serious mental illness in the past year. People with serious mental illness are more likely to be unemployed, arrested, and/or face inadequate housing compared to those without mental illness.

Serious Emotional Disturbance

The term serious emotional disturbance (SED) is used to refer to children and youth who have had a diagnosable mental, behavioral, or emotional disorder in the past year, which resulted in functional impairment that substantially interferes with or limits the child's role or functioning in family, school, or community activities. A Centers for Disease Control and Prevention (CDC) review of population-level information found that estimates of the number of children with a mental disorder range from 13 to 20%, but current national surveys do not have an indicator of SED.

Substance Use Disorders

Substance use disorders occur when the recurrent use of alcohol and/or drugs causes clinically significant impairment, including health problems, disability, and failure to meet major responsibilities at work, school, or home.

In 2014, about 21.5 million Americans ages 12 and older (8.1%) were classified with a substance use disorder in the past year. Of those, 2.6 million had problems with both alcohol and drugs, 4.5 million had problems with drugs but not alcohol, and 14.4 million had problems with alcohol only.

Co-Occurring Mental and Substance Use Disorders

The coexistence of both a mental health and a substance use disorder is referred to as co-occurring disorders.

According to SAMHSA's 2014 National Survey on Drug Use and Health (NSDUH), approximately 7.9 million adults had co-occurring disorders in 2014. During the past year, for those adults surveyed who experienced substance use disorders and any mental illness, rates were highest among adults ages 26 to 49 (42.7%). For adults with past-year serious mental illness and co-occurring substance use disorders, rates were highest among those ages 18 to 25 (35.3%) in 2014.

Severe Mental Illness Tied to Higher Rates of Substance Use

NIH study shows that certain protective factors do not exist in those with severe mental illness

People with severe mental illness such as schizophrenia or bipolar disorder have a higher risk for substance use, especially cigarette smoking, and protective factors usually associated with lower rates of substance use do not exist in severe mental illness, according to a new study funded by the National Institute on Drug Abuse (NIDA), part of the National Institutes of Health.

Estimates based on past studies suggest that people diagnosed with mood or anxiety disorders are about twice as likely as the general population to also suffer from a substance use disorder. Statistics from the 2012 National Survey on Drug Use and Health indicate close to 8.4 million adults in the United States have both a mental and substance use disorder. However, only 7.9 percent of people receive treatment for both conditions, and 53.7 percent receive no treatment at all, the statistics indicate.

Studies exploring the link between substance use disorders and other mental illnesses have typically not included people with severe psychotic illnesses.

In the current study, 9,142 people diagnosed with schizophrenia, schizoaffective disorder, or bipolar disorder with psychotic features, and 10,195 controls matched to participants according to geographic region, were selected using the Genomic Psychiatry Cohort program. Mental disorder diagnoses were confirmed using the Diagnostic Interview for Psychosis and Affective Disorder (DI-PAD), and controls were screened to verify the absence of schizophrenia or bipolar disorder in themselves or close family members. The DI-PAD was also used for all participants to determine substance use rates.

Compared to controls, people with severe mental illness were about 4 times more likely to be heavy alcohol users (four or more drinks per day); 3.5 times more likely to use marijuana regularly (21 times per year); and 4.6 times more likely to use other drugs at least 10 times in their lives. The greatest increases were seen with tobacco, with patients with severe mental illness 5.1 times more likely to be daily smokers. This is of concern because smoking is the leading cause of preventable death in the United States.

In addition, certain protective factors often associated with belonging to certain racial or ethnic groups—or being female—did not exist in participants with severe mental illness. In the general population, women have lower substance use rates than men, and Asian-Americans have lower substance use rates than white Americans, but these differences are absent among people with severe mental illness. Among young people with severe mental illness, the smoking rates were as high as smoking rates in middle-aged adults, despite success in lowering smoking rates for young people in the general population."

Previous research has shown that people with schizophrenia have a shorter life expectancy than the general population, and chronic cigarette smoking has been suggested as a major contributing factor to higher morbidity and mortality from malignancy as well as cardiovascular and respiratory diseases. These new findings indicate that the rates of substance use in people with severe psychosis may be underestimated, highlighting the need to improve the understanding of the association between substance use and psychotic disorders so that both conditions can be treated effectively.

Section 33.2

Study Parses Comorbidity of Cannabis Use and Social Anxiety

This section includes text excerpted from "Study Parses Comorbidity of Cannabis Use and Social Anxiety," National Institute on Drug Abuse (NIDA), October 25, 2013.

A recent large-scale epidemiological study sheds light on the relationship between cannabis use disorder (CUD) and social anxiety disorder (SAD). The findings affirmed that a significant portion of individuals with CUD also have SAD, and showed that comorbid SAD is associated with greater severity of cannabis-related problems. Moreover, almost all individuals with both CUD and SAD had at least one additional clinically significant psychiatric disturbance.

The researchers say that their findings highlight the importance of assessing CUD patients for SAD. Their evidence suggests that SAD can be both a contributing cause and a consequence of CUD, and that treating both disorders may be a key to helping patients recover from each.

A Common Comorbidity

Dr. Julia D. Buckner at Louisiana State University, Dr. Richard G. Heimberg at Temple University, Dr. Franklin Schneier at Columbia University, and Dr. Carlos Blanco's team at the New York State Psychiatric Institute analyzed data from the National Epidemiologic Survey on Alcohol and Related Conditions (NESARC). Their results confirmed previous observations that patients with CUD experience high rates of SAD.

Of the 43,093 respondents to the survey, 3,297 (7.6 percent) reported having had drug problems consistent with CUD at some time in their lives. Of those with CUD, 340 (10.3 percent) also reported having had, at some time in their lives, social anxiety that was severe enough to warrant a clinical diagnosis of SAD.

Given these numbers, Dr. Buckner says, assessing CUD patients for SAD can facilitate treatment for many. Identifying and treating comorbid SAD can remove an obstacle to recovery from substance abuse. "For example, research suggests that socially anxious people may be less likely to participate in group therapy or seek a sponsor. Also, higher levels of anxiety at the end of CUD treatment have been shown to lead to a higher rate of relapse into cannabis use and related problems," she says.

The Order of Maladies

Over 80 percent of the NESARC respondents with CUD? SAD comorbidity reported that their SAD preceded their CUD, and 15 percent reported CUD onset before SAD onset. Based on this observation, Dr. Buckner and colleagues suggest that two alternative pathways can lead to CUD?SAD comorbidity.

In both pathways, CUD and SAD promote and exacerbate each other. In the more common one, individuals develop CUD as an adverse consequence of self-medicating to ease their social anxiety. In the alternative pathway, uncontrolled cannabis use generates social difficulties and anxiety that develop into SAD.

From a clinical perspective, the researchers say, it will be important to determine whether different pathways indeed exist, because the two groups may respond differently to treatment. For example, those who develop CUD as a result of relying on cannabis to manage their anxiety may benefit from skills to help them better manage their anxiety. In contrast, those who develop SAD as a result of CUD-related impairment may benefit first from strategies to help them better manage their social difficulties and other cannabis-related problems.

SAD and Cannabis Use Severity

Further analysis suggested that people with CUD and SAD experience more cannabis-related problems than those with only CUD. Among NESARC respondents with CUD, 21 percent of those who met the diagnostic criteria for cannabis dependence—which requires compulsive use of the drug and drug-related psychological or physiological problems—also had SAD. In contrast, the rate of SAD among those who met the criteria for cannabis abuse—which specifies only periodic cannabis use and does not require physiological problems—was 8.5 percent.

After controlling statistically for the effects of gender, race, and other psychiatric comorbidities, the researchers estimated that an individual with cannabis dependence had 1.6 times higher odds of comorbid SAD, compared to an individual with cannabis abuse.

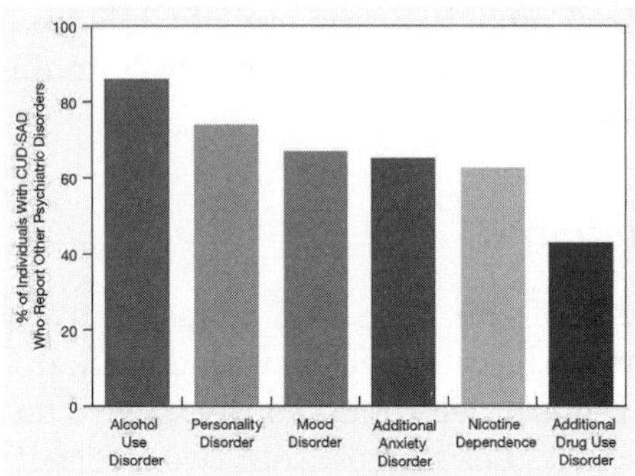

Figure 33.1. *Individuals With Both Cannabis Use and Social Anxiety Disorders Reported High Rates of Additional Psychiatric Problems*

Compounded Comorbidities

The patient with CUD and SAD probably has other psychiatric problems as well, the NESARC data suggest. More than 99 percent of the respondents who reported CUD-SAD also reported symptoms meeting the diagnostic criteria for at least one additional psychiatric disorder (see Figure 33.1). More than 98 percent had experienced another Axis I disorder (e.g., other substance use disorder, mood disorder, or anxiety disorder), and about 73 percent had experienced an Axis II personality disorder (e.g., obsessive-compulsive, paranoid, avoidant, antisocial, schizoid). The CUD-SAD group's odds for reporting a third comorbidity were over 7 times higher than those of respondents who had CUD without SAD.

Not surprisingly, individuals with CUD-SAD reported poorer overall health than those with CUD alone. Just over half rated their health status as excellent or very good, compared to 60 percent of those with CUD alone.

In the National Epidemiologic Survey on Alcohol and Related Conditions, more than 99 percent of respondents who reported symptoms meeting diagnostic criteria for both disorders also qualified for at least one additional psychiatric diagnosis.

The graphic shows a bar chart with 6 bars representing the percentage of patients with co-occurring cannabis use disorder and social anxiety disorder who report another psychiatric disorder. The bars are: Alcohol Use Disorder 86 percent, Personality Disorder 74 percent, Mood Disorder 67 percent, Additional Anxiety Disorder 65 percent, Nicotine Dependence 63 percent, and Additional Drug Use Disorder 43 percent.

Clinical Implications

"In drug treatment settings, anxiety in general, but SAD in particular, can often be overlooked because providers are focused on substance use," says Dr. Buckner. However, addressing patients' social anxiety in treatment can enhance their chances for successful recovery from substance abuse, as well as improve their general quality of life. A finding that a patient with CUD has comorbid SAD can also alert clinicians to a high likelihood of other comorbid problems.

"The relationships among anxiety disorders and substance use disorders are complex and merit this kind of attention, given how commonly they co-occur," says Dr. Naimah Weinberg from NIDA's Division of Epidemiology, Services, and Prevention Research. "This type of study, with the power to focus on a particular anxiety disorder and type of substance dependence, helps refine our understanding of these complex relationships. If the results can be replicated, particularly by prospective studies, this may offer an opportunity for intervention with high-risk youth to prevent the development of substance use disorders."

Section 33.3

Link between Marijuana Use and Psychiatric Disorders

This section includes text excerpted from "Is There a Link between Marijuana Use and Psychiatric Disorders?" National Institute on Drug Abuse (NIDA), March 2016.

Is There a Link between Marijuana Use and Psychiatric Disorders?

Several studies have linked marijuana use to increased risk for psychiatric disorders, including psychosis (schizophrenia), depression, anxiety, and substance use disorders, but whether and to what extent it actually causes these conditions is not always easy to determine. The amount of drug used, the age at first use, and genetic vulnerability have all been shown to influence this relationship. The strongest evidence to date concerns links between marijuana use and substance use disorders and between marijuana use and psychiatric disorders in those with a preexisting genetic or other vulnerability.

Research using longitudinal data from the National Epidemiological Survey on Alcohol and Related Conditions examined associations between marijuana use and mood and anxiety disorders and substance use disorders. After adjusting for various confounding factors, no association between marijuana use and mood and anxiety disorders was found. The only significant associations were increased risk of alcohol use disorders, nicotine dependence, marijuana use disorder, and other drug use disorders.

Recent research has found that marijuana users who carry a specific variant of the *AKT1* gene, which codes for an enzyme that affects dopamine signaling in the *striatum*, are at increased risk of developing psychosis. The striatum is an area of the brain that becomes activated and flooded with dopamine when certain stimuli are present. One study found that the risk for psychosis among those with this variant was seven times higher for daily marijuana users compared with infrequent- or non-users.

Another study found an increased risk of psychosis among adults who had used marijuana in adolescence and also carried a specific variant of the gene for catechol-O-methyltransferase (COMT), an enzyme that degrades neurotransmitters such as dopamine and norepinephrine. Marijuana use has also been shown to worsen the course of illness in patients who already have schizophrenia. As mentioned previously, marijuana can also produce an acute psychotic reaction in non-schizophrenic users, especially at high doses, although this fades as the drug wears off.

Inconsistent and modest associations have been reported between marijuana use and suicidal thoughts and attempted suicide among teens. Marijuana has also been associated with an *amotivational syndrome*, defined as a diminished or absent drive to engage in typically rewarding activities. Because of the role of the endocannabinoid system in regulating mood and reward, it has been hypothesizes that brain changes resulting from early use of marijuana may underlie these associations, but more research is needed to verify that such links exist and better understand them.

Adverse Consequences of Marijuana Use

Acute (Present during Intoxication)

- Impaired short-term memory
- Impaired attention, judgment, and other cognitive functions
- Impaired coordination and balance
- Increased heart rate
- Anxiety, paranoia
- Psychosis (uncommon)

Persistent (lasting longer than intoxication, but may not be permanent)

- Impaired learning and coordination
- Sleep problems

Long-term (cumulative effects of repeated use)

- Potential for marijuana addiction
- Impairments in learning and memory with potential loss of IQ

- Increased risk of chronic cough, bronchitis
- Increased risk of other drug and alcohol use disorders
- Increased risk of schizophrenia in people with genetic vulnerability

Section 33.4

Prevention of Substance Abuse and Mental Illness

This section includes text excerpted from "Prevention of Substance Abuse and Mental Illness," Substance Abuse and Mental Health Services Administration (SAMHSA), November 23, 2015.

Overview

Mental and substance use disorders can have a powerful effect on the health of individuals, their families, and their communities. In 2014, an estimated 9.8 million adults aged 18 and older in the United States had a serious mental illness, and 1.7 million of which were aged 18 to 25. Also 15.7 million adults (aged 18 or older) and 2.8 million youth (aged 12 to 17) had a major depressive episode during the past year. In 2014, an estimated 22.5 million Americans aged 12 and older self-reported needing treatment for alcohol or illicit drug use, and 11.8 million adults self-reported needing mental health treatment or counseling in the past year. These disorders are among the top conditions that cause disability and carry a high burden of disease in the United States, resulting in significant costs to families, employers, and publicly funded health systems. By 2020, mental and substance use disorders will surpass all physical diseases as a major cause of disability worldwide.

In addition, drug and alcohol use can lead to other chronic diseases such as diabetes and heart disease. Addressing the impact of substance use alone is estimated to cost Americans more than $600 billion each year.

Preventing mental and/or substance use disorders and related problems in children, adolescents, and young adults is critical to Americans' behavioral and physical health. Behaviors and symptoms that signal the development of a behavioral disorder often manifest two to four years before a disorder is present. In addition, people with a mental health issue are more likely to use alcohol or drugs than those not affected by a mental illness. Results from the 2014 NSDUH report showed that of those adults with any mental illness, 18.2% had a substance use disorder, while those adults with no mental illness only had a 6.3% rate of substance use disorder in the past year. If communities and families can intervene early, behavioral health disorders might be prevented, or symptoms can be mitigated.

Data have shown that early intervention following the first episode of a serious mental illness can make an impact. Coordinated, specialized services offered during or shortly after the first episode of psychosis are effective for improving clinical and functional outcomes.

In addition, the Institute of Medicine and National Research Council's Preventing Mental, Emotional, and Behavioral Disorders Among Young People report – 2009 notes that cost-benefit ratios for early treatment and prevention programs for addictions and mental illness programs range from 1:2 to 1:10. This means a $1 investment yields $2 to $10 savings in health costs, criminal and juvenile justice costs, educational costs, and lost productivity.

Continuum of Care

A comprehensive approach to behavioral health also means seeing prevention as part of an overall continuum of care. The Behavioral Health Continuum of Care Model recognizes multiple opportunities for addressing behavioral health problems and disorders. Based on the Mental Health Intervention Spectrum, first introduced in a 1994 Institute of Medicine report, the model includes the following components:

- **Promotion**—These strategies are designed to create environments and conditions that support behavioral health and the ability of individuals to withstand challenges. Promotion strategies also reinforce the entire continuum of behavioral health services.
- **Prevention**—Delivered prior to the onset of a disorder, these interventions are intended to prevent or reduce the risk of developing a behavioral health problem, such as underage alcohol use, prescription drug misuse and abuse, and illicit drug use.

- **Treatment**—These services are for people diagnosed with a substance use or other behavioral health disorder.
- **Recovery**—These services support individuals' abilities to live productive lives in the community and can often help with abstinence.

Risk and Protective Factors

People have biological and psychological characteristics that can make them vulnerable or resilient to potential behavioral health problems. Individual-level protective factors might include a positive self-image, self-control, or social competence.

In addition, people do not live in isolation, they are part of families, communities, and society. A variety of risk and protective factors exist within each of these environmental contexts.

Evidence-Based Practices

Experts attest that an optimal mix of prevention interventions is required to address substance use issues in communities, because they are among the most difficult social problems to prevent or reduce. SAMHSA's program grantees should consider comprehensive solutions that fit the particular needs of their communities and population, within cultural context, and take into consideration unique local circumstances, including community readiness. Some interventions may be evidence-based, while others may document their effectiveness based on other sources of information and empirical data.

Early intervention also is critical to treating mental illness before it can cause tragic results like serious impairment, unemployment, homelessness, poverty, and suicide. The Community Mental Health Services Block Grant (MHBG) directs states to set aside 5% of their MHBG allocation, which is administered by SAMHSA, to support evidence-based programs that address the needs of individuals with early serious mental illness, including psychotic disorders.

Prevention Strategies

Many prevention approaches, such as selective prevention strategies, focus on helping individuals develop the knowledge, attitudes, and skills they need to make good choices or change harmful behaviors. Many of these strategies can be classroom-based.

Universal prevention approaches include the use of environmental prevention strategies, which are tailored to local community characteristics and address the root causes of risky behaviors by creating environments that make it easier to act in healthy ways. The successful execution of these strategies often involves lawmakers, local officials, and community leaders, as well as the acceptance and active involvement of members from various sectors of the community (such as business, faith, schools, and health). For example, the use of this type of strategy may offer fewer places for young people to purchase alcohol, so consuming alcohol becomes less convenient; therefore, less is consumed.

Environmental change strategies have specific advantages over strategies that focus exclusively on the individual. Because they target a much broader audience, they have the potential to produce widespread changes in behavior at the population level. Further, when implemented effectively, they can create shifts in both individual attitudes and community norms that can have long-term, substantial effects. Strategies that target the environment include:

- Communication and education
- Enforcement

Cultural Awareness and Competency

Improving cultural and linguistic competence is an important strategy for addressing persistent behavioral health disparities experienced by diverse communities, including the lesbian, gay, bisexual, and transgender population and racial and ethnic minority groups. These diverse populations tend to have less access to prevention services and poorer behavioral health outcomes.

Cultural and linguistic competence includes, but is not limited to, the ability of an individual or organization to interact effectively with people of different cultures. To produce positive change, prevention practitioners must understand the cultural and linguistic context of the community, and they must have the willingness and skills to work within this context.

For diverse populations to benefit from prevention and early intervention programs, SAMHSA ensures that culture and language be considered at every step when developing and then implementing these programs. In addition, the SAMHSA Center for the Application of Prevention Technologies lists the elements of a culturally competent prevention system. With regard to the development of a culturally diverse workforce, the *Now Is The Time:* Minority Fellowship Program–Youth expands on the existing Minority Fellowship program to support master's level-trained behavioral health providers in the fields of psychology, social work, professional counseling, marriage and family therapy, and nursing. In addition, SAMHSA supports the *Now Is The Time:* Minority Fellowship Program–Addiction Counselors, which supports students pursuing master's level degrees in addiction/substance abuse counseling as well as the Minority Fellowship Program whose purpose is to reduce health disparities and improve healthcare outcomes of racially and ethnically diverse populations by increasing the number of culturally competent behavioral health professionals available to underserved populations in the public and private nonprofit sectors.

Community Coalitions

Community coalitions are increasingly used as a vehicle to foster improvements in community health. A coalition is traditionally defined as "a group of individuals representing diverse organizations, factions or constituencies who agree to work together to achieve a common goal." Community coalitions differ from other types of coalitions in that they include professional and grassroots members committed to work together to influence long-term health and welfare practices in their community. Additionally, given their ability to leverage existing resources in the community and convene diverse organizations, community coalitions connote a type of collaboration that is considered to be sustainable over time.

The federal government has increasingly used community coalitions as a programmatic approach to address emerging community health issues. Community coalitions are composed of diverse organizations that form an alliance in order to pursue a common goal. The activities of community coalitions include outreach, education, prevention, service delivery, capacity building, empowerment, community action, and systems change. The presumption is that successful community coalitions are able to identify new resources to continue their activities and sustain their impact in the community over time. Given the large investment in community coalitions, researchers are beginning to systematically explore the factors that affect the sustainability of community coalitions once their initial funding ends.

The Office of National Drug Control Policy (ONDCP) and the SAMHSA Center for Substance Abuse Prevention (CSAP) support Drug-Free Communities (DFC) Support Program grants, which were created by the Drug-Free Communities Act of 1997 (Public Law 105-20). The DFC Support Program has two goals:

- Establish and strengthen collaboration among communities, public and private non-profit agencies, as well as federal, state, local, and tribal governments to support the efforts of community coalitions working to prevent and reduce substance use among youth
- Reduce substance use among youth and, over time, reduce substance abuse among adults by addressing the factors in a community that increase the risk of substance abuse and promoting the factors that minimize the risk of substance abuse

Long-term analyses suggest a consistent record of positive accomplishment for substance use outcomes in communities with a DFC grantee from 2002 to 2012. The prevalence of past 30-day use of alcohol, tobacco, and marijuana declined significantly among both middle school and high school students. The prevalence of past 30-day alcohol use dropped the most in absolute percentage point terms, declining by 2.8 percentage points among middle school students and declining by 3.8 percentage points among high school students. The prevalence of past 30-day tobacco use declined by 1.9 percentage points among middle school students, and by 3.2 percentage points among high school students from DFC grantees' first report to their most recent report. Though significant, the declines in the prevalence of past 30-day marijuana use were less pronounced, declining by 1.3 percentage points among middle school students and by 0.7 percentage points among high school students.

Chapter 34

Substance Abuse and Suicide Prevention

Substance Abuse Prevention is Suicide Prevention

Drug poisoning deaths have increased 120 percent in recent years–from 17,415 in 2000 to 38,329 in 2010. The majority (58 percent) of the drug deaths involved pharmaceuticals, and 75 percent of those deaths involved prescription pain relievers. In 2010, U.S. emergency departments treated 202,000 suicide attempts in which prescription drugs were used as the means, 33,000 of which were narcotic pain relievers.

The suicide and substance abuse prevention fields need to align their efforts to promote healthy individuals and healthy communities.

Many of the factors that increase the risk for substance abuse, such as traumatic experiences, also increase the risk for suicidal thoughts and behaviors, and substance abuse, like mental health problems, is linked with a several-fold increase in suicide risk.

There is hope, however: Prevention works, treatment is effective, and recovery is possible. Life skills that support effective problem-solving

---

This chapter contains text excerpted from the following sources: Text under the heading "Substance Abuse Prevention is Suicide Prevention" is excerpted from "Substance Abuse Prevention is Suicide Prevention," WhiteHouse.gov, September 10, 2013; Text under the heading "Substance Use Disorders and Suicide" is excerpted from "2012 National Strategy for Suicide Prevention: Goals and Objectives for Action," U.S. Department of Health and Human Services (HHS), September 2012. Reviewed April 2016.

and emotional regulation, connections with positive friends and family members, and social support can protect individuals from both substance abuse and suicide. Treatment and support are important precursors for recovery from substance abuse as well as recovery from suicidal thoughts.

In September 2012, a newly revised National Strategy for Suicide Prevention (NSSP) was released by the National Action Alliance for Suicide Prevention (Action Alliance) in conjunction with the Office of the Surgeon General. The Action Alliance is a public-private partnership, jointly launched in 2010 by the Secretaries of Health and Human Services and Defense, envisioning a Nation free from the tragic experience of suicide. The connection between suicide prevention and the prevention and treatment of substance abuse is either implicit or explicit in each of the 13 goals of the NSSP, as it should be. Recognizing this, the NSSP calls for several actions, including:

- Train staff in substance abuse treatment settings to ask their clients and patients *directly* and in a *non-judgmental way* whether they are having thoughts of suicide or think things would be better if they were dead. Ask on intake and periodically throughout the course of treatment, and ask in a way that opens the door for a truthful response.
- Work with individuals, families and other social groups, and communities to reduce access to drugs, especially access to lethal quantities of drugs among individuals at increased risk for suicide. This includes reducing stocks of medications kept in the home, locking up commonly abused medications, and encouraging the proper disposal of unused and unneeded prescription drugs, a key component of the *2013 National Drug Control Strategy.*

Substance Use Disorders and Suicide

Alcohol and drug abuse are second only to depression and other mood disorders as the most frequent risk factors for suicide. According to data from the National Violent Death Reporting System (NVDRS), in 2008 alcohol was a factor in approximately one-third of suicides reported in 16 states. Opiates, including heroin and prescription painkillers, were present in 25.5 percent of suicide deaths, antidepressants in 20.2 percent, cocaine in 10.5 percent, marijuana in 11.3 percent, and amphetamines in 3.4 percent.

Suicide is a leading cause of death among people with substance use disorders (SUDs). Substance use may increase the risk for suicide by intensifying depressive thoughts or feelings of hopelessness while at the same time reducing inhibitions to hurting oneself. Alcohol and some drugs can cause a "transient depression," heighten impulsivity, and cloud judgment about long-term consequences of one's actions.

About 8.5 percent of U.S. adults are estimated to have an alcohol use disorder, which includes alcohol dependence and alcohol abuse. About one-fourth of all the suicides in the United States are estimated to occur among individuals with alcohol use disorders. Acute (e.g., binge drinking episodes) and chronic use of alcohol are associated with suicidal behaviors. Among individuals with alcohol use disorders, suicide frequently takes place within the context of a major depression and interpersonal stressors. Aggression, impulsivity, hopelessness, and partner-relationship disruptions are also risk factors. Studies have shown that depression is present in 45 percent to more than 70 percent of those with alcohol and substance use disorders who die by suicide.

Although less is known about the relationship between suicide risk and other drug use, the number of substances used seems to be more predictive of suicide than the types of substances used. Findings from a few initial studies suggest that treatment of drug abuse may help reduce the risk for future suicidal behaviors.

SUDs and chronic substance use can lead to consequences and losses that contribute to suicide risk factors. Individuals in treatment for substance use disorders and/or transitioning between levels of care may be especially vulnerable. A large number of people in treatment have co-occurring mental disorders that increase suicide risk, particularly mood disorders. At the time these individuals enter treatment, their substance abuse may be out of control, they may be experiencing a number of life crises, and they may be at peaks in depressive symptoms.

In addition, mental disorders associated with suicidal behaviors, such as mood disorders, PTSD, anxiety disorders, and some personality disorders, often co-occur among people who have been treated for substance use disorders. Crises that are known to increase suicide risk, such as relapse and treatment transitions, may occur during treatment. According to one study, compared with the general population, individuals treated for alcohol abuse or dependence have a 10 times greater risk of eventually dying by suicide. Among those who inject drugs, the risk is about 14 times greater than in the general population.

More is known about the factors that increase the risk of suicidal behaviors among this population than about the factors that may be protective. SUDs share many risk factors with suicide: family history of suicide or child abuse; history of mental disorders, particularly mood disorders; history of or family history of addiction; impulsiveness; feelings of isolation; barriers to mental health and/or treatment; relational, social, work, or financial losses; physical illness/chronic pain; access to lethal methods; and prejudice associated with asking for help.

Perceiving that there are clear reasons to live is thought to be an important protective factor in this group. Other protective factors may include: a child at home and/or childrearing responsibilities; an intact marriage; a trusting relationship with a counselor, physician, or other service provider; employment; religious attendance and/or belief in religious teachings against suicide; and an optimistic or positive outlook. Sobriety can be a protective factor, along with attendance of mutual support group meetings.

Part Five

Drug Abuse Treatment and Recovery

Chapter 35

Recognizing Drug Use

Chapter Contents

Section 35.1

Signs of Drug Use

This section contains text excerpted from the following sources: Text beginning with the heading "Substance Use Disorders" is excerpted from "Mental Health and Substance Use Disorders," U.S. Department of Health and Human Services (HHS), May 31, 2013; Text under the heading "What Are Signs of Drug Use in Adolescents, and What Role Can Parents Play in Getting Treatment?" is excerpted from "What Are Signs of Drug Use in Adolescents, and What Role Can Parents Play in Getting Treatment?" National Institute on Drug Abuse (NIDA), January 2014; Text under the heading "The Signs" is excerpted from "Join the Voices for Recovery," Substance Abuse and Mental Health Services Administration (SAMHSA), September 2013.

Substance Use Disorders

Substance use disorders can refer to substance use or substance dependence. Symptoms of substance use disorders may include:

- Behavioral changes, such as:
    - Drop in attendance and performance at work or school
    - Frequently getting into trouble (fights, accidents, illegal activities)
    - Using substances in physically hazardous situations such as while driving or operating a machine
    - Engaging in secretive or suspicious behaviors
    - Changes in appetite or sleep patterns
    - Unexplained change in personality or attitude
    - Sudden mood swings, irritability, or angry outbursts
    - Periods of unusual hyperactivity, agitation, or giddiness
    - Lacking of motivation
    - Appearing fearful, anxious, or paranoid, with no reason

- Physical changes, such as:
    - Bloodshot eyes and abnormally sized pupils
    - Sudden weight loss or weight gain
    - Deterioration of physical appearance
    - Unusual smells on breath, body, or clothing
    - Tremors, slurred speech, or impaired coordination
- Social changes, such as:
    - Sudden change in friends, favorite hangouts, and hobbies
    - Legal problems related to substance use
    - Unexplained need for money or financial problems
    - Using substances even though it causes problems in relationships

What Are Signs of Drug Use in Adolescents, and What Role Can Parents Play in Getting Treatment?

If an adolescent starts behaving differently for no apparent reason—such as acting withdrawn, frequently tired or depressed, or hostile—it could be a sign he or she is developing a drug-related problem. Parents and others may overlook such signs, believing them to be a normal part of puberty.

Other signs include:

- a change in peer group
- carelessness with grooming
- decline in academic performance
- missing classes or skipping school
- loss of interest in favorite activities
- changes in eating or sleeping habits
- deteriorating relationships with family members and friends

Parents tend to underestimate the risks or seriousness of drug use. The symptoms listed here suggest a problem that may already have become serious and should be evaluated to determine the underlying cause—which could be a substance abuse problem or another mental health or medical disorder. Parents who are unsure whether their child is abusing drugs can enlist the help of a primary care physician, school guidance counselor, or drug abuse treatment provider.

The Signs

To reduce the impact of behavioral health conditions, it's important to know the signs of mental and/or substance use disorders. The most common signs and symptoms of mental health problems among adults include:

- Confused thinking;
- Prolonged depression (sadness or irritability);
- Feelings of extreme highs and lows;
- Excessive fears, worries, and anxieties;
- Social withdrawal;
- Dramatic changes in eating or sleeping habits;
- Strong feelings of anger;
- Delusions or hallucinations;
- Growing inability to cope with daily problems and activities;
- Suicidal thoughts;
- Denial of obvious problems;
- Numerous unexplained physical ailments; and
- Substance abuse.

The most frequently displayed signs of a substance use disorder among adults include:

- Bloodshot eyes and abnormally sized pupils;
- Changes in appetite or sleep patterns;
- Sudden weight loss or weight gain;
- Deterioration of physical appearance;
- Unusual smells on breath, body, or clothing;
- Tremors, slurred speech, or impaired coordination;
- Drop in attendance and performance at work or school;

- Unexplained need for money or financial problems;
- Engaging in secretive or suspicious behaviors;
- Sudden change in friends, favorite hangouts, and hobbies;
- Frequently getting into trouble (fights, accidents, illegal activities);
- Unexplained change in personality or attitude;
- Sudden mood swings, irritability, or angry outbursts;
- Periods of unusual hyperactivity, agitation, or giddiness;
- Lack of motivation; and
- Appearing fearful, anxious, or paranoid, with no reason.

Section 35.2

Am I Drug Addicted?

This section includes text excerpted from "What to Do If You Have a Problem with Drugs: For Adults," National Institute on Drug Abuse (NIDA), January 2016.

How Do I Know If I Am Addicted?

If you can't stop taking a drug even if you want to, or if the urge to use drugs is too strong to control, even if you know the drug is causing harm, you might be addicted. Here are some questions to ask yourself:

1. Do you think about drugs a lot?
2. Did you ever try to stop or cut down on your drug usage but couldn't?
3. Have you ever thought you couldn't fit in or have a good time without the use of drugs?
4. Do you ever use drugs because you are upset or angry at other people?

5. Have you ever used a drug without knowing what it was or what it would do to you?
6. Have you ever taken one drug to get over the effects of another?
7. Have you ever made mistakes at a job or at school because you were using drugs?
8. Does the thought of running out of drugs really scare you?
9. Have you ever stolen drugs or stolen to pay for drugs?
10. Have you ever been arrested or in the hospital because of your drug use?
11. Have you ever overdosed on drugs?
12. Has using drugs hurt your relationships with other people?

If the answer to some or all of these questions is yes, you might have an addiction. People from all backgrounds can get an addiction. Addiction can happen at any age, but it usually starts when a person is young.

Anyone Can Become Addicted to Drugs

Through scientific advances, we know more than ever about how drugs work in the brain. We also know that drug addiction can be successfully treated to help people stop abusing drugs and lead productive lives. If you think you might be addicted, seek the advice of your doctor or an addiction specialist.

Why Can't I Stop Using Drugs on My Own?

Repeated drug use changes the brain, including parts of the brain that enable you to exert self-control. These and other changes can be seen clearly in brain imaging studies of people with drug addictions. These brain changes explain why quitting is so difficult, even if you feel ready.

Chapter 36

Responding to Drug Abuse Emergencies

Five Essential Steps for First Responders

Overdose is common among persons who use illicit opioids such as heroin and among those who misuse medications prescribed for pain, such as oxycodone, hydrocodone, and morphine. The incidence of opioid overdose is rising nationwide. For example, between 2001 and 2010, the number of poisoning deaths in the United States nearly doubled, largely because of overdoses involving prescription opioid analgesics. This increase coincided with a nearly fourfold increase in the use of prescribed opioids for the treatment of pain.

To address the problem, emergency medical personnel, healthcare professionals, and patients increasingly are being trained in the use of the opioid antagonist naloxone hydrochloride (naloxone or Narcan), which is the treatment of choice to reverse the potentially fatal respiratory depression caused by opioid overdose. (Note that naloxone has no effect on non-opioid overdoses, such as those involving cocaine, benzodiazepines, or alcohol.)

Based on current scientific evidence and extensive experience, the steps outlined below are recommended to reduce the number of deaths resulting from opioid overdoses.

This chapter includes text excerpted from "Opioid Overdose Toolkit," Substance Abuse and Mental Health Services Administration (SAMHSA), 2014.

Step 1: Call for Help (DIAL 911)

An Opioid Overdose Needs Immediate Medical Attention.

An essential step is to get someone with medical expertise to see the patient as soon as possible, so if no EMS or other trained personnel are on the scene, dial 911 immediately. All you have to say is: "Someone is not breathing." Be sure to give a clear address and/or description of your location.

Step 2: Check for Signs of Opioid Overdose

Signs of **Overdose**, which often results in death if not treated, include:

- Face is extremely pale and/or clammy to the touch
- Body is limp
- Fingernails or lips have a blue or purple cast
- The patient is vomiting or making gurgling noises
- He or she cannot be awakened from sleep or is unable to speak
- Breathing is very slow or stopped
- Heartbeat is very slow or stopped.

Signs of **Overmedication**, which may progress to overdose, include:

- Unusual sleepiness or drowsiness
- Mental confusion, slurred speech, intoxicated behavior
- Slow or shallow breathing
- Pinpoint pupils
- Slow heartbeat, low blood pressure
- Difficulty waking the person from sleep.

Because opioids depress respiratory function and breathing, one telltale sign of a person in a critical medical state is the "death rattle." If a person emits a "death rattle"—an exhaled breath with a very distinct, labored sound coming from the throat—emergency resuscitation will be necessary immediately, as it almost always is a sign that the individual is near death.

Step 3: Support the Person's Breathing

Ideally, individuals who are experiencing opioid overdose should be ventilated with 100% oxygen before naloxone is administered so as to reduce the risk of acute lung injury. In situations where 100% oxygen is not available, rescue breathing can be very effective in supporting respiration. Rescue breathing involves the following steps:

- Be sure the person's airway is clear (check that nothing inside the person's mouth or throat is blocking the airway).
- Place one hand on the person's chin, tilt the head back and pinch the nose closed.
- Place your mouth over the person's mouth to make a seal and give 2 slow breaths.
- The person's chest should rise (but not the stomach).
- Follow up with one breath every 5 seconds.

Step 4: Administer Naloxone

Naloxone (Narcan) should be administered to any person who shows signs of opioid overdose, or when overdose is suspected. Naloxone injection is approved by the FDA and has been used for decades by emergency medical services (EMS) personnel to reverse opioid overdose and resuscitate individuals who have overdosed on opioids.

Naloxone can be given by intramuscular or intravenous injection every 2 to 3 minutes. The most rapid onset of action is achieved by intravenous administration, which is recommended in emergency situations. The dose should be titrated to the smallest effective dose that maintains spontaneous normal respiratory drive.

Opioid-naive patients may be given starting doses of up to 2 mg without concern for triggering withdrawal symptoms.

The intramuscular route of administration may be more suitable for patients with a history of opioid dependence because it provides a slower onset of action and a prolonged duration of effect, which may minimize rapid onset of withdrawal symptoms.

Duration of Effect. The duration of effect of naloxone is 30 to 90 minutes, and patients should be observed after this time frame for the return of overdose symptoms. The goal of naloxone therapy should be to restore adequate spontaneous breathing, but not necessarily complete arousal.

More than one dose of naloxone may be needed to revive someone who is overdosing. Patients who have taken longer-acting opioids may require further intravenous bolus doses or an infusion of naloxone.

Comfort the person being treated, as withdrawal triggered by naloxone can feel unpleasant. As a result, some persons become agitated or combative when this happens and need help to remain calm.

Safety of Naloxone. The safety profile of naloxone is remarkably high, especially when used in low doses and titrated to effect. When given to individuals who are not opioid-intoxicated or opioiddependent, naloxone produces no clinical effects, even at high doses. Moreover, while rapid opioid withdrawal in tolerant patients may be unpleasant, it is not life-threatening.

Naloxone can safely be used to manage opioid overdose in pregnant women. The lowest dose to maintain spontaneous respiratory drive should be used to avoid triggering acute opioid withdrawal, which may cause fetal distress.

Step 5: Monitor the Person's Response

All patients should be monitored for recurrence of signs and symptoms of opioid toxicity for at least 4 hours from the last dose of naloxone or discontinuation of the naloxone infusion. Patients who have overdosed on long-acting opioids should have more prolonged monitoring.

Most patients respond by returning to spontaneous breathing, with minimal withdrawal symptoms. The response generally occurs within 3 to 5 minutes of naloxone administration. (Rescue breathing should continue while waiting for the naloxone to take effect.

Naloxone will continue to work for 30 to 90 minutes, but after that time, overdose symptoms may return. Therefore, it is essential to get the person to an emergency department or other source of medical care as quickly as possible, even if he or she revives after the initial dose of naloxone and seems to feel better.

Signs of Opioid Withdrawal. The signs and symptoms of opioid withdrawal in an individual who is physically dependent on opioids may include, but are not limited to, the following: body aches, diarrhea, tachycardia, fever, runny nose, sneezing, piloerection, sweating, yawning, nausea or vomiting, nervousness, restlessness or irritability, shivering or trembling, abdominal cramps, weakness, and increased blood pressure. In the neonate, opioid withdrawal may also include convulsions, excessive crying, and hyperactive reflexes.

Naloxone-Resistant Patients. If a patient does not respond to naloxone, an alternative explanation for the clinical symptoms should be considered. The most likely explanation is that the person is not overdosing on an opioid but rather some other substance or may even be experiencing a non-overdose medical emergency. A possible explanation to consider is that the individual has overdosed on buprenorphine, a long-acting opioid partial agonist. Because buprenorphine has a higher affinity for the opioid receptors than do other opioids, naloxone may not be effective at reversing the effects of buprenorphine-induced opioid overdose.

In all cases, support of ventilation, oxygenation, and blood pressure should be sufficient to prevent the complications of opioid overdose and should be given priority if the response to naloxone is not prompt.

Summary

Do's and Don'ts in Responding to Opioid Overdose

- **DO** support the person's breathing by administering oxygen or performing rescue breathing.
- **DO** administer naloxone.
- **DO** put the person in the "recovery position" on the side, if he or she is breathing independently.
- **DO** stay with the person and keep him/ her warm.
- **DON'T** slap or try to forcefully stimulate the person—it will only cause further injury. If you are unable to wake the person by shouting, rubbing your knuckles on the sternum (center of the chest or rib cage), or light pinching, he or she may be unconscious.
- **DON'T** put the person into a cold bath or shower. This increases the risk of falling, drowning or going into shock.
- **DON'T** inject the person with any substance (salt water, milk, "speed," heroin, etc.). The only safe and appropriate treatment is naloxone.
- **DON'T** try to make the person vomit drugs that he or she may have swallowed. Choking or inhaling vomit into the lungs can cause a fatal injury.

Note: All naloxone products have an expiration date, so it is important to check the expiration date and obtain replacement naloxone as needed.

Chapter 37

Drug Abuse Intervention

Web-Based Intervention Strengthens Drug Abuse Treatment

A new study shows that incorporating the web-based Therapeutic Education System (TES) intervention in the treatment of drug abuse can not only help people stop using drugs, but can also keep them in treatment longer. TES is a web-based version of the Community Reinforcement Approach plus Contingency Management, a packaged approach with demonstrated efficacy. The National Institute on Drug Abuse (NIDA), part of the NIH, funded this study.

TES consists of 62 interactive modules that teach patients how to achieve and maintain abstinence from drug use and includes prize-based motivational incentives to encourage adherence to treatment. Patients given TES were less likely to drop out of treatment than those in the control group. Also, the web-based intervention helped patients stay abstinent from drug use, even those who were not abstinent at the beginning of the study. With such findings, web-based interventions like TES are promising additions to drug abuse treatment.

This chapter contains text excerpted from the following sources: Text under the heading "Web-Based Intervention Strengthens Drug Abuse Treatment" is excerpted from "Web-Based Intervention Strengthens Drug Abuse Treatment," National Institute on Drug Abuse (NIDA), April 4, 2014; Text beginning with the heading "Brief Intervention Helps Adolescents Curb Substance Use" is excerpted from "Brief Intervention Helps Adolescents Curb Substance Use," National Institute on Drug Abuse (NIDA), January 2, 2013.

Brief Intervention Helps Adolescents Curb Substance Use

Two Hour-Long Sessions a Week Apart Reduce Symptoms of Substance Abuse or Dependence.

Drug- and alcohol-involved middle and high school students markedly reduced their substance use following two 60-minute sessions that combined motivational interviewing (MI) and cognitive behavioral therapy. The students also reported significantly fewer substance-related symptoms of substance use disorders during the 6 months after the intervention compared with the 6 months before it. Adding a separate 1-hour MI-based session with a parent or primary caregiver enhanced the beneficial effects.

Dr. Ken C. Winters and colleagues at the University of Minnesota Medical School, in Minneapolis, conducted the trial with 315 adolescent and parent/caregiver pairs. Their findings strengthen evidence, which has been inconsistent in smaller trials, that brief interventions can help adolescents move away from drug use.

Motivating Behavior Change

The Minnesota researchers designed their intervention to help teenagers who abuse drugs, drink heavily, or drink in binges, but are not physically dependent and can largely control their intake. Nationally, an estimated 25 percent of 12- to 18-year-olds meet these criteria for "moderate" substance involvement. (See Figure 36.1)

The manualized intervention consists of two meetings with a therapist, 7 to 10 days apart. In the first session, therapist and teen discuss the teen's substance use, examine the pros and cons of use, discuss the teen's willingness to change, and identify goals for behavior change. In the second session, the two review the teen's progress toward achieving the goals, identify high-risk situations associated with drug-use triggers, generate strategies to deal with peer pressure, and negotiate long-term goals related to substance use. A third, parent-only session, which was offered to 123 families, involved the therapist and parent discussing how to improve communication with the teen and to support the teen's intervention goals.

To test the intervention, Dr. Winters and colleagues recruited Twin Cities students who had been referred for a substance abuse assessment in their public schools. The researchers assessed the students and randomly assigned those having at least a mild substance use problem to receive the intervention; an enhanced version of the intervention that added a third session, between a therapist and parent/

caregiver; or an assessment only, no treatment. The therapists typically met the students in their schools and the parents in their homes.

Six months later, compared to when they entered the trial:

- Treated adolescents reported using alcohol on fewer of the past 90 days, while the untreated adolescents reported increased days of alcohol use.
- Treated and untreated youths both reported fewer days of cannabis use during the past 90 days, but the treatment group's reductions were significantly greater.
- Treated and untreated youths both reported fewer symptoms of alcohol abuse and dependence during the past 60 days, but the treated group's relief was significantly greater.

Also at the 6-month follow-up, half of the treated adolescents reported having been abstinent from marijuana for the past 3 months, and half reported having been abstinent from alcohol for the past 3 months, compared to 37 percent and 26 percent, respectively, of untreated students.

Teens whose parents received a counseling session made still larger gains, which included significantly greater reductions in cannabis abuse and dependence disorders compared to the untreated teens. More than 60 percent of this group reported having been abstinent from cannabis for 90 consecutive days at their follow-up interview.

The teens' before-and-after self-reports indicated that the intervention strengthened their motivation to resist drugs and enhanced their success in resisting situational triggers for drug use (e.g., peer pressure, boredom). Teens whose parents attended a session in the enhanced intervention also benefited from improved parenting practices and utilized more community counseling and mental health services during the 6-month follow-up than untreated teens. The researchers suggest that the parent sessions contributed to the intervention's efficacy mainly by enhancing parents' recognition of their children's problems and motivating parents to arrange additional counseling.

Teen-Brain Friendly

Moderate substance use can influence relationships, neurological development, educational attainment, and interpersonal functioning. Typically, adolescents who abuse substances but do not meet criteria for substance use disorders are less likely than nonusers to fully engage in family and school life. As they bond and socialize with like-minded peers, these teens often initiate other problem behaviors, such as delinquency. When faced with difficulties, they may intensify substance use rather than learning healthy coping skills. Because these teens are not yet dependent, however, brief intervention may suffice to put them back on track.

Teens naturally desire independence and individuation, which generates conflict with adults. "Motivational interviewing disarms that tension by focusing on the teen and adjusting the direction of treatment to his or her interests, goals, and motivation level. Rather than telling teens they must stop using drugs, therapists discuss the adolescents' current problems and realistic goals for their immediate future. This sparks thoughts about change," says Dr. Winters. Brief interventions are a good fit for adolescents because teens have difficulty envisioning a treatment that involves many steps, let alone a complete lifestyle change, he adds.

A Place for Brevity

Currently, only 10 percent of teens who need treatment for substance use problems receive it, according to the Substance Abuse and Mental Health Services Administration (SAMHSA). Because most teens who abuse substances fall into the moderate use category, effective brief interventions potentially could go far toward making up the gap between treatment need and availability.

"Dr. Winters' and colleagues' brief intervention benefits youth with a lower level of substance use," says Dr. Jessica Campbell Chambers of NIDA's Division of Clinical Neuroscience and Behavioral Research. "Adolescent substance use problems are quite diverse, so clinicians need an array of therapies."

Dr. Winters concurs that youth with more severe drug use problems require more help. When assessment results identify moderate substance use, but therapy sessions uncover deeper problems, such as more severe drug use or co-occurring mental disorders, therapists should refer individuals for additional treatment, says Dr. Winters.

Despite the documented positive impact of brief interventions, little is known about how these programs reduce youth substance use. "Identifying this treatment's particular mechanism of action—what is driving its beneficial effects—would be very valuable, because researchers could then increase its therapeutic potency," says Dr. Campbell Chambers.

Chapter 38

Medical Professionals Need to Identify Substance Use Disorders

What Role Can Medical Professionals Play in Addressing Substance Abuse (including Abuse of Prescription Drugs) among Adolescents?

Medical professionals have an important role to play in screening their adolescent patients for drug use, providing brief interventions, referring them to substance abuse treatment if necessary, and providing ongoing monitoring and follow-up. Screening and brief interventions do not have to be time-consuming and can be integrated into general medical settings.

- *Screening*. Screening and brief assessment tools administered during annual routine medical checkups can detect drug use before it becomes a serious problem. The purpose of screening is to look for evidence of any use of alcohol, tobacco, or illicit drugs or abuse of prescription drugs and assess how severe the problem is. Results from such screens can indicate whether a

---

This chapter includes text excerpted from "Principles of Adolescent Substance Use Disorder Treatment: A Research-Based Guide," National Institute on Drug Abuse (NIDA), January 2014.

more extensive assessment and possible treatment are necessary. Screening as a part of routine care also helps to reduce the stigma associated with being identified as having a drug problem.

- *Brief Intervention.* Adolescents who report using drugs can be given a brief intervention to reduce their drug use and other risky behaviors. Specifically, they should be advised how continued drug use may harm their brains, general health, and other areas of their life, including family relationships and education. Adolescents reporting no substance use can be praised for staying away from drugs and rescreened during their next physical.
- *Referral.* Adolescents with substance use disorders or those that appear to be developing a substance use disorder may need a referral to substance abuse treatment for more extensive assessment and care.
- *Follow-up.* For patients in treatment, medical professionals can offer ongoing support of treatment participation and abstinence from drugs during follow-up visits. Adolescent patients who relapse or show signs of continuing to use drugs may need to be referred back to treatment.
- *Before prescribing medications that can potentially be abused,* clinicians can assess patients for risk factors such as mental illness or a family history of substance abuse, consider an alternative medication with less abuse potential, more closely monitor patients at high risk, reduce the length of time between visits for refills so fewer pills are on hand, and educate both patients and their parents about appropriate use and potential risks of prescription medications, including the dangers of sharing them with others.

Chapter 39

Detoxification

Introduction to Detoxification

Detoxification is a set of interventions aimed at managing acute intoxication and withdrawal. It denotes a clearing of toxins from the body of the patient who is acutely intoxicated and/or dependent on substances of abuse. Detoxification seeks to minimize the physical harm caused by the abuse of substances. The acute medical management of life threatening intoxication and related medical problems generally is not included within the term detoxification.

The Washington Circle Group (WCG), a body of experts organized to improve the quality and effectiveness of substance abuse prevention and treatment, defines detoxification as "a medical intervention that manages an individual safely through the process of acute withdrawal." The WCG makes an important distinction, however, in noting that "a detoxification program is not designed to resolve the longstanding psychological, social, and behavioral problems associated with alcohol and drug abuse." The consensus panel supports this statement

---

This chapter contains text excerpted from the following sources: Text beginning with the heading "Introduction to Detoxification" is excerpted from "Detoxification and Substance Abuse Treatment," Substance Abuse and Mental Health Services Administration (SAMHSA), September 11, 2015; Text beginning with the heading "Patients Addicted to Opioid Painkillers Achieve Good Results With Outpatient Detoxification," is excerpted from "Patients Addicted to Opioid Painkillers Achieve Good Results With Outpatient Detoxification," National Institute on Drug Abuse (NIDA), February 11, 2015.

and has taken special care to note that detoxification is not substance abuse treatment and rehabilitation.

The consensus panel built on existing definitions of detoxification as a broad process with three essential components that may take place concurrently or as a series of steps:

- *Evaluation* entails testing for the presence of substances of abuse in the bloodstream, measuring their concentration, and screening for co-occurring mental and physical conditions. Evaluation also includes a comprehensive assessment of the patient's medical and psychological conditions and social situation to help determine the appropriate level of treatment following detoxification. Essentially, the evaluation serves as the basis for the initial substance abuse treatment plan once the patient has been withdrawn successfully.
- *Stabilization* includes the medical and psychosocial processes of assisting the patient through acute intoxication and withdrawal to the attainment of a medically stable, fully supported, substance-free state. This often is done with the assistance of medications, though in some approaches to detoxification no medication is used. Stabilization includes familiarizing patients with what to expect in the treatment milieu and their role in treatment and recovery. During this time practitioners also seek the involvement of the patient's family, employers, and other significant people when appropriate and with release of confidentiality.
- *Fostering the patient's entry into treatment* involves preparing the patient for entry into substance abuse treatment by stressing the importance of following through with the complete substance abuse treatment continuum of care. For patients who have demonstrated a pattern of completing detoxification services and then failing to engage in substance abuse treatment, a written treatment contract may encourage entrance into a continuum of substance abuse treatment and care. This contract, which is not legally binding, is voluntarily signed by patients when they are stable enough to do so at the beginning of treatment. In it, the patient agrees to participate in a continuing care plan, with details and contacts established prior to the completion of detoxification.

All three components (evaluation, stabilization, and fostering a patient's entry into treatment) involve treating the patient with compassion and understanding. Patients undergoing detoxification need to know that someone cares about them, respects them as individuals, and has hope for their future. Actions taken during detoxification will demonstrate to the patient that the provider's recommendations can be trusted and followed.

Detoxification as Distinct From Substance Abuse Treatment

Detoxification is a set of interventions aimed at managing acute intoxication and withdrawal. Supervised detoxification may prevent potentially life-threatening complications that might appear if the patient were left untreated. At the same time, detoxification is a form of palliative care (reducing the intensity of a disorder) for those who want to become abstinent or who must observe mandatory abstinence as a result of hospitalization or legal involvement. Finally, for some patients it represents a point of first contact with the treatment system and the first step to recovery. *Treatment/rehabilitation*, on the other hand, involves a constellation of ongoing therapeutic services ultimately intended to promote recovery for substance abuse patients.

Guiding Principles Recognized by the Consensus Panel

1. Detoxification does not constitute substance abuse treatment but is one part of a continuum of care for substance-related disorders.
2. The detoxification process consists of the following three sequential and essential components:
    - Evaluation
    - Stabilization
    - Fostering patient readiness for and entry into treatment

A detoxification process that does not incorporate all three critical components is considered incomplete and inadequate by the consensus panel.

1. Detoxification can take place in a wide variety of settings and at a number of levels of intensity within these settings. Placement should be appropriate to the patient's needs.
2. Persons seeking detoxification should have access to the components of the detoxification process described above, no matter what the setting or the level of treatment intensity.

3. All persons requiring treatment for substance use disorders should receive treatment of the same quality and appropriate thoroughness and should be put into contact with a substance abuse treatment program after detoxification, if they are not going to be engaged in a treatment service provided by the same program that provided them with detoxification services. There can be "no wrong door to treatment" for substance use disorders.

4. Ultimately, insurance coverage for the full range of detoxification services is cost-effective. If reimbursement systems do not provide payment for the complete detoxification process, patients may be released prematurely, leading to medically or socially unattended withdrawal. Ensuing medical complications ultimately drive up the overall cost of health care.

5. Patients seeking detoxification services have diverse cultural and ethnic backgrounds as well as unique health needs and life situations. Organizations that provide detoxification services need to ensure that they have standard practices in place to address cultural diversity. It also is essential that care providers possess the special clinical skills necessary to provide culturally competent comprehensive assessments. Detoxification program administrators have a duty to ensure that appropriate training is available to staff.

6. A successful detoxification process can be measured, in part, by whether an individual who is substance dependent enters, remains in, and is compliant with the treatment protocol of a substance abuse treatment/rehabilitation program after detoxification.

Overarching Principles for Care During Detoxification Services

- Detoxification services do not offer a "cure" for substance use disorders. They often are a first step toward recovery and the "first door" through which patients pass to treatment.
- Substance use disorders are treatable, and there is hope for recovery.
- Substance use disorders are brain disorders and not evidence of moral weaknesses.

- Patients are treated with respect and dignity at all times.
- Patients are treated in a nonjudgmental and supportive manner.
- Services planning is completed in partnership with the patient and his or her social support network, including such persons as family, significant others, or employers.
- All health professionals involved in the care of the patient will maximize opportunities to promote rehabilitation and maintenance activities and to link her or him to appropriate substance abuse treatment immediately after the detoxification phase.
- Active involvement of the family and other support systems while respecting the patient's rights to privacy and confidentiality is encouraged.
- Patients are treated with due consideration for individual background, culture, preferences, sexual orientation, disability status, vulnerabilities, and strengths.

Challenges to Providing Effective Detoxification

It is an important challenge for detoxification service providers to find the most effective way to foster a patient's recovery. Effective detoxification includes not only the medical stabilization of the patient and the safe and humane withdrawal from drugs, including alcohol, but also entry into treatment. Successfully linking detoxification with substance abuse treatment reduces the "revolving door" phenomenon of repeated withdrawals, saves money in the medium and long run, and delivers the sound and humane level of care patients need. Studies show that detoxification and its linkage to the appropriate levels of treatment lead to increased recovery and decreased use of detoxification and treatment services in the future.

In addition, recovery leads to reductions in crime, general healthcare costs, and expensive acute medical and surgical treatments consequent to untreated substance abuse. While detoxification is not treatment per se, its effectiveness can be measured, in part, by the patient's continued abstinence.

Another challenge to providing effective detoxification occurs when programs try to develop linkages to treatment services. A study conducted for the Substance Abuse and Mental Health Services Administration highlights the pitfalls of the service delivery system. According to the authors, each year at least 300,000 patients with substance use disorders or acute intoxication obtain inpatient detoxification in general hospitals while additional numbers obtain detoxification in other settings. Only about one-fifth of people discharged from acute care hospitals for detoxification receive substance abuse treatment during that hospitalization.

Moreover, only 15 percent of people who are admitted through an emergency room for detoxification and then discharged receive any substance abuse treatment.

Finally the average length of stay for people undergoing detoxification and treatment in 1997 was only 7.7 days. Given that "research has shown that patients who receive continuing care have better outcomes in terms of drug abstinence and readmission rates than those who do not receive continuing care," the report authors conclude that there is a pronounced need for better linkage between detoxification services and the treatment services that are essential for full recovery.

Reimbursement systems can present another challenge to providing effective detoxification services. Third-party payors sometimes prefer to manage payment for detoxification separately from other phases of addiction treatment, thus treating detoxification as if it occurred in isolation from addiction treatment. This "unbundling" of services has promoted the separation of all services into somewhat scattered segments. In other instances, some reimbursement and utilization policies dictate that only "detoxification" currently can be authorized, and "detoxification" for that policy or insurer does not cover the nonmedical counseling that is an integral part of substance abuse treatment.

Many treatment programs have found substance abuse counselors to be of special help with resistant patients, especially for patients with severe underlying shame over the fact that their substance use is out of control. Yet some payors will not reimburse for nonmedical services such as those provided by these counselors, and therefore the use of such staff by a detoxification or treatment service may be impossible, in spite of the fact that they are widely perceived as useful for patients.

Payors are gradually beginning to understand that detoxification is only one component of a comprehensive treatment strategy. Patient placement criteria, such as those published by the American Society of Addiction Medicine (ASAM) in the Patient Placement Criteria, Second Edition, Revised, have come to the fore as clinicians and insurers try to reach agreements on the level of treatment required by a given patient, as well as the medically appropriate setting in which the treatment services are to be delivered. Accordingly, the TIP offers suggestions for resolving conflicts as well as clearly defining terms used in patient placement and treatment settings as a step toward clearer understanding among interested parties.

Patients Addicted to Opioid Painkillers Achieve Good Results with Outpatient Detoxification

A recent NIDA-funded clinical trial indicates that a significant portion of individuals who are addicted to opioid painkillers may initiate and maintain abstinence with a brief but intensive outpatient detoxification treatment followed by opioid antagonist therapy using naltrexone. Patients in the trial achieved higher abstinence rates than are typically obtained with detoxification regimens. The duration of a taper with buprenorphine/naloxone (Bp/Nx) was a determinative factor in patients' success, with longer tapers yielding greater abstinence.

Dr. Stacey Sigmon and colleagues at the University of Vermont in Burlington enrolled 70 adults who were addicted to opioid painkillers into a double-blind, randomized clinical trial that involved a three-step detoxification process:

- Stabilization on a Bp/Nx (Suboxone) dosage that suppresses withdrawal symptoms, craving, and use of illicit opioid painkillers
- Gradual tapering of the Bp/Nx dose to zero over 1, 2, or 4 weeks
- Transition to the opioid antagonist naltrexone once a patient provides opioid-negative urine samples and reports no opioid use within the past 24 hours

The trial participants also received twice-weekly behavioral therapy using the evidence-based Community Reinforcement Approach and underwent thrice-weekly staff-observed urinalysis testing. Supplementary nonopioid medications were used as needed to treat breakthrough withdrawal symptoms.

The patients randomly assigned to the 4-week Bp/Nx taper provided the highest percentage of illicit opioid–free urine samples during the 12-week trial. Of these 22 patients, 63 percent were abstinent at the 5-week mark, and 50 percent were still opioid-abstinent at the end of the 12-week trial. In contrast, 29 percent of each of the two groups receiving shorter tapers provided drug-free urine samples at 5 weeks, and 20 percent or less of each provided drug-free samples at 12 weeks. Similar findings were seen with adherence to naltrexone ingestion and treatment retention.

Working Parts

Although many patients who are dependent on opioids will benefit from long-term maintenance therapy with methadone or buprenorphine, the Vermont study suggests that there may be a meaningful subset of individuals who can obtain good outcomes with more time-limited approaches, Dr. Sigmon says.

"Detoxification is typically associated with high relapse rates and return to opioid abuse," Dr. Sigmon says. "However, some data also suggest that if you do it right, outpatient detoxification can be effective. The inclusion of naltrexone therapy is likely extremely important to help prevent resumption of illicit opioid use following detoxification."

Dr. Sigmon notes that outpatient detoxification may be particularly appropriate for patients who present for treatment with less severe opioid dependence. In this trial, consistent with previous research, stabilization on a lower dose of buprenorphine—an indicator of less severe dependence—was associated with a favorable treatment response. "This finding may hold particular relevance for prescription opioid abusers, many of whom are younger and have briefer histories of opioid dependence, less severe other drug use, less IV use, and greater psychosocial stability than past generations of primary heroin abusers," says Dr. Sigmon.

Although their study design did not permit them to measure the impacts of the treatment regimen's intensive behavioral therapy and naltrexone maintenance, the researchers believe that both were instrumental to their patients' positive outcomes. The behavioral therapy, delivered by master's-level therapists, included counseling on how to handle withdrawal and avoid relapse, strengthen social networks, and find healthy recreational activities. The patients were also offered individually tailored sessions focused on their particular needs, from employment to managing depression.

Naltrexone is a nonopioid medication that blocks the receptors where opioids bind and exert their effects. A patient undergoing treatment for opioid addiction who slips and takes an opioid drug doesn't get the expected high or euphoria. Naltrexone can be taken long term to prevent resumption of opioid use after detoxification.

The Vermont team's finding that longer Bp/Nx tapers enhance patients' outcomes is consistent with some, although not all, previous studies on detoxification. Dr. Sigmon says that more gradual Bp/Nx tapering may more completely suppress opioid withdrawal symptoms, thereby reducing patient discomfort and risk for relapse to opioids.

Dr. Will Aklin, acting chief in NIDA's Behavioral and Integrative Treatment Branch, says that the current rates of opioid painkiller misuse and dependence have strained treatment resources and challenged researchers and clinicians to fashion effective therapies for a population that is at significant risk for overdose and death. The Vermont team's findings represent a meaningful advance toward meeting that challenge, Dr. Aklin says.

He adds that future studies might investigate how innovative approaches for delivering medications and new technology to remotely support and monitor abstinence could complement the intensive detoxification regimen developed by Dr. Sigmon's team. "This is especially important in rural or other resource-constrained settings, where community-based treatment centers can benefit from such complementary programs," says Dr. Aklin.

Chapter 40

Treatment Approaches for Drug Addiction

Chapter Contents

Section 40.1

Treatment for Drug Addiction Overview

This section includes text excerpted from "DrugFacts: Treatment Approaches for Drug Addiction," National Institute on Drug Abuse (NIDA), January 2016.

What Is Drug Addiction?

Drug addiction is a chronic disease characterized by compulsive, or uncontrollable, drug seeking and use despite harmful consequences and changes in the brain, which can be long lasting. These changes in the brain can lead to the harmful behaviors seen in people who use drugs. Drug addiction is also a relapsing disease. Relapse is the return to drug use after an attempt to stop.

The path to drug addiction begins with the voluntary act of taking drugs. But over time, a person's ability to choose not to do so becomes compromised. Seeking and taking the drug becomes compulsive. This is mostly due to the effects of long-term drug exposure on brain function. Addiction affects parts of the brain involved in reward and motivation, learning and memory, and control over behavior.

Addiction is a disease that affects both the brain and behavior.

Can Drug Addiction Be Treated?

Yes, but it's not simple. Because addiction is a chronic disease, people can't simply stop using drugs for a few days and be cured. Most patients need long-term or repeated care to stop using completely and recover their lives.

Addiction treatment must help the person do the following:

- stop using drugs
- stay drug-free
- be productive in the family, at work, and in society

Principles of Effective Treatment

Based on scientific research since the mid-1970s, the following key principles should form the basis of any effective treatment program:

- Addiction is a complex but treatable disease that affects brain function and behavior.
- No single treatment is right for everyone.
- People need to have quick access to treatment.
- Effective treatment addresses all of the patient's needs, not just his or her drug use.
- Staying in treatment long enough is critical.
- Counseling and other behavioral therapies are the most commonly used forms of treatment.
- Medications are often an important part of treatment, especially when combined with behavioral therapies.
- Treatment plans must be reviewed often and modified to fit the patient's changing needs.
- Treatment should address other possible mental disorders.
- Medically assisted detoxification is only the first stage of treatment.
- Treatment doesn't need to be voluntary to be effective.
- Drug use during treatment must be monitored continuously.
- Treatment programs should test patients for HIV/AIDS, hepatitis B and C, tuberculosis, and other infectious diseases as well as teach them about steps they can take to reduce their risk of these illnesses.

How Is Drug Addiction Treated?

Successful treatment has several steps:

- detoxification (the process by which the body rids itself of a drug)
- behavioral counseling
- medication (for opioid, tobacco, or alcohol addiction)

- evaluation and treatment for co-occurring mental health issues such as depression and anxiety
- long-term follow-up to prevent relapse

A range of care with a tailored treatment program and follow-up options can be crucial to success. Treatment should include both medical and mental health services as needed. Follow-up care may include community- or family-based recovery support systems.

How Are Medications Used in Drug Addiction Treatment?

Medications can be used to manage withdrawal symptoms, prevent relapse, and treat co-occurring conditions.

Withdrawal. Medications help suppress withdrawal symptoms during detoxification. Detoxification is not in itself "treatment," but only the first step in the process. Patients who do not receive any further treatment after detoxification usually resume their drug use. One study of treatment facilities found that medications were used in almost 80 percent of detoxifications.

Relapse prevention. Patients can use medications to help re-establish normal brain function and decrease cravings. Medications are available for treatment of opioid (heroin, prescription pain relievers), tobacco (nicotine), and alcohol addiction. Scientists are developing other medications to treat stimulant (cocaine, methamphetamine) and cannabis (marijuana) addiction. People who use more than one drug, which is very common, need treatment for all of the substances they use.

- **Opioids:** Methadone (Dolophine®, Methadose®), buprenorphine (Suboxone®, Subutex®), and naltrexone (Vivitrol®) are used to treat opioid addiction. Acting on the same targets in the brain as heroin and morphine, methadone and buprenorphine suppress withdrawal symptoms and relieve cravings. Naltrexone blocks the effects of opioids at their receptor sites in the brain and should be used only in patients who have already been detoxified. All medications help patients reduce drug seeking and related criminal behavior and help them become more open to behavioral treatments.
- **Tobacco:** Nicotine replacement therapies have several forms, including the patch, spray, gum, and lozenges. These products are available over the counter. The U.S. Food and Drug

Administration (FDA) has approved two prescription medications for nicotine addiction: bupropion (Zyban®) and varenicline (Chantix®). They work differently in the brain, but both help prevent relapse in people trying to quit. The medications are more effective when combined with behavioral treatments, such as group and individual therapy as well as telephone quitlines.

- **Alcohol:** Three medications have been FDA-approved for treating alcohol addiction and a fourth, topiramate, has shown promise in clinical trials (large-scale studies with people). The three approved medications are as follows:
    - **Naltrexone** blocks opioid receptors that are involved in the rewarding effects of drinking and in the craving for alcohol. It reduces relapse to heavy drinking and is highly effective in some patients. Genetic differences may affect how well the drug works in certain patients.
    - **Acamprosate (Campral®)** may reduce symptoms of long-lasting withdrawal, such as insomnia, anxiety, restlessness, and dysphoria (generally feeling unwell or unhappy). It may be more effective in patients with severe addiction.
    - **Disulfiram (Antabuse®)** interferes with the breakdown of alcohol. Acetaldehyde builds up in the body, leading to unpleasant reactions that include flushing (warmth and

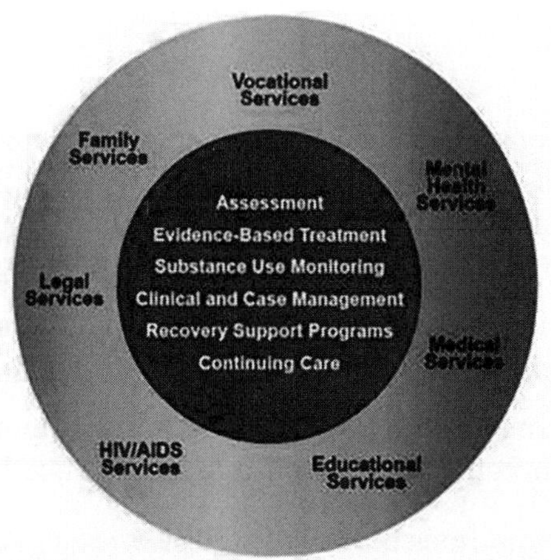

Figure 40.1. *Components of Comprehensive Drug Addiction Treatment*

redness in the face), nausea, and irregular heartbeat if the patient drinks alcohol. Compliance (taking the drug as prescribed) can be a problem, but it may help patients who are highly motivated to quit drinking.

- **Co-occuring conditions:** Other medications are available to treat possible mental health conditions, such as depression or anxiety, that may be contributing to the person's addiction.

How Are Behavioral Therapies Used to Treat Drug Addiction?

Behavioral therapies help patients:

- modify their attitudes and behaviors related to drug use
- increase healthy life skills
- persist with other forms of treatment, such as medication

Patients can receive treatment in many different settings with various approaches.

Outpatient behavioral treatment includes a wide variety of programs for patients who visit a behavioral health counselor on a regular schedule. Most of the programs involve individual or group drug counseling, or both. These programs typically offer forms of behavioral therapy such as:

- cognitive-behavioral therapy, which helps patients recognize, avoid, and cope with the situations in which they are most likely to use drugs
- multidimensional family therapy—developed for adolescents with drug abuse problems as well as their families—which addresses a range of influences on their drug abuse patterns and is designed to improve overall family functioning
- motivational interviewing, which makes the most of people's readiness to change their behavior and enter treatment
- motivational incentives (contingency management), which uses positive reinforcement to encourage abstinence from drugs

Treatment is sometimes intensive at first, where patients attend multiple outpatient sessions each week. After completing intensive treatment, patients transition to regular outpatient treatment, which meets less often and for fewer hours per week to help sustain their recovery.

Inpatient or residential treatment can also be very effective, especially for those with more severe problems (including co-occurring disorders). Licensed residential treatment facilities offer 24-hour structured and intensive care, including safe housing and medical attention. Residential treatment facilities may use a variety of therapeutic approaches, and they are generally aimed at helping the patient live a drug-free, crime-free lifestyle after treatment. Examples of residential treatment settings include:

- Therapeutic communities, which are highly structured programs in which patients remain at a residence, typically for 6 to 12 months. The entire community, including treatment staff and those in recovery, act as key agents of change, influencing the patient's attitudes, understanding, and behaviors associated with drug use.
- Shorter-term residential treatment, which typically focuses on detoxification as well as providing initial intensive counseling and preparation for treatment in a community-based setting.
- Recovery housing, which provides supervised, short-term housing for patients, often following other types of inpatient or residential treatment. Recovery housing can help people make the transition to an independent life—for example, helping them learn how to manage finances or seek employment, as well as connecting them to support services in the community.

Is Treatment Different for Criminal Justice Populations?

Scientific research since the mid-1970s shows that drug abuse treatment can help many drug-using offenders change their attitudes, beliefs, and behaviors towards drug abuse; avoid relapse; and successfully remove themselves from a life of substance abuse and crime. Many of the principles of treating drug addiction are similar for people within the criminal justice system as for those in the general population. However, many offenders don't have access to the types of services they need. Treatment that is of poor quality or is not well suited to the needs of offenders may not be effective at reducing drug use and criminal behavior.

In addition to the general principles of treatment, some considerations specific to offenders include the following:

- Treatment should include development of specific cognitive skills to help the offender adjust attitudes and beliefs that lead to drug abuse and crime, such as feeling entitled to have things one's own way or not understanding the consequences of one's behavior. This includes skills related to thinking, understanding, learning, and remembering.

- Treatment planning should include tailored services within the correctional facility as well as transition to community-based treatment after release.
- Ongoing coordination between treatment providers and courts or parole and probation officers is important in addressing the complex needs of offenders re-entering society.

Challenges of Re-entry

Drug abuse changes the function of the brain, and many things can "trigger" drug cravings within the brain. It's critical for those in treatment, especially those treated at an inpatient facility or prison, to learn how to recognize, avoid, and cope with triggers they are likely to be exposed to after treatment.

How Many People Get Treatment for Drug Addiction?

According to SAMHSA's National Survey on Drug Use and Health, 22.5 million people (8.5 percent of the U.S. population) aged 12 or older needed treatment for an illicit drug or alcohol use problem in 2014. Only 4.2 million (18.5 percent of those who needed treatment) received any substance use treatment in the same year. Of these, about 2.6 million people received treatment at specialty treatment programs.

Points to Remember

- Drug addiction can be treated, but it's not simple. Addiction treatment must help the person do the following:
    - stop using drugs
    - stay drug-free
    - be productive in the family, at work, and in society
- Successful treatment has several steps:
    - detoxification
    - behavioral counseling
    - medication (for opioid, tobacco, or alcohol addiction)

- evaluation and treatment for co-occurring mental health issues such as depression and anxiety
- long-term follow-up to prevent relapse

- Medications can be used to manage withdrawal symptoms, prevent relapse, and treat co-occurring conditions.
- Behavioral therapies help patients:
  - modify their attitudes and behaviors related to drug use
  - increase healthy life skills
  - persist with other forms of treatment, such as medication
- People within the criminal justice system may need additional treatment services to treat drug use disorders effectively. However, many offenders don't have access to the types of services they need.

Section 40.2

Medication and Counseling Treatment

This section contains text excerpted from the following sources: Text in this section begins with excerpts from "Medication and Counseling Treatment," Substance Abuse and Mental Health Services Administration (SAMHSA), September 28, 2015; Text under the heading "Naloxone" is excerpted from "Naloxone," Substance Abuse and Mental Health Services Administration (SAMHSA), March 3, 2016.

Medication-assisted treatment (MAT) is the use of medications with counseling and behavioral therapies to treat substance use disorders and prevent opioid overdose.

Medication-Assisted Treatment (MAT) is the use of medications, in combination with counseling and behavioral therapies, to provide a "whole-patient" approach to the treatment of substance use disorders. Research shows that a combination of medication and therapy can successfully treat these disorders, and for some people struggling with addiction, MAT can help sustain recovery.

MAT is primarily used for the treatment of addiction to opioids such as heroin and prescription pain relievers that contain opiates. The prescribed medication operates to normalize brain chemistry, block the euphoric effects of alcohol and opioids, relieve physiological cravings, and normalize body functions without the negative effects of the abused drug. Medications used in MAT are approved by the U.S. Food and Drug Administration (FDA), and MAT programs are clinically driven and tailored to meet each patient's needs. Combining medications used in MAT with anxiety treatment medications can be fatal. Types of anxiety treatment medications include derivatives of Benzodiazepine, such as Xanax or valium.

Opioid Treatment Programs (OTPs)

Opioid treatment programs (OTPs) provide MAT for individuals diagnosed with an opioid use disorder. OTPs also provide a range of services to reduce, eliminate, or prevent the use of illicit drugs, potential criminal activity, and/or the spread of infectious disease. OTPs focus on improving the quality of life of those receiving treatment.

OTPs must be accredited by a SAMHSA-approved accrediting body and certified by SAMHSA. The Division of Pharmacologic Therapies (DPT), part of the SAMHSA Center for Substance Abuse Treatment (CSAT), oversees accreditation standards and certification processes for OTPs.

Federal law requires patients who receive treatment in an OTP to receive medical, counseling, vocational, educational, and other assessment and treatment services, in addition to prescribed medication. The law allows MAT professionals to provide treatment and services in a range of settings, including hospitals, correctional facilities, offices, and remote clinics.

Counseling and Behavioral Therapies

Under federal law, MAT patients must receive counseling, which could include different forms of behavioral therapy. These services are required along with medical, vocational, educational, and other assessment and treatment services.

MAT Effectiveness

In 2013, an estimated 1.8 million people had an opioid use disorder related to prescription pain relievers, and about 517,000 had an opioid use disorder related to heroin use. MAT has proved to be clinically effective and to significantly reduce the need for inpatient detoxification services for these individuals. MAT provides a more comprehensive, individually tailored program of medication and behavioral therapy. MAT also includes support services that address the needs of most patients.

The ultimate goal of MAT is full recovery, including the ability to live a self-directed life. This treatment approach has been shown to:

- Improve patient survival
- Increase retention in treatment
- Decrease illicit opiate use and other criminal activity among people with substance use disorders
- Increase patients' ability to gain and maintain employment
- Improve birth outcomes among women who have substance use disorders and are pregnant

Research also shows that these medications and therapies can contribute to lowering a person's risk of contracting HIV or hepatitis C by reducing the potential for relapse.

Unfortunately, MAT is greatly underused. For instance, according to SAMHSA's Treatment Episode Data Set (TEDS) 2002-2010, the proportion of heroin admissions with treatment plans that included receiving medication-assisted opioid therapy fell from 35% in 2002 to 28% in 2010. The slow adoption of these evidence-based treatment options for alcohol and opioid dependence is partly due to misconceptions about substituting one drug for another. Discrimination against MAT patients is also a factor, despite state and federal laws clearly prohibiting it. Other factors include lack of training for physicians and negative opinions toward MAT in communities and among health care professionals

MAT and Patient Rights

SAMHSA's Partners for Recovery Initiative produced a brochure designed to assist MAT patients and to educate and inform others. This Medication-Assisted Treatment Know Your Rights Brochure–2009 presents and explains the federal laws that prohibit discrimination against individuals with disabilities and how they protect people receiving MAT for opioid addiction.

Under the Confidentiality Regulation, 42 Code of Federal Regulations (CFR) 2, personally identifiable health information relating to substance use and alcohol treatment must be handled with a higher degree of confidentiality than other medical information.

Medications Used in MAT

FDA has approved several different medications to treat opioid addiction and alcohol dependence.

A common misconception associated with MAT is that it substitutes one drug for another. Instead, these medications relieve the withdrawal symptoms and psychological cravings that cause chemical imbalances in the body. MAT programs provide a safe and controlled level of medication to overcome the use of an abused opioid. And research has shown that when provided at the proper dose, medications used in MAT have no adverse effects on a person's intelligence, mental capability, physical functioning, or employability.

Medications used in MAT for opioid treatment can only be dispensed through a SAMHSA-certified OTP. Some of the medications used in MAT are controlled substances due to their potential for misuse. Drugs, substances, and certain chemicals used to make drugs are classified by the Drug Enforcement Administration (DEA) into five distinct categories, or schedules, depending upon a drug's acceptable medical use and potential for misuse.

Opioid Dependency Medications

Methadone, buprenorphine, and naltrexone are used to treat opioid dependence and addiction to short-acting opioids such as heroin, morphine, and codeine, as well as semi-synthetic opioids like oxycodone and hydrocodone. People may safely take medications used in MAT for months, years, several years, or even a lifetime. Plans to stop a medication must always be discussed with a doctor.

Methadone

Methadone tricks the brain into thinking it's still getting the abused drug. In fact, the person is not getting high from it and feels normal, so withdrawal doesn't occur.

Pregnant or breastfeeding women must inform their treatment provider before taking methadone. It is the only drug used in MAT approved for women who are pregnant or breastfeeding.

Buprenorphine

Like methadone, buprenorphine suppresses and reduces cravings for the abused drug. It can come in a pill form or sublingual tablet that is placed under the tongue.

Naltrexone

Naltrexone works differently than methadone and buprenorphine in the treatment of opioid dependency. If a person using naltrexone relapses and uses the abused drug, naltrexone blocks the euphoric and sedative effects of the abused drug and prevents feelings of euphoria.

Opioid Overdose Prevention Medication

FDA approved naloxone, an injectable drug used to prevent an opioid overdose. According to the World Health Organization (WHO), naloxone is one of a number of medications considered essential to a functioning healthcare system.

Alcohol Use Disorder Medications

Disulfiram, acamprosate, and naltrexone are the most common drugs used to treat alcohol use disorder. None of these drugs provide a cure for the disorder, but they are most effective in people who participate in a MAT program.

Disulfiram

Disulfiram is a medication that treats chronic alcoholism. It is most effective in people who have already gone through detoxification or are in the initial stage of abstinence. This drug is offered in a tablet form and is taken once a day. Disulfiram should never be taken while intoxicated and it should not be taken for at least 12 hours after drinking alcohol. Unpleasant side effects (nausea, headache, vomiting, chest pains, difficulty breathing) can occur as soon as ten minutes after drinking even a small amount of alcohol and can last for an hour or more.

Acamprosate

Acamprosate is a medication for people in recovery who have already stopped drinking alcohol and want to avoid drinking. It works to prevent people from drinking alcohol, but it does not prevent withdrawal symptoms after people drink alcohol. It has not been shown to work in people who continue drinking alcohol, consume illicit drugs, and/or engage in prescription drug misuse and abuse. The use of acamprosate typically begins on the fifth day of abstinence, reaching full effectiveness in five to eight days. It is offered in tablet form and taken three times a day, preferably at the same time every day. The medication's side effects may include diarrhea, upset stomach, appetite loss, anxiety, dizziness, and difficulty sleeping.

Naltrexone

When used as a treatment for alcohol dependency, naltrexone blocks the euphoric effects and feelings of intoxication. This allows people with alcohol addiction to reduce their drinking behaviors enough to remain motivated to stay in treatment, avoid relapses, and take medications.

MAT Medications and Child Safety

It's important to remember that if medications are allowed to be kept at home, they must be locked in a safe place away from children. Methadone in its liquid form is colored and is sometimes mistaken for a soft drink. Children who take medications used in MAT may overdose and die.

Naloxone

Naloxone is a medication approved by the U.S. Food and Drug Administration (FDA) to prevent overdose by opioids such as heroin, morphine, and oxycodone. It blocks opioid receptor sites, reversing the toxic effects of the overdose. Naloxone is administered when a patient is showing signs of opioid overdose. The medication can be given by intranasal spray, intramuscular (into the muscle), subcutaneous (under the skin), or intravenous injection.

Naloxone is also added to buprenorphine to decrease the likelihood of diversion and misuse of the combination drug product.

A doctor can prescribe naloxone to patients who are in medication-assisted treatment (MAT), especially if the patient is taking medications used in MAT or considered a risk for opioid overdose. Candidates for naloxone are those who:

- Take high doses of opioids for long-term management of chronic pain
- Receive rotating opioid medication regimens

- Have been discharged from emergency medical care following opioid poisoning or intoxication
- Take certain extended-release or long-acting opioid medications
- Are completing mandatory opioid detoxification or abstinence programs

Pregnant women can be safely given naloxone in limited doses under the supervision of a doctor.

A doctor or pharmacist can show patients, their family members, or caregivers how to administer naloxone. Intravenous injection every two to three minutes is recommended in emergencies.

Patients given an automatic injection device or nasal spray should keep the item available at all times. Medication should be replaced when the expiration date passes.

Naloxone is effective if opioids are misused in combination with other sedatives or stimulants. It is not effective in treating overdoses of benzodiazepines or stimulant overdoses involving cocaine and amphetamines.

Section 40.3

Treatment for Methamphetamine Addiction

This section includes text excerpted from "Methamphetamine," National Institute on Drug Abuse (NIDA), September 2013.

What Treatments Are Effective for People Who Abuse Methamphetamine?

The most effective treatments for methamphetamine addiction at this point are behavioral therapies, such as cognitive-behavioral and contingency-management interventions. For example, the Matrix Model, a 16-week comprehensive behavioral treatment approach that combines behavioral therapy, family education, individual counseling, 12-Step support, drug testing, and encouragement for non-drug-related activities, has been shown to be effective in reducing methamphetamine abuse. Contingency management interventions, which provide tangible incentives in exchange for engaging in treatment and maintaining abstinence, have also been shown to be effective. Motivational Incentives for Enhancing Drug Abuse Recovery (MIEDAR), an incentive based method for promoting cocaine and methamphetamine abstinence, has demonstrated efficacy in methamphetamine abusers through NIDA's National Drug Abuse Clinical Trials Network.

Although medications have proven effective in treating some substance use disorders, there are currently no medications that counteract the specific effects of methamphetamine or that prolong abstinence from and reduce the abuse of methamphetamine by an individual addicted to the drug. NIDA has made research in the development of medications to treat addiction to stimulants and other drugs a priority, however. One approach being tried is to target the activity of glial cells. A drug called AV411 (ibudilast) that suppresses the neuroinflammatory actions of glial cells has been shown to inhibit methamphetamine self-administration in rats and is now being fast-tracked in clinical trials to establish its safety and effectiveness in humans with methamphetamine addiction.

Also under study are approaches that use the body's immune system to neutralize the drug in the bloodstream before it reaches the brain. These approaches include injecting a user with antimethamphetamine antibodies or with vaccines that would stimulate the body to produce its own such antibodies. Researchers have begun a clinical study to establish the safety of an antimethamphetamine monoclonal antibody known as mAb7F9 in human methamphetamine users.

Section 40.4

Vaccines For Drug Abuse

This section contains text excerpted from the following sources: Text in this section begins with excerpts from "A Vaccine for Drug Abuse? Maybe Someday," National Institute on Drug Abuse (NIDA), January 8, 2014; Text beginning with the heading "Vaccines to Treat Addiction—Basic Questions and Answers" is excerpted from "Dr. Thomas Kosten Q & A: Vaccines To Treat Addiction," National Institute on Drug Abuse (NIDA), June 11, 2015.

You've likely gotten vaccines for many different diseases, like measles, hepatitis B, and tetanus. But NIDA researchers hope that someday a vaccine will help people avoid drug abuse too.

New research has already led to a heroin vaccine that works by tricking the body's immune system into thinking heroin is a bacteria or virus. Immune cells attack the drug and block it from entering the brain. That way, heroin can't cause its addictive effects, such as the first rush of euphoria.

It has only been tested in animals so far, but such a vaccine could be vital in helping those who are trying to stop using heroin. By blocking the drug's effects, the vaccine could cause heroin to lose its power over the person. As one researcher says, the vaccine would not necessarily stop the person from craving the drug, but it could help the person stay strong in moments when they're feeling very tempted.

Researchers are working to create vaccines for other drugs, like cocaine.

Drug abuse vaccines are still a long way from being approved for people, and there are still a lot of questions about how they could be used. For instance, will only people already addicted to the drug get vaccinated? Could they also keep a person from starting to use a drug in the first place? Whatever the answer, vaccines offer a promising new way to fight drug abuse and addiction.

Vaccines to Treat Addiction—Basic Questions and Answers

What Is the Basic Idea behind Antidrug Vaccines?

The fundamental approach underlying an antidrug vaccine is the same as for a vaccine against a pathogenic virus or bacterium: You inject a person with an antigen, which is an agent that will stimulate production of antibodies.

In an antidrug vaccine, the antigen consists of the target drug linked to a large carrier protein such as tetanus toxoid or cholera toxin. The carrier protein is necessary because the drug molecule by itself is too small to stimulate antibody production. The carrier protein triggers production of antibodies that target the drug as well. If the vaccinated person subsequently takes the drug, these antibodies bind it and prevent it from entering the brain and other organs. The person doesn't get high from the drug and is shielded from its other harmful effects.

What Happens to the Drug after the Antibody Binds It?

That depends on the particular drug. In the case of cocaine, an enzyme is naturally present in the blood that breaks down the drug. The enzyme, called cholinesterase, increases the cocaine vaccine's effectiveness, because in addition to inactivating the drug, it also frees up antibody to bind more drug.

For other drugs, such as methamphetamine and nicotine, the drug is metabolized when it passes through the liver. That process also frees up antibody, but it doesn't assist those vaccines' efficiency as much as cholinesterase does the cocaine vaccine's. The reason is that it only happens in the liver, instead of throughout the bloodstream, and it takes time for the drug-antibody complex to reach the liver.

Would a Single Treatment with an Antidrug Vaccine Be Enough?

No. Booster shots will be required.

For an antidrug vaccine to be effective, the antibody response to it must be substantially greater than that typically produced by an infectious-disease vaccine. The antidrug vaccines we are developing stimulate production of 100 to 1,000 times more antibody than is produced with a typical vaccine against an infectious disease. After the initial vaccination, antibody levels rise and stay very high for 2 to 3 months. Each booster will push the antibody levels back up for another 2 to 3 months. The antibody levels may stay up for a longer time after each booster shot, as occurs with the tetanus vaccine. But they certainly will not last for years and will drop off to undetectable levels within 9 to 12 months.

What Are the Potential Risks of the Antidrug Vaccination?

The primary risk is that a user takes a large amount of the drug to try to override the vaccine. The antibodies act like a sponge that keeps the drug in the blood stream and prevents it from rapidly entering the brain and causing the euphoria the user seeks. But a full sponge is leaky, and so at high doses, some amounts of the drug are regularly coming off the antibodies. The drug enters the brain and other organs, albeit slowly, and even though the person doesn't get high, it may produce harmful effects. In the case of stimulants, for example, these might include anxiety, paranoia, or even cardiovascular events. In fact, these toxic effects may be worsened because the organs are being exposed to higher amounts of the drug.

Section 40.5

Addressing Co-Occurring Disorders in Different Settings

This section includes text excerpted from "Co-Occuring Disorders," Substance Abuse and Mental Health Services Administration (SAMHSA), March 8, 2016.

Co-occurring Disorders

The coexistence of both a mental health and a substance use disorder is referred to as co-occurring disorders.

People with mental health disorders are more likely than people without mental health disorders to experience an alcohol or substance use disorder. Co-occurring disorders can be difficult to diagnose due to the complexity of symptoms, as both may vary in severity. In many cases, people receive treatment for one disorder while the other disorder remains untreated. This may occur because both mental and substance use disorders can have biological, psychological, and social components. Other reasons may be inadequate provider training or screening, an overlap of symptoms, or that other health issues need to be addressed first. In any case, the consequences of undiagnosed, untreated, or undertreated co-occurring disorders can lead to a higher likelihood of experiencing homelessness, incarceration, medical illnesses, suicide, or even early death.

People with co-occurring disorders are best served through integrated treatment. With integrated treatment, practitioners can address mental and substance use disorders at the same time, often lowering costs and creating better outcomes. Increasing awareness and building capacity in service systems are important in helping identify and treat co-occurring disorders. Early detection and treatment can improve treatment outcomes and the quality of life for those who need these services.

Addressing Co-Occurring Disorders in Different Settings

SAMHSA offers guidance aimed at helping practitioners improve services to people with co-occurring disorders in the following social service settings:

- Co-occurring Disorders in the Criminal Justice System
- Co-occurring Disorders and Homelessness
- Co-occurring Disorders and Primary Care
- Co-occurring Disorders Among Veterans and the Military Community

Co-Occurring Disorders in the Criminal Justice System

Many people in the criminal justice system have co-occurring disorders. Providing integrated treatment to address mental and substance use disorders can lead to positive outcomes such as reduced substance use and arrests.

Failure to effectively screen and assess inmates with co-occurring disorders is a major concern in the criminal justice system. As part of the full protocol, an effective screening process should include the following:

- Routine screening at entry points to criminal justice settings
- Use of standardized instruments that include cut-off points to determine whether a person should be referred for a follow-up assessment

- Trained staff to administer the screening instruments and refer people for assessment
- A response for incarcerated people experiencing a behavioral health crisis, such as intoxication or drug use that requires medical attention, or if an individual is experiencing suicidal thoughts
- Healthcare records being maintained by the agency conducting the screening

Co-occurring Disorders and Homelessness

Co-occurring disorders are common among people experiencing homelessness. This population often has a variety of issues that require services beyond behavioral health treatment, such as life skills development, employment assistance, and housing.

While treating people experiencing homeless who are suffering from co-occurring disorders through integrated care is important to recovery, few have access to it. People experiencing homelessness may be isolated or have little to no access to health and behavioral health services, and therefore their health issues may go undiagnosed or untreated. This can lead to chronic homelessness and further deterioration in physical and behavioral health, as well as social and economic functioning.

One way to improve access to integrated care for people experiencing homelessness is to implement integrated screening and assessment throughout the homeless system of care. Integrated screening determines the likelihood that people experiencing homelessness may or may not have co-occurring disorders or whether co-occurring disorders are influencing their presenting signs, symptoms, or behaviors. Assessment is an ongoing process of collecting and organizing clinical information, and interpreting the information on the basis of diagnostic criteria and professional judgment.

Co-Occurring Disorders and Primary Care

People who receive primary care often may have multiple health issues, including co-occurring disorders. Integrating behavioral and primary care is especially important to meeting their needs.

People with co-occurring disorders may seek primary care services first before seeking behavioral health services. As a result, primary care practitioners have unique opportunities to identify people with co-occurring disorders through screening. Screening for co-occurring disorders in primary care settings can assist practitioners in recognizing and addressing conditions early. Screening also can serve as a baseline to measure clinical progress.

A variety of screening and assessment tools are available for primary care practitioners. These screening and assessment tools can help determine if the need for further assessment is necessary, provide background on a client's substance use and mental health disorders and the severity, and estimate how effective they respond to interventions.

Co-Occurring Disorders Among Veterans and the Military Community

Co-occurring disorders, such as post-traumatic stress disorder (PTSD) and substance use, is prevalent among veterans and the military community. According to the Veterans Affairs Department (VA), approximately one-third of veterans seeking treatment for substance use disorders also met the criteria for PTSD.

Veterans and service members benefit from integrated care for mental and substance use disorders. However, some veterans may not seek medical treatment for one of many reasons, including a fear of being treated differently.

To promote wellness among veterans, service members, and their families, practitioners are encouraged to collaborate with other organizations to develop a training plan in effective integrated care techniques. The following organizations provide guidance on treating PTSD and substance use disorders:

- PTSD: National Center for PTSD offers a continuing education course for practitioners on Managing PTSD and Co-occurring Substance Use Disorders.
- The VA provides VA/DOD Clinical Practice Guidelines for Management of PTSD and Acute Stress Reaction, which offers guidance on screening, assessment, and treatment of PTSD and substance use disorders.
- The Alcohol Research & Health Journal of the National Institute on Alcohol Abuse and Alcoholism (NIAAA) provides recommendations from the Institute of Medicine (IOM) for implementing quality care for individuals with co-occurring disorders.
- The National Institute on Drug Abuse (NIDA) provides some guidance on how comorbid conditions should be treated.

Practitioner Competencies for Treating Co-Occurring Disorders

States working to improve treatment for people with co-occurring disorders have established practitioner competencies that define roles and create a common framework for working collaboratively across social service systems. These competencies have been developed as guidelines or checklists for clinical supervisors to use when assessing practitioner performance in providing integrated services. The competencies can be incorporated into existing job descriptions, training plans, supervision meetings, personal evaluation, and credentialing and licensure.

Chapter 41

Supporting Substance Abuse Recovery

Chapter Contents

Section 41.1

Mutual Support Groups

This section includes text excerpted from "Substance Abuse in Brief Fact Sheet," Substance Abuse and Mental Health Services Administration (SAMHSA), 2008. Reviewed April 2016.

Introduction to Mutual Support Groups

Mutual support (also called self-help) groups are an important part of recovery from substance use disorders (SUDs). Mutual support groups exist both for persons with an SUD and for their families or significant others and are one of the choices an individual has during the recovery process. This section will help healthcare and social service providers understand the effect of mutual support groups on recovery, become familiar with the different types of mutual support groups available, and make informed referrals to such groups.

Mutual support groups are nonprofessional groups comprising members who share the same problem and voluntarily support one another in the recovery from that problem. Although mutual support groups do not provide formal treatment, they are one part of a recovery-oriented systems-of-care approach to substance abuse recovery. By providing social, emotional, and informational support for persons throughout the recovery process, mutual support groups help individuals take responsibility for their alcohol and drug problems and for their sustained health, wellness, and recovery. The most widely available mutual support groups are 12-Step groups, such as Alcoholics Anonymous (AA), but other mutual support groups such as Women for Sobriety (WFS), SMART Recovery® (Self-Management and Recovery Training), and Secular Organizations for Sobriety/Save Our Selves (SOS) are also available.

12-Step Groups

Twelve-Step groups emphasize abstinence and have 12 core developmental "steps" to recovering from dependence. Other elements of 12-Step groups include taking responsibility for recovery, sharing personal narratives, helping others, and recognizing and incorporating into daily life the existence of a higher power. Participants often maintain a close relationship with a sponsor, an experienced member with long-term abstinence, and lifetime participation is expected. AA is the oldest and best known 12-Step mutual support group. There are more than 100,000 AA groups worldwide and nearly 2 million members. The AA model has been adapted for people with dependence on drugs and for their family members. Some groups, such as Narcotics Anonymous (NA) and Chemically Dependent Anonymous, focus on any type of drug use. Other groups, such as Cocaine Anonymous and Crystal Meth Anonymous, focus on abuse of specific drugs. Groups for persons with co-occurring substance use and mental disorders also exist (e.g., Double Trouble in Recovery; Dual Recovery Anonymous).

Other 12-Step groups—Families Anonymous, Al-Anon/Alateen, Nar-Anon, and Co-Anon—provide support to significant others, families, and friends of persons with SUDs. Twelve-Step meetings are held in locations such as churches and public buildings. Metropolitan areas usually have specialized groups, based on such member characteristics as gender, length of time in recovery, age, sexual orientation, profession, ethnicity, and language spoken. Attendance and membership are free, although people usually give a small donation when they attend a meeting.

Meetings can be "open" or "closed"—that is, anyone can attend an open meeting, but attendance at closed meetings is limited to people who want to stop drinking or using drugs. Although meeting formats vary somewhat, most 12-Step meetings have an opening and a closing that are the same at every meeting, such as a 12-Step reading or prayer. The main part of the meeting usually consists of

1. members sharing their stories of dependence, its effect on their lives, and what they are doing to stay abstinent,
2. the study of a particular step or other doctrine of the group, or
3. a guest speaker.

Twelve-Step groups are not necessarily for everyone. Some people are uncomfortable with the spiritual emphasis and prefer a more secular approach. Others may not agree with the 12-Step philosophy that addiction is a chronic disease, thinking that this belief can be a self-fulfilling prophesy that weakens the ability to remain abstinent. Still others may prefer gender specific groups.

Mutual support groups that are not based on the 12-Step model typically do not advocate sponsors or lifetime membership. These support groups offer an alternative to traditional 12-Step groups, but the availability of in-person meetings is more limited than that of 12-Step programs. However, many offer literature, discussion boards, and online meetings.

Women for Sobriety

WFS is the first national self-help group solely for women wishing to stop using alcohol and drugs. The program is based on Thirteen Statements that encourage emotional and spiritual growth, with abstinence as the only acceptable goal. Although daily meditation is encouraged, WFS does not otherwise emphasize God or a higher power. The nearly 300 meetings held weekly are led by experienced, abstinent WFS members and follow a structured format, which includes reading the Thirteen Statements, an introduction of members, and a moderated discussion.

Smart Recovery

SMART Recovery helps individuals become free from dependence on any substance. Dependence is viewed as a learned behavior that can be modified using cognitive-behavioral approaches. Its four principles are to

1. Enhance and maintain motivation to abstain,
2. cope with urges,
3. manage thoughts, feelings, and behaviors, and
4. balance momentary and enduring satisfactions.

At the approximately 300 weekly group meetings held worldwide, attendees discuss personal experiences and real-world applications of these SMART Recovery principles. SMART Recovery has online meetings and a message board discussion group on its Web site.

Secular Organization for Sobriety / Save Our Selves

SOS considers recovery from alcohol and drugs an individual responsibility separate from spirituality and emphasizes a cognitive approach to maintaining lifelong abstinence. Meetings typically begin with a reading of the SOS Guidelines for Sobriety and introductions, followed by an open discussion of a topic deemed appropriate by the members. However, because each of the approximately 500 SOS groups is autonomous, the meeting format may differ from group to group.

LifeRing Secular Recovery

Originally part of SOS, LifeRing is now a separate organization for people who want to stop using alcohol and drugs. The principles of LifeRing are sobriety, secularity, and self-help. LifeRing encourages participants to develop a unique path to abstinence according to their needs and to use the group meetings to facilitate their personal recovery plan. LifeRing meetings are relatively unstructured; attendees discuss what has happened to them in the past week, but some meetings focus on helping members create a personal recovery plan. Although there are fewer than 100 meetings worldwide, LifeRing has a chat room, e-mail lists, and an online forum that provide additional support to its members.

Effectiveness of Mutual Support Groups

Research on mutual support groups indicates that active participation in any type of mutual support group significantly increases the likelihood of maintaining abstinence. Previous research has shown that participating in 12-Step or other mutual support groups is related to abstinence from alcohol and drug use. An important finding is that these abstinence rates increase with greater group participation. Persons who attend mutual support groups have also been found to have lower levels of alcohol- and drug-related problems. Another benefit of mutual support group participation is that "helping helps the helper." Helping others by sharing experiences and providing support increases involvement in 12-Step groups, which in turn increases abstinence and lowers binge drinking rates among those who have not achieved abstinence.

Facilitating Mutual Support Group Participation

If a healthcare or social service provider suspects that a patient or client has an SUD, the provider should ensure that the client receives formal treatment. Once the client receives formal treatment—or if he or she refuses or cannot afford treatment—the provider's next step is to facilitate involvement in a mutual support group. Matching clients to treatment based solely on gender, motivation, cognitive impairment, or other such characteristics has not been proved to be effective. Clients who are "philosophically well matched" to a mutual support group are more likely to actively participate in that group. Thus, the best way to help a client benefit from mutual support groups is to encourage increased participation in his or her chosen group. Providers can increase their knowledge of mutual support groups, and thus their ability to make informed referrals, by doing the following:

- Become familiar with the different types of support groups and their philosophies. Most groups' Web sites describe their philosophies and have online publications.
- Determine which groups are active locally. Most groups' Web sites have meeting locator services.
- Find out about the different types of meetings available within local mutual support groups (e.g., which meetings are for women only).
- Establish contacts in local mutual support groups. AA and NA in particular have committees whose members work with healthcare and social service providers to get clients to meetings and to provide information to providers.
- Attend open meetings to expand knowledge of mutual support groups and how local meetings are conducted.

Understanding the needs and beliefs of clients with SUDs helps providers make informed referrals. Providers should find out clients' experiences with mutual support groups, their concerns and misconceptions about mutual support groups, and their personal beliefs. Persons who agree with the group's belief system are more likely to participate and, thus, more likely to have better outcomes. For example, having strong religious beliefs is related to greater participation in the spiritually based 12-Step programs and WFS.

In contrast, religiosity was less effective in increasing participation in SMART Recovery groups and decreased participation in SOS. Whether the client is participating in medication-assisted treatment (MAT) is another consideration when making a referral to a mutual support group, because some groups may be more supportive of MAT than others. For example, individuals being treated with methadone for opioid dependence may be more comfortable attending a meeting of Methadone Anonymous, whose members understand the benefits of opioid pharmacotherapy.

To improve the client's chances of attending a meeting, providers can:

- Present more than one choice when making referrals and encourage clients to attend several meetings before making any judgments about the groups. Clients should be encouraged to attend different groups until they find one in which they are comfortable.

- Initiate the first conversation between a client and a support group contact person. Having a mutual support group member speak to a client by phone during the office visit may increase the likelihood that the client will attend the support group meeting.
- Refer family members or others who may be affected by the client's substance use. Their involvement may encourage participation by providing social support.

Once clients are attending a group they are comfortable with, the provider should actively encourage the clients' support group experiences by scheduling follow-up visits to talk about their experiences and providing positive feedback. Clients should be asked about details—how many meetings are they attending, do they have a sponsor, are they abstinent. Gentle, positive encouragement will likely increase participation. Providers should watch for signs of an impending relapse, such as a reluctance to discuss group participation or periods of extreme stress. By offering knowledgeable advice and informed referrals and taking an ongoing, active interest in clients' support group experiences, providers can make a difference in their clients' recovery.

Section 41.2

Peer Recovery Support Services

This section includes text excerpted from "Peer Support and Social Inclusion," Substance Abuse and Mental Health Services Administration (SAMHSA), July 2, 2015.

Peer Support and Social Inclusion

By sharing their experiences, peers bring hope to people in recovery and promote a sense of belonging within the community.

Peer support services are delivered by individuals who have common life experiences with the people they are serving. People with mental and/or substance use disorders have a unique capacity to help each other based on a shared affiliation and a deep understanding of this experience. In self-help and mutual support, people offer this support, strength, and hope to their peers, which allows for personal growth, wellness promotion, and recovery.

Research has shown that peer support facilitates recovery and reduces healthcare costs. Peers also provide assistance that promotes a sense of belonging within the community. The ability to contribute to and enjoy one's community is key to recovery and well-being. Another critical component that peers provide is the development of self-efficacy through role modeling and assisting peers with ongoing recovery through mastery of experiences and finding meaning, purpose, and social connections in their lives.

SAMHSA's Recovery Community Services Program (RCSP) advances recovery by providing peer recovery support services across the nation. These services help prevent relapse and promote sustained recovery from mental and/or substance use disorders.

Through the RCSP, SAMHSA recognizes that social support includes informational, emotional, and intentional support. Examples of peer recovery support services include:

- Peer mentoring or coaching—developing a one-on-one relationship in which a peer leader with recovery experience encourages, motivates, and supports a peer in recovery
- Peer recovery resource connecting—connecting the peer with professional and nonprofessional services and resources available in the community
- Recovery group facilitation—facilitating or leading recovery-oriented group activities, including support groups and educational activities
- Building community—helping peers make new friends and build healthy social networks through emotional, instrumental, informational, and affiliation types of peer support

Community Living and Participation

Recovery for individuals with behavioral health conditions is greatly enhanced by social connection. Yet, many people with mental and/or substance use disorders are not fully engaged in their communities either through personal relationships, social events, or civic activities. Unfortunately, many individuals often remain socially isolated and excluded. Negative perceptions, prejudice, and discrimination contribute to the social exclusion of people living with behavioral health disorders.

People living with mental and/or substance use conditions can increase social connections greatly when they have access to recovery-oriented services and establish positive relationships with family and friends. Greater social connections lead to improved economic, educational, recreational, and cultural opportunities that are generally available.

In a socially inclusive society, people in recovery have the opportunity and necessary supports to contribute to their community as citizens, parents, employees, students, volunteers, and leaders. Prevention activities help create communities in which people have an improved quality of life that includes healthier environments at work and in school, and supportive neighborhoods and work environments. Social connections and understanding also help people in recovery from addictions benefit from alcohol- and tobacco-free activities in the community.

Section 41.3

Recovery Services

This section includes text excerpted from "Recovery and Recovery Support," Substance Abuse and Mental Health Services Administration (SAMHSA), October 5, 2015.

Overview of Recovery and Recovery Support

The adoption of recovery by behavioral health systems in recent years has signaled a dramatic shift in the expectation for positive outcomes for individuals who experience mental and/or substance use conditions. Today, when individuals with mental and/or substance use disorders seek help, they are met with the knowledge and belief that anyone can recover and/or manage their conditions successfully. The value of recovery and recovery-oriented behavioral health systems is widely accepted by states, communities, healthcare providers, peers, families, researchers, and advocates including the U.S. Surgeon General, the Institute of Medicine, and others.

SAMHSA has established a working definition of recovery that defines recovery as a process of change through which individuals improve their health and wellness, live self-directed lives, and strive to reach their full potential. Recovery is built on access to evidence-based clinical treatment and recovery support services for all populations.

SAMHSA has delineated four major dimensions that support a life in recovery:

Health—overcoming or managing one's disease(s) or symptoms—for example, abstaining from use of alcohol, illicit drugs, and non-prescribed medications if one has an addiction problem—and, for everyone in recovery, making informed, healthy choices that support physical and emotional well-being

- **Home**—having a stable and safe place to live
- **Purpose**—conducting meaningful daily activities, such as a job, school volunteerism, family caretaking, or creative endeavors, and the independence, income, and resources to participate in society
- **Community**—having relationships and social networks that provide support, friendship, love, and hope

Hope, the belief that these challenges and conditions can be overcome, is the foundation of recovery. A person's recovery is built on his or her strengths, talents, coping abilities, resources, and inherent values. It is holistic, addresses the whole person and their community, and is supported by peers, friends, and family members.

The process of recovery is highly personal and occurs via many pathways. It may include clinical treatment, medications, faith-based approaches, peer support, family support, self-care, and other approaches. Recovery is characterized by continual growth and improvement in one's health and wellness that may involve setbacks. Because setbacks are a natural part of life, resilience becomes a key component of recovery.

Resilience refers to an individual's ability to cope with adversity and adapt to challenges or change. Resilience develops over time and gives an individual the capacity not only to cope with life's challenges but also to be better prepared for the next stressful situation. Optimism and the ability to remain hopeful are essential to resilience and the process of recovery.

Because recovery is a highly individualized process, recovery services and supports must be flexible to ensure cultural relevancy. What may work for adults in recovery may be very different for youth or older adults in recovery. For example, the promotion of resiliency in young people, and the nature of social supports, peer mentors, and recovery coaching for adolescents and transitional age youth are different than recovery support services for adults and older adults.

The process of recovery is supported through relationships and social networks. This often involves family members who become the champions of their loved one's recovery. They provide essential support to their family member's journey of recovery and similarly experience the moments of positive healing as well as the difficult challenges. Families of people in recovery may experience adversities in their social, occupational, and financial lives, as well as in their overall quality of family life. These experiences can lead to increased family stress, guilt, shame, anger, fear, anxiety, loss, grief, and isolation. The concept of resilience in recovery is also vital for family members who need access to intentional supports that promote their health and well-being. The support of peers and friends is also crucial in engaging and supporting individuals in recovery.

Recovery Support

SAMHSA established the Recovery Support Strategic Initiative to promote partnering with people in recovery from mental and substance use disorders and their family members to guide the behavioral health system and promote individual, program, and system-level approaches that foster health and resilience (including helping individuals with behavioral health needs be well, manage symptoms, and achieve and maintain abstinence); increase housing to support recovery; reduce barriers to employment, education, and other life goals; and secure necessary social supports in their chosen community.

Recovery support is provided through treatment, services, and community-based programs by behavioral healthcare providers, peer providers, family members, friends and social networks, the faith community, and people with experience in recovery. Recovery support services help people enter into and navigate systems of care, remove barriers to recovery, stay engaged in the recovery process, and live full lives in communities of their choice.

Recovery support services include culturally and linguistically appropriate services that assist individuals and families working toward recovery from mental and/or substance use problems.

They incorporate a full range of social, legal, and other services that facilitate recovery, wellness, and linkage to and coordination among service providers, and other supports shown to improve quality of life for people in and seeking recovery and their families.

Recovery support services also include access to evidence-based practices such as supported employment, education, and housing; assertive community treatment; illness management; and peer-operated services. Recovery support services may be provided before, during, or after clinical treatment or may be provided to individuals who are not in treatment but seek support services. These services, provided by professionals and peers, are delivered through a variety of community and faith-based groups, treatment providers, schools, and other specialized services. For example, in the United States there are 22 recovery high schools that help reduce the risk environment for youth with substance use disorders. These schools typically have high retention rates and low relapse rates. The broad range of service delivery options ensures the life experiences of all people are valued and represented.

Cultural Awareness and Competency

Supporting recovery requires that mental health and addiction services:

- Be responsive and respectful to the health beliefs, practices, and cultural and linguistic needs of diverse people and groups
- Actively address diversity in the delivery of services
- Seek to reduce health disparities in access and outcomes

Cultural competence describes the ability of an individual or organization to interact effectively with people of different cultures. To produce positive change, practitioners must understand the cultural context of the community they serve, and have the willingness and skills to work within this context. This means drawing on community-based values, traditions, and customs, and working with knowledgeable people from the community to plan, implement, and evaluate prevention activities.

Individuals, families, and communities that have experienced social and economic disadvantages are more likely to face greater obstacles to overall health. Characteristics such as race or ethnicity, religion, low socioeconomic status, gender, age, mental health, disability, sexual orientation or gender identity, geographic location, or other characteristics historically linked to exclusion or discrimination are known to influence health status.

SAMHSA is committed to addressing these health disparities by providing culturally and linguistically appropriate prevention, treatment, and recovery support programs. This commitment is reinforced through the agency's disparity impact strategy that monitors programs and activities to ensure that access, use, and outcomes are equitable across racial and ethnic minority groups.

The SAMHSA Office of Behavioral Health Equity (OBHE) works to reduce mental health and substance use disparities among diverse racial and ethnic populations, as well as lesbian, gay, bisexual, and transgender (LGBT) populations. OBHE was established to improve access to quality care and in accordance with section 10334(b) of the Affordable Care Act of 2010, which requires six agencies under the Department of Health and Human Services (HHS) to establish an office of minority affairs.

Chapter 42

Know Your Rights When in Recovery from Substance Abuse

The Federal Non-Discrimination Laws That Protect You

Q: I am in recovery from substance abuse, but I still face discrimination because of my addiction history. Does any law protect me?

A: Yes. Federal civil rights laws prohibit discrimination in many areas of life against qualified "individuals with disabilities." Many people with past and current alcohol problems and past drug use disorders, including those in treatment for these illnesses, are protected from discrimination by:

- The Americans with Disabilities Act (ADA)
- The Rehabilitation Act of 1973
- The Fair Housing Act (FHA) and
- The Workforce Investment Act (WIA)

This chapter includes text excerpted from "Know Your Rights," Substance Abuse and Mental Health Services Administration (SAMHSA), January 17, 2012. Reviewed April 2016.

Who Is Protected?

The non-discrimination laws discussed below protect individuals with a "disability."

- Under these Federal laws, an individual with a "disability" is someone who –
  - has a current "physical or mental impairment" that "substantially limits" one or more of that person's "major life activities," such as caring for one's self, working, etc.
  - has a record of such a substantially limiting impairment *or*
  - is regarded as having such an impairment.
- Whether a particular person has a "disability" is decided on an individualized, case-by-case basis.
- Substance use disorders (addiction) are recognized as impairments that can and do, for many individuals, substantially limit the individual's major life activities. For this reason, many courts have found that individuals experiencing or who are in recovery from these conditions are individuals with a "disability" protected by Federal law.
- To be protected as an individual with a "disability" under Federal non-discrimination laws, a person must show that his or her addiction substantially limits (or limited, in the past) major life activities.
- People wrongly believed to have a substance use disorder (in the past or currently) may also be protected as individuals "regarded as" having a disability.

Who Is Not Protected?

- People who currently engage in the illegal use of drugs are not protected under these non-discrimination laws, except that individuals may not be denied health services (including drug rehabilitation) based on their current illegal use of drugs if they are otherwise entitled to those services.
- People whose use of alcohol or drugs poses a direct threat—a significant risk of substantial harm—to the health or safety of others are not protected.
- People whose use of alcohol or drugs does not significantly impair a major life activity are not protected (unless they show they have a "record of" or are "regarded as" having a substance use disorder—addiction—that is substantially limiting).

What Is, and Is Not, Illegal Discrimination?

- Discriminating against someone on the basis of his or her disability—for example, just because he has a past drug addiction or she is in an alcohol treatment program—may be illegal discrimination. Discrimination means treating someone less favorably than someone else because he or she has, once had, or is regarded as having a disability.
- Acting against a person for reasons other than having a disability is not generally illegal discrimination, even if the disability is related to the cause of the adverse action.

For instance, it is not likely to be ruled unlawful discrimination if someone in substance abuse treatment or in recovery is denied a job, services, or benefits because he

- does not meet essential eligibility requirements
- is unable to do the job
- creates a direct threat to health or safety by his behavior, even if the behavior is caused by a substance use disorder
- violates rules or commits a crime, including a drug or alcohol-related one, when that misconduct is cause for excluding or disciplining anyone doing it.

Since the basis for the negative action in these cases is not (or not solely) the person's disability, these actions do not violate Federal non-discrimination laws.

Employment

Q: Are people in treatment for or in recovery from substance use disorders protected from job discrimination?

A: The answer in many cases is "yes." The Americans with Disabilities Act and the Rehabilitation Act prohibit most employers from refusing to hire, firing, or discriminating in the terms and conditions of employment against any qualified job applicant or employee on the basis of a disability.

- The ADA applies to all State and local governmental units, and to private employers with 15 or more employees.
- The Rehabilitation Act applies to Federal employers and other public and private employers who receive Federal grants, contracts, or aid.

Rights: In general, these employers –

- May not deny a job to or fire a person because he or she is in treatment or in recovery from a substance use disorder, unless the person's disorder would prevent safe and competent job performance.
- Must provide "reasonable accommodations," when needed, to enable those with a disability to perform their job duties. Changing work hours to let an employee attend treatment is one kind of a reasonable accommodation. (But if an accommodation would cause the employer undue hardship—significant difficulty or expense—it is not required.)
- Must keep confidential any medical-related information they discover about a job applicant or employee, including information about a past or present substance use disorder.

Limits: The non-discrimination laws protect only applicants and employees qualified for the job who currently are not engaging in the illegal use of drugs.

- "Qualified" means that a person meets the basic qualification requirements for the job, and is able to perform its essential functions—fundamental duties—with or without a reasonable accommodation.
- Remember: people who pose a direct threat to health or safety, or have committed misconduct warranting job discipline, including termination, are not protected.

Medical Inquiries and Examinations

As a general rule, employers:

- May not use information they learn about an individual's disability in a discriminatory manner. They may not deny or treat anyone less favorably in the terms and conditions of employment if he or she is qualified to perform the job.
- Must maintain the confidentiality of all information they obtain about applicants' and employees' health conditions, including addiction and treatment for substance use disorders.

Before making a job offer, employers may not ask:

- Questions about whether a job applicant has or has had a disability, or about the nature or severity of an applicant's disability. Pre-offer medical examinations also are illegal.

- Whether a job applicant is or has ever abused or been addicted to drugs or alcohol, or if the applicant is being treated by a substance abuse rehabilitation program, or has received such treatment in the past.

Employers may ask job applicants:

- Whether the applicant currently is using drugs illegally
- Whether the applicant drinks alcohol
- Whether the applicant can perform the duties of the job.

After making a job offer, employers may:

- Make medical inquiries and require an individual to undergo a medical examination (including ones that reveal a past or current substance use disorder), as long as all those offered the position are given the same exam.
- Condition employment on the satisfactory results of such medical inquiries or exams.

After employment begins, employers may make medical inquiries or require an employee to undergo a medical examination, but only when doing this is job-related and justified by business necessity.

Such exams and inquiries may be permitted if the employer has a reasonable belief, based on objective evidence, that an employee has a health (including substance use-related) condition that impairs his or her ability to perform essential job functions, or that poses a direct threat to health or safety.

Workplace Drug Testing

- Employers are permitted to test both job applicants and employees for illegal use of drugs, and may refuse to hire—or may fire or discipline—anyone whose test reveals such illegal use.
- Employers may not fire or refuse to hire any job applicant or employee solely because a drug test reveals the presence of a lawfully used medication (such as methadone).
- Employers must keep confidential information they discover about an employee's use of lawfully prescribed medications.

Medical Leave

Q: Do I have the right to take medical leave from my job if I need it for substance abuse treatment?

A: Yes, in many workplaces, you do.

Rights: The Family and Medical Leave Act (FMLA) gives many employees the right to take up to 12 weeks of unpaid leave in a 12-month period when needed to receive treatment for a "serious health condition"—which, under the FMLA, may include "substance abuse." The leave must be for treatment; absence because of the employee's use of the substance does not qualify for leave.

- The FMLA covers Federal, State, and local Government employers, public and private elementary and secondary schools, and private employers with 50 or more employees.
- To be eligible for leave under FMLA, you must have been employed by a covered employer for at least 12 months, worked at least 1,250 hours during the 12 months immediately before the leave, and work at a worksite where there are at least 50 employees or within 75 miles of that site.
- FMLA makes it illegal for employers to deny leave to or take action against an employee for requesting or taking leave.
- In some circumstances, denying an employee leave for substance use treatment may constitute a violation of the ADA or the Rehabilitation Act.

Limits: Neither the FMLA nor Federal non-discrimination laws make it illegal for an employer to fire or discipline an employee for a legitimate non-discriminatory reason, even when the employee is granted or entitled to leave under these laws or under the employer's personnel policy. This means an employee who violates workplace rules or who uses drugs illegally still can be fired for those reasons.

Job Training

Q: I need job training and placement services. Can I be denied that help because of my substance use history?

A: No, not in public (governmental) job training and placement programs, nor in private job placement services that receive Federal financial assistance.

The Workforce Investment Act (WIA) provides financial assistance for job training and placement services for many people through the One-Stop Career Center system. Section 188 of WIA and the other non-discrimination laws discussed in this brochure prohibit most job training and placement service providers from denying services to, or discriminating in other ways against, qualified applicants and recipients on the basis of disability—including people with past or current substance use disorders—who otherwise:

- meet the eligibility requirements for these services *and*
- are currently not using drugs illegally.

Housing

Q: Am I also protected from discrimination when it comes to renting or buying housing?

A: The Fair Housing Act (FHA) makes discrimination in housing and real estate transactions illegal when it is based on a disability. The FHA protects people with past and current alcohol addiction and past drug addiction—although other Federal laws sometimes limit their rights. The FHA does not protect people who currently engage in illegal drug use.

Rights: Landlords and other housing providers may not refuse to rent or sell housing to people in recovery or who have current alcohol disorders, and may not discriminate in other ways against them in housing transactions solely on the basis of their disability. It is also illegal to discriminate against housing providers (such as sober or halfway houses for people in recovery) because they associate with individuals with disabilities.

Limits on Public Housing Eligibility: Federal law limits some people's eligibility for public and other federally assisted housing because of past or current substance use-related conduct. The Quality Housing and Work Responsibility Act:

- requires public housing agencies, Section 8, and other federally assisted housing providers to exclude:
    - Any person evicted from public, federally assisted, or Section 8 housing because of drug-related criminal activity (including possession or sale). This bar ordinarily lasts for 3 years after the individual's eviction. A public housing agency can lift or shorten that time period if the individual successfully completes a rehabilitation program.
    - Any household with a member who is abusing alcohol or using drugs in a manner that may interfere with the health, safety, or right to peaceful enjoyment of the premises by

other residents. Exceptions can be made if the individual demonstrates that he or she is not currently abusing alcohol or using drugs illegally and has successfully completed a rehabilitation program.

- permits applicants for public housing to be denied admission if a member of the household has engaged in any drug-related criminal activity (or certain other criminal activity) within a "reasonable time" of the application.

Government Services and Programs

Q: Government benefits and services are crucial to my getting treatment and staying in recovery. Do Federal laws protect me from discrimination in these areas?

A: Yes. The Americans with Disabilities Act and Rehabilitation Act prohibit disability-based discrimination by Federal, State, or local governmental agencies in any of their "services, programs, or activities." These include Government –

- services (such as health or social services and education and training programs)
- benefit programs (such as welfare or child-care assistance) and other forms of financial assistance (such as student loans)
- other Government activities, such as zoning or occupational licensure.

Rights: If you are "qualified"—that is, you meet the essential eligibility requirements of the service, program, or activity—you may not be denied the opportunity to participate in or receive benefits from these and other public services, benefit programs, or governmental activities because of your disability.

Limits on Rights and Opportunities Due to Drug Convictions:

1. Public Assistance and Food Stamps: Drug Felony Ban–The Federal welfare law (the Personal Responsibility and Work Opportunity Act of 1996) imposes a lifetime ban on Federal cash assistance and food stamps for anyone convicted of a drug-related felony (including possession or sale) after August 22, 1996. However, States may "opt out" of or modify this Federal rule:

   - 12 States do not impose this ban.

- 21 other States have modified the ban, and allow people who get treatment, show they are rehabilitated, or meet other requirements to become eligible again.

2. Education: Student Loans and Aid—The Higher Education Act of 1998 makes students convicted of drug offenses (including possession or sale) ineligible for federally funded student loans, grants, or work assistance.
    - Ineligibility lasts for varying lengths of time, depending on the type of drug offense and if it is a repeat offense.
    - This bars students from getting federally funded education loans or aid in college, and in many other educational and training programs.
    - States cannot "opt out" of or otherwise modify this Federal rule.
3. Driver's Licenses – The Department of Transportation (DOT) Appropriation Amendment offers Federal financial incentives to States that agree to revoke or suspend, for at least 6 months, the driver's license of anyone convicted of a drug offense (including not only drug-related driving offenses, but also those involving drug possession or sale).
    - Many States choose not to opt out of this law.

Private Educational, Health Care, and Other Facilities

Q: Do private educational institutions, service providers, and other facilities also have to comply with Federal non-discrimination laws protecting people with disabilities?

A: A large number do.

- The Americans with Disabilities Act requires "public accommodations" as well as Government agencies to comply with its non-discrimination requirements. Public accommodations are private facilities that provide goods or services to the public. They include:
    - schools and universities
    - hospitals, clinics, and health care providers
    - social service agencies such as homeless shelters, day care centers, and senior centers.

- Private service providers that receive Federal grants, contracts, or aid must comply with the same non-discrimination requirements under the Rehabilitation Act and the Workforce Investment Act, when it applies.

Rights: In offering or providing their goods or services, public accommodations (and other private entities covered by the Rehabilitation Act or WIA) must not discriminate against individuals on the basis of their past, current, or perceived disability. This means they must ensure that individuals with disabilities:

- enjoy the equal opportunity to participate in or benefit from the facility's goods and services
- receive goods or services in the most integrated setting possible. Segregating or providing different services to people with disabilities generally is not allowed.

How You Can Protect Your Rights

Q: Is there anything I can do to protect my rights under these Federal non-discrimination laws?

A: Yes. If you believe you are being or have been discriminated against because of your past or current alcohol disorder or past drug use disorder, you can challenge the violation of your rights in two ways:

- You may file a complaint with the Office of Civil Rights, or similar office, of the Federal agency(s) with power to investigate and remedy violations of the disability discrimination laws. Key ones are listed below. You do not need a lawyer to do this. Filing with the Government can be faster and easier than a lawsuit and get you the same remedies. However, the deadline for filing these complaints can be as soon as 180 days after the discriminatory act–or even sooner, with Federal employers–so always check. The Federal agencies listed can tell you the deadlines and other requirements for filing discrimination complaints.
- In most (but not all) cases, you also may file a lawsuit in Federal or State court, in addition to or instead of filing an administrative complaint. Deadlines for lawsuits vary from 1 to 3 years following the discriminatory act.
- You must file employment discrimination claims under the ADA with the U.S. Equal Opportunity Employment Commission

(EEOC). You may not file a lawsuit first or instead of filing with the EEOC.

If your complaint is upheld, the persons or organizations that discriminated against you may be required to correct their actions and policies, compensate you, or give you other relief.

Chapter 43

Employee Assistance Programs (EAPs) for Substance Abuse

How Does an EAP Support Your Drug-Free Workplace Program?

Since EAP services typically mirror the components of a drug-free workplace program, putting an EAP in place may go a long way towards building your drug-free workplace program. However, if you rely on the EAP for your policy development, supervisor training and employee education, you must be sure that the EAP provider is qualified to deliver these services as part of a drug-free workplace program. Not all EAP providers are experienced in training supervisors on how to make referrals to drug testing, which is significantly different from making referrals to an EAP.

On the other hand, an EAP offers other valuable services to the organization that go beyond those of a drug-free workplace program. An EAP can complement and support your drug-free workplace program in a unique way. By encouraging employees to seek assistance with a variety of emotional issues and day-to-day problems, employee assistance professionals are in a position to identify employees who have

---

This chapter includes text excerpted from "Drug-Free Workplace Advisor," U.S. Department of Labor (DOL), 2008. Reviewed April 2016.

developed problems with drugs and/or alcohol before there are problems at work. Furthermore, an EAP gives supervisors tools for dealing with troubled employees, while allowing them to remain focused on employees' work performance, rather than on employees' personal lives.

The EAP component of a drug-free workplace program maximizes the health and efficiency of the workforce while conveying a caring attitude on the part of the employer. Organizations that have EAPs as part of their drug-free workplace program have adopted a prevention and treatment approach to alcohol and drug problems. This means that employees are encouraged to come forward on their own to seek help, and those who are identified as using prohibited drugs are offered treatment and education. By addressing personal problems early, EAPs can help prevent employees from starting to use alcohol or drugs in misguided attempts to relieve pressure and stress. The EAP can help to properly assess and refer the employee who has problems to the most appropriate level of help.

The EAP supports three important ideas in a drug-free workplace:

1. Employees are a vital part of business and valuable members of the team.
2. It is better to offer assistance to employees than to fire them.
3. Recovering employees can, once again, become productive and effective members of the workforce.

Including an EAP as part of your drug-free workplace reflects a concern about the well being of employees and represents a distinctly different approach from that of "test and terminate". Employers who adopt the "test and terminate" approach attempt to achieve a drug-free workplace by eliminating and discarding drug-using employees without offering treatment or opportunities for recovery.

In addition to offering an EAP, employers can choose to help employees by allowing a reasonable period of time off the job to participate in treatment as well as adequate benefits coverage for the treatment of addiction. Even in the absence of a formal EAP, employers may make such benefits available and maintain a list of qualified therapists and treatment facilities that specialize in the treatment of alcoholism and drug addiction.

What Are the Goals of an EAP?

Employers implement EAPs to accomplish a variety of goals:

- Identify employee personal problems at an early stage before there is a serious impact on the job

- Motivate employees to seek help through easy access to assessment and referral
- Direct employees to the best source of help and high-quality providers
- Limit health insurance costs through early intervention
- Reduce workers' compensation claims by encouraging easy access to help
- Decrease employee turnover
- Offer an alternative to firing valuable employees
- Provide employees with support and demonstrate that a company is a caring employer

What Are the Essential Components of an EAP?

An EAP should include these essential components:

- A policy statement that defines how employees access the EAP, the services provided and how confidentiality is protected.
- Consultation and training services for supervisors and managers on how to manage and refer troubled employees to the EAP.
- Promotional activities to ensure the EAP is highly visible and easily accessible to employees.
- Educational programs for employees on relevant issues such as alcohol and drug addiction.
- Problem identification and referral services provided directly to individual employees (and often to family members).
- Identification and maintenance of a current, annotated directory of qualified providers of treatment or assistance to enable prompt referral of employees to appropriate resources.

Some EAPs also offer short-term counseling by licensed professionals.

What Services Does an EAP Offer?

EAPs provide services to a variety of "customers" within the work organization. EAPs provide distinct but complementary services to each customer group--the employer or work organization, the supervisors/managers and the employees.

Organizational services include:

- Assistance in developing alcohol and drug policies
- Consultation regarding legal compliance issues
- Design and selection of health benefit plans
- Evaluation of health care providers
- Compliance with drug-free workplace policies

Guidance to managers and supervisors includes:

- How to make supervisor referrals based on declining job performance
- Separating performance issues from behavioral health issues
- Determining the need to intervene with troubled employees
- Following up on an employee's progress

Assistance provided directly to individual employees includes:

- General information and referral resources
- Crisis intervention
- Easy access to help
- Timely problem identification
- Short-term problem resolution
- Substance abuse assessments
- Referral for diagnosis and treatment or other kinds of help
- Follow-up contacts or sessions to provide support
- Educational seminars and workshops

In addition to addressing alcohol and drug addiction problems and at no additional cost, most EAPs also help employees with:

- Marital/relationship problems
- Job stress
- Childcare issues
- Grief
- Financial problems

- Legal concerns
- Eldercare issues

How Does an EAP Help Employees?

EAPs target both:

1. Employees whose performance shows a pattern of decline which is not readily explained by job circumstances, and
2. Employees who are aware of personal problems that may or may not be affecting their performance.

Any employee can seek assistance from the EAP to get information or to discuss a personal problem. Approximately four to six percent of employees will contact the EAP on their own every year. In fact, most employees who use the EAP seek these services on their own. However, employees with job performance problems who do not contact the EAP are of most concern to supervisors. When a supervisor refers a troubled employee to the EAP, the supervisor does not have to wait until the problem is job threatening. Having an EAP allows supervisors to combine their offers of assistance with early disciplinary measures to help restore performance.

The EAP systematically and effectively approaches workplace and personal problems. The employee assistance professional meets privately with the employee, discusses the issues with the employee and helps identify the problem. The EAP then explores available options and refers the employee to appropriate resources that may be available in the community or professional services covered under the employee benefit plan.

Most EAPs offer services not only to employees but also to their dependent family members. This proves to be a wise investment because the work performance of an employee can be affected when a parent, spouse or child is abusing alcohol and other drugs.

How Does an EAP Work?

Employees can directly access the EAP voluntarily or be referred by their supervisor in cases of job-performance problems. When an employee uses EAP services voluntarily, there is no need for involvement on the part of the supervisor. However, when a supervisor refers an employee to the EAP because of job performance, the offer of help may be combined with progressive discipline, and the supervisor will need to continue to monitor the employee's performance.

How Is Confidentiality Protected?

Employees will support and have faith in your program only if their confidentiality is protected. The assurance of confidentiality means that an employee's private and personal information will not be released to anyone other than with whom the employee confides.

The following are several areas of the program where employees may have concerns about their privacy:

- What will the supervisor disclose if the employee has a performance problem that may be due to the use of alcohol and/or drugs?
- What will the supervisor disclose if the employee comes forward on his or her own and discloses that he or she has a problem?
- What will be released if the employee uses the EAP?
- Who will get the information?
- What will be released if the employee sees the EAP in response to a supervisor referral?

As with any performance problem, the employee needs to be aware that the issue of his/her performance problems will not be made public. Although his/her supervisors may share information about disciplinary action with other managers or the Human Resources Department, all information about performance issues, constructive confrontation and disciplinary actions should be maintained in the employee's personnel file. In addition, access should be strictly limited to those in management with a need to know.

The EAP should assure employees that their personal information and details of their personal problems will not go beyond the EAP. Private conversations with the EAP should not be shared with supervisors and EAP records must be kept completely separate from personnel records. These records should be protected by the EAP's confidentiality policy and should not be released without the employee's expressed, written permission.

In some instances, it may be in the employee's best interest for information to be shared; however, this information should not be shared without a written release. Some examples of circumstances when an employee may request release of information include:

- Releasing information so that benefits can be accessed or insurance companies can conduct reviews. Usually, if reimbursement is requested from a third party payer, the request contains a waiver of confidentiality.

- Releasing information regarding EAP participation if the employee was referred by the supervisor based on declining job performance.
- Releasing information to support a request for accommodation or recovery support.
- Releasing information of assessment, evaluation and follow-through following a positive drug test when the employee will be given an opportunity to return to the job.
- Releasing information according to company policy for verification for treatment release time, leave requests and disability.

There also are limited areas where state laws require disclosure. These are circumstances where someone is in imminent danger, such as in cases of:

- child abuse
- elder abuse
- serious threats of homicide or suicide

The EAP policy must be very clear about the limits of what information can be shared and with whom it can be shared. If an employee chooses to tell coworkers about his or her private concerns, that is a personal decision. However, when an employee tells a supervisor something in confidence, the supervisor is obligated to protect that disclosure.

Chapter 44

Drug Abuse Treatment in the Criminal Justice System

Drug Abuse Treatment

Treatment offers the best alternative for interrupting the drug use/criminal justice cycle for offenders with drug problems. Jail or prison should be a place where people can get the help they need, and offenders should ask if treatment is available. Untreated substance using offenders are more likely to relapse into drug use and criminal behavior, jeopardizing public health and safety and taxing criminal justice system resources. Additionally, treatment consistently has been shown to reduce the costs associated with lost productivity, crime, and incarceration caused by drug use.

Scientific research shows that treatment can help many drug using offenders change their attitudes, beliefs, and behaviors; avoid relapse; and successfully remove themselves from a life of substance use and crime. Treatment can cut drug use in half, decrease criminal activity, and reduce arrests. It is true that legal pressure might be needed to get a person into treatment and help them stay there. Once in a

---

This chapter contains text excerpted from the following sources: Text beginning with the heading "Drug Abuse Treatment" is excerpted from "Drug Addiction Treatment in the Criminal Justice System," National Institute on Drug Abuse (NIDA), April 2014; Text beginning with the heading "Drug Courts" is excerpted from "Drug Courts," National Institute of Justice (NIJ), March 16, 2015.

treatment program, however, even those who are not initially motivated to change can become engaged in a continuing treatment process. In fact, research suggests that mandated treatment can be just as effective as voluntary admission to rehab centers.

Drug abuse treatment can be incorporated into criminal justice settings in a variety of ways. These include:

- Treatment as a condition of probation
- Drug courts that blend judicial monitoring and sanctions with treatment
- Treatment in prison followed by community-based treatment after discharge
- Treatment under parole or probation supervision.

Why Family Support Is Critical

Drug use often leads to violence; separation of parents and children; loss of jobs; feelings of hopelessness; serious money problems; single parenthood and worry over childcare needs; harmful relationships; emotional and behavioral difficulties in children; and dangerous driving that can result in the death of the drug user, family members, or innocent travelers on the road.

In 2007, 53 percent of prisoners in Federal and State prisons reported having children under the age of 18. Children with parents who use drugs and abuse alcohol are widely considered at high risk for a range of physical and behavioral problems, including substance use. Juvenile justice systems are also affected; as many as two-thirds of juveniles who have been detained may have a substance use disorder.

Effective treatment decreases future drug use and drug-related criminal behavior, and can improve a person's relationship with his or her family. In addition, the family needs tools and support to help deal with the offender's incarceration, rehabilitation, and loss of income.

More Treatment Is Needed

Many prisons are not making treatment a priority, despite clear benefits to offenders, their families, and communities shown in multiple studies. A 2004 survey showed that 40 percent of State and 49 percent of Federal inmates took part in some kind of drug program, but most were self-help or peer counseling groups. Only 15 percent of State prisoners and 17 percent of Federal prisoners took part in drug treatment programs with a trained professional.

Coordination between criminal justice professionals, substance abuse treatment providers, and other social service agencies can improve outcomes for people with substance use problems. By working together, the criminal justice and treatment systems can optimize resources to benefit the health, safety, and well-being of these offenders, their families, and their communities.

Treatment Principles: An Overview

Principles for Drug Abuse Treatment for Criminal Justice Populations: A Research-Based Guide provides research-based principles of addiction treatment. The 13 principles are:

1. **Drug addiction is a brain disease that affects behavior.** It affects people both physically and mentally. It can alter the brain and body chemistry for months or even years after a person stops using, so relapse is often part of the recovery process. It should be treated like any other disease.
2. **Recovery from drug addiction requires effective treatment, followed by management of the problem over time.** Drug users cannot alter their behavior without taking care of their addiction. Treatment that starts in prison or jail must continue after release. Treatment and recovery is hard work that must continue throughout a user's life.
3. **Treatment must last long enough to produce stable behavioral change.** Without the right treatment, most drug users will use again once they return to their neighborhoods, even though drugs might put them right back in prison. Treatment should last long enough (90 days or more) to help drug users learn to manage their own drug problems.
4. **Assessment is the first step in treatment.** Drug users need to be examined by a doctor. The doctor might prescribe medicine, and will look for other possible problems, such as depression and anxiety, or medical conditions such as hepatitis, tuberculosis, or HIV/AIDS.
5. **Tailoring services to fit the needs of the individual is an important part of effective drug use treatment for criminal justice populations.** Each drug user has different needs regarding addiction counseling and treatment. The best approaches take each person's age, gender, ethnicity, culture, and needs into account.

6. **Drug use during treatment should be carefully monitored.** Individuals recovering from drug addiction sometimes return to drug use, called relapse. Testing for continued drug use is an important part of treatment.

7. **Treatment should target factors that are associated with criminal behavior.** Offenders often have patterns of behavior, attitudes, and beliefs that support a "criminal" lifestyle. Treatment that helps offenders avoid negative thinking patterns can be effective.

8. **Criminal justice supervision should incorporate treatment planning for drug using offenders, and treatment providers should be aware of correctional supervision requirements.** It is important that corrections personnel work with treatment providers to make sure the individual treatment plan meets the needs of both the offender and the institution.

9. **Continuity of care is essential for drug users re-entering the community.** People who start receiving treatment while incarcerated need to continue treatment after release.

10. **A balance of rewards and sanctions encourages pro-social behavior and treatment participation.** During treatment, it is important that both positive and negative behaviors are recognized.

11. **Offenders with co-occurring drug use and mental health problems often require an integrated treatment management approach.** Drug treatment can sometimes help people who have depression or other mental health problems. It is important that these issues are addressed in treatment programs.

12. **Medications are an important part of treatment for many drug using offenders.** Medicines like methadone have been shown to help reduce heroin use. Medicines for mental health issues can also be used as part of treatment.

13. **Treatment planning for drug using offenders who are living in or re-entering the community should include strategies to prevent and treat serious, chronic medical conditions, such as HIV/AIDS, hepatitis B and C, and tuberculosis.** Drug users and offenders are more likely to have infectious diseases like HIV/AIDS, hepatitis, and

tuberculosis. People seeking treatment should be tested for these diseases and receive counseling on risky behaviors and seeking medical advice.

Where to Get Treatment Information

When a drug user is arrested, he or she should ask if treatment is available. The websites listed below can offer information on treatment in your area.

- U.S. Department of Health and Human Services, Substance Abuse and Mental Health Services Administration Substance Abuse Treatment Facility Locator (searchable directory of alcohol and drug treatment programs) www.findtreatment.samhsa.gov or call the Treatment Helpline at 1-800-662-4357
- National TASC/Treatment Accountability for Safer Communities (offers leadership, advocacy, and policy recommendations for innovative treatment and recovery supports that result in opportunities for justice-involved individuals with behavioral health needs to achieve healthy and productive lives with their families and communities) www.nationaltasc.org
- National Institute on Drug Abuse, Principles of Adolescent Substance Use Disorder Treatment: A Research-Based Guide

Drug Courts

Drug courts are specialized court docket programs that target criminal defendants and offenders, juvenile offenders, and parents with pending child welfare cases who have alcohol and other drug dependency problems.

As of June 2014, the estimated number of drug courts operating in the U.S. is over 3400. More than half target adults, including DWI (driving while intoxicated) offenders and a growing number of Veterans; others address juvenile, child welfare, and different case types.

Types of Drug Court

- Adult Drug Courts
- Adult Drug/DWI
- Juvenile Drug Courts
- Family
- DWI
- Veterans
- Tribal
- Co-Occurring

- Reentry
- Federal Drug
- Campus
- Federal Veterans

The Drug Court Model

Although drug courts vary in target population, program design, and service resources, they are generally based on a comprehensive model involving:

- Offender screening and assessment of risks, needs, and responsivity.
- Judicial interaction.
- Monitoring (e.g., drug testing) and supervision.
- Graduated sanctions and incentives.
- Treatment and rehabilitation services.

Drug courts are usually managed by a nonadversarial and multidisciplinary team including judges, prosecutors, defense attorneys, community corrections, social workers and treatment service professionals. Support from stakeholders representing law enforcement, the family and the community is encouraged through participation in hearings, programming and events like graduation.

Part Six

Drug Abuse Testing and Prevention

Chapter 45

Effective Public Health Responses to Drug Abuse

Strengthen Efforts to Prevent Drug Use in Our Communities

Preventing drug use before it starts is a fundamental element of the National Drug Control Strategy. As noted in the introduction, there has been overall progress in reducing illicit drug use among young people, including youth (ages 12-17) and young adults (ages 18-25). Data from the 2013 NSDUH show a decline in the rate of current illicit drug use since 2002 among youth (from 11.6 percent to 8.8 percent), including declines in the rates of current nonmedical use of prescription–type drugs and the nonmedical use of pain relievers. This trend is also reflected in the results of the 2014 MTF study, which shows that overall drug use in the past year among 8th, 10th, and 12th graders was generally lower in 2014 compared to 2001. MTF also indicates positive trends in reduced use for marijuana, alcohol, and tobacco.

However, while progress has been made in a number of areas among youth, the overall rates of use of drugs and alcohol and tobacco among adolescents remain concerning, especially as we learn more about the negative effects of illicit substances and alcohol on the developing brain. The rate of past month illicit drug use among the nation's

---

This chapter includes text excerpted from "National Drug Control Strategy," WhiteHouse.gov, 2015.

young people rapidly escalates as they move through adolescence, from 2.3 percent of 12-year-olds to over 24 percent of 20-year-olds. Furthermore, MTF shows that historically when the perceptions of harm related to drug use decrease, rates of drug use are likely to subsequently increase. As shown in the chart below, over the five-year period between 2009 and 2014 among 12th graders, there has been a 40 percent drop in the perceived risk of occasional use of marijuana, accompanied by a 7 percent increase in past year use of marijuana.

The nation's vitality and ability to succeed globally depends on the ability of the next generation to succeed academically, achieve their ambitions, and live healthy, productive lives. Drug use among youth and its impact on their academic achievement are linked. For example, marijuana use is associated with cognitive impairment, including lower IQs among people who use marijuana early and persistently over the long-term; students with an average grade of "D" or lower are more likely to be substance users compared to students whose grade average is better than "D;" and higher levels of substance use were reported by students who were involved in truancy.

Substance use appears to contribute to college students skipping more classes, spending less time studying, earning lower grades, dropping out of college, or being unemployed after college or some combination of these factors. Alcohol consumption among youth is also known to impact academic achievement; it can cause problems with short-term memory and other brain functions and undermine the efficiency and effectiveness of study time. It has been observed that alcohol-related differences in sleep patterns contribute to greater daytime sleepiness and, consequently, lower grades. Finally, college students who drink excessively tend to spend less time studying and skip more of their classes.

Fortunately, by working together, we can improve academic performance and reduce substance use among students by implementing evidence-based practices that address both issues simultaneously and comprehensively. The Strategic Prevention Framework is an evidence-based process that states can use to inform policies and programs and introduce change at the community-level.

The Framework employs the following 5-step process to guide states, jurisdictions, tribes, and communities in the selection, implementation, and evaluation of effective, culturally appropriate, and sustainable prevention activities: (1) assess needs, current resources, and community readiness; (2) build capacity; (3) develop a plan to address state, local, and tribal needs; (4) implement the plan; and (5) evaluate implementation. By using this framework and bringing together willing partners, community coalitions can foster the development of comprehensive prevention approaches. Research investments lead to more robust understanding of causal factors. When schools are included in the coalition activities, we can also help achieve our nation's academic goals and make sure every child in America has access to a world-class education and a chance to succeed.

Principle: A National Prevention System Must Be Grounded at the Community Level

Effective substance use prevention must bring together state and local sectors to assess illicit substance use issues and challenges and develop comprehensive, multi-sector approaches to reduce use and its consequences. The formation of strong partnerships coupled with understanding the needs of the community will support the development of successful strategies to address community-level challenges. These partnerships are also uniquely poised to identify emerging threats.

Action Item: Collaborate with States to Support Communities

The need for comprehensive prevention programming is critical to ensure a healthy and safe Nation. While progress has been made in reducing tobacco use and binge drinking, youth today are faced with challenges including messages about marijuana use and the dangers of non-medical use of prescription and other illicit drugs. The Administration continues to support efforts to meet these challenges and prevent illicit drug use before it starts. The U.S. Department of Education has focused on keeping students safe and improving their learning environments. In FY 2014, School Climate Transformation grants to school districts provided support to 71 school districts in 23 states, Washington, D.C., and the U.S. Virgin Islands. The grants help schools develop, enhance, or expand systems of support for implementing evidence-based, multi-tiered behavioral frameworks for improving behavioral outcomes and learning conditions for students.

In FY 2014, SAMHSA provided funding to 50 states, eight territories, and one tribe in support of substance use prevention initiatives. Specifically, states use the Substance Abuse Prevention and Treatment Block Grant Prevention Set-Aside to fund substance misuse prevention programs; the Prevention Set-Aside is the sole Federal source of substance use prevention funding available to all states and territories. Additionally, SAMHSA's Strategic Prevention Framework State Incentive Grant program supports states in using a data-driven decision-making process that includes assessing needs to guide the implementation of evidence-based strategies.

Action Item: Promote Prevention in the Workplace

The workplace is an important place for employees to receive information on illicit substance use prevention. It is an opportunity to encourage and educate employees on relevant materials and resources available to them and their families. Workplace programs also play a key role in promoting safe and productive work environments.

The Division of Workplace Programs at SAMHSA is responsible for two principal activities mandated by Executive Order 12564 and Public Law 100-71. These are oversight of the Federal Drug-Free Workplace Program to eliminate illicit drug use within Executive Branch agencies and the regulated industry; and oversight of the National Laboratory Certification Program, which certifies laboratories to conduct forensic drug testing for Federal agencies, Federally-regulated industries, and the private sector. The program is further supported by the Workplace Helpline, a toll-free telephone service (800-WORKPLACE) for business and industry that answer questions about drug testing in the workplace.

In addition, the Department of Transportation (DOT) regulates a strong industry-based drug and alcohol testing program that conducted approximately 3.1 million drug screenings in the first 6 months of 2014. This Federal testing program protects public health and safety by ensuring that safety-sensitive transportation employees in the aviation, trucking, railroad, mass transit, pipeline, and other transportation industries are screened for substance use issues. While ensuring public health and safety, the DOT process allows an individual to return to safety-sensitive work after he or she tests negative on a return-to-duty test, thereby providing an incentive for successful completion of treatment. The DOT program is a model for other programs in the U.S. and internationally as an effective tool for accurate testing, deterrence, and recovery.

Principle: Prevention Efforts Must Encompass the Range of Settings in Which Young People Grow Up

Implementing effective prevention approaches for youth requires paying special attention to the sectors that influence young people's lives. By working together states, communities, schools, parents, and health professionals can use evidence-based prevention programs and policies to make a positive impact on youth drug use.

Action Item: Strengthen the Drug-Free Communities Support Program

Coalitions across the United States are rallying to address the drug trends unique to their communities. Since the program's inception, DFC grantees have targeted areas that cover 37 percent of the U.S. population. DFC-funded coalitions are required to work with various sectors of their community to identify local drug problems and implement comprehensive strategies to create community-level change. The contributions of community coalitions constitute a critical part of the Nation's drug prevention infrastructure. DFC-funded community coalitions are a catalyst for creating local change where drug problems manifest.

Findings from the 2013 DFC National Cross site Evaluation indicate that prevalence of youth substance use has declined significantly in DFC-funded programs. Prevalence of past 30-day use declined significantly between the first and the most recent data reports across all substances (alcohol, tobacco, marijuana) and school levels (middle and high school). Collectively the data suggest DFC grantees' activities are associated with positive outcomes among youth in DFC communities.

Between February 2013 and August 2013, DFC grantees distributed more than 1.5 million prevention materials; reached over 600,000 people with special events; held direct face-to-face information sessions with more than 230,000 attendees; trained over 350,000 youth, parents, and community members; recognized more than 9,000 businesses for compliance (or noncompliance) with local ordinances; and were instrumental in educating on more than 500 laws or policies.

Action Item: Leverage and Evolve the Above the Influence (ATI) Brand to Support Teen Prevention Efforts

The Above the Influence (ATI) campaign, introduced in 2005, is dedicated to demonstrating the power of young people living "above the influence" of drugs and alcohol. To ensure the continuation of the ATI brand after Congressional funding was discontinued, ONDCP transitioned ATI to The Partnership for Drug-Free Kids (The Partnership). The Partnership has maintained and expanded its direct outreach to teens in social media, including through Facebook, Tumblr, Twitter, and Instagram. The Partnership has maintained ATI-related toolkits and resources that provide support to community organizations working to engage their youth in drug and alcohol prevention efforts.

Action Item: Support Mentoring Initiatives, Especially Among At-Risk Youth

Mentoring initiatives focused on young people and vulnerable groups are an important component of a comprehensive approach to prevention that includes families, communities, schools, and states. Mentoring provides support to youth with structured activities and often includes a focus on achieving life and career goals. ONDCP partners with both Federal agencies and community-based organizations to promote support for mentoring initiatives, for example: the Department of Defense (DoD) Education Activity, Students against Destructive Decisions (SADD), the Mentor Foundation USA, U.S. Department of Agriculture's (USDA) 4-H Program, and U.S. Department of Education's 21st Century Community Learning Centers Program.

The Administration's My Brother's Keeper initiative has taken steps and inspired others to ensure that all young people can reach their full potential—including through mentoring that will help our youth find opportunities for career growth and skill building. The initiative has brought together Federal, state, tribal, and community partners to build on successes and promising ideas and implement strategies which have been shown to have the greatest impact at key moments in the lives of the Nation's young people. In addition, the White House Council on Women and Girls works across departments and agencies to provide a coordinated response to issues that have a distinct impact on the lives of women and girls, as part of the Administration's broader focus on expanding opportunity for each American.

Action Item: Mobilize Parents to Educate Youth to Reject Drug Use

Parents play a critical role in reducing substance use among youth, and many underestimate the power they have to influence their children to make sound decisions. It is important to continue to provide resources and materials for parents to educate them on the dangers of illicit drug use. ONDCP continues to collaborate with organizations and Federal partners to build the capacity of parents to support their youth. Helping parents understand the nexus between improving academic achievement and reducing substance use is vital to ensure every child can pursue a healthy and productive life.

In recognition of National Substance Abuse Prevention Month, ONDCP hosted a twitter chat with youth and parents focusing on experiences and strategies that can be used to keep youth drug free. In addition, SAMHSA released two new products as part of the "Talk. They Hear You." campaign. One product is a new public service announcement encourages American Indian and Alaskan Native parents and caregivers to talk to their young people as early as 9 years old. A second product introduced a role-playing mobile application designed to teach parents and caregivers how to effectively use a conversation to influence their child's behavior and attitudes toward alcohol. In addition, the National Institute on Drug Abuse's (NIDA) Family Check-Up is a program that provides practical, evidence-based information to promote good communication between parents and children.

Developing good communication skills helps parents stay aware of what is happening in their children's lives, catch problems early, support positive behavior, and prevent illicit drug use. The Drug Enforcement Administration's (DEA) Demand Reduction Program supports national efforts to reduce the demand for drugs by educating parents and youth about the dangers associated with using illegal drugs and misusing prescription and over-the-counter drugs.

Principle: Develop and Disseminate Information on Youth Drug, Alcohol, and Tobacco Use

A key element of creating a safe, healthy, and drug free environment is the dissemination of accurate information on drug use. It is especially important to share information regarding the impact of substance use on young people including school-aged children. As noted earlier, the apparent effects of drug use on these children is concerning (i.e., long-term effect on IQ, diminished academic achievement, and altered brain function). With sound information dissemination communities, parents, schools, and healthcare providers can better prevent use before it starts and intervene early, when necessary.

Action Item: Support Substance Abuse Prevention on College Campuses

Drug use and its consequences affect every sector of society and hampers the ability of young people to reach their full potential. Approaches that keep young people from using drugs and alcohol, identify risky behaviors, treat those with substance use disorders, and support individuals in recovery are vital to maintaining safe and healthy campus communities in the United States. The Administration has also launched the "It's On Us" initiative—an awareness campaign to help put an end to sexual assault on college campuses, which is often related to substance use.

In 2014, SAMHSA awarded 23 grants under its Minority Serving Institutions (MSIs) Partnerships with Community-Based Organizations (CBOs) grant program. The purpose of this illicit substance use prevention education and testing program is to equip and empower MSIs located in communities at the highest risk of substance abuse, HIV, and Hepatitis-C (HCV) infections with evidence-based prevention methodologies. The goals of the program are to: 1) increase access to comprehensive, integrated substance abuse, HIV, and HCV prevention services on the grantees' campuses and/or institutions and surrounding community; and 2) achieve normative and environmental changes to prevent and/or reduce substance use problems as risk factors for the transmission of HIV/AIDS among African-American, Hispanic/Latino, Asian American/Pacific Islander), and American Indian/Alaska Natives young adult (ages 18-24) populations on campus.

The National Institute on Alcohol Abuse and Alcoholism (NIAAA) supports studies to better understand both individual and environmental approaches to prevention and treatment for college students that are necessary to reduce harmful drinking and its consequences. Working with researchers in the college drinking field, NIAAA is developing a research-based, interactive, user-friendly decision tool and guide to help colleges and universities select appropriate strategies to meet their alcohol intervention goals. In 2015, the College Alcohol Interventions Matrix (College-AIM) will be launched to help college leadership select effective interventions. NIAAA's Clinician's Guide: Helping Patients Who Drink Too Much is another important resource for use with this age group; the Guide is an alcohol screening tool that healthcare practitioners can use with individuals aged 18 and older, including young adults and college students.

Action Item: Expand Research on Understudied Substances

It is important to monitor substance use trends in the community continually in order to adapt to emerging needs. NIDA's prevention program supports large surveys and surveillance networks to monitor drug-related issues and trends locally and nationally such as the emergence of synthetic drugs and e-cigarettes. NIDA also supports an enhanced understanding of prevention approaches by identifying and characterizing human candidate genes that influence risk for substance use disorders. NIAAA supports research on preventing and reducing underage drinking, recognizing the harmful effects of alcohol use among young people, and the connection between early initiation of alcohol use and future substance use problems.

NIDA recently launched an innovative National Drug Early Warning System (NDEWS) to monitor emerging trends related to illicit drug use and to identify increased use of synthetic drugs such as methamphetamine and New Psychoactive Substances (NPS). NDEWS will generate critical information about new drug trends in specific locations around the country so rapid, informed, and effective public health and prevention-focused responses can be developed and implemented precisely where and when they are needed. In addition, NIDA's intramural research program (IRP) recently established a Designer Drug Research Unit (DDRU) to help address the problem of synthetic drugs including NPS. NPS are marketed as safe, cheap, and legal alternatives to illicit drugs like marijuana, cocaine, and ecstasy. The DDRU collects, analyzes, and disseminates current information about the pharmacology and toxicology of newly emerging synthetic drugs. This information can be used to inform public health and prevention oriented responses.

Action Item: Prepare a Report on the Health Risks of Youth Substance Use

The Department of Health and Human Services (HHS) continues to implement the National Prevention Council Action Plan that outlines the Federal government's commitment to implementing the Nation's first ever National Prevention Strategy. This Action Plan focuses on a number of public health issues important to the Nation. Preventing illicit substance use is one of the Action Plan's key priorities and identifies several recommendations including: creating environments that empower young people not to drink or use other drugs; identifying alcohol and other drug use disorders early and providing early intervention and referral to treatment; and educating healthcare professionals on proper opioid prescribing and reducing inappropriate access to and use of prescription drugs.

Principle: Criminal Justice Agencies and Prevention Organizations Must Collaborate

Bringing together all sectors in a community to work together towards a common goal is an important component in developing effective approaches to reduce drug use. When public health, public safety, and school sectors share information and work together they are able to have a more complete view of the challenges and are better equipped to develop more comprehensive solutions.

Action Item: Provide Information on Effective Prevention Strategies to Law Enforcement

Participation by law enforcement professionals in prevention activities in schools, community settings, and organizations is an essential component of regional efforts to reduce illicit drug use and make communities safer places in which to live. Twenty of the 28 High Intensity Drug Trafficking Areas (HIDTAs) are engaged in activities that connect law enforcement with community-based prevention efforts through mentoring, role modeling, and life skills education. For example, the Central Florida HIDTA has partnered with the Orange County Drug Free Coalition in an initiative to engage, advocate, inform, and bring awareness of alcohol and illicit substance use issues among Central Florida youth to build a healthy, safe, and drug-free community. A report funded by the National Institute of Justice (NIJ) of the Department of Justice (DOJ) identifies regional efforts supported by HIDTAs to reduce illegal prescription drug demand through training, education, and drug take-back programs. ONDCP is additionally working to expand prevention activities to all 28 HIDTAs.

The New York National Guard Counterdrug Civil Operators partnered with the NY State Office of Alcohol and Substance Abuse and their Prevention Resource Centers (PRC). These PRCs are located around the state and serve as a focal point for coalitions and community-based organizations to obtain resources, technical assistance, training, and assessment data. Civil Operators coordinate and synergize local education authorities and community initiatives. Serving in this role allows alignment of efforts between law enforcement and community prevention entities, and leverage of National Guard resources supporting Federal, state, tribal, and local law enforcement agencies to aid community coalitions in gathering timely and relevant substance use data to create comprehensive strategies that address local drug problems.

Action Item: Enable Law Enforcement Officers to Participate in Community Prevention Programs in Schools, Community Coalitions, Civic Organizations, and Faith-Based Organizations

Collaboration with multiple sectors of the community is vitally important to community change. To address the number of messages youth face today promoting substance use, we must work together to encourage a safe and healthy nation free from addiction and violence. To support this goal, the Office of Juvenile Justice and Delinquency

Prevention (OJJDP) of the Department of Justice (DOJ) is partnering with the Department of Education and SAMHSA to coordinate grant programs that fund communities and local education agencies to improve school climate and respond early to the mental health/substance use disorder needs for at-risk youth.

To improve academic achievement among youth, collaboration and coordination among schools, mental health/substance use disorder specialists, law enforcement and juvenile justice officials must help students succeed in school and prevent negative outcomes for youth and communities. The National Association of School Resource Officers continues to focus on substance use prevention in school settings. Relevant and current culturally appropriate training on prevention programs and evidence-based programs will educate officers on best practices to implement programs in school settings.

Action Item: Strengthen Prevention Efforts Along the Southwest Border

ONDCP has engaged with the U.S. Border Health Commission to promote improved and culturally appropriate prevention, screening, brief intervention, and referral to treatment (SBIRT). ONDCP coordinated with the U.S. Border Health Commission to support substance abuse training for promotores along the border. With the collaborative work of SAMHSA, the U.S. Border Health Commission has set the ground-work for a train-the-trainer model to expand the capacity for promotores along the U.S.-Mexico border.

These trainings focus on how to conduct screenings and make referrals to appropriate care for persons with substance use disorders within their communities. The training efforts took place along each of the 10 border cities with an estimated total of 250 to 300 promotores trained upon completion. These train-the-trainer efforts were based on the Mental Health Gap Action Program (mhGAP) Intervention Guide for mental, neurological, and substance use disorder in non-specialized health settings developed by the World Health Organization and adapted by SAMHSA.

Chapter 46

Drug Abuse Prevention Begins at Home

Chapter Contents

Section 46.1

Talking to Your Child about Drugs

This section contains text excerpted from the following sources: Text beginning with the heading "The Basics" is excerpted from "Talk to Your Kids about Tobacco, Alcohol, and Drugs," Office of Disease Prevention and Health Promotion (ODPHP), February 24, 2016; Text beginning with the heading "Talking to Your Kids—Communicating the Risks" is excerpted from "Marijuana: Facts Parents Need to Know," National Institutes on Drug Abuse (NIDA), March 2014.

The Basics

Talk to your child about the dangers of tobacco, alcohol, and drugs. Knowing the facts will help your child make healthy choices.

What Do I Need to Say?

When you talk about tobacco, alcohol, and drugs:

- Teach your child the facts.
- Give your child clear rules.
- Find out what your child already knows.
- Be prepared to answer your child's questions.
- Talk with your child about how to say "no."

When Should I Start Talking with My Child?

Start early. By preschool, most children have seen adults smoking cigarettes or drinking alcohol, either in real life, on TV, or online.

Make sure your child knows right from the start that you think it's important to stay safe and avoid drugs.

Here are more reasons to start the conversation early:

- Almost 9 out of 10 smokers start smoking before they turn 18.
- Many kids start using tobacco by age 11 and are addicted by age 14.

- By the time they are in 8th grade, most children think that using alcohol is okay.
- At age 12 or 13, some kids are already using drugs like marijuana or prescription pain relievers.

What If My Child Is Older?

It's never too late to start the conversation about avoiding drugs. Even if your teen may have tried tobacco, alcohol, or drugs, you can still talk about making healthy choices and how to say "no" next time.

What Do I Need to Know about Prescriptions and Other Medicines?

When you talk to your child about the dangers of drugs, don't forget about drugs that may already be in your home. Prescription drugs are the third most commonly abused substances by teens age 14 and older (after marijuana and alcohol).

Prescription or over-the-counter (OTC) drug abuse is when a person:

- Takes too much of a prescription or OTC drug
- Takes a prescription drug prescribed to someone else
- Uses a prescription or OTC drug to get high

When not taken safely, prescription and OTC medicines can be just as addictive and dangerous as other drugs.

Commonly abused prescription or OTC drugs include:

- Pain killers, like Vicodin, OxyContin, or codeine
- Medicines used for anxiety or sleep problems, like Valium or Xanax
- Medicines that treat ADHD (attention deficit hyperactivity disorder), like Adderall or Ritalin

Make sure to talk to your kids about the dangers of prescription drug abuse.

Set a good example for your kids – never take someone else's prescription medicine or give yours to anyone else. Keep track of the medicines in your home and store them in a locked cabinet.

Why Do I Need to Talk to My Child?

Research shows that kids do listen to their parents. Children who learn about drug risks from their parents are less likely to start using drugs.

When kids choose not to use alcohol or drugs, they are also less likely to:

- Have serious trouble in school
- Get hurt in a car accident
- Be a victim of crime
- Have a problem with addiction as an adult
- If you don't talk about it, your child may think it's okay to use alcohol and other drugs.

Take Action!

Talk with your child about tobacco, alcohol, and drugs today – and keep the conversation going.

Talk with Your Child Early and Often

Start conversations about your values and expectations while your child is young. Your child will get used to sharing information and opinions with you. This will make it easier for you to continue talking as your child gets older.

Here are some tips:

- Use everyday events to start a conversation. For example, if you see a group of kids smoking, talk about how tobacco harms the body.
- Give your child your full attention. Turn off your TV, radio, cell phone, and computer, and really listen.
- Try not to "talk at" your child. Encourage your child to ask questions. If you don't know the answer to a question, look it up together.

Teach Your Child the Facts

Your child needs to know how drugs can harm the brain, affect the body, and cause problems at home and in school. Kids who know the facts are more likely to make good choices.

- If your child likes sports, focus on how smoking can affect athletic performance. Or you can say that tobacco causes bad breath and yellow teeth.
- Remind your child that alcohol is a powerful drug that slows down the body and brain.
- Tell your child how other drugs – like steroids, marijuana, and prescription medicines – affect the brain and body.

Set Clear Rules for Your Child

Not wanting to upset their parents is the number one reason kids give for not using drugs. Your child will be less tempted to use tobacco, alcohol, and drugs if you explain your rules clearly.

Here are some things to keep in mind when you talk to your child:

- Explain that you set rules to keep your child safe.
- Tell your child you expect her not to use tobacco, alcohol, or drugs.
- Let your child know what will happen if he breaks the rules.
- Praise your child for good behavior.

Help Your Child Learn How to Say "No."

Kids say that they use alcohol and other drugs to "fit in and belong" with other kids. That's why it's important for parents to help children build the confidence to make a healthy choice when someone offers tobacco, drugs, or alcohol.

Set a Good Example

- If you smoke, try to quit.
- If you drink alcohol, don't drink too much or too often.
- If you use drugs, find a treatment program near you.
- Use prescription and over-the-counter medicines safely.
- Never drink or use drugs and drive.

What If I've Used Drugs in the Past?

Be honest with your child, but don't give a lot of details.

Get Help If You Need It

If you think your child may have a drug or alcohol problem, get help.

Talking to Your Kids—Communicating the Risks

Why Do Young People Use Marijuana?

Children and teens start using marijuana for many reasons. Curiosity and the desire to fit into a social group are common ones. Some teens have a network of friends who use drugs and urge them to do the same (peer pressure). Those who have already begun to smoke cigarettes or use alcohol—or both—are at heightened risk for marijuana use as well. And children and teens who have untreated mental disorders (such as ADHD, conduct disorder, or anxiety) or who were physically or sexually abused are at heightened risk of using marijuana and other drugs at an early age.

For some, drug use begins as a means of coping—to deal with anxiety, anger, depression, boredom, and other unpleasant feelings. But in fact, being high can be a way of simply avoiding the problems and challenges of growing up. Research also suggests that family members' use of alcohol and drugs plays a strong role in whether children/teens start using drugs. Parents, grandparents, and older brothers and sisters are models that children follow.

So indeed, all aspects of a teen's environment—home, school, and neighborhood—can influence whether they will try drugs.

How Can I Prevent My Child from Using Marijuana?

There is no magic bullet for preventing teen drug use. But research shows parents have a big influence on their teens, even when it doesn't seem that way! So talk openly with your children and stay actively engaged in their lives. To help you get started, below are some brief summaries of marijuana research findings that you can share with your kids to help them sort out fact from myth, and help them make the soundest decisions they can. These facts were chosen because they reflect the questions and comments that we receive from teens every day on our teen Web site and blog—what teens care about. Following this brief summary of research evidence, FAQs and additional resources are provided to equip you with even more information.

Did You Know

- **Marijuana can be addictive.** Repeated marijuana use can lead to addiction—which means that people often cannot stop when they want to, even though it undermines many aspects of their lives. Marijuana is estimated to produce addiction in approximately 9 percent, or about 1 in 11, of those who use it at least once. This rate increases to about 1 in 6, or 17 percent, for users who start in their teens, and 25–50 percent among daily users. Moreover, 4.3 million of the more than 7.3 million people who abused or were addicted to any illegal drug in 2012 were dependent on marijuana. And among youth receiving substance abuse treatment, marijuana accounts for the largest percentage of admissions: 74 percent among those 12–14, and 76 percent among those 15–17.

- **Marijuana is unsafe if you are behind the wheel.** Marijuana compromises judgment and affects many other skills required for safe driving: alertness, concentration, coordination, and reaction time. Marijuana use makes it difficult to judge distances and react to signals and sounds on the road. Marijuana is the most commonly identified illegal drug in fatal accidents (showing up in the bloodstream of about 14 percent of drivers), sometimes in combination with alcohol or other drugs. By itself, marijuana is believed to roughly double a driver's chances of being in an accident, and the combination of marijuana and even small amounts of alcohol is even more dangerous—more so than either substance by itself.

- **Marijuana is associated with school failure.** Marijuana has negative effects on attention, motivation, memory, and learning that can persist after the drug's immediate effects wear off—especially in regular users. Someone who smokes marijuana daily may be functioning at a reduced intellectual level most or all of the time. Recent research even suggests that people who begin using marijuana heavily as teens may permanently lose an average of 8 points in IQ by mid-adulthood. Compared with their nonsmoking peers, students who smoke marijuana tend to get lower grades and are more likely to drop out of high school. Long-term marijuana users report decreased overall life satisfaction, including diminished mental and physical health, memory and relationship problems, lower salaries, and less career success.

- **High doses of marijuana can cause psychosis or panic during intoxication.** Although scientists do not yet know whether the use of marijuana causes mental illness, high doses can induce an acute psychosis (disturbed perceptions and thoughts, including paranoia) or panic attacks. In people who already have schizophrenia, marijuana use can worsen psychotic symptoms, and evidence so far suggests there is a link between early marijuana use and an increased risk of psychosis among those with a preexisting vulnerability for the disease.

Section 46.2

Protecting Your Children from Prescription Drugs in Your Home

This section contains text excerpted from the following sources: Text beginning with the heading "Keep Young Children Safe from Poisoning" is excerpted from "Tips to Prevent Poisonings," Centers for Disease Control and Prevention (CDC), November 24, 2015; Text beginning with the heading "How to Dispose of Unused Medicines" is excerpted from "How to Dispose of Unused Medicines," U.S. Food and Drug Administration (FDA), June 4, 2015.

Keep Young Children Safe from Poisoning

Be Prepared

Put the poison help number, 1-800-222-1222, on or near every home telephone and save it on your cell phone. The line is open 24 hours a day, 7 days a week.

Be Smart about Storage

- Store all medicines and household products up and away and out of sight in a cabinet where a child cannot reach them.
- When you are taking or giving medicines or are using household products:
  - Do not put your next dose on the counter or table where children can reach them—it only takes seconds for a child to get them.
  - If you have to do something else while taking medicine, such as answer the phone, take any young children with you.

- Secure the child safety cap completely every time you use a medicine.
- After using them, do not leave medicines or household products out. As soon as you are done with them, put them away and out of sight in a cabinet where a child cannot reach them.
- Be aware of any legal or illegal drugs that guests may bring into your home. Ask guests to store drugs where children cannot find them. Children can easily get into pillboxes, purses, backpacks, or coat pockets.

Other Tips

- Do not call medicine "candy."
- Identify poisonous plants in your house and yard and place them out of reach of children or remove them.

What to Do If A Poisoning Occurs

- Remain calm.
- Call 911 if you have a poison emergency and the victim has collapsed or is not breathing. If the victim is awake and alert, dial 1-800-222-1222. Try to have this information ready:
    - the victim's age and weight
    - the container or bottle of the poison if available
    - the time of the poison exposure
    - the address where the poisoning occurred
    - Stay on the phone and follow the instructions from the emergency operator or poison control center.

How to Dispose of Unused Medicines

Is your medicine cabinet full of expired drugs or medications you no longer use? How should you dispose of them?

Many community-based drug "take-back" programs offer the best option. Otherwise, almost all medicines can be thrown in the household trash, but consumers should take the precautions described below.

A small number of medicines may be especially harmful if taken by someone other than the person for whom the medicine was prescribed.

Many of these medicines have specific disposal instructions on their labeling or patient information leaflet to immediately flush them down the sink or toilet when they are no longer needed.

Drug Disposal Guidelines and Locations

The following guidelines were developed to encourage the proper disposal of medicines and help reduce harm from accidental exposure or intentional misuse after they are no longer needed:

Follow any specific disposal instructions on the prescription drug labeling or patient information that accompanies the medicine. Do not flush medicines down the sink or toilet unless this information specifically instructs you to do so.

Take advantage of programs that allow the public to take unused drugs to a central location for proper disposal. Call your local law enforcement agencies to see if they sponsor medicine take-back programs in your community. Contact your city's or county government's household trash and recycling service to learn about medication disposal options and guidelines for your area.

Transfer unused medicines to collectors registered with the Drug Enforcement Administration (DEA). Authorized sites may be retail, hospital or clinic pharmacies, and law enforcement locations. Some offer mail-back programs or collection receptacles ("drop-boxes").

If no disposal instructions are given on the prescription drug labeling and no take-back program is available in your area, throw the drugs in the household trash following these steps:

1. Remove them from their original containers and mix them with an undesirable substance, such as used coffee grounds, dirt or kitty litter (this makes the drug less appealing to children and pets, and unrecognizable to people who may intentionally go through the trash seeking drugs).
2. Place the mixture in a sealable bag, empty can or other container to prevent the drug from leaking or breaking out of a garbage bag.

FDA's Ilisa Bernstein, Pharm.D., J.D., offers a few more tips:

- Scratch out all identifying information on the prescription label to make it unreadable. This will help protect your identity and the privacy of your personal health information.
- Do not give your medicine to friends. Doctors prescribe medicines based on your specific symptoms and medical history.

Something that works for you could be dangerous for someone else.

- When in doubt about proper disposal, ask your pharmacist.
- Bernstein says the same disposal methods for prescription drugs could apply to over-the-counter drugs as well.

Why the Precautions?

Some prescription drugs such as powerful narcotic pain relievers and other controlled substances carry instructions for flushing to reduce the danger of unintentional use or overdose and illegal abuse.

For example, the fentanyl patch, an adhesive patch that delivers a potent pain medicine through the skin, comes with instructions to flush used or leftover patches. Too much fentanyl can cause severe breathing problems and lead to death in babies, children, pets and even adults, especially those who have not been prescribed the medicine.

"Even after a patch is used, a lot of the medicine remains in the patch," says Jim Hunter, R.Ph., M.P.H., an FDA pharmacist. "So you wouldn't want to throw something in the trash that contains a powerful and potentially dangerous narcotic that could harm others."

Environmental Concerns

Some people are questioning the practice of flushing certain medicines because of concerns about trace levels of drug residues found in surface water, such as rivers and lakes, and in some community drinking water supplies.

"The main way drug residues enter water systems is by people taking medicines and then naturally passing them through their bodies," says Raanan Bloom, Ph.D., an environmental assessment expert at FDA. "Many drugs are not completely absorbed or metabolized by the body and can enter the environment after passing through wastewater treatment plants."

"While FDA and the Environmental Protection Agency take the concerns of flushing certain medicines in the environment seriously, there has been no indication of environmental effects due to flushing," Bloom says.

"Nonetheless, FDA does not want to add drug residues into water systems unnecessarily," adds Hunter.

FDA reviewed drug labels to identify products with disposal directions recommending flushing down the sink or toilet. This continuously updated listing can be found at FDA's Web page on Disposal of Unused Medicines.

Disposal of Inhaler Products

Another environmental concern involves inhalers used by people who have asthma or other breathing problems, such as chronic obstructive pulmonary disease. Traditionally, many inhalers have contained chlorofluorocarbons (CFCs), a propellant that damages the protective ozone layer. CFCs have been phased out of inhalers and are being replaced with more environmentally friendly inhaler propellants.

Read handling instructions on the labeling of inhalers and aerosol products, because they could be dangerous if punctured or thrown into a fire or incinerator. To ensure safe disposal that complies with local regulations and laws, contact your local trash and recycling facility.

Section 46.3

Information for Parents about Club Drugs

This section includes text excerpted from "Tips for Parents: The Truth About Club Drugs," Federal Bureau of Investigation (FBI), August 19, 2014.

What Are Raves?

"Raves" are high energy, all-night dances that feature hard pounding techno-music and flashing laser lights. Raves are found in most metropolitan areas and, increasingly, in rural areas throughout the country. The parties are held in permanent dance clubs, abandoned warehouses, open fields, or empty buildings.

Raves are frequently advertised as "alcohol free" parties with hired security personnel. Internet sites often advertise these events as "safe" and "drug free." However, they are dangerously over crowded parties where your child can be exposed to rampant drug use and a high-crime environment. Numerous overdoses are documented at these events.

Raves are one of the most popular venues where club drugs are distributed. Club drugs include MDMA (more commonly known as

"Ecstasy"), GHB and Rohypnol (also known as the "date rape" drugs), Ketamine, Methamphetamine (also known as "Meth"), and LSD.

Because some club drugs are colorless, odorless, and tasteless, they can be added without detection to beverages by individuals who want to intoxicate or sedate others in order to commit sexual assaults.

Rave promoters capitalize on the effects of club drugs. Bottled water and sports drinks are sold at Raves, often at inflated prices, to manage hyperthermia and dehydration. Also found are pacifiers to prevent involuntary teeth clenching, menthol nasal inhalers, surgical masks, chemical lights, and neon glow sticks to increase sensory perception and enhance the Rave experience.

Cool down rooms are provided, usually at a cost, as a place to cool off due to increased body temperature of the drug user.

Don't risk your child's health and safety. Ask questions about where he or she is going and see it for yourself.

What Are Club Drugs?

1. **Methylenedioxymethamphetamine (MDMA)**

Street names: Ecstasy, E, X, XTC, Adam, Clarity, Lover's Speed

An amphetamine-based, hallucinogenic type drug that is taken orally, usually in a tablet or capsule form.

Effects:

- Lasts 3-6 hours.
- Enables dancers to dance for long periods of time.
- Increases the chances of dehydration, hyper tension, heart or kidney failure, and increased body temperature, which can lead to death.
- Long-term effects include confusion, depression, sleep problems, anxiety, paranoia, and loss of memory.

2. **Gamma-hydoxybutyrate (GHB)**

Street names: Grievous Bodily Harm, G, Liquid Ecstasy, Georgia Home Boy

A central nervous system depressant that is usually ingested in liquid, powder, tablet, and capsule forms.

Effects:

- May last up to 4 hours, depending on the dose used.

- Slows breathing and heart rates to dangerous levels.
- Also has sedative and euphoric effects that begin up to 10-20 minutes from ingestion.
- Use in connection with alcohol increases its potential for harm.
- Overdose can occur quickly-sometimes death occurs.

3. **Methamphetamine**

Street names: Speed, Ice, Chalk, Meth, Crystal, Crank, Fire, Glass

A central nervous system stimulant, often found in pill, capsule, or powder form, that can be snorted, injected, or smoked.

Effects:

- Displays signs of agitation, excited speech, lack of appetite, and increased physical activity.
- Often results in drastic weight loss, violence, psychotic behavior, paranoia, and sometimes damage to the heart or nervous system.

4. **Ketamine**

Street names: Special K, K, Vitamin K, Cat Valium

An injectable anesthetic used primarily by veterinarians, found either in liquid form or as a white powder that can be snorted or smoked, sometimes with marijuana.

Effects:

- Causes reactions similar to those of PCP, a hallucinatory drug.
- Results in impaired attention, learning, and memory function. In larger doses, it may cause delirium, amnesia, impaired motor function, high blood pressure, and depression.

5. **Rohypnol**

Street names: Roofies, Rophies, Roche, Forget-me Pill

Tasteless and odorless sedative, easily soluble in carbonated beverages, with toxic effects that are aggravated by concurrent use of alcohol.

Effects:

- Can cause anterograde amnesia, which contributes to Rohypnol's popularity as a "date rape" drug.
- Can cause decreased blood pressure, drowsiness, visual disturbances, dizziness, and confusion.

6. **Lysergic Acid Diethylamide (LSD)**

Street names: Acid, Boomers, Yellow Sunshines

Hallucinogen that causes distortions in sensory perception, usually taken orally either in tablet or capsule form. Often sold on blotter paper that has been saturated with the drug.

Effects:

- Are often unpredictable and may vary depending on dose, environment, and the user.
- Causes dilated pupils, higher body temperature, increased heart rate and blood pressure, sweating, dry mouth, and tremors.
- Can cause numbness, weakness, and nausea.
- Long-term effects may include persistent psychosis and hallucinogenic persisting perception disorder, commonly known as "flashbacks."

Know the Signs

Effects of stimulant club drugs, such as MDMA and Methamphetamine:

- Increased heart rate
- Convulsions
- Extreme rise in body temperature
- Uncontrollable movements
- Insomnia
- Impaired speech
- Dehydration
- High blood pressure
- Grinding teeth

Effects of sedative/hallucinogenic club drugs, such as GHB, Ketamine, LSD, and Rohypnol:

- Slow breathing
- Decreased heart rate (Except LSD)
- Respiratory problems
- Intoxication
- Drowsiness
- Confusion
- Tremors
- Nausea

Effects common to all club drugs can include anxiety, panic, depression, euphoria, loss of memory, hallucinations, and psychotic behavior. Drugs, traces of drugs, and drug paraphernalia are direct evidence of drug abuse. Pacifiers, menthol inhalers, surgical masks, and other such items could also be considered indicators.

Where Do You Go for Help?

If you suspect your child is abusing drugs, monitor behavior carefully. Confirm with a trustworthy adult where your child is going and what he or she is doing. Enforce strict curfews. If you have evidence of club drug use, approach your child when he or she is sober, and if necessary, call on other family members and friends to support you in the confrontation.

Once the problem is confirmed, seek the help of professionals. If the person is under the influence of drugs and immediate intervention is necessary, consider medical assistance. Doctors, hospital substance programs, school counselors, the county mental health society, members of the clergy, organizations such as Narcotics Anonymous, and rape counseling centers stand ready and waiting to provide information and intervention assistance.

Section 46.4

Family-Based Intervention for Teenage Drug Abuse

This section includes text excerpted from "Principles of Adolescent Substance Use Disorder Treatment: A Research-Based Guide," National Institute on Drug Abuse (NIDA), January 2014.

Family-Based Approaches

Family-based approaches to treating adolescent substance abuse highlight the need to engage the family, including parents, siblings, and sometimes peers, in the adolescent's treatment. Involving the family can be particularly important, as the adolescent will often be living with at least one parent and be subject to the parent's controls, rules, and/or supports.

Family-based approaches generally address a wide array of problems in addition to the young person's substance problems, including family communication and conflict; other co-occurring behavioral, mental health, and learning disorders; problems with school or work attendance; and peer networks. Research shows that family-based treatments are highly efficacious; some studies even suggest they are superior to other individual and group treatment approaches. Typically offered in outpatient settings, family treatments have also been tested successfully in higher-intensity settings such as residential and intensive outpatient programs. Below are specific types of family-based treatments shown to be effective in treating adolescent substance abuse.

Brief Strategic Family Therapy (BSFT)

BSFT is based on a family systems approach to treatment, in which one member's problem behaviors are seen to stem from unhealthy family interactions. Over the course of 12–16 sessions, the BSFT counselor establishes a relationship with each family member, observes how the members behave with one another, and assists the family in changing negative interaction patterns. BSFT can be adapted to a broad range of family situations in various settings (mental health clinics, drug abuse treatment programs, social service settings, families' homes) and treatment modalities (as a primary outpatient intervention, in combination with residential or day treatment, or as an aftercare/continuing-care service following residential treatment).

Family Behavior Therapy (FBT)

FBT, which has demonstrated positive results in both adults and adolescents, combines behavioral contracting with contingency management to address not only substance abuse but other behavioral problems as well. The adolescent and at least one parent participate in treatment planning and choose specific interventions from a menu of evidence-based treatment options. Therapists encourage family members to use behavioral strategies taught in sessions and apply their new skills to improve the home environment. They set behavioral goals for preventing substance use and reducing risk behaviors for sexually transmitted diseases like HIV, which are reinforced through a contingency management (CM) system. Goals are reviewed and rewards provided at each session.

Functional Family Therapy (FFT)

FFT combines a family systems view of family functioning (which asserts that unhealthy family interactions underlie problem behaviors) with behavioral techniques to improve communication, problem-solving, conflict resolution, and parenting skills. Principal treatment strategies include

1. engaging families in the treatment process and enhancing their motivation for change and
2. modifying family members' behavior using CM techniques, communication and problem solving, behavioral contracts, and other methods.

Multidimensional Family Therapy (MDFT)

MDFT is a comprehensive family- and community-based treatment for substance-abusing adolescents and those at high risk for behavior problems such as conduct disorder and delinquency. The aim is to foster family competency and collaboration with other systems like school or juvenile justice. Sessions may take place in a variety of locations, including in the home, at a clinic, at school, at family court, or in other community locations. MDFT has been shown to be effective even with more severe substance use disorders and can facilitate the reintegration of substance abusing juvenile detainees into the community.

Multisystemic Therapy (MST)

MST is a comprehensive and intensive family- and community-based treatment that has been shown to be effective even with adolescents whose substance abuse problems are severe and with those who engage in delinquent and/or violent behavior. In MST, the adolescent's substance abuse is viewed in terms of characteristics of the adolescent (e.g., favorable attitudes toward drug use) and those of his or her family (e.g., poor discipline, conflict, parental drug abuse), peers (e.g., positive attitudes toward drug use), school (e.g., dropout, poor performance), and neighborhood (e.g., criminal subculture). The therapist may work with the family as a whole but will also conduct sessions with just the caregivers or the adolescent alone.

Chapter 47

Drug Testing

Chapter Contents

Section 47.1

Overview of Drug Testing

This section contains text excerpted from the following sources: Text under the heading "Brief Description" is excerpted from "Drug Testing," National Institute on Drug Abuse (NIDA), September 2014; Text beginning with the heading "What Testing Methods Are Available?" is excerpted from "Frequently Asked Questions About Drug Testing in Schools," National Institute on Drug Abuse (NIDA), September 2014.

Brief Description

Some schools, hospitals, and places of employment conduct drug testing. There are a number of ways this can be done, including: pre-employment testing, random testing, reasonable suspicion/cause testing, post-accident testing, return to duty testing, and follow up testing. This usually involves collecting urine samples to test for drugs such as marijuana, cocaine, amphetamines, PCP, and opiates.

What Testing Methods Are Available?

There are several testing methods currently available that use urine, hair, oral fluids, and sweat. These methods vary in cost, reliability, drugs detected, and detection period. Schools can determine their needs and choose the method that best suits their requirements, as long as the testing kits are from a reliable source.

Which Drugs Can Be Tested For?

Various testing methods normally test for a "panel" of five to ten different drugs. A typical drug panel tests for marijuana, cocaine, opioids (including the prescription pain relievers OxyContin and Vicodin), amphetamines, and PCP. If a school has a particular problem with other drugs, such as MDMA, GHB, or steroids, they can include testing for these drugs as well. It is also possible to screen for synthetic cannabinoids, commonly known as spice and K2.

What about Alcohol?

Alcohol is a drug, and its use is a serious problem among young people. However, alcohol does not remain in the blood long enough for most tests to detect most recent use. Breathalyzers, oral fluid tests, and urine tests can only detect use within the past few hours. The cutoff is usually detection of the presence of alcohol for the equivalent of a blood alcohol content greater than 0.02 percent (20mg/1dL). Teens with substance use problems are often polydrug users (they use more than one drug) so identifying a problem with an illicit or prescription drug may also suggest an alcohol problem.

How Accurate Are Drug Tests? Is There a Possibility a Test Could Give a False Positive?

Tests are very accurate but not 100 percent accurate. Usually samples are divided so that if an initial test is positive a confirmation test can be conducted. Federal guidelines are in place to ensure accuracy and fairness in drug testing programs.

Section 47.2

Home Use Drug Testing

This section includes text excerpted from "Drugs of Abuse Home Use Test," U.S. Food and Drug Administration (FDA), June 5, 2014.

Drugs of Abuse Home Use Test

What Do These Tests Do?

These tests indicate if one or more prescription or illegal drugs are present in urine. These tests detect the presence of drugs such as marijuana, cocaine, opiates, methamphetamine, amphetamines, PCP, benzodiazepine, barbiturates, methadone, tricyclic antidepressants, ecstasy, and oxycodone.

The testing is done in two steps. First, you do a quick at-home test. Second, if the test suggests that drugs may be present, you send the sample to a laboratory for additional testing.

What Are Drugs of Abuse?

Drugs of abuse are illegal or prescription medicines (for example, Oxycodone or Valium) that are taken for a non-medical purpose. Non-medical purposes for a prescription drug include taking the medication for longer than your doctor prescribed it for or for a purpose other than what the doctor prescribed it for. Medications are not drugs of abuse if they are taken according to your doctor's instructions.

What Type of Test Are These?

They are qualitative tests — you find out if a particular drug may be in the urine, but not how much is present.

When Should You Do These Tests?

You should use these tests when you think someone might be abusing prescription or illegal drugs. If you are worried about a specific drug, make sure to check the label to confirm that this test is designed to detect the drug you are looking for.

How Accurate Are These Tests?

The at-home testing part of this test is fairly sensitive to the presence of drugs in the urine. This means that if drugs are present, you will usually get a preliminary (or presumptive) positive test result. If you get a preliminary positive result, you should send the urine sample to the laboratory for a second test.

It is very important to send the urine sample to the laboratory to confirm a positive at-home result because certain foods, food supplements, beverages, or medicines can affect the results of at-home tests. Laboratory tests are the most reliable way to confirm drugs of abuse.

Many things can affect the accuracy of these tests, including (but not limited to):

- the way you did the test
- the way you stored the test or urine
- what the person ate or drank before taking the test

- any other prescription or over-the-counter drugs the person may have taken before the test

Note that a result showing the presence of an amphetamine should be considered carefully, even when this result is confirmed in the laboratory testing. Some over-the-counter medications will produce the same test results as illegally-abused amphetamines.

Does a Positive Test Mean That You Found Drugs of Abuse?

No. Take no serious actions until you get the laboratory's result. Remember that many factors may cause a false positive result in the home test.

Remember that a positive test for a prescription drug does not mean that a person is abusing the drug, because there is no way for the test to indicate acceptable levels compared to abusive levels of prescribed drugs.

If the Test Results Are Negative, Can You Be Sure That the Person You Tested Did Not Abuse Drugs?

No. No drug test of this type is 100% accurate. There are several factors that can make the test results negative even though the person is abusing drugs. First, you may have tested for the wrong drugs. Or, you may not have tested the urine when it contained drugs. It takes time for drugs to appear in the urine after a person takes them, and they do not stay in the urine indefinitely; you may have collected the urine too late or too soon. It is also possible that the chemicals in the test went bad because they were stored incorrectly or they passed their expiration date.

If you get a negative test result, but still suspect that someone is abusing drugs, you can test again at a later time. Talk to your doctor if you need more help deciding what steps to take next.

How Soon after a Person Takes Drugs, Will They Show up in a Drug Test? And How Long after a Person Takes Drugs, Will They Continue to Show Up in a Drug Test?

The drug clearance rate tells how soon a person may have a positive test after taking a particular drug. It also tells how long the person may continue to test positive after the last time he or she took the drug. Clearance rates for common drugs of abuse are given below. These are only guidelines, however, and the times can vary significantly from these estimates based on how long the person has been taking the drug, the amount of drug they use, or the person's metabolism.

How Do You Do a Drugs of Abuse Test?

These tests usually contain a sample collection cup, the drug test (it may be test strips, a test card, a test cassette, or other method for testing the urine), and an instruction leaflet or booklet. It is very important that the person doing the test reads and understands the instructions first, before even collecting the sample. This is important because with most test kits, the result must be visually read within a certain number of minutes after the test is started.

You collect urine in the sample collection cup and test it according to the instructions. If the test indicates the preliminary presence of one or more drugs, the sample should be sent to a laboratory where a more specific chemical test will be used order to obtain a final result. Some home use kits have a shipping container and pre-addressed mailer in them. If you have questions about using these tests, or the results that you are getting, you should contact your healthcare provider.

Chapter 48

Drug Abuse Testing and Prevention in Schools

Chapter Contents

Section 48.1

Drug Testing in Schools

This section includes text excerpted from "Frequently Asked Questions About Drug Testing in Schools," National Institute on Drug Abuse (NIDA), September 2014.

Do All Schools Conduct Drug Testing?

Following models established in the workplace, some schools have initiated random drug testing and/or reasonable suspicion/cause testing. This usually involves collecting urine samples to test for drugs such as marijuana, cocaine, amphetamines, PCP, and opioids (both heroin and prescription pain relievers).

In random testing, schools select one or more students to undergo drug testing using a random process (like flipping a coin). Legally, only students who participate in competitive extracurricular activities (including athletics and school clubs) can be subject to random drug testing.

In reasonable suspicion/cause testing, a student can be asked to provide a urine sample, if the school suspects or has evidence they are using drugs. Such evidence might include direct observations made by school officials, physical symptoms of being under the influence, and/or has patterns of abnormal or erratic behavior.

Why Do Some Schools Conduct Random Drug Tests?

Schools that have adopted random student drug testing seek to decrease drug use among students via two routes. First, they hope random testing will serve as a deterrent and give students a reason to resist peer pressure to take drugs. Secondly, drug testing can identify teens who have started using drugs and would be good targets for early intervention, as well as identify those who already have drug problems, so they can be referred for treatment. Using drugs not only interferes with a student's ability to learn, but it can also disrupt the teaching environment, affecting other students as well.

Is Student Drug Testing Effective?

Drug testing should never be undertaken as a stand-alone response to a drug problem. If testing is done, it should be a component of broader prevention, intervention, and treatment programs, with the common goal of reducing students' drug use.

If a Student Tests Positive for Drugs, Should That Student Face Disciplinary Consequences?

The primary purpose of drug testing is not to punish students who use drugs but to prevent drug abuse and to help students already using become drug-free. If a student tests positive for drugs, schools can respond to the individual situation. If a student tests positive for drug use but has not yet progressed to addiction, the school can require counseling and follow-up testing. For students diagnosed with addiction, parents and a school administrator can refer them to effective drug treatment programs to begin the recovery process.

Why Test Teenagers at All?

Adolescents' brains and bodies are still developing, and this makes them especially vulnerable to the harmful effects of drug use. Most teens do not use drugs, but for those who do, it can lead to a wide range of adverse effects on their behavior and health.

Short term: Even a single use of an intoxicating drug can affect a person's judgment and decision making—resulting in accidents, poor performance in school or sports activities, unplanned risky behavior, and the risk of overdosing.

Long term: Repeated drug use can lead to serious problems, such as poor academic outcomes, mood changes (depending on the drug: depression, anxiety, paranoia, psychosis), and social or family problems caused or worsened by drugs.

Repeated drug use can also lead to the disease of **addiction**. Studies show that the earlier a teen begins using drugs, the more likely he or she will develop a substance use disorder or addiction. Conversely, if teens stay away from drugs while in high school, they are less likely to develop a substance use disorder later in life.

How Many Students Actually Use Drugs?

Drug use among high schools students has dropped significantly since 2001. In December, the 2013 Monitoring the Future study of 8th, 10th, and 12th graders showed that drug use was down from 31.8 percent in 2001 to 28.4 percent. While drug use is still below that from 2001, it has been increasing over the last several years largely due to increased marijuana use.

About 50 percent of 12th graders say that they've used any illicit drug at least once in their lifetime, and over 35 percent report using marijuana in the last year. Abuse and misuse of prescription drugs are also high—for example, in 2013, 7.4 percent of high school seniors reported nonmedical use of the prescription stimulant Adderall in the past year.

Can Students "Beat" the Tests?

Many drug-using students are aware of techniques that supposedly detoxify their systems or mask their drug use. Popular magazines and Internet sites give advice on how to dilute urine samples, and there are even companies that sell clean urine or products designed to distort test results. A number of techniques and products are focused on urine tests for marijuana, but masking products increasingly are becoming available for tests of hair, oral fluids, and multiple drugs.

Most of these products do not work, are very costly, are easily identified in the testing process, and need to be on hand constantly due to the very nature of random testing. Moreover, even if the specific drug is successfully masked, the product itself can be detected, in which case the student using it would become an obvious candidate for additional screening and attention. In fact, some testing programs label a test "positive" if a masking product is detected.

Is Random Drug Testing of Students Legal?

In June 2002, the U.S. Supreme Court broadened the authority of public schools to test students for illegal drugs. Voting 5 to 4 in Pottawatomie County v. Earls, the court ruled to allow random drug tests for all middle and high school students participating in competitive extracurricular activities. The ruling greatly expanded the scope of school drug testing, which previously had been allowed only for student athletes.

Just Because the U.S. Supreme Court Said Student Drug Testing for Adolescents in Competitive Extracurricular Activities Is Constitutional, Does That Mean It Is Legal in My City or State?

A school or school district that is interested in adopting a student drug testing program should seek legal expertise so that it complies with all federal, state, and local laws. Individual state constitutions may dictate different legal thresholds for allowing student drug testing. Communities interested in starting student drug testing programs should become familiar with the law in their respective states to ensure proper compliance.

What Has Research Determined about the Utility of Random Drug Tests in Schools?

Research in this area shows mixed results, however study authors generally agree that student drug testing should not be a stand-alone strategy for reducing substance use in students, and that school climate (the quality and character of school life) is an important factor for achieving positive results in drug prevention programs.

- A NIDA-funded study published in 2013 found significant associations between both random and for-cause student drug testing and use of marijuana or other drugs. The authors note that while drug testing was associated with moderately lower marijuana use, it was also associated with higher use of other illicit drugs.
- A study published in 2013 found that perceived school climate was associated with reduced likelihood of marijuana and cigarette initiation and cigarette escalation, and that student drug testing was not associated with improved drug use outcomes. The authors conclude that improving school climates is a promising strategy for preventing student substance use, while testing is a relatively ineffective drug-prevention policy.
- A study published in 2012 found that students subject to mandatory random student drug testing reported less substance use than comparable students in high school without such testing. The study found no impact of randing drug testing on intention to use substances, perceived consequences of substance use, participation in covered activities, or school connectedness.

- Results from a study published in 2012 indicate that drug testing is primarily effective at deterring substance use for female students in schools with positive climates. The authors conclude that drug testing should not be implemented as a stand-alone strategy for reducing substance use, and that school climate should be considered before implementing drug testing.
- A NIDA-funded study published in 2012 showed little empirical evidence supporting or refuting the efficacy of random student drug testing in schools.
- A NIDA-funded study published in 2007 found that student athletes who participated in randomized drug testing had overall rates of drug use similar to students who did not take part in the program, and in fact some indicators of future drug use increased among those participating in the drug testing program.

Section 48.2

Drug Use Prevention Education in Schools

This section includes text excerpted from "Alcohol or Other Drug Use Prevention," Centers for Disease Control and Prevention (CDC), 2015.

Health Education

Among classes or courses in which alcohol or other drug use prevention was taught:

- The mean number of hours of required instruction teachers provided on alcohol or other drug use prevention was 3.8 among elementary school classes, 5.9 among middle school courses, and 7.4 among high school courses.
- The percentage that provided students with the opportunity to practice communication, decision making, goal-setting, or refusal skills related to alcohol or other drug use prevention decreased from 68.7% in 2006 to 55.9% in 2014.

- During the two years before the study, 27.9% of health education classes or courses had a teacher who received professional development on alcohol or other drug use prevention, and 30.4% of classes or courses had a teacher who wanted professional development on this topic.

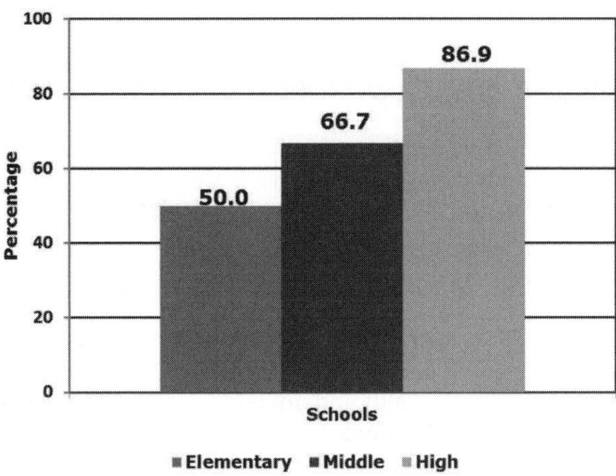

Figure 48.1. *Percentage of Schools in Which Students are Required to Receive Instruction on Alcohol or Other Drug Use Prevention, by School Level*

Family Engagement and Community Involvement

Table 48.1. Percentage of Schools That Had Students' Families or Community Members Help Develop, Communicate, or Implement Alcohol Use or Illegal Drug Use Prevention Policies or Activities,* SHPPS 2000, 2006, and 2014

Topic	2000	2006	2014	Trend
Alcohol use				
Students' families	45.4	35.1	16.1	Decreased
Community members	53.1	47	24.4	Decreased
Illegal drug use				
Students' families	46.1	36.9	18.1	Decreased
Community members	55.6	49.9	26.2	Decreased

**During the two years before the study.*

Employee Wellness

- 73.2% of nonpublic schools offered health insurance coverage for alcohol or other drug use treatment to faculty and staff.
- 91.6% of nonpublic schools do not require drug testing of any faculty and staff prior to employment, and 88.0% do not require drug testing of any faculty and staff periodically while employed.

Health Services and Counseling, Psychological, and Social Services

Table 48.2. Percentage of Middle and High Schools Providing Alcohol or Other Drug Use Prevention Services in One-on-One or Small-Group Sessions and Alcohol or Other Drug Use Treatment Services

Service	At school by health services or mental health and social services staff	Through arrangements with organizations or professionals not on school property
Alcohol or other drug use prevention*	32.8	38.5
Alcohol or other drug use treatment†	23.7	24.7

Provided to students. †Provided to students or families.

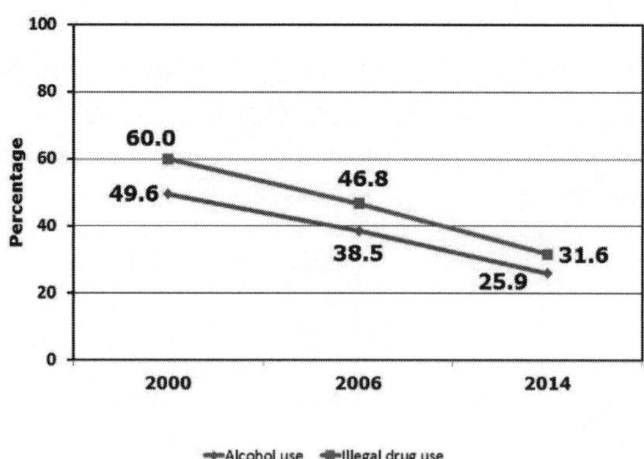

Figure 48.2. *Percentage of Schools That Have or Participate in a Community-based Alcohol or Illegal Drug Use Prevention Program, 2000, 2006, and 2014*

Healthy and Safe School Environment (Includes Social and Emotional Climate)

- Among the 97.1% schools in which students receive a student handbook, code of conduct, or other document that outlines school policies, rules, regulations and standards for behavior that students are expected to follow, 89.3% informed students about rules related to alcohol use and 91.4% informed students about rules related to illegal drug possession or use.
- 58.4% of schools post signs marking a drug-free zone.
- 8.6% of middle schools and 26.6% of high schools conduct any drug testing on students.
- Among the 35.7% of schools that had one or more school health councils, committees, or teams, 60.5% addressed alcohol or other drug use prevention.

Chapter 49

Preventing Drug Abuse in the Workplace

Chapter Contents

Section 49.1

Drug-Free Workplace Policies

This section contains text excerpted from the following sources: Text beginning with the heading "Drug-Free Workplace Toolkit" is excerpted from "Drug-Free Workplace Toolkit," Substance Abuse and Mental Health Services Administration's (SAMHSA), November 2, 2015; Text under the heading "Drug Testing and Workplace Issues" is excerpted from "Drug Testing," National Institute on Drug Abuse (NIDA), September 2014.

Drug-Free Workplace Toolkit

The Drug-free Workplace Toolkit provides information to help employers develop and sustain successful drug-free workplace programs.

Use the Drug-free Workplace Toolkit to support workplace health and safety by creating and maintaining drug-free workplace policies and programs. These policies and programs may include preventing the misuse and abuse of alcohol, tobacco, and other drugs; addressing substance misuse within the context of workplace health and wellness programs; and providing intervention services for employees and for their families.

Why a Drug-Free Workplace?

If you have legal requirements for a drug-free workplace policy and program and comply with those requirements, you will reduce the chances that your organization will experience legal issues. First, you will be meeting the requirements of the law. Second, you will be able to reduce drug-related accidents and the liability issues and lawsuits that can arise from such accidents.

In addition to meeting the legal requirements, consider putting in place a drug-free workplace policy and program that addresses the specific issues and needs in your workplace. Issues and needs can be identified by assessing your workplace. This approach increases the likelihood that you will achieve positive results in the form of reduced drug use and related problems.

Components of a Drug-Free Workplace

Drug-free workplace programs can help employers create safe, cost-effective, and healthy workplaces. Most successful drug-free workplace programs have five key components:

- A written policy
- Employee education
- Supervisor training
- An employee assistance program (EAP)
- Drug testing

Written Policy

A clearly written policy forms the foundation of your drug-free workplace program. At minimum, your policy should include:

- The rationale for the policy, such as organizational goals and compliance with laws or regulations
- Expectations for compliance, including who, what, when, and where
- Assistance options to support employees in following the policy
- Consequences for violating the policy

Employee Education

Employees at all levels should be prepared for the implementation of the drug-free workplace policy and program. Everyone in the organization needs information about the problems associated with substance misuse. Be sure to provide education and training that reinforces healthy attitudes and behaviors and deepens awareness on how substance misuse can affect employee health and employment.

Supervisor Training

Customized training for supervisors can help maximize the effectiveness of your drug-free workplace policy and program. Supervisors should be well-informed about the policy and program and be aware of legally sensitive areas. They must also be trained on how to document potential problems in a fair and systematic manner, honor confidentiality, and refer employees to appropriate services. Supervisors may also need training on how to help employees reintegrate into the workplace after receiving services.

Employee Assistance Programs (EAPs)

EAPs are designed to help employees with personal problems that may affect their job performance. Although some EAPs focus on problems related to alcohol and other drugs, most address a range of issues and can provide a variety of services.

Two professional associations—the International Employee Assistance Professionals Association (EAPA) and the Employee Assistance Trade Association (EASNA)—have developed certification procedures for EAP providers.

Drug Testing

Drug testing is one way to protect your workplace from the negative effects of substance misuse. Conducting drug testing may help your organization comply with federal regulations or insurance carrier requirements. It can improve workplace safety and reduce costs from misuse of alcohol and other drugs in the workplace. A drug-testing program can also deter employees from coming to work unfit for duty.

Brief Description

Some schools, hospitals, and places of employment conduct drug testing. There are a number of ways this can be done, including: pre-employment testing, random testing, reasonable suspicion/cause testing, post-accident testing, return to duty testing, and follow up testing. This usually involves collecting urine samples to test for drugs such as marijuana, cocaine, amphetamines, PCP, and opiates.

Drug Testing and Workplace Issues

According to recent data, 67.9 percent of all adult illegal drug users are employed full or part time, as are most binge and heavy alcohol users.1 Studies show that when compared with non-substance users, substance using employees are more likely to:

- Change jobs frequently
- Be late to or absent from work
- Be less productive

- Be involved in a workplace accident and potentially harm others
- File a workers' compensation claim.

Employers who have implemented drug-free workplace programs have important experiences to share.

- Employers with successful drug-free workplace programs report improvements in morale and productivity, and decreases in absenteeism, accidents, downtime, turnover, and theft.
- Employers with long-standing programs report better health status among employees and family members and decreased use of medical benefits by these same groups.
- Some organizations with drug-free workplace programs qualify for incentives, such as decreased costs for workers' compensation and other kinds of insurance.

Section 49.2

Drug Testing in the Workplace

This section includes text excerpted from "Drug Testing," Substance Abuse and Mental Health Services (SAMHSA), February 11, 2015.

Workplace Drug-Testing Programs

Workplace drug-testing programs are designed to detect the presence of alcohol, illicit drugs, or certain prescription drugs. Drug testing is a prevention and deterrent method that is often part of a comprehensive drug-free workplace program. Both federal and non-federal workplaces may have drug testing programs in place.

Any workplace drug-testing program should comply with applicable local, state, and federal laws.

Conducting Drug Tests

Federal agencies must use certified labs and follow other guidelines for drug testing. Learn more about drug-free workplace resources for federal agencies.

Before beginning drug testing, ask the following questions and consider how they will affect your testing program. Be sure to address each question in your drug-free workplace policy.

- Who receives testing?
- When are the drug tests given?
- Who conducts the testing?
- What substances are tested for?
- Who pays for the drug testing?
- What steps are taken to ensure the accuracy of the drug tests?
- What are the legal rights of employees who receive a positive test result?

Tests may be done by a trained collector who visits your workplace to collect specimens, or employees may go to a certified laboratory. To ensure accuracy, the specimen's chain of custody must be continuous from receipt until disposal.

Develop a system to protect the confidentiality of employee drug-testing records. Select a person within your organization who will be responsible for receiving employee drug test results, and make sure that the person is aware of confidentiality protocols. Explain the relationship of the drug testing program to your organization's employee assistance plan (EAP), if one is offered. Let employees know how drug-testing results can be used to inform their treatment, rehabilitation, and re-integration into the workplace.

Types of Drug Tests

Drug tests vary, depending on what types of drugs are being tested for and what types of specimens are being collected. Urine, hair, saliva (oral fluid), or sweat samples can be used as test specimens.

In federally regulated programs, only urine samples are collected, although the Secretary of Health and Human Service has released proposed guidelines for the inclusion of oral fluid specimens.

Tests are commonly used for five categories of drugs:

- Amphetamines
- Cocaine
- Marijuana
- Opiates
- Phencyclidine(PCP)

Additional categories may include barbiturates, Benzodiazepines, ethanol (alcohol), hydrocodone, MDMA, methadone, methaqualone, or propoxyphene.

Random tests are the most effective for deterring illicit drug use. Employers conduct random tests using an unpredictable selection process.

Drug testing may also be used in the following set times or circumstances:

Pre-Employment Tests

You can make passing a drug test a condition of employment. With this approach, all job candidates will receive drug testing prior to being hired.

Annual Physical Tests

You can test your employees for alcohol and other drug use as part of an annual physical examination. Be sure to inform employees that drug-testing will be part of the exam. Failure to provide prior notification is a violation of the employee's constitutional rights.

For-Cause and Reasonable Suspicion Tests

You may decide to test employees who show discernible signs of being unfit for duty (for-case testing), or who have a documented pattern of unsafe work behavior (reasonable suspicion testing.) These kinds of tests help to protect the safety and wellbeing of the employee and other co-workers.

Post-Accident Tests

Testing employees who were involved in a workplace accident or unsafe practices can help determine whether alcohol or other drug use was a contributing factor to the incident.

Post-Treatment Tests

Testing employees who return to work after completing a rehabilitation program can encourage them to remain drug-free.

Test Results

Ensuring the accuracy of drug-testing results is critical. Using an HHS-certified laboratory to test the specimens and a Medical Review Officer (MRO) to interpret the test results will help prevent inaccurate testing. MROs are licensed physicians who receive laboratory results and have knowledge of substance use disorders and federal drug-testing regulations. MROs are trained to interpret and evaluate test results together with the employee's medical history and other relevant information.

A negative test result does not indicate that an employee has never used alcohol or illicit drugs, nor is it a guarantee against future use.

Federal employees or employees in safety- and security-sensitive industries regulated by the Department of Defense (DOD) or the Department of Transportation (DOT) who show positive test results have the right to have the specimen tested by a second HHS-certified laboratory. Although a second test is not required, all employers should include this right in their drug-testing programs.

Depending on the workplace and the circumstances, employees who test positive may be referred to EAPs, into treatment, or for disciplinary action.

Chapter 50

Social Media and Substance Misuse Prevention

Developing a Social Media Plan to Support Substance Misuse Prevention Efforts

It wasn't so long ago that the idea of creating a website for your prevention program or organization was new and exciting, with so much to learn and do to make it happen. Today, static websites no longer make the grade. With the advent of social media, such as *Facebook* and *YouTube*, people increasingly expect opportunities to comment, share, discuss, and collaborate online.

Yet there are hundreds of social media options to choose from, with new sites and features popping up all the time. While the rapid pace of technology may make the thought of jumping on board the social media train feel daunting, a well-conceived plan can help ensure a smooth ride. To develop this plan, you will need to take a step back and think through why and how you intend to use social media to support your prevention efforts. Once you have a solid plan in place, you can board that train and feel confident that it will take you where you want to go!

This chapter includes text excerpted from "Developing a Social Media Plan to Support Substance Misuse Prevention Efforts," Substance Abuse and Mental Health Services Administration (SAMHSA), September 24, 2015.

A social media communications plan should include the following six steps:

Step 1. Establish Goals

What do you hope to achieve by using social media? Try to think broadly about this, considering both short- and long-term goals. For example, you may consider adding a blog to your website to share updates about current prevention activities. The possibilities are endless!

The world of social media offers you the capacity for ongoing communication, collaboration, and even social change. As your understanding of and comfort using social media deepen, consider its potential to influence—not just connect with—community members. For example, you might engage local youth in helping to shape the online conversation about drug use and prevention in your community. Or you might use social media to raise awareness about and gather signatures petitioning for a much-needed policy change to support prevention efforts.

Step 2. Clarify Roles

Who should participate in your social media efforts? Include folks who are experienced, motivated, and able to dedicate their time to both planning and implementing your social media strategies. Who are the recognized "early technology adopters" in your agency? Who's logging onto Facebook or Twitter in their spare time or blogging about their recent trip abroad? Who might be new to social media, but ready and willing to learn more? As you identify these individuals, consider what each person brings to the table. Tech experience? Design know-how? Comfort "speaking" online?

And, if you have any connections with young people, be sure to include them in your social media planning! Growing up immersed in high-tech devices and online forums that support near constant communication and information exchange, today's youth are being referred to as digital natives. They are fluent in the language of technology, well-versed in the practices of social media, and eager for more. They are likely to possess just the knowledge and talent you need to get your social media efforts up and running.

Step 3. Develop an Image

How will you present yourself online? Communications materials (logos, mission statements, or brochures) that work well in print don't always transfer well to the world of social media. To create a more social media-savvy image:

- **Develop a brief and memorable acronym or nickname to use online.** Many prevention programs and organizations come with lengthy, descriptive titles that lose their punch online. They also take up too much "digital real estate." Twitter messages, or "tweets," must be 140 characters or less. You don't want to use up the bulk of your tweet simply stating your name!
- **Simplify your language.** Remove formal language and excess jargon. Mission and vision statements that make sense in grant proposals and progress reports can appear awkward online. Consider reworking these for use in more casual, conversational online forums.
- **Think visual.** The virtual world is a visual world. Consider using a creative and colorful logo, icon, or photograph to represent your program and/or organization. Once you feel good about your image, use it widely and consistently across all of your social media platforms. In other words, do some branding!

Step 4. Select Tools

The world of social media is expansive. Platforms include social networking sites such as *Facebook*; blogs such as *Blogger*; microblogs such as *Twitter* and *Tumblr*; and image and video sharing sites such as *Flickr*, *Vimeo*, and *YouTube*. Each serves a different purpose, and choosing the right platform—given your target audience and goals—is critical.

When selecting a platform, first zero in on whom you want to reach (be very specific). Then figure out the best way to reach them. Talk to members of your target audience to find out which social media tools they prefer and how they use them. Think carefully about the kind of information you want to share and how you want your audience to use it.

Then you want to match your message to the proper communication channel. For example:

- If you want to offer lengthy updates or provide detailed information about specific topics, add a blog to your website.
- If you have a great set of photos or compelling videos from recent events, post them on photo and video sharing sites.

- If you need to communicate urgently or frequently with program participants about ongoing tasks and projects, try texting or tweeting them.

Keep in mind that these tools have incredible overlap. Use this overlap to your advantage. Provide links to all that you do, everywhere you do it.

Step 5. Determine Content

Social media is all about interaction. Any content posted to these sites will—by definition—invite commentary. Rich online discussion means welcoming many points of view, including those you or your organization may not agree with. Think carefully about which messages you feel comfortable opening up to unpredictable responses and be prepared to handle a wide range of questions and comments. Using social media in the world of prevention may be challenging, but the pay-off in terms of community reach and engagement can be significant!

Tips for Inviting Interaction

- **Mix it up.** Share information and ideas in as many ways as possible—use text, photos, drawings, slides, and video. Don't be afraid to experiment!
- **Make it count.** Give people something to talk about by posting content that is engaging and thought-provoking. Ask yourself, would you respond to what you just posted?
- **Think small.** You may be hoping for big results in the end, but small steps can get you there. Remember that each and every comment, "like," and "tweet" you get brings you closer to your goals.
- **Be present.** Make sure that program representatives routinely monitor and actively participate in your social media efforts. Social media requires frequent content updates.
- **Stay current.** Social media tools are continually evolving, with new tricks of the trade popping up often. Visitors—particularly youth—will be quick to notice if your social media efforts are out of date.
- **Don't talk at people.** Engage your audience. Invite responses and encourage people to interact with one another as well as

with program/organization representatives. Think of your messages as magnets: opportunities to attract people and draw them into conversations.

- **Show more than you tell.** Thoughtful and engaging messages are important, but never underestimate the value of images in the virtual world. Capitalize on the visual nature of social media to capture and keep people's attention.
- **Be positive—sure of yourself and affirming of others.** Create safe and comfortable spaces for people to come together online. Think carefully about what you want to say and how you want to say it, and establish policies that support open and honest—yet civil and respectful—interactions. With each positive social media action you take, you are building social capital for your program and organization.

Step 6. Evaluate and Refine Efforts

Monitor your social media efforts and work toward improving your messages and overall approach over time. Pay careful attention to the concrete numbers: How many people have "friended" or "liked" your program? How many comments have you received on your latest blog entry? Did more people participate in a program or show up to an event after you started using social media for publicity? How many tweets are exchanged among program staff and the community?

And, since social media is all about interaction, look closely at the nature of the input and feedback you are receiving. What seems to be working well? Do more of that! What is not working very well? Think about how you can modify your approach. Down the road, consider how to assess whether your social media efforts are having a real impact on knowledge, attitudes, and behaviors in the community.

Give it Some Time

Don't be discouraged if your social media efforts are not immediately rewarded—this is perfectly normal. Allow for a learning curve, as well as time to build and expand your online presence. It won't happen overnight, but it will happen. With careful planning and preparation, social media tools can help you establish a compelling online identity, publicize your prevention activities, spread your prevention messages, and both build and maintain relationships with colleagues and community members.

Chapter 51

Federal Drug Abuse Prevention Campaigns

Chapter Contents

Section 51.1

National Campaigns: An Overview

This section includes text excerpted from "Substance Misuse Prevention Media Campaigns," Substance Abuse and Mental Health Services Administration (SAMHSA), September 24, 2015.

National Campaigns

Prescription Drug Misuse and Abuse

- The AWARxE Prescription Drug Safety Program is designed to spread awareness about prescription drug misuse and abuse. It offers tips for understanding prescription information, safely acquiring and administering medications, and properly disposing of unused medications. The campaign also encourages people to share their personal stories about prescription drug misuse and connects website users with prescription drug awareness events happening across the United States.
- Up and Away and Out of Sight is an educational program to remind families of the importance of safe medicine storage. It is an initiative of PROTECT, in partnership with the Centers for Disease Control and Prevention (CDC), the Consumer Healthcare Products Association Educational Foundation among others. The campaign encourages adults to keep medicine out of reach of small children and to teach children about medicine safety. Other tips include never telling a child that medicine is candy, (even if having trouble administering medicine) and instructing guests to keep purses, bags, and coats containing medication out of sight. Parents and caregivers can take a pledge on the campaign website to keep medication up and away from children. Those who take the pledge are encouraged to share it with friends and family via social media and email. The website is also available in Spanish.

Public Health

- Above the Influence, created as part of the National Youth Anti-Drug Media Campaign, aims to help teens stand up to peer pressure and other influences that encourage the use of drugs and alcohol. Through television commercials, Internet advertising, and regular communication with teens via Facebook, this educational campaign encourages teens to be aware and critical of all messages they receive about drugs and alcohol. Acknowledging that the campaign provides one of many messages teens receive about alcohol and drug use, the website urges teens to review sources of information to check the facts and make informed decisions.

- NIDA for Teens: The Science Behind Drug Abuse is a campaign geared toward adolescents ages 11 to 15 years. It uses a blog, videos, and drug factsheets to educate youth, parents, and teachers about the science behind drug misuse. The campaign website contains information on a wide array of substances, including emerging drug trends. The blog contains celebrity stories about the dangers of substance misuse, answers to real questions from teens, and information about how the brain works and the effects of drugs on the brain.

Underage Drinking

- SAMHSA's "Talk. They Hear You" Public service announcement campaign encourages parents and caregivers to talk to their children about the dangers of alcohol. It is designed to increase parents' awareness and understanding of underage drinking, and to help them engage in thoughtful conversations on the topic with the young people in their lives. Resources available in English and in Spanish include information on the consequences of underage drinking, advice for answering difficult questions that children may ask about alcohol, and sample text messages that parents can send to their children reminding them not to drink.
- SAMHSA's "Too Smart to Start" public education initiative aims to stimulate conversations between youth and adults on the harms of underage alcohol use, and to create an environment where youth, parents, and the general public see underage drinking as harmful. The Too Smart to Start website includes separate sections for youth; teens; and families, educators, and community leaders, each with its own set of information and engagement tools.
- "We Don't Serve Teens" developed by the Federal Trade Commission, provides materials for high schools, colleges, social

services organizations, and alcohol industry members to spread the message that providing alcohol to teens is unsafe, illegal, and irresponsible. Campaign materials include press releases, letters to the editor, radio public services announcements, and buttons to add to websites. The campaign website also includes facts about underage drinking, alcohol laws by state, and media literacy tools.

Section 51.2

Drug Abuse Prevention Programs

This section contains text excerpted from the following sources: Text beginning with the heading "High Intensity Drug Trafficking Areas (HIDTA) Program" is excerpted from "High Intensity Drug Trafficking Areas (HIDTA) Program," WhiteHouse.gov, March 1, 2015; Text under the heading "National Drug & Alcohol Facts Week" is excerpted from "National Drug & Alcohol Facts Week," National Institute on Drug Abuse (NIDA), July 24, 2015.

High Intensity Drug Trafficking Areas (HIDTA) Program

The High Intensity Drug Trafficking Areas (HIDTA) program, created by Congress with the Anti-Drug Abuse Act of 1988, provides assistance to Federal, state, local, and tribal law enforcement agencies operating in areas determined to be critical drug-trafficking regions of the United States.

The purpose of the program is to reduce drug trafficking and production in the United States by:

- Facilitating cooperation among Federal, state, local, and tribal law enforcement agencies to share information and implement coordinated enforcement activities;
- Enhancing law enforcement intelligence sharing among Federal, state, local, and tribal law enforcement agencies;
- Providing reliable law enforcement intelligence to law enforcement agencies needed to design effective enforcement strategies and operations; and

- Supporting coordinated law enforcement strategies which maximize use of available resources to reduce the supply of illegal drugs in designated areas and in the United States as a whole.

There are currently 28 HIDTAs, which include approximately 17.2 percent of all counties in the United States and a little over 60 percent of the U.S. population. HIDTA-designated counties are located in 48 states, as well as in Puerto Rico, the U.S. Virgin Islands, and the District of Columbia.

Each HIDTA assesses the drug trafficking threat in its defined area for the upcoming year, develops a strategy to address that threat, designs initiatives to implement the strategy, proposes funding needed to carry out the initiatives, and prepares an annual report describing its performance the previous year. A central feature of the HIDTA program is the discretion granted to the Executive Boards to design and implement initiatives that confront drug trafficking threats in each HIDTA. The program's 59 Intelligence and Investigative Support Centers help HIDTA's identify new targets and trends, develop threat assessments, de-conflict targets and events, and manage cases.

HIDTA Activities

The HIDTA program funds 737 initiatives throughout the country, including:

- Enforcement initiatives comprising multi-agency investigative, interdiction, and prosecution activities;
- Intelligence and information-sharing initiatives;
- Support for programs that provide assistance beyond the core enforcement and intelligence and information-sharing initiatives; and
- Drug use prevention and drug treatment initiatives.

Today, prevention and treatment initiatives are an integral part of the HIDTA program. Currently, 22 regional HIDTA programs support prevention initiatives across the country, including the 5 SWB HIDTA regions. The HIDTA members work with community-based coalitions and adhere to evidence-based prevention practices, such as community mobilization and organizational change. For example:

- SCOPE (Safe and Competent Opioid Prescribing Education) of Pain initiative, sponsored by the New England HIDTA in partnership with the Boston University School of Medicine, provides continuing education opportunities to Physicians.

- A program funded by the Northwest HIDTA in Skagit County, Washington, is a multidisciplinary partnership of community coalitions, law enforcement, tribal, medical health providers and other agencies that provides prevention programs to the Hispanic student population in several schools.
- In 2014, the latest year for which we have complete information, the Washington/Baltimore HIDTA funded 10 state and local agencies that provided successful drug treatment services to 462 individuals with the goal of reducing their rate of recidivism. The declines in individuals arrested, the number of arrests, and the number of charges, were substantially lower than among the group that was unsuccessful. These programs are seeing more clients with a primary diagnosis of heroin addiction and require more resources such as medication assisted treatment as well as a full continuum of services from outpatient didactic treatment to long-term residential services.

The HIDTA program also supports several key domestic projects. These national level initiatives are administered by the National HIDTA Assistance Center (NHAC) and overseen by the HIDTA Directors Committee. These programs are the Domestic Highway Enforcement (DHE) program; the National Methamphetamine and Pharmaceuticals Initiative (NMPI); and the National Marijuana Initiative (NMI).

Drug trafficking is a significant problem in Indian Country, and ONDCP has made it a priority to collaborate with tribal leadership and enhance law enforcement and prevention responses. There are currently six HIDTA programs collaborating in enforcement operations and training with Tribal Nations. They are located in the states of Arizona, New Mexico, New York, Oklahoma, Oregon, and Washington.

National Drug and Alcohol Facts Week

What is National Drug & Alcohol Facts Week^{SM}?

National Drug & Alcohol Facts Week^{SM} links students with scientists and other experts to counteract the myths about drugs and alcohol that teens get from the internet, TV, movies, music, or from friends.

It was launched in 2010 by scientists at the National Institute on Drug Abuse (NIDA) to stimulate educational events in communities so teens can learn what science has taught us about drug abuse and addiction. The National Institute of Alcohol Abuse and Alcoholism became a partner starting in 2016, and alcohol has been added as a topic area for the week. NIDA and NIAAA are part of the National Institutes of Health.

What happens during National Drug & Alcohol Facts Week^SM?

National Drug & Alcohol Facts Week^SM is an opportunity for teens to **SHATTER THE MYTHS**^TM, SM about drugs and drug abuse. In community and school events all over America, teens, scientists and other experts come together for an honest conversation about how drugs affect the brain, body and behavior. In school assemblies, after school clubs, athletic events, and other venues, students are able to ask experts questions about drugs, and discuss NIDA materials designed for teens.

How can I plan an event for National Drug & Alcohol Facts Week^SM?

Check out the *National Drug & Alcohol Facts Week*^SM Website (teens.drugabuse.gov/national-drug-alcohol-facts-week) for more information. NIDA offers an online toolkit with lots of suggestions on how to plan events, how to find experts who can participate, and how to connect with NIDA staffers who can help. The site also tells you how to register your event, and how to get free materials for teens, including the National Drug & Alcohol IQ Challenge quiz, and our popular *SHATTER THE MYTHS*^TM, SM booklet.

Why Celebrate National Drug & Alcohol Facts Week^SM?

About a third of high school seniors report using an illicit drug sometime in the past year; about 5 percent of seniors report nonmedical use of potentially addictive prescription painkillers; and more than 20 percent report smoking marijuana in the past month. Many teens are not aware of the risks to their health, to their success in school and the dangers while driving under the influence. When teens are given the scientific facts about drugs, they can be better prepared to make good decisions for themselves and they can share this information with others.

Who are the Federal Partners for National Drug & Alcohol Facts Week^{SM}?

NIDA and NIAAA have many federal, state and local partners working together to get the facts about drugs to teens in communities all over America. Partners include the Substance Abuse and Mental Health Services Administration, the White House Office of National Drug Control Policy, the Office of Safe and Healthy Students in the U.S. Department of Education and the Drug Enforcement Administration in the U.S. Department of Justice.

Section 51.3

New Funding Proposed to Address the Prescription Opioid Abuse and Heroin Use Epidemic

This section includes text excerpted from "Fact Sheet: President Obama Proposes $1.1 Billion in New Funding to Address the Prescription Opioid Abuse and Heroin Use Epidemic," WhiteHouse.gov, February 2, 2016.

Prescription drug abuse and heroin use have taken a heartbreaking toll on too many Americans and their families, while straining resources of law enforcement and treatment programs. More Americans now die every year from drug overdoses than they do in motor vehicle crashes. New data from the Centers for Disease Control and Prevention (CDC) show that opioids—a class of drugs that include prescription pain medications and heroin—were involved in 28,648 deaths in 2014. In particular, CDC found a continued sharp increase in heroin-involved deaths and an emerging increase in deaths involving synthetic opioids, such as fentanyl.

The President has made clear that addressing the opioid overdose epidemic is a priority for his Administration and has highlighted tools that are effective in reducing drug use and overdose, like evidence-based prevention programs, prescription drug monitoring, prescription drug take-back events, medication-assisted treatment and the overdose reversal drug naloxone. Under the Affordable Care Act, substance use disorder services are essential health benefits that are required to be covered by health plans in the Health Insurance Marketplace. The law also required that covered substance use disorder benefits are comparable to medical and surgical benefits.

The President's FY 2017 Budget takes a two-pronged approach to address this epidemic. First, it includes $1 billion in new mandatory funding over two years to expand access to treatment for prescription drug abuse and heroin use. This funding will boost efforts to help individuals with an opioid use disorder seek treatment, successfully complete treatment, and sustain recovery. This funding includes:

- $920 million to support cooperative agreements with States to expand access to medication-assisted treatment for opioid use disorders. States will receive funds based on the severity of the epidemic and on the strength of their strategy to respond to it. States can use these funds to expand treatment capacity and make services more affordable.
- $50 million in National Health Service Corps funding to expand access to substance use treatment providers. This funding will help support approximately 700 providers able to provide substance use disorder treatment services, including medication-assisted treatment, in areas across the country most in need of behavioral health providers.
- $30 million to evaluate the effectiveness of treatment programs employing medication-assisted treatment under real-world conditions and help identify opportunities to improve treatment for patients with opioid use disorders.

This investment, combined with other efforts underway to reduce barriers to treatment for substance use disorders, will help ensure that every American who wants treatment can access it and get the help they need.

Second, the President's Budget includes approximately $500 million—an increase of more than $90 million—to continue and build on current efforts across the Departments of Justice (DOJ) and Health and Human Services (HHS) to expand state-level prescription drug overdose prevention strategies, increase the availability of medication-assisted treatment programs, improve access to the overdose-reversal drug naloxone, and support targeted enforcement activities. A portion of this funding is directed specifically to rural areas, where rates of overdose and opioid use are particularly high. To help further expand access to treatment, the Budget includes an HHS pilot project for nurse practitioners and physician assistants to prescribe buprenorphine for opioid use disorder treatment, where allowed by state law.

Building on Actions to Address the Opioid Epidemic

In October 2015, the President announced a number of new public and private sector actions to address this issue, including a Presidential Memorandum on prescriber training and opioid use disorder treatment. He also announced a commitment by more than 40 provider groups that more than 540,000 healthcare providers will complete training on appropriate opioid prescribing in the next two years. After just over three months, these groups reported that more than 66,000 providers have completed prescriber training to date, putting them on target to meet their goal.

In December, the President signed a bipartisan budget agreement with more than $400 million in funding specifically to address the opioid epidemic, an increase of more than $100 million over the previous year. The agreement also revised a longstanding ban on using federal funds to support syringe service programs, which can help reduce the transmission of HIV and viral hepatitis by confronting one major source of the outbreaks: injection drug use, including opioids.

These actions build on efforts that began in 2010 when the President released his first National Drug Control Strategy, which emphasized the need for action to address opioid use disorders and overdose while ensuring that individuals with pain receive safe, effective treatment. In 2011, the White House released its national Prescription Drug Abuse Prevention Plan, which outlined goals for addressing prescription drug abuse and overdose.

Since then, the Administration has supported and expanded efforts to prevent drug use, pursue "smart on crime" approaches to drug enforcement, improve prescribing practices for pain medication, increase access to treatment, work to reduce overdose deaths, and support the millions of Americans in recovery:

Community Prevention and Overdose Response

- The Office of National Drug Control Policy (ONDCP), in collaboration with the Substance Abuse and Mental Health Services Administration (SAMHSA), supports local Drug-Free Communities coalitions to reduce youth substance use through evidence-based prevention. In recent years, hundreds of these coalitions have specifically focused on prescription drug misuse issues in their areas.

- With support from the Administration, prescriber education programs have been developed to teach medical professionals skills such as how to start a conversation with patients about their substance use; managing pain appropriately; and treating patients using opioids more safely. In response to a Presidential Memorandum, federal agencies are leading the way by making certain that their workforce is properly trained. In addition, ten states have passed legislation requiring training for prescribers.
- In FY 2016, HHS will implement the $10 million Strategic Prevention Framework for Prescription Drugs to raise awareness about the dangers of misusing prescribed medications and to work with pharmacy and medical communities to address the risks of overprescribing to young adults. The FY 2017 Budget continues this effort.
- With support from the Department of Justice (DOJ) and other funders, 49 states have established Prescription Drug Monitoring Programs to help prescribers identify potential opioid misuse issues—up from 30 states at the start of the Administration.
- The federal government is expanding access to prescription drug monitoring program data throughout federal agencies. The Department of Defense's (DoD) Pharmacy Data Transaction Service automatically screens all new medication orders against a patient's computerized medication history and permits DoD physicians to monitor for concerning drug usage patterns. The Indian Health Service has successfully piloted integrating this data into their electronic systems, and a pilot to integrate data into the workflow of physicians in the DoD health system is slated to launch in 2016.
- Through the National Take Back Days to remove unused prescription drugs from communities, the Drug Enforcement Administration (DEA) has collected more than 5.5 million pounds of medication. DEA also finalized a new rule making it easier for communities to establish ongoing drug take-back programs.
- ONDCP has worked with federal, state, and local government agencies and other stakeholders to expand access to the lifesaving opioid overdose reversal drug naloxone, including equipping first responders. Today, hundreds of law enforcement agencies across the country carry and are trained to administer naloxone. Additionally, prior to 2012, just six states had any laws that

expanded access to naloxone or limited criminal liability for persons who took steps to assist an overdose victim. Today, 46 states and the District of Columbia have enacted statutes that expand access to naloxone or provide "Good Samaritan" protections for possession of a controlled substance if emergency assistance is sought for a victim of an opioid overdose.

- The Department of Veteran Affairs (VA) supports the Opioid Overdose Education and Naloxone distribution program to help Veterans at risk of an opioid overdose. This program is a key objective of VA's safety initiatives. In the less than two years since the program was implemented, over 12,000 Veterans have received a naloxone kit, and there have been 141 reported reversals as of December 2015.
- In September 2015, CDC launched a $20 million Prescription Drug Overdose: Prevention for States initiative in 16 states to expand their capacity to put prevention into action in communities nationwide and encourage education of providers and patients about the risk of prescription drug overdose. In 2016, the initiative received a further increase of $50 million dollars to expand these state prevention activities to a national scale.
- The DOJ Bureau of Justice Assistance released a Law Enforcement Naloxone Toolkit to support law enforcement agencies in establishing naloxone programs. The toolkit has been downloaded more than 2,200 times in the last year.
- DOD is ensuring that opioid overdose reversal kits and training are available to every first responder on military bases or other areas under its control.
- In 2016, SAMHSA will provide a total of $12 million specifically to increase use of the overdose reversal drug naloxone. States can use these funds to purchase naloxone, equip first responders with naloxone, and provide training on other overdose death prevention strategies. The FY 2017 Budget will continue these investments and includes an additional $10 million to address opioid overdose in rural areas, including through expanding access to naloxone.
- In November 2015, the President signed bipartisan legislation, the Protecting Our Infants Act, to help identify evidence-based approaches to care for mothers and their newborns affected by the opioid epidemic.

- In December 2015, the Indian Health Service (IHS) and the Bureau of Indian Affairs announced a new partnership to reduce opioid-related overdoses among American Indians and Alaska Natives. In 2016, the more than 90 IHS pharmacies will dispense naloxone to as many as 500 BIA Office of Justice Services officers and will train these first responders to administer emergency treatment to people experiencing an opioid overdose.
- Using the most recent scientific evidence, the CDC has been working with clinical experts and other stakeholders to develop guidelines on prescribing opioids for chronic pain. The guidelines will be used to help improve the way opioids are prescribed and help providers offer safer, more effective chronic pain treatment, while reducing opioid misuse, abuse and overdose.
- Using its fast-track and priority review systems, FDA recently approved for the first time a nasal spray version of naloxone hydrochloride, providing an easy to administer way to deliver this lifesaving drug. The National Institute on Drug Abuse helped develop this product through a partnership to apply new technology towards developing interventions for opioid overdose.

Treatment

- In FY 2016, SAMHSA will support grants to 22 States to support medication-assisted treatment for opioid use disorders in high need communities. The FY 2017 Budget will expand the number of States that will receive funding to 45.
- In 2016, the Health Resources and Services Administration will award up to $100 million to Health Centers across the country to improve and expand the delivery of substance use disorder services, with a focus on medication-assisted treatment for opioid use disorders.
- HHS Secretary Burwell announced that the Department will engage in rulemaking related to the prescribing of buprenorphine-containing products approved by the FDA for treatment of opioid dependence to expand access to medication-assisted treatment for opioid use disorders. HHS will take a strategic approach in order to minimize diversion and ensure evidence-based treatment.
- In conjunction with the Budget rollout, HHS also will release Medicaid guidance to States on best practices for addressing the

opioid epidemic focused on Medicaid pharmacy benefit management strategies to manage and monitor prescription opioid prescribing, cover medication-assisted treatment, and increase the use of the overdose reversal drug naloxone.

Enforcement and Supply Reduction

- The White House Office of National Drug Control Policy's High Intensity Drug Trafficking Areas program is funding an unprecedented network of public health and law enforcement partnerships to address the heroin threat across 15 states.
- DEA has deployed a 360 Strategy targeting the opioid epidemic through coordinated law enforcement operations, diversion control and partnerships with community organizations following enforcement operations.
- DOJ's enforcement efforts include targeting the illegal opioid supply chain, thwarting doctor-shopping attempts, and disrupting so-called "pill mills."
- DOJ has cracked down on those who use the Internet to illegally buy and sell controlled substances.
- DEA agents and investigators are integrating with other federal, state, and local law enforcement officers in 66 Tactical Diversion Squads stationed across 41 states, Puerto Rico, and the District of Columbia. Outcomes of this effort include the largest pharmaceutical-related takedown in the DEA's history in an operation that resulted in 280 arrests.
- Since 2007, through the Merida Initiative, the Department of State has been working with the Government of Mexico to help build the capacity of Mexico's law enforcement and justice sector institutions to disrupt drug trafficking organizations and to stop the flow of illicit drugs including heroin from Mexico to the United States.

Section 51.4

PEERx Prescription Drug Abuse Prevention Campaign

This section includes text excerpted from "Help Prevent Teen Prescription Drug Abuse," National Institute on Drug Abuse (NIDA), March 23, 2016.

Help Prevent Teen Prescription Drug Abuse

Prescription drug abuse among teens is a significant problem affecting communities nationwide. Results from NIDA's 2014 Monitoring the Future survey of teen drug use showed a number of worrying issues:

- Nonmedical use of prescription drugs remains high, while teens' perception of the risk of such abuse is low.
- 13.9% of high school seniors used a prescription drug for nonmedical reasons or one that was not prescribed for them in the past year.
- After alcohol, tobacco, and marijuana, prescription and over-the-counter medications account for most of the top drugs abused by 12th graders in the past year, with Adderall and Vicodin being the most commonly abused prescription drugs.

Prescription Drugs and the Brain

This class of drugs targets the central nervous system and includes medications used to treat pain (e.g., Vicodin, OxyContin), ADHD (e.g., Adderall), and anxiety and sleep disorders (e.g., Xanax, Valium). Taken as intended, prescription drugs safely treat specific mental or physical symptoms.

However, when taken in unmanaged doses or by someone without a prescription, these medications may affect the brain in ways similar to illegal drugs. Ritalin, for example, increases alertness, attention, and energy in a way similar to cocaine—by boosting the amount of the neurotransmitter dopamine released in the brain. Similarly, prescription opioid pain relievers such as OxyContin attach to the same cell receptors targeted by illegal opioids like heroin. When abused, these drugs can lead to a large increase in the amount of dopamine in the brain's reward pathway. Repeatedly seeking to experience that pleasurable feeling can lead to addiction. Abuse of opioids can also affect areas of the brain that control breathing, causing it to slow down significantly and potentially causing death (a fatal overdose). When abused, opioids can also cause drowsiness and constipation.

The Problem among Teens

Teens may abuse prescription painkillers like Vicodin or OxyContin for a number of reasons, such as to get "high" or to counter anxiety, pain, or sleep problems. Fueled by academic pressure, teens are also abusing stimulants such as Adderall and Ritalin—a.k.a. "study drugs"—with the intent to improve their concentration, energy, and focus. A dangerous misconception is that these drugs are safer to abuse than illegal drugs because they are prescribed by doctors. Another misconception is that they improve cognitive performance in people who don't actually have an attention disorder.

Help Teens Make Smart Decisions

In response to this serious public health issue, NIDA developed PEERx, an online educational campaign to discourage abuse of prescription drugs among teens. A component of the NIDA for Teens program, PEERx provides science-based resources—in an engaging format—for teens and teen leaders, counselors, and educators to encourage discussions about this important issue.

PEERx offers a variety of free resources, including the Choose Your Path interactive videos that allow teens to assume the role of the main character and make decisions about whether to abuse prescription drugs. After each scene, the viewer selects what the main character will do next and sees the results of each decision. Another resource, the PEERx Activity Guide, can be used to plan events in schools and communities. The partner toolkit and fact sheets about prescription drugs are other helpful resources to supplement your efforts.

Through the PEERx initiative, NIDA is reaching out to help stop prescription drug abuse among teens. "Prescription drug abuse is not new, but it does deserve continued vigilance," says NIDA Director Nora D. Volkow, M.D. "It is imperative that as a Nation we make ourselves aware of the consequences associated with the abuse of these medications."

Part Seven

Additional Help and Information

Chapter 52

Glossary of Terms Related to Drug Abuse

addiction: A chronic, relapsing disease, characterized by compulsive drug seeking and use accompanied by neurochemical and molecular changes in the brain.

agitation: A restless inability to keep still. Agitation is most often psychomotor agitation, that is, having emotional and physical components. Agitation can be caused by anxiety, overstimulation, or withdrawal from depressants and stimulants.

agonist: A chemical compound that mimics the action of a natural neurotransmitter and binds to the same receptor on nerve cells to produce a biological response.

amphetamine: A stimulant drug with effects similar to cocaine.

amyl nitrite: A yellowish oily volatile liquid used in certain diagnostic procedures and prescribed to some patients for heart pain. Illegally diverted ampules of amyl nitrite are called "poppers" or "snappers" on the street.

anabolic/androgenic steroids: Male hormones, principally testosterone, that are partially responsible for the tremendous developmental changes that occur during puberty and adolescence. Male hormones can accelerate growth of muscle, bone, and red blood cells; decrease body fat; enhance neural conduction (anabolic effects); and produce

---

This glossary contains terms excerpted from documents produced by several sources deemed reliable.

changes in primary and secondary sexual characteristics (androgenic effects).

anabolic effects: Drug-induced growth or thickening of the body's nonreproductive tract tissues—including skeletal muscle, bones, the larynx, and vocal cords—and a decrease in body fat.

analgesics: A group of medications that reduce pain.

analog: A chemical compound that is similar to another drug in its effects but differs slightly in its chemical structure

antagonist: A drug that binds to the same nerve cell receptor as the natural neurotransmitter but does not activate the receptor, instead blocking the effects of another drug.

barbiturate: A type of central nervous system (CNS) depressant often prescribed to promote sleep.

behavioral treatments: A set of treatments that focus on modifying thinking, motivation, coping mechanisms, and choices made by individuals.

benzodiazepine: A type of CNS depressant often prescribed to relieve anxiety. Valium® and Xanax® are among the most widely prescribed benzodiazepine medications.

blackout: A blackout is a period of amnesia or memory loss, typically caused by chronic, high-dose substance abuse. The person later cannot remember the blackout period. Blackouts are most often caused by sedative-hypnotics such as alcohol and the benzodiazepines.

brainstem: The lower portion of the brain. Major functions located in the brainstem include those necessary for survival, e.g., breathing, heart rate, blood pressure, and arousal.

buprenorphine: A partial opioid agonist for the treatment of opioid addiction that relieves drug cravings without producing the "high" or dangerous side effects of other opioids.

cannabinoid receptor: The receptor in the brain that recognizes and binds cannabinoids that are produced in the brain (anandamide) or outside the body (for example, THC and cannabidiol).

cannabinoids: Chemicals that bind to cannabinoid receptors in the brain. They are found naturally in the brain (anandamide) and are also chemicals found in marijuana (for example, THC and CBD).

cannabis: The botanical name for the plant that produces marijuana.

CD4+ T Cells: A type of cell involved in protecting against viral, fungal, and protozoal infections. These cells normally stimulate the immune response, signaling other cells in the immune system to perform their special functions.

CNS depressants: A class of drugs (also called sedatives and tranquilizers) that slow CNS function; some are used to treat anxiety and sleep disorders (includes barbiturates and benzodiazepines).

cocaine: A highly addictive stimulant drug derived from the coca plant that produces profound feelings of pleasure.

cognitive: Pertaining to the mind's capacity to understand concepts and ideas.

comorbidity: The occurrence of two disorders or illnesses in the same person, either at the same time (co-occurring comorbid conditions) or with a time difference between the initial occurrence of one and the initial occurrence of the other (sequentially comorbid conditions).

comprehensive continuous integrated system of care (CCISC): A theoretical method for bringing the mental health and substance abuse treatment systems (and other systems, potentially) into an integrated planning process to develop a comprehensive, integrated system of care.

concomitant treatment: Treatment of two or more mental or physical disorders at the same time.

constricted pupils (pinpoint pupils): Pupils that are temporarily narrowed or closed. This is usually a sign of opioid abuse.

convulsions: A symptom of a seizure, characterized by twitching and jerking of the limbs. A seizure is a sudden episode of uncontrolled electrical activity in the brain. If the abnormal electrical activity spreads throughout the brain, the result may be loss of consciousness and a grand mal-seizure

co-occurring disorders (COD): It refers to co-occurring substance use (abuse or dependence) and mental disorders. Clients said to have COD have one or more mental disorders as well as one or more disorders relating to the use of alcohol and/or other drugs.

counter transference: The feelings, reactions, biases, and images from the past that the clinician may project onto the client with COD.

crack: Slang term for a smokeable form of cocaine.

craving: A powerful, often uncontrollable desire for drugs.

culturally: competent treatment Biopsychosocial or other treatment that is adapted to suit the special cultural beliefs, practices, and needs of a client.

dependence: A physiological state that can occur with regular drug use and results in withdrawal symptoms when drug use is abruptly discontinued.

depression: A disorder marked by sadness, inactivity, difficulty with thinking and concentration, significant increase or decrease in appetite and time spent sleeping, feelings of dejection and hopelessness, and, sometimes, suicidal thoughts or an attempt to commit suicide.

detoxification: A process of allowing the body to rid itself of a drug while managing the symptoms of withdrawal; often the first step in a drug treatment program.

dopamine: A neurotransmitter present in regions of the brain that regulate movement, emotion, motivation, and the feeling of pleasure.

drug: A chemical compound or substance that can alter the structure and function of the body. Psychoactive drugs affect the function of the brain.

drugged driving: Driving a vehicle while impaired due to the lingering, intoxicating effects of recent drug use.

euphoria: A feeling of well-being or elation

fentanyl: A medically useful opioid analog that is 50 times more potent than heroin.

hallucinogens: A diverse group of drugs that alter perceptions, thoughts, and feelings. Hallucinogenic drugs include LSD, mescaline, PCP, and psilocybin (magic mushrooms).

hepatitis C virus (HCV): A virus that causes liver inflammation and disease. Hepatitis is a general term for liver damage and hepatitis C is the most common type of hepatitis found among those with HIV.

heroin: A synthetic opioid related to morphine. It is more potent than morphine and is highly addictive.

highly active antiretroviral therapy (HAART): A combination of three or more antiretroviral drugs used in the treatment of HIV infection and AIDS.

hormone: A chemical substance formed in glands in the body and carried by the blood to organs and tissues, where it influences function, structure, and behavior.

hyperthermia: A potentially dangerous rise in body temperature.

hypothalamus: A part of the brain that controls many bodily functions, including feeding, drinking, body temperature regulation, and the release of many hormones.

inhalant: Any drug administered by breathing in its vapors. Inhalants commonly are organic solvents, such as glue and paint thinner, or anesthetic gases, such as ether and nitrous oxide.

injection drug use (IDU): Act of administering drugs directly into a vein using a hypodermic needle and syringe. Injection drug users (IDUs) are individuals that abuse drugs in this way.

lysergic acid diethylamide (LSD): A hallucinogenic drug that acts on the serotonin receptor.

major depressive disorder: A mood disorder having a clinical course of one or more serious depression episodes that last 2 or more weeks. Episodes are characterized by a loss of interest or pleasure in almost all activities; disturbances in appetite, sleep, or psychomotor functioning; a decrease in energy; difficulties in thinking or making decisions; loss of self-esteem or feelings of guilt; and suicidal thoughts or attempts.

mania: A mood disorder characterized by abnormally and persistently elevated, expansive, or irritable mood; mental and physical hyperactivity; and/or disorganization of behavior.

marijuana: A drug, usually smoked but can be eaten, that is made from the leaves of the cannabis plant. The main psychoactive ingredient is THC.

medication: A drug that is used to treat an illness or disease according to established medical guidelines. If the medication contains one or more controlled substances, it must be prescribed by a licensed physician.

methadone: A long-acting opioid agonist medication shown to be effective in treating heroin addiction.

methamphetamine: An addictive, potent stimulant drug that is part of the larger class of amphetamines.

methylphenidate (Ritalin®/Concerta®): A CNS stimulant that has effects similar to, but more potent than, caffeine and less potent than amphetamines. It has a notably calming and "focusing" effect on patients with ADHD, particularly children.

motivational enhancement therapy (MET): A systematic form of intervention designed to produce rapid, internally motivated change.

MET does not attempt to treat the person, but rather mobilize his or her own internal resources for change and engagement in treatment.

naloxone: An opioid receptor antagonist that rapidly binds to opioid receptors, blocking heroin from activating them.

naltrexone: An opioid antagonist medication that can only be used after a patient has completed detoxification. Naltrexone is not addictive or sedating and does not result in physical dependence; however, poor patient compliance has limited its effectiveness.

neonatal abstinence syndrome (NAS): NAS occurs when heroin from the mother passes through the placenta into the baby's bloodstream during pregnancy, allowing the baby to become addicted along with the mother. NAS requires hospitalization and treatment with medication (often a morphine taper) to relieve symptoms until the baby adjusts to becoming opioid-free.

neuron (nerve cell): A unique type of cell found in the brain and throughout the body that specializes in the transmission and processing of information.

neurotransmitter: A chemical that acts as a messenger to carry signals or information from one nerve cell to another.

nicotine: The addictive drug in tobacco. Nicotine activates a specific type of acetylcholine receptor.

nitrites: A special class of inhalants that act primarily to dilate blood vessels and relax the muscles. Whereas other inhalants are used to alter mood, nitrites are used primarily as sexual enhancers.

noradrenaline: A neurotransmitter that is made in the brain and influences, among other things, the function of the heart.

norepinephrine: A neurotransmitter present in regions of the brain that affect heart rate and blood pressure.

opioid: A natural or synthetic psychoactive chemical that binds to opioid receptors in the brain and body.

opioid use disorder: A problematic pattern of opioid drug use, leading to clinically significant impairment or distress that includes cognitive, behavioral, and physiological symptoms as defined by the new Diagnostic and Statistical Manual of Mental Disorders, 5th edition (DSM-V) criteria.

partial agonist: A substance that binds to and activates the same nerve cell receptor as a natural neurotransmitter but produces a diminished biological response.

physical dependence: An adaptive physiological state that occurs with regular drug use and results in a withdrawal syndrome when drug use is stopped; usually occurs with tolerance.

placebo: An inactive substance (pill, liquid, etc.), which is administered to a comparison group, as if it were therapy, but which has no therapeutic value other than to serve as a negative control.

polydrug abuse: The abuse of two or more drugs at the same time, such as CNS depressants and alcohol.

posttraumatic stress disorder (PTSD): A disorder that develops after exposure to a highly stressful event (e.g., wartime combat, physical violence, or natural disaster). Symptoms include sleeping difficulties, hypervigilance, avoiding reminders of the event, and re-experiencing the trauma through flashbacks or recurrent nightmares.

prescription drug abuse: The use of a medication without a prescription; in a way other than as prescribed; or for the experience or feeling elicited.

propofol: A common type of anesthetic used for surgery.

psychedelic drug: A drug that distorts perception, thought, and feeling. This term is typically used to refer to drugs with actions like those of LSD.

psychoactive: Having a specific effect on the brain.

psychosis: A mental disorder (e.g., schizophrenia) characterized by delusional or disordered thinking detached from reality; symptoms often include hallucinations.

psychotherapeutics: Drugs that have an effect on the function of the brain and that often are used to treat psychiatric/neurologic disorders; includes opioids, CNS depressants, and stimulants.

relapse: In drug abuse, relapse is the resumption of drug use after trying to stop taking drugs. Relapse is a common occurrence in many chronic disorders, including addiction, that require behavioral adjustments to treat effectively.

route of administration: The way a drug is put into the body. Drugs can enter the body by eating, drinking, inhaling, injecting, snorting, smoking, or absorbing a drug through mucous membranes.

rush: A surge of euphoric pleasure that rapidly follows administration of a drug.

salvia: An herb in the mint family native to southern Mexico that is used to produce hallucinogenic experiences.

schizophrenia: A psychotic disorder characterized by symptoms that fall into two categories: (1) positive symptoms, such as distortions in thoughts (delusions), perception (hallucinations), and language and thinking and (2) negative symptoms, such as flattened emotional responses and decreased goal-directed behavior.

sedatives: Drugs that suppress anxiety and promote sleep; the NSDUH classification includes benzodiazepines, barbiturates, and other types of CNS depressants.

self-medication: The use of a substance to lessen the negative effects of stress, anxiety, or other mental disorders (or side effects of their pharmacotherapy). Self-medication may lead to addiction and other drug- or alcohol-related problems.

serotonin: A neurotransmitter used in widespread parts of the brain, which is involved in sleep, movement and emotions

Spice/K2: Dried plant material containing synthetic (or designer) cannabinoid compounds that produce mind-altering effects as well as other compounds that vary from product to product.

stimulants: A class of drugs that elevates mood, increases feelings of well-being, and increases energy and alertness. These drugs produce euphoria and are powerfully rewarding. Stimulants include cocaine, methamphetamine, and methylphenidate (Ritalin).

tetrahydrocannabinol (THC): Delta-9-tetrahydrocannabinol; the main psychoactive ingredient in marijuana, which acts on the brain to produce marijuana's psychoactive effects.

tobacco: A plant widely cultivated for its leaves, which are used primarily for smoking; the tabacum species is the major source of tobacco products.

withdrawal: A variety of symptoms that occur after use of an addictive drug is reduced or stopped.

Chapter 53

Glossary of Street Terms for Drugs of Abuse

Abyssinian Tea: Khat

Acid: LSD

Adam: Ecstasy (MDMA)

African Salad: Khat

Ah-pen-yen: Opium

Amidone: Methadone

Angel Dust: PCP

Aunti Emma: Opium

Aunti: Opium

Barbs: Barbiturates

barbs: Depressants

Beans: Ecstasy (MDMA)

Beautiful: 2,5-Dimethoxy-4-(n)-propylthiophenethylamine

Bennies: Amphetamines

Benzos: Benzodiazepines

Big H: Narcotics

Big O: Opium

Black Beauties: Amphetamines

Black Beauties: Stimulants

Black Mamba: K2/"Spice"

Black Pill: Opium

Black Tar: Heroin

Black Tat: Narcotics

Block Busters: Barbiturates

Blotter Acid: LSD

Blue: Morphine

Blue Mystic: 2,5-Dimethoxy-4-(n)-propylthiophenethylamine

Blunts: Marijuana

This glossary contains terms excerpted from documents produced by several sources deemed reliable.

Boat: PCP

Bold: Inhalants

Bombay Blue: K2/"Spice"

Boom: Marijuana

Bromo: 4-Bromo-2,5-dimethoxyphenethylamine

Brown Sugar: Narcotics

Bud: Marijuana

Buttons: Peyote and mescaline

Cactus: Peyote and mescaline

candy: Depressants

Cat Tranquilizer: Ketamine

Cat Valium: Ketamine

Catha: Khat

CCC: Dextromethorphan

Chalk: Methamphetamine

Chandoo: Opium

Chandu: Opium

Chat: Khat

Chinese Molasses: Opium

Chinese Tobacco: Opium

Chocolate Chip Cookies: Methadone

Christmas Trees: Barbiturates

Chronic: Marijuana

Circles: Rohypnol

Clarity: Ecstasy (MDMA)

Cloud Nine: Bath salts (synthetic cathinones)

Coca: Cocaine

Coke: Cocaine

Crack: Cocaine

Crank: Amphetamines or methamphetamine

Crystal: Phencyclidine (PCP)

D: Hydromorphone

Dex: Dextromethorphan

Dillies: Hydromorphone

Dopium: Opium

Dots: LSD

Dover's Powder: Opium

Downers: Depressants

Dream Gun: Opium

Dream Stick: Opium

Dreamer: Morphine

Dreams: Opium

Drone: Bath salts (synthetic cathinones)

Dust: Hydromorphone

DXM: Dextromethorphan

E: Ecstasy (MDMA)

Easing Powder: Opium

Easy Lay: Gamma-hydroxybutyric acid (GHB)

Embalming Fluid: PCP

Emsel: Morphine

Fake Weed: K2/"Spice"

Fi-do-nie: Opium

First Line: Morphine

Fizzies: Methadone

Flake: Cocaine

Footballs: Hydromorphone

Forget Pill: Rohypnol

Forget-Me-Pill: Rohypnol

Foxy: 5-methoxy-N,N-diisopropyl-tryptamine

Foxy methoxy: 5-methoxy-N,N-diisopropyltrypt-amine

G: Gamma-hydroxybutyric acid (GHB)

Gangster: Marijuana

Ganja: Marijuana

Gee: Opium

Genie: K2/"Spice"

Georgia Home Boy: Gamma-hydroxybutyric acid (GHB)

GHB: Gamma-hydroxybutyric acid

Glass: Methamphetamine

God's Drug: Morphine

God's Medicine: Opium

Go-Fast: Methamphetamine

Gondola: Opium

Goof Balls: Barbiturates

Goop: Gamma-hydroxybutyric acid (GHB)

Goric: Opium

Grass: Marijuana

Great Tobacco: Opium

Grievous Bodily Harm: Gamma-hydroxybutyric acid (GHB)

Guma: Opium

Hash: Marijuana

Hashish: Cannabis

Herb: Marijuana

Hillbilly Heroin: Narcotics

Hop/hops: Opium

Horse: Heroin

Hows: Morphine

i: 4-Iodo-2,5-dimethoxyphenethylamine

Ice: Amphetamines or methamphetamine

Jet K: Ketamine

Joint: Marijuana

Joy Plant: Opium

Juice: Hydromorphone or steroids

Junk: Narcotics

Kat: Khat

Kicker: Oxycodone

Kif: Marijuana

Kit Kat: Ketamine

La Rocha: Rohypnol

laughing gas: Inhalants

lean: Narcotics

Liquid Ecstasy: Gamma-hydroxybutyric acid (GHB)

Liquid X: Gamma-hydroxybutyric acid (GHB)

Lover's Speed: Ecstasy (MDMA)

Lunch Money Drug: Rohypnol

M.S.: Morphine

Magic Mushrooms: Psilocybin

Maria Pastora: *Salvia divinorum*

Maria: Methadone

Mary Jane: Marijuana

MDMA: Ecstasy

Mellow Yellow: LSD

Meow Meow: Bath salts (synthetic cathinones)

Mesc: Peyote and mescaline

Meth: Methamphetamine

Mexican Valium: Rohypnol

MPTP (New Heroin): Narcotics

Midnight Oil: Opium

Mira: Opium

Mister Blue: Morphine

Morf: Morphine

Morpho: Morphine

Mud: Narcotics

Mushrooms: Psilocybin

O: Opium

Oat: Khat

OC: Oxycodone

O.P.: Opium

Ope: Opium

Ox: Oxycodone

Oxy: Oxycodone

Oxycotton: Narcotics

Pastora: Methadone

Pen Yan: Opium

Perc: Oxycodone

Peyoto: Peyote and mescaline

phennies: Depressants

Pin Gon: Opium

Pingus: Rohypnol

Pinks: Barbiturates

Poor Man's PCP: Dextromethorphan

poppers: Inhalants

Pot: Marijuana

Pox: Opium

Purple: Ketamine

R2: Rohypnol

red birds: Depressants

Red Devils: Barbiturates

reds: Depressants

Reds & Blues: Barbiturates

Reefer: Marijuana

Reynolds: Rohypnol

Roach: Rohypnol

Roach 2: Rohypnol

Roaches: Rohypnol

Roachies: Rohypnol

Roapies: Rohypnol

Robo: Dextromethorphan

Robutal: Rohypnol

Rochas Dos: Rohypnol

Rocket Fuel: PCP

Roids: Steroids

Rojo: Dextromethorphan

Roofies: Rohypnol

Rophies: Rohypnol

Ropies: Rohypnol

Roples: Rohypnol

Row-Shay: Rohypnol

Roxy: Oxycodone

Ruffies: Rohypnol

Rush: Inhalants

Sally-D: *Salvia divinorum*

Scoop: Gamma-hydroxybutyric acid (GHB)

Shermans: PCP

Shrooms: Psilocybin

Sinsemilla: Marijuana

Sippin Syrup: Narcotics

Ska: Heroin

Skee: Opium

Skittles: Dextromethorphan

Skunk: Marijuana

Smack: Heroin or hydromorphone

Snow: Cocaine

Special K: Ketamine

Special La Coke: Ketamine

Spectrum: 4-Bromo-2,5-dimethoxyphenethylamine

Speed: Amphetamines or methamphetamine

Spice: K2

Street Methadone: Methadone

Super Acid: Ketamine

Super K: Ketamine

Supergrass: PCP

Tic Tac: PCP

Tina: Methamphetamine

tooies: Depressants

Toonies: 4-Bromo-2,5-dimethoxyphenethylamine

Toxy: Opium

Toys: Opium

Triple C: Dextromethorphan

Tripstay: 2,5-Dimethoxy-4-(n)-propylthiophenethylamine

Tweety-Bird Mescaline: 2,5-Dimethoxy-4-(n)-propylthiophenethylamine

2C-B, Nexus: 4-Bromo-2,5-dimethoxyphenethylamine

2C-I : 4-Iodo-2,5-dimethoxyphenethylamine

2C-T-7: 2,5-Dimethoxy-4-(n)-propylthiophenethylamine

2's: 4-Bromo-2,5-dimethoxyphenethylamine

T7: 2,5-Dimethoxy-4-(n)-propylthiophenethylamine

Unkie: Morphine

Uppers: Amphetamines

Vanilla Sky: Bath salts (synthetic cathinones)

Velvet: Dextromethorphan

Venus: 4-Bromo-2,5-dimethoxyphenethylamine

Vitamin K: Ketamine

Wafer: Methadone

Weed: Marijuana

When-shee: Opium

Whippets: Inhalants

White Lightning: Bath salts (synthetic cathinones)

Window Pane: LSD

Wolfies: Rohypnol

Yellow Jackets: Barbiturates

yellows: Depressants

Ze: Opium

Zero: Opium

Zohai: K2/"Spice"

Zoom: PCP

Chapter 54

Directory of State Substance Abuse Agencies

Alabama
Division of Mental Health and Substance Abuse Services
Alabama Department of Mental Health
P.O. Box 301410
Montgomery, AL 36130-1410
Fax: 334-242-0725
Website: www.mh.alabama.gov/sa
E-mail: Alabama.DMH@mh.alabama.gov

Alaska
Division of Behavioral Health
Alaska Department of Health and Social Services
P.O. Box 110620
Juneau, AK 99811-0620
Toll-Free: 877-266-4357 (Hotline)
Phone: 907-465-5808
Fax: 907-465-2185
Website: dhss.alaska.gov/dbh/Pages/default.aspx
E-mail: randall.burns@alaska.gov

Information in this chapter was compiled from various sources deemed reliable. All contact information was verified and updated in April 2016.

Arizona
Behavioral Health Services
Arizona Department of Health Services
801 E Jefferson St.
Phoenix, AZ 85034
Phone: 602-364-4558
Fax: 602-364-4570
Website: www.azdhs.gov
E-mail: DCW@azahcccs.gov

Arkansas
Division of Behavioral Health Services
Arkansas Department of Human Services
305 S. Palm St.
Little Rock, AR 72205
Phone: 501-686-9164
TDD: 501-686-9176
Fax: 501-686-9182
Website: humanservices.arkansas.gov/dbhs/Pages/default.aspx
E-mail: tommie.waters@arkansas.gov

Colorado
Office of Behavioral Health
Department of Human Services
3824 W. Princeton Cir.
Denver, CO 80236-3111
Phone: 303-866-7400
Fax: 303-866-7428
Website: www.colorado.gov/cs/Satellite/CDHS-BehavioralHealth/CBON/1251578892077
E-mail: cdhs.communications@state.co.us

Connecticut
Department of Mental Health and Addiction Services
P.O. Box 341431
Hartford, CT 06134
Toll-Free: 800-446-7348
Phone: 860-418-7000
TDD: 860-418-6707
Website: www.ct.gov/dmhas

Delaware
Division of Substance Abuse and Mental Health
Community Mental Health and Addiction Services
1901 N. DuPont Hwy
New Castle, DE 19720
Toll-Free: 800-652-2929 (Helpline—Delaware Only)
Phone: 302-255-9399
Fax: 302-255-4427
Website: www.dhss.delaware.gov/dsamh/index.html
E-mail: DHSS@state.de.u

District of Columbia
Department of Health
Addiction Prevention and Recovery Administration (APRA)
70 N St. N.E.
Washington, DC 20002
Phone: 202-727-8857
Fax: 202-727-0092
Website: dbh.dc.gov/page/apra
E-mail: doh@dc.gov

Florida
Substance Abuse Program Office
Florida Department of Children and Families
1317 Winewood Blvd.
Bldg. 6, Rm. 334
Tallahassee, FL 32399-0700
Phone: 850-487-2920
Fax: 850-414-7474
Website: www.myflfamilies.com/service-programs/substance-abuse
E-mail: Jayme.Carter@myflfamilies.com

Georgia
Division of Addictive Diseases
Department of Behavioral Health and Developmental Disabilities
Two Peachtree St. N.W.
24th Fl.
Atlanta, GA 30303-3171
Toll-Free: 800-715-4225 (Hotline)
Phone: 404-657-2331
Fax: 404-657-2256
Website: dbhdd.georgia.gov/addictive-diseases
E-mail: David@dbhdd.ga.gov

Hawaii
Alcohol and Drug Abuse Division
Hawaii Department of Health
601 Kamokila Blvd.
Rm. 360
Kapolei, HI 96707
Phone: 808-692-7506
Fax: 808-692-7521
Website: health.hawaii.gov/substance-abuse
E-mail: webmail@hawaii.gov

Idaho
Division of Behavioral Health
Department of Health and Welfare
P.O. Box 83720
Boise, ID 83720-0036
Toll-Free: 800-922-3406 (Screening/Referral)
Phone: 208-334-6997
Website: www.healthandwelfare.idaho.gov
E-mail: DPHInquiries@dhw.idaho.govQ

Illinois
Division of Alcoholism and Addiction
Department of Human Services
100 W. Randolph
Ste. 5-600, Chicago, IL 60601
Toll-Free:800-843-6154 (Help Line)
Phone: 312-814-3840
Toll-Free TTY:800-447-6404 (Help Line)
Fax: 312-814-2419
Website: www.dhs.state.il.us/page.aspx?item=29725
E-mail: DHSWebBits@illinois.gov

Indiana
Division of Mental Health and Addiction
Family and Social Services Administration
P.O. Box 7083
Indianapolis, IN 46207-7083
Toll-Free: 800-901-1133
Phone: 317-233-4454
Fax: 317-233-4693
Website: www.in.gov/fssa/dmha/index.htm
E-mail: pla8@pla.in.gov

Iowa
Division of Behavioral Health
Department of Public Health
Lucas State Office Building
321 E. 12th St.
Des Moines, IA 50319-0075
Toll-Free: 866-227-9878
Phone: 515-281-4417
Fax: 515-281-4535
Website: www.idph.iowa.gov
E-mail: PLPublic@idph.iowa.gov

Kansas
Community Services and Programs
Department for Aging and Disability Services New England State Office Building
503 S. Kansas Ave.
Topeka, KS 66603-3404
Phone: 785-296-4986
Fax: 785-296-0557
Website: www.dcf.ks.gov/Pages/Default.aspx
E-mail: Amy.Neuman@dcf.ks.gov

Kentucky
Cabinet for Health and Family Services
Department for Behavioral Health, Developmental, and Intellectual Disabilities
100 Fair Oaks Ln., 4E-B
Frankfort, KY 40621
Phone: 502-564-4527
TTY: 502-564-5777
Fax: 502-564-5478
Website: chfs.ky.gov/dbhdid
E-mail: Sherry.Carnahan@ky.gov

Louisiana
Office of Behavioral Health
Department of Health and Hospitals
P.O. Box 629
Baton Rouge, LA 70821-0629
Phone: 225-342-9500
Fax: 225-342-5568
Website: www.dhh.louisiana.gov/index.cfm/subhome/10/n/6
E-mail: gary.balsamo@la.gov

Maine
Substance Abuse and Mental Health Services
Department of Health and Human Services
41 Anthony Ave.
#11 State House Stn
Augusta, ME 04333-0011
Phone: 207-287-2595
Fax: 207-287-4334
Website: www.maine.gov/dhhs/samhs/osa
E-mail: osa.ircosa@maine.gov

Maryland
Alcohol and Drug Abuse Administration
Department of Health and Mental Hygiene Spring Grove Hospital Center Vocational Rehabilitation Building
55 Wade Ave.
Rm. 216
Catonsville, MD 21228
Phone: 410-402-8600
Fax: 410-402-8601
Website: dhmh.maryland.gov
E-mail: DHMH.ADAA_info@maryland.gov

Massachusetts
Bureau of Substance Abuse Services
Health and Human Services
250 Washington St.
Boston, MA 02108-4609
Toll-Free: 800-327-5050 (Helpline)
Phone: 617-624-5171
Toll-Free TTY: 888-448-8321 (Helpline)
Fax: 617-624-5395
Website: www.mass.gov/dph/bsas
E-mail: DLSfeedback@state.ma.us

Michigan
Office of Recovery Oriented Systems of Care
Department of Community Health
320 S. Walnut St.
Lansing, MI 48913
Phone: 517-373-4700
TTY/TTD: 517-373-3573
Fax: 517-335-2121
Website: www.michigan.gov/mdhhs
E-mail: MDCH-BSAAS@michigan.gov

Minnesota
Alcohol and Drug Abuse Division
Department of Human Services
P.O. Box 64977
Saint Paul, MN 55164-0977
Phone: 651-431-2460
Toll-Free TTY/TDD: 800-627-3529
Fax: 651-431-7449
Website: mn.gov/dhs
E-mail: dhs.adad@state.mn.us

Mississippi
Bureau of Alcohol and Drug Services
Mississippi Department of Mental Health
1101 Robert E. Lee Bldg.
239 N. Lamar St.
Jackson, MS 39201
Toll-Free: 877-210-8513 (Helpline)
Phone: 601-359-1288
TDD: 601-359-6230
Fax: 601-359-6295
Website: www.dmh.ms.gov/alcohol-and-drug-services
E-mail: kimela.smith@dmh.state.ms.us

Missouri
Division of Behavioral Health
Missouri Department of Mental Health
P.O. Box 687
Jefferson City, MO 65102
Toll-Free: 800-575-7480
Phone: 573-751-4942
Fax: 573-751-7814
Website: www.dmh.mo.gov/ada
E-mail: dbhmail@dmh.mo.gov

Montana
Addictive and Mental Disorders Division
Department of Public Health and Human Services
P.O. Box 202905
Helena, MT 59620-2905
Phone: 406-444-3964
Fax: 406-444-9389
Website: www.dphhs.mt.gov/amdd
E-mail: hhsamdemail@mt.gov

Nebraska
Division of Behavioral Health
Department of Health and Human Services
P.O. Box 95026
Lincoln, NE 68509-5026
Toll-Free: 888-866-8660 (Helpline)
Phone: 402-471-8553
Fax: 402-471-9449
Website: www.dhhs.ne.gov/Behavioral_Health
E-mail: DHHS.BehavioralHealthDivision@Nebraska.Gov

Nevada
Substance Abuse Prevention and Treatment Agency
Department of Health and Human Services
4126 Technology Way
2nd Fl.
Carson City, NV 89706
Phone: 775-684-4190
Fax: 775-684-4185
Website: www.hhs.gov/asl
E-mail: MHDS@mhds.nv.gov

New Hampshire
Bureau of Drug and Alcohol Services
Department of Health and Human Services
105 Pleasant St.
Concord, NH 03301
Toll-Free: 800-804-0909
Phone: 603-271-6738
Fax: 603-271-6105
Website: www.dhhs.nh.gov/dcbcs/bdas/index.htm

New Jersey
Division of Addiction Services
Department of Human Services
222 S. Warren St.
Trenton, NJ 08625
Toll-Free: 800-238-2333 (Hotline)
Phone: 609-292-5760
Fax: 609-292-3816
Website: www.state.nj.us/humanservices/das/home
E-mail: dmhas@dhs.state.nj.us

New Mexico
Behavioral Health Services Division
Human Services Department
P.O. Box 2348
Santa Fe, NM 87504
Toll-Free: 800-362-2013
Phone: 505-476-9266
Fax: 505-476-9277
Website: www.hsd.state.nm.us/bhsd
E-mail: kylerb.nerison@state.nm.us

New York
New York State Office of Alcoholism and Substance Abuse Services
1450 Western Ave.
Albany, NY 12203-3526
Toll-Free: 877-846-7369 (Hotline)
Phone: 518-473-3460
Fax: 518-457-5474
Website: www.oasas.ny.gov
E-mail: communications@oasas.ny.gov

North Carolina

Department of Health and Human Services
Division of Mental Health, Developmental Disabilities, and Substance Abuse Services
2001 Mail Service Center
Raleigh, NC 27699-2001
Toll-Free: 800-662-7030
Phone: 919-733-4670
Fax: 919-733-4556
Website: www.dhhs.state.nc.us/mhddsas
E-mail: david.aaron@dhhs.nc.gov

North Dakota

Division of Mental Health and Substance Abuse Services
Department of Human Services
Prairie Hills Plaza 1237 W. Divide Ave., Ste. 1C
Bismarck, ND 58501-1208
Toll-Free: 800-755-2719 (North Dakota only)
Phone: 701-328-8920
Fax: 701-328-8969
Website: www.nd.gov/dhs/services/mentalhealth
E-mail: dhsmhsas@nd.gov

Ohio

Ohio Department of Mental Health and Addiction Services
30 E. BRd. St.
36th Fl.
Columbus, OH 43215-3430
Toll-Free: 877-275-6364
TTY: 614-752-9696
Toll-Free TTY: 888-636-4889
Fax: 614-752-9453
Website: mha.ohio.gov
E-mail: askODMH@mh.ohio.gov

Oklahoma

Oklahoma Department of Mental Health and Substance Abuse Services
P.O. Box 53277
Oklahoma City, OK 73152-3277
Toll-Free: 800-522-9054
Phone: 405-522-3908
TDD: 405-522-3851
Fax: 405-522-3650
Website: ok.gov/odmhsas
E-mail: Kendale.Williams@bbhl.ok.gov

Oregon

Addictions and Mental Health Division
Oregon Health Authority
500 Summer St. N.E.
Salem, OR 97301-1079
Phone: 503-945-5763
Toll-Free TTY: 800-375-2863
Fax: 503-378-8467
Website: www.oregon.gov/oha/amh/Pages/index.aspx
E-mail: Amh.web@state.or.us

Pennsylvania

Department of Drug and Alcohol Programs
Pennsylvania Department of Health
02 Kline Plaza
Ste. B
Harrisburg, PA 17104-1579
Phone: 717-783-8200
Fax: 717-787-6285
Website: www.health.state.pa.us/bdap
E-mail: ancatalano@pa.gov

Rhode Island
Department of Behavioral Healthcare
Developmental Disabilities and Hospitals
Barry Hall Bldg. 14 Harrington Rd.
Cranston, RI 02920
Phone: 401-462-2339
Fax: 401-462-3204
Website: www.bhddh.ri.gov
E-mail: linda.reilly@bhddh.ri.gov

South Carolina
Department of Alcohol and Other Drug Abuse Services
P.O. Box 8268
Columbia, SC, 29202
Phone: 803-896-5555
Fax: 803-896-5557
Website: www.daodas.org

South Dakota
Division of Community Behavioral Health
Department of Social Services
c/o 700 Governor's Dr.
Pierre, SD 57501
Toll-Free: 800-265-9684
Phone: 605-773-3123
Fax: 605-773-7076
Website: dss.sd.gov/behavioralhealth
E-mail: infoMH@state.sd.us

Tennessee
Division of Substance Abuse Services
Department of Mental Health and Substance Abuse Services
601 Mainstream Dr.
Nashville, TN 37243
Toll-Free: 800-560-5767
Phone: 615-532-6500
Website: www.tn.gov/mental
E-mail: OC.TDMHSAS@tn.gov

Texas
Mental Health and Substance Abuse Division
Department of State Health Services
P.O. Box 149347
Austin, TX 78714-9347
Toll-Free: 866-378-8440
Phone: 512-206-5000
Fax: 512-206-5714
Website: www.dshs.state.tx.us/MHSA
E-mail: contact@dshs.state.tx.us

Utah
Division of Substance Abuse and Mental Health
Utah Department of Human Services
195 N. 1950 W.
2nd Fl.
Salt Lake City, UT 84116
Phone: 801-538-3939
Fax: 801-538-9892
Website: www.dsamh.utah.gov
E-mail: dsamhwebmaster@utah.gov

Vermont
Division of Alcohol and Drug Abuse Programs
Department of Health
P.O. Box 70, Drawer 27
Burlington, VT 05402-0070
Phone: 802-651-1550
Fax: 802-651-1573
Website: healthvermont.gov/adap/adap.aspx
E-mail: AHS.VDHADAP@state.vt.us

Virginia
Office of Substance Abuse Services
Department of Behavioral Health and Developmental Services
P.O. Box 1797
Richmond, VA 23218-1797
Phone: 804-786-3906
TDD: 804-371-8977
Fax: 804-786-9248
Website: www.dbhds.virginia.gov
E-mail: OIG@oig.sc.gov

Washington
Division of Behavioral Health and Recovery Services
Department of Social and Health Services
P.O. Box 45330
Olympia, WA 98504-5330
Toll-Free: 877-301-4557
TTY: 206-461-3219 (Help Line)
Toll-Free TTY: 800-833-6384
Fax: 360-586-0341
Website: www.dshs.wa.gov/bha
E-mail: DASAInformation@dshs.wa.gov

West Virginia
Division of Alcoholism and Drug Abuse
Bureau for Behavioral Health and Health Facilities
350 Capitol St., Rm. 350
Charleston, WV 25304
Phone: 304-356-4811
Fax: 304-558-1008
Website: www.dhhr.wv.gov/bhhf/Sections/programs/ProgramsPartnerships/AlcoholismandDrugAbuse/Pages/default.aspx
E-mail: DHHRSecretary@wv.gov

Wisconsin
Department of Health Services
Bureau of Prevention, Treatment, and Recovery
P.O. Box 7851
Madison, WI 53707-7851
Phone: 608-266-2717
Fax: 608-266-1533
Website: www.dhs.wisconsin.gov/aoda/index.htm
E-mail: DHSWEBMAILDMHSAS@dhs.wisconsin.gov

Wyoming
Behavioral Health Division
Mental Health and Substance Abuse Services Department of Health
6101 Yellowstone Rd., Ste. 220
Cheyenne, WY 82002
Toll-Free: 800-535-4006
Phone: 307-777-6494
Fax: 307-777-5849
Website: www.health.wyo.gov/mhsa
E-mail: wdh@state.wy.us

Chapter 55

Directory of Organizations Providing Information about Drug Abuse

Government Organizations

Centers for Disease Control and Prevention (CDC)
1600 Clifton Rd.
Atlanta, GA 30333
Toll-Free: 800-CDC-INFO (800-232-4636)
Website: www.cdc.gov
E-mail: cdcinfo@cdc.gov

Drug Enforcement Administration (DEA) Office of Diversion Control
8701 Morrissette Dr.
Springfield, VA 22152
Toll-Free: 800-882-9539
Website: deadiversion.usdoj.gov
E-mail: DEA.Registration.Help@usdoj.gov

National Criminal Justice Reference Service (NCJRS)
P.O. Box 6000
Rockville, MD 20849-6000
Toll-Free: 800-851-3420
Phone: 301-519-5500
TTY: 301-947-8374
Fax: 301-519-5212
Website: www.ncjrs.gov
E-mail: askojp@ncjrs.gov

National Institute on Alcohol Abuse and Alcoholism (NIAAA)
Toll-Free: 888-MY-NIAAA (888-696-4222)
Website: www.niaaa.nih.gov
E-mail: niaaaweb-r@exchange.nih.gov

Information in this chapter was compiled from various sources deemed reliable. All contact information was verified and updated in April 2016.

National Institute on Drug Abuse (NIDA)
6001 Executive Blvd.
Rm. 5213, MSC 9561
Bethesda, MD 20892-9561
Website: www.drugabuse.gov
E-mail: media@nida.nih.gov

New York State Office of Alcoholism and Substance Abuse Services (OASAS)
1450 Western Ave.
Albany, NY 12203-3526
Phone: 518-473-3460
Website: www.oasas.ny.gov
E-mail: communications@oasas.ny.gov

Office of Juvenile Justice and Delingquency Prevention (OJJDP)
810 Seventh St. N.W.
Washington, DC 20531
Toll-Free: 800-638-8736

Office of National Drug Control Policy (ONDCP)
Website: www.whitehouse.gov/ondcp

Substance Abuse and Mental Health Services Administration (SAMHSA)
P.O. Box 2345
Rockville, MD 20847-2345
Phone: 877-SAMHSA-7 (877-726-4727)
Fax: 240-221-4292
Website: www.samhsa.gov
E-mail: SAMHSAInfo@samhsa.hhs.gov

U.S. Department of Education
550 12th St. S.W.
10th Fl.
Washington, DC 20202-6450
Fax: 202-485-0013
Website: www2.ed.gov/about/offices/list/oese/oshs/index.html
E-mail: OESE@ed.gov

U.S. Department of Labor
200 Constitution Ave., N.W.
Washington, DC 20210
Toll Free:1-866-487-2365
Email: webmaster@dol.gov
Website: webapps.dol.gov/elaws/drugfree.htm

Private Organizations

American Society of Addiction Medicine
4601 N. Park Ave.
Upper Arcade, Ste. 101
Chevy Chase, MD 20815-4520
Phone: 301-656-3920
Fax: 301-656-3815
Website: www.asam.org
E-mail: email@asam.org

Co-Anon Family Groups World Services
P.O. Box 12722
Tucson, AZ 85732-2722
Toll-Free: 800-898-9985
Phone: 520-513-5028
Website: www.co-anon.org
E-mail: info@co-anon.org

Cocaine Anonymous World Services
P.O. Box 492000
Los Angeles, CA 90049-8000
Phone: 310-559-5833
Fax: 310-559-2554
Website: www.ca.org
E-mail: cawso@ca.org

Community Anti-Drug Coalitions of America
625 Slaters Ln., Ste. 300
Alexandria, VA 22314
Toll-Free: 800-542-2322
Phone: 703-706-0560
Fax: 703-783-0318
Website: www.cadca.org
E-mail: jjoisten@cadca.org

Narconon International
Phone: 800-775-8750
Website: www.narconon.org
E-mail: info@
narcononarrowhead.org

Narcotics Anonymous
P.O. Box 9999
Van Nuys, CA 91409
Phone: 818-773-9999
Fax: 818-700-0700
Website: www.na.org
E-mail: fsmail@na.org

National Center on Addiction and Substance Abuse at Columbia University
633 Third Ave., 19th Fl.
New York, NY 10017-6706
Phone: 212-841-5200
Website: www.casacolumbia.org
E-mail: KKeneipp@
casacolumbia.org

National Council on Alcoholism and Drug Dependence, Inc. (NCADD)
217 Broadway
Ste. 712
New York, NY 10007
Toll-Free Hope Line: 800-NCA-CALL (800-622-2255)
Phone: 212-269-7797
Fax: 212-269-7510
Website: www.ncadd.org
E-mail: national@ncadd.org

National Families in Action
P.O. Box 133136
Atlanta, GA 30333-3136
Phone: 404-248-9676
Website: www.nationalfamilies.
org
E-mail: nfia@nationalfamilies.org

The Partnership at Drugfree.org
352 Park Ave. S.
9th Fl.
New York, NY 10010
Phone: 212-922-1560
Fax: 212-922-1570
Website: www.drugfree.org
E-mail: webmail@drugfree.org

Students Against Destructive Decisions (SADD)
255 Main St.
Marlborough, MA 01752
Toll-Free: 877-SADD-INC
(877-723-3462)
Fax: 508-481-5759
Website: www.sadd.org
E-mail: info@sadd.org

Index

Page numbers followed by 'n' indicate a footnote. Page numbers in *italics* indicate a table or illustration

B

C

D

E

F

G

H

I

J

K

L

M

N

O

P

Q

R

S

T

U

V

X

Y

Z